THIRD EDITION

Political Economy and the Changing Global Order

EDITED BY

Richard Stubbs

Geoffrey R.D. Underhill

OXFORD
UNIVERSITY PRESS

OXFORD
UNIVERSITY PRESS

8 Sampson Mews, Suite 204, Don Mills, Ontario M3C 0H5
www.oupcanada.com

Oxford University Press is a department of the University of Oxford.
It furthers the University's objective of excellence in research, scholarship,
and education by publishing worldwide in

Oxford   New York
Auckland   Cape Town   Dar es Salaam
Hong Kong   Karachi   Kuala Lumpur   Madrid   Melbourne   Mexico City   Nairobi   New Delhi   Shanghai   Taipei   Toronto

With offices in
Argentina   Austria   Brazil   Chile   Czech Republic   France   Greece   Guatemala   Hungary   Italy   Japan   Poland   Portugal
Singapore   South Korea   Switzerland   Thailand   Turkey   Ukraine   Vietnam

Oxford is a trade mark of Oxford University Press
in the UK and in certain other countries

Published in Canada
by Oxford University Press

Library and Archives Canada
Cataloguing in Publication

Political economy and the changing global order / edited by Richard Stubbs and Geoffrey R. D. Underhill. -- 3rd ed.

Includes bibliographical references and index.
ISBN–13: 978-0-19-541989-4

1. International economic relations.
2. Economic history—1990-.
3. World Politics—1989-
I. Stubbs, Richard
II. Underhill, Geoffrey R. D.

HF1359.P65 2005   337
C2005-901837-2

8 9 10 – 18 17 16

Cover Image: Corbis/Global Concepts
Cover Design: Joan Dempsey
This book is printed on permanent (acid-free) paper ∞
Printed in Canada

MIX
Paper from
responsible sources
FSC
www.fsc.org   **FSC® C004071**

In Memory of Susan Strange 1923–1998

Contents

III Regional Dynamics

IV Responses to Globalization

Abbreviations

ABF   Asian Bond Fund

ACCS   advanced capitalist countries

ACT UP   AIDS Coalition to Unleash Power

ADB   Asian Development Bank

AEC   ASEAN Economic Community

AFTA   ASEAN Free Trade Area

AICMA   All India Carpet Manufacturers Association

AMF   Asian Monetary Fund

AMUE   Association for Monetary Union in Europe

APEC   Asia-Pacific Economic Co-operation

APT   ASEAN + 3 (China, Japan, South Korea)

ASEAN   Association of Southeast Asian Nations (Brunei Darussalam, Cambodia, Indonesia, Laos, Malaysia, Myanmar, Philippines, Singapore, Thailand, Vietnam)

ASEM   Asia–Europe Meeting

ATTAC   Association pour une Taxation des Transactions financières pour l'Aide aux Citoyens

AU   African Union

AUC   United Self-Defence Forces of Colombia

BIS   Bank for International Settlements

BSE   bovine spongiform encephalopathy

BTAS   bilateral trade agreements

CAP   Common Agricultural Policy (EU)

CCP   Chinese Communist Party

CDA   Christlich Demokratische Arbeitnehmerschaft (Christian Democratic Employees, Germany)

CDM   clean development mechanism

CEC   Commission for Environmental Co-operation (NAFTA)

CEE   Central and Eastern Europe

CEO   chief executive officer

CEP   Comprehensive Economic Partnership

CEPC   Carpet Export Promotion Council (India)

CESDP   Common European Security and Defence Policy (EU)

CFSP   Common Foreign and Security Policy (EU)

CGM   critical globalization movement

CIS   Commonwealth of Independent States

CITES   Convention on International Trade in Endangered Species

COMECON   Council for Mutual Economic Assistance (Soviet Union)

COMESA   Common Market for Eastern and Southern Africa

CPE   comparative political economy

CTE   Committee on Trade and Environment (WTO)

CTM   Confederación des Trabajadores de México

CTOC   Convention against Transnational Organized Crime (UN)

CUFTA   Canada–US Free Trade Agreement

DNS   domain name system

EBRD   European Bank for Reconstruction and Development

EC   European Community

ECA   Economic Commission for Africa (UN)

ECB   European Central Bank

ECJ	European Court of Justice	ICANN	International Corporation for Assigned Names and Numbers
ECOWAS	Economic Community of West African States	ICFTU	International Confederation of Free Trade Unions
EES	European Employment Strategy	IETF	Internet Engineering Task Force
EFF	Electronic Frontiers Foundation	IFIS	international financial institutions
EFTA	European Free Trade Association	ILO	International Labour Organization
ELN	National Liberation Army (Colombia)	IMF	International Monetary Fund
EMES	emerging market economies	EPC	Intellectual Property Committee (US)
EMU	Economic and Monetary Union	IPE	international political economy
EP	European Parliament	IPR	intellectual property right
EPZ	export processing zone	IR	international relations
ERT	European Round Table of Industrialists	ISO	International Standards Organization
ESF	European Social Forum	ISP	Internet service provider
EU	European Union	IT	information technology
FARC	Revolutionary Armed Forces of Colombia	ITO	International Trade Organization
FDI	foreign direct investment	IWS	industrial welfare state
FDP	Free Democratic Party (Germany)	JSEPA	Japan–Singapore Economic Partnership Agreement
FIES	foreign-invested enterprises (China)	KMP	Peasant Movement of the Philippines
FLG	Financial Leaders Group	KRRS	Karnataka State Farmers' Association (India)
FOIL	Forum of Indian Leftists	LDCS	less-developed countries
FSC	foreign sales corporation	MAI	Multilateral Agreement on Investment
FSU	former Soviet Union	MANTHOC	Movimiento de Adolescentes y Niños Trabajadores Hijos de Obreros Cristianos
FTAS	free trade agreements		
FTAA	Free Trade Area of the Americas		
FZLN	Frente Zapatista de Liberación Nacional (Mexico)	MBA	Master of Business Administration
GATS	General Agreement on Trade in Services	MDGS	Millennium Development Goals
		MERCOSUR	Mercado Común del Sur
GATT	General Agreement on Tariffs and Trade	METI	Ministry of Economy, Trade and Industry (Japan)
GDP	gross domestic product	MFN	most favoured nation
GMOS	genetically modified organisms	MITI	Ministry of International Trade and Industry (Japan)
GNP	gross national product		
G-7	Group of Seven (United States, Japan, Germany, Britain, France, Canada, Italy)	MNCS	multinational corporations
		MNE	multinational enterprise
G-8	Group of Eight (G-7 plus Russia)	MOF	Ministry of Finance (Japan)
G-20	Group of Twenty	MST	Movemento sem Terra (Brazil)
HIPCS	heavily indebted poor countries	NAAEC	North American Agreement on Environmental Co-operation
HST	hegemonic stability theory		
HTTP	Hyper Text Transfer Protocol	NAFTA	North American Free Trade Agreement
IBRD	International Bank for Reconstruction and Development (World Bank)		
		NATS	Niños y Adoloscentes Trabajadores

NEPAD	New Partnership for Africa's Development	SEZS	Special Economic Zones (China)
NGO	non-governmental organization	SME	socialist market economy
NIEO	New International Economic Order	SMES	small and medium-sized enterprises
NIES-4	newly industrialized economies of Hong Kong, Taiwan, South Korea, Singapore	SMP	Single Market Program (EU)
		SPS	sanitary and phytosanitary measures
		SSL	Secure Sockets Layer
NTBS	non-tariff barriers	TABD	Transatlantic Business Dialogue
ODA	overseas (or official) development assistance	TBTS	technical barriers to trade
		TCP/IP	Transmission Control Protocol/Internet Protocol
OECD	Organization for Economic Co-operation and Development	TINA	there is no alternative
		TLD	top-level domain
OEM	original equipment manufacturing	TMT	top management team
OPEC	Organization of Petroleum Exporting Countries	TNCS	transnational corporations
		TRIMS	trade-related investment measures
PGA	Peoples' Global Action against 'Free' Trade and the World Trade Organization	TRIPS	Agreement on Trade-Related Aspects of Intellectual Property Rights
		TVES	township and village enterprises (China)
PhRMA	Pharmaceutical and Research Manufacturers of America	UN	United Nations
PMT	Programa Muchacha Trabajador (Peru)	UNCTAD	United Nations Conference on Trade and Development
PPMS	product and processing methods	UNFCCC	United Nations Framework Convention on Climate Change
PRSPS	poverty reduction strategy programs		
PT	Worker's Party (Brazil)	UNSNA	United Nations System of National Accounts
PTAS	preferential trade agreements		
R&D	research and development	USTR	United States Trade Representative
RMB	renminbi (Chinese currency, the yuan)	VERS	voluntary export restraints
RTAS	regional trade agreements	WEF	World Economic Forum
SAA	South African Airways	WHO	World Health Organization
SACCS	South Asian Coalition on Child Servitude	WID	Women in Development
		WSF	World Social Forum
SACU	Southern Africa Customs Union	WSSD	World Summit on Sustainable Development
SADC	South African Development Community		
SADCC	Southern African Development Coordination Conference	WTO	World Trade Organization
		WWF	World Wide Fund for Nature (World Wildlife Fund)
SAPS	structural adjustment programs	WWW	World Wide Web
SDRS	Special Drawing Rights		

Preface

The first edition of this book (1994) was prompted by the need to introduce students to the rapid changes taking place in the global economy, often referred to as 'globalization', as well as to associated regional and national developments. The second edition (2000) examined the consolidation of this process at the turn of the millennium and reflected on its apparent vulnerability in the shadow of the Asian crisis. The pace of change has not abated since then. The European Union has expanded, many of the East Asian economies have rebounded from the crisis of 1997–8, and China has been transformed by remarkable economic growth. At the same time, difficulties in moving forward the World Trade Organization's new Doha Round of multilateral trade talks have underscored the apparent unpredictability of changes to the global economic order. Certainly, the need to understand the major trends in the global economy and their impact on the lives of millions of people around the world is just as compelling as it was when we published the first two editions. As a result, when we were asked by Laura Macleod at Oxford University Press Canada to put together a third edition of this book we agreed to take on the task. The decision was made easier by the encouragement of colleagues and students who found the first two editions valuable in coming to grips with the major issues in international political economy.

As with the second edition, the contributions to this volume examine how the economic global order is unfolding and how it will evolve over the next decade or so. Once again, we emphasize the linkages between the political and economic domains, on the one hand, and between the domestic and international domains, on the other. We focus on conceptualizing the state and its role in the international political economy, on the increasing importance of non-state actors, and on the growing influence of both public and private forms of transnational governance. We draw attention to the complex interaction of political authorities and the market structures in the global system, identifying the causes of changing economic structures in the political conflicts that take place at the individual, national, regional, and international levels of analysis. The book is organized to reflect both the issue-structure of the international political economy and the global, regional, and state levels at which these issues are debated and contested.

While this third edition of the book has roughly the same format as the first two editions, the content has changed substantially. Nearly two-thirds of the chapters are new, having been written especially for this volume, while the remaining chapters are revised and updated—in most cases significantly. Following the successful approach used in assembling the first two editions we asked each contributor, while keeping the student readership in mind, to develop an argument that briefly explores a specific aspect of the global political economy. Once again we are extremely grateful for the unfailing co-operation of our contributors as we put the collection together. We are also grateful to the seven reviewers in Europe, Canada, and the US who analyzed the second edition and provided many helpful suggestions, most of them now implemented, on how we could improve the volume. Of course, despite the size of the volume and the number of chapters, we have not been able to cover everything and we are very conscious of the fact that specialists in one field or another inevitably will feel that we have been neglectful.

Many of our colleagues have once again been a major source of advice, support, and encouragement. We would especially like to thank Marshall Beier, Philip G. Cerny, William D. Coleman, Eric Helleiner, Richard Higgott, Robert O'Brien, Lou Pauly, Tony Porter, Susan Sell, and Grace Skogstad; we are sure to have missed a number. Our thanks also to the new contributors who have so successfully broadened the scope of the book. We would like to thank the reviewers on both sides of the Atlantic for their constructive comments, our many colleagues around the world and their students who used the first two editions of the book and offered their advice, and our own students who read many of the chapters as they came in and offered their thoughts. As usual we owe a special thanks to Gerald Bierling, Mara Giannotti, and Emile Yesodharan for helping to get the manuscript ready for the publishers. At Oxford University Press Canada we would like to acknowledge the work of Rachael Cayley, Laura Macleod, Phyllis Wilson, and our editor, Richard Tallman.

As with the first two editions, we hope that this collection contributes as much to scholarship as to teaching in the field of IPE.

Richard Stubbs
Geoffrey R.D. Underhill
February 2005

Part I

Understanding the Changing Global Order

Introduction

Conceptualizing the Changing Global Order

Geoffrey R.D. Underhill

Political power and wealth creation have been intimately intertwined throughout the history of the modern international system.[1] In a now classic article, Jacob Viner invoked the example of the seventeenth and eighteenth centuries when the view was strongly held that 'wealth and power are each proper ultimate ends of national policy; [and] there is a long run harmony between these ends'.[2] Whether there is harmony or tension between the two in the formation of state policies, political conflict in the international system has continued to focus on these two interrelated elements of power, wealth, and their relative distribution, thereby attracting the attention of international relations scholars. Of course, the historical setting of this conflict has undergone dramatic changes since the decline of the mercantilist system to which Viner was referring. At that time, most European absolutist monarchies saw control over both foreign and domestic economic relations as intimately related to their centralization of power.

The most recent expression of the complex relationship between power and wealth (or more specifically, between the political and economic domains) in international politics is the link between political authority, on the one hand, and the system of production and distribution of wealth referred to as the market economy, on the other. Let us first of all make an important distinction with regard to the 'market'. Historically, markets have always existed in one form or another as economic exchange relationships ('trade') among individuals, enterprises, or communities. However, the general notion of a market as a localized pattern of exchange should be distinguished from the particular form of market economy or system, with its origins in the Industrial Revolution, which we know today.[3]

This market system, characterized by industrial capital, lies at the heart of the phenomenon analyzed by the classical political economists (Smith, Ricardo) and by Marx (see Chapter 1), wherein owners of capital, workers, and intermediaries are all linked in social relationships via a complex pattern of political and market institutions. These generate investment capital for the production of commodities and facilitate the circulation of money for the purchase of goods/services, land, labour, and, of course, money itself. In the mercantilist period and before, there were markets, but there was no market *system* based on capital investment and industrial production; the market did not form the basis of economic and social relationships to the extent it does today. Until the Industrial Revolution and its aftermath, most domestic economies were scarcely integrated either internally or internationally; they consisted of essentially local markets, their development spatially limited by technology and the subsistence nature of agriculture.[4]

This market economy began to emerge in the second half of the eighteenth century and went through its 'classical' phase in the mid- to late nineteenth century.[5] National economies integrated internally as well as outwardly with the structures of international commerce. Even the market system has undergone profound transformations since its inception, with the collapse of laissez-faire in the 1930s and the construction of the post-war mixed economy system, which in turn underwent significant transformations from the 1970s (see Introduction to Part II). These transformations in the market system have all been intimately bound up with important changes in the political domain. Not surprisingly, therefore, it has become largely accepted by most scholars in political economy, whether domestic or international, that there is an intimate and reciprocal connection between the control of significant resources in the market economy and the exercise of political power, even in democratic societies; changes in the nature of economic structures are bound up with political and social changes in the society in question. There is, however, considerable debate concerning the substance of this relationship and how to think about it.

The essays in this volume demonstrate why it is important to consider the relationship between the political and economic domains, between economic structures and political interaction, in contemporary international context. This is the central question of the discipline of *international political economy*. This introduction aims to demonstrate how one might meaningfully think about this relationship.

On the whole, and despite a diversity of perspectives, the contributors to this volume generally share three fundamental premises. The first is that the political and economic domains cannot be separated in any meaningful sense. When the two domains are separated in our understanding of the world around us, important errors of analysis and policy are likely to result. This implies that the dynamics of economic and security issues, of government and the market, are intimately bound up with each other in international politics, a premise that contrasts with the assumptions of traditional approaches to the discipline of international relations.

The second premise confronts a widely held intellectual orthodoxy in our societies that leaps from the pages of almost every newspaper or popular publication on the economy, as well as from the pages of economics textbooks. Most accounts of economic issues portray the state and the market

as operating in contrasting realms, their dynamics conflicting with one another. The authors in this volume in their own ways challenge this assumption, insisting that economic structures are not the result of the spontaneous interaction of individual economic agents, even in a market setting where political authorities may refrain from direct intervention in economic decision-making. The structures of the market and of the larger political economy are inherently contestable, and this is demonstrated by the way they have developed over time. If the principal focus of political conflict, at either the domestic or the international level, concerns who gets what, when, and how, and if setting out the rules and framework of the market in large part determines just this, then *political interaction is the means by which economic structures, in particular the structures of the market, are established and in turn transformed.*

Understanding the global political economy therefore involves overcoming orthodoxy and understanding markets and political authorities as part of the same, integrated ensemble of governance, not as contrasting principles of social organization. Political interaction is therefore as central to economic development (or lack thereof) as the process of economic competition itself, and of course asymmetries of power abound. This point is elaborated further in Chapter 1 of this volume (Krätke and Underhill), which charts the emergence of the field and shows how it is broader than traditional political science and international relations.

There is, then, a two-way or reciprocal relationship between politics and formal political authorities, on the one hand, and economic structures and institutions, on the other, in the changing global order. As will be discussed later, this implies a two-way relationship between the *structures* of global markets and the *agents* of political and economic interaction that constitute them. Let us also bear in mind that any particular economic arrangement, whether mercantilism, Communist central planning, or industrial capitalism, is far from neutral in its effects on access to political resources. Only after major political conflict did the structures of the industrial market economy emerge, first in late eighteenth- and early nineteenth-century Britain[6] and eventually along distinctive national lines in Europe and elsewhere. At the same time, the process of developing a market economy resulted in profound social transformations, which in turn altered the distribution of political resources within the societies affected. By the middle of the nineteenth century the market was developing into a pattern of transnational relations, a complex that transcended borders as much as it altered social structures and relations among states.

The same could be said of the construction of the post-World War II economic order and its rapid transformation in recent years. A market is a political device to achieve certain outcomes, conferring relative benefits on some and costs on others in both political and economic terms; it is, in essence, a political institution that plays a crucial role in structuring society and international politics. The changing market structure gives rise to new patterns of economic and political forces.

The rules of the market economy, then, even in the international domain, are created and enforced through the resolution (or lack thereof) of political conflict among competing interests. Referring to the rise of the international market economy, Karl Polanyi put it in the following manner:

> the gearing of markets into a self regulatory system of tremendous power was not a result of the inherent tendency of markets towards excrescence, but rather the effect of highly artificial stimulants administered to the body social in order to meet a situation which was created by the no less artificial phenomenon of the machine.[7]

Looking at the relationship between the political and economic domains with respect to the international system is a complex task. This task is difficult enough in a domestic political setting, but when one takes into account the international setting, one encounters the twin problems of *anarchy* (lack of overarching political authority) and *levels of analysis*. This brings one to the third shared premise of the volume, and another confrontation

with orthodoxy: traditional international relations approaches have emphasized a clear distinction between the dynamics of politics at the domestic and international realms, yet the authors here challenge this in important ways.

As the economies of the market system become increasingly internationalized (perhaps a more appropriate term is interpenetrated or *trans*nationalized[8]) and thereby increasingly outside the direct control of individual states, the more it becomes necessary to understand the interaction of domestic and international levels of analysis. States remain the principal (and, indeed, the only legal) decision-makers in the anarchic international order, and they continue to respond to essentially domestic political constituencies. But they are far from possessing all the political and economic resources to continue meaningfully to shape the direction of political and economic development in line with national preferences.[9] With the transnationalization of economic decision-making, what were once essentially matters of domestic politics have now spilled over and become contentious in relations among states and other actors in the international system.

Indeed, careful research reveals that the distinction between the domestic and international levels of analysis is in a strict sense artificial: sometimes useful for understanding a complex situation, but not necessarily corresponding to a real state of affairs. Human associations, corporations, markets, and governmental institutions all may spill across borders; what one government, actor, or group does often affects the options and actions of others. We live in an international system characterized by a high degree of interdependence among states and their societies, at least a high degree in relative historical terms.

Therefore, the third shared premise of this volume is the intimate connection between domestic and international levels of analysis. The global political economy (and international politics as a whole) cannot meaningfully be packaged into a separate 'international' realm of politics, structured by the principle of anarchy, which generates the behaviour of an arrangement of 'units' (states) in relation to a particular distribution of power.[10] In fact, the international system is much more akin to a 'state-society complex',[11] spanning domestic and international levels of analysis, with the institutions and agencies of the state at its core. 'Levels of analysis' is an analytical tool useful only to denote the different patterns of institutional arrangements (local, domestic, interstate) that can be found in the global system. The international level of analysis, taken on its own, cannot properly be regarded as the source of an explanation: there is only one 'politics', with the state as the primary focus of political conflict in a larger state-society complex. The state manages the constraints of the domestic and international domains through domestic policy-making and intergovernmental bargaining, the one being intimately embedded in the other. This in turn implies that a vast array of different sorts of agents or actors are part of global political processes focused on the institutions of political authority, states in particular.[12]

Another way of putting this is to consider the international domain as reflecting the specific balance of social forces of the most powerful states as this balance becomes projected into the international system:

> to say anything sensible about the *content* of international economic orders . . . it is necessary to look at how power and legitimate social purpose become fused to project political authority into the international system.[13]

So this book is about the relationship between the political and economic domains, between states and markets, and how that relationship plays itself out across borders. In fact, the fundamental problematic of international political economy has been described by two theorists of quite differing perspectives, Robert Gilpin and Immanuel Wallerstein, in roughly similar terms:[14] the interaction of a transnational market economy with a system of competitive states (which, for the record, often co-operate on matters related to the maintenance of a transnational economy). The book will attempt to conceptualize (in Part I) and analyze (in Part II) the principal issues around which this interaction takes place. Part III will examine the

dynamics of particular regions, while the chapters in Part IV review the responses of both state and non-state actors to what has been named, for better or for worse, *globalization*.

The structure of this book, divided into sections on theory, global issues, regional dynamics, and strategies and responses, represents a commitment to highlight the relationship among levels of analysis. To this end, the volume has sought to include the expertise of specialists in comparative and regional political economy where appropriate. The contributors will put forward a diversity of views, but they all tend to share the premises referred to above. It is most important to draw the connections among the structure of the economic domain, the (politicized) interests of the social groups and actors who participate in this structure (the *structure-agent* question), and the patterns of political conflict and change that take place within a particular set of domestic and international institutions. These institutions tend to 'load the dice' in political conflict, enhancing the political resources of some states, groups, or actors as opposed to others. The question of institutions is important in the changing global order, as institutions struggle to keep up with rapid, underlying changes in the international system.

Theoretical Debates in the Literature

One contribution of a volume such as this is to provide the student with a guide to the theoretical debates in the literature of the discipline. Many texts have adopted the 'three models' or 'ideologies' approach, looking at liberal, Marxist, and realist (sometimes called economic nationalist/mercantilist) approaches as competing models of world order. The authors then tend to settle for one or another approach, or aim for some sort of synthesis, or worse, simply despair at their incompatibility. However, this traditional presentation of the debates in the literature yields rather stale and, indeed, rigid categories, given the diversity *within* each and the cross-fertilization among them. There is a tendency to reduce theoretical discussion in IPE to competing and mutually exclusive, even irreconcilable, ideologies.

One problem is that there are perspectives beyond these three, such as postmodernism,[15] environmentalism (see Chapter 5 by Helleiner and Chapter 17 by Bernstein), and feminism (see Chapter 6 by Whitworth and Chapter 18 by Marchand). Most importantly, this focus on competing ideological paradigms severs the connection between the material economic interests of actors or groups and the ideas they espouse: for example, while some might benefit from regulation, powerful firms with a strong competitive position in the international economy tend to argue for relatively unregulated or 'liberal' international conditions that allow them to take unimpeded advantage of their market power. Unless this connection between policy preferences (as expressed in ideas) and concrete economic interests is maintained, the debate becomes detached from the real world of political conflict over who gets what, when, and where: Robert Cox has gone so far as to assert that 'Theory is always *for* someone and *for* some purpose.'[16]

It is nonetheless difficult to avoid discussing these three approaches—so much contemporary theory either derives from or reacts against them. It is, however, possible to escape the traditional procedure of comparing 'incompatible' models with one another, which only leads to the sterile conclusion that there is little agreement and, consequently, very little real progress on what matters most: deepening theoretical understanding. The purpose of this section, then, is critically to assess how *adequately* each deals with the central theoretical *issues* in international political economy, the better to indicate the direction for further progress.

These fundamental theoretical problems or issues have been hinted at above. International political economy is concerned first of all with the relationship between the economic and political domains across territorial boundaries. Second, attention should be drawn to the role of the state as the focus of decision-making in a system of competitive states that is, in turn, interdependent with a transnational market economy: how political agency and economic competition in a certain structural and institutional setting in turn contribute to the dynamics of change. Understanding

the role of the state-as-agent must go beyond glib pronouncements on the 'national interest'. How, and in whose interest, the 'national interest' is determined is precisely the problem. To be sure, dominant socio-economic interests with substantial political resources heavily influence the outcome of policies made in the name of the state. But it is crucial to understand that in the context of a transnational market economy, these dominant domestic groups extend across borders, becoming transnational, and thus have relationships with similar interests in other states, usually precisely because of market relationships.

This implies a third theoretical problem that must be addressed: the linkage between the domestic and international domains (or levels of analysis), given that political-economic processes clearly cut across the lines of political decision-making constituted by the institutional structures of the state. Situating the state and economic interests within this vast 'state-society complex'[17] that we call the global order will be a crucial problem for any theoretical approach. This implies focusing on the nature and political consequences of interdependence among states and their societies.[18]

Interdependence deserves some brief explanation. It was defined by Nye and Keohane as mutual but unequal dependence among states and their societies.[19] At one level this implies that what one state in the system does in some way affects the options of at least some of the others.[20] For example, aggressive behaviour by one country might cause others to reassess their security policies, or protectionist trade policies might cause a commensurate reaction. But interdependence means more than this: it also refers to how states and their societies are linked through (among other factors) the interactions and structures of the market, which in turn affects the politics of the state in the domestic and international contexts. Patterns of interdependence affect patterns of conflict and co-operation in the international system, and indeed within domestic societies, by helping to define who gets what, when, and how. Interdependence and transnationalization affect the politics at both levels. The state very often faces political or economic constituencies that are, in the traditional sense, domestic, but where many of the dominant interests are in important respects transnational economic actors and can, therefore, elude state policy tools to a considerable degree.

Once again, the role of the state is highlighted, making the state perhaps the central theoretical question. Just how one characterizes and assesses the state in IPE is critical, and the discussion of interdependence raises a fourth question—which actors are relevant to a discussion of global order? The ties of interdependence that operate through the changing structures of the market underscore the importance of considering how *non-state actors* affect the politics of the state, and how this in turn has an impact on the political economy of the global system.[21] If this is the case, is it relevant to conceive of the state as a unified rational actor making clear choices among rationally determined alternatives, as in much of the traditional literature on international relations? The discussion of interdependence above would imply this to be a somewhat misleading account. Instead, one must consider the state as *a key decision-making institution-as-agent at the core of the state-society complex*. Successful theories of IPE need to account for the relationship between the political power exercised through and on behalf of state authority in international and domestic politics, on the one hand, and constituent interests and agents of the wider social whole in which the institutions of the state are embedded, on the other.

Finally, there will be methodological issues, in particular concerning the role of structure in theoretical explanations: the structure-agent problem. The theoretical problems outlined above constantly emphasize the *interactive relationships* between elements of the IPE: between domestic and international levels of analysis; between economic issues and political conflict; and between institutional patterns and economic structures, on the one hand, and the politics that takes place within them, on the other. Interactive relationships are developmental (or *dialectical*) processes. Explanations based primarily on an analysis of structure (and structure is a static concept in and of itself), deriving political outcomes from structural patterns, will have difficulty explaining historical change in the

IPE. Theory must do more than highlight the patterns (structures) in a system and their consequences; it must also explain how agents in interactive relationships, through the medium of political conflict, lead to changes in the structures themselves. Theories that focus primarily on structure[22] will tend to suffer from deterministic predictions about the direction of change because they leave out the complex interrelationships, or 'process variables',[23] that govern change.

A similar set of problems arises with respect to rational choice models of analysis. Many perspectives in IPE theory portray actors (usually the state) in international politics as unitary and rational, maximizing their power, wealth, or some other utility function in a setting characterized by the absence of an overarching political authority (anarchy). However, the idea of a clear choice between defined alternatives tends to break down as it becomes evident that states, as 'decision-makers', are the scene of political conflict that often proves inconclusive. States have legal decision-making power in international and (depending on constitutional arrangements) domestic affairs, and are units in this sense. They are not, however, unified and single-purpose decision-makers because of the ways in which an array of competing coalitions of social forces are integrated into the policy process of the state itself. State policies are likely to be ambivalent on most issues, and international agreements consist of a complex mixture of co-operative and conflictual behaviour. The rational choice/unitary state device may well be useful for clarifying a complex situation in a set of international negotiations, for example, but it does not necessarily enhance a general theory of international politics. A broader, more fluid notion of the politics of state decision-making in a global context is needed. *Non*-decisions may result from a failure, deliberate or otherwise, to put certain issues on the political agenda. Indeed, powerful interests in society may even succeed in 'capturing' parts of the policy-making machinery of the state—so-called public purpose may come to serve blatantly private ends.

Furthermore, interdependence among states and their societies means that domestic political conflict and intergovernmental politics become intertwined, which further erodes the rational actor perspective. The state emerges as a social entity caught in a web of pressures and constraints at the domestic and international levels, among the most important of which is the transnational market economy. The relationship between the state and the decision-making environment is an interactive one where the rationality of cause and effect is difficult to discern. While rational choice methodologies are highly suggestive of the incentives facing agents or of bargaining dynamics in conflictual situations, they need to be combined with broader historical and contextual understanding.

Contrasting Theoretical Approaches: A Critical Examination

This discussion will make much more sense if it is related specifically to the theoretical literature in IPE. Here we will look at how these points apply to the various approaches that have evolved over time. We can evaluate them in terms of how well they deal with the theoretical issues we have identified as central concepts in IPE. Based on this critical analysis of these competing perspectives, we will develop some broad parameters for an approach to the discipline of IPE. It is not the intention to produce a single, coherent theoretical approach, but rather to suggest directions for further exploration that are likely to prove fruitful. A number of these questions are also discussed, in different ways, in the essays in this collection, particularly in Part I.

The generalizations arrived at in theoretical inquiry, it should be emphasized, are best understood in relation to empirical research into specific issue-areas in IPE (money, trade, environment) and specific historical circumstances. A concept 'attains precision only when brought into contact with a particular situation which it helps to explain—a contact which also helps develop the meaning of the concept.'[24] Theory cannot meaningfully be understood in a vacuum, devoid of empirical context; 'theoretically informed' empirical analysis has been the aim of most contributions to this volume. If theory does not successfully enhance our understanding of complex 'real-world' phenomena, it risks becoming an exercise in intellectual fantasy.

The Realist Tradition

The realist tradition in international relations theory has dominated the relatively young discipline in the post-war period, usurping the place liberal idealism held in the interwar years. This longevity is a tribute to the explanatory power of the approach. In its traditional guise realism was not a coherent theory as such, but it provided a flexible tool for understanding the dynamics and content of relations among states, particularly as far as issues of peace and war were concerned. The central feature of the realist model is the competitive dynamic of the system of states where no overarching authority or government exists. The preservation of sovereignty by national communities organized into states and the competition this engenders within an international system in the absence of higher political authority are fundamental facts of international politics, and this can be borne out by historical analysis. In time, the realist tradition evolved into *neo-realism*, to which the work of Kenneth Waltz was central.[25] This was an attempt to take the basic principles of the realist tradition and to construct a coherent explanatory theory of the dynamics of international politics; it did not stand the test of time well.

The traditional realist approach adapts itself to include economic issues on the agenda of international politics by relating economic power to issues of national security[26] in a context of competition among states under conditions of anarchy. Economic issues are considered secondary to the preservation of national independence. In this sense, states may sacrifice much in terms of economic rationality to preserve their socio-economic and territorial integrity, but the power necessary for that preservation could not be attained without adequate capacity to generate wealth.

However, traditional realism assumes that the political and economic domains are essentially separate. Hans Morgenthau stated this explicitly in his classic *Politics among Nations*:

Intellectually, the political realist maintains the autonomy of the political sphere, as the economist, the lawyer, the moralist maintain theirs. He thinks in terms of interest defined in terms of power, as the economist thinks in terms of utility; the lawyer the conformity of action with legal rules; the moralist the conformity of action with moral principles. . . . [T]he political realist asks 'How does this policy affect the power of the nation?'[27]

For traditional realists, international politics was largely about the struggle for power and the skill of statesmen at reaching a workable power balance that provided for systemic stability and the successful management of inevitable conflicts of national interest. International politics became for realists a world apart, divorced from the day-to-day interaction of socio-economic groups and institutions common to domestic politics. In making this questionable distinction, many post-war realists seemed to forget that among the most vital political issues in either the domestic or the international domain was the question of material life: who gets what, when, and where. If politics is not about what goes into people's pockets or purses, then it is difficult to imagine the content of political conflict in a domestic or international context. That this conflict periodically erupts into violence, which in the international system we call war, is no more surprising than social unrest or civil war at the domestic level. States, after all, are institutions through which particular social groups defend (internally and externally) their power and the particular structures of the society they represent.

Realism, then, assumed the primacy of the political over the economic domain, as well as a separation of the domestic and international realms. Political conflict among or within states could influence the economy, and economic factors might well constrain state decision-makers, but as Morgenthau emphasized, the laws and dynamics of each were separate.

This assumption is problematic: careful research demonstrates that the political economy is an integrated whole, embedding normative, economic, legal, and political dynamics together. It makes little sense to speak of the laws of the economic sphere when the outcome of political conflict over time largely contributed to the establishment of these laws in the first place, and the laws of the economic sphere are constantly contested by those socio-economic groups who find them to their relative or even absolute disadvantage; they may even resort to violence to this end. By the same token, the security framework of the international system is established by states to preserve their individual patterns of socio-economic order. The Cold War was as good an illustration of this as any other: two contrasting socio-economic systems confronted each other, organized into security blocs. E.H. Carr, long associated with the realist school but occupying a subtle niche in the lexicon of international relations theory, argued that socio-economic questions were an integral part of the problem of international security.[28]

Another assumption of traditional realism concerned its conceptualization of the state. The approach was quite correct to draw attention to the importance of the state in international politics, but the state was most often seen as a unified actor making rational calculations with a view to maximizing power and security in a world characterized by the absence of overarching authority structures.

But if the state makes calculations of interest defined in terms of power, this assumes that the state has a single-minded capacity to make such calculations in the first place. In the face of stark choices concerning the survival of the state in the international system, this view may be relatively accurate, but this situation occurs relatively infrequently. Defining the national interest where less desperate issues are involved may not be so clear-cut. Even in national security crises there is considerable evidence that states are far from unified in their decision-making processes.[29] A question arises as to how the national interest is generated, particularly where economic choices are concerned. The view of the state as a unified rational actor is not particularly helpful when state decision-making structures are revealed to be fragmented and often poorly co-ordinated, and when coalitions of socio-economic interests, with power and influence over some issues but not others, compete to alter state policies to their own advantage.

We may summarize the points with respect to the key theoretical issues made so far. (1) The realist approach assumes a separation of the economic and political domains, which sharply reduces the scope of its analysis as a comprehensive theory of international relations. (2) Security is regarded as the primary issue-area in international politics,[30] which fits poorly with the fundamental assumptions of the discipline of international political economy. On the contrary, it has been argued that security has much to do with the very economic question of who gets what, when, and how. (3) The state is portrayed as a unified and autonomous rational actor, an assumption that has been revealed as problematic. In this sense, the importance of non-state actors is usually overlooked and the relationship between the state and non-state actors in state decision-making processes receives little attention (though need not be excluded from analysis).

While the traditional realist approach was a flexible heuristic device permitting much rich historical understanding of the competitive dynamics of the system of states, and for understanding the difficult foreign policy choices facing states on matters of international security, a coherent theory it was not. This perception led to the steady emergence of what came to be called the *neo-realist* or *structural realist* approach, encapsulated in the works of Waltz, who was immensely if briefly influential in the period of the 1980s and the American 'new Cold War' policy of the Reagan era. He emphasized the importance of the anarchic *structure* of the international system as a determinant of behaviour and outcomes in international politics. The competitive pressures of a system characterized by anarchy, with states as the basic units, would lead to a persistently conflictual interaction and behaviour based on the principle of self-preservation. The distribution of power among the units under conditions of anarchy essentially deter-

mined what states could and would do in their quest for self-help and security. These competitive dynamics tended towards self-sufficiency and a low degree of interdependence (a theoretical prediction at extraordinary variance with any available evidence drawn from any one of the last four centuries!) and to the long-term preservation of the system itself, if not necessarily each and every one of the states constituting it.

Waltz was therefore engaged in an attempt to create a coherent account of systemic dynamics in international politics, and as such it made the dubious assumption that the dynamics of the domestic level were contrary to and indeed of little relevance to the dynamics of international politics. Waltz's theory, logically consistent as it may have been, was embarrassingly short-lived in terms of its perceived ability to explain the ongoing dynamics of the very international politics it claimed to understand so well. When the bipolar power structures of the Cold War world collapsed for reasons almost entirely related to the dynamics of *domestic* developments inside the former Soviet Union (under the leadership of Mikhail Gorbachev) and the Berlin Wall separating East from West came down following unsustainable *internal* social unrest across the former Soviet bloc, it was clear that a theory of the international that pointedly ignored the *interaction* of the domestic and system levels of analysis was problematic.

Neo- or structural realism had its IPE counterpart, the theory of hegemonic stability, wherein neo-realist system-level analysis and more liberal notions of the advantages of the market coexist somewhat uneasily.[31] The idea that a hegemon might provide some of the political preconditions for a liberal economic order ('hegemonic stability') was originally put forward by Charles Kindleberger (1973) in relation to the international monetary system,[32] well before Waltz's *Theory of International Politics* (1979). Several authors projected this into Waltz's systemic framework, providing a neo-realist approach to international economic relations. They postulated that an international market economy, institutionalized in international economic 'regimes' characterized by liberal norms and rules,[33] would constitute a *public good* for all nations in the system because a liberal market order ensured the greatest economic benefit for the greatest number (see discussion of liberal approaches below). They also recognized that the anarchic international system provides infertile ground for the degree of co-operation necessary to sustain liberal economic regimes.

Consequently, a dominant power or 'hegemon' must be able and willing to bear the 'cost' of providing the 'public good' of a liberal market economy and a correspondingly 'strong' liberal international economic regime. In this way, a political framework is provided for the market despite the anarchic nature of international relations. To tie the theory into its neo-realist assumptions, the existence of a liberal economic order is essentially a function of the distribution of power among states in the system, with a hegemonic distribution being the most propitious ground for the emergence of a liberal market system.[34]

As the hegemonic power declines, however, the established liberal order may well come under pressure and indeed unravel entirely as the weakening hegemon becomes less and less willing or able to bear the costs of openness (costs such as keeping its market open to others in times of economic crisis). Furthermore, the economic success of others, made possible by the liberal order maintained by the dominant state, will slowly challenge the hegemon's position and, therefore, undermine the liberal character of international regimes.

The theory of hegemonic stability suffered from the same sorts of inadequacies as its neo-realist system-level partner. It is empirically inaccurate in the first place in its portrayal of historical developments in the post-war period, and this problem is dealt with at length in the introduction to Part II of this volume. On a more general note, the *existence* of a dominant power (in what should be a self-evident proposition) tells us little about its motivations, liberal or otherwise (see Chapter 31 by Moon). A systemic-level theory says little about the *content* of relations among states because it does not cut across levels of analysis. An understanding of the social and economic foundations of power is

crucial to understanding the motivations of a dominant country in the international system. The feature of anarchy and the distribution of power among states are of course important, but these do not 'cause' the interactions between states in any real sense. 'Levels of analysis' as a concept simply denotes the various *institutional patterns* or layers within which political conflict is organized. Politics is a continuum across various institutional layers that constitute a social whole—the state-society complex—and the state is the most important of these institutions. It is a decision-making forum within and around which the politics of the international system takes place, providing an institutional bridge between the domestic and the international.

If we are to understand how states manage the constraints of the domestic and international domains, we must understand the politics of the state itself, situated as it is between domestic and international society. If the state is a prime decision-maker, this requires some notion of how the economic interests involved in the transnational market economy become articulated in the politics of the state. We need to disaggregate the state to understand its politics, focusing on the preferences and political resources of social groups and, of course, market actors (largely, but not exclusively, firms) to understand how particular material interests are articulated politically. With the disaggregation of the state and an emphasis on social groups and actors, an understanding of the nature and effects of evolving patterns of interdependence on international politics is a crucial concern. The state appears as the most important decision-making forum in the international political economy, but it is far from the only actor of consequence.

Liberal Approaches

A political strain of liberal international theory, and derived from this an economic strain, can be identified. We shall be more interested in the economic strain, but we must begin with a brief account of political liberalism in international theory.[35] The underlying assumption of political liberalism is the intrinsic value of individuals as the primary actors in the international system. Liberalism is thus permeated with a concern for enhancing the freedom and welfare of individuals; it proposes that humankind can employ reason better to develop a sense of harmony of interest among individuals and groups within the wider community, domestic or international. Thus liberalism has as a goal the harmonization of conceptions of self-interest *through political action*. Progress towards this goal is 'seen in terms of possibility rather than certainty',[36] and the definition of what constitutes the proper goal of such political action (what constitutes 'progress') is inherently contestable.[37]

In the international sphere, these goals are realized through the promotion of liberal democracy, through international co-operation, law, and institutions, and through social integration and technological development. It is fairly easy to see how the economic variant fits into this general picture. The maximization of individual economic welfare is a very important aspect of the enhancement of individual freedoms. States can direct their policies towards this goal through co-operation to realize mutually beneficial economic gains for their peoples.

Therefore, if realism is a political theory of relations among states, then economic liberalism, especially in its neo-classical variant,[38] has become a theory of the interaction of individuals in the economic sphere. This involves understanding the structure of comparative advantage and the international division of labour in a market economy consisting of producers and consumers who exist, somewhat incidentally, in different political systems. Some of these political entities may be closed to the market, but this is the result of political suppression of the natural propensity of individuals to truck, barter, and trade. Furthermore, if individuals are indeed offered the freedom to interact as economic agents, this is likely to ensure the most beneficial distribution of welfare among individuals of the international system. It is the task of the state as rational actor to recognize the advantages of the international market as yielding the greatest

good for the greatest number, and to respond by reducing or eliminating 'artificial' political impediments to 'natural' patterns of exchange. What is more, an assumption of the economic liberal approach is that the market will achieve this *automatically*—markets are self-regulating if individuals are left largely to their own economic devices. Many liberals also maintain that the transactions associated with the international market economy will build patterns of interdependence that will increase the incentives for international co-operation among states: in short, policies aimed at enhancing trade may contribute to international peace. Liberalism has a political program for the international system that emphasizes the market, the role of co-operative international institutions, international law, and national self-determination coupled with electoral democracy.

At first glance the liberal theory appears to be in sharp contrast to traditional realism (especially the optimism of liberalism as against the pessimism of the realists). However, when it comes to IPE they are often two sides of the same coin with their shared emphasis on the separation of the economic and political domains, each with its own laws and dynamics. Many realists are economic liberals in their understanding of the international economy, but they will be sceptical of the possibility of achieving a liberal system, and especially liberal international institutions, under conditions of international anarchy.[39]

How successful is the liberal approach at addressing the theoretical issues outlined? In the first place, the separation of markets from politics, from their political and institutional setting, misunderstands what a market actually is. It is not a natural phenomenon resulting from spontaneous interactions among individuals; it is instead a complex political institution for producing and distributing material and political resources. As such, it is relatively advantageous for some and rather bad news for others, depending on the historical circumstances of individuals in their socio-economic context. The institutions of the market are as much part of the governance of our societies as are the institutions of the state, and the two are essentially integrated functions in the global system. If markets are properly understood as political institutions, the assumption that they are automatic or 'self-regulating' breaks down—it becomes clear that markets, like any other political arrangement, are contestable and open to manipulation by those who have the power to do so. Indeed, it is extremely difficult to find historical examples of markets that function as economists assume they do.

Second, it is difficult to understand the behaviour of economic agents, whether individuals or firms, outside their socio-political context. Economic agents do not just react to a series of uniform market incentives: markets differ from sector to sector or country to country; socio-cultural institutions and political conflict shape the pattern of market institutions and vice versa; 'economic' issues are intimately interconnected with other aspects of human existence. In sum, it is essentially a cliché to assert that economic agents interact as members of a social whole that is greater than the sum of its parts.

A third point is that the economic liberal perspective is ahistorical (the separation of markets from politics leads to this). There have always been markets in the sense of local exchanges of goods and services, but the market system or economy is a relatively recent development.[40] Liberalism therefore fails to account for the history of political conflict that led to the emergence of the institutions of the market and neglects the ongoing political conflict that has altered the institutions of the market over time. The institutions of nineteenth-century laissez-faire contrast greatly with those of the post-war mixed economy, and since the 1970s rapid changes have been underway (see introduction to Part II). The changing patterns of market institutions have altered the distribution of gains and losses, the pattern of political resources, and the political preferences of players in the game.

Fourth, the liberal perspective is an economic reductionist approach. By this we mean that liberal economists ultimately focus on a feature of economic structure, the pattern of comparative advantage among economic agents, as a source of explanation. The complexity and political content of international economic relations are reduced to a reflection of the international division of labour, or market structure, as individual utility maximizers interact within its confines. By separating our understanding of the state from that of the economy, and of the individual from society, there can be no successful theory of politics or of the state and we cannot understand the ways in which the state and market are integrated parts of the same socio-political dynamics.

Yet, as has been emphasized, it is precisely a political theory of the market that is required. Without a theory of political conflict and the state, we cannot understand how the market structure changes over time. Theories based on structure as a pattern or matrix of relationships in a system—an essentially static concept—run the risk of *tautology*.[41] The structure of comparative advantage certainly does shape and constrain the interactions among actors. However, the emergence and transformation of comparative advantage, of the structure itself, requires explanation. Change is an open-ended political process that takes place within a particular structural setting but with the potential to alter structure itself. Structures are politically contestable in the sense that they confer advantages on some and disadvantages on others.[42]

Radical Approaches

The principal strength of Marxist analysis and most other radical approaches to international political economy is that they focus precisely on the connection between the social and economic structures of the capitalist economic system, on the one hand, and the exercise of political power in the international system, on the other.[43] Within domestic political systems, the capitalist system of production entrenches the dominance of one class over another: the state is the *capitalist* state. As the economy becomes internationalized, this class dominance projects itself into international politics. The political organization of the international system reflects the power relations of the transnational market economy. This manifests itself both in competition among states in the international system and in the co-operative processes represented by international economic regimes. For some traditional Marxists, the spread of capitalism touches off a process of economic and political development in less-developed parts of the globe as capitalist firms, often supported by their home states, seek profitable opportunities for investment abroad. Dependency theorists saw the flaw of this approach and pointed instead to the likelihood of core and periphery areas of the global economy remaining distinct despite incorporation into the capitalist world economy. Johann Galtung, for example, developed a structural theory of *imperialism*, hypothesizing that the mutually beneficial political and economic relationships between elites in core and periphery countries would maintain the structural pattern of dependency in the global economy.[44]

There is considerable risk when one attempts to generalize about this diverse range of theories, but most do share some essential characteristics. The approaches tend to be based on an analysis of the socio-political *effects* of economic structure and therefore do not adequately deal with the relationship between structure and agency. In this sense, most are reductionist like the liberal approach. This is not surprising; Marx regarded his work as a critique of the classical liberal political economists, and thus he focused on a similar set of intellectual problems. Politics in the domestic and international domains tends to be reduced to a function of the capitalist production structure and the division of society into classes, which is in turn a result of the individual's relationship to the means of production.[45] Yet the theories are weak on explaining just how this relationship between political power and economic structure is articulated; 'there is an essential, missing ingredient—a theory of how structures themselves originate, change, work, and reproduce themselves.'[46] Once again, what is needed is a theory of politics in the wider sense of the word.

Antonio Gramsci, the Italian Marxist of the interwar period, attempted to develop a more agent-centric and therefore political explanation of the relationship between economic structure and political processes at domestic and international levels of analysis. He sought to explain the relative durability and legitimacy of the capitalist system, despite its clear inequalities and historical tendency to periodic major crises such as the 1930s Depression. How could such a system be simultaneously oppressive and unstable on the one hand, yet enduring and resilient on the other? Surely it must satisfy enough of the people enough of the time. Gramsci postulated that the political dynamics of the state were important: to be sure, class domination existed, but it was a series of complex political compromises between capitalists, workers, small landholders, and so on. These political compromises at the heart of the state are what rendered the market and capitalist system of production essentially legitimate instruments of governance. In this sense he sought to avoid the problem of economic reductionism and to resolve in important ways the structure-agent problem.

The pioneering Robert Cox sought to project this basic model into theories of the international system.[47] Cox also followed Gramsci by emphasizing the power of ideas and knowledge structures and the ways in which they emerged from the material interests of different constituent elements of the capitalist system. Control over ideas is central to legitimizing and maintaining the fundamentally conflictual socio-economic structures of global capitalism. In this way Cox and other *neo-Gramscian* scholars sought to avoid the problem of economic reductionism referred to above, drawing on Gramsci himself as well as Karl Polanyi, Fernand Braudel,[48] and other social theorists, and in the process overcame many of the limitations of liberalism, Marxism, and realism. Thus the radical tradition was adapted to deal better with the structure-agent problem and to understand better the role of the state as political forum and agent in the *structuration* of global economic order. The neo-Gramscian approach provides a flexible analytical tool of considerable promise for our understanding of international political economy across levels of analysis. Patterns of global order are directly related to the balance of social forces of the system, particularly those in the dominant states. While the traditional Marxist preoccupation with class conflict may be overemphasized in the work of many neo-Gramscian scholars, the approach also permits a focus on the fragmented and often conflictual relationships *within* the capitalist or business class itself, which are so crucial to the nature of global economic order. Indeed if Marx was correct and capitalist producers do have overwhelming structural power in the establishment of the socio-political order, then it is not surprising that the role of the corporate sector is central to the policies of states and of global economic regimes in trade, finance, environment, development, and the like.

Towards a Theory of IPE

This review of the theoretical literature has been necessarily brief, leaving out many of the subtleties and much of the variety of all the approaches covered. It has also neglected the growing literature on feminist approaches, environmentalist approaches, and the postmodern theorists who have built on the work of the French historian Michel Foucault, among others. The final task is to build on this necessarily incomplete discussion and to lay down the building blocks of a successful approach to understanding the discipline of international political economy. The aim is to highlight the factors that need to be considered by theorists if a successful approach to the discipline is to emerge. Certainly one would not wish to rule out the possibilities for cross-fertilization offered by the various perspectives put forward by the contributors to this book. So far, this introduction has necessarily been more concerned with critique (what *not* to do in IPE theory) than with advancing a coherent alternative. What follows is an attempt to draw out the implications of the critique, with a view to allowing contributors to the work at hand to address these points in their own individual ways and in relation to their particular topics.

The three interrelated theoretical problems we have highlighted in IPE are, first, the relationship of the economic and political domains—in a contemporary context, this means politics and markets. Second, the levels of analysis problem must be addressed: how do the politics and economic structures of the domestic and international domains relate to each other? Third, implied by the second, there is the problem of the state: what is it, what is its role, and how is it situated in relation to domestic and international levels of analysis?[49] In turn, these three points imply the importance of what has been identified as the structure-agent problem, and the question of actors: what kinds of actors and what relationships among them need to be accounted for in our conceptual framework for understanding IPE.

Of these theoretical questions or problems, the problem of the state ties them all together: the socio-economic tensions of changing global capitalism highlight the role of state policy-making processes as the site of struggles for influence within advanced capitalist society. The state emerges as the political focus for the process of adjustment and change. In short, the politics of the state mediates between the economic and political domains, among different types of actors, and between the domestic and international levels of analysis, and contains the key to understanding structure and agency. Understanding the state—what it is, what it does, and where it fits in Cox's state-society complex—is in a way *the* problem of international political economy.

Most of the theories of international politics and political economy we have reviewed above suffer from one or both of the following difficulties: 'either they derive the state itself—its structure and autonomous character—from other social structures [the economy, the anarchic structure of the international system]; or they tend to reify the state, virtually personifying it, by giving it the character of a conscious, rational agent.'[50] They do not see the politics of societies, economies, and, indeed, the international system as coming together in the processes constituted by the integrated state-market itself.

So how do we make sense of the state, and thereby of the levels of analysis problem, the relationship of politics to markets, and the structure-agent problem? We need a link between the state, economic structure, and broader notions of politics. That link is the perceived *self-interest of agents or actors*, whether individuals, formal or informal groups, the corporate economic entities known as firms, or states. The relationship between individual self-interest and the collective needs of the community is precisely the philosophical problem that inspired Adam Smith to write the classic text in political economy, *Inquiry into the Nature and Causes of the Wealth of Nations*, published in 1776.[51] We must begin developing an understanding of the 'state-society complex', the integrated state-market package that comprises the international political economy, by analyzing the structure of economic relations (production and the market) as it becomes increasingly transnationalized. Part of this analysis involves recognizing how economic structure constrains yet is part of the broader politics of distributional and other conflicts. In doing so, we see the material self-interest of political economic agents, and of key social groups, at domestic and international levels of analysis. In turn, we must analyze the effects this transnationalization of structure has on the perceived interests of actors. The state and the social institutions of the market in which it is embedded[52] together constitute the governance of global society.

In this sense, and despite criticisms above of 'structuralism' in international relations theory, structure *is* part of a successful theory of international political economy. It is what one means by 'structure' in the first place,[53] and how one employs structure in a theory, that is important. Structure is not a causal variable—in and of itself it does not explain outcomes. Structure *does* inform one of the terms under which the political interactions of particular agents or groups occur at a particular time in history.

It is worth taking a moment to focus on the structure-agent problem in brief. We should remind ourselves that the distinction between structure and agents (either individual or collective/institutional) is essentially abstract and therefore artificial in the first place. It may be perfectly useful in helping us to conceive of the relationship of individual agents to the wider whole around them, but it remains artificial: structure and agency

are not different things at all; each makes little sense without the other when we consider concrete reality around us. The individual (or institutional) actor-as-agent no more exists in isolation from its socially constructed reality than structure can emerge and develop without agency. By the same token, structures make little sense in historical analysis unless they are conceived as dynamic. Structure is conceived as a *process*, set in motion by agents, whether individual or collective actors (such as the state), over time. The conflicts of interest among agents in a particular structural setting give structure its real, dynamic qualities. Self-interest, constrained by the peculiarities of historically contingent structure, provides the motive (including normative bases) for agency to move from the potential to the actual and explains how structure-as-process is in a constant state of flux. The nature of the structure—and the differential power, costs, and/or benefits it confers on those in contrasting structural positions—is the constant subject of dispute among agents interacting in the context of the institutions of governance (formal and informal) of the international political economy, most importantly the state. In this sense we can view the ongoing process of globalization as a structural change: (1) generated by the agency of ongoing conflicts of perceived self-interest among social forces through the practices of individual agents; (2) generated by the agency of firms as bearers of competitive relations in the contingent structures of the market; (3) and generated in the institutionalized context of the policy process of states and regimes, in which the agency of firms and social forces are expressed in the practices of individuals and are engaged as constituent interests. The state-market condominium emerges as an integrated but evolving mechanism of governance with institutional nodal points or sites for the process of structural change.

The self-interest of agents will be reflected in their policy preferences as a function of their place in a particular structure. Indeed, different economic sectors with contrasting economic structures and dynamics will require specific analysis.[54] A number of different strategies may be open to any one set of actors, but it is not difficult to understand that a national industrial sector with structural features such as relatively small, uncompetitive firms and little integration into the international economy (in other words, essentially dependent on domestic markets and domestically based production units) will have different preferences from a sector dominated by firms with multinational production strategies heavily dependent on international trade for profitability. The former might prefer the protection of national authorities; the latter is likely to prefer more liberal international economic regimes so as freely to move goods and capital from one national economy to another.[55] Thus, one set of domestic-international linkages consists of the ties between respective actors in national economies and transnational markets, or the lack thereof.

Next, we must understand how these material economic interests, expressed as policy preferences and representing a diverse range of state and non-state actors, are articulated politically within the political institutions of the global system. By institutions we mean essentially the state, but also intergovernmental bargaining and international institutionalized behaviour (regimes) in a setting characterized by anarchy through which the politics of the state is projected into the international domain. Political articulation, or how interests are organized and institutionalized, is the link between economic structure and the politics (agency) of the state and political economy (both domestic and international domains).

The questions are: How unified are these coalitions of interests? How well can they assert themselves? What kind of political resources do they have, given the pattern of state and international institutions and economic structures that act as constraints and opportunities for the agents involved? 'These sets of constraints and opportunities in effect form structured fields of action upon and within which agents make choices.'[56] It makes a difference whether a particular coalition of interests, with a given set of policy preferences, enjoys not just market but also political power within the state. Unless they have sufficient institutionalized political resources, they are unlikely to have much impact on state policy. Institutions do load the

dice; groups that are economically powerful but divided internally may prove impotent.

By the same token, a coalition or group that is powerful within a particular state, but a state with little ability to project its choices into the processes of intergovernmental bargaining and regime formation, will have little impact outside its domestic setting. As the economic structure or market becomes increasingly transnationalized, these coalitions of interests within relatively impotent states may find their choices severely constrained (unless, of course, they have a strong competitive position in the market itself). They often have a lot to lose and may initiate successful state strategies to adjust to the new structural parameters, or they may find themselves facing economic and political decline or elimination. This is a problem not just for groups of economic interests but also for the state, which is accountable to these political constituencies. In today's increasingly global economy, one can perceive a growing tension between the domestic economic constituencies on which the state is ultimately dependent for its power and legitimacy, and the increasingly transnational nature of the economy and economic problems facing governments. The transnationalization of economic structures has reduced the economic space controlled by the state and intensified the competition its domestic economic constituency has to bear. This is the crux of the management problems of the contemporary international political economy. It implies a pressing need for co-operative management structures in the anarchic international setting, but the political constituencies and institutions of such co-operation are relatively underdeveloped. Once again the state emerges as the crucial nodal point for political conflict over structure and institutions.

By the same token, the transnationalization of economic structure has not taken place in a political vacuum. This will be emphasized by a considerable number of contributions in this volume. The interests of firms with multinational production strategies and access to international capital markets have found expression in the policies of, in particular, the United States (see Chapter 12 by Sell). This provides some insight into the real underpinnings and impact of American 'hegemony': the interests of transnational capital have been best articulated politically within the US state. They have pressed, whenever the opportunity presented itself, for more market-oriented international economic regimes, often overcoming stiff domestic and international opposition. The structural changes that intergovernmental negotiations have produced in money, finance, and trade in the postwar period furnish much of the substance of the contributions to this volume. The point here is to emphasize the two-way relationship between the domestic and international domains and between markets and politics. The political choices of important actors or groups, well placed politically within the more powerful states of the international system, are projected into the international domain. This leads to a restructuring of the market and institutions of international economic management, and in turn feeds back into the domestic politics of countries in the system. In this way, liberalization and 'marketization' intensify the competitive pressures on domestic firms, which use their political resources to press for policies that will manage the new situation. Whether the political strategies they choose to manage economic change are successful or not remains an open question.

One final point is worth restating. The role of politics (agency), as opposed to structure, as a determinant of outcome has constantly been emphasized. This holds whether we refer to the economic structure of markets and production, as stressed by liberals and Marxists, or the structural features of the competitive system of states (the institutional setting of anarchy), as emphasized by the neo-realists. This point highlights the role of process variables over structural variables in IPE theory. Politics constitutes a two-way relationship between structure and agents in a particular institutional setting. Politics shapes structure at the same time as structure shapes and constrains the options of political actors pursuing their preferences. The politics of the state is the principal linkage between the domestic and international levels of analysis. 'The impact of structure lies not in some inherent, self-contained quality, but in the way a given structure at specific historical moments helps one set of opinions prevail over another.'[57] It is not structure in and of itself that is important but the politics that takes place within it. The changing structure of the international economy and the regimes/institutional patterns that mediate it are shaped by the political conflicts occurring at domestic, transnational, and international levels of analysis, and vice versa.[58] There is a two-way relationship between structure and process, domestic and international, mediated by changing institutional patterns.

The exercise of power in the international political economy therefore takes place in a setting characterized by the complex interdependence among states, their societies, and economic structures at domestic and international levels of analysis. This occurs largely through an integrated system of governance operating simultaneously through the mechanisms of the market and the multiple sovereignties of a system of competitive states. Interdependence, as well as anarchy, is an integral part of the international environment within which states attempt to promote their 'sovereign' interests and those of their domestic constituencies: 'Viewing the international system as a web of interdependencies necessitates a focus on the linkages among actors'[59] and political interaction is the substance of these linkages. The outcome is determined by the complex interaction of systemic and domestic structural and process variables. We live in a system of multiple state sovereignties 'which is interdependent in its structure and dynamics' with the transnational market economy, 'but not reducible to it'.[60]

Notes

1. I wish to acknowledge with gratitude those who have contributed many helpful comments on earlier drafts and other works that became part of this Introduction: Brian Burgoon, Barry Buzan, Philip G. Cerny, Jerry Cohen, Daniel Drache, Stephen Gill, Eric Helleiner, Richard Higgott, Helen Milner, Tony Porter, Susan Sell, the late Susan Strange, my co-editor, Richard Stubbs, and the many students over the years with whom I have developed these ideas. Of course, I alone am responsible for any failings or shortcomings.

2. Jacob Viner, 'Power versus Plenty as Objectives of Foreign Policy in the Seventeenth and Eighteenth Centuries', *World Politics* 1, 1 (1948–9): 10.

3. Karl Polanyi made this distinction particularly clear in his classic work, *The Great Transformation* (Boston: Beacon Press, 1944).

4. See Herman Schwartz, *States versus Markets: History, Geography, and the Development of the International Political Economy*, 2nd edn (London: Macmillan, 2000), esp. chs 1–2.

5. Fernand Braudel, followed by Immanuel Wallerstein, would dispute this understanding of the emergence of the market economy. Both see the capitalist 'world-economy' as emerging in Europe during the 'long' sixteenth century. See, for example, Immanuel Wallerstein, *The Modern World System: Capitalist Agriculture and the Origins of the European World-Economy in the 16th Century* (New York: Academic Press, 1974). However, their conception of capitalism appears to be based on the notion of market exchange and division of labour as opposed to the system of industrial production based on capital investment that emerged with the Industrial Revolution.

6. Polanyi, *The Great Transformation*.

7. Ibid, 57.

8. *International* denotes relations among states as units; *transnational* implies a more complex pattern of relationships across borders involving the interpenetration of economies and societies, which is not necessarily limited to state-to-state

relations in the formal sense of the term.

9. Susan Strange, *The Retreat of the State: The Diffusion of Power in the World Economy* (Cambridge: Cambridge University Press, 1996).

10. See chapters by Waltz (excerpts from Kenneth Waltz, *Theory of International Politics* [Reading, Mass.: Addison-Wesley, 1979]), in Robert O. Keohane, ed., *Neorealism and Its Critics* (New York: Columbia University Press, 1986), esp. ch. 4, 'Political Structures', 81-97.

11. Robert Cox, 'Social Forces, States, and World Orders: Beyond International Relations Theory', ibid., 205.

12. See Richard Higgott, Geoffrey R.D. Underhill, and Andreas Bieler, eds, *Non-State Actors and Authority in the Global System* (London: Routledge, 2000).

13. John Gerard Ruggie, 'International Regimes, Transactions, and Change: Embedded Liberalism in the Postwar Economic Order', in Stephen D. Krasner, ed., *International Regimes* (Ithaca, NY: Cornell University Press, 1983), 198.

14. Robert Gilpin, *The Political Economy of International Relations* (Princeton, NJ: Princeton University Press, 1987), 11; Immanuel Wallerstein, *The Capitalist World-Economy* (Cambridge: Cambridge University Press/Maison des Sciences de l'Homme, 1979), 273.

15. See Richard Devetak, 'Postmodernism', in Scott Burchill and Andrew Linklater, eds, *Theories of International Relations* (London: Macmillan, 1996), 179–209.

16. Cox, 'Social Forces, States, and World Orders', 207; emphasis in original.

17. Ibid., 205.

18. Robert O. Keohane and Joseph Nye, *Power and Interdependence: World Politics in Transition* (Boston: Little, Brown, 1977); Helen Milner, 'The Assumption of Anarchy in International Relations Theory: A Critique', *Review of International Studies* 17, 1 (Jan. 1991): 67–85; Geoffrey R.D. Underhill, 'Industrial Crisis and International Regimes: France, the EEC, and

International Trade in Textiles 1974–1984', *Millennium: Journal of International Studies* 19, 2 (Summer 1990): 185–206.

19. See Keohane and Nye, *Power and Interdependence*, 8–11.

20. This is akin to the concept of 'strategic interdependence' developed by Schelling. See Milner, 'The Assumption of Anarchy'.

21. See Higgott et al., eds, *Non-State Actors*.

22. It depends, of course, on how one conceives of structure. Some see it primarily as a pattern of relationships that *structure* the overall system, and this is roughly the definition adopted here. Others, for example Robert Cox and Fernand Braudel, see structure as a more holistic concept, or *historical structure*, the totality of social, economic, and political relationships and processes in particular historical circumstances.

23. See Peter Gourevitch, 'The Second Image Reversed: The International Sources of Domestic Politics', *International Organization* 32, 4 (Autumn 1978): esp. 900–7.

24. Robert Cox paraphrasing Antonio Gramsci in 'Gramsci, Hegemony, and International Relations: An Essay in Method', *Millennium: Journal of International Studies* 12, 2 (1983): 162.

25. Waltz, *Theory of International Politics*.

26. See Klaus Knorr, 'Economic Interdependence and National Security', in Knorr and Frank N. Trager, eds, *Economic Issues and National Security* (Lawrence: University Press of Kansas, Regent's Press/National Security Education Program, 1977), 1–18; also Barry Buzan, *People, States and Fear*, 2nd edn (Boulder, Colo.: Lynne Rienner, 1991), ch. 6.

27. Hans J. Morgenthau, *Politics among Nations: The Struggle for Power and Peace* (New York: Alfred A. Knopf, 1956), 10–11. Not all traditional realists put forward as narrow a view of politics as Morgenthau in this passage. E.H. Carr, *The Twenty Years' Crisis 1919–1939: An Introduction to the Study of International Relations* (London: Macmillan, 1939), has a view of international politics that includes economic issues as relevant to political interaction in the international domain. The classical realist tradition of the Greek Thucydides, the Italian Renaissance writer Machiavelli, and the French Enlightenment philosopher Jean-Jacques Rousseau offers rich perspectives for the study of politics at the international and domestic levels of analysis.

28. For a recent analysis of the work of E.H. Carr, see Charles Jones, *E.H. Carr and International Relations: A Duty to Lie* (Cambridge: Cambridge University Press, 1998).

29. Graham Allison, *Essence of Decision* (Boston: Little, Brown, 1971), called even this into question through his analysis of decision-making in the 1962 Cuban Missile Crisis.

30. Unless more elaborate concepts such as 'economic security' are elaborated; see B. Buzan, O. Waever, and J. de Wilde, *Security: A New Framework for Analysis* (Boulder, Colo.: Lynne Rienner, 1997); and Buzan, *People, States, and Fear*, ch. 6.

31. Perhaps the clearest explanation of the theory of hegemonic stability can be found in Robert Gilpin, *Global Political Economy: Understanding the International Economic Order* (Princeton, NJ: Princeton University Press, 2001). For a critique, see, among others, Isabelle Grunberg, 'Exploring the "Myth" of Hegemonic Stability', *International Organization* 44, 4 (Autumn 1990): 431–77; Underhill, 'Industrial Crisis and International Regimes', 186–92.

32. Charles Kindleberger, *The World in Depression 1929–39* (Berkeley: University of California Press, 1973).

33. 'International regimes' is a term that refers to the formal and informal aspects of institutionalized co-operation and conflict in international politics. For the classic definition, see Stephen D. Krasner, 'Structural Causes and Regime Consequences: Regimes as Intervening Variables', in Krasner, ed., *International Regimes*, 2. In IPE, we are largely concerned with international economic regimes.

34. While the theory of hegemonic stability does have a distinctively realist flavour about it, this emphasis on a unipolar order contradicts the insistence by many traditional realists on the need for a *balance* of power to maintain a stable

order in the international system.

35. The following account of the principal features of liberal political theory in international relations is drawn from Mark Zacher and Richard Mathew, 'Liberal International Theory: Common Threads, Divergent Strands', in Charles Kegley, ed., *Realism and the Neoliberal Challenge: Controversies in International Relations Theory* (New York: St Martin's Press, 1994). See also the account of the emergence of classical and radical political economy in Chapter 1 of this volume.

36. Ibid., 2–3.

37. In important respects the liberal approach does not as such constitute an *explanation* of the international system, of 'why it is the way it is'. Liberalism's explanatory tools cannot be separated from its normative and strongly prescriptive principles. The differing conceptions of 'progress' promoted by liberals are bound to be socially embedded in the sense that they are likely to be perceived as more advantageous to the material interests of some social groups/individuals as opposed to others. The ideas of political liberalism are generally associated, for example, with the historical emergence of merchant classes and industrial capital in modern Europe, and have undergone changes with the subsequent emergence of liberal democracies.

38. See Chapter 1 concerning the emergence of the neo-classical approach to economics.

39. Robert Gilpin put this quite candidly in *The Political Economy of International Relations*, 25.

40. Polanyi, *The Great Transformation*.

41. In other words, the derivation of causes from a definition or description of the effects, and vice versa: the structure of comparative advantage cannot be explained through an analysis of the division of labour because the one derives from the other by definition.

42. I refer once again to the discussion of the role of structure and political process by Gourevitch, 'The Second Image Reversed', 900–7. See also Philip G. Cerny, *The Changing Architecture of Politics: Structure, Agency, and the Future of the State* (London: Sage, 1990), esp. 'Epilogue'.

43. This is discussed at greater length in Chapter 1.

44. Johann Galtung, 'A Structural Theory of Imperialism', *International Journal of Peace Research* 8 (1971): 81–118.

45. Marx himself was ambivalent on this issue and there are two strains 'at war' in his work. One is his analysis of the laws of capitalist economic development by focusing on the structural contradictions or tensions of the system and its inherently unstable nature, an approach that risks reducing social and political phenomena to effects of structure. The second is his close attention to the historical political and social conflicts, dominated by class struggle, which led to the emergence and development of capitalism over time, thus emphasizing the role of agency in structural change.

46. Cerny, *The Changing Architecture of Politics*, 15.

47. For a collection of Cox's work, see R. Cox, with T. Sinclair, *Approaches to World Order* (Cambridge: Cambridge University Press, 1996).

48. Polanyi, *The Great Transformation*; Fernand Braudel, *Capitalism and Material Life* (London: Weidenfield and Nicolson, 1973); Braudel, *The Wheels of Commerce* (London: Collins, 1982). The neo-Gramscian approach, or *transnational historical materialism*, is developed more systematically elsewhere. See Robert Cox, *Production, Power, and World Order* (New York: Columbia University Press, 1987); Stephen Gill, ed., *Gramsci, Historical Materialism, and International Relations* (Cambridge: Cambridge University Press, 1993).

49. For a comprehensive attempt to deal with these problems in a contemporary context, especially the problem of the state, see Cerny, *The Changing Architecture of Politics*.

50. Ibid., 12.

51. This point is argued cogently by Claudio Napoleoni in *Smith, Ricardo, Marx: Observations on the History of Economic Thought* (Oxford: Basil Blackwell, 1975), particularly 25–31.

52. See John Lie, 'Embedding Polanyi's Market Society', *Sociological Perspectives* 34, 2 (1991): 219–35.

53. For example, the distinction between economic structure in the Marxist or liberal sense of the

term, as opposed to political structure in the neo-realist literature. See note 22 above.

54. The value of a sectoral approach was highlighted by Susan Strange in 'The Study of Transnational Relations', *International Affairs* 52, 3 (July 1976): 341–5, and re-emphasized by Helen Milner, *Resisting Protectionism: Global Industries and the Politics of International Trade* (Princeton, NJ: Princeton University Press, 1988), esp. 14–17, and by Underhill, 'Industrial Crisis and International Regimes', 188–92.

55. Of course, the preferences of governments are an important variable here. State authorities might be powerful enough to impose preferences and strategies on actors or groups of actors, or at least to constrain sharply the options of some over others.

56. Cerny, *The Changing Architecture of Politics*, 233.

57. Gourevitch, 'The Second Image Reversed', 904.

58. This notion that theory must account for the ways in which structures themselves are pro-duced and transformed is akin to Giddens's notion of structure as process or *structuration*. See Anthony Giddens, *Central Problems of Social Theory: Action, Structure, and Contradiction in Social Analysis* (London: Macmillan, 1979). These points were raised comprehensively by Cerny, *Changing Architecture*, and have been adopted to an extent by the constructivist variant of international theory. See Alexander Wendt, 'The Agent-Structure Problem in International Relations Theory', *International Organization* 41, 3 (Summer 1987): 355–70.

59. Milner, 'The Assumption of Anarchy', 84; in this article Milner deals particularly well with the issue of anarchy and interdependence.

60. Theda Skocpol and Ellen Kay Trimberger, 'Revolutions and the World-Historical Development of Capitalism', in Barbara Hockey Kaplan, ed., *Social Change in the Capitalist World Economy* (London: Sage, 1978), 132.

Suggested Readings

Burchill, Scott, and Andrew Linklater, eds. *Theories of International Relations*. London: Macmillan, 1996.

Buzan, Barry, O. Waever, and J. de Wilde. *Security: A New Framework for Analysis*. Boulder, Colo.: Lynne Rienner, 1997.

Carr, Edward Hallet. *The Twenty Years' Crisis 1919–1939: An Introduction to the Study of International Relations*. London: Macmillan, 1939.

Cerny, Philip G. *The Changing Architecture of Politics: Structure, Agency and the Future of the State*. London: Sage, 1990.

Cox, Robert. *Production, Power, and World Order*. New York: Columbia University Press, 1987.

———. with T. Sinclair. *Approaches to World Order*. Cambridge: Cambridge University Press, 1996.

Gill, Stephen, ed. *Gramsci, Historical Materialism, and International Relations*. Cambridge: Cambridge University Press, 1993.

Morgenthau, Hans J. *Politics among Nations: The Struggle for Power and Peace*. New York: Alfred A. Knopf, 1956.

Polanyi, Karl. *The Great Transformation*. Boston: Beacon Press, 1944.

Rosenau, James N., and Ernst-Otto Czempiel, eds. *Governance without Government: Order and Change in World Politics*. Cambridge: Cambridge University Press, 1992.

Schwartz, Herman M. *States versus Markets: The Emergence of a Global Economy*, 2nd edn. London: Macmillan/Palgrave, 2000.

Strange, Susan. *States and Markets*, 2nd edn. Oxford: Basil Blackwell, 1994.

———. *The Retreat of the State*. Cambridge: Cambridge University Press, 1996.

Underhill, Geoffrey R.D. *Industrial Crisis and the Open Economy*. London: Macmillan, 1998.

Chapter 1

Political Economy
The Revival of an 'Interdiscipline'

Michael R. Krätke and Geoffrey R.D. Underhill

Political Economy: What's in a Name?

Political economy is a venerable intellectual tradition that has undergone a recent revival. It was the name given to a version of social science prevailing in Europe until late in the nineteenth century, closely linked to its progenitor, moral (meaning social and political) philosophy. Its roots lie deep in the liberal Enlightenment that emerged across Europe in the seventeenth and eighteenth centuries, but it was given particular vigour through such figures of the 'Scottish Enlightenment' as David Hume, James Steuart, and Adam Smith in the latter half of the eighteenth century.

In the 1870s, political economy informed every budding civil servant or member of the political and economic elites how to run the affairs of state. The social movements of the French Revolution and in Britain during the 1820s brought forth a wave of radical or 'popular' political economy upon which Marx built his 'critique', challenging the very bases of modern civil society (private property, capital, market exchange, money). Legislation in Britain and elsewhere was subject to heated debates (the 'general glut' debate concerning the possibility of general crisis; the banking-currency school controversy about the nature of money and credit; the debate on free trade; the debate on the freedom of the labour 'market'). All were fought in public as well as in academic publications, and because many of the leading political economists were politicians as well (famously, the free-trade advocate David Ricardo), there was no clear-cut divide between 'academic' and 'political' debates.

Drawing attention to the potential social conflicts that would result from underlying socio-economic relationships dividing society into classes, political economy was designated the 'dismal science'. Long before Marx, political economists were accused of inciting class struggle. From the 1870s on, several political economists provided the core of what was to become—and was immediately proclaimed as—a 'pure theory' of political economy comparable to a social physics or mechanics, focusing on the analysis of market exchange under the hypothetical conditions of 'absolute [perfect] competition'. The idea was to develop a more optimistic and 'pure' science of economics free of its roots in social and political analysis. This emergence of modern 'neo-classical' economics as orthodoxy marked a divide between analysis of (conflictual) political and social relationships, on the one hand, and the analysis of (harmonious) market exchange, on the other, but true political economists rebelled against this division in a series of revivals in the twentieth century, preferring to see the patterns of market exchange as an integral part of broader social and political phenomena.

At the same time, the analytical techniques of 'utilitarian calculus' and marginal utility theory based on the utility or 'pleasure'-maximizing behaviour of self-interested 'rational economic man', which came to be employed in economic 'science', have also heavily influenced the emergence of other social sciences, especially sociology, political science, and international relations. The so-called 'rational choice' approach is very much an offspring of neo-classical economics, analyzing politics and political interactions as 'markets'. These approaches are at odds with broader institutional or historically based approaches to these disciplines, which maintain their (often tenuous) links with classical political economy. However, given that political economy was itself a compromise between these various modes of analysis, there is no reason why they cannot complement each other if the intention to do so is present.

On the other hand, political economy is back in economics as well. Since the 1970s there is an ongoing revolt uniting all sorts of dissidents—Keynesians, institutionalists, Marxists, Ricardians—against the mainstream. History, evolution, time, space, and various social relationships in economic theorizing have returned to the agenda of critical economists, symbolized by the student protests in 2000 against the 'autism' of established neo-classical economics.[1]

Political economy today has come to have at least four meanings, and students should be careful to identify the version with which they are dealing because mainstream economists, critical economists, and political scientists mean quite different things when they use the same term 'political economy'. First, many economists still use the term to denote the study of economic policy issues *within* economics. Political economy in this sense is the application of neo-classical analysis to specific policy issues, wherein analysts attempt to identify optimal policy solutions for key variables such as inflation or unemployment. Second, what is called the 'economic theory of politics' is little more than the strict application of the concepts and analytical methods of neo-classical economics to the realm of political interactions and bargaining, which are consequently transformed into something looking very much like a 'market'. Neo-classical techniques are employed to determine how policy decisions are taken, given stylized conflicts among identifiable actors. Third, the name 'political economy' is used as a rallying cry by heterodox economists, indicating a more or less radical critique of the allegedly 'unpolitical' mainstream economics. Various strands of heterodox economics may be lumped together under this heading, including post-Keynesian, neo-Ricardian, Marxian and neo-

Marxian, Austrian school (von Hayek), and institutionalist and neo-institutionalist traditions. More specifically, the term 'political economy' is in use to denote 'radical economics', a potential amalgam of Marxian economics plus some feminism, ecology, or postmodernism. Finally, political economy indicates the recent rediscovery by political scientists of the importance of economic issues and, in particular, of the political nature allegedly of 'economic' facts, structures, and processes. This has led to a series of efforts to reoccupy what was once a no-man's land between the realms of economics and political science. In this respect, the term also indicates the revivalist move *across* disciplinary boundaries—and the venture into a new 'inter-discipline'—which is the subject of this chapter.

This chapter will develop several central points concerning political economy and its revival. It will begin by reviewing the origins of political economy in the 'classical' period of the Enlightenment, then follow the progress of the debate through the emergence of radical or 'critical' political economy and the eventual emergence of the separate disciplines of economics and political science/international relations. The chapter will then turn to the contemporary revival of political economy as a study with domestic (comparative) and international aspects focused on the relationship of national political economies to the very political process of global economic integration. The chapter will conclude by examining the crucial question of the relationship between political authority and markets, and how the political institutions of the state are embedded in the market as a thoroughly social phenomenon.

The overall argument of the chapter is that political economy should remain in touch with its classical and radical roots. Successful approaches to political economy do not embrace a series of 'sub-fields' but rather constitute an inter-discipline, however difficult a project that might be. As emphasized in the Introduction to this volume, political economy consists of analyzing a set of socio-political relationships that can be summarized as follows: (1) there is a systematic and reciprocal relationship between the political and economic domains; (2) as the ways in which societies produce and distribute their means of subsistence and surpluses changes, so the nature and structure of the societies themselves will evolve over time; (3) there is a dynamic and systematic relationship between the changing structures of production and exchange, on the one hand, and the forms that political authority and governance will take over time, on the other. Therefore the political institutions we call states are embedded in the social relationships around which production and exchange are organized, and the state and the market, as in the classical period, should be conceptualized as forming a single, integrated ensemble of governance.

The Life and Times of Classical and Radical Political Economy

Political economy preceded the social sciences as we know them today. When it emerged in the seventeenth century, social science research had to be disentangled from philosophical and, especially, pre-scientific theological thinking. Political economy was both a science and a practice based on a new sort of knowledge and inquiry, but it lacked all the features of the 'disciplinary' social sciences we know today. To this pre-disciplinary stage we nonetheless owe a number of innovations crucial to contemporary social science, such as statistics ('Political Arithmetick') or the invention of macroeconomic models depicting the interdependencies among producers, workers, taxation, and demand and supply, beginning with the 'Tableaux économiques' of the French physiocrats in the eighteenth century. Last and certainly not least, the classical political economists were the first to envisage 'economic laws' or dynamics and a long-run evolution of human societies during which the basic features of economic, social, and political life changed in relation to each other.

Classical political economy was also very political from its beginnings. Building on Aristotle and the Greek philosophers, classical political economists initially thought in terms of 'art'—the art of running a large (family) household or estate, and

the various rights and obligations within/between a family and its (bonded) labourers. Political economy, as the classics conceived it, also had to deal with a series of *new* phenomena—the rise of the modern state, the development of 'national economies', and the rapid expansion of a world economy that had not previously existed. The preeminent scholars of classical political economy—from William Petty at the end of the seventeenth century to Karl Marx in the second half of the nineteenth century—were well aware of the radical changes in the economy and society of their own time. The medieval world had come to an end and there were commercial, financial, and industrial revolutions of an unforeseen scale and scope.

Political economists therefore variously investigated, propagated, and criticized the new social and economic order of modern (mercantile and later industrial) capitalism as it emerged. Its virtues and associated ideas of political and economic freedoms had to be propagated and defended against the prevailing ideas of the *ancien régime* and absolute monarchy, and its prerequisites had to be created. These consisted of private property rights for all (not just for the landowning Church, aristocracy, or monarch), including the patents associated with intellectual property rights; market systems as opposed to religious or monarchical edict; national and international monetary systems directed to the needs of commerce; a credit and banking system free of religious restraints on 'usury'; and new forms of private enterprise, e.g., 'limited liability' and joint-stock ownership. All had to be constructed, institutionalized, and enforced together with the basic institutions of the modern state that associated itself with emerging capitalism through new forms of taxation, public money, and, not least, the public debt. Deeply involved as they were in this historical process of transition towards modern capitalism, classical political economists shared an overtly political conception of their science.

The movement may be regarded as beginning with the mid-eighteenth-century physiocrats in France, including Antoine Mirabeau and their inspiration, François Quesnay.[2] They regarded agricultural *production* (as opposed to commercial *transactions*) and the land as the foundation of value creation. Production was in turn tied to a series of interdependent relationships in society: they were the first to see a political economy as a circular flow of production, employment, and consumption oiled by money as a medium, with manufactures and luxury goods as incidental 'sterile' extras. Interdependence in economic terms meant social and political interdependence, though not necessarily on equal terms. This idea of circular flow governed by a series of natural laws (the *Tableaux économiques*) remains central to all contemporary economic thought, although industry and service production have long supplanted agriculture in theory and practice as the focus of analysis. The physiocrats also gave birth to the idea that the best prices were likely to emerge if individuals were allowed to compete freely, revealing a self-regulating natural order.

The central place of manufactures and commerce in the political economy was a crucial development of later political economists, particularly those of the Scottish Enlightenment. James Steuart maintained the ancient notion of 'oeconomy' as the 'art of providing for all the wants of a family, with prudence and frugality', and asserted the analogy—'what oeconomy is in a family, political oeconomy is in a state'—and thus distinguished the private from the 'publick'.[3] David Hume made a central contribution concerning the role of money in the circular economic flow of commerce and price levels (the quantity theory of money), and its international payments dimensions (the price-specie flow mechanism of the gold standard), both central planks in our understanding of the relationship between prices, money, and (domestic/international) economic activity.[4]

Adam Smith, just a few years later, saw it as 'a branch of the science of a statesman or legislator'—the science that should teach how to enlarge the 'wealth of nations' and how 'to enrich both the people and the sovereign'.[5] Smith deserves further mention as the key figure in the movement, recognized as such by Hume in his praiseworthy preface to *Wealth of Nations* (1776). Smith's seminal contribution was in understanding that the sophisticated

development of the division of labour in industry lay at the root of greater economic efficiency and, therefore, greater levels of wealth and prosperity for all.[6] High levels of specialization could increase productivity and the surpluses a society could produce—thus disputing the physiocrats' claim concerning agriculture in political economy and implying that a deep, mature economy based on highly developed manufactures and elaborate commercial interaction was to be encouraged.

Furthermore, Smith developed a number of important arguments in favour of enforcing market mechanisms as promoting a better pattern of distribution and greater levels of wealth than the seventeenth- and eighteenth-century mercantilist system dominated by monarch, Church, and state-sponsored merchant oligopoly. Deliberate changes in the functioning and structures of economic interdependencies presaged more harmonious social and political relationships and greater benefits for all, employing human greed as a route to collective improvement. As he famously argued, we do not owe our good meals to the charity of the butcher, but to his desire for self-enrichment.[7] As individuals pursue their own best interests motivated by greed, they unwittingly realize an important public good—a more productive society with a broader division of labour and more for all. In this way he argued against the restrictive practices in the labour market of the craft guilds, who (often through inherited membership) controlled for their members' benefit the quantity and price of labour in crucial activities, and the prerogatives of royal and other commercial monopolies set by political fiat, which institutionalized the privileges of the powerful and impaired adjustment to economic change. Competition would lower prices and free resources for investment.

Furthermore, he was underpinning some of the crucial liberal Enlightenment arguments about personal *political* freedoms. Freedom of private property, unencumbered by fear of arbitrary seizure, was associated with freedom to choose one's occupation and enjoy the fruit of one's labour. Doing so would enhance both wealth and equality. Labour, capital, and their skilful employment were the source of wealth in society, not inherited riches and privilege. This implied that ordinary people had a worth of their own, associating economic and political freedoms or 'natural rights' as one. Despite this optimistic doctrine, Smith remained sceptical about the power of commercial interests and argued that intervention was needed to ensure that restrictive practices and self-interested behaviour of the commercial classes were curbed and regulated to ensure market-based outcomes and benefits.

David Ricardo took Smith's work in a systematic and coherent direction and developed now familiar techniques of deductive economic reasoning under strict and highly abstract assumptions. His aim was to demonstrate the advantages of government policies promoting the new market principles, for example, in taxation and international trade. Societies at the time were deeply divided along class lines—and political economists were searching for 'laws' governing their conflicts of interest and betterment of the situation. At the same time, Jean-Baptiste Say attempted to demonstrate systematically his law that 'supply creates its own demand' (Say's Law), by which he meant that the wages from employment for a given level of production would result in sufficient purchasing power to see that it was sold—an early demonstration of the principle of economic equilibrium.

This turn towards abstract reasoning proved influential and linked up with Jeremy Bentham's 'utilitarian calculus' in moral philosophy: people are assumed to be rational and to pursue a self-interested agenda of 'utility maximization' ('utility' standing variously for pleasure, wealth, happiness, profit) in interaction with others. The question, as Smith had seen, was how this pursuit of self-interest might add up to a beneficial outcome for the social whole (or not). Liberal ideas concerning harmony of interests and economic equilibrium combined with the new 'science' in a heady idealism that often conflicted with observable realities. John Stuart Mill, writing as the Ricardian consensus concerning the 'basic principles' and 'true laws' was collapsing, explicitly made the distinction between

production, ruled by 'natural and universal laws' (like the 'law of diminishing returns'), and distribution, ruled by custom and hence subject to change and political strife.

Finally, there was Marx, who coined the term 'classical political economy'. He clearly belongs to the classical tradition, but as its greatest critic he also goes far beyond it. The critical or radical political economy tradition he founded aimed to debunk liberal idealism and expound the real, inner mechanisms of capitalism as well as its intrinsic tendencies (or 'laws of motion'). Marx's critique was not just political and ethical—demonstrating, he hoped, the historical limits of modern capitalism—but also 'economic'. He extended Mill's arguments concerning strife associated with distribution to the functioning of capitalist production and exchange itself. Capitalism was a contested and complex system of social relations involving fundamental power relationships between the 'economic classes' of modern society. Without the modern state and modern law, without politics, the highly artificial institutions of modern capitalism could not last a day.

Marx represented a turning point. His revolutionary critique stimulated many to intensify the search for 'pure science' removed from the complexities of history and socio-political interaction, generating 'Economics' as opposed to the older and discredited term, 'Political Economy'. The utilitarian calculus fostered the 'marginal revolution' based on (often highly algebraic) marginal utility analysis as a sort of anatomy of market transactions. This generated Leon Walras's mathematical 'general equilibrium model' demonstrating in the abstract that the interdependent economic flows could result in a long-run balance between demand and supply factors. Alfred Marshall's *Principles of Economics*, first published in 1890, replaced Mill's 1848 *Principles of Political Economy* as the leading and standard textbook and for over 50 years retained this position in the English-speaking world. Political economy was 'purified' and professional economists forgot about history, politics, and conflicts of social life. Their concern was to analyze 'universal' patterns of market exchange proper as applied to both economic and social life, and to demonstrate the attainability of equilibrium yielding 'Pareto optimal' levels of general welfare, where no one person can be better off without someone else being worse off.[8] The new orthodoxy also implied the emergence of a *separate* study of society (sociology) and of politics (political science and international relations). These separate disciplinary tracks have been maintained to this day.

How is the tradition of classical political economy relevant today? The heritage appears split between those who claim eternal 'laws' of economics as natural or, in a flight of modesty, laws of 'rational behaviour'. Others—like Sismondi, Jones, Mill, and Marx—focus more on the historical, transient, contested, and hence *political* nature of all economic processes. Smith was no true believer in the liberal Utopia of a market unbound: the furies of private interests would always disturb the markets, which had to be regulated to make them work. Political economy informs us not to take 'economic man' for granted, but to study the social relationships behind the division between private interests and the public or 'common' good. Individuals and economic relationships, thus 'laws', are in fact highly contestable, generated by society through social and political interaction, not as assumed by mainstream economics. Political economists like Karl Polanyi and Albert Hirschman do not take any 'universal' market behaviour for granted, and they take issue with the notion of the 'neutrality' of money. Money and credit involve exchange and power relationships (different classes do different things with it) anchored in social practices and beliefs (confidence), which can be a source of instability and even crisis: money is only stable as long as collective human behaviour makes it so. In stark contrast to mainstream economics, political economists study market competition in time and space: economic agents (e.g., firms) have a history and their interaction is often cyclical and uncertain.

Last but not least, political economists in the classical tradition are preoccupied with the study of

the interaction between political and economic processes. The tradition understood that systems of production changed symbiotically with patterns of classes in society and patterns of governance, requiring a theory of history. Adam Smith realized that a better relationship between private pursuit of self-interest and collectively acceptable outcomes in terms of state and market required carefully contrived conditions enforced by political authorities not beholden to the whims of the rich and powerful. The interaction between states and markets is a misleading formula if each represents a competing logic: power on the one side, rational exchange behaviour on the other. Private property and market exchange also involve power structures underpinned by the political and social arrangements maintained through our institutions of governance. Understanding how and why markets are politically made and determined, as well as how and why states are made up of and determined by peculiar economic institutions of their own making, allows political economists to overcome the oversimplified state-market divide. In this respect, Karl Polanyi's seminal study on the Great Transformation has been a source of inspiration cherished by many political economists ever since its first publication in 1944.[9]

A Tale of Two Revivals: International and Comparative Political Economy

This section[10] traces the revival of political economy within the broad discipline of political science. In the post-war period social science began a rapid and rather exaggerated process of specialization, and much concerning the interrelationships and shared heritage of these subjects was lost. The re-emergence of political economy refers to a process of reintegrating what had been somewhat arbitrarily split up: though specialization resulted from the laudable pursuit of better expertise, it had important opportunity costs for our understanding of the world around us. Furthermore, as the global economy became increasingly integrated, the traditional distinction between the study of things international and things domestic began to break down. As the political and economic domains stubbornly revealed themselves to be closely interdependent, there was a re-examination of disciplinary specialization.

Classical political economy had always been preoccupied with the domestic and world economies. Although only fragments, such as Ricardo's theory of comparative advantage, survive in orthodox economics, classical political economists had been very much concerned with the contrast between the wealth of some nations and the poverty of others. The decline of the Spanish empire, the Dutch miracle of the seventeenth century, the rise of Britain to industrial and commercial supremacy, the capitalist development of backward countries like Russia were all topics of heated debate among political economists. So the beginning of a revival of political economy had two dimensions or sources in the literature: comparative political economy (CPE), which seeks to analyze and explain the similarities and/or differences among national and/or regional variants of political economy, and international political economy (IPE), which analyzes the relationships among the various national/regional components of the global system. Each of these dimensions began to approach the other within political science/international relations.

One might begin with the work of Richard Cooper, an economist,[11] who was particularly influential in inducing political science/international relations scholars, including comparative foreign policy analysts, to consider the observable fact of *interdependence* and what it meant for our understanding of the world around us. Increasingly, foreign affairs would be understood in relation to the tensions between domestic considerations and relations with other states and their own domestic dynamics. This blurred the levels-of-analysis distinction through the work of a range of scholars (for example, James Rosenau).[12]

A further step was the emergence in the late 1960s of the debate about 'transnational relations', wherein *inter*national was placed in opposition to the more sophisticated concept of *trans*national relationships (see also the Introduction to Part I). Interdependence among states and their societies[13] was central to this debate, highlighting the role of both *non*-state and *sub*-state actors of a private or public nature. Such concepts greatly expanded the empirical terrain on which the nascent IPE/CPE would operate.

There were disputes about basic assumptions of agency and method. Cooper's article was an early application of methodologically individualist rational choice to IPE, an application that became particularly influential when applied to game theory and the transaction cost economics of Nobel Prize-winner Ronald Coase[14] and others. Axelrod's innovative use of game theory and Keohane's use of transaction cost logic were particularly useful examples, as was Mancur Olson's application of his own 'public goods' approach in his *Rise and Decline of Nations*.[15] These more formal and quantitative rational choice contributions under the 'positive political economy' label represent a growing direct overlap of neo-classical economics and IPE.[16]

Meanwhile, 1970s monetary turbulence, the rise of the Euromarkets, and the expansion of international trade signalled a transformation at domestic and international levels. Trade and financial policies had always been highly charged politically, both *within* and *among* states in the system, proving fertile ground for interdisciplinary sectoral research projects, e.g., the team under Andrew Shonfield at the Royal Institute for International Affairs (Chatham House) that included Susan Strange, perhaps the most renowned of all the IPE 'revival' generation.[17] B.J. Cohen represents one of the rare cases of an economist who came in from the cold of the dismal science—producing his seminal *Organizing the World's Money* (1977).[18] A healthy literature developed in various issue-areas on emerging co-operative 'international regimes'.[19]

Comparative and international political economy began increasingly to overlap. The economic historian Charles Kindleberger developed his explanation of the collapse of the international monetary system in the 1930s in terms of domestic policy failures and the need for a political stabilizer for international markets, spawning the often misunderstood 'hegemonic stability' hypothesis,[20] which was further pursued by Robert Gilpin, who started as a specialist in French public policy.[21] Further contributions from comparative political economists followed, including Peter Katzenstein's *Between Power and Plenty*[22] on diverse national responses to the 1970s oil shocks, and the work of Peter Gourevitch and John Zysman.[23] Comparative specialists recognized that the phenomenon of deepening European and global integration forced them to reassess their approach to their subject, linking the crisis of welfare states variously to systemic or national-level developments: it was increasingly difficult to remain a country specialist without absorbing the impact of structural changes in the global economy—the debates about corporatism and the role of organized interests were forced to 'go global'.[24] Comparativists (the 'developmental state' debate) were also busy analyzing the difficulties of developing political economies at the domestic level as global integration pressures mounted.[25] While some IPE specialists had always anchored global generalizations in specific sectoral and, indeed, country cases, IPE and CPE needed each other as much as ever, coming together in a synthesis through the work of scholars such as Philip Cerny.[26]

The radical tradition in international political economy must not be neglected, especially as it kept alive assumptions about the interdependent nature of the political and economic domains. Indeed, over time the radical and the 'orthodox' have moved closer together.[27] Radical contributions stemming from Marx and Lenin can be split a number of ways, with the work of Sutcliffe and Owen or Kubalkova and Cruickshank standing out as sound texts.[28] Considerable innovation occurred with the emergence of the 'French Regulation' school led by Michel Aglietta and including well-known scholars such as Robert Boyer and Alain Lipietz,[29] and the revival of empirical work in the Marxist school.[30] Perhaps the most obvious of the long-standing radical contributions to IPE is that of dependency theorists, with variants ranging from world systems theory developed by Immanuel Wallerstein and others[31] to explanations emphasiz-

ing domestic factors.[32] The insights of dependency theorists concerning uneven development and inequality have been difficult to ignore, and despite ongoing discomfort the mainstream has increasingly accepted some of the basic observations of dependency theorists. Finally, Robert Cox was the author of an important innovation bridging international relations/international political economy and the domestic level of analysis in important respects. His 'neo-Gramscian' approach,[33] resolutely post-structuralist in its theory, has been embraced in whole or in part by a sizable proportion of IPE specialists. Cox also served as a reminder to link political economy to its historical roots as he drew heavily on Marx, Gramsci, and Karl Polanyi, and history as represented by Fernand Braudel. His conceptual devices cross levels of analysis and admit the relevance of a wide range of public and private actors and, crucially, the relationships among them in a pattern of global governance. The emphasis on the transnationalization of class and (related) corporate power was also developed by the 'Amsterdam School',[34] as well as by scholars such as Stephen Gill at York University in Canada.[35]

The emergence of IPE has paralleled wider developments in the social sciences. In this sense, 'new' issues have made their way onto the agenda, prompting renewed consideration of conceptual approaches as well. Of particular note is the rise of feminist scholarship and work on the environment—heralding feminist and 'green' approaches to IPE. Both have moved rapidly from arguing the need to find a place in CPE/IPE scholarship to showing how these approaches might be included on the agenda through theory and empirical case research (see especially Chapters 5, 6, and 18 in this volume). IPE and CPE scholarship is now rich and varied. Different perspectives and scholars emphasize different aspects of the normative agenda, and much of the underlying debate is ultimately about values, not simply analysis and research tools.[36] Yet mainstream (international) economics and (international) political economy remain in mutual neglect or even denial. Hardly anyone, perhaps with the remarkable exception of the pioneer Susan Strange, has ever complained.[37]

Whither Political Economy?

The emerging political economy approaches were increasingly resisting disciplinary straitjackets and reaching across boundaries towards economics and, in particular, the classical roots. Research into social and economic interdependence across political boundaries threw into question the levels-of-analysis assumptions of comparative politics and international relations. It brought to the fore the question of which actors and what issues are of central importance. By examining the constraints of economic structure and the impact of political interaction on the changing economic scene, it highlighted the role of structure versus agency in this process of transformation (for an account of these theoretical issues, see the Introduction to this volume). In time, inquiry settled on a move away from a focus on 'government' towards a focus on the looser concept of 'governance'.[38] This once again expanded the range of issues on the table.

In other words, emergence of political economy was a reawakening and relinking with the broad if not always coherent tradition of social science scholarship from the French physiocrats onward, via Smith, Marx, Keynes, Polanyi, and the pioneers of the contemporary period. This welcome ecumenism has become characterized by a concern with how the pieces of the global puzzle fit together: the social, the normative, the formal and institutionalized, the public and the private, the local and the global. This requires specialized research employing diverse techniques but based on a broad understanding of the nature of political authority and underlying socio-economic structures in a variety of settings.

It is arguable that despite this welcome diversity in *approach*, political economy has come to settle around a set of core questions and empirically verifiable assumptions concerning the nature of the social whole. Given arguments about roots, a useful starting point is Adam Smith himself,[39] who was strongly aware that, historically, evolving ways in which who gets what, when, and how lend form and substance (sometimes rather unpleasant) to society and to its more formal institutions of governance, and who has power over whom. In this he shared much with his eventual critic, Marx. Smith observed an ongoing tension between the private interests of individuals and the needs of the wider community—a tension between the pursuit of self-interest and the public good. This leads to the first core issue: how has this tension been resolved in particular periods of history? One might disagree with Smith's market-based proposal, but his core question remains relevant in our increasingly transnational political economy, with the lines of institutionalized authority becoming more blurred all the time.

This leads to a crucial second core assumption—that there is a systematic and reciprocal relationship between the political and the economic domains. Systems of production and exchange are deeply embedded and indeed underpin the evolving characteristics of our societies. Building on the concern with history within both classical and radical political economy, a third assumption is that, over time, a systematic but not always linear relationship exists between the changing ways in which societies organize production and exchange, on the one hand, and emerging patterns of governance, on the other.

These core issues can be formulated in contemporary terms. We now have a market-based social system, indeed, an increasingly global one, but not always the carefully contrived conditions Smith recommended. The market has furthermore proved less stable, less equal, and less harmonious in operation than he and many of his successors thought would be the case; hence, radical critique. Power is clearly not the sole preserve of the formal institutions that pretend to monopolize it, particularly states—private market power is very much part of the pattern of governance we experience. The core issues noted above all focus on the reciprocal relationship between economic structures of the market and political authority (loosely defined) in the ongoing and accelerating process of global change,[40] and political authority is today largely represented by the state. This means we should focus on the *contemporary state-market relationship* in this period of global economic integration and changing forms of governance: what we think a state is, what we think a market is, and how, if at all, they are or should be related. The central focus on the contemporary state-market relationship leaves ample room for normative concerns such as who should get what and how, the appropriate nature of governance, and guidance as to how we might improve the global order.

If the relationship between political authority and markets is the core question, the argument here is that the discipline must move beyond mere invocation in terms of dealing with it. For too long, scholars have either merely invoked the interrelationship in terms of mutual effects (i.e., economic liberal or realist approaches) or assumed it. Either way, the relationship has not been adequately conceptualized. Politics and markets, as most IPE/CPE literature insists, are interdependent, but their interdependency is usually depicted as a simple dichotomy: states *versus* markets, each following contrasting and antagonistic logic (political power *versus* rational, self-interested action) and always pulling in opposite directions. In the conventional view, states and markets are ruled by contrasting values, and the processes in each domain remain distinct. This state-market tug-of-war is deeply rooted in the nineteenth-century disciplinary split between economics and political science. Accordingly, the dichotomy view, still prevailing in contemporary political economy, does not overcome the conceptual divide between politics and economics. In fact, it reproduces their unhappy divorce.

This dichotomy view has a number of disadvantages. First, it is based on formulas that lack explanatory accuracy because of empirically inaccurate analytical differentiation. To invoke 'markets' as an abbreviation for the structure and logic of development of contemporary economies is wide of the mark. Modern capitalist economies are structured by firms, which internally are not markets but power hierarchies.[41] Furthermore, modern economies comprise a variety of markets, among them the markets for the 'fictitious commodities' such as human labour, land or natural resources, money and capital. These are also essentially social

power structures that yield a range of potential conflicts requiring political resolution (e.g., between employers and employees, landowners and land users, creditors and debtors, investors and capital users). These are not 'markets' in the abstract but distinct or specific markets and market systems as social entities. States, on the other hand, as political economists should see them, are economic *organizations* of a peculiar, political kind and origin. They have acquired a series of 'monopolies' that are either directly economic (power of taxation, monopoly of money) or central to modern economic life, like the 'monopoly of legitimate violence' and the 'monopoly of law'. States are in this sense the institutions that act as a forum to settle the political conflicts generated in the social domain of the market.

Second, the state-market dichotomy explains a number of phenomena rather poorly. For instance, why do successful and ostensibly mobile market agents not *consistently* take the 'exit option' but, in many instances, choose to remain wedded to enduring state-market configurations (viz. Japan)? Or why have persistent predictions of a 'retreat of the state'[42] and race-to-the-bottom regulatory competition failed to materialize under the pressures of global market integration? Or again, why do some economies display an outstanding adaptive capacity to external pressures at one time, but despite continuity in institutional structure and even personnel, demonstrate incapacity at another time? What is more, the state-market dichotomy presents a distorted view of business strategies and the process of competition as consisting solely of the deployment of firms' relative capacities in terms of organization, innovation, and capital. Thus, *political* resources deployed in the policy processes—the ability to shape the terms of competition in line with the preferences of private actors—are discounted as an add-on extra, good if one can have it, instead of seen as integral to the very nature of inter-firm competition itself.

So how might we transform political economy into a true inter-discipline in touch with its classical roots, overcoming the states *versus* markets dichotomy and bringing together political scientists and heterodox economists who still remain in a tacit state of mutual negligence and ignorance? A lead is provided by the literature on institutional economics. Douglass North argued that the ways in which markets are structured, the sorts of values embedded in the prevailing regulatory systems, and which actors/organizations are able to develop within the prevailing incentives make all the difference to outcomes.[43] In this view, the institutions of the market and the institutions of the policy process are integrated into the notion of what a market is. Markets cannot thrive without the reduction of transaction costs that governance provides. But it is insufficient to import techniques of economics (in this case, the transaction cost approach) into political science or vice versa. We must fully recognize the implications of such formulations and think of the market setting as part of a wider process that includes the crucial functions that states and firms, as institutions, both perform, along with the functions and actions of other social constituents.

Let us take one recent proposal to replace the dichotomy with a broader concept[44] linking state and market in the process of governance. Remembering the classical economists, we can conceive of states and their political conflicts as active constituents of the marketplace, and of market actors and their constituencies as participants in the wider process of governance. Rethinking the state-market relationship, we focus on the process of regulation taking place on markets, within firms, and in interactions between firms, as well as among other, compound market actors. Apparently, the regulatory processes at the (trans)national level are as much a part of business strategies as the game of investment and marketing. Firms simultaneously deploy their political and competitive resources to achieve the outcomes they seek. The preferences of powerful coalitions of market agents are integrated into the policy process. States and markets can be regarded as parts of an integrated ensemble of governance, the *state-market condominium* wherein the identifiable parts of the whole cannot be conceptualized or analyzed in isolation from each other.

Change occurs simultaneously through the process of economic competition among firms, on the one hand, and the policy and regulatory processes mediated by the institutions of the state, on the other. Market agents enhance or protect their position and prosperity by making simultaneous calculations through their business strategies, deploying in parallel their competitive (investment, technology, productivity, organization, labour skills) and political (in the policy processes of the state and in less formal institutional settings) resources. This is clearly visible in corporatist systems in Western Europe, where even labour is integrated into both state policy processes and the strategic decision-making of firms, and in the close integration of private firms/associations into the system of bureaucratic management that characterizes the economic development process in Japan and other parts of Asia. The point is less obvious to observers of Anglo-Saxon political economies, where the independence of the private sector appears more marked than in other societies. But the considerable evidence of 'regulatory capture' of the agencies of governance in the US economy should indicate the need to avoid the stereotypes developed, particularly in the economics literature.

Of course, this conceptualization of states and markets appears counter-intuitive in the present global era increasingly dominated by private-sector market processes. The case also appears difficult to support in view of the existence of multiple sovereignties in the global economy, which firms are supposedly trying to circumvent. Our contemporary experience of modern capitalism and the prevalence of economic modes of analysis engrave on our intellects the idea of the state-market dichotomy. Yet it is precisely against this sort of orthodoxy that political economy teaches us to rebel. There is nothing surprising in the idea that a transnational market structure, or indeed any market, should have multiple institutional nodes exercising authority in different ways and even with different functions. The analogy of a federal system or of the European Union is useful here: different layers of political institutions can fulfill the 'state' function over time and we should not misconceive the identifiable institutional/organizational structures of the state as a phenomenon external to the dynamics of the market.

The state-market condominium model facilitates understanding of the role of 'non-state' private interests, integrated into the complex institutional fabric of the state, in driving the process of global integration. As the pattern of material interests in national political economies has become more transnational, so the state has changed. Over the past three decades, the state has become far more a facilitator of global market processes than a protector of domestic market structures and interests (see Chapter 26 by Cerny). The pattern of political authority becomes more transnational in symbiosis with the transformation of the market. The state has progressively delegated a number of tasks either to private bodies or to institutions of international co-operation, though it maintains its functions in terms of domestic political legitimacy and all the tensions that entails. In this sense what we have seen is not so much a retreat of the state in the face of market forces, but a transformation of the state in symbiosis with the transformation of economic structures. This argument also implies that the state could claw back (at a cost!) its authority should political and market circumstances make this a desirable policy option. Political agency, depending on the balance of social forces and their organizational and institutional capacities, can be deployed to liberalize or indeed to invoke closure, as has happened many times in history—humankind does have free will where the market is concerned. It should be clear that the form and functions of the state will continue to evolve, as they have in the past. The question, then, is not why the state is in retreat, but how long the current form of state-market condominium is sustainable in the face of the increased volatility of the global markets.

Conclusion

This chapter has demonstrated that, in addition to flourishing, comparative and international political economy have come of age in an emerging synthesis. Forms of academic specialization were failing to address, let alone answer, important questions. This synthesis was as much a revival of older traditions as a new development, but it was no less welcome for that.

Yet the political economy revival initially failed to grapple successfully with the conceptual puzzle of the state-market relationship. We have argued here for a conceptual leap that would generate a genuine political economy approach: the adoption of the state-market condominium model. We are all political and economic agents at one and the same time, whatever the historical context. This argument is important because it re-establishes the role of agency, the capacity to make normatively informed policy choices concerning the nature and direction of the current global transformation. We need to focus on determining the political constituencies that need to be challenged in order to correct the balance of costs and benefits of aspects of global economic integration, particularly the problem of inequality and poverty.

The state-market condominium model therefore operationalizes political economy and infuses the global economic development process with agency. There is room for discretionary policy and action, even for the relatively vulnerable. We can, at least to a limited degree, affect the norms and values underpinning global order. As long as we see only a tug-of-war between the state and the market, then the benefits of one will be overshadowed by the costs of the other. The point is that they exist in symbiosis. The argument also demonstrates the real importance of Strange's insistence that we should focus not on states and markets as such, but on the interaction of *political authority* and the *market*. Political authority is not just vested in the formal institutions of states and their offshoots of governance, such as international regimes, but is also present in the agents of the market as part of the state-market condominium. The market *is* governance, even as it appears to work in mysterious, private ways.

Notes

1. See E. Fullbrook, ed., *The Crisis in Economics* (London: Routledge, 2003).
2. See H. Landreth, *History of Economic Thought* (Boston: Houghton Mifflin, 1976), 24–9.
3. See J. Steuart, *An Inquiry into the Principles of Political Economy* (New York: Augustus M. Kelley, 1967 [1767]), 1–2.
4. See David Hume, *Of Interest, Of Money and Of the Balance of Trade*, in E. Rotwein, ed., *David Hume: Writings on Economics* (Madison: University of Wisconsin Press, 1970 [1752]).
5. See Adam Smith, *An Inquiry into the Nature and Causes of the Wealth of Nations* (New York: Modern Library, 1937 [1776]), 375.
6. Ibid., Book I, chs 1–3.
7. Robert Heilbroner, ed., *The Essential Adam Smith* (Oxford: Oxford University Press, 1986), 168–71.
8. Landreth, *History of Economic Thought*, 408–11.
9. K. Polanyi, *The Great Transformation* (Boston: Beacon Press, 1957 [1944]).
10. This and the following section of this chapter draw heavily on Underhill, 'State, Market, and Global Political Economy: Genealogy of an (Inter-?)discipline', *International Affairs* 76, 4 (Oct. 2000): 805–24.
11. Richard N. Cooper, *The Economics of Interdependence* (New York: McGraw-Hill, 1968).
12. James N. Rosenau, ed., *Domestic Sources of Foreign Policy* (New York: Free Press, 1967).
13. Robert O. Keohane and Joseph Nye, *Power and Interdependence: World Politics in Transition* (Boston: Little, Brown, 1977), 8–11.
14. Ronald Coase, 'The Problem of Social Cost', *Journal of Law and Economics* 3 (1960): 1–44.
15. Robert Axelrod, *The Evolution of Co-operation* (New York: Basic Books, 1984); Robert O. Keohane, *After Hegemony: Co-operation and Discord in the World Political Economy* (Princeton, NJ: Princeton University Press, 1984); M. Olson, *The Rise and Decline of Nations* (New Haven: Yale University Press, 1982).
16. J. Alt and K. Schepsle, *Perspectives on Positive Political Economy* (Cambridge: Cambridge University Press, 1990); Dani Rodrik, *Has Globalization Gone Too Far?* (Washington: Institute for International Economics, 1997).
17. A. Shonfield, V. Curzon, et al., *Politics and Trade*, vol. 1, and Susan Strange, *International Monetary Relations*, vol. 2, of *International Economic Relations of the Western World 1959–1971*, ed. A. Shonfield (Oxford: Oxford University Press, 1976). For a critical assessment and further development of the work of Susan Strange, see A. Verdun and T. Lawton, eds, *Strange Power* (Aldershot: Ashgate, 2000)
18. Benjamin J. Cohen, *Organizing the World's Money* (New York: Basic Books, 1977)
19. Starting with, among others, Keohane and Nye, *Power and Interdependence*, and S. Krasner, ed., *International Regimes* (Ithaca, NY: Cornell University Press, 1983).
20. Charles Kindleberger, *The World in Depression 1929–39* (Berkeley: University of California Press, 1973).
21. Robert Gilpin, *US Power and the Multinational Corporation: The Political Economy of Foreign Direct Investment* (New York: Basic Books, 1975).
22. Peter J. Katzenstein, ed., *Between Power and Plenty: Foreign Economic Policies of Advanced Industrial States* (Madison: University of Wisconsin Press, 1978).
23. See Peter Gourevitch, *Politics in Hard Times* (Ithaca, NY: Cornell University Press, 1986); J. Zysman, *Governments, Markets, and Growth* (Ithaca, NY: Cornell University Press, 1983).
24. See Justin Greenwood and Henry Jacek, eds, *Organized Business and the New Global Order* (London: Routledge, 2000).
25. See P. Evans and J.D. Stephens, 'Studying Development Since the Sixties: The Emergence of a New Comparative Political Economy', *Theory and Society* 17 (1988): 713–45.
26. On the state in the global economy, see P. Cerny, *The Changing Architecture of Politics: Structure, Agency, and the Future of the State* (London: Sage,

1990); on finance, see Cerny, ed., *Finance and World Politics: Markets, Regimes, and States in the Post-Hegemonic Era* (Aldershot: Edward Elgar, 1993).

27. The influence of radical political economy on Cerny's work is a good example of the ways in which radical insights have affected a range of scholars.

28. Bob Sutcliffe and Roger Owen, eds., *Studies in the Theory of Imperialism* (London: Longman, 1972); V. Kubalkova and A. Cruickshank, *Marxism and International Relations* (Oxford: Clarendon Press, 1985).

29. M. Aglietta, *A Theory of Capitalist Regulation* (London: New Left Books, 1979). The school is covered well in the review article by Alain Noël, 'Accumulation, Regulation, and Social Change: An Essay on French Political Economy', *International Organization* 41, 2 (Spring 1987): 303–33.

30. See Peter Burnham, 'Open Marxism and Vulgar International Political Economy', *Review of International Political Economy* 1, 2 (Summer 1994): 221–31.

31. See Christopher Chase-Dunn, *Global Formation: Structures of the World Economy* (Oxford: Blackwell, 1989).

32. Henrique Cardoso and Enzo Falletto, *Dependency and Development in Latin America* (Berkeley: University of California Press, 1979).

33. See Robert W. Cox, with T. Sinclair, *Approaches to World Order* (Cambridge: Cambridge University Press, 1996); Cox, *Production, Power, and World Order* (New York: Columbia University Press, 1987).

34. See the widely cited Kees van der Pijl, *The Making of the Atlantic Ruling Class* (London: Verso, 1984), and, more recently, van der Pijl, *Transnational Classes and International Relations* (London: Routledge, 1998).

35. Stephen Gill, ed., *Gramsci, Historical Materialism, and International Relations* (Cambridge: Cambridge University Press, 1993).

36. See Susan Strange, *States and Markets* (Oxford: Blackwell, 1988), ch. 1.

37. See Susan Strange, *Authority and Markets: Susan Strange's Writings on International Political Economy* (London: Palgrave Macmillan, 2002), and especially her classic article, 'International Economics and International Relations: A Case of Mutual Neglect', *International Affairs* 46, 2 (Apr. 1970): 304–15.

38. The concept of 'governance' helped to overcome the gap between formal and informal frameworks of 'government', and is nicely outlined in James Rosenau and Ernst-Otto Czempiel, eds, *Governance without Government: Order and Change in World Politics* (Cambridge: Cambridge University Press, 1992).

39. See Andrew Skinner, 'Introduction' to Adam Smith, *The Wealth of Nations* (London: Penguin, 1970 [1776]); Heilbroner, ed., *The Essential Adam Smith.*

40. The point Susan Strange made so long ago in 'The Study of Transnational Relations', *International Affairs* 52, 3 (July 1976): 333–45.

41. See Oliver Williamson, *Markets and Hierarchies* (New York: Free Press, 1975). Williamson recognizes the point but does not bring it alive politically and in social terms.

42. Such as that propounded by Susan Strange in *The Retreat of the State* (Cambridge: Cambridge University Press, 1996).

43. D.C. North, *Institutions, Institutional Change, and Economic Performance* (Cambridge: Cambridge University Press, 1990), 109.

44. See Geoffrey R.D. Underhill, 'States, Markets, and Governance for Emerging Market Economies', *International Affairs* 79, 4 (July 2003): 755–81.

Suggested Readings

Canterbery, E.R. *A Brief History of Economics*. Singapore and London: World Scientific Publishing, 2001.

Caporaso, J.A., and D.P. Levine. *Theories of Political Economy*. Cambridge: Cambridge University Press, 1992.

Evans, P., and J.D. Stephens. 'Studying Development Since the Sixties: The Emergence of a New Comparative Political Economy', *Theory and Society* 17 (1988): 713–45.

Fullbrook, E., ed. *The Crisis in Economics*. New York and London: Routledge, 2003.

Goodin, R.E., and H.D. Klingemann, eds. *A New Handbook of Political Science*. Oxford and New York: Oxford University Press, 1996.

Heilbroner, R., ed. *The Essential Adam Smith*. Oxford University Press, 1986.

Lane, J.E., and S.O. Ersson. *Comparative Political Economy*. London: Pinter, 1990.

Marx, K. *Grundrisse*. Harmondsworth: Penguin Books, 1993 [written 1857–61].

Polanyi, K. *The Great Transformation*. Boston: Beacon Press, 1957 [1944].

Przeworski, A. *The State and the Economy under Capitalism*. New York: Harwood Academic Publishers, 1990.

Smith, A. *An Inquiry into the Nature and Causes of the Wealth of Nations*. London: Dent, 1970 [1776].

Steuart, J. *An Inquiry into the Principles of Political Economy*. New York: Augustus Kelley, 1967 [1767].

Strange, S. *Authority and Markets: Susan Strange's Writings on International Political Economy*. London: Palgrave Macmillan, 2002.

Tabb, W. *Reconstructing Political Economy*. London and New York: Routledge, 1999.

Winch, D. *Adam Smith's Politics*. Cambridge: Cambridge University Press, 1978.

Chapter 2

Problems of Power and Knowledge in a Changing World Order

Robert W. Cox

Theory concerning human affairs is not cumulative and progressive. Theory follows history, so that when the structures and problems of one era give place to emerging new structures and new problems there is a challenge for theory to respond. This is most notably the case with regard to world politics. The concepts and categories that became conventional following World War II are now widely challenged by recent history.

Established bodies of knowledge have their own inertia. They represent a considerable investment of time and effort—not to be cast away lightly. Furthermore, even while recognizing that the circumstances that validated established knowledge have changed, ingenious thinkers may adapt accustomed mental frameworks to new circumstances and new perceptions of threats to security without basically changing them. One form of 'realism' maintains that the basic structure of world order is unchanged since Thucydides wrote about the Peloponnesian War. Even though certain theorems of power relations may be abstracted from the flow of history, they can never be more than explanatory hypotheses, possibly helpful in interpreting specific situations but not to be represented as the universal truth of power politics. The flow of history is constantly producing power structures that shape and constrain actions and outcomes in different historical epochs.

It takes the shock of awareness that global power relations have significantly altered to call into question the conventional thinking and to stimulate the development of alternative forms of knowledge. Old realities remain. The state may retreat[1] with respect to some of its erstwhile functions, but it assumes new functions. Economic globalization does not bring about the disappearance of the state any more than *real socialism* brought about its 'withering away'. States make the framework for globalization. But states can also become agencies for bringing the global economy under social control. The state remains a site of struggle for those who would challenge the social consequences of globalization. History does not end with globalization of the economy and liberal political structures.

For three decades and more, knowledge in the sphere of world politics was built predominantly with reference to the Cold War. 'Neo-realism', the influential theoretical construct of that period, was a problem-solving form of knowledge applicable to the rivalry of two superpowers.[2] It was generally adequate to that specific purpose. Its limitation was that anything not pertaining to the superpower struggle tended to be ignored.

Of course, for the great mass of humankind other considerations were paramount: physical survival in conditions of hunger, disease, violent conflicts, and, at a more spiritual level, the denial of cultural identity. These were subordinated to the global power struggle, or, insofar as they became disruptive, were linked instrumentally to the interests of the two superpowers. Two competing forms of homogenization—world capitalism and world communism, respectively picturing themselves as the free world and national liberation—were the only games admitted. Once the overarching control of the Cold War was lifted, the underlying but obscured diversity of the human situation became apparent. Neo-realism lost its monopoly of explaining the world and of proposing action.[3]

Sources of Globalization

During the Great Depression of the 1930s, states became the agents of economic revival and the defenders of domestic welfare and employment against disturbances from the outside world. Corporatism, the union of the state with productive forces at the national level, became, under various names, the model of economic regulation; and economic nationalism with the 'beggar-my-neighbour' practices it involved was its counterpart in international economic relations. Following World War II, under US hegemonic leadership, the Bretton Woods system attempted to strike a balance between the liberal world market and the domestic responsibilities of states. States became in principle accountable to agencies of an international economic order—the International Monetary Fund (IMF), the World Bank, and the General Agreement on Tariffs and Trade (GATT)—in regard to trade liberalization and exchange rate stability and convertibility, and were also granted facilities and time to make adjustments in their national economic practices so as not to have to sacrifice the welfare of domestic groups. This balanced compromise between defence of welfare and a liberal international economic order sustained three decades of growth and social progress; but a crisis in the post-war order came about during the years 1968–75. From then until the present, the balanced compromise shifted towards allowing deregulated markets free rein. Domestic economies became subordinated to the perceived exigencies of the world market with growing disparity between rich and poor, gradual erosion of the social protections introduced during the post-war decades, and increased threats to the environment. States willy-nilly became more effectively accountable to forces inherent in the global economy; and they were constrained to mystify this accountability in the eyes and ears of their own publics through the new vocabulary of globalization, interdependence, and competitiveness.

The Structures of Globalization

The crisis of the post-war order expanded the breadth and depth of a global economy that exists alongside and incrementally supersedes the classical international economy.[4] The global economy is the system generated by globalizing production and global finance. Global production is able to make use of the territorial divisions of the international economy, playing off one territorial jurisdiction against another so as to maximize reductions in costs, savings in taxes, avoidance of anti-pollution regulation, control over labour, and guarantees of political stability and favour. Global finance has achieved a virtually unregulated 24-hour-a-day network. The collective decision-making of global finance is centred in world cities rather than states—New York, Tokyo, London, Paris, Frankfurt—and extends by computer terminals to the rest of the world.

The two components of the global economy are in latent contradiction. Global production requires a certain stability in politics and finance in order to expand. Global finance has the upper hand because its power over credit creation determines the future of production; but global finance is in a parlously fragile condition. A concatenation of calamitous circumstances could bring it down—a number of corporate failures combined with government debt defaults or a cessation of lending by leading creditors and international institutions like the IMF. The major crises of the world economy in recent years have been debt crises of this kind—the Mexican crises of the 1980s and early 1990s and the Asian crisis of the later 1990s. Up to now governments have not been able to devise any effectively secure scheme of regulation for global finance. Each crisis so far has been met with an ad hoc solution.

The myth of the free market is that it is self-regulating. As Karl Polanyi demonstrated, enforcement of market rules required the existence of military or police power.[5] The fact that this force may rarely have to be applied helps to sustain the myth but does not dispense with the necessity of the force in reserve. Globalization in the early twenty-first century also depends on the military-territorial power of an enforcer. That enforcer is the US military.

The role of enforcer is, however, beset by a contradiction. The US projection of military power on the world scale has become more salient, monopolistic, and unilateral while the relative strength of US productive capacity has declined.[6] This in turn rests on the contradiction that the United States consumes more than its own production can pay for because foreigners are ready to accept a flow of dollars, which has made the United States into the world's biggest debtor nation. As foreigners came to finance the difference between US consumption and the economy's ability to pay, the hegemonic system of the post-war period was becoming transformed into a tributary system.

There is, in effect, no explicit political or authority structure for the global economy. There is, nevertheless, something that could be described by the French word *nébuleuse* or by the notion of 'governance without government'.[7] There is a transnational process of consensus formation among the official caretakers of the global economy. It has generated consensual guidelines, underpinned by an ideology of globalization, that are transmitted into the policy-making channels of national governments and big corporations. Part of this consensus-formation process has taken place through unofficial forums like the Trilateral Commission and the annual world economic conferences at Davos, Switzerland. Part of it goes through official bodies like the Organization for Economic Co-operation and Development (OECD), the Bank for International Settlements, the IMF, and the G-7 major economic powers (now the G-8 with the inclusion of Russia). These have shaped the discourse within which policies have been defined, as well as the terms and concepts that have circumscribed what can be thought and done. They have also tightened the transnational networks that have linked policy-making from country to country.

Some of the political structures underpinning the global economic order have, however, been vulnerable to the social tensions and inequities economic liberalism produced. In Argentina, Brazil, and South Korea revolt against the attempt to entrench the global economic order has generated popular resistance to the domination of global finance and resulted in changes of political regime. Reactions to the onward sweep of globalization have also led other states to make prudent efforts to acquire and retain a degree of national or regional defensive capability in the realm of finance.

The structural power of the United States in global finance is based on the role of the US dollar as the principal world currency, the global predominance of American financial markets, and US control of the International Monetary Fund and its predominant influence in the other international economic institutions. Following World War II, the United States, as hegemonic power, was the principal source of credit for the rest of the world. However, during the period from 1977 to 1981 the United States transformed itself into the single largest consumer of international credit. First Japan, and subsequently China, took the place of the United States as principal supplier of credit.[8] The status of the dollar as world currency has given the United States the unique privilege of being able to borrow from foreigners in its own currency, which means that any depreciation of that currency (which was indeed occurring as this book was going to press) will both reduce the value of US debt and increase the competitiveness of US exports.

This structural power in global finance has enabled the United States to shape the global economy by influencing other states to bring their economic practices into conformity with an American concept and practice of global capitalism and by propagating a common way of thinking about economic matters, what in French is called *la pensée unique*. (The English term 'neo-liberalism' fails to capture the irony of the French.)

Both in Europe and in Asia, states have looked to regional financial arrangements as a defence against the structural power of the US dollar. The adoption of the euro by European countries, the establishment of the European Central Bank, and the prospect of further integration of European financial markets are de facto steps towards independence from the rule of the dollar and towards the consolidation of a plural world in finance. In the East Asian financial crisis of 1997–8 the United States rejected a Japanese initiative for a regional solution and managed the crisis in such a way that European and American firms were able to buy up Asian assets at fire-sale prices while Asian populations suffered economic disaster.[9] It shook Asian confidence in the benign nature of US hegemonic power and reinforced the determination of Asian governments to obstruct the foreign buyout of national economies and to encourage regional protection against dependence on US financial dominance.

China has become the new focus for Asian economic regionalism. Both China and Japan have been diversifying their trade and capital flows towards other Asian countries as a hedge against too much dependence on the US market. Together with countries of Southeast Asia they have agreed to create a virtual Asian monetary fund independent from the IMF in order to be able to guard against a future Asian currency crisis like that of 1997. Of course, the weakness of Asian regionalism, as of the euro area, lies in the lack of a central political authority over finance. Yet in both cases the movement is sustained and impelled forward by the experience of US unilateralism.

If there is to be a solution to the problems generated by economic globalization it is unlikely to be a return to post-war practices. It would more likely have to be a new concept of economy less resource-depleting and -polluting, more oriented towards the basic material needs of people that advanced technology makes possible with a smaller proportion of workers, and with much greater emphasis on the more neglected labour-intensive tasks of satisfying social and human needs for health, education, child and elder care, and conviviality. This, of course, implies a radical reorienting of social values, including the way in which different kinds of work are valued. States will most likely have to regulate and legitimate these new practices; but it seems clear that action by the state will only be triggered by bottom-up pressure of citizen activism.

The Changing Structure of World Politics

Out of the crisis of the post-war order, a new global political structure is emerging, requiring a new and more complex view of political reality. In this complex realism at the beginning of the twenty-first century there are three major configurations of power:

- The first is what is often now called the 'American empire', or increasingly simply 'Empire'. It differs from the imperialism of the nineteenth and early twentieth centuries, which meant political and administrative control of overseas territories—or, in the case of Russia, overland territories. The new 'Empire' penetrates through the borders of formally sovereign states to control their actions from within by compliant elites in both public and private spheres. It penetrates first into the principal allies of the United States but also into many other countries where US interests wield influence. Transnational corporations influence domestic policy in countries where they are located; and economic ties influence local business elites. Military co-operation among allies facilitates integration of military forces under leadership of the core of 'Empire'. Co-operation among intelligence services gives predominance to the security concerns of the imperial leadership. The media generalize an ideology that propagates imperial values and justifies the expansion of 'Empire' as beneficial to the whole world. Economic systems of the component territories of 'Empire' are restructured into one vast market for capital, goods, and services. In the imagined future of 'Empire' the 'hard power' of military dominance and economic coercion is both maintained and transcended by the 'soft power' of attraction and emulation.[10] 'Empire' constitutes a movement towards convergence in political, economic, and social practices and in basic cultural attitudes—a movement tending to absorb the whole world into one *civilization*.[11]

- The second configuration is the persistence of the Westphalian interstate system that was inaugurated in Europe in the seventeenth century and spread throughout the world during the period of European dominance. The sovereign state, though weakened, remains a hardy structure. Sovereignty has a dual aspect. One aspect is the autonomy of each sovereign state in the society of nations. The other is the authority of each state within its own territory and population. Both aspects are protected by the principle of non-intervention in the internal affairs of other states. Both external and internal sovereignty remain a defence against absorption into 'Empire'. The two fronts on which the residue of the Westphalian order confronts the impact of 'Empire' are, first, the defence of the interstate system and its creations, international law and the United Nations; and second, the strengthening of links between citizens and political authorities. These protect national autonomy in economic and social organization, and thus, by extension, sustain a plural world of coexisting cultures and civilizations. The governing principles of the Westphalian world are pluralism and a continuing search for consensus. The US adventure in Iraq appears to challenge this order, but the difficulties that followed invasion may reinforce Westphalian instincts once again as intervention proves highly costly to those who would initiate it.

- The third configuration is what is often called 'civil society' or sometimes the 'social movement'. This exists both within states and transnationally. This configuration of forces has become more evident in recent decades, initially in a movement for an alternative to the economic globalization of transnational corporate power and then as a direct confrontation of 'Empire' in the popular mobilization against the Anglo-American invasion of Iraq. 'Civil society' differs from both 'Empire' and the state system in that it functions as a decentred network rather than as a disciplined hierarchical structure. Modern information technology in the forms of the Internet and the cellphone has helped it to develop and to mobilize for action. The 'social movement' operates as gadfly and opposition within states and within 'Empire'. It has an ambiguous relationship with the state system, contesting the state's repressive powers but also seeking to strengthen it as a system responsive to popular pressures. Its diversity and popular basis are totally opposed to the centralizing and homogenizing force of 'Empire'.

Behind and below these three rival configurations of power lies a covert world including organized crime, 'terrorist' organizations, intelligence services, mercenary forces, illegal financial circuits, arms dealers, the drug trade and the sex trade, and sundry religious cults. This covert world functions in the interstices of the three overt configurations of power. Some of its component elements, like 'terrorist' networks, conspire to subvert and destroy established powers. Other components, like organized crime, are parasitical upon established power and live in symbiosis with it. The covert world is always present in some measure. Its expansion signals trouble for established order—a loosening of confidence in the security that established power is supposed to ensure for people in general.[12]

Each of the three power configurations is rooted in a different view of the whole—'Empire' sees the whole as a convergent and ultimately homogeneous world society; the state system as the vision of a plural world with social, economic, and cultural diversity and a commitment to seeking consensus; and the social movement as a process of building world order from the bottom up. The three configurations overlap geographically. They are not confined by boundaries. They have points of geographical concentration but are in contest everywhere asserting rival claims to legitimacy; while the expansion of the covert world, in both its subversive and parasitical aspects, undermines legitimacy everywhere.

Empire and Terror

It is easy to accept the phenomenon of 'Empire' as the main fact about the present state of world affairs; but it is important to look critically at its origins and prospects. The analogy is often made rhetorically with Rome—the United States as the new Rome. The aura of Rome's Empire endured for a thousand years, far outlasting the decline of Roman power. Barbarian armies invaded the Roman Empire not to destroy it but to merge with it and take power within it. Spiritual forces from the Middle East penetrated throughout the Empire and took the institutional form of Rome in the Catholic Church. The successor political authorities invoked the legitimacy of Rome.

The parallel doesn't work for America. American power has provoked an affirmation of *difference* on the part of other peoples. They do not strive to merge into a homogenized imperial whole. They prize their own distinctiveness. US influence had a benign quality, often welcomed abroad, in the decades following World War II. It is now regarded abroad with great suspicion. American values do not now, if they ever did, inspire universal endorsement as a basis for social and political life. Once widely admired, if not emulated, they have become more contested and more ambiguous. The terms 'democracy' and 'liberation' have become transformed to mean the domination of markets and military occupation. Even the seductiveness of American material culture turns to irony. Much has been made of America's 'soft power': that America's appeal to others may be stronger than the 'hard power' of military and economic coercion. The relationship between 'hard power' and 'soft power', however, has been inverse rather than complementary. The aggressive application of 'hard power' in the opening years of the twenty-first century has dissipated the gains that American 'soft power' made in the post-World War II era.

The American 'Empire' may appear as the predominant military and economic force in the world. It is less stable and less durable than first appears. US unilateralism and its use of 'coalitions of the willing' in impatience with opposition by the majority of states and peoples have divorced the exercise of American power from the legitimacy of universal consent. The American public's sustained support for US military intervention abroad is questionable. The ability of American forces to construct viable administrations or 'democratic' successor regimes in occupied territories has become very doubtful.

The Al-Qaeda attack of 11 September 2001 (9/11 in popular discourse) against the World Trade Center in New York and the Pentagon in Washington and the US response to it, with invasions first of Afghanistan and then Iraq, made the duality of 'terror' and 'Empire' salient in the consciousness of people throughout the world. 'Terrorism', in its twenty-first-century form, is a reaction to 'Empire'; and the expansion of 'Empire' is a response to 'terrorism'. To escape from this dialectic is a challenge to the world.

After the 9/11 attacks, a US President, the legitimacy of whose election was questionable, gained a new instantaneous legitimacy through the patriotic rallying of the American people behind his proclaimed 'war on terror'. That regained legitimacy was put in question internationally and also within the United States as the justifications given for the invasion of Iraq were discredited (no Iraqi weapons of mass destruction, no Iraqi links to Al-Qaeda), as the ability of the United States to sustain a long occupation became questionable, and as the vision of grateful 'liberated' peoples faded into armed uprising.

'Empire' may be a fantasy for a certain ideologically driven US political elite that is not shared unequivocally by US military leaders anxious to conserve their forces. Likewise, the public at large may have little taste for an extended aggressive war and long-term occupation abroad, although the November 2004 US election could be seen as casting doubt on this premise. In addition, American corporate power would prefer to achieve global hegemony by other than military means.

The State System

The state system, though weakened, is a more durable structure. It is challenged by 'Empire' but is self-consciously resisting its own demise. Where it has been weakened is when the United Nations, which is the institutional embodiment of the state system in our time, has been seen to have become an agency of American power.[13] The strength of the United Nations lies in a perception that no single dominant power can control it, that its decisions depend on a process of consensus in which all powers have a voice, if not in practice an equal one.

An imbalance in the state system arises when one 'hyper-power' (to borrow the terminology of French diplomacy) has overwhelming military and economic clout and other powers lack credible capacity for collective military action and financial independence. This situation undermines the effectiveness of the United Nations as the instrument for achieving consensus in the management of conflict. The restoration of the United Nations—and more broadly the process of multilateralism—will depend on overcoming that imbalance. It can happen only when the major states acquire effective military and economic capacity, underwritten by financial independence; and when the United States decides to play a role as one state among others, albeit the most powerful one.

Civil Society and the Social Movement

At the base of the emerging structure of world order are social forces. The old social movements—trade unions and peasant movements—have suffered setbacks under the impact of globalization, but the labour movement, in particular, has a background of experience in organization and ideology that can still be a strength in shaping the future. New social movements converging around specific sets of issues—environmentalism, feminism, and peace—have grown to a different extent in different parts of the world. More amorphous and ephemeral movements—'people power'—have arisen where political structures are both repressive and fragile. In the Philippines and subsequently in Indonesia they have overthrown governments but perhaps not fundamentally changed structures of power.

The social movement is a different kind of power compared to either 'Empire' or the state system. It is non-territorial, or rather trans-territorial, and it is non-hierarchical and non-bureaucratic. It takes the form of a fluid network composing, decomposing, and recomposing in reaction to deeply felt popular concerns. The weakness of the social movement is the obverse of its strength; its non-hierarchical character makes it difficult to coordinate action and define clear objectives and leaves it open to infiltration by extremist elements and *agents provocateurs*. But the social movement has been developing its means of co-ordinating action and articulating alternative perspectives for the world. The creation of the World Social Forum and its regional counterparts has provided an embryo institutional structure.

Identity, Class, and Civilization

Social movements evoke particular identities—ethnic, nationalist, religious, gender. The newly affirmed identities have substantially displaced class as the focus of social struggle, but, like class, they derive their force from resentment against exploitation. The disparate nature of identities, however, means that particular resentments can be manipulated into conflict one with another. The danger of authoritarian populism, of reborn fascism, is particularly great where political structures are crumbling and no common material basis of resentment becomes a uniting force. 'People power' can move to the right as well as to the left.

For people in the richer countries the nation-state has become a less central feature of their identity (with the notable exception of the United States), while in some poorer countries nationalism has become more virulent and aggressive. Social and economic cleavages remain fundamental as economic globalization accentuates polarization between rich and poor in all parts of the world. However, these cleavages are less frequently expressed as social class identities and more often as gender, race or ethnicity, religion, organizational affiliation, or a consciousness of historical griev-ance and humiliation.

Popular resistance becomes effective when it unites the various alienated groups into a coherent force and is able to articulate a clear alternative to the prevailing social and political order. In doing this, the social movement is engaging in a struggle for the transformation of civilization. We should not picture civilizations as fixed entities con-fronting one another in a 'clash' but rather consid-er all civilizations as being in process of transfor-mation both from internal contradictions and from external encounters.[14] This process of transforma-tion, together with the problematic of coexistence among civilizations, could be the foundation of a future knowledge of world order.

The key problem in understanding such a plural world of coexisting civilizations is to be able to enter into the mental framework of people who see the world differently from the way we do (who-ever 'we' are), people who have different percep-tions of reality. 'Reality' is historically and socially constructed, and is thus different for different civi-lizations, not a universal given. (This, it should be said, does not mean adopting other civilizational perspectives or rationalities, only understanding them.) Following from empathetic understanding of others is the need to work towards finding common ground among these different realities as a basis for some degree of tolerance within a world of differences.

Values

The social movement impacts upon the realm of values. It expresses people's inherent values and is part of the process of transforming values. It has raised consciousness of the position of women in society and of the threats of environmental degra-dation. It has championed peace and opposed aggression. It has put a higher value on life than on profit.

Civil society in Western Europe has by and large come to imagine that Europe as a whole has transcended former conflicts among European nations, accepting cultural diversity in the European whole while remaining suspicious of centralizing authority. Consensus is achieved through a cautious elaboration of *trans*national law and institutions. Furthermore, the emerging European entity and its component national iden-tities tend to envisage a *world* political order in sim-ilar fashion as the search for consensus and the elaboration of *inter*national law. This is not just a matter of moral preference. It is *realpolitik*. It is the interest of the European entity and of its compo-nent parts to shape world order in this manner so as to preserve the autonomy of Europe and of its component states in world politics.

The United States, meanwhile, has been moving in an opposite direction, towards a unipo-lar concept of world power in which the United States has emerged from the global conflicts of World War II and the Cold War as the paragon of economic, social, and political order with a mission to transmit its values and its order to the rest of the world, both for the benefit of other peoples and to ensure the security of its own way of life. In part, this evolution in American values has been encour-aged by the collapse of Soviet power and the vision that this has left the American way as the 'end of history' beyond which no fundamental change is conceivable. In part, it arises from the domestic shift in power within the United States from the northeast, with its historic links to Europe and European thought, to a southwest more susceptible to the idea of American 'exceptionalism',[15] more troubled by the historical divides of race and immi-gration, and more impregnated by the certainties of Christian fundamentalism as to the absolute and evident nature of good and evil.

This conviction of being the bearers of an exceptional historic mission has led American lead-ership to refuse to ratify the Kyoto Accord on envi-ronmental protection, the treaty to abolish the use of land mines, and the International Criminal Court. American 'exceptionalism' affirms in prac-tice that the United States is not a state like all the others and that American officials, the agents of this special responsibility, cannot be subject to other than US law. Europeans and Americans have been drawn towards two fundamentally different visions of world order.

In the balance of world forces, Western Europe may be weakened in the present by its military posture relative to the United States and in the long term by demographic decline; but European values are strengthened by the fact that the idea of a plural world is congenial to people in other parts of the world and their governments—to Russia, which like Europe is threatened by demographic decline, and to China and India and other Asian countries with growing populations and resentment against the universalist pretensions of America. The European perspective is also attractive to Latin Americans, who see themselves as reluctant members of an American 'Empire'. American unilateral commitment to Israel in the conflict over Palestine has antagonized more than just the Arab and Islamic world. Beyond the way these sentiments are reflected through the state system, the mobilized global social movement has articulated opposition in civil society to the vision of 'Empire'. To borrow the American usage, this attractiveness of European values is Europe's 'soft power'.

The state system remains the most feasible means for restoring legitimacy in global governance. The primary challenge is to induce the American 'hyper-power' to abandon the mirage of 'exceptionalism' and bring the United States back into membership along with other states in a community of nations. The diplomacy of other powers may have some small influence to this end; but the outcome will depend most of all on how Americans in the aggregate come to see the world. The social movement has a role to play in the transformation of American opinion and in challenging the state system to transform itself into a mechanism for working collectively on the salient problems affecting the condition of the world's peoples.

The Salient Problems of World Order

A newspaper reader or television viewer in the Western world in the early twenty-first century might expect to see 'terrorism' listed as the pre-eminent problem of world order. What is called 'terrorism' today has been a constant feature of political life throughout history as a symptom of persistent and unresolved conflicts. 'Terrorism' has been the tactic of the weaker party challenging the legitimacy of established order. The new thing about 'terrorism' in the twenty-first century is that it has acquired a global dimension. Global 'terrorism' came about as a challenge to 'Empire'. It is an epiphenomenon, a secondary symptom, of the salient problems inherent in the expansion of 'Empire'.

The Biosphere

Primary among these problems is the health of the biosphere. We are now increasingly aware that humanity is only one part of nature and that, within nature, humanity is interdependent with other forms of life and life-sustaining substances. A series of concerns have driven home the implications of that interdependence: the hole in the ozone layer, global warming, the decline of biodiversity, the decline of fish stocks, environmental pollution, and catastrophic weather patterns. The irruption of non-human nature into human politics arouses awareness that human survival is at stake, if not tomorrow then in a longer run that cannot be ignored.

Globalization is driven by global competitiveness, and the counterpart to competitiveness is consumer demand. The prevailing model of demand derived from the affluent societies spurs continuing expansion of existing production patterns, which are accompanied by depletion of natural resources and pollution. The implications to be drawn are (1) that the affluent societies will have to change their patterns of consumption and production if they are to become compatible with biospheric survival; (2) that this radically altered behaviour in affluent societies should serve as an alternative model for progress in the less affluent; and (3) that the now affluent societies pioneering an alternative social economy should aid the less affluent to develop in this different way.

Western electoral democracies confront this issue with difficulty because of the power of entrenched interests in the status quo. An alternative vision of economy is most likely to be advanced through civil society. The social movement can put pressure on states to regulate pollutants and the consumption of energy and resources in the interest of all. The very nature of this task defies exceptions—and exceptionalism. It concerns the whole planet. It requires regulation of the whole in which all participate and share responsibility.

Global Social Equity

The second salient problem is to bring about a reasonable degree of equity in the conditions of life of people around the world. In the past, capitalism in the leading countries has been legitimated by legislation guaranteeing a minimal economic and social security, including health and education, and providing orderly means for settlement of social conflicts. Latterly, governments have been cutting back on these guarantees—which have been the social achievement of reformist politics over decades—in an effort to subordinate everything to the market. The legitimacy of the economic system is threatened when these 'acquired rights' are eroded. What is true in the nation is true of the global economy. Global capitalism of the kind forced upon poor countries through the 'structural adjustment' imposed by the power of the so-called 'Washington Consensus'—the consensus of the IMF, World Bank, and US Treasury—has widened the gap between rich and poor and deprived countries of control over their own economies.[16] This consequence of global capital has produced the 'anti-globalization' movement in civil society that has confronted the managers of the global economy at every summit meeting since the 'battle of Seattle' of November 1999.[17] Legitimacy requires that global economic management subordinate the absolute claims of market logic to an assurance of social equity.

Domination Through Finance

The United States finances its massive trade and budget deficits, which include the cost of its military adventures, by an equally massive inflow of foreign capital. This is what has enabled government and people in the United States to command the resources of the rest of the world and to pay for the building and use of its own military power. This American 'structural power' in finance is a major reason for the lopsidedness of the state system and for the expansion of 'Empire' with its dialectical twin 'global terrorism'. A restoration of the state system as the mechanism for managing world affairs in a plural world order would depend in large measure on achieving some balance in global finance, the sinews of power.

Power, Knowledge, and Consciousness

The way people think about the world is the fundamental condition for world order. The basic choice here is between the vision of one homogeneous world to be shaped into one civilization and a plural world of coexisting civilizations. It is a choice between, on the one hand, a fundamentalist drive towards an absolutist moral unity and, on the other, an expectation of diversity with tolerance and a willingness to confront the frustrations of a search for consensus on divisive issues.

'Empire' offers the illusion of a uniform patented form of democracy and human rights under a colossal power that of its very nature contains its own contradiction: the repressive force necessary to maintain it constitutes an overwhelming threat to freedom and dissent.

Conclusion

The challenges of recent history have stimulated thinking about world order. IPE, which was initially limited to introducing an economic dimension alongside the military and diplomatic chronicle of events, gradually broadened its scope to put its emphasis on the frameworks or historical structures within which human activity takes place and on the processes of change in these frameworks. The emerging multiplicity of identities is an indication of the complexity of these processes. Complexity requires an integrated form of knowledge that spans the whole range of problems affecting human physical and psychic well-being. It also requires self-criticism, reflexivity, awareness of how one's own position in time and place and in society affects one's perspective on the world.

Notes

1. Susan Strange, *The Retreat of the State: The Diffusion of Power in the World Economy* (Cambridge: Cambridge University Press, 1996).

2. On the distinction between problem-solving and critical theory, see Robert W. Cox, 'Social Forces, States, and World Orders: Beyond International Relations Theory', in Cox, with Timothy J. Sinclair, *Approaches to World Order* (Cambridge: Cambridge University Press, 1996).

3. For a discussion of neo-realism, see Robert O. Keohane, ed., *Neorealism and Its Critics* (New York: Columbia University Press, 1986).

4. Bernadette Madeuf and Charles-Albert Michalet, 'A New Approach to International Economics', *International Social Science Journal* 30, 2 (1978): 253–84.

5. Karl Polanyi, *The Great Transformation: The Political and Economic Origins of Our Time* (Boston: Beacon Press, 1957), esp. ch. 12.

6. Two contributions giving opposite views of US 'decline' are Paul Kennedy, *The Rise and Fall of the Great Powers* (New York: Random House, 1987), and Joseph S. Nye Jr, *Bound to Lead: The Changing Nature of American Power* (New York: Basic Books, 1990). There is little disagreement about the basic facts: the decline of US productivity relative to European and Japanese productivity, and the extent of functional illiteracy and non-participation in economically productive work among the US population. The debate is mainly between optimists and pessimists with respect to whether these conditions can be reversed. See Kennedy, '"Fin-de-siècle" America', *New York Review of Books*, 28 June 1990.

7. The title of a book edited by James Rosenau and E.-O. Czempiel (Cambridge: Cambridge University Press, 1992). Susan Strange, *Casino Capitalism* (Oxford: Basil Blackwell, 1986), 165–9, argued that effective regulation over finance is unlikely to be achieved through international organization and that only the US government, by intervening in the New York financial market, might be capable of global effectiveness. But, she added, US governments had behaved unilaterally and irresponsibly in this matter and showed no signs of modifying their behaviour.

8. Susan Strange, 'Finance, Information and Power' (1990), in Roger Tooze and Christopher May, eds, *Authority and Markets: Susan Strange's Writing on International Political Economy* (London: Palgrave Macmillan, 2000), 80, 100; Eric Helleiner, *States and the Reemergence of Global Finance: From Bretton Woods to the 1990s* (Ithaca, NY: Cornell University Press, 1994), 13–14, 183–5; Randall D. Germain, *The International Organization of Credit: States and Global Finance in the World Economy* (Cambridge: Cambridge University Press, 1997), 78, 110–11, 165n., 168.

9. Chalmers Johnson, *Blowback: The Costs and Consequences of American Empire* (New York: Henry Holt, 2000), 221–9; Joseph E. Stiglitz, *Globalization and Its Discontents* (New York: Norton, 2002), 89–132.

10. The concept of 'soft power' comes from Nye, *Bound to Lead*, 32, which he defines as the 'intangible power resources such as culture, ideology and institutions' or those aspects of a dominant power that are attractive to people beyond its borders. Nye was arguing against the thesis that American hegemony was in decline as a result of the rising costs and waning usefulness of military power. 'Hard power' includes the capability for economic as well as military coercion.

11. Two recent books discuss the emergence of this latent force. Martin Shaw, *Theory of the Global State: Globality as an Unfinished Revolution* (Cambridge: Cambridge University Press, 2000); Michael Hardt and Antonio Negri, *Empire* (Cambridge, Mass: Harvard University Press, 2000). Shaw focuses on the political and institutional aspects of the emergence of the 'global state' in a spirit of benign inevitability. Hardt and Negri look more to cultural and knowledge aspects and to a dialectic in which the 'multitude'—a post-Marxist name for all those subject to power—will ultimately overcome 'transcendence' whether in the form of God, the state, or 'Empire'. A liberal imperialist perspective that justifies 'Empire' as the enforcer of moral law and human rights is the theme of Michael Ignatieff, *Empire Lite: Nation-building in Bosnia, Kosovo and Afghanistan* (Toronto: Penguin Canada, 2003).

12. The covert world is discussed more fully in Robert W. Cox, *The Political Economy of a Plural World: Critical Reflections on Power, Morals and Civilization* (London: Routledge, 2002), ch. 7.

13. That perception emerged during the Clinton presidency and Madeleine Albright's tenure as Secretary of State. It appeared in the US veto of the candidacy of Boutros Boutros-Ghali for a second term as Secretary-General of the United Nations, a reappointment supported by all members of the Security Council but the United States, and the subsequent election of Kofi Annan as the candidate favoured by the United States. US dominance in the United Nations was also evident in the inability of the United Nations, reflecting US (and also French and British) reluctance, to prevent the genocide in Rwanda. In contrast, the refusal by the Security Council to endorse the invasion of Iraq by US and British forces can be seen as a *prise de conscience* of the danger to the United Nations of succumbing to overt US unilateralism.

14. Dieter Senghaas, *The Clash within Civilizations* (London: Routledge, 1998).

15. Seymour Martin Lipset, *American Exceptionalism: A Double-edged Sword* (New York: Norton, 1997).

16. See Chapter 4 by Mittelman.

17. The 'battle in Seattle' refers to the anti-globalization, anti-multinational corporation demonstrations from a variety of civil society groups that paralyzed the World Trade Organization conference in Seattle, 30 November–3 December 1999.

Suggested Readings

Braudel, Fernand. 'History and the Social Sciences: The *longue durée*', in Braudel, *On History*, trans. Sarah Matthews. Chicago: University of Chicago Press, 1980.

Capra, Fritjof. *The Web of Life*. New York: Doubleday Anchor Books, 1996.

Cox, Robert W., with Michael G. Schechter. *The Political Economy of a Plural World: Critical Reflections on Power, Morals and Civilization*. London: Routledge, 2002.

Guéhenno, Jean-Marie. *La fin de la démocratie*. Paris: Flammarion, 1993.

Morin, Edgar. *Science avec conscience*. Paris: Fayard, 1982.

Waldrop, M. Mitchell. *Complexity: The Emerging Science at the Edge of Order and Chaos*. New York: Touchstone, 1992.

Web Sites

European Union: www.europa.eu.int/
International Monetary Fund: www.imf.org
Organization for Economic Co-operation and Development: www.oecd.org/home/
World Bank: www.worldbank.org/
World Trade Organization: www.wto.org/

Chapter 3

Globalization: The Long View

Herman M. Schwartz

What is globalization, and how should we think about it?[1] This chapter will contrast states and markets before and after 1500 to answer these questions. It uses economic development and the welfare state to illustrate how globalization works. Both discussions make clear that, contrary to many contemporary arguments, globalization is not particularly novel, is not a purely quantitative phenomenon, cannot be explained by dichotomizing or polarizing either states and markets or 'international' and 'domestic' markets as analytic categories, and is not a 'once only' transformation. Instead, globalization is the simultaneous expansion of, on the one hand, states characterized by unmediated relations between states and their citizens, and, on the other, of markets characterized by profit accumulation rather than just the exchange of goods for immediate consumption, and by exchanges mediated by money. Globalization thus involves continuous changes in two major social relations that affect nearly all other social relations. While globalization involves states, they are not the only focus of analysis. A wide range of relevant actors constitute globalization from the bottom up. States are both embedded in social structures these actors create and help to create those social structures themselves.

The Beginnings of Globalization

Globalization is certainly not something intrinsically new, because global trade is old, as are quite extensive empires. Exchanges of goods, people, and cultural and technical knowledge in the Eurasian/African land mass have been going on for centuries. Imperial Rome engaged in long-distance trade with ancient China 2,000 years ago, and indigenous people in the Americas also had an active continent-scale trade. But if globalization is not particularly new, neither is it particularly old, because globalization implies connections and dynamics that amount to more than these ancient, but fairly simple, exchanges of people and goods, and more than geographically extensive systems of political control. While long-distance trade moved luxuries that were important to a thin layer of elites, this trade did not significantly affect the lives of the mass of people. The masses grew what they ate and wove what they wore.

Rapid technological change, particularly in telecommunications, and rapid increases in the quantity of money, people, firms, and goods on the move globally also lead many analysts to focus on the last few decades. The quantity of money, etc. on the move globally is in many instances higher today than in the period before the 1850s, though not during the *belle époque* just prior to World War I.[2] While the *quantity* of goods and people moving long distances surely matters, globalization also possesses an inner dynamic that involves political and economic social relations. It is not just a quantitative phenomenon. The dynamics creating today's growing volume of exchanges are the same as those that emerged in the fifteenth century to drive quantitatively much lower levels of trade. This dynamic differs *qualitatively* from the dynamics that characterized ancient exchanges and empires.

Finally, globalization cannot be understood by positing states and markets as separate and conflicting realms, or domestic and international markets as inherently separate sets of exchanges.[3] Thus approaches that explicitly or implicitly begin with the state-market distinction are problematic. First, states and markets are mutually constituting. Practically, markets need state-sanctioned violence (e.g., social order imposed over a specific territory, establishment of property rights) to come into being, because traditional markets are oriented around exchange rather than profit, and most pre-modern actors did not need access to the market to survive. States had to force peasants into profit-oriented markets. Markets also rely on enforceable contracts, but ultimately it is state-sanctioned violence that makes contracts enforceable. Practically, states need revenues to function. Both theory and history show that, in the absence of formal and functioning states, actors in the market will pay specialists in the use of violence—mafias—to enforce contracts and assure property rights, and actors with a comparative advantage in the use of force are equally willing to extort a share of production from direct producers. Thus, for example, mafias proliferated in Russia consequent to the collapse of the Soviet state and the re-emergence of markets. Naturally, some contestation always occurs over the precise share going to each, and actors on both sides sometimes make disastrous mistakes. Second, an ever-deepening division of labour and the consequent reduction in transport and transaction costs mean that local and global prices and production are always connected. Moreover, in the pre-railroad era, the high cost of inland transport often made the 'overseas' or 'international' market more accessible than a largely non-integrated 'national' market. State policy recognized and reinforced this reality by encouraging economic expansion overseas through colonization and imperialism.

The Divide between the Local and the Global

The nature of globalization can be understood better by contrasting politics and the economy before the fifteenth century with politics and the economy after that date. This meander through the past is useful because the fundamental nature of globalization in the past is essentially similar to globalization today. Understanding how states decisively and successfully shifted to unmediated relations with their subjects, and how economies got reoriented away from subsistence production with barter and towards accumulation of capital and exchanges mediated by money helps us to see how globalization operates today.

Pre-globalization *states* were 'mediated'. The central state did not have direct contact with the population living on the state's territory. Instead, the state essentially 'subcontracted' the administration of law and the collection of taxes to local elites, usually large landowners. These landowners mediated relations between the population and the state. Mediation placed severe limits on the degree to which the state could control its people, law, or revenues. By contrast, pre-globalization *economies* were unmediated. People had direct access to the means of survival—they grew their own food, wove their own clothing, and made many of their own tools. While they rarely had title to the land they farmed, their usage rights gave them unmediated access to that land and complicated large landowners' ability to use or sell that land. The lack of mediation placed severe limits on market pressures to increase productivity. Globalization is thus a process characterized by two fundamental, ongoing changes that began in the fifteenth century: less and less mediation between states and citizens and more and more mediation of social relations between people by money.

After 1400 the fundamental nature of both states and economies in some Western European countries changed in ways that made it possible for those states to project the new forms of state and economy onto the rest of the world. These new forms eventually connected most economic activity around the globe and subjected most of people's lives to the logic of markets, where the purpose of exchange was profit rather than barter. These developments also gave people direct relationships with the machinery of the state and tied all states up into one system of interstate relations. All three features enabled states and economies to overcome some fundamental limits on their ability to transcend their locality and thus become global. These limits were both technological—inefficient communication and transportation technologies—and social—nothing forced people and enterprises to constantly improve productivity, little motivated people to produce the behaviours the state desired, and little forced states to improve their administrative practices.

Transportation and communication technologies limited pre-globalization states' span of control. In an era when nearly everyone walked and food was transported mostly by wagon or on people's backs, it was difficult to project military force more than 50–60 miles in any direction from a town. Thus, in 1490, the average diameter of most European states and most Chinese 'counties'—the basic imperial administrative unit—was about 100 miles. Princes (or a county administrator) could exercise direct authority over a territory this size, because its borders were about two 20-mile hikes in any given direction or one day's horseback ride.[4]

Central elites generally ruled larger territories—empires—indirectly. Controlling larger units forced princes to mediate their rule through other people, namely local elites. Central elites relied on local elites to run their own, peripheral bits of the empire. Central elites tried to bind those local elites to the centre through a common ideology, culture, or provision of a larger share of the pie than those elites could get on their own. Thus the city of Rome extended Roman citizenship to peripheral elites first in the Italian peninsula and later to the rest of the republic/empire, while also giving those elites access to an expanded supply of slaves. But ancient empires fell apart with considerable frequency because distant intermediaries controlling local populations tended to be unreliable and self-serving.

Why did mediation make states unstable? The local elites who mediated the connections between local populations, mostly peasants, and the central state could exercise greater control over those populations and the resources they generated than could the central state. Mediation thus left imperial states vulnerable to three different threats. First, because peripheral elites controlled local resources, they might acquire enough money and weapons from those sources to make a bid to displace central elites, as Roman generals based in Gaul often did. Second, local elites might inadvertently provoke peasant rebellions by squeezing peasants too hard. These rebellions often spread to other parts of the empire. Third, central elites' efforts to tax peasants directly to reduce the threat posed by local elites' military and financial power might provoke local elites to rebel rather than suffer domination. The new states that emerged in Western Europe after 1400 successfully built government bureaucracies that displaced local elites, securing the central state's unmediated access to the population.

High transportation and communication costs before 1400 also limited economic activity. Virtually the entire economy revolved around the production of agricultural goods for food or clothing. People directly produced most of what they ate and wore, bartering excess production in local market towns. The absence of a larger market limited the division of labour. Nothing forced peasants to increase productivity levels because they produced what they ate and did not have to earn cash in a market to feed themselves. In turn, low productivity in food production limited the available surplus, again constraining new opportunities. Meanwhile, long-distance trade mostly involved luxuries. This trade was socially important but not critical to the survival of the population. Even if transportation costs were lower, however, and there was more trade, most peasants would not have engaged in much productivity-enhancing investment. Their self-sufficiency meant that they could always survive without access to the market.

Furthermore, the intersection of political power and property rights around landownership and labour also deterred productivity-enhancing investment. Generally, either the empire or local elites had legal ownership of land, peasants, or slaves. Political power grew directly from this ownership. For local elites, landownership conveyed the right to make and enforce local law. If those elites didn't control land, they couldn't extract rent from peasants; if they couldn't extract rents they couldn't build and supply their private armies; and without private armies anyone could take away their power to extract rents from peasants. Local elites thus assured their continued legal control over land through laws that prevented land sales (entailment) and instead mandated that land pass to the oldest (usually male) child.

By the same token, imperial elites strove to secure the emperor's ownership rights over all land, and thus his right to allocate land to compliant local elites. This right would strip local elites of their ability to raise their own armies against the emperor. But an open land market would also threaten the centre's control over local elites. The absence of an open land market in most places meant that nobles often were better off squeezing more rent from peasants than they were trying to increase productivity. Even during the so-called agricultural revolution that started in Holland and Britain in the fifteenth century, after globalization started, agricultural productivity roughly rose by only 0.25 per cent each year. In contrast, post-Industrial Revolution economies generally experienced annual productivity gains 10 times as high over the past two centuries in their core technologies.

The old empires thus saw constant tension between central and local control over these key resources. Overly high levels of local control caused empires to break apart. Overly strenuous efforts by central elites to remove local elites and get unmediated access to peasants provoked local elites to rebel. Meanwhile, unmediated access to land and food meant no one had much incentive to pursue sustained productivity gains or sustained investment. What caused local and central elites in Western Europe to break out of this ancient cycle and start the process of globalization? How did states decisively and successfully shift to unmediated relations with their subjects? How did economies get reoriented away from subsistence with barter and towards accumulation of capital and exchanges mediated by money?

The Historical Shift to Globalization

The short answer to these very complicated questions is that Europe combined three factors found elsewhere to a lesser degree or not all at once. These three factors answer the questions: Why this kind of state? Why many states and not one empire? Why this kind of market? First, Western European states were simultaneously backward and advanced in terms of their administrative and military technologies. Backwardness made it difficult for any one state to overwhelm the others and create an empire like that in China or India. Superior naval military technologies, however, allowed them to project force into the Americas and Indian Ocean. Europeans couldn't dominate each other but they could use violence to take what they wanted from many of their global neighbours. They organized this theft through state-chartered companies, such as the Dutch and British East India Companies or the Hudson's Bay Company, which established economic and military control in vast areas of British North America prior to US or Canadian independence. These corporations merged trade and violence in one organization. Jan Coen, Director-General of the Dutch East India Company, noted that violence was part of the 'means of production' for spices and other goods from Asia: 'Trade in Asia must be maintained under the protection of our own weapons; and [these weapons] have to be paid for from the profits of trade. We can't trade without war, nor make war without trade.'[5]

This organized theft provided some European states with unmediated access to the cash they needed to build bureaucracies, while constant war provided a strong incentive to build strong domestic bureaucracies. These centrally controlled bureaucracies then undercut the power local elites gained from mediating relations between the state and peasants. The new bureaucracies gave the state direct access to tax revenues from peasants and enabled the state to transform peasants into citizens loyal to the central state. Unmediated access to cash outside their realms enabled European princes to construct unmediated access to cash inside their realms, and consequently the form of the modern state developed. States' global involvements shaped their internal development.

Second, the absence of successful empire-building within Europe meant constant warfare prevailed in Europe. Theft overseas made it possible to finance these constant, and constantly more expensive, wars. The rising cost of war forced a search for more money, and for more efficient ways of fighting. Self-sustaining military competition widened rather than narrowed the military gap between a few European states and the rest of the world. This gap permitted those states to construct large-scale empires *outside* Europe, and thus ultimately led to the diffusion of European state forms to the rest of the world. Areas outside Europe that successfully imitated European state-building—like Japan and Turkey—were able to survive the European onslaught, but by doing so they reproduced European state forms. Areas that unsuccessfully imitated Europe—nearly the whole of Africa and the Middle East—were colonized and then had ineffective versions of the European state form pressed upon them after decolonization. This generated our modern state system.

The first two differences generated states and the state system. What about markets? The third critical difference was the consolidation of the open market for land and labour that had been emerging in Britain during the sixteenth century as a consequence of conflicts between central and local elites. This occurred after the English Civil War (1642–8).[6] In Britain, the emergence of an open land market forced both workers and owners into constant competition to buy access to that land. Workers and tenant farmers had to increase their work effort or be fired and starve. Owners had to accumulate capital or risk having their land bought out by someone with more capital. The new land market rested on new kinds of 'absolute' property rights that gave one person the right to sell land. Elsewhere in Europe, war's insatiable demand for revenue forced many monarchs to concede similar absolute property rights to the

local nobility in exchange for rights to tax the population. During the next few centuries, capitalist markets, which had profit accumulation as their central purpose, replaced exchange markets, which had had subsistence as their central purpose. This generated our modern market economy, in which exchange for profit dominates virtually all activity people undertake.

Europe thus gave birth to modern states, with unmediated relations between states and citizens, and to modern markets, with their constant pressure to increase productivity and output and the mediation of social relations through cash purchases. Constant conflict among states and constant competition among firms translated both of these large-scale systems to the rest of the world in several spasms of expansion. More activities in more areas became subjected to market logic, forcing people always to work for money and to buy more and more of the goods and services they required rather than directly produce them. States developed more technologies for controlling and taxing their populations using the combination of bureaucratic surveillance and the inculcation of self-control. People found themselves 'caged'—compelled by the logic of the situation to continue conforming to demands from the state and markets in their own self-interest.[7]

Why did the state system and markets for profit expand into the rest of the world, and what did this mean for the possibility for economic and political development inside and outside of Europe? The rapid expansion of industry inside Europe strongly shaped development outside Europe in the direction of raw material extraction, while interstate competition for access to or control over those resources strongly shaped political development. Both forces intersected in the nature and interests of local elites in countries and colonies outside Western Europe. Those local elites could get relatively wealthy by exporting raw materials to Europe; on the other hand, the choice not to export exposed them to the risk of incursions by European states and settlers in pursuit of those same raw materials. The same dilemma confronts poorer countries today, except that they have added cheap clothing and cheap workers to their list of exports, supplementing traditional staples like sugar, cocoa, and spices.

Economic globalization accelerated after the Industrial Revolution in Britain (c. 1750–1850) and its echoes 50 years later in the United States and Northwestern Europe. In both instances, the introduction of steam power and complicated machinery to manufacturing processes enormously increased demand for raw materials and set the pattern for similar processes in the twentieth and twenty-first centuries. Nineteenth-century manufacturing largely involved the transformation of agricultural raw materials into food and clothing or the transformation of minerals into simple metals. British cotton textile production doubled every 10 years from 40 million yards of fabric equivalent in 1785 to over 2 billion yards in 1850, with proportionate increases in raw cotton imports.[8] Mechanization of woollen production in the 1830s meant demand for wool also doubled about every 13 years, from 4,400 tons in 1820 to 214,000 tons in 1913. All of the cotton and 80 per cent of the wool had to be imported.

The Industrial Revolution also created a new and rapidly expanding urban proletariat that could not grow its own food (and thus had to work for wages and acquire goods in the market, mediated through money). Britain's population nearly quadrupled over the course of the nineteenth century, from 10.2 million people in 1801 to 37 million in 1901, even as about 20 million people emigrated from Britain. By 1900 Britain imported 84 per cent of its wheat, 37 per cent of its beef, 47 per cent of its mutton, nearly 100 per cent of its sugar, and 53 per cent of its dairy and poultry products. By 1914 Britain imported roughly 60 per cent of its total calories, and Germany about one-fifth.[9] Total world trade—mostly manufactured exports from Western Europe and raw material exports from European colonies—rose from $7.3 billion in 1820 to $236.3 billion in 1913, in constant 1990 US dollars.[10]

Because industrializing Europe could not produce enough raw materials and foods, these had to be grown elsewhere. European demand for cotton, wool, and wheat (among many other things) thus sparked a global expansion of capitalist agricultural production oriented towards export markets. World wheat acreage expanded 78 per cent from 1885 to 1929, with virtually all of this growth occurring outside Western Europe. Just as textile and garment assembly moved offshore to low-wage countries in the late twentieth century, large parts of agricultural production moved to settler colonies with cheap land in the nineteenth century. And just as offshore producers of garments have driven down the real price of clothing in the past 30 years, driving onshore producers out of business, the nineteenth century's new agricultural exporters drove down the cost of food and raw materials in Europe, forcing peasants off the land. Overall, world crop production expanded by 50 per cent from 1840 to 1880, with half of this in North America and Australia,[11] where settlers could easily dominate and destroy small indigenous populations and where strong state institutions were both built by or borrowed from the British.

Where did the workers come from for these new production zones? Initially Europeans took roughly 14 million slaves from Africa, but after 1800 Europe supplied about 50 million voluntary migrants while Asia supplied an additional 50 million voluntary, but mostly indentured, workers. These migrants left Europe, India, and China because falling prices for imported agricultural goods pushed them out of a peasant livelihood in their own countries; simultaneously, all the new places producing exports needed so many workers that wages there were uniformly higher. Thus, virtually all European emigrants went to high-wage areas like the United States, Canada, and Argentina. Chinese and Indian emigrants went to tropical areas (like Malaysia, Sri Lanka, East Africa, and the Caribbean) where relatively higher wages enabled some to repay their indenture debt. Much the same is happening today, with migrants flowing from low-wage to high-wage areas, but in manufacturing instead of agriculture. Workers flow from rural areas to local export-processing zones, and often thence into what are low-wage sectors of rich-country economies but nonetheless high-wage areas relative to their original economies. Thus Mexicans flow from poor states in Mexico to low-wage manufacturing work in the border zone with the United States, and then hop the border to work in gardening, restaurants, and meat-packing.

Just as Europe and Japan supplied much of the capital for Southeast Asian industrialization in the 1990s, and US capital powered much of Latin American industrialization in the 1970s, Britain lent most of the money that capitalized nine-teenth-century agricultural development in new states in the America and elsewhere. And just as in contemporary Latin America and Southeast Asia, this huge inflow of capital created an over-supply of output from these new producers. In turn, this oversupply caused export prices to drop, making it difficult for these new states to pay back foreign debt and causing the occasional international financial crisis. Just as falling prices for wool and wheat triggered a series of develop-ing-country defaults in the 1890s, falling prices for toys and clothing helped trigger the 1997 Asian financial crisis.

If local elites in would-be developing countries wanted to get rich, the only game in town was exporting to Britain, and the only way to export in large quantities was to construct some reasonable facsimile of both modern states and modern mar-kets. Thus these local elites pursued what we would today call 'neo-liberal reforms'.[12] The states they controlled created property rights in land to make land alienable (saleable); they legalized mort-gages on land so producers could borrow money to capitalize their operations; and they created open labour markets by eliminating the more obvious forms of coerced labour and slavery and helping to organize the flow of migrants. Generally, they cre-ated production systems dedicated to a handful of exports oriented towards rich-country markets. Growth in their economies was almost totally reliant on growth in the rich industrial countries—were it not for industrialized countries' growth, after all, these peripheral economies would have essentially remained subsistence economies. An overwhelming reliance on one or two exports was not unique to poor countries in this first round of

economic growth. Iowa and Kansas were as reliant on a handful of export crops as were Argentina and Malaya—perhaps even more so. For all these agri-cultural exporters the issue was whether they could overcome this reliance and generate new exports and a more diversified local economy.

States played the crucial role in determining whether this economic diversification occurred.[13] Generally speaking, states enjoying a benign secu-rity environment—most of Latin America, for example—tended to continue producing agricul-tural exports for industrial countries. They had no pressing need for revenues or industry to fight off aggressive neighbours. Colonies, of course, had little say in the matter. Economies that did not diversify, that remained pure exporters of raw materials, proved extraordinarily vulnerable to declining relative demand for their exports. After the first century of industrialization, rich economies increasingly consumed manufactured goods made of other manufactured goods, decreas-ing the share of raw materials in total consumption. Consumers spent more money on cars, made up of metal manufactures, rather than clothes, made of fibres. The falling income elasticity of demand for raw materials in general produced lower prices for raw materials, slower growth in raw materials exports, and an acute vulnerability to foreign debt crises. In the late twentieth century, few countries would voluntarily opt for this policy choice. But in the nineteenth century the consequences of this choice were not obvious, and virtually all states chose to specialize in raw materials exports, and imperial administrations forced virtually all colonies to focus on natural resource exploitation.

By contrast, states with predatory Europeans as neighbours or unwelcome guests—Germany, Russia, Japan, China, Turkey, Austria-Hungary—opted for significant, if not always successful, inter-vention in their economies in an effort to promote industrialization. These states borrowed money abroad to channel capital to state-owned firms or firms so closely linked to the state that they might as well have been state-owned. They sheltered new local industry from foreign competition, invested heavily in education, freely stole foreign production technologies and patents, and aggressively promoted manufactured exports as well as agricultural exports. To do this, industrializing states had to create professional bureaucracies, conscript large numbers of peasants into the military (often the school of first resort), and increase their ability to turn peasants into citizens and then directly tax those citizens.

Economic and military competition between states outside Europe thus worked just like competition among European states to create new states with an unmediated relationship between themselves and their citizens and more pervasive markets mediated by money. As in earlier centuries, continued competition helped spread the modern forms of state and market. This competition also drove the diffusion of the physical and cultural infrastructure that supported both the military and the market: the use of money to mediate an increasing percentage of interactions between human beings, telecommunications, modern mechanized transport, English as a lingua franca, and the standardization of weights, measures, and the interfaces where people met machines and machines met machines.[14] All this in turn made it increasingly easy to make and trade goods in a global market, as well as to loan money. It also lowered barriers for people emigrating away from low wages resulting from low production prices in the home country and facilitated the conscription imposed by increasingly intrusive states.

The diffusion of the modern state and market also had some seemingly paradoxical effects. First, while the old system of mediated politics exposed people to abuse by local elites, it also obliged local elites to shelter their clients from economic shocks, lest those clients turn against local elites. But as states displaced local elites and built an increasingly unmediated relationship between themselves and citizens, people lost the protection local elites used to offer in economic downturns. The separation of most people from the land meant that few had the opportunity to turn to subsistence production in times of economic hardship—and economic crises are endemic to capitalist economies. The average person thus felt the risks of unemploy-

ment, bad health, and poverty more acutely. But the lack of mediation exposed states to citizen demands for shelter from market pressures. And states' successes at getting unmediated access to (male) citizen bodies, for example, through conscription, inadvertently reinforced political demands for state intervention to buffer those citizens from market forces and to give them (mostly males) the vote. Both conscription and then real war enabled voting citizens to demand what we now term the welfare state, while pushing states into providing a wide range of cash transfers and public services. In particular, the extraordinarily high body count of World War I gave surviving citizens a robust moral claim on states.

Even before that, though, most Western European states realized that they needed to assure citizens of some minimum level of health care and income in order to get an adequate supply of healthy soldiers.[15] These states thus began to pay baby bonuses to mothers ('pro-natalist' policies), created public health systems, and started up pension systems for those few workers lucky enough to survive to retirement age. The expansion of volatile capitalist markets thus provoked a whole range of state welfare interventions to tame the effects of that volatility. In turn, these interventions made it possible for markets based on profit accumulation to survive politically by taming citizen reactions against market volatility.[16] The welfare state also made it possible for the market to continue expanding into new areas of life, as we will see.

Second, both the interstate system and the market were somewhat unstable. High levels of competition meant high levels of conflict, and increased conflict in both markets and diplomacy risked quite severe consequences. Both the interstate system and the market came crashing down in the first half of the twentieth century. In 1914, alarmed by what appeared to be Russia's rising power, Germany provoked a European war that soon involved everyone.[17] World War I, whose unsettled resolution in 1918 sowed the seeds for a second, truly global war that began in the 1930s, undid several centuries of European global expansion. Extraordinary death rates forced European states into conscripting their colonial populations for combat in Europe and elsewhere, setting in motion the same kinds of demands for the vote and equality that conscription had started in Europe 30 years earlier. Returning colonial soldiers staffed liberation movements run by leaders educated in the universities of the colonial powers. Meanwhile, enfeebled European states had neither the strength nor the will to successfully hang on to their colonies, though some tried. Some empires floated promises of decolonization in the 1930s, and from 1946 through the late 1960s there was a massive transfer of power from European colonial administrations to newly independent states.

The similar instability of the market also helped expand state intervention to control the market. The volatile 1920s and economic catastrophe of the 1930s Great Depression, when unemployment rose above 20 per cent in many countries and many farmers lost their land, gave rise to massive and pervasive state intervention to temper the market for the sake of political stability and military security. Following bankruptcies of private providers and breakdowns in service, states everywhere nationalized infrastructure services—telecommunications, rail and air transport, and finance—while regulating agricultural prices and wages. After World War II, the rich states began providing tertiary education for free, or at a great subsidy, began providing public housing or housing subsidies, and, as women entered the labour force, expanded the pro-natalist policies of the nineteenth century to encompass a whole range of health and child-care services. Post-war economic stability, high growth rates, and low unemployment foreclosed a political future in which states exerted complete control over the economy, however. Instead, manufacturing enjoyed an unparalleled period of prosperity as workers flush with cash and largely relieved of the fear of unemployment cheerfully acquired expensive consumer durables, such as automobiles, TVs, and refrigerators, on credit. Thus equipped, European workers soon spurned the advances of Communist parties.

Was the Post-World War II Period Different?

The post-World War II period is usually seen as a period in which globalization stopped. Overseas capital flows, which had amounted to between 5 and 10 per cent of British GDP, largely evaporated as investors feared default and states regulated capital outflows. International migration to the western hemisphere fell from its pre-1914 peak of 1.7 million people to fewer than 100,000 annually. And, after 1930, trade collapsed by two-thirds. States regulated trade to initiate or accelerate local industrialization, while the European empires imposed strict preferences for trade within their own empires.

But 'paused' might be a better word to describe the onward march of globalization during this period, particularly as political and economic developments in the Great Depression and in the 25 years after World War II laid the foundations for a renewed expansion of state and market. Neither decolonization nor the vast expansion of welfare transfers and services after World War II stopped the two long-term trends discussed above. Quite the contrary. Decolonization created many more states, each of which aspired to the level of control European states possessed over their own citizens and which thus began the process of gaining unmediated access to those citizens. Nuclear weapons and the US occupation of Germany and Japan prevented the kind of chaos that occurred after World War I. But the post-World War II period was not devoid of interstate competition. Instead, this competition largely took economic forms. Almost everyone outside the United States tried to catch up to the United States by resurrecting the techniques that European states had used in the nineteenth century to pursue industrialization. Europeans and Asians exported in order to get rich, and by exporting they, in combination with the United States, increased the share of trade in total world production from about 8 per cent in 1950 to 24 per cent in 2003.

Efforts at industrialization in some peripheral economies attracted renewed flows of capital from rich countries, particularly as states in those countries began removing capital controls in the 1970s. By 1979 would-be industrializers in the periphery had borrowed US$830 billion (in 2002 dollars). By 2003 their debt had tripled to US$2,650 billion. To service this increased debt, would-be and successful industrializers aggressively promoted exports. Would-be exporters' willingness to supply new places from which to export met a demand by rich-country producers for new places from which to export. Rich-country firms in industries where labour costs were crucial responded to high-wage, high-tax, high-regulation environments in their home markets by shifting low-skill, labour-intense production offshore to export processing zones (EPZs) in low-wage, low-regulation former colonies. Rich states encouraged and organized this shift to keep firms profitable by rearranging tax codes, subsidizing relocation, and expanding the scope of free-trade treaties. These EPZs relied heavily on young female workers, usually the daughters of small peasant family farmers. So whether or not EPZ-based industrialization strategies worked in terms of economic development, they also pulled millions of women out of households and into the market economy and into urban areas.

Peripheral countries' efforts at industrialization, and rich-country firms' efforts to find cheap labour, also helped restart international migration flows. From 1965 to 2000 the global stock of migrants (people living in a country different from their country of birth) rose by approximately 100 million people to 175 million.[18] Workers in EPZs acquired the social and work skills, the cash, and sometimes the language skills they needed to migrate to the home country of the multinational firms that employed them. In turn, migration increased both their exposure to cash-mediated market exchanges and those of their families. Migrants by definition lived apart from their extended social network at home and had to buy more services and goods that they would have perhaps acquired in non-cash exchanges at home. But migrants also monetized their original societies. Migrants typically save huge proportions of their earnings—10 to 20 per cent—and remit those savings back home to their families. This enables those families to acquire a bigger share of their goods and services from the cash economy. Peripheral efforts at industrialization thus expanded international flows of people, capital, and goods, deepening the influence of the market on those societies.

In the rich countries, the welfare state turned out to be an unwitting agent for further globalization as well. This expansion laid the groundwork for further expansion of the market into areas of social life that previously had been either insulated from or untouched by market forces. Welfare state expansion also pulled more and more people into an unmediated relationship with the state. As in the periphery, both trends disproportionately affected women. Welfare states after World War II expanded or created three crucial services that helped propel women into the market. First, women gained access to free (or cheap) university education. By increasing women's human capital, education increased both the financial and emotional incentives for women to work. Labour force participation by college-educated European women aged 25–39 (those born after universalization of higher education) runs 20 to 30 percentage points higher than for those women who have only completed the minimum compulsory public education.[19] Second, many states either directly provided child care and (sometimes) elder care or provided cash transfers to subsidize the purchase of these services. This increased women's ability to balance babies and bosses, albeit only imperfectly. Third, the expansion of university education, health services, and child care/elder care created millions of jobs for women in these new 'caring' sectors of the economy. Caring thus came out of the house and into the market.

The welfare state thereby provided motive, means, and opportunity for increased labour force participation by married women with children.[20] In the US, labour force participation of married women with children under the age of 18 rose from 45 per cent in 1975 to 70 per cent in 2000; in Britain, 24 per cent of married women worked for wages in 1950, but by 1998, 74 per cent were in the workforce.[21] By contrast, countries with lower rates of university education for women and lower levels of public or publicly subsidized child care have substantially lower rates of female labour market participation. Rather than impeding the growth of the market, the welfare state proved to be a necessary step in the expansion of the market. Many formerly household services moved into the public domain, and thence into cash-mediated production, partly at states' behest, and partly at women's.

If the post-war welfare state helped to pull rich-country women into the open labour market, globalization, understood narrowly as increased trade, helped to push them. Competition from low-wage (women) workers in poor countries undercut wage levels for low-skill male workers in rich countries. Falling wages for those male workers made it impossible to maintain a family on just one (male) wage. In the US, the real wage for males with only a high school education fell 17 per cent from 1979 to 1995, while high school-educated females saw a slight increase.[22] By 1998, 57 per cent of working women married to men in the lowest wage quintile earned an hourly wage higher than that of their husbands, as compared to only 7 per cent of women married to men with wages in the top quintile, and 31 per cent of the women in the lowest group earned 50 per cent more than their husbands did.[23]

Towards the Future: More of the Same

How, then, should we think and not think about globalization? Clearly, we should not think about globalization as a new process, in which novel electronic technologies triggered an unexpected rise in global trade and capital flows. Nor is it a process in which a reified international market wrestles a weakening state for control of the domestic economy. Instead, individual actors caged within states and firms are respectively locked into a relentless search for power and revenues, and power and profits. The existence of each set of actors is conditioned on the presence of the other. Each makes specific and contingent alliances to advance mutual interests. These alliances produce the variation we

can observe among different political economies, but the underlying causal force is systemic—the inability of any organization to avoid competition. The last 500 years have seen two parallel and continual, if not continuous, processes that comprise globalization. First, states swept away the local elites that previously had mediated their access to peasants and replaced those elites with bureaucracies that regulate ever-increasing aspects of citizens' lives. Second, more and more of people's time, social life, and economic activity is mediated through money rather than by the direct exchanges and barter that characterized the peasant economies of the pre-globalization era.[24]

Nothing suggests that either trend will abate. The relocation of some state activities to supranational bodies like the European Union and the United Nations merely recreates the older conflict between central states and local elites at a new level. The core constitutional issue confronting the European Union, after all, is whether it is a union of states (a loose federation, in which the new EU state's power is mediated through the old states) or a new state (in which the EU has direct power of taxation, conscription, and regulation). Similarly, the basic premise of the United Nations is sovereign equality—its members are all recognized states—and its peacekeeping operations are aimed at the rehabilitation of failed states, not their replacement by something else.

The constant expansion of the market geographically and socially also looks robust. The last 20 years have seen the expansion of low-cost manufacturing (think: beanie babies) to the one billion people living in China and the expansion of low-cost service-sector production (think: call centres) to India's one billion people. Compared to this, the withdrawal of much economic activity from Africa over the past 30 years looks less significant in economic terms. In the rich countries, the welfare state has changed in directions that also magnify unmediated state power and market-mediated logics—and it has often done so in response to popular demands. Just as states helped make markets in agriculture and manufacturing in the past, they are making markets in services now. More welfare services are produced under market conditions, e.g., through subcontracting, private production, or competition among public providers. More and more, the payout level of the single largest welfare state transfer payment, the old age pension, is based on individuals' prior performance in the wage market. And more and more, European states are looking for incentives to get women to have more babies, which is to say, they are expanding the number of policies affecting the rate at which new citizens are produced. Continued globalization—the direct intrusion of the state into the lives of people constituted as self-regulating citizens, and the increasing mediation of all social life through monetized exchanges—is thus both the past and the future.

Notes

1. A more extensive treatment can be found in Herman Schwartz, *States vs. Markets: Emergence of a Global Economy* (Basingstoke: Palgrave, 2000). Thanks to Shelley Hurt and Alethia Jones for many useful comments.

2. See Paul Hirst and Grahame Thompson, *Globalization in Question: The International Economy and the Possibilities of Governance* (Cambridge: Polity Press, 1996), for a thorough discussion of relative magnitudes; also Jeffrey Williamson and Kevin O'Rourke, *Globalization and History: The Evolution of a Nineteenth-Century Atlantic Economy* (Cambridge, Mass.: MIT Press, 1999).

3. See Chapter 1, by Michael Krätke and Geoffrey Underhill, for a longer discussion of this point. Fernand Braudel's *Civilization and Capitalism, 15th to the 18th Century*, 3 vols (New York: Harper and Row, 1985), provides 1,500 pages of examples.

4. Michael Mann, *The Sources of Social Power*, vol. 1 (Cambridge: Cambridge University Press, 1986), 136; Charles Tilly, *Coercion, Capital, and European States* (Cambridge: Basil Blackwell, 1990), 45. A state with a 100-mile diameter has a land mass equal to Kuwait, half of the Netherlands, or double that of Connecticut.

5. 'International Trade: 1614: The East India Companies', *The Economist*, 31 Dec. 1999.

6. Robert Brenner, *Merchants and Revolution: Commercial Change, Political Conflict, and London Overseas Traders, 1550–1653* (London: Verso, 2003); Richard Lachman, *From Manor to Market: Structural Change in England, 1536–1640*

(Madison: University of Wisconsin Press, 1987).

7. Max Weber, *The Protestant Ethic and the Spirit of Capitalism* (New York: Routledge, 1992 [1930]); Mann, *Sources of Social Power*.

8. B.R. Mitchell, *International Historical Statistics, Europe: 1750–1988* (New York: Stockton Press, 1992).

9. Avner Offer, *The First World War: An Agrarian Interpretation* (Oxford: Clarendon Press, 1989), 25, 81; Eric Hobsbawm, *Age of Capital, 1848–1875* (New York: Scribner, 1975), 179.

10. Angus Maddison, *Monitoring the World Economy, 1820–1992* (Paris: OECD, 1995), 236–9.

11. Harriet Friedmann, 'World Market, State and Family Farm', *Comparative Studies in Society and History* 20, 3 (1978): 546.

12. See, for example, the chapters in this volume by Phillips (23), Cerny (26), Baker (29), and Freyberg-Inan (30).

13. Alexander Gerschenkron, *Economic Backwardness in Historical Perspective* (Cambridge, Mass.: Belknap, 1962); David Waldner, *State Building and Late Development* (Ithaca, NY: Cornell University Press, 2000); Linda Weiss and John Hobson, *States and Economic Development: A Comparative Historical Analysis* (Cambridge: Polity Press, 1995).

14. Consider the standardization of the controls for driving cars or of 'plug-and-play' computer equipment.

15. Jytte Klausen, *War and Welfare: Europe and the US* (New York: St Martin's Press, 1998).

16. See, of course, Karl Polanyi, *The Great Transformation* (New York: Farrar and Rinehart, 1944).

17. Dale Copeland, *Origins of Great Power War* (Ithaca, NY: Cornell University Press, 2000).

18. Jeffrey G. Williamson, *The Political Economy of World Mass Migration: Comparing Two Global Centuries* (Washington: American Enterprise Institute Press, 2004), Table 10.1.

19. Ingrid Jönsson, 'Women and Education in Europe', *International Journal of Contemporary Sociology* 36, 2 (1999): 145–62. Men's participation rates are almost identical for all educational levels.

20. Childless and unmarried women had always worked at rates close to those of men.

21. Anne Winkler, 'Earnings of Husbands and Wives in Dual Income Families', US Bureau of Labor Statistics, *Monthly Labor Statistics* (Apr. 1998): 42–8; Dora L. Costa, 'From Mill Town to Board Room: The Rise of Women's Paid Labor', *Journal of Economic Perspectives* 14, 4 (Fall 2000): 106.

22. Richard Freeman, 'The New Inequality in the United States', in Albert Fishlow and Karen Parker, eds, *Growing Apart: The Causes and Consequences of Global Wage Inequality* (New York: Council on Foreign Relations, 1999), 23.

23. Winkler, 'Earnings of Husbands and Wives in Dual-Earner Families', 46.

24. Georg Simmel, *The Philosophy of Money*, ed. David Frisby (London: Routledge, 1978).

Suggested Readings

Braudel, Fernand. *Civilization and Capitalism, 15th to the 18th Century*, 3 vols. New York: Harper and Row, 1985.

Chaudhury, K.N. *Trade and Civilization in the Indian Ocean*. New York: Cambridge University Press, 1985.

Mann, Michael. *Sources of Social Power: From the Earliest Times to 1760*, 2 vols. New York: Cambridge University Press, 1986.

Shonfield, Andrew. *Modern Capitalism: The Changing Balance of Public and Private Power*. New York: Oxford University Press, 1966.

Williamson, Jeffrey, and Kevin O'Rourke. *Globalization and History: The Evolution of a Nineteenth-Century Atlantic Economy*. Cambridge, Mass.: MIT Press, 1999.

Chapter 4

Globalization and Its Critics

James H. Mittelman

If globalization confers unparalleled benefits, as its torchbearers hold, then why does it produce increasing disenchantment, as at the 'battle in Seattle', a large-scale protest at the 1999 meeting of the World Trade Organization (WTO), followed by demonstrations in several cities on five continents?[1] Embedded in this broad question are specific issues: Precisely what do globalizers promise, and what do their critics allege?

In the growing debate, answers to these questions necessarily avoid a bipolar separation of pro-globalization and anti-globalization forces. A caricatured representation of a contest between two apparently irreconcilable sides impoverishes social criticism and obscures multiple positions along a spectrum, best explained by first making clear in this chapter the meanings of globalization. Then the promises and the counterweight of seven different critiques will be presented. There is contestation not only between the celebrants of globalization and the critics but also among the seven clusters of criticism. And no cluster is monolithic—each one subsumes its own heterodoxies.

Whereas the criticism emerges from varied standpoints, is there common ground? Do globalization critics agree in any measure? What can be learned from the similarities and differences in the critical discourses? In this examination of the discursive strategies of the enthusiasts of globalization and its critics, the conclusion will provide indications, albeit tentative, of the directions in which the structure of globalization is headed.

What Is Globalization?

There are three possibilities for conceptualizing globalization. Simply put, it is often understood as an increase in interconnections or growing interdependence on a world scale. In this manner, globalization is deemed to be a surge in global flows, such as investment, migration, and consumer goods, facilitated by new technologies, especially in communications and transportation. Probing further, scholars have defined globalization as a compression of time and space. Events in one part of the world can instantly affect what takes place in distant locales.[2] (For example, a steep fall in the value of Asian currencies during the 1997–8 financial crisis immediately rippled to Brazil, Russia, and South Africa.) These definitions are helpful as far as they go; however, they are devoid of power relations.

Arguably, a more useful avenue of inquiry is to approach globalization as a historical structure of material power. It is a historical transformation in the economy in that livelihoods and modes of existence change; in politics, the locus of power gradually shifts above and below territorial states, forming a multi-level system; and in culture, an erosion of certain lifeways and the emergence of new hybrid forms occur, as with the rise of Singlish, a syncretic language widely spoken in Singapore. With this definition in mind, let us turn to the potential benefits of globalization.

Promises

The promises of contemporary globalization are embodied in a set of ideas and a policy framework. The predominant ideas or shared meanings about world order from the 1980s to the twenty-first century have been neo-liberal and centre on heightened integration in the world market. When transmitted transnationally, these meanings help to maintain and reproduce a social order, especially, as Antonio Gramsci taught us, by eliciting consent from both dominant and subordinate groups.[3] Not only may entrenched meanings support the continuity of a given order, but inasmuch as they contain the capacity to create and invent new ways of life, universalizing values also bear potential as transforming agents.

A group of intellectuals associated with philosopher-economist Friedrich von Hayek and his colleagues at the University of Chicago drew on classical political economists like Adam Smith and propounded a belief in self-running markets and faith in the beneficial role of competition. Popularized and put into practice by Ronald Reagan and Margaret Thatcher in the 1980s, the neo-liberal formula has projected a win-win scenario, particularly with the multiplier effects on people's livelihoods and the prospect for poverty reduction. The radical agenda set by Reagan and Thatcher included a shift away from national Keynesianism; and since the public sector does not compete for profits, its scope, especially social spending, had to be reduced. The sponsors of neo-liberalism have also promised advancements in technology, gains in productivity, new jobs, and the spread of knowledge and information to all who would adhere to its principles. Moreover, the purveyors of this set of ideas have contended that by generating material well-being, neo-liberalism will solve social ills.

That said, neo-liberal globalization offers an image of world order with normative appeal for all those who want to ascend the global hierarchy of power and privilege. This is an ethical claim with real implications for distributive justice and social organization. The expansion of markets is deemed to be natural and inevitable, while existing social arrangements within which economies are partially embedded are treated as chains that need to be unshackled. Projecting a vision in which the peoples of the world increasingly relate to each other only as individuals, Margaret Thatcher declared: 'There is no such thing as society, only individual men and women and their families.' From this grandiloquent perspective, neo-liberalism is a means to free the market from social and political control.

The core ideas and norms are thus encapsulated in a policy framework. Its bedrock is deregulation, liberalization, and privatization—a prescription administered by international economic institutions, such as the WTO, the World Bank, and the International Monetary Fund (IMF), as well as bilateral agencies and regional organizations. This model is implemented and customized in different locales and formed the 'Washington Consensus', a way to reorganize economies and societies around neo-liberal principles. However, the presumed consensus has run aground on the shoals of the ascendance of state-led economies in Asia that did not follow the path set by neo-liberal devotees, the debacle of 'shock therapy' of market reforms in the former Soviet Union and parts of Eastern Europe, the 1997–8 Asian financial crisis in which IMF advice contributed to the descending spiral, and the 2001 Argentine collapse wherein the neo-liberal blueprint clearly accelerated the downturn. The cumulative impact of these experiences has led to attempts to reconstruct consensus, such as at the 2002 United Nations Conference on Financing for Development in Monterrey, Mexico.

Towards this end, a complex of research institutions and think-tanks in Washington, DC, seek to refurbish discourses about neo-liberal policies. The mission of these groups is to bridge public education and policy formulation. Also, leading public intellectuals who offer policy advice propel new currents of ideological discourse. Among them are journalists, such as Thomas Friedman in the United States and John Micklethwait and Adrian Woodridge in Britain, and celebrity economists, like Jagdish Bhagwati, who acknowledge some of neo-liberalism's downsides but do not depart from its fundamental premises.[4] So, too, ideas are diffused and honed in policy arenas—for example, at the World Economic Forum, a private gathering that meets each year, usually in Davos, Switzerland, and brings together the world's leading CEOs, heads of state, cabinet ministers, journalists, and select intellectuals. Other structures involved in the dissemination of neo-liberal tenets are schools and universities through their curricula in business and commerce. MBA programs serve as a vital mechanism in the transnational spread of a distinctive combination of values and hence for the emergence of a common framework among policy-makers in diverse countries. Indeed, many MBA-toting ministers and senior bureaucrats have been trained in economics at elite universities in the United States.

A Conundrum of Criticism

A range of cataclysmic events—financial collapses, radical market reforms, and clashes between demonstrators and police at international summits—along with the formation of resistant organizations like the World Social Forum, founded to think about alternatives to neo-liberal globalization, have elicited diverse critical appraisals. Some of them are internal to the dominant paradigm and others fall outside it. There are also scripts that overlap this heuristic, put forward by critics who straddle the inside-outside distinction.

Holders of State Power

Although states possess different quanta of power and are in varied positions vis-à-vis the dynamics of globalization, some resist its pressures. France exemplifies a resistant state insofar as it maintains much regulation, generous welfare provisions (in schooling, health care, vacations, retirement, and unemployment entitlements), and a large government-run infrastructure, such as its reliable subways and rail networks. Its detractors point to a relatively high unemployment rate (at present, 9.5 per cent), a substantial government deficit, frequent strikes and demonstrations impeding daily life, if not rendering it chaotic, and labyrinthine labour legislation, banking codes, and an educational system that discourages innovation. Faced with the Anglo-American model of neo-liberalism and urged to adopt 'the American solution', President Jacques Chirac responded that his country has a global sense of itself and will fight to maintain a way of life: 'France', he said, 'intends to remain France.'[5] This nationalist backlash is emerging from some power-holders in both the developed and developing worlds.

Brazil's former president, Fernando Henrique Cardoso, candidly stated that he did not rule Brazil, because globalization is swallowing national states. He also noted that the 'increase in inequality and exclusion that globalization fuels is intricate and difficult to counter.' Moreover, according to Cardoso, 'globalization is inevitable, as are its consequences, its disasters, exclusion and social regression.'[6]

Going further, Malaysia's former prime minister, Mahathir Mohamad, complained that in just a few weeks his state lost the economic gains of 40 years of political independence when currency speculators suddenly moved their money out of Southeast Asian countries. The value of Malaysia's currency, the ringgit, tumbled by 40 per cent, and the meltdown of the stock market resulted in as much as a 70 per cent decline. Mahathir pointed to the lack of regulation and the ways in which global capital has spun out of control. He verbally attacked 'the present rules in which we had no say in their formulation, i.e., if there are rules at all.'[7] To curb 'hot money' (rapid transfers of capital in and out of Malaysia) and the offshore trading of the ringgit, Mahathir applied selective capital controls on 1 September 1998; however, some investors negotiated around these regulations, which were lifted on 15 February 1999, when a more modest 'repatriation levy' was introduced.[8]

In short, the power-holders cited above—Chirac, Cardoso, and Mahathir—allege that globalization has three shortcomings: it erodes national culture, excludes many from its benefits, and is lacking in effective governance. Not surprisingly, principal officers at interstate institutions share elements of the statist critique.

Interstate Institutionalists

Internal to the neo-liberal paradigm is sharp criticism from international institutions. Viewing globalization mainly as an increase in flows and as a route to poverty reduction, the Secretary-General of the United Nations, Kofi Annan, and the heads of its affiliated agencies have often expressed moral outrage at the dynamics of inclusion and exclusion inscribed in globalization. James Wolfensohn, while president of the World Bank, presented a vision shared by diverse critics of globalizing forces: '[O]ur challenge is to make globalization an instrument of opportunity and inclusion.'[9] Yet the debate goes beyond so much forehead-slapping. At issue is not rhetorical behaviour but the actual impact of the policies of international economic institutions, seen by many critics as instruments of globalization, a theme to which we will return.

Just as the World Bank has assessed its own performance in regard to making globalization a more inclusive phenomenon, the Independent Evaluation Office of the IMF has reviewed the Fund's role and also generated a self-evaluation process.[10] Although the IMF is often regarded as stubborn in its adherence to neo-liberal formulations, its public self-criticism candidly acknowledges mistakes in remedies prescribed for crises in Indonesia, Korea, and Brazil. The findings of the evaluation note several limitations.

The assessment of the IMF's actions undertaken by the Independent Evaluation Office points out that in pre-crisis surveillance, the IMF was more successful at diagnosing macroeconomic vulnerabilities than in bringing to light the risks coming from the financial sector and corporate balance sheets and identifying the ways in which government added to those weaknesses. Another shortcoming, according to the report, was the IMF's reluctance to stimulate broad policy debates. In other words, greater transparency could have helped catch the burgeoning problems. While the scope of the financing project was too small in Korea, the IMF's part in co-ordinating the involvement of the private sector, especially in Korea and Brazil, was constrained by the shareholder governments, which had reservations about the use of non-market instruments.

A larger problem was the failure to develop a comprehensive strategy and communicate the logic of the program. Hence, a lack of focus on reforms in the banking sector resulted in diminishing confidence and non-implementation of policies. The IMF's own operations suffered from inadequate staff resources and insufficient up-to-date knowledge. Finally, difficulties arose in efforts to collaborate with other international financial institutions, especially the World Bank. To learn from its mistakes, the IMF calls for improvement in pre-crisis surveillance, making assessments more available to the public, co-operating more fully with other international and non-governmental organizations (NGOs), adjusting program design during a crisis, giving more emphasis to human resource development, and strengthening the Fund's role as a crisis co-ordinator.[11]

Neo-Liberal Reformers

A reformist position is advanced by Joseph Stiglitz, a former senior vice-president and chief economist at the World Bank and co-recipient of the 2001 Nobel Prize in Economic Sciences.[12] He contends that the IMF has repeatedly adopted misguided and hypocritical policies—a 'one-size-fits-all' approach that reflects a dogmatic adherence to ideology. It follows that the problem is not just international economic institutions themselves, in which finance ministers, shareholders, and trade ministers purport to speak for their countries, but the dominant mindsets about globalization: the culprit is the ideology of market fundamentalism, and the international institutions suffer from a democratic deficit. Lacking transparency, the policy framework—from capital market liberalization to substantial bailouts—serves the rich and ultimately contributes to global instability.

Stiglitz holds that, on balance, the IMF has failed to achieve macroeconomic success, has contributed to rising poverty in many countries, and is insensitive to inequality. He maintains that the Fund's recipes are ill-advised, for development must be home-grown. Unlike shock therapy, as in

Russia, a co-ordinated and gradualist policy of opening to the market, adopted in China, has much to commend it. A balanced encounter with globalization must be negotiated and gauged in terms of a specific context. Stiglitz calls for debt forgiveness and a multi-faceted system of reform, including interventions to correct large externalities stemming from risks in the capital market, bankruptcy provisions, reduced reliance on bailouts, banking regulation, more extensive safety nets, and a reconsideration of basic economic principles. Although Stiglitz calls for a social transformation, the meaning is unspecified. He does not flesh out this notion. For him, the task, at bottom, is to *manage* problems. Presto, deep structural transformations are converted into managerial issues.

A like-minded exemplar of the reformist critique, the billionaire investor, speculator, and philanthropist George Soros, identifies the structure of the global capitalist system as the locus of the problem. The difficulty is a defective market mechanism—that is, unstable financial markets, the failure of politics, and the 'erosion of moral values'.[13] Emphasizing the 'universal idea' of fallibility, Soros lambastes conventional economic theory for its presupposition that the market, left to its own devices, tends towards equilibrium. He adds that the capitalist system is characterized by the defects of market mechanisms, as evidenced in the Asian financial crisis, Russia, and the overall reverse flow of capital from the periphery to the centre. The root issue is that market values have weakened civic values and that the political process has not controlled the excesses of the market. The inefficiency of the political process works in favour of market fundamentalism, which undermines democracy.

For Soros, the remedy is to reclaim the institutions of representative democracy and recapture civic virtue.[14] Rejecting the ideology of untrammelled individualism and the imposition of market values, Soros wants to check the disintegration of the global capitalist system. He would reform globalization so that it becomes a socially oriented process. The way to do so, Soros believes, is by buttressing Special Drawing Rights (SDRs) so that developing countries have a more substantial reserve of foreign exchange and by making international assistance more effective for helping the poor. The antidote is not to dismantle international economic institutions but to fix them—for example, by establishing a special independent board to help implement SDRs and by making these bodies more socially responsible and oriented to welfare. Soros's call is thus for a more effective multilateralism and greater equity in the distribution of goods and services.[15] Commendably, this judgement reaches deeper than symptoms, searches for underlying causes, and touches on power relations, though in a manner that differs markedly from rival critiques of globalization.

Free-Market Advocates

Like Stiglitz and Soros, proponents of a self-running market seek to stabilize capitalism. Like Soros, they probe the nature of capitalism itself, but their reading and conclusions differ from those of the reformers. And unlike the reformers, the free-marketers' critique veers outside the standard neo-liberal paradigm.

Advocates of the free market, such as Lowell Bryan and Diana Farrell, express their unshaken belief that globalizing capitalism facilitates the transfer of savings from the developed countries and their innovative production technologies throughout the world.[16] This transfusion can reinvigorate growth in the developed economies, some of which have experienced stagnation in recent years. It is greater exposure to competition that increases productivity levels. The mobility of capital enables the market to break down the barriers to the gains of globalization and establishes the conditions for the acceleration of cross-border flows. Hence, best-practice transplants attract enormous movements of capital and multiply opportunities so long as the forces of economic globalization are unleashed. The engines, including transnational corporations and the skills revolution furthered by education, are catalysts for capital mobility. Yet the participants who distort global capital markets are national governments, which underwrite risk, impose regulatory measures, mint money, and borrow funds. Even developed countries, including the United States, formerly the world's leading creditor nation, are expanding their debt capacities relative to the size of their economies, leading to the possibility of severe market crises on a worldwide basis.

The answer is an open, global system in which each participant is liable for risk. Unshackle the forces of globalization by removing market restrictions, with the United States in its leading role as champion of a transition to an open, world economy. In Bryan and Farrell's view, there needs to be a shift to thinking about the world 'as one open, global system under no one's control but with a global market as its center which will have increasing power to motivate businesses to become more productive and to motivate governments to dismantle restrictive regulation, cut unsustainable deficits, and pursue sound fiscal and monetary policy.'[17] From this perspective, power cannot go back to the conditions of Bretton Woods when the World Bank and IMF were launched.

In another assessment, Milton Friedman put it bluntly when he contended that if there had been no IMF, there would have been no crisis in the Asian economies in the late 1990s.[18] Hence, some advocates of free markets draw the conclusion that international economic institutions cannot be reformed; they must be abolished if there is to be global economic stability and steady growth.

Populists

Opposed to free trade are many populist politicians. In the United States, they include Patrick Buchanan and Ross Perot, a candidate in the 1992 presidential election. In other countries, nationalists such as Jean-Marie Le Pen in France and Pauline Hanson of Australia have also expressed distress over globalization. Although the contexts vary, sources of disillusionment include the loss of jobs, especially with outsourcing to countries

where the cost of labour is cheaper than at home, and immigration. Illegal migrants are especially blamed for eroding national culture. Rallying these criticisms, politicians on the political right have attracted support from elements of organized labour, the unemployed, and the underemployed, many of whom have felt the pinch of reductions in social policy and rollbacks in the welfare state. In the United States and Europe, these groups are also backed by certain movements based in religion and neo-fascism.

Protectionists hence criticize transnational corporations for transferring jobs overseas, and want to institute measures to insulate the national economy from the world market, such as high barriers to restrict imports. These critics also seek to preserve traditional solidarities. In their ranks, xenophobic tendencies invoke a sense of nativism and aim to repeal or revise regional schemes like the North American Free Trade Agreement on the grounds that they jeopardize job security and weaken sovereignty. Some ultranationalists further claim that the United Nations and other international organizations are a precursor to world government. Right-wing nationalist politics thus embraces the principle of sovereignty, and would build a fortress around territorially bound notions of the state, thereby calling for the restructuring of globalization.

Anarchists

Unlike the populists on the right, contemporary anarchists contest hierarchical organizations, including powerful states and transnational corporations. Anarchists are against institutionalized oppression embodied not only in capitalism but similarly in the authoritarian tendencies of socialism. An understanding of politics based on class struggle is faulted for notions such as the dictatorship of the proletariat and the Leninist vanguard party. Non-governmental organizations as well are often deemed as expressions of hierarchies given to reformist politics.

Given these sensibilities, anarchists call for

small-scale, self-governing bodies. Eventually, they may join together and form networks or federations. The goal is local autonomy, grassroots democracy, and compact communities. The political forms are to be decentralized, co-operative, and voluntary associations, as established during the Spanish Civil War. In fact, the tactic of affinity groups, deployed by North American anarchists in recent years, is adapted from the legacy of Spanish anarchism, the idea being that they form sectors with different styles, embrace varied aims, and range in their attitudes about the use of violence. These groups are loosely connected, even leaderless, and mostly willing to join together for particular actions. Direct Action Movement, Anti-Capitalist Convergence, People's Global Action, and the Black Bloc are all influenced by anarchism and have been involved in protesting globalization.[19]

Frequently identified as militants, participants in anarchist groups hold that there is no 'black bloc organization'. A standing body between protests does not exist. Rather, these protestors self-identify as an ad hoc collection of individuals whose actions are contingent and who form a transitory group, though part of the stream of the more than century-old anarchist movement. There are different interpretations of whether a bloc actually constitutes an organizational form: even if activists who subscribe to its philosophy do not join, or do so only on a temporary basis, is the anarchist movement itself a kind of organization?

Socialists

In some respects complementary to, yet also diverging from, anarchist positions, socialist perspectives centre on revisiting the ideas of capitalism and reconstituting the globalizing system. The challenge is to rethink and extend Marxist understanding. Socialists offer vigorous critiques of globalizing capitalism and probe the parameters within which national and international institutions operate.[20] Historicizing globalization to situate it in the development of capitalism, socialists have sought to identify fundamental shifts since 1970, especially the end of the post-war era of national

Keynesianism, the collapse of the Bretton Woods system of fixed exchange rates that accompanied the rise of the neo-liberal regime, and the fall of the Soviet Union.

A historical materialist framework is structural in ways that the other clusters of criticism are not. In diverse accounts, emphasis is given to the continuities between the history of imperialism and contemporary globalization. A central theme is structural power—not merely imbalances at a world level but the relations among *both* states, including interstate institutions, and transnational classes. This conceptualization is decidedly reflexive on the interactions of ideas like neo-liberalism and interests.

Today, many socialists want to end global governance through interstate institutions—the WTO, the World Bank, and the IMF—and transnational corporations. They seek to engineer an ideological shift towards the priorities of the nascent global justice movement. While supporting certain reformist measures, socialists deem it more important to establish control over market forces—regarded by Marxists as a matter of transforming social relations.

From this standpoint, there is a focus on the dialectic of globalization and marginalization, a dynamic with severe consequences for both enclaves in the West (e.g., indigenous peoples in North America, migrants, and impoverished people in regions such as Appalachia in the United States) and the so-called developing world.[21] Several developing countries are small and fragile actors that have experienced a reduction in policy latitude and an erosion of sovereignty, including over natural resources, and of local ownership in their national economies. The vulnerabilities of the South are sustained by multiple mechanisms (e.g., loan conditionalities, fluctuations in commodity prices and terms of trade, and the volatility of short-term capital flows), thought to be systemic in nature and driven by the relations of domination and subordination among social forces. Hence, socialist perspectives peer into relational, not only gradational, divisions, and, while favouring alterations in institutional arrangements,

they take as their objective transforming the hierarchies and norms that are being institutionalized.

Resistance

Having sketched seven clusters of critique and
noted some of the overlap among them, it is important to reflect on how they are implicated in practice. Whereas globalization begets both accommodation and resistance, it is the latter that substantially embraces critical thinking and attempts to implement aspects of it. But inasmuch as resistance is
multi-faceted, its dynamics can be difficult to grasp.

Myriad forms of resistance to globalization are
based in, but not limited to, place—a distinct physical setting. Yet resistance is also dispersed and spa-
tialized through networks, some of which may be
submerged.[22] Or resistance to neo-liberal globalization may even be formless. Moreover, just as there
is resistance to hegemony, so there are hegemonic
tendencies within resistance. Not only is there
power to resist, but power within resistance may
suppress subgroups and dissent.

Resistance, then, is about power relations. To
underline my point, it may be read as not only a
response to but also an integral part of globalization
itself. Not surprisingly, the least understood type of
resistance is the more hidden, sometimes subsur-
face, micro variant that emerges in various locales.
Micro-resistance refers to countless diverse acts and
beliefs that send forth ripples of doubt and questions concerning the viability and sustainability of
neo-liberal globalization. The importance of the distinction between micro- and *macro-resistance* to
neo-liberal globalization is that public debates, as
represented in the media, and most scholarly discourse focus on the latter in the guise of street
protests, movements, networks, and sometimes
state policies, as with French subsidies for their cultural industries. Nonetheless, the micro variant is
the prevailing pattern in many parts of the world
and entwines with the latter in ways that have not
adequately been understood. The interplay between
the micro and macro are displayed when the
former, often in the cultural and symbolic realms,
provides inspiration, energy, and communication

for the more visible and institutional phases of
political resistance.[23] In practice, they meld in intricate and varied ways.

The fluid blending of micro- and macro-resistance to neo-liberal globalization is exemplified in
Japan. At Ritsumeikan University in Kyoto, where I
taught in 2000, my students carried out team
research. In a fascinating project on globalization
and Japanese women, students interviewed and
distributed a questionnaire to prostitutes, host-
esses, and ethnic Korean and Japanese feminists.[24]
The interviews and survey tapped attitudes on
global flows that directly affect women, especially
the transnational sex industry. A Japanese professor
introduced the research team to an activist whose
work with the transnational NGO End Child
Prostitution in Asian Tourism probes networks that
operate across borders, as evident in Osaka
Prefecture. The students found that child prostitutes profess to be proud that they are feeding their
families and that in some cases, such as Meiji-era
Japan as well as in parts of contemporary Southeast
Asia, national development strategies have promoted prostitution. The sex industry today, the students argued, 'is a part of the larger problem of how
to moderate the sometimes cruel process of the
[sic] globalization.' The research team concluded
on an optimistic note, holding that heightened
market integration has the potential to advance
women's interests and human rights, but there is a
need to adapt the Japanese economy, which 'is
starting to change if not crumble', to globalization.

Two other groups of students chose topics pertaining to food, also a fundamental matter of vital
bodily forces. In recent decades, the marketplace for
food has changed substantially, with national and
then global products supplanting local goods, altering price structures and consumption patterns,
being integrated into a system of worldwide trade,
and fundamentally affecting health. With a premoni-
tion about this, the student research teams prepared
papers on 'The Resistance to Genetically Modified
Foods in Japan' and 'WTO and Farming Product
(Rice)'.[25] The former paper shows that despite the
Japanese government's support for the biotechnology industry's efforts to redesign plants using genes

from other organisms, including different species, certain Japanese food companies felt obliged to address public concerns through either official pronouncements or altered policies on genetically modified products. For example, in 1997, Taishi Food Industry stated that 'we never use GM [genetically modified] crops as raw materials.' Similarly, in 1999, Kikkoman, the largest soy sauce company in Japan, changed the soybeans in its 'marudaizu' series and labelled its non-genetically modified products. The pressure came not from large-scale public demonstrations, but from expressions of concern shared by consumers, especially the Consumers Union of Japan, and dairy farmers. Not stridently voiced, but easily elicited in interviews, the apprehension centres on uncertainty over safety, the ethical question of tampering with nature, and media coverage and advertisements regarding genetically modified foods.

Similarly, the other research paper details a quiet form of resistance, in this case by Japanese farmers and consumers. Not surprisingly, Japanese rice growers are against liberalization because they do not want to face stiff international competition. Also, opening to the global market is perceived as a threat to their identity, connections to nature, and cultural and spiritual heritage, of which rice is a principal part. Competition from overseas and mechanized technology portend the demise of family farming, as well as the lifeways and values attendant to it. For many Japanese consumers, the taste of foreign rice is unappealing. Moreover, the pesticides applied in countries with little regulation present health risks. At bottom, the issues concerning governmental policy and the WTO's promotion of liberalization are matters of cultural dignity, food security, and environmental protection.

Taken together, the students' incisive research on these themes identifies a key and untheorized pattern. Although Japan has not experienced conspicuous confrontations over neo-liberal globalization, there is substantial and highly varied resistance to it. The resistance meshes several forms, some of them different from the Western varieties, which, it is worth emphasizing, are also diverse. The students show that reservations about globalization are enacted in ways of life,

though not as any one cluster of critics would have it. As such, the students have provided important pointers for empirical research on the less evident resistance to the dark side of globalization, blurring some of the ingrained categories employed by both the champions and critics of globalization. There are cross-cutting criticisms in the personal as well as public realms, sometimes mediated in complex ways. Practically speaking, these mediations take the form of embryonic efforts to build nodes of resistance and alliances, including transnational efforts to thrust out of the local sphere and to join separate issues such as peace, the environment, labour, and gender.

Common and Uncommon Ground

The sheer heterogeneity of the seven critiques and resistances to neo-liberal globalization is quite clear. But is there any common ground in these expressions of disenchantment? Rhetorically, the array of critics and resisters share a professed commitment to the pursuit of human freedom and development—a classical theme enunciated more than two millennia ago by Aristotle and one that sits well with contemporary populists as well as others across the spectrum. Likewise, many critics now emphasize poverty reduction, due not solely to altruism but also the self-interested recognition that an impoverished populace forms a reserve for recruiting terrorists. There is overall agreement on the need to dispense with the *pensée unique*, the singularity of thinking about the ordering of economy, politics, and society embodied in the frayed Washington Consensus. Given the proven failings of the latter, there tends to be a growing appreciation of the need for plural forms and a synthesis of principles, including elements of liberalism (particularly free speech, human rights, and diversity) and opportunities for social equity, though policy strategists map divergent paths towards this outcome.

Various critics want to transform but not stop globalization. Thus the competing agendas share a key point: the contemporary era is marked by a bundling of globalization and neo-liberalism. But what inference may be drawn from this convergence? And what is meant by transformation? Some observers clearly favour tightening the bundle and others favour an unbundling. Indeed, it is intriguing to contemplate what globalization would be like without neo-liberalism.

Here is where the axes of power grind out contention among the disenchanted. Some critics argue that neo-liberal globalization can be reformed; others claim that its central institutions must be demolished. For instance, the former are prepared to give more seats for decision-makers in international institutions to developing countries, and others maintain that these institutions exist only to cushion the jarring effects of globalizing capitalism, an inherently unjust system that cannot be rescued. At stake, then, is democratic control. Some critics support measures to extend the reach of the institutions that enact neo-liberal policies while calling for greater accountability. The attention of others is riveted on the ways in which undemocratic institutions exercise social domination and depoliticize issues by propagating a neo-liberal ethic and technocratic discourse. A crucial role continues to be played by the state, usually seen as either a potential instrument for alleviating social problems or as a constellation of coercive power. The debate is between those who regard the state as too controlling and others who deem it as lacking control in relation to the market. The former call for deregulation; the latter, re-regulation.

Ultimately, these debates come down to different visions of human solidarity. In a globalizing era, what is the glue that holds society together, and what scale of community is appropriate? Along with the search for principles to help imagine options and guide policy after 9/11 and following the 2003 Anglo–American invasion of Iraq, the foremost conflict surrounds attempts to link neo-liberal globalization and US empire.

Beyond the New Globalization

If globalization is a historical structure of material power, then it cannot be fixed and invariant. In this evolving structure, there are continuities and discontinuities between the old and the new. To grasp this shift, I now want to draw from the plethora of criticism and train my own critical lens on our times.

In the interregnum between the old and the new, the main trajectory is a change in emphasis from *multilateral* to *militarized* globalization, with transformative possibilities. These are not discrete and mutually exclusive patterns. Their elements may coexist as parts of a contradictory whole that embody varying aspects of globalization and different mixes of consent and coercion.

From the 1970s until 11 September 2001, world order was based on a preponderance of consensus, especially among dominant classes, along with the periodic application of brute force. Built on a Westphalian model of formal equality among sovereign states, multilateral globalization adopted both the principle of territoriality and the material capabilities of globalizing capitalism. The interstate system thus interacted with transnational processes, especially in the economic and cultural spheres. Not only has there been enormous structural inequality among states themselves, but also globalizing markets produced increasing polarization among the rich and the poor, in some cases leading to heightened state repression, as in certain Middle Eastern countries. Emblematic of severe transnational problems prior to the attacks on New York and Washington in September 2001 was a rapid rise in global environmental harms, including global warming, the hole in the ozone layer, and the loss of biodiversity.

Post-9/11, the pendulum in global hegemony swung from consent towards coercion. The ratio is inverted. As noted, following the Asian financial crisis, the shock of market reforms in Russia and elsewhere, the Argentine debacle, and diminishing confidence in international economic institutions, the Washington Consensus needed reworking, as evidenced by blistering criticism from even major beneficiaries of globalization, such as Soros, and neo-classical economists themselves, including insiders like Stiglitz. Clearly, a more coerced, less consensual framework became ascendant. Washington increasingly relied on its military power and covert agencies relative to more subtle forms of domination.

In 2003, when its allies in the UN Security Council threatened to veto US policy on Iraq, Washington renounced the use of the veto power on the ground that it does not need permission to go it alone. President Bush's decision to wage war resulted in the removal of Saddam Hussein, yet the United States had to return to the Security Council to seek legitimacy, troops, and money, demonstrating that unilateralism does not preclude multilateral initiatives. US unilateralist policies contain elements of multilateralism partly because unilateralism is not in the interest of either American or global capital. Unilateralism is self-centered and adopts a short-run perspective, while the dominant fractions of capital are extroverted and take a longer view. Unilateralism, including the war in Iraq, is a retreat from the professed ideal of self-regulating globalization. To maintain a neo-liberal world economy, multilateral political co-operation, at least among the principal actors, is needed. Overall, the trend suggests that a series of trade wars *and* military wars based on pre-emptive policies and, following Afghanistan and Iraq, ongoing 'regime change' may well mark the coming phase of globalization. In this sense, *unilateral globalization*, especially when militarized, is a quagmire if not an oxymoron. The two strands of *the new globalization*—unilateralism and free markets—are incommensurate.

Militarized globalization is thus characterized by both interstate war, as in Iraq, and an erosion of the Westphalian system, with the territorial state facing mounting pressure from the disciplinary power of markets, regionalizing processes, and civil society. The attempt to universalize US-led globalization has contributed mightily to the surge in micro- and macro-resistance.

The resistance offers alternative futures, but they are more of a potential than a set of lived practices. There are many voices, sometimes at odds with one another; different visions; and no lack of concrete proposals.[26] The centrepiece is a new normative architecture—an ethics based on concerns about social justice and equity. There are also calls to relax the Westphalian system without at all diminishing state capacity to regulate capital and strengthen social policies. In an extension of Karl Polanyi's insight about the double movement (the expansion of the market and the counterthrust from social forces seeking self-protection), *democratic globalization* would entail re-embedding the economy in society.[27] And it is about building a counter-hegemony: an order that is tolerant of differences, seeks new ways to reconcile them in an open and participatory manner, and embraces a dispersion of power. Currently, the three patterns—multilateral, militarized, and democratic globalization—intersect and compete, their different logics colliding with one another. The outcome will form the basis of the coming world order.

Notes

1. This chapter draws on previously published research: James H. Mittelman, *The Globalization Syndrome: Transformation and Resistance* (Princeton, NJ: Princeton University Press, 2000); Mittelman, *Whither Globalization? The Vortex of Knowledge and Ideology* (London: Routledge, 2004). I owe a debt of gratitude to Priya Dixit for stellar research assistance.

2. Anthony Giddens, *The Consequences of Modernity* (Cambridge: Polity Press, 1990); David Harvey, *The Condition of Postmodernity* (Oxford: Basil Blackwell, 1990); Roland Robertson, *Globalization: Social Theory and Global Culture* (Newbury Park, Calif.: Sage, 1992); Anthony Giddens, *Runaway World: How Globalization Is Reshaping Our Lives* (New York: Routledge, 2000).

3. Antonio Gramsci, *Selections from Prison Notebooks,* trans. and ed. Quintin Hoare and Geoffrey Nowell Smith (London: Lawrence and Wishart, 1971).

4. Thomas L. Friedman, *The Lexus and the Olive Tree: Understanding Globalization* (New York: Farrar, Straus and Giroux, 1999); John Micklethwait and Adrian Wooldridge, *A Future Perfect: The Challenge and Hidden Promise of*

Globalization (New York: Crown Business, 2000); Jagdish Bhagwati, *In Defense of Globalization* (New York: Oxford University Press, 2004).

5. As quoted in Charles Trueheart, 'French Hold Proudly Fast to Benevolent Central Rule', *Washington Post*, 14 July 1997.

6. As quoted in Paulo Moreira Leite, 'Males Globalizados', trans. Lillian Duarte, *Veja* 29, 9 (28 Feb.): 24–5.

7. As quoted in Abdul Kadir Jasin and Syed Nazri, 'No Choice but To Accept Globalisation', *New Straits Times* (Kuala Lumpur), 25 Oct. 1997. Also Mahathir Mohamad, *Islam and the Muslim Ummah: Selected Speeches of Dr. Mahathir Mohamad*, ed. Hashim Makaaruddin (Kuala Lumpur: Pelanduk Publications (M) Sdn Bhd, 2000).

8. Mustapha Mohamed, 'Globalisation: A Malaysian View', in Nik Mustapha Nik Hassan and Mazilan Musa, eds, *The Economic and Financial Imperatives of Globalisation: An Islamic Response* (Kuala Lumpur: Institute of Islamic Understanding Malaysia, 2000), 6–8.

9. As quoted in William Pfaff, 'Globalization Is Discredited', *Japan Times*, 29 Feb. 2000.

10. Nicholas Stern, *A Strategy for Development* (Washington: World Bank, 2000); World Bank, *Globalization, Growth, and Poverty: Building an Inclusive World Economy* (Washington and New York: World Bank and Oxford University Press, 2002); *International Monetary Fund, IMF and Recent Capital Account Crises: Indonesia, Korea, Brazil* (Washington: IMF, 2003).

11. IMF, *IMF and Recent Capital Account Crises.*

12. See Joseph E. Stiglitz, *Globalization and Its Discontents* (New York: Norton, 2002); for further evaluation of this book, see my review in *New Political Economy* 9, 1 (Mar. 2004): 129–33.

13. George Soros, *The Crisis of Global Capitalism: Open Society Endangered* (New York: Public Affairs, 1998), xxiii.

14. Ibid., 200.

15. George Soros, *George Soros on Globalization* (New York: Public Affairs, 2002).

16. Lowell Bryan and Diana Farrell, *Market Unbound:*

Unleashing Global Capitalism (New York: John Wiley, 1996).

17. Ibid., 252–3.

18. 'Is It Doing More Harm or Has the IMF Cured Asia?', *New Straits Times* (Kuala Lumpur), 26 Apr. 1998.

19. I am drawing on Mark Rupert, 'Anticapitalist Convergence: Anarchism, Socialism, and the Global Justice Movement', in Manfred B. Steger, ed., *Rethinking Globalism* (Lanham, Md: Rowman and Littlefield, 2004), 121–35; Barbara Epstein, 'Anarchism and the Anti-Globalization Movement', *Monthly Review* 53, 4 (Sept. 2001): 1–14.

20. For example, William K. Tabb, *The Amoral Elephant: Globalization and Social Justice in the Twenty-First Century* (New York: Monthly Review Press, 2001); Leslie Sklair, *Globalization: Capitalism and Its Alternatives*, 3rd edn (Oxford: Oxford University Press, 2002).

21. A leading critic in the South is Walden Bello, whose books include *Deglobalization: Ideas for a New World Economy* (London: Zed Books, 2002).

22. Margaret E. Keck and Kathryn Sikkink, *Activists beyond Borders: Advocacy Networks in International Politics* (Ithaca, NY: Cornell University Press, 1998); Alberto Melucci, 'The Symbolic Challenge of Contemporary Movements', *Social Research* 52, 4 (Winter 1985): 789–816.

23. Alberto Melucci, *Challenging Codes: Collective Action in the Information Age* (New York: Cambridge University Press, 1996).

24. This account originally appeared in my 'Globalization Debates: Bringing in Microencounters', *Globalizations* 1, 1 (Aug. 2004): 24–37. Hirokai Ikeda, Reis Lopez Rello, and Janne-Magnus Lundh, 'Globalization's Effects on Japanese Women and Their Reactions' (2000), unpublished.

25. Sanri Arai, Yoshinobu Inou, Makikio Otsuki, Mari Takayangi, and Naoyuki Yamagishi, 'The Resistance to Genetically Modified Foods in Japan: A Case Study of the Resistance to Globalization' (2000), unpublished; Ayako Kontani, Takahiro Kawada, and Tomohiro Uemura, 'WTO and

Farming Product (Rice)' (2000), unpublished.

26. See, for example, Richard Sandbrook, ed., *Civilizing Globalization: A Survival Guide* (Albany: State University of New York Press, 2003).

27. Karl Polanyi, *The Great Transformation: The Political and Economic Origins of Our Time* (Boston: Beacon Press, 1957). I have provided more detail about the meaning of democratic globalization in *The Globalization Syndrome* and *Whither Globalization?*

Suggested Readings

Cheru, Fantu. *African Renaissance: Roadmaps to the Challenge of Globalization*. London: Zed Books, 2002.

Dicken, Peter. *Global Shift: Reshaping the Global Economic Map in the 21st Century*, 4th edn. New York: Guilford, 2003.

McMichael, Philip. *Development and Social Change: A Global Perspective*, 3rd edn. Thousand Oaks, Calif.: Pine Forge Press, 2004.

Mittelman, James H. *Wither Globalization? The Vortex of Knowledge and Ideology*. London: Routledge, 2004.

Robertson, Roland, and Kathleen White, eds. *Globalization: Critical Concepts in Sociology*, 4 vols. London: Routledge, 2003.

Sassen, Saskia. *Losing Control? Sovereignty in an Age of Globalization*. New York: Columbia University Press, 1996.

Scholte, Jan Art. *Globalization: A Critical Introduction*. New York: St Martin's Press, 2000.

Web Sites

Attac International (alternative globalization): www.attac.org/indexfla

No Logo (anti-corporate): www.nologo.org

International Monetary Fund: www.imf.org

World Bank: www.worldbank.org

World Economic Forum: www.weforum.org

World Social Forum 2004 (Mumbai, India): www.wsfindia.org/anotherworld.php

World Social Forum 2003 (Porto Alegre, Brazil): www.portoalegre2003.org/publique/index02I.htm

World Trade Organization: www.wto.org

Chapter 5

Alternatives to Neo-Liberalism?
Towards a More Heterogeneous Global Political Economy

Eric Helleiner

In the early 1980s, a remarkable revolution in economic policy was launched within the global political economy. Governments across the world began to embrace more liberal policies that soon freed up market forces, both at the international and domestic levels, to a much greater degree than at any point in the post-1945 era. This 'neo-liberal' policy revolution swept across Western and Southern countries, and then became almost globally dominant by the early 1990s when ex-Eastern bloc countries embraced free-market reforms.

This revolution now seems to be running out of steam. Public officials at international conferences declare that the neo-liberal 'Washington Consensus' is passé, while activists across the world mobilize confidently behind the slogan 'Another World is Possible'. This backlash against neo-liberalism is often analyzed by IPE scholars through interest-based analytical frameworks that map the various economic groups affected negatively by neo-liberal reforms. But the statements of these public officials and activists suggest that an important dimension of the backlash is ideational. What, then, are the ideologies prominent within the emerging opposition movement to neo-liberalism? What kind of alternative economic visions are being proposed by the increasingly influential critics of the global neo-liberal economic order?

Transnational Social Movements and Global Alternatives to Neo-Liberalism

To answer these questions, it is useful to begin by examining the ideas of the transnational social movements that have been among the most prominent opponents of neo-liberal policies. By the early to mid-1990s they had already begun to emerge as important critics of neo-liberal economic policies through their co-ordinated campaigns against International Monetary Fund (IMF) and World Bank programs.[1] More recently, transnational social movements are credited with helping to stop a number of major neo-liberal initiatives at the international level. One of these was the proposed Multilateral Agreement on Investment (MAI). This liberal international investment treaty began to be negotiated by the Organization for Economic Co-operation and Development (OECD) governments in 1995, but it was abandoned by 1998 in part because of large-scale opposition generated by transnational activists. The unravelling of the MAI negotiations was soon followed by collapse of the initiative to launch a new international round of trade negotiations in 1999 in Seattle. Once again, many observers argue that protests against the talks by transnational social movements, on the streets of Seattle and elsewhere, played a key role in producing this outcome. Since 'the battle in Seattle' the presence of large groups of protestors associated with transnational social movements has become a permanent feature of most major international economic summits. Their prominence at these events has attracted unprecedented public attention to these meetings and has encouraged broader criticism of the neo-liberal policy agenda.[2]

What kind of alternative economic order do these transnational social movements want? They are often described as an 'anti-globalization movement', but the term is misleading for two reasons. Many groups are not opposed to economic globalization itself but simply to the kind of globalization that neo-liberals endorse; that is, a globalization process driven and organized by free markets. They are also not a single movement, but rather represent various transnational groups with diverse world views. This diversity is worth exploring briefly.

Some of the participants are inspired by ideologies that have acted as important challenges to economic liberalism in the past. Many, for example, are 'embedded liberals' who worry that the neo-liberal policy revolution is rolling back various forms of social protection against unregulated capitalism introduced during the post-war era. The post-war Bretton Woods order endorsed international economic liberalism but only to the extent that it was compatible with strong welfare states and activist macroeconomic management designed to promote full employment. Contemporary embedded liberals believe that advocates of neo-liberal policies are making a grave mistake of forgetting that unregulated free markets can result in social and economic upheavals of the kind experienced during the Great Depression of the 1930s.[3]

Others are guided by the structuralist ideology that held a prominent place among Southern policy-makers during the post-war years. This ideology—which represents a modern version of the nineteenth-century economic nationalism advocated by Frederich List—holds that free trade in an unequal world will keep poorer countries in a subordinate position by inhibiting indigenous industrialization and locking them into a position as dependent commodity exporters. Its supporters advocate tariff protection and state subsidies to support local firms to become competitive in world markets. During the 1980s and 1990s, these kinds of policies were swept away by neo-liberal reformers, who viewed them as inefficient and as a constraint on individual freedom. From a Listian or structuralist standpoint, neo-liberal policies represented a new form of 'free-trade imperialism' imposed by rich countries.[4]

Marxism also retains some influence among more radical groups within transnational social movements. The collapse of the Eastern bloc, of course, dealt a severe blow to the political influence of Marxism at the level of state policy-making, but various strands of Marxism have remained influential among activist groups. Particularly prominent within the transnational movements have been ideas that build on the analysis of Antonio Gramsci, a prominent Italian Marxist from the interwar period. Neo-Gramscians view the neo-liberal policy revolution as a new stage in the evolution of global capitalism in which an emerging transnational capitalist class is seeking to reinforce its dominance vis-à-vis subordinate groups. By freeing markets domestically and internationally, this class is encouraging and intensifying the worldwide spread of capitalist exploitation as a means of bolstering its social position.[5]

In addition to these 'traditional' critics of economic liberalism, many within the transnational social movements are inspired by economic ideologies that were less prominent in the past. One of these is environmental activism. Transnational activists in the green movement have played a lead role in developing new critiques of neo-liberal policies through their involvement with campaigns against the policies of the IMF, World Bank, and World Trade Organization (WTO) as well as through such bodies as The Other Economic Summit and the International Forum on Globalization.[6] Their principal concern—described in more detail below—is that the global spread of free markets is undermining local diversity and autonomy in ways that are socially and environmentally destructive. Similar critiques have also been put forward by indigenous peoples, who have emerged in important roles within transnational activist networks against neo-liberalism.[7]

Activists in the transnational feminist movements have also emerged as prominent critics of neo-liberal policies. They highlight how women often bear the brunt of the social costs associated with the introduction of free-market reforms. Cutbacks to the public sector—particularly in areas such as education, health care, and other social services—often mean that the unpaid, predominantly female sector of the economy picks up the burden. Domestic deregulation has further promoted the 'feminization of poverty' by encouraging more insecure, non-union, poorly paid work in sectors of the economy where female employment is high. The introduction of free trade policies has also created similar kinds of jobs in export-processing zones, which draw disproportionately on women workers, and it has often displaced female-dominated subsistence agriculture in favour of male-dominated export-oriented farming.[8]

Given the diversity of views among the various transnational movements opposing neo-liberalism, the project of agreeing on a unified alternative global economic order is a difficult and controversial one. The most ambitious effort to work towards greater consensus involved the creation of the World Social Forum (WSF), which met for the first time in March 2001 at Porto Alegre, Brazil. The meeting's slogan was 'Another World is Possible' and it was timed to coincide with the annual World Economic Forum that had for years brought together political and business elites in the luxury Swiss resort of Davos. Indeed, at the first meeting, a 90-minute satellite debate was conducted between several delegates attending each of the two meetings. The first WSF meeting was considered an enormous success, attracting roughly 15,000 people from 120 countries, including many of the figures who had played a leading role in mobilizing transnational opposition to neo-liberalism over the past decade. The number of participants has grown considerably at the subsequent annual meetings.

Although the first meeting ended with a collective 'call for mobilization' it is interesting that subsequent meetings of the WSF chose not endorse a common statement.[9] A number of analysts have noted how participants in the Forum are divided between groups that seek to reform the existing global economic order and those hoping for more radical change.[10] From the former camp, we hear calls for reforms that include: the introduction of a Tobin tax on international financial transactions, the forgiveness of Southern external debt, the incorporation of labour and environmental standards within international trade agreements, and the democratization of the IMF and World Bank. The general thrust of these proposals is reminiscent of the calls for a New International Economic Order during the 1970s, which offered the most coherent global alternative to the emerging neo-liberal global project at the time. The New International Economic Order (NIEO) was put forward by thinkers associated with Southern structuralist thought and found support among many Northern embedded liberals.[11] In the transnational movements of today, the same two groups generally support the reforms mentioned above. These proposals also attract the support of reformist elements in the feminist and green movements.

These kinds of reforms to global capitalism are rejected by the more radical wings of these movements as well as by many neo-Marxists. In the 1970s, neo-Marxists from the dependency school led the critique of the NIEO from the left, arguing that what was needed was a sharper break from world capitalism via national 'de-linking'. Today, many of the critics of global reform favour what Walden Bello has called a 'deglobalization' strategy.[12] Instead of reforming the IMF, World Bank, and WTO, they favour the abolition of these institutions and the strengthening of the capacity of national and subnational local communities to determine their economic destiny. From this perspective, global rules and institutions should be endorsed only if they reinforce national and/or local self-reliance and diversity. These groups are more generally sceptical of the project to construct a single alternative global economic vision to neo-liberalism, arguing that it will suppress important differences and inevitably privilege one voice over others. Their political project is sometimes summarized as a strategy of 'the one no, and the many yeses'.[13]

Challenging Neo-Liberalism at the Regional Level

While activists in transnational social movements engage in debates about the desirability of outlining a single global economic vision, other critics of neo-liberalism are focusing on the construction of an alternative economic order at the regional level. This thinking is most fully developed in the European context, where a regional integration project has intensified dramatically since the mid-1980s. In some ways, this project has been a neo-liberal one involving not just the full liberalization of the flow of goods, people, and capital but also the creation of common currency managed on a very neo-liberal basis. But supporters of European integration have also included many opponents of neo-liberalism.

Embedded liberals, in particular, have supported the project on the grounds that it represents a way to defend their values in an era of globalization. In their view, the economic globalization trend promoted by neo-liberals has made the task of defending their principles at the national level increasingly difficult. The experience of the French socialist government in 1981–3 is often cited to make this point. When that government pursued a strategy of 'Keynesianism in one country', it soon experienced an enormous balance-of-payment crisis that prompted it to abandon the policy within two years. Many embedded liberals concluded from this experience that their values could only be defended in a Europe-wide political setting.

The lead advocate of this view was Jacques Delors, who had been Finance Minister in the French government and then held the post of President of the European Commission between 1985 and 1994. He and others promoted the idea of a 'social Europe' in which European economic integration would be paralleled by various region-wide forms of intervention in the market.[14] One such intervention was the introduction of a common Social Charter in 1989 that guarantees workers' rights across the European economic space. Environmentalists and feminists have also been successful in pressing for some common environmental standards and measures to promote gender equity at the EU level. In addition, the European Union redistributes a considerable amount of money from wealthy regions of Europe to poorer ones. Even the creation of a common currency is seen by some critics of neo-liberalism as a positive first step towards Europe-wide activist macroeconomic management.[15] And, more generally, the common market space is subject to region-wide democratic governance in the form of various European political institutions that have been strengthened since the mid-1980s.

All of these features make European economic integration a very different phenomenon from the kind of neo-liberal model of regional integration embodied in a document such as the North American Free Trade Agreement (NAFTA). This is not to say that the European Union represents a successful alternative regional economic model. Embedded liberals, as well as many feminists and environmentalists, are often highly critical of the European Union, arguing that the features mentioned above are quite inadequate and subject to various weaknesses. In addition, as the number of countries joining the European Union has grown in recent years, these features of regional integration have also been subject to increasing strain.

But it is worth noting that these features of Europe's regional integration have posed an ideological challenge to neo-liberalism not just within Europe but beyond the region as well. The EU has increasingly acted as an important alternative model of regional economic integration that has inspired critics of neo-liberalism in other regions such as North America. Equally important, as its power in global economic diplomacy has grown, the EU has sometimes chosen to project these alternative values globally. The EU has, for example, been supportive of initiatives to bring environmental and labour laws into the WTO. Decisions to prioritize food safety issues over free trade principles in cases involving the importation of hormone-treated beef and the use of genetically modified organisms have had an especially high profile.

A different kind of ideological challenge to neo-liberalism is increasingly being promoted at the regional level in East Asia. In that region, the goal has been to defend the kind of Listian economic nationalism embodied in the East Asian 'developmental state'. This model of economic development has many supporters in the region; indeed, East Asia was more insulated than most regions from the neo-liberal economic revolution during the 1980s and early 1990s for this very reason. During the 1997–8 regional financial crisis, however, neo-liberals—particularly from the US and the IMF—attempted to discredit the East Asian 'developmental state' by associating it with 'crony capitalism'.

This strategy met much resistance and some of it was channelled into support for initiatives to build closer regional co-operation. Most notably, at the height of the crisis, Japan proposed the creation of an Asian Monetary Fund that would enable countries in the region to avoid having to accept the neo-liberal advice of the IMF and the US. Although the AMF proposal was shot down by strong opposition from the United States (as well as that of several East Asian countries initially nervous about Japanese intentions in the region), the idea of fostering closer regional financial co-operation as a means of insulating the distinctive East Asian development model from future US and IMF pressure has not died. Since Japan's initial proposal, East Asian governments have quietly launched a number of more limited efforts to strengthen regional co-operation of this kind.[16]

As in Europe, regional co-operation is increasingly seen in East Asia as a means to defend a set of values that do not fit the neo-liberal paradigm. Interestingly, in both cases, this defence has also sometimes been couched in 'civilizational' terms. Some East Asian leaders have argued that neo-liberal economics is not compatible with 'Asian values' that stem from deeply rooted Confucian traditions.[17] These traditions are said to have fostered the distinctive political economy tradition that is reflected in the 'developmental state' model of economic growth. Similarly, some European thinkers have suggested that neo-liberalism is an Anglo-American ideology that is alien to the more collectivist political economy traditions of continental Europe. As the EU's trade commissioner put it, one of the EU's goals in international trade negotiations involves defending 'specific traits of European civilization—the insistence on high quality foodstuffs, cultural identity in a world without barriers and a reluctance to see some activities reduced to a commercial footing'.[18]

These 'civilizational' claims are highly controversial, but they are interesting politically because they represent a new kind of challenge to neo-liberal thought. By claiming that perspectives on political economy are rooted in deep-seated values distinct to certain cultures and civilizations, they challenge the universalistic claims of neo-liberalism. The clear message of this line of argument is that neo-liberalism reflects the values and traditions of a foreign civilization, usually identified as an Anglo-American one. These arguments are also interesting because they appeal to tradition and culture—rather than secular reason—as their inspiration for thinking about issues of political economy. One further example of this phenomenon is the rise of the Islamic economics movement, which has become increasingly influential across the Middle East and parts of Asia during the last two decades. Its advocates promote the incorporation of Islamic religious values into economic life through such measures as the prohibition of interest payments.[19] This approach to political economy is once again presented as an alternative to neo-liberalism that is distinctive to particular cultural regions.

Challenging the Cult of Impotence: Economic Alternatives at the National Level

Alternatives to neo-liberalism have emerged not just at the global and regional levels. Some critics of the current ideology have concentrated on the national level as the central location at which an alternative economic order can be built. The neo-liberal TINA (there is no alternative) thesis suggests that the nation-state has become an increasingly powerless political entity in this age of globalization. This 'cult of impotence', as one author describes it, assumes that global market forces will force a convergence of national economic policies towards a neo-liberal model.[20] These critics suggest otherwise.

Many have called attention to the considerable room for manoeuvre that nation-states continue to have to pursue alternative economic policies within the current global economy. One line of argument has highlighted how the disciplining power of global financial markets is easily overstated. Countries with generous welfare states need not fear capital flight as long as this spending is not financed with large budget deficits.[21] Others have pointed to the endurance, and even strengthening, of social democratic corporatist arrangements in various countries. In an age of globalization, these nation-wide planning mechanisms can help to facilitate the kind of rapid technological and economic change that is useful for national firms to compete successfully while preserving 'embedded liberal values'.[22]

Advocates of the 'Third Way' have also suggested that national governments can retain an activist policy orientation at the microeconomic level by investing in infrastructure and education. Transnational corporations, it is argued, will respond positively to these kinds of interventions in the market by bringing high-wage and high-skill jobs to countries pursuing this policy agenda. The resulting wealth generated can, in turn, help to finance generous social service programs. This new justification for an activist state in a globalized economy was embraced by many prominent national politicians, ranging from Tony Blair and Bill Clinton to Fernando Cardoso, who sought to distance themselves from neo-liberalism during the 1990s.[23]

Others highlight how the embrace of Listian economic nationalist policies also remains a viable option within the global economy. I have already described the persistence of a commitment to the practices of the developmental state in East Asia. During the 1997–8 Asian crisis, some governments in the region showed interest not just in Japan's AMF proposal but also in national-level responses to the pressure exerted by the United States and the IMF to introduce more neo-liberal policy. The most prominent was Malaysia, which introduced national controls on the cross-border movement of financial capital as a means of preserving national policy autonomy during the crisis.[24] The potential usefulness of such capital controls was supported by the fact that countries such as China and Taiwan, which were quite insulated from the crisis, had never abandoned these kinds of controls.

Many Northern governments also continue to intervene within their domestic economies in various ways to promote the competitiveness of nationally based firms, contrary to neo-liberal orthodoxy. In some cases, the intervention is designed to promote the development and success of strategic and high-technology sectors. But equally important has been the staunch defence, via protectionism and subsidization, of the domestic agriculture sector as well as 'sunset' industries such as textiles and clothing. These measures directly challenge neo-liberal principles and highlight the extent to which the post-Keynesian policy revolution was far from complete even in its heyday. They also play a significant role in undermining the broader legitimacy of the global neo-liberal order. Poorer countries that are pressured to adopt radical economic liberalization and deregulation strategies are right to point out that the Northern countries applying this pressure have refused to embrace these same policies.[25]

These various examples represent cases where policy-makers are departing from neo-liberal principles without challenging the ongoing involvement of their countries in the global economy. More radical critics of neo-liberalism, however, argue that the national state should be used to refocus the national economy in a more inward-looking and self-reliant direction. Interestingly, advocates of this strategy can be found on both the left and the right. On the left, I have already mentioned Walden Bello's advocacy of a strategy of 'deglobalization' for Southern countries. From his perspective, the reorientation of the domestic economy on a more self-reliant basis via trade and capital controls would be part of a broader economic project involving land reform and domestic economic redistribution. Similar ideas have been put forward by some Northern, radical critics of neo-liberalism.[26]

'Deglobalizers' at the national level also exist on the right of the political spectrum. Their central goal is not domestic redistribution but rather the defence of national sovereignty and identity. These right-wing nationalists have emerged in most OECD countries in recent years, including the US, where Pat Buchanan has emerged as one of their more vocal spokespersons. In his 1998 book *The Great Betrayal: How American Sovereignty and Social Justice are Being Sacrificed to the Gods of the Global Economy*, Buchanan argues that 'free trade is shredding the society we grew up in and selling out America's sovereignty' and that the US is becoming 'a colony to the world'.[27] These sentiments resonate with strands of American society that have long been attracted to isolationist ideas.

The prospect of the rise of both left-wing and right-wing 'deglobalizers' within the US is quite worrying to advocates of global open markets. After all, the neo-liberal policy revolution worldwide has been strongly supported by the US. If this support were to wane, the future of the global economy could become much more fragile than the TINA thesis suggests. Already, this support has diminished in some areas with the new focus on security issues in US foreign policy since 11 September 2001. If this support continues to diminish, new uncertainties and instabilities in global economic relations could occur. These, in turn, might encourage other governments to begin to protect and defend their countries' national economic interests via more interventionist means designed to insulate themselves from this uncertainty and instability.

Economic Localism: Green Alternatives to Neo-Liberalism

'Deglobalization' has been put forward as an alternative to global neo-liberalism not just at the national level but also at the local level. This 'localist' alternative is promoted above all by the 'greens' mentioned above. The greens are often seen primarily as an environmental movement but their desire to protect local diversity and autonomy in the face of globalization pressures reflects their deeper critique of what they perceive as the alienating effects and rootlessness of large-scale economic life in the industrial age.

Inspired by thinkers such as Mahatma Gandhi and E.F. Schumacher, they argue that large-scale economies are governed by anonymous market forces and distant bureaucracies—both governmental and corporate—that undermine a sense of genuine participation and democracy.[28] In this context, they believe that economic life becomes detached from meaningful social and environmental values. While large-scale economies may produce higher economic growth, the greens argue that they will not necessarily foster human development in a broader sense for this reason. Out of these beliefs has come the greens' well-known slogan, 'think globally, act locally'.

The phrase 'act locally' is a call for, among other things, the decentralization of economic life. Smaller-scale economic settings will, in their view, be more compatible with democratic values, environmental sensibilities, and the cultivation of a sense of community membership and spiritual well-being. Gandhi himself advocated a loose confederation of self-governing villages whose economies were geared towards local self-sufficiency. Most greens today, however, have less ambitious objectives and instead support various voluntarist economic initiatives that foster a degree of local economic autonomy and self-reliance parallel to the 'mainstream' global economy. One example is the creation of community-shared agricultural schemes that encourage people to purchase more of their food from local farmers by fostering a longer-term relationship with them. Another is the voluntary simplicity movement that seeks to encourage local consumption and a rejection of the consumerist and materialist values of the global economy. The greens have also supported 'buy local' campaigns, the creation of local producer and consumer co-operatives, and the growth of community-based credit unions.

Among the most innovative of these localist initiatives has been the creation of subnational 'local currencies'.[29] Since the early 1980s, hundreds of these currencies have been created by local communities across the world. They provide a means of exchange that can only be used among the members of the currency network. Because they are not convertible into the national currency, these currencies foster intra-community trade and help to keep money within the local setting. In a broader sense, these forms of money are viewed by their proponents as a means to re-embed monetary relations within a meaningful social context. Indeed, they sometimes encourage trade to be denominated according to alternative theories of value—such as labour time—that may reflect community priorities instead of pure market logic.

It is worth noting that none of these localist initiatives is designed to produce an entirely self-reliant locally oriented economy. It is expected that participants will continue to participate in the mainstream global economy. The goal is simply to carve out spaces in which local factors of production are used more actively in ways that cultivate a self-reliant, democratic, and environmentally sustainable ethic within a local community context. The 'turn towards the local', in other words, usually involves only a kind of partial de-linking from the neo-liberal global economy.[30]

Although the greens are strong opponents of neo-liberalism, these various localist economic initiatives also make considerable use of small-scale markets. The transparency and efficiency of these markets are often celebrated by greens as supportive of their vision of local communities in which power is decentralized and individual freedom and creativity flourish. Moreover, they see this scale of market as more likely to be embedded within local community values and relationships. For this reason, the greens' localist agenda exists in an uneasy relationship with neo-liberal economic priorities. The greens see themselves as a movement working against the neo-liberal globalization agenda. And they do represent a radical challenge to this agenda at the global level through their rejection of worldwide economic integration and their value system that prioritizes community values and environmental sensibilities, often in quite alternative ways. At the same time, however, the greens' enthusiasm for small-scale markets and voluntary initiatives in a local community context, as well as their often strongly anti-statist stance, can sometimes dovetail with neo-liberal goals at the local level in terms of scaling back the role of government and delegating social welfare functions to local civil society groups. For example, some neo-liberal governments are beginning to look favourably on local currency networks as a vehicle through which welfare payments and services can be channelled.[31]

If the greens think 'small is beautiful', why do they also endorse the idea of 'thinking globally'? This phrase is meant partly to encourage localist activists to retain strong links to ideas and groups beyond their local community to avoid the danger of their local setting becoming too stagnant, parochial, and perhaps even repressive. It also reflects their recognition that localism is inadequate to address existing and large-scale environmental problems at the global level in the short to medium term, despite all its potential environmental benefits over the longer run. Indeed, their decentralist project may make these problems worse in the short term by increasing the collective action dynamics and leaving unaddressed existing global disparities of power and wealth that contribute to these problems. For this reason, they believe localism must be combined with some kind of wider global frame of reference for political action. This wider frame is also seen to be necessary because the greens' localist agenda can increasingly be thwarted by powerful global actors and forces—from global market forces to the rules of the WTO—that have emerged in this era of globalization. In order to defend the ability of localist strategies to survive, the greens recognize the necessity for political mobilization beyond the local setting.

'Think globally' has one further and final meaning that is sometimes forgotten. René Dubos, who is usually credited with originating the slogan 'think globally, act locally', hoped that its first part would act as a caution to those engaging in the practice of politics above the local level. Having participated in many international environmental conferences and initiatives, he had become deeply sceptical of solutions from distant bureaucracies and diplomats who had little knowledge of the diversity, distinctiveness, and complexity of local environments and peoples. His call to 'think globally' was thus designed to encourage green activists working at the global level to develop a humble awareness of the complex diversity of the world and to favour locally developed initiatives and knowledge over strategies for reform proposed by faraway planners.[32]

Conclusion

There are few historical precedents to the worldwide scope and dramatic nature of the neo-liberal economic revolution launched in the early 1980s. The closest parallel was the triumph of the nineteenth-century free trade movement during the 1850s and 1860s when governments across much of the world embraced more liberal trade policies. In that earlier era, the liberal economic revolution soon provoked a political backlash. It appears that a similar phenomenon is taking place in the contemporary age.

In both eras, the backlash is/was driven partly by various groups whose material interests had been adversely affected by liberal economic policies. At the same time, however, ideational factors are/were also significant. In the late nineteenth and early twentieth centuries, economic liberals found themselves challenged ideologically by advocates of various alternative world views, most prominently Listian economic nationalism, Marxism, and embedded or welfare-state liberalism. These ideologies played an important role in influencing the

subsequent course of the global political economy. Indeed, by the early post-1945 years, they had come to define the content of economic policymaking in the three major political-economic regions of the world at the time: the East (Marxism), the South (Listian economic nationalism/structuralism), and the West (embedded liberalism).

In the current era, I have shown how these same three ideological challenges have vigorously re-emerged, although they have been reformulated in various ways. But new ones, such as the ideas associated with green, feminist, and 'civilizational' thought, have also become quite influential. An equally interesting feature of the opposition to neoliberalism is its multi-level nature. There is little consensus on the question of whether an alternative economic project is best built at the global, regional, national, or local level. Because of this diversity, it is difficult to predict the specific ways in which the ideational dimension of the backlash against neo-liberalism will influence the course of future developments in the global political economy. But one more general conclusion can be reached from this analysis. The political backlash against neo-liberalism is likely to result in a much more heterogeneous global political economy that is no longer characterized by the kind of worldwide uniformity of economic practice that was ushered in by the neo-liberal revolution.

Notes

For their support of this research, I am grateful to the Social Sciences and Humanities Research Council of Canada and Canada Research Chair Program.

1. See, e.g., R. O'Brien et al., *Contesting Global Governance: Multilateral Economic Institutions and Global Social Movements* (Cambridge: Cambridge University Press, 2000).

2. See, e.g., J. Seoane and E. Taddei, 'From Seattle to Porto Alegre: The Anti-Neoliberal Globalization Movement', *Current Sociology* 50 (2002): 99–122.

3. For a discussion of the contemporary relevance of 'embedded liberalism', see Jonathan Kirshner, 'Keynes, Capital Mobility and the Crisis of Embedded Liberalism', *Review of International Political Economy* 6 (1999): 313–37.

4. For an analysis of the enduring significance of this Listian or structuralist position, see H.-J. Chang, *Kicking Away the Ladder: Development Strategy in Historical Perspective* (London: Anthem Press, 2002).

5. See, e.g., Robert Cox, with Timothy J. Sinclair, *Approaches to World Order* (Cambridge:

Cambridge University Press, 1996); Stephen Gill, *Power and Resistance in the New World Order* (New York: Palgrave, 2003).

6. See, e.g., Paul Ekins, ed., *The Living Economy: A New Economics in the Making* (London: Routledge and Kegan Paul, 1986); John Cavanagh et al., *Alternatives to Economic Globalization* (San Francisco: Berrett-Koehler, 2002).

7. See, e.g., Bice Maiguaschca, 'The Transnational Indigenous Movement in a Changing World Order', in Y. Sakamoto, ed., *Global Transformation* (Tokyo: United Nations University, 1994).

8. See, e.g., M. Marchand and A. Runyan, eds, *Gender and Global Restructuring* (London: Routledge, 2000).

9. For the 'Call for Mobilization', see F. Houtart and F. Polet, eds, *The Other Davos* (London: Zed Books, 2001), 122–4. It was endorsed by hundreds of organizations at the end of the first WSF and called for various economic policy initiatives at the international level, including:
   - the introduction of the Tobin tax on international financial transactions;
   - the cancellation of the external debt of Southern countries;
   - an end to the 'interference in national policy' by international economic institutions such as the IMF, World Bank, and WTO;
   - the requirement that transnational corporations uphold ILO-defined workers' rights;
   - the creation of an international trading system that guaranteed 'full employment, food security, fair terms of trade and local prosperity' and respected international human rights and multilateral environmental agreements;
   - the endorsement of the principle that seeds and genetic stocks are the heritage of humanity, and the banning of the use of transgenics and patenting of life;
   - the freer movement of people across borders.

10. See, e.g., Seoane and Taddei, 'From Seattle to Porto Alegre'; Michael Hardt, 'Today's Bandung?', *New Left Review* 14 (2002): 112–18; Emir Sader, 'Beyond Civil Society: The Left after Porto Alegre', *New Left Review* 17 (2002): 87–99.

11. See, e.g., Craig Murphy, *The Emergence of the NIEO Ideology* (Boulder, Colo.: Westview Press, 1984).

12. Walden Bello, *Deglobalization: Ideas for a New World Economy* (New York: Zed Books, 2002).

13. See, e.g., Naomi Klein, 'Reclaiming the Commons', *New Left Review* 9 (2001): 81–9.

14. See, e.g., George Ross, *Jacques Delors and European Integration* (New York: Oxford University Press, 1995).

15. See, e.g., T. Notermans, ed., *Social Democracy and Monetary Union* (New York: Berghahn, 2001).

16. See, e.g., Saori Katada, 'Japan and East Asian Monetary Regionalisation', *Geopolitics* 7 (2002): 85–112.

17. See, e.g., J.B. Rosser and M. Rosser, 'Islamic and Neo-Confucian Perspectives on the New Traditional Economy', *Eastern Economic Journal* 24 (1998): 217–27.

18. Quoted in Patti Goff, 'It's Got to be Sheep's Milk or Nothing!: Geography, Identity, and Economic Nationalism', in E. Helleiner and A. Pickel, eds, *Economic Nationalism in a Globalizing World* (Ithaca, NY: Cornell University Press, 2004).

19. See Rosser and Rosser, 'Islamic and Neo-Confucian Perspectives'.

20. Linda McQuaig, *The Cult of Impotence: Selling the Myth of Powerlessness in the Global Economy* (Toronto: Viking, 1998).

21. See, e.g., Layna Mosely, *Global Capital and National Governments* (Cambridge: Cambridge University Press, 2003).

22. See, e.g., G. Garrett, *Partisan Politics in the Global Economy* (Cambridge: Cambridge University Press, 1998).

23. See, e.g., Anthony Giddens, *The Third Way* (Oxford: Polity Press, 1998). See also Robert Reich, *The Work of Nations* (New York: Knopf, 1991).

24. Mark Beeson, 'Mahathir and the Markets: Globalisation and the Pursuit of Economic Autonomy in Malaysia', *Pacific Affairs* (Fall 2000): 335–51.

25. See, e.g., Oxfam, *Rigged Rules and Double Standards: Trade, Globalisation and the Fight*

against Poverty (London: Oxfam, 2002).

26. See, e.g., Gordon Laxer, 'Radical Transformative Nationalisms Confront the US Empire', *Current Sociology* 51 (2003): 133–52

27. Pat Buchanan, *The Great Betrayal* (New York: Little, Brown, 1998), 44, 68.

28. See S. Kumar, 'Gandhi's *Swadeshi*: The Economics of Permanence', in J. Mander and E. Goldsmith, eds, *The Case against the Global Economy and the Case for a Turn Toward the Local* (San Francisco: Sierra Club, 1996); E.F. Schumacher, *Small is Beautiful* (London: Blond and Briggs, 1973); E.

Helleiner, 'IPE and the Greens', *New Political Economy* 1 (1996): 59–78.

29. See, e.g., E. Helleiner, 'Think Globally, Transact Locally: Green Political Economy and the Local Currency Movement', *Global Society* 14 (2000): 35–52.

30. Quote from the title of Mander and Goldsmith, *The Case against the Global Economy*.

31. Helleiner, 'Think Globally'.

32. Réné Dubos, *Celebrations of Life* (New York: McGraw-Hill, 1981), 82-3.

Suggested Readings

Bello, Walden. *Deglobalizatioin: Ideas for a New World Order*, new updated edition. New York: Zed Books, 2004.

Helleiner, Eric, and Andreas Pickel, eds. *Economic Nationalism in a Globalizing World*. Ithaca, NY: Cornell University Press, 2004.

Houtart, Francois, and Francois Polet, eds. *The Other Davos*. London: Zed Books, 2001.

Oxfam. *Rigged Rules and Double Standards: Trade, Globalisation and the Fight against Poverty*. London: Oxfam, 2002.

Web Sites

Development Alternatives with Women in a New Era: www.dawn.org.fj

International Forum on Globalization: www.ifg.org

Third Way: www.progressive-governance.net

World Social Forum: www.forumsocialmundial.org.br

Chapter 6

Theory and Exclusion
Gender, Masculinity, and International Political Economy

Sandra Whitworth

In women's studies, a good piece of conventional wisdom holds that it is simply not enough to
'add women and stir'. In political science,
women are just now being added, and the field
has hardly begun to stir. —Nannerl Keohane[1]

Stop the whining and just get on with it. —
Susan Strange[2]

Once one views international relations
through the lens of sex and biology, it never
again looks the same. It is very difficult to
watch Muslims and Serbs in Bosnia, Hutus
and Tutsis in Rwanda, or militias from Liberia
and Sierra Leone to Georgia and Afghanistan
divide themselves up into what seem like
indistinguishable male-bonded groups in
order to systematically slaughter one another,
and not think of the chimps at Gombe. —
Francis Fukuyama[3]

If masculine privilege is so all-pervasive and
absolute, we must ask . . . why it is that men
live substantially shorter lives than women,
kill themselves at rates vastly higher than
women, absorb close to 100 per cent of the
fatal casualties of society's productive labour,
and direct the majority of their violence
against 'their own' ranks. . . . They surely
deserve more sustained, non-dogmatic attention than . . . every feminist theorist I have
encountered grants them. —Adam Jones[4]

Several years ago, when a previous version of this
chapter was written for the first edition of the
volume at hand, it was appropriate to note that
Nannerl Keohane's statement was perhaps even truer
of the discipline of international relations (IR) than it
was of political science. In the years since the 'new
women's movement' emerged in the late 1960s,
progress had been made by at least some feminist
academics in incorporating analyses of women and
gender relations into traditional areas of academic
study, but the same could not be said of a feminist
international relations theory. Indeed, of the little
work that had been done on women and international relations to that point, one shared observation
was that IR, of all the social science disciplines, had
been one of the most resistant to incorporating feminist analyses of women and gender relations.[5]

My argument then focused on the extent to
which, despite how much contemporary work
within international political economy (IPE) converged with the kinds of questions feminists have
raised, there was a disturbing silence on the part of
IPE scholars when it came to questions of gender.[6]
Like mainstream IR before it, IPE had rarely
acknowledged, much less analyzed, how female
subordinations are created and sustained both
nationally and internationally.[7] This absence is
important because many IPE scholars have taken it
as part of their project to explore the social and
political complex as a whole rather than its separate parts.[8] This is not merely an empirical claim,
but a political one as well. As Craig Murphy and
Roger Tooze note, many authors within the 'new'

IPE 'are more concerned with the involvement in the global political economy of people who are often ignored because they are considered less powerful.'[9] By this view, I argued, the continued invisibility of women and gender within IPE could no longer be sustained.

Today, the terrain is in some ways dramatically different, and in other ways it remains very much the same. Most feminist contributions to IR and IPE go far beyond the simple liberal notion of adding women to the mix, and it is certainly true that the field has finally begun to stir—though, as the quotations above indicate, not always in ways we may have anticipated. On the one hand, there has been a virtual explosion of literature within the realms of gender and IR and of gender and IPE in both journals and monographs, with institutional acknowledgement in the form of a journal, *International Feminist Journal of Politics*, as well as the continued success of the 'feminist theory and gender studies' section at the International Studies Association, which draws some of the largest audiences throughout that professional association's annual meetings.

On the other hand, feminist interventions have elicited a range of responses from the rest of our field. Some have tried to interject attention to women or to gender, and while too often this remains a token and largely unintegrated venture, it has sometimes gained more visibility than in the past. At the same time, however, others, such as Susan Strange in her call to feminists to 'stop whining' and Francis Fukuyama in his use of chimp behaviour to illustrate his agreement with '*the* feminist view'[10] that a world run by women would be less aggressive, competitive, and violent, have offered up baffling accounts of feminism that only serve to underline the extent to which this literature remains almost entirely unread and unheard by too many scholars within both IR and IPE.[11]

Others seem to take more seriously the feminist IR literature—insofar as they actually read it—but see in that literature a threat to traditional sites of power and so reproduce the backlash we have witnessed over the past decade against a whole host of social justice issues, including affirmative action, human rights for gays and lesbians, anti-racist activism, pay equity, and, of course, feminism. In each, the form of the argument is the same, with 'new' issues consistently depicted as redirecting attention or resources away from more traditional concerns or groups. In IR we have seen this most recently in Adam Jones's celebrated[12] lament that feminist attention to women within IR has detracted attention away from the usually more important concerns facing men.

This chapter will attempt, first, to situate the emergence of the feminist IR literature within the field of IR and will note the ways in which many of the questions raised by feminists have paralleled those raised by international political economists. It will then argue, following the work of V. Spike Peterson, that the contemporary structural crisis of capitalism and, in conjunction with that crisis, the feminist and critical analyses made of it constitute in part a crisis of masculinity.[13] Peterson points out that, seen in this light, reactions of continued silence, as well as those seeking to reassert and reprivilege traditional understandings of naturalized forms of masculinism, are responses to the 'deeply disturbing' attempts to 'disrupt' what is understood to be natural. As Peterson writes:

> Gender is conventionally invisible because the *longue durée* of masculinism obscures the power required to institutionalise, internalise, and reproduce gender hierarchy and its associated oppressions. In this sense, gender is hard to see because it is so taken for granted. But gender also resists visibility and critique due to its pervasiveness and our personal investments: it is not only 'out there' structuring activities and institutions, and 'in our heads' structuring discourse and ideologies; it is also 'in here'—in our hearts and bodies—structuring our intimate desires, our sexuality, our self-esteem and our dreams. As a consequence, our investments in gendered selves fuel heroic and self-sacrificing as well as despotic and self-serving actions.[14]

Gender, in short, informs all that we do. It is, therefore, imperative that we interrogate gender when we explore questions of IR and IPE.

International Relations and Feminism

One of the reasons that feminist issues have been raised only quite recently within the study of international relations has to do with the very different concerns of IR and feminism. International relations is a subfield of political science, and is much younger than its parent discipline. A product of the twentieth century, mainstream IR was born in the interwar period and located primarily in the United States.[15] It was created in large part to serve the needs of government, specifically the American government, in training diplomatic and government personnel and answering the 'What should we do?' questions about important diplomatic and strategic issues of the time. More than most other social science disciplines, mainstream IR has had an intimate relationship with government, both through the funding of IR research institutes and in the regular exchange of academic and government personnel. As Stanley Hoffmann notes, 'IR academics and researchers operate not merely in the corridors but also in the kitchens of power.'[16]

Informed by this goal of serving government, scholars of mainstream international relations have taken as their central concerns the causes of war and the conditions of peace, order, and security.[17] Such inquiry appears to be antithetical to the study of women. The 'high politics' of international security policy is, as J. Ann Tickner writes, 'a man's world, a world of power and conflict in which warfare is a privileged activity' and from which women traditionally have been excluded.[18]

Much of international relations theorizing, moreover, posits a separation between inside and outside, community and anarchy. It is argued that while one may appropriately raise questions of ethics and politics when examining relations within civil society, such questions are irrelevant outside, in the society of nations, where it is appropriate to ask only how rational states may enhance their power within an anarchic system.[19]

Apparently absent from the particular substantive concerns of IR, in fact or by definition, the suggestion that women or gender relations should be examined in international relations is often met with, at best, incredulity or, at worst, hostility.

In contrast to the field of international relations, contemporary feminism has its roots in a social movement: the women's liberation movement. It represents a protest against prevailing gender-based power structures and against accepted societal norms and values concerning women and men. Feminists have expressed this protest in a variety of ways, with some demanding that women be allowed to join the spheres in which only men, historically, have been permitted and others demanding more dramatic and fundamental social change. Whatever its different prescriptions, however, feminism is a politics of protest directed at transforming the historically unequal power relationships between women and men.[20] As a politics of protest, feminism clearly follows a different path from that of IR. It is concerned with those 'inside' questions often defined as irrelevant to the study of international relations. That IR and feminism may be antithetical, then, does not follow merely from their apparently different substantive concerns, but more importantly from their normative and political predispositions: mainstream IR has been aimed primarily at maintaining the (international) status quo while feminism aims at precisely the opposite. It is little wonder that studies of women and international relations do not proliferate.

Feminism and IPE: Affinities?

From the preceding sketch, it should be clear that many of the issues raised by feminists about IR have previously been or are currently being raised by specialists in IPE. While the political motivations often are quite different, political economists share a dissatisfaction with the emphasis of mainstream IR on questions of 'high politics', its lack of theorizing about the relationship between domestic and international politics, the inappropriate and usually untenable separation of 'politics' and 'economics', and the failure to assess co-operation and interdependence to the same degree that it has anarchy.[21]

International political economists have approached their critique of IR in a variety of ways. Some have sought to enlarge the number of relevant actors through adding firms, international organizations, and sometimes even social movements to the usual consideration of state behaviour and consequences of state action. Others have focused instead on the addition of new issues, arguing that trade and monetary concerns are as important in their own right as military and strategic ones. Still others examine new forms of behaviour, whether examples of co-operation or the intersubjectively shared norms associated with regimes and rule-governed activities within international relations.[22]

More recently, some IPE work has moved well beyond simply 'adding in' actors and issues to a far more profound ontological and epistemological challenge to the discipline. As Stephen Gill observes, 'we may be in the throes of an ontological change or shift: a redefinition of understandings and experiences that form basic components of lived reality. This includes mental frameworks—for example, the way that we think about social institutions and forms of political authority.'[23] Such an account suggests that critical and Gramscian IPE is beginning to address how, as Mark Laffey writes, 'social subjects understand themselves and their relations to social structures, structures which are in turn constituted in and by social practices informed by intersubjective understandings.'[24] Not only does such a move create more 'spaces' for a discussion of women or gender within IR and IPE, but feminist approaches in all of their guises are centrally involved in a project that reveals both the complexities and deep-seatedness of some of our most fundamental and naturalized 'mental frameworks'.[25]

Feminists Examine IR

Feminist analysts share with IPE scholars many of their epistemological strategies.[26] Like liberal political economists, for example, numerous feminists have sought to introduce women as a new actor or issue within IR and IPE. This work seeks to document the under-representation of women in traditional areas of international relations activities, or conversely, to show how women do participate in international relations. For example, much of the early work on women and development was written from this perspective and aimed at demonstrating how women were involved in the development process and the manner in which this involvement had been ignored previously by development researchers and practitioners. Ester Boserup's pioneering book, *Woman's Role in Economic Development*,[27] documented women's economic contributions in the Third World, and from Boserup's own and later work we now know that women constitute 60 to 80 per cent of the agricultural workforce in Africa and Asia and more than 40 per cent in Latin America.[28] Development planners ignored these facts because they assumed that women in the developing world were involved primarily in household chores and tasks. As such, the policies that they produced tended to bypass women workers, fundamentally misunderstanding the economic processes they were supposedly analyzing and thereby exacerbating women's inequality rather than alleviating it.[29] By showing women's true role in developing societies, Boserup and her colleagues created the basis for Women in Development (WID) programs and departments in almost all major international development agencies. The WID agenda has been to take women into account in the formulation and implementation of development policies around the world.

While the collection of information about women's roles in development and other issue-areas of relevance to IPE is useful and important, a number of criticisms of this approach have emerged. These parallel the criticisms made of liberal political economy more generally and suggest that the collection of empirical information about women is made at the expense of any assessment of the structural features of relations of inequality between women and men.[30] Implicit in a liberal analysis, the critics argue, is the assumption that the inclusion of women into areas previously denied them will eliminate gender inequalities. By contrast, feminists who attempt to introduce analyses of class or patriarchy argue that inequalities are a defining characteristic of the very structures in which women might participate, and as such their participation alone will not change this fundamental fact.

Theorists who have focused on patriarchy, described variously as standpoint theorists or radical feminists, suggest that the relations of inequality observed within both the study and practice of international relations reflect the simple fact that both of these represent the viewpoint of men over that of women.[31] These feminists argue that women have a unique perspective, different from that of men, and that this perspective should be given a voice within many of the decisions associated with international relations. By this view, women tend to be more nurturing and pacifistic than men and thus should be brought into international relations not on equity grounds but to allow women's more peaceful views some influence. The fact that recent Nobel Peace Prize winners include Wangari Maathai, Shirin Ebadi, and Jody Williams underscores this point. Accordingly, a feminist reformulation of notions such as power, security, and national interest—in which, from a 'feminine' perspective, 'power' is defined as empowerment and 'security' as including development and ecological concerns—is an important first step towards a better understanding of women and international relations.

Other authors focused instead on the dynamic of class and gender oppression. They (and others) argue that analyses presuming a single 'feminine' perspective essentialize and universalize the category of 'woman' (and 'man') at the expense of other forms of domination.[32] Analyses like those of Maria Mies or Gita Sen and Caren Grown have assessed the impact of the changing international division of labour on women and the ways in which women's subordination is sustained under different historical modes of production, with forms of domination associated with class relations taking advantage of, and building on, pre-existing relations of domination between women and men.[33] For example, with the introduction of private property during the colonial period, women tended to suffer more than men because they lost completely their access to traditional land-use rights.[34] Likewise, as production

shifts to the export sector during the forms of structural adjustment we are witnessing today, it is again women who are moving into these poorly paid positions with little or no opportunities to improve wages or benefits and the prospect of only short-term, limited employment.[35] The point here, of course, is that class and gender oppression work together rather than separately.

These demonstrations of the way sex and class oppression are linked improve yet again on the previous analyses outlined above, but they, too, have been subject to criticism. Primarily, the concern is that analyses of gender must examine as well how racist ideologies and practices figure into these issues. Many feminists argue also that gender oppression is sustained as much by the ideas surrounding certain practices, the self-understandings reproduced through institutional as well as individual action, as by those practices themselves. Informed by these kinds of concerns, feminists from a variety of perspectives have sought to explore how gender—understood as the prevailing assumptions concerning women and men, their roles in family and society, even what it means to be a man or woman, masculine or feminine—affects and is affected by the practices of international relations. As Chandra Talpade Mohanty writes:

> The idea I am interested in invoking here is not 'the work that women do' or even the occupations that we/they happen to be concentrated in, but rather the ideological construction of jobs and tasks in terms of notions of appropriate femininity, domesticity, (hetero)sexuality, and racial and cultural stereotypes.[36]

Cynthia Enloe provides one of the most sustained accounts of how gender figures within IPE. She examines a whole series of issues, including tourism, foreign domestic servants, and export processing zones, and the manner in which particular 'packages of expectations' associated with masculine and feminine behaviour are used to sustain and legitimize certain practices within IR. She notes, for example, the manner in which developing countries are increasingly relying on tourism as a source of foreign exchange and the profoundly gendered nature of the tourism industry. As Enloe writes: 'On the oceans and in the skies: the international business travelers are men, the service workers are women.'[37] This includes not only flight attendants and chambermaids, but the burgeoning market for prostitutes within the sex tourism industry.

Enloe's project is not simply to recount the places in which women find themselves, however, but rather to provide some insight into 'how' this has happened. How particular material conditions join together with existing assumptions and ideas about women and men is made clear in the following passage:

> To succeed, sex tourism requires Third World women to be economically desperate enough to enter prostitution; having done so it is made difficult to leave. The other side of the equation requires men from affluent societies to imagine certain women, usually women of colour, to be more available and submissive than the women in their own countries. Finally, the industry depends on an alliance between local governments in search of foreign currency and local and foreign business men willing to invest in sexualized travel.[38]

Understood in this way, not only are the activities of women placed within the realm of international relations, but they are understood in specific ways because of the particular material conditions and ideas associated with their activities: in this case, women's economic desperation is joined with the eroticization of racist stereotypes. The entire scenario works only if all of these factors are considered together and not separately.

Developing countries' search for foreign exchange also leads Enloe to examine multinational corporations and export processing zones (EPZS). She outlines in detail the various practices used, first, to recruit young women into the assembly lines of EPZS, and then the ways in which their continued docility is ensured until that time that they are pushed out of such employment.[39] This is achieved not only through assumptions around women's 'cheaper' labour (both real and imagined), through which multinational corporations (MNCs) are enticed in the first place, but more importantly by sustaining a vision of the female worker as a member of a large family—a family ruled by fathers and brothers/supervisors and managers. These women, moreover, because of prevailing social attitudes about the role of young women, are employable for only a few short years, after which time they may return to their family homes in rural areas or turn to prostitution in the larger urban centres in which they find themselves.

Finally, Enloe draws a series of links between the adoption of IMF austerity measures and the capacity of women to respond to those measures. She argues that a government's ability to maintain its legitimacy depends at least in part on the capacity of families to tolerate those measures, specifically on the capacity of women to stretch their budgets, to continue to feed, clothe, and care for their families. This may include severe domestic financial management as well as travelling abroad as foreign domestic servants, often with the requirement that a significant proportion of their salaries be repatriated back to the home country. As Enloe argues, IMF austerity measures depend on these women and the choices they are forced to make.

> Thus the politics of international debt is not simply something that has an impact on women in indebted countries. The politics of international debt won't work in their current form unless mothers and wives are willing to behave in ways that enable nervous regimes to adopt cost-cutting measures without forfeiting their political legitimacy.[40]

A dynamic is set up around ideas about what women will and will not do, the actual material conditions of their lives, and the policies produced by international organizations and foreign governments. This dynamic both sustains and is dependent on assumptions about the appropriate roles and qualities of women, and women of particular races, in specific times and places.

When women do travel abroad to work as foreign domestic servants, they often face unregulated and unsupervised workplace environments with less than subsistence wages, in countries where labour and citizenship rights are differentially applied, and in some instances they are subject to sexual and physical assault. Yet, assumptions about work, familial relations, and race are again used to justify lower pay and different rights from those of other workers. The terms of work are shaped in part by the fact that foreign domestic servants are employed in the home and perform work (child-rearing, housecleaning, cooking, and so on) that is not normally recognized as such. Ideologies about 'family' join with assumptions around race, and as Abigail Bakan and Daiva Stasiulis note, 'racialized images of womanhood play an important role in justifying to employers why non-white women of colour are "naturally" suited for childcare and housework.'[41]

The point here, of course, is that pressures to work as a foreign domestic servant derive in part from the pressures of the global capitalist system, the structural adjustment policies imposed by international financial institutions, and the historical legacy of imperialism and colonialism in many developing countries. Those pressures not only depend on women acting in a certain way, as Enloe describes, but, once having decided to work as a foreign domestic servant, a woman is involved in a complex of issues that includes assumptions about femininity, citizenship, and the transformation of a 'family home' into a workplace, and all of these are informed by gendered and racialized attitudes.[42] Or, as Jan Jindy Pettman more bluntly states: 'Domestic service has long been the site for "close encounters" between colonising and coloniser women.'[43]

International organizations more generally are also involved in promoting and sustaining assumptions around gender relations. Marilyn Waring has documented in considerable detail how women and women's work are made almost completely invisible within the United Nations System of National Accounts (UNSNA). This invisibility is important, she argues, because national governments and international agencies decide what is important, both politically and economically, based in part on the various measures found within the UNSNA—for example, when aid donors use the UNSNA to decide which countries are the most 'needy' and which projects are the most important; when governments determine economic policy priorities based on UNSNA figures; and when multinational corporations decide where, whether, and how to invest internationally based on what is recorded in the UNSNA.[44] More importantly, Waring notes, the meanings associated with women's work are fundamentally affected: women, by virtue of their absence in standard measures of work, are understood not to be involved in productive activities, despite the fact that they may be collecting food and fuel and caring for children and home from well before dawn to well after dusk. This has an impact on those women's lives, for the absence of women and women's work from these figures, and from the meaning of work at all, makes it very convenient to ignore their interests, concerns, and demands and, as Enloe has noted, to 'cheapen' the various forms of work that women are involved in.

Chandra Talpade Mohanty develops the notion of the meanings attached to women's work in specific locales even further. In her analysis of the lacemakers of Narsapur and electronics workers in Silicon Valley, she notes how gender and race and caste-based ideologies inform understandings of work, workers, and leisure-time activities. Seclusion and purdah, she notes, are a sign of higher status, and lacemaking in Narsapur came to be associated with higher-caste women but was linked also to the assumption that these women were just sitting in the house. As Mohanty writes, 'The caste-based ideology of seclusion and purdah was essential to the extraction of surplus value.'[45] But she goes further:

> Ideologies of seclusion and the domestication of women are clearly sexual, drawing as they do on masculine and feminine notions of protectionism and property. They are also heterosexual ideologies, based on the normative

definition of women as wives, sisters, and mothers—always in relation to conjugal marriage and the 'family'.[46]

This same dynamic is at work, she argues, in Silicon Valley, where the work done by Third World women is described as 'easy as a recipe', tedious, and a 'supplementary activity for women whose main tasks were mothering and housework'.[47] 'There is a clear connection between low wages and the definition of the job as supplementary', Mohanty writes, 'and the fact that the lifestyles of people of color are defined as different and cheaper.'[48]

In addition to analyzing the assumptions about women and work, some feminist analyses explore also the ways in which particular assumptions about men are embedded within the practices associated with work. This is well illustrated by the efforts of international organizations such as the ILO to promote protective legislation for women during pregnancy.[49] Such legislation is usually aimed at prohibiting heavy lifting during pregnancy or removing women from workplaces in which they might be exposed to substances hazardous to their pregnancy, such as lead or benzene. Such protection is, of course, laudable in many respects. As Zillah Eisenstein notes, pregnancy is engendered; women do, or may, bear children. This fact already structures their choices within the labour force, and protective legislation that recognizes pregnancy may protect some women from further discrimination based on it.[50] But at the same time, a number of tensions emerge, one of which is that protective legislation that removes women from reproductive health hazards leaves men subject to those same hazards.

As early as 1860, the reproductive effects on men exposed to lead were documented with indications that their wives had a very high incidence of spontaneous abortion. More recently, lead and other substances have been linked to low sperm counts, childhood cancers, heart defects, genetic damage to sperm, and chromosonal aberrations.[51] With the assumption that only women play an important enough role in reproduction to require

protection, it becomes clear that men's role in reproduction does not entitle them to any sort of special consideration—they become, in effect, invisible. In short, women are recognized not as workers, but only insofar as they are child-bearers, and men are ignored insofar as they are involved in reproduction. Men are in both a privileged and invisible position through this sort of protective legislation: privileged because it is normally men with whom women are compared, and invisible because they do not exist outside of this category, that of the 'normal' worker.

Conclusion

The above examples illustrate briefly the ways in which quite traditional IPE issues, such as debt management, export processing zones, divisions of labour, and protective labour legislation are informed by assumptions around gender. More specifically, what they illustrate is how 'ideas about the "naturalness" of forms of gender inequality are integral to understanding how the international economy functions.'[52] It is this naturalness that V. Spike Peterson argues is being challenged, both by feminist analyses and by the structural transformations of the global political economy that many of those feminists seek to analyze. Thus, not only are IR and IPE experiencing a renewed 'theoretical effervescence',[53] as was discussed above, but dramatic changes within the so-called 'real world' have produced a crisis in both our thinking and our practices around international relations. The end of the Cold War, economic realignments, and many of the other issues raised by the authors in this volume suggest that, at the very least, the ways in which gender relations are maintained and constructed will be made clear, for it is in periods of crisis that prevailing notions become threatened. As Peterson writes:

> gender is hard to see and critique because it orders 'everything' and disrupting that order feels threatening—not only at the 'level' of institutions and global relations but also in

relation to the most intimate and deeply etched beliefs/experiences of personal (but relentlessly gendered) identity. Yet, however much we are uncomfortable with challenges to gender ordering, we are in the midst of them. Failure to acknowledge and address these challenges both impairs our under-

standing of the world(s) we live in and sustains relations of domination.[54]

Feminist interrogations of gender thus can, and should, become a regular feature of the landscapes of both IR and IPE.

Notes

1. Nannerl O. Keohane, 'Speaking from Silence: Women and the Science of Politics', in E. Langland and W. Cove, eds, *A Feminist Perspective in the Academy* (Chicago: University of Chicago Press, 1981), 87.

2. Susan Strange, Presidential Address to the International Studies Association, 1995. Though these comments were deleted from the published version of her address, Strange's remarks are reported in Craig Murphy, 'Seeing Women, Recognizing Gender, Recasting International Relations', *International Organizations* 50, 3 (Summer 1996): 532.

3. Francis Fukuyama, 'Women and the Evolution of World Politics', *Foreign Affairs* (Sept.–Oct. 1998): 33.

4. Adam Jones, 'Does "Gender" Make the World Go Round? Feminist Critiques of International Relations', *Review of International Studies* 22, 4 (Oct. 1996): 423–4.

5. Fred Halliday, 'Hidden from International Relations: Women and the International Arena', *Millennium* 17, 3 (Winter 1988): 419. See also other essays in this special edition of *Millennium*.

6. This argument is made about critical international relations theory in my 'Gender in the International Paradigm Debate', *Millennium* 18, 2 (Summer 1989): 265-72.

7. Paraphrased from Nancy Fraser, 'What's the Critical Theory? The Case of Habermas and Gender', in S. Benhabib and D. Cornell, eds, *Feminism and Critique* (Minneapolis: University of Minnesota Press, 1987), 31.

8. Robert W. Cox, 'Social Forces, States and World Order: Beyond International Relations Theory', in R.O. Keohane, ed., *Neorealism and Its Critics* (New

York: Columbia University Press, 1986), 208.

9. Craig N. Murphy and Roger Tooze, 'Introduction', in Murphy and Tooze, eds, *The New International Political Economy* (Boulder, Colo.: Lynne Rienner, 1991), 6.

10. Fukuyama, 'Women and the Evolution of World Politics', 27; emphasis added.

11. As Murphy pointed out, much of the work that Strange described as 'whining' was in fact doing the very empirical research that Strange seemed to be calling for. See also J. Ann Tickner, 'You Just Don't Understand: Troubled Engagements between Feminists and IR Theorists', *International Studies Quarterly* 41, 4 (Dec. 1997): 6111–32, and the dialogue that followed with interventions by Robert O. Keohane, 'Beyond Dichotomy: Conversations between International Relations and Feminist Theory', Marianne H. Marchand, 'Different Communities / Different Realities / Different Encounters: A Reply to J. Ann Tickner', and J. Ann Tickner, 'Continuing the Conversation . . .', *International Studies Quarterly* 42, 1 (Mar. 1998): 193–210.

12. Jones's essay won the British International Studies Association graduate student essay prize for 1996. It is worth noting that Jones's general point is a good one; that is, that analyses concerned with gender need to address prevailing assumptions of both men and women and the effects that those assumptions have. It is a point made by numerous feminist scholars. As Jan Jindy Pettman writes, IR ensures that 'most men and all women are erased from view.' Jan Jindy Pettman, *Worlding Women: A Feminist International Politics* (New York: Routledge,

1996), viii; see also selections from my own *Feminism and International Relations* (Basingstoke: Macmillan, 1994), esp. ch. 5.

13. V. Spike Peterson, 'Whose Crisis? Early and Postmodern Masculinism', in Stephen Gill and James H. Mittelman, eds, *Innovation and Transformation in International Studies* (Cambridge: Cambridge University Press, 1997), 185–201.

14. Ibid., 199.

15. See Stanley Hoffman, 'An American Social Science: International Relations', *Daedalus* 106, 3 (1977): 41–60.

16. Ibid., 49, 58.

17. K.J. Holsti, *The Dividing Discipline: Hegemony and Diversity in International Theory* (Boston: Allen & Unwin, 1985), ch. 1.

18. J. Ann Tickner, 'Hans Morgenthau's Principles of Political Realism: A Feminist Reformulation', *Millennium* 17, 3 (Winter, 1988): 429.

19. R.B.J. Walker, 'Sovereignty, Security and the Challenge of World Politics', *Alternatives* 15, 1 (1990): 3–28.

20. Chris Weedon, *Feminist Practice and Poststructuralist Theory* (Oxford: Basil Blackwell, 1987), 1; see also Rosalind Delmar, 'What Is Feminism?', in Juliet Mitchell and Ann Oakley, eds, *What Is Feminism?* (New York: Pantheon Books, 1986), 8. Alison M. Jagger, *Feminist Politics and Human Nature* (Sussex: Harvester Press, 1983), provides an excellent account of some of the different approaches to feminism.

21. For general explorations of this theme, see George T. Crane and Abla Amawi, *The Theoretical Evolution of International Political Economy* (New York: Oxford University Press, 1991), esp. 3–33; Stephen Gill and David Law, *The Global Political Economy: Perspectives, Problems and Policies* (Baltimore: Johns Hopkins University Press, 1988), 3–24.

22. Ibid.

23. Stephen Gill, 'Transformations and Innovations in the Study of World Order', in Gill and Mittelman, eds, *Innovation and Transformation in International Studies*, 7.

24. Mark Laffey, 'Ideology and the Limits of Gramscian Theory in International Relations',

paper presented to the annual meeting of the International Studies Association, 1–4 Apr. 1998, 2 and *passim*.

25. See also Anne Sisson Runyan and V. Spike Peterson, 'The Radical Future of Realism: Feminist Subversions of IR Theory', *Alternatives* 16 (1991).

26. For reviews of feminist scholarship within international relations, see Jacqui True, 'Feminism', in Scott Burchell and Andres Linklater, *Theories of International Relations* (New York: St Martin's Press, 1996), 210–51; Jill Steans, *Gender and International Relations: An Introduction* (New Brunswick, NJ: Rutgers University Press, 1998).

27. Ester Boserup, *Women's Role in Economic Development* (London: George Allen and Unwin, 1970).

28. Asoka Bandarage, 'Women in Development: Liberalism, Marxism and Marxist-Feminism', *Development and Change* 15 (1984): 497.

29. Ibid. See also Barbara Rogers, *The Domestication of Women: Discrimination in Developing Countries* (New York: St Martin's Press, 1979).

30. In terms of women and development, this critique is made by Lourdes Bernia and Gita Sen, 'Accumulation, Reproduction, and Women's Role in Economic Development: Boserup Revisited', *Signs* 7, 2 (1981): 279–98.

31. See, for example, Tickner, 'Hans Morgenthau's Principles of Political Realism'.

32. Lynne Segal, *Is the Future Female?* (London: Virago Press, 1987).

33. Maria Mies, *Patriarchy and Accumulation on a World Scale: Women in the International Division of Labour* (London: Zed Books, 1986); Gita Sen and Caren Grown, *Development, Crises and Alternative Visions: Third World Women's Perspectives* (New York: Monthly Review Press, 1986). This section draws on Abigail Bakan, 'Whither Woman's Place? A Reconsideration of Units of Analysis in International Political Economy', paper presented at the annual meetings of the Canadian Political Science Association, Victoria, BC, May 1990.

34. Sen and Grown, *Development, Crises and Alternative Visions*, 30–1.

35. Ibid., 37.

36. Chandra Talpade Mohanty, 'Women Workers and Capitalist Scripts: Ideologies of Domination, Common Interests, and the Politics of Solidarity', in M. Jacqui Alexander and Mohanty, eds, *Feminist Genealogies, Colonial Legacies, Democratic Futures* (New York: Routledge, 1997), 6.

37. Cynthia Enloe, *Bananas, Beaches and Bases: Making Feminist Sense of International Politics* (London: Pandora, 1989), 33.

38. Ibid., 36–7.

39. Ibid., ch. 7.

40. Ibid., 185.

41. Abigail B. Bakan and Daiva Stasiulis, 'Foreign Domestic Worker Policy in Canada and the Social Boundaries of Modern Citizenship', in Bakan and Stasiulis, eds, *Not One of the Family: Foreign Domestic Workers in Canada* (Toronto: University of Toronto Press, 1997), 12 and *passim*. See also Kimberly A. Chang and L.H.M. Ling, 'Globalization and Its Intimate Other: Filipina Domestic Workers in Hong Kong', in M.H. Marchand and A.S. Runyan, eds, *Gender and Global Restructuring* (London: Routledge, 2000), 27–43.

42. Bakan and Stasiulis, 40–3 and *passim*.

43. Pettman, *Worlding Women*, 189.

44. Marilyn Waring, *If Women Counted: A New Feminist Economics* (San Francisco: Harper, 1988), 2; Marilyn Waring, *Three Masquerades: Essays on Equality, Work and Human Rights* (Toronto: University of Toronto Press, 1997), ch. 2.

45. Mohanty, 'Women Workers and Capitalist Scripts', 13.

46. Ibid.

47. Ibid., 15–16.

48. Ibid., 17. See also Eileen Boris and Elisabeth Prügl, *Homeworkers in Global Perspective* (New York: Routledge, 1996).

49. This is drawn from my *Feminism and International Relations*, ch. 5.

50. Zillah Eisenstein, *The Female Body and the Law* (Berkley: University of California Press, 1988), 204–6.

51. Michael J. Wright, 'Reproductive Hazards and "Protective" Discrimination', *Feminist Studies* 5, 2 (Summer 1979): 303.

52. Jill Krause, 'The International Dimension of Gender Inequality and Feminist Politics: A "New Direction" for International Political Economy?', in John Macmillan and Andrew Linklater, eds, *Boundaries in Question: New Directions in International Relations* (London: Pinter, 1995), 130.

53. Yosef Lapid, 'The Third Debate: On the Prospects of International Theory in a Post-Positivist Era', *International Studies Quarterly* 33 (1989): 238.

54. Peterson, 'Whose Crisis?', 199.

Suggested Readings

Alexander, M. Jacqui, and Chandra Talpade Mohanty. *Feminist Genealogies, Colonial Legacies, Democratic Futures*. New York: Routledge, 1997.

Marchand, Marianne, and Anne Sisson Runyan, eds. *Gender and Global Restructuring: Sightings, Sites and Resistances*. New York: Routledge, 2000.

Peterson, V. Spike. *A Critical Rewriting of Global Political Economy: Integrating Reproductive, Productive and Virtual Economies*. London: Routledge, 2003.

Tickner, J. Ann. *Gendering World Politics*. New York: Cambridge University Press, 2001.

Web Sites

Coalition Against Trafficking in Women:
www.catwinternational.org/

Gender, Science and Technology:
www.ifias.ca/GSD/GSDinfo.html

International Labour Organization, Women and
Gender Issues:
www.ilo.org/public/english/140femme/index.htm

International Organization Migration (IOM)
Trafficking Project: www.focus-on-trafficking.net/

Regional Summit on Foreign Domestic Workers, Sri
Lanka:
caramasia.gn.apc.org/Regional_Summit_MainPage.htm

Third World Network, Gender Issues and Women's
Rights: www.twnside.org.sg/women.htm

UNIFEM: www.unifem.org/

Women in Development Network:
www.focusintl.com/widnet.htm

Part II

Global

Issues

Introduction

Global Issues in Historical Perspective

Geoffrey R.D. Underhill

Although World War II is slowly sinking deeper into our past, it remains one of the most important punctuation marks in human history in terms of both economic and security matters, to say nothing of its effects on human life. It is difficult to understand the contemporary period without at least some reference to the new beginning that war constituted. This introduction seeks to explain how the initially established post-war order became transformed into the global state-market system we know today.[1]

While the war itself was experienced in different ways in various parts of the globe, it was the first genuinely global conflict. In dramatic and asymmetrical ways it altered the balance of power and the distribution of wealth among territories of the globe, undermining the dominance of Europe. The US and Canada, along with Australia and New Zealand, were almost alone among developed nations to emerge unscathed by the physical destruction, but the war had served its purpose for them as history's most successful industrial development policy.

While one would not wish to underestimate the continuities between the interwar and post-war worlds, to a considerable extent there was an opportunity to begin afresh combined with a strong sense that this time things *had* to be done better. The interwar period had been a disaster in terms of international economic management, and there was a determination not to repeat the perceived mistakes. If the war was not a 'full stop' as punctuation marks go, it came close.

This of course makes the post-war period a fascinating laboratory in international and comparative political economy. Through careful historical analysis it is possible to chart the emergence and transformation of an order, to identify causal factors, and to determine the distribution of costs and benefits, all from a relatively clear starting point.

Although today one is inclined to think in terms of a *global* order, until the collapse of the Soviet bloc in 1989 there were in fact *two* orders organized into separate security blocs. The politics of security in the Cold War evolved around the protection of and competition between these two distinct forms of political economy. We are concerned here with the so-called 'Western' order, as opposed to the centrally planned economies of the Soviet bloc. This Western order was dominated by the advanced market economies. In reality it was not much of a 'bloc'; there was a wide variety of national patterns of development, economic policies, and economic structures among the states in the system, including the developing world. National economic strategies ranged from the relatively laissez-faire approach of the Americans to the more interventionist approach of Japan and several Western European states.

There remains no doubt, however, that the greatest beneficiary of the events of the war was the United States. Its economy emerged as the most competitive and advanced and as the principal source of capital for economic development elsewhere. Seldom, in historical terms, has a country been as dominant, at least economically, as the United States in 1945. The USSR emerged from the war as a military colossus, but it was an economic cripple devastated by invasion and occupation, having paid the heaviest cost of all the wartime allies.[2]

Therefore, any historical account of the post-war international political economy must explain the role of America in the fashioning and transformation of the global economic order. Nonetheless, several myths have established themselves in the literature on post-war international economic relations: myths about the character of the order itself and about ways of explaining its emergence. These myths are encapsulated in hegemonic stability theory (HST): that the United States used its dominant position to the benign purpose of leading other countries towards the benefits of a liberal world order. As American decline set in from the 1970s, this liberal order has become frayed and more difficult to maintain.[3] If it is fairly evident that the US played a central role in the planning and implementation of the post-war world, what precisely was that role and how do we understand it?

Liberalization cannot be explained in the state-centric terms of the realist school and HST. To explain the long gestation of our current liberal world economy, one must turn to the underlying socio-economic dimensions of the political economy and the deep socio-political dynamics of structural change in global markets, often beginning at the national level.[4] The theory turns out to be a refuge for apologists seeking to square the undoubted liberal idealism of much US policy throughout the post-war period with the considerable vagaries of the actual content of policy since the 1970s in particular, and who share a clear view that US power is by definition benign.[5]

This argument can be developed by exposing three important and interrelated myths. The first is that the United States was a *consistent* sponsor of liberalization and that it got its way through its hegemonic position in the post-war order. In reality, the era of liberalization did not correspond to the putative period of hegemony, and the US was as inconsistent as the rest in promoting it.[6] Progress towards liberalization has in fact accelerated during the period of relative American economic decline.

The second myth is that the role of the United States in the politics of the world economy is essentially reducible to the role of the US 'state-as-actor'. The role of social coalitions or private corporate actors in domestic and international policy processes, across the global political economy, must also be taken into account; decisions and compromises made by private economic agents *interacting* with political authorities and agencies have driven changes in market structure. Finally, there is the myth that the US hegemon necessarily acted in an enlightened fashion, leading often recalcitrant horses to the waters of liberalization and gently persuading them of the benefits for all concerned of a long drink. This in turn implies that the decline of the United States is largely responsible for many of the difficulties encountered in the last two decades, leading the Americans to behave in a more self-serving manner. However, US leadership on liberalization, when it occurred, was quite naturally self-interested, as were the very deviations from liberal multilateralism that the United States has sponsored in a fairly regular fashion since imposing unilateral restrictions on agricultural trade and textile imports in the mid-1950s.

To summarize, the US state was often ambivalent about liberalization. Sometimes it experienced difficulties in persuading sceptical domestic interests of the bounties of international competition to the extent of violating its international commitments. Sometimes domestic firms sought radical freedom from government guidance at home and abroad and this met determined international resistance, and the pursuit of liberalization might destabilize relations with important allies. Liberalization did occur, but for reasons only partially related to US state power and purpose, and the liberalization of trade followed a different path from the liberalization of the financial system. This process of liberalization has greatly intensified competition among producers, which in turn has enhanced the political and economic instability associated with ongoing market-led adjustment. Whether political systems can withstand these pressures over time is an open question, especially where the spate of financial and monetary crises is concerned.

This introduction, in tandem with much of the rest of the volume, is therefore quite deliberately revisionist. The main focus is on the global regimes for money, finance, and trade, as these constitute the framework of the international political economy. The aim is not to cover all the details or issues, but to provide the reader with a broad background for understanding the subsequent contributions to this volume. I will deal first with the financial and monetary system, demonstrating that early post-war US dominance of the international monetary system did not lead to a liberalized system of global finance; globalization came later and for reasons linked less to state power and more to the interests of New York and London financiers, among others. The second section focuses on trade and will indicate once again that the development of liberal trade regimes corresponded not to US dominance but to relative decline, and was linked less to exertions of state power than to structural developments in the global economy, which first came to fruition within the United States and spread to Europe and Asia.

Money, Payments, and Finance in Historical Perspective

The planning began as Anglo-American wartime collaboration, with substantial input from the Canadian government,[7] in what came to be known as the Bretton Woods process.[8] Bretton Woods was about the monetary and payments system and the financial order, and agreement was reached in 1944. Money and finance were seen as crucial because the monetary regime provides a backdrop for the settlement of trade accounts and other transactions across state boundaries. A parallel series of conferences on the trade regime culminated in the Havana Charter of 1948, which will be dealt with later.

The monetary and financial system would largely determine the overall nature of the global economic order. Control over the circulation of money (or lack thereof) was considered to shape the possibilities in other issue-areas. At stake was the very nature of the economic order. How market oriented should it be? What kind of role should state authorities have? How could the pitfalls of pre-war laissez-faire and the eruption of economic nationalism that characterized the breakdown of the pre-war market system be avoided? The answers to these and other questions would largely determine the relative distribution of benefits, and costs, in the post-war era.

In the end the answers were not always clear, and sometimes the answers initially provided were altered as the system evolved. Right from the start there was considerable conflict within the US administration over the proper role of the market versus public institutions, and conflict existed as well between the government and the business community, and even within the business community, over the appropriate extent of openness and market orientation of the international system under negotiation.[9] The US Treasury Department, which handled the Bretton Woods monetary negotiations, strongly supported a monetary and financial order based on the involvement of public multilateral institutions in managing exchange rates, payments systems, capital flows, and domestic adjustment to disequilibrium in the system. In short, the aim was 'to drive the usurious money lenders from the temple of international finance'.[10] The British delegation, headed by John Maynard Keynes, was no less emphatic in this regard. This was not just a matter of self-interest with regard to a war-weary British economy. It was considered that volatile short-term capital flows had contributed substantially to the interwar period of economic disaster.

Public multilateral institutions—the International Monetary Fund (IMF) in the short term and the World Bank in the long term—were therefore to provide a cushion to help states adjust to balance-of-payments and economic development problems. The system, while it placed greater constraints on countries in deficit as opposed to surplus economies, was to permit them to square the maintenance of a stable (fixed-rate) exchange rate mechanism and payments system with the goals of domestic economic development. As this was the dawn of the era of post-war welfare states, domestic socio-political stability was perceived, quite rightly, as a crucial ingredient of international co-operation on monetary and trade issues. Unless states, within certain agreed limits, could pursue their own socio-economic aspirations in keeping with internal democratic (or otherwise) debate, the pressures of international economic interdependence would have an adverse effect on the prospects for co-operation anyway.

The agreement signed at Bretton Woods provided for a *fixed but flexible system* of exchange rates. Adjustment to imbalances that might emerge was to be eased through the right to draw foreign exchange on fairly liberal terms (at least initially) from the IMF. Longer-term economic development and reconstruction would be financed by the World Bank, officially known as the International Bank for Reconstruction and Development (IBRD). States agreed that controls on the short-term flows of capital across borders were a necessary and desirable part of the system. A stable monetary and payments system compatible with domestic policy goals was furthermore seen as a necessary precondition for the successful liberalization of trade, judged by most to be desirable. Keynes had long maintained that an open trading system, with the constant adjustment to a changing international division of labour that this implied, would soon collapse in the presence of volatile short-term capital flows that could skew the exchange rate and adjustment process and undermine the aspirations of domestic populations. Liberal trade and the integrity of the fixed exchange rate system would be facilitated by a relatively closed financial system.[11]

Someone had to pay for the resources the system required. As the only major creditor country, the US, not surprisingly, was somewhat ambivalent about providing the funds to finance everyone else's adjustment to the consequences of the war. Indeed, conservative congressmen, powerful elements of the American business community, and officials in the Department of State combined forces to push through alterations to the plan in the negotiations and in the implementation process.[12] This reduced the resources of the IMF and World Bank to nowhere near the level required for the scale of payments problems linked with wartime devastation and the extraordinary competitive edge of American industry—the total amount of IMF quotas was set at $8.8 billion and IBRD resources at $10.2 billion (a lot for an individual, little for a world economy). Furthermore, most countries could not afford to pay their quotas in the first place. Yet, somehow, if the global economy was to be resurrected in a way that would ensure continued co-operation, money had to be introduced to the system to facilitate the process of international exchange upon which recovery depended. If the IMF/IBRD could not provide it, someone would have to, and the only available candidate was the US Treasury. Furthermore, American industry needed overseas customers to maintain the levels of economic activity wartime production had hitherto provided, while Europe and Asia needed capital goods for reconstruction to regenerate their domestic economies. There was a common interest to be exploited.

The more rapidly Europe recovered, the more glaring the imbalances became between the United States and the rest as recovery sucked in imports that no one could pay for, at least in the short term.[13] When the payments crisis of the winter of 1946–7 erupted, wartime controls had to be extended, limiting trade to an elaborate system of barter. The likelihood of a liberal system of trade and convertible currencies seemed distant indeed.

As Britain's balance of payments collapsed under the pressure, an opportunity to accelerate liberalization presented itself, which the new officials of the Truman administration did not miss. In 1945, Britain had approached America for a loan, and the terms obliged Britain to make sterling convertible and help promote a liberal trade regime.[14] Probably neither side fully appreciated the desperate nature of the payments crises. The view from the US was often rather short-sighted: American business saw opportunities in a more liberal system, and some US officials were convinced that recovery would be facilitated by a greater role for the market. The British reluctantly agreed to the main American conditions. In return, the Americans would provide $3.75 billion, which the UK hoped to use to restore monetary reserves.

Implemented in 1947, the move was an abject failure. Intended to accelerate the introduction of the Bretton Woods agreement by reducing the transition period, the effect was to kill the accord altogether. Within about six weeks the British Treasury's reserves were exhausted, and exchange and currency controls were reimposed. Britain had been the most competitive of the European economies, so the problem was serious and general.

Clearly the problems of post-war reconstruction were greater than anticipated. More money (or 'liquidity', as it is referred to by economists) was required in the system if a virtuous circle of international trade and payments was to be established in the world economy. The resources of the World Bank ($10.2 billion) were dwarfed by the scale of the problem, as were those of the IMF ($8.8. billion). The inappropriate conditions of the American loan made the US case for the free market look increasingly self-interested. Further attempts by the erstwhile US hegemon to use aid as a lever would be met with the increasing resolve of Europeans to pursue their own particular national economic strategies as a *prerequisite* to eventual liberalization. Not surprisingly, exertions of raw American power had provided infertile ground for multilateral co-operation. The European Payments Union, set up in 1950 and lasting to 1958, remained a poor substitute for US-led global multilateralism and reflected European determination to go their own way.[15] The dream of a relatively open monetary, payments, and financial order dominated by the Bretton Woods institutions appeared dead. Unlike the apocryphal death of Mark Twain, the death of Bretton Woods was far from exaggerated. Transitional arrangements would persist; the IMF was sidelined, the World Bank marginalized, eventually to become a long-term lender to the emerging ex-colonies and other less-developed countries (LDCs). Virtually all currencies were subject to exchange controls and seldom were directly convertible into dollars, and trade remained heavily protected.

Direct US provision of liquidity was substituted for the role the Fund was supposed to play through what came to be called the Marshall Plan (officially, the European Recovery Program), cer-

tainly among the most brilliant developments in US post-war diplomacy. It was a plan of aid to European economies that they would administer themselves in co-operation with each other under specified conditions. The aid would fill the payments gap with billions of liquid dollars. The idealism of the US move was obvious, but this should not entirely cloak the shrewd self-interest of US policy-makers. The Marshall Plan aid, at approximately $18 billion,[16] essentially gave Europeans the resources they needed to purchase the American capital and agricultural goods required for reconstruction. Occupied Japan benefited from equivalent largesse after the outbreak of the Korean War. The resulting exports to Europe helped compensate for the substantial reduction in economic activity in the US economy, which it was feared would follow the winding down of wartime production. It was hoped in vain that the aid program would provide leverage over the Europeans as well—aid recipients were banned from drawing on the IMF.[17] Marshall Plan aid furthermore was extensively supplemented by Korean War rearmament. Rearmament, including US military assistance to allies, accelerated the supply of dollar liquidity and stimulated economies, especially that of West Germany, and had the same function as Marshall Plan aid for US allies in Asia.[18]

The problem was to persuade Congress that US generosity was as good for America as fiscal conservatives saw it to be for thankless (and state-interventionist) Europeans, including the British with their reviled imperial preference system of trade discrimination. The growing perceived Soviet threat to Western European security was instrumental in helping the US administration to extract the funding. Marshall Plan aid became America's first Cold War policy, Korean War rearmament the second. When eventually, in 1958, European countries were sufficiently recovered to allow the relatively free convertibility of their national currencies with the dollar, what had emerged was a 'key currency system' or 'dollar standard'.[19]

There were some apparent similarities with the original Bretton Woods plan, such as the fixed-price convertibility of the dollar into gold and the pegging of other currencies in terms of the dollar and the right of countries to control capital flows. Despite this, the international monetary and payments system built on this new key currency foundation was not regulated by the Bretton Woods institutions but by the American Treasury and the Federal Reserve.[20] The growing pool of dollars in foreign hands, not the meagre resources of the IMF, oiled the wheels of international commerce, and so the international monetary system hinged on confidence in the US dollar. As the economist Robert Triffin pointed out at the time,[21] this posed a dilemma that would eventually lead to instability and the collapse of the system. The world economy needed an ample supply of dollar liquidity to ensure growth and trade, yet the more dollars there were the more doubtful would be the ability of the US to honour its pledge to convert unlimited amounts of dollars to gold on demand at the fixed price of $35 an ounce. The payments system and exchange rate mechanism were therefore at the mercy of unilateral US willingness and capacity to manage the dollar in keeping with the needs of a stable international system: some combination of maintaining the international trade competitiveness of American industry and service sectors and controlling the capital outflows linked to private overseas investment and government expenditure.

America had become the world's banker, largely replacing the multilateral institutions of the Bretton Woods agreements, with all the privileges and responsibilities that entailed. The system of fixed exchange rates would collapse if these privileges and responsibilities were not exercised with caution. However, it is a cliché to assert that US domestic pressures, as opposed to the exigencies of international co-operation, were always likely to overshadow the dollar system.

The post-convertibility world of the 1960s was not, then, the Bretton Woods system at all, nor was it as stable as the notion of benign hegemonic stability implies. There was a persistent element of crisis as the American keeper of the key currency responded more to its domestic preferences than to the imperatives of international stability.[22] First, the US commitment to the Cold War led to military and other government expenditures overseas,

which swelled the dollar holdings of foreigners, many of whom cashed them in for gold at the official rate, depleting the Treasury's gold stocks. Second, European and Asian economies recovered and came to compete with the US on more equal terms. Slowly the seemingly invincible US trade surplus began to dwindle. Finally, the international activities of American corporations completed the picture. Through foreign direct investment in dollars, American firms contributed to the outflow, and the administration was understandably reticent to curtail this activity.[23] Eventually these firms began even to raise capital (in dollars) overseas as their bankers followed them in their international exploits. Dollar-based capital markets emerged in the City of London, which allowed the private sector to expand the supply of dollars once again through the credit multiplier of bank lending. It was all unregulated by US monetary or supervisory authorities, with the British turning a blind eye in the hope of rejuvenating the City through offshore banking.[24]

Eventually, a lack of trade competitiveness and accelerating financial outflows meant that the foreign holdings of dollar IOUs severely overshadowed US gold stocks. No one really believed the dollar was worth what the system maintained it was, either in terms of gold or other currencies. Speculation began sporadically in the early and mid-1960s, reaching a fever pitch in 1968 and again in 1971.

The problem was what to do about it. Numerous stopgap measures were negotiated multilaterally,[25] but the fundamental problem was one of American adjustment to declining competitiveness and financial outflows. The Vietnam War, with its domestic inflationary pressures and vast overseas military expenditures, distorted the US economy while boosting the development of Asian economies, which eventually emerged as important competitors for US industry. However, as the US controlled unilaterally the key to the system, the dollar, there was little others could do to compel American adjustment. The US was equally unwilling to restrain the overseas activities of its multinational firms and financial institutions or to reduce overseas military expenditures. Eventually, short-term capital flows overwhelmed the financial capacity of governments to maintain the pegged system, precipitating its collapse.

Characteristically, the American government chose a unilateral approach to the problem, an approach hardly the stuff of benign hegemony. In August 1971, the Nixon administration sought to free itself from the constraints of the exchange rate mechanism, breaking the link with gold and allowing the dollar to float. Despite attempts to resurrect the pegged system with greater flexibility, by 1973 most countries had to accept a floating currency. The onset of economic crisis and greater international economic disorder associated with the OPEC oil price rise made international co-operation to reform the system difficult.

The vast pool of Eurodollars on international capital markets had given rise to short-term capital flows that swamped governments and central banks in their attempts to maintain currency parities. As private firms began to enjoy the unrestricted transnational financial game, they increased the pressure on their governments to ease restrictions on business activity, especially financial institutions, and to deregulate domestic markets. Thus in the 1970s financial deregulation was added to the emergence of floating currencies. This trend accelerated in the 1980s and lay behind the global integration of financial markets, building on the offshore Euromarkets.

The problems of the pegged system were more closely linked to the policy of dollars on the loose and US failure to adjust internally than to the pressures of the fixed rates. Nonetheless, the touted *object* of the deregulation of the exchange rate mechanism was to regain the national policy-making autonomy restricted by the obligations of a fixed-rate system. Contrary to expectations, the collapse of fixed exchange rates, combined with the increased volume and volatility of private financial flows, effectively jeopardized the capacity of governments to pursue the independent policy goals so cherished in the post-war period while maintaining the ties of economic interdependence that were so costly to break. By abandoning fixed exchange rates, international monetary governance was left increasingly to market forces to the detriment of state capacity to manage the domestic macro economy in line with domestic preferences and imperatives. Governments would henceforth find it more difficult to pursue social and economic policies at variance with the preferences of market players (see Chapter 10 by Webb).

A further result of the state retreat from international monetary management was to accelerate the growth of the capital markets, which had undermined the fixed-rate system in the first place.[26] American capital controls were removed in the late 1960s, and in 1979 the UK government followed. Most other major Western countries and many LDCs have since conformed under pressure from private lobbies and other states. Similar pressures from financial sectors have led to comprehensive programs of domestic financial deregulation and a corresponding cross-border integration of capital markets in a process of globalization. This liberalization of capital flows and global financial integration has removed many of the last vestiges of domestic policy-making autonomy, completing the transformation of the post-war global order (see Chapter 8 by Pauly, Chapter 9 by Story, and Chapter 10 by Webb) in a way that had little to do with US decline. This more 'marketized' financial order, in combination with the liberalization of trade, permits owners of capital to seek their preferred investment climate among a variety of economies in terms of lower inflation, more advantageous interest rates, less restrictive rules on wage rates, hiring practices, and other aspects of government regulation.

In this sense, financial market integration meant that major investors were no longer restricted to opportunities in their respective home countries or equally restrictive conditions elsewhere. Deregulation and liberalization have produced a dynamic conferring greater freedoms on private corporate actors in the international political economy. That is what the creation of a more liberal or 'marketized' economic order is all about, and this represents a dramatic reversal both of the intentions of the post-war planners and in the balance of public and private in domestic and international economic management. This financial globalization was caused by the unplanned emergence of the dollar standard, the incompatible objectives of states in international monetary relations, the rise of the Euromarkets, and consistent private lobbying for financial liberalization. The policies of democratic states must increasingly conform to the exigencies of the international market order, making international constraints difficult to square with the demands of many domestic socio-political constituencies. The consistent outbreak of episodes of financial crisis has not helped matters, particularly for fragile emerging market economies.

Trade Issues and the Post-War Order

The post-war monetary system provided the backdrop for the international trade regime. The development of the trading order was also a long and difficult story, which conforms little to traditional accounts of the role of the US and the causes of liberalization.

Negotiations took place during and after the war, culminating in the Havana Conference of 1948. While most parties agreed that protectionism had been a negative aspect of interwar economic relations, there was a lack of agreement on the timing, extent of, and preconditions necessary for liberalization. Given the extraordinary international competitiveness of the America economy and the US worry about a possible post-war slump following the winding down of war production, it is not surprising that the Americans tended to see access to foreign markets through multilateral trade liberalization as a prerequisite for full employment and future growth. The much more vulnerable British and Europeans saw things rather differently. Their delicate balance-of-payments positions, their need for substantial imports of capital goods and food, and their crippled manufacturing capacity linked to wartime devastation meant that they tended to see a move towards reconstruction and full employment as a necessary precondition of trade liberalization.[27]

In the end, however, all revealed themselves ambivalent about the liberalization of trade. US trade policy historically had been characterized by

high tariffs, and the Americans continued to be cautious for a number of reasons: most of the firms in the American economy were domestically oriented, with no desire to see their markets threatened by foreign competition; those firms that were export-oriented were far from convinced that other countries would play the liberalization game fairly and allow highly competitive US producers into domestic markets (the classic argument of protectionists in liberal clothing); and the US government was ambivalent because it had to strike a balance between these different perceptions of national self-interest. Furthermore, the US Congress was jealous of its trade policy-making prerogatives and was suspicious by nature of international institutions that might diminish this constitutional right in any way. Nonetheless, the administration consistently maintained that reciprocity and non-discrimination in trade relations would form a foundation for mutual benefits from international trade in a climate of ongoing liberalization.[28]

European countries and less-developed countries (Latin America and the emerging ex-colonies) were likewise sceptical about liberalization, but for different reasons. In the British case, there was an understandable loyalty to the countries of the imperial preference system, which had stood by Britain in the dark days of the war prior to Soviet and American entry into the conflict. Europeans generally were aware that their devastated economies could not cope with liberalization, which meant direct competition with the US. The potential effects of a liberal international trade regime on employment and domestic social stability, in view of the legacy of the interwar depression, were ominous. Europeans were also toying with the idea of a comprehensive system of regional economic integration, which the US encouraged in its own way. The LDCs were worried about the effects of trade liberalization on their development prospects.

All agreed on the need for some sort of stable system of multilateral rules and norms to reduce to a minimum the arbitrariness and unpredictability of national practices. What was needed, then, was a compromise. The underlying principles promoted by the Americans (reciprocity and non-discrimination) were readily enough adopted, but there were various opt-outs and caveats in the Havana Charter and a transition period of uncertain length, with a view to permitting adjustment prior to the cold shower of trade competition through liberalization. Once again, states sought to ensure that the international order would be largely compatible with domestically formulated social and economic policy objectives and sufficient national decision-making autonomy.

The resulting 1948 Havana agreement to form the International Trade Organization (ITO) was therefore a compromise for the long-term achievement of non-discriminatory and liberalized international trading relations in both services and industry, preserving the right of states to opt out, for example, when experiencing balance-of-payments difficulties. It also provided for a dispute-settlement mechanism with the legal powers to question national trade policies should they be deemed in violation of the principles and rules underpinning the ITO. Its principles encapsulated the broad agreement that full employment was to be fully compatible with the emergence of the new rules of international trade. The ITO Charter also incorporated a 1947 interim agreement that codified the ITO rules and trade product categories and provided a legal framework for negotiations on liberalization, an agreement called the General Agreement on Tariffs and Trade (GATT, since 1994 the World Trade Organization or WTO).

The ITO was never ratified by the American Congress, and therefore the trade pillar of the Bretton Woods order was abandoned from the start. The defection of the US business community was crucial to this failure. Some appear to have favoured continued US protectionism through tariffs; others felt the Charter did little to promote access to foreign markets for American firms, with too many opt-outs and caveats to the accord and not enough firm commitment to the systematic removal of barriers, especially those posed by the British imperial preference system.[29] The US Congress continued to provide a brake on attempts to proceed to a more liberal order.[30]

The Americans and their partners turned to the interim GATT of 1947, which contained the essential rules of the failed ITO. GATT remained provisional, an executive agreement stripped of most ITO institutional substance, but it did provide a set of rules and a sufficient basis for intergovernmental co-operation.[31]

Over time, GATT developed its rules and became more intrusive on sovereignty. With limited progress in the 1950s and early 1960s, economic recovery and reconstruction in Europe and elsewhere provided a firm foundation for substantial agreement. The US provided crucial leadership in this regard by launching the Kennedy Round of negotiations (1963–7), seeking to benefit from a perceived competitive edge in international competition and to tie the emerging European Union (EU) into the global trade regime. Major tariff cuts resulted, and the efforts were continued in more difficult economic circumstances in the Tokyo Round (1974–9).[32] These two rounds of tariff cuts brought tariffs on manufactured goods to near-negligible levels and set out the major lines of conflict for the Uruguay Round, in particular the EU–US dispute over agriculture, the (somewhat waning) demands from LDCs for preferential treatment, and the 'back-door protectionism' of non-tariff barriers. The Uruguay Round success cemented these developments and extended, gingerly in most cases, liberalization and rule-making to agriculture, trade in services, intellectual property issues, and foreign investment protection (see Chapter 12 by Sell). These efforts were continuing at the time of writing in the context of the latest Doha Round, where a major confrontation between developed and developing countries had emerged to stall the talks.

It should be clear that the US failed to persuade others of the bounties of liberalization until relatively late in the day, and the erstwhile liberal champion itself had been ambivalent about thoroughgoing trade liberalization for compelling domestic reasons. Substantive moves towards liberalization were not underway until American dominance was declining in late 1960s. Despite relative American industrial decline and the rise of new producers such as China, the process continues. Furthermore, the drive for liberalization was never a policy of self-denial by the hegemon—it was more an off-on instrument of national policy in a limited but progressively growing range of producer and service sectors than an enlightened blueprint for global economic order and prosperity. When liberalization began in earnest, it was a longer and more arduous process involving complex domestic and international compromises for all parties concerned. Raw assertions of state power were never successful in the construction of a liberal trade order.[33] Only when domestic conditions were simultaneously right in the EU, the United States, and Japan could the regime move towards substantive liberalization and the development of the dispute-settling role originally foreseen in the Havana Charter.

It should also be emphasized that the process of trade liberalization was not simply a matter of state policies and decision-making, though these helped. Private-sector actors played a key role in accepting and indeed promoting policies aimed at a more liberal trading order, and the process was underpinned by the emergence of transnational economic structures.[34] Governments were often only the legal surrogates for private coalitions of liberal or protectionist interests. While the 1947 rules of the trading order were crucial foundations, strategic decisions by private firms (often despite state protectionism) led to the web of international economic interdependence upon which liberalization was built. As prosperity grew and domestic firms became more oriented towards international trade and investment, the domestic support for liberalization strengthened.[35] It was very much a bottom-up process where non-state actors embedded in national policy processes played a central role.

For all the progress, protectionist pressures have not disappeared by any means. In fact, the adjustment process associated with tariff cuts and other forms of liberalization have consistently forced many industrial sectors in industrialized economies on the defensive, leading to the implementation of various 'new protectionist' non-tariff barriers (NTBs) such as voluntary export restraints (VERs) and 'orderly marketing arrangements'.[36] The

US has been as guilty as any on this score, often leading the pack, pushed by narrow sectional interests with power in the Congress. By the late 1990s, the US steel industry was once again lobbying against imports from a range of competing producers as recessionary conditions hit in the wake of the Asian financial crisis and the bursting of the 'dot-com' bubble. In 2001 the incoming Bush administration was quick to impose new steel tariffs, eventually declared illegal by the WTO. Though there has been much change, especially in Latin America (see Chapter 23 by Phillips), LDCs have historically seen their fundamental economic weakness as a handicap in accepting a liberal order, and the confrontations of the Doha Round illustrate the point.

On the whole, however, the perceived costs of a return to a closed system are now seen to be high, not least because a substantial coalition of the private interests across a range of countries that participate in the policy process identify their continued profitability with improved access to foreign markets. Many even have multinational production strategies and substantial networks of intra-firm trade, moving intermediary as well as finished goods across borders to benefit from the most advantageous mix of factor and input costs available. For example, it was estimated as far back as the 1980s that some 60 per cent of US imports derived not from traditional cross-border trading between national producers but from intra-firm and intra-industry trade carried out by transnational corporations (TNCs) within their own company structure.[37] The integrated production strategies of TNCs have had an important impact on trade balances, often displacing domestic production to overseas locations where it is reimported as foreign value-added products.

While the rise of highly competitive newly industrialized countries (the first of which was Japan in the 1950s, with China now to the fore) and the rise of regional integration projects (see Chapter 20 by Hveem), such as the European Union, the Canada–US/North American Free Trade Agreement, and MERCOSUR, have complicated the multilateral picture, the worst fears of free traders have yet to materialize. Defensive regional blocs currently seem unlikely,[38] and new forms of protectionism have not led to a repudiation of the GATT/WTO regime. The Doha Round attempts to build on the successful Uruguay Round establishment of the WTO, which greatly expanded the liberalization agenda. As in the past, the trade regime continues to be a mixture of liberal principles combined with protectionist reflexes. Conflict will be ongoing as states with different patterns of competitive advantage and different policy mixes confront each other on old and new issues, but few contemplate a return to the pre-GATT era.

Conclusion

This introduction has highlighted a number of interrelated points about the post-war order. Although this has been a story of liberalization, probably more far-reaching than many post-war planners thought possible, the explanation provided here has contrasted with much of the more state-centric IPE literature. In particular, while American leadership was important at crucial junctures, the evolution of the system cannot be explained by the exercise of US power alone.

In the first place, the period of greatest American dominance was the most illiberal. US attempts to apply leverage of various kinds failed to persuade the Europeans and Japanese in turn to accept the American vision. In contrast, the period of relative US decline has seen dramatic developments with respect to liberalization in trade, but especially in the monetary and financial order. Like most countries, the US has remained ambivalent about the liberalization of trade, pursuing tariff cuts and the elimination of discrimination in a self-interested fashion and displaying reticence to remove barriers, even easy readiness to erect new ones, when domestic sectors appeared threatened.

Perhaps most importantly, the achievement of a liberal order in trade and finance is as much a market phenomenon as it is a matter for state decision-making. The transnationalization of American and other firms created its own policy dynamic over time with states and market actors integrated in ongoing dialogue for the governance of the global economy. The growing patterns of interdependence, while far from eliminating conflicts of interest in the system, fostered a constituency of economic agents dependent on cross-border transactions. The GATT/WTO regime provided a relatively orderly framework in which states could negotiate openness where support was forthcoming, while they responded with at least equal vigour to more vulnerable constituencies (such as farmers) seeking continued protection. The underlying social and economic interest base behind state policies were a more important variable than the power of individual states.

This introduction has sought to allay other myths as well. It has been argued, for example, that the Bretton Woods plan was not implemented. The short-lived fixed-rate system after convertibility in 1958 was, in contrast, a key currency system, the dollar standard. This afforded the US considerable discretion over the international monetary system: the world's currency system was manipulated through US monetary policy, and this was perhaps the principal source of American influence in international economic relations. The move to floating currencies has not necessarily diminished this power because US policy can manipulate the value of the world's main fiduciary asset, the dollar. The establishment of the euro, the fruit of European Monetary Union, is slowly changing the situation in trade and in international bond markets, but that will take some time.[39]

What this introduction has left out is addressed in the upcoming chapters, but two final questions invite reflection. In the first place the successful pursuit of liberalization has elevated the liberal creed to a doctrine. The case for the ongoing liberalization of economic relations has been accepted rather uncritically, either *faut de mieux* or because of its perceived benefits. The liberal case is fairly clear: a market-oriented order leads to a more efficient allocation of resources and therefore provides the key to future economic growth and prosperity. The logical conclusion of this is the effective removal of public authorities from the economic domain and the removal of embedded barriers to market transactions, including the protective social policies and other restrictive practices that have accompanied the success of many post-war economies. Yet this brief history has illustrated that even the most liberal designs will meet obstacles as vested interests resist the pressures of the market.

Nonetheless, this liberal creed should be questioned for a number of important reasons related to what the post-war planners were trying to do in the first place and to the increasing frequency of financial crisis in the contemporary global economy. They were trying to find an alternative to laissez-faire, which had proved so problematic in the inter-war period, leading to the Great Depression. The market proved unsustainable as the principal arbiter of economic decision-making and led to an outbreak of economic nationalism that greatly exacerbated the crisis at the time. For all the failures of post-war multilateral co-operation, one is pushed to conclude that John Maynard Keynes and Harry Dexter White, respectively the British and American negotiators at Bretton Woods, addressed these problems with a considerable degree of wisdom, a commodity often in shorter supply than base self-interest in international relations. They realized that political authority would lose its legitimacy where the market ran rampant, leading to a general and very undesirable failure of international co-operation altogether. A proper role for public authority is a prerequisite for a sustainable economic order.[40]

Little in contemporary experience would lead one to question these lessons, and yet an incautious liberal creed has come to dominate much thinking on these matters. It should be observed, however, that as liberalization has proceeded, especially in the domain of finance, economic growth has become more problematic and economic cycles more volatile. The golden age of post-war growth occurred *prior* to the dramatic liberalization of trade and finance in the 1970s and 1980s. Furthermore, some of the main post-war success stories, such as Japan, France, and Germany (despite their considerable difficulties in the late 1990s), or more recent successes like Korea and now China, are not necessarily the most liberal. One would not wish to imply simple cause and effect here, but despite anticipated howls of protest from many economists there is at least reason to pause for reflection on these issues.

Second, it is not clear that continued liberalization of the global economic order is politically sustainable, at least unless approached with considerable caution. The removal of trade barriers intensifies competition and requires constant industrial restructuring and rapid economic change. The market is probably the most efficient tool of social engineering, but its results can be unpredictable, wasteful, and unsettling. The liberalization of the financial order is more disquieting.[41] The excessive freedom and volatility of capital markets and financial flows threaten investment, payments equilibrium, and the ability of national communities to attain their collective aspirations. The Asian and Argentine crises have threatened some of the most noteworthy successes in the developing world, and the new financial order has forced deflationary strategies on many unwilling governments, much like the nineteenth-century classical gold standard. Although in the developed world, which arguably benefits most from liberalization given its strong position in open market competition, firms and citizens have apparently learned to cope, the experiences of the developing world are more difficult and the Doha Round conflict may signal reduced acceptance of the liberal approach.

Of course, one would not wish to call into question the institutionalization of international co-operation that has developed in the post-war era, whatever the policy pursued. Yet might one conclude that multilateral rules to attenuate conflict and foster some sense of fairness across levels of development are almost certainly more important than liberalization per se? If co-operation can indeed bring sustained benefits, then its participants must find the outcome, not just the promise, legitimate in one way or another.

Notes

1. The author would like to thank Peter Burnham, Susan Strange, and the many students over the years who have contributed to this essay.

2. See estimates of Soviet military and economic resources by American intelligence in Walter Lafeber, *America, Russia, and the Cold War 1945–1984*, 5th edn (New York: Alfred A. Knopf/Newberry Award Records, 1985), 26–7, 49–50.

3. Robert Gilpin, *Global Political Economy: Understanding the International Economic Order* (Princeton NJ: Princeton University Press, 2001). Gilpin is an eminent exponent of HST.

4. For two approaches that address these underlying dimensions in different ways, see Herman Schwartz, *States versus Markets: History, Geography, and the Development of the International Political Economy* (New York: St Martin's Press, 1994), esp. chs 3, 8–10, a remarkable and under-rated study; Robert W. Cox, *Production, Power, and World Order* (New York: Columbia University Press, 1987).

5. For a critical analysis of the motivations behind HST, see Isabelle Grunberg, 'Exploring the Myth of Hegemonic Stability', *International Organization* 44, 4 (Autumn 1990): 431–78.

6. Bruce Moon, in Chapter 31, reinforces this point in the specific context of the US political economy.

7. See Thomas Keating, *Canada and World Order: The Multilateralist Tradition in Canadian Foreign Policy* (Toronto: McClelland & Stewart, 1993), esp. chs 1–2.

8. For detailed accounts of the negotiations and aftermath, see Richard Gardner, *Sterling-Dollar Diplomacy in Current Perspective* (New York: Columbia University Press, 1981); Armand van Dormael, *Bretton Woods: Birth of a Monetary System* (London: Macmillan, 1978).

9. See Gardner, *Sterling-Dollar Diplomacy*; Fred Block, *The Origins of International Economic Disorder* (Berkeley: University of California Press, 1977), esp. chs 1–5; and the very important work by Marcello de Cecco: 'Origins of the Post-war Payments System', *Cambridge Journal of Economics* 3 (1979): 49–61, and 'International Financial Markets and US Domestic Policy since 1945', *International Affairs* 52, 3 (July 1986): 381–99.

10. Henry Morgenthau, US Treasury Secretary, as quoted in Gardner, *Sterling-Dollar Diplomacy*, 76.

11. See Eric Helleiner, *States and the Re-emergence of Global Finance: From Bretton Woods to the 1990s* (Ithaca, NY: Cornell University Press, 1994).

12. Block, *International Economic Disorder*, ch. 3; de Cecco, 'Origins of the Post-war Payments System'; de Cecco, 'International Financial Markets'.

13. See Alan S. Milward, *The Reconstruction of Western Europe 1945–1951* (London: University Paperbacks/Methuen, 1984), ch. 1 and Conclusion.

14. See Block, *International Economic Disorder*, ch. 3; Peter Burnham, *The Political Economy of Post-war Reconstruction* (London: Macmillan, 1990), ch. 3 (esp. p. 51, quote from Will Clayton, US State Department: 'if you succeed in doing away with Empire preference . . . it may well be that we can afford to pay a couple of billion dollars for it.').

15. See Burnham, *Political Economy of Post-war Reconstruction*, ch. 5; William Diebold, *Trade and Payments in Western Europe* (Washington: Council on Foreign Relations, 1952).

16. There is considerable controversy over the eventual size of the aid package. The original budgetary request in the congressional legislation was for $17 billion (Block, *International Economic Disorder*, 87), but it seems accurate to say that the total was over $20 billion. See Fred Hirsch and Peter Oppenheimer, 'The Trial of Managed Money: Currency, Credit, and Prices 1920–1970', in C.M. Cipolla, ed., *The Fontana Economic History of Europe* (Glasgow: Collins/Fontana, 1976), 626.

17. Block, *International Economic Disorder*, 111–12.

18. See Richard Stubbs, 'War and Economic Development: Export-oriented Industrialization in East and South-east Asia', *Comparative Politics* 31, 3 (Apr. 1999): 337–55.

19. The term 'dollar standard' is borrowed from Richard Gardner. Let us also be reminded that while convertibility was an aspect of liberalization, the global financial order remained segmented along national lines. Globalization would have to wait.

20. See de Cecco, 'Origins of the Post-war Payments System'; de Cecco, 'International Financial Markets'.

21. Robert Triffin, *Gold and the Dollar Crisis: The Future of Convertibility* (New Haven: Yale University Press, 1961).

22. See Susan Strange, *International Monetary Relations*, vol. 2 of Andrew Shonfield, ed., *International Economic Relations of the Western World 1959–1971* (Oxford: Oxford University Press, 1976).

23. Block, *International Economic Disorder*, chs 6–7, offers a good analysis of the growth and management of the American payments deficit.

24. See Michel Aglietta, 'The Creation of International Liquidity', and David T. Llewelyn, 'The Role of International Banking', in Loukas Tsoukalis, ed., *The Political Economy of International Money* (London: Sage, 1985).

25. See Strange, *International Monetary Relations*.

26. See G.R.D. Underhill, ed., *The New World Order in International Finance* (London: Macmillan, 1997), esp. ch. 1.

27. See Gardner, *Sterling-Dollar Diplomacy*, chs 6, 8, 14, 17.

28. Certainly it seems fair to say that the US government was more concerned with discriminatory trade practices than liberalization per se. See Gerard and Victoria Curzon, 'The Management of Trade Relations in the GATT', in Andrew Shonfield, ed., *International Economic Relations of the Western World 1959–1971*, vol. 1, *Politics and Trade* (Oxford: Oxford University Press, 1976), 143–67.

29. See Gardner, *Sterling-Dollar Diplomacy*, 372–80. These criticisms were levelled at the Charter despite the admission of the US government that 'if we want to be honest with ourselves, we will find that many of the sins that we freely criticize other countries for practising have their counterpart in the United States.' Quote from Will Clayton, Asst. Sec. of State for Economic Affairs, ibid., 378.

30. Curzon, 'Management of Trade Relations', 148.

31. Ibid., 146. The US Congress remained distinctly cool towards the GATT for many years; in fact, it was not until 1968 that the US government felt bold enough to request from Congress permanent authorization for the US financial contribution to the GATT secretariat (Gardner, *Sterling-Dollar Diplomacy*, xxv–xxvi). Furthermore, the US unilaterally exempted agriculture from GATT provisions in 1955 and initiated such discriminatory practices as voluntary export restraints on cotton textile exports from Japan as early as 1956.

32. See Gilbert Winham, *International Trade and the Tokyo Round Negotiations* (Princeton, NJ: Princeton University Press, 1986).

33. See Shonfield, Curzon, et al., *Politics and Trade*, 39, 48–9.

34. See G.R.D. Underhill, *Industrial Crisis and the Open Economy* (London: Macmillan, 1998), where this argument is taken up in detail.

35. See Helen Milner, *Resisting Protectionism: Global Industries and the Politics of International Trade* (Princeton, NJ: Princeton University Press, 1988).

36. For an in-depth study of VERs in the textile case, see Underhill, *Industrial Crisis and the Open Economy*.

37. Robert Gilpin, *The Political Economy of International Relations* (Princeton, NJ: Princeton University Press, 1987), 254.

38. See W.D. Coleman and G.R.D. Underhill, eds, *Regionalism and Global Economic Integration* (London: Routledge, 1998).

39. See Kenneth Dyson, ed., *European States and the Euro* (Oxford: Oxford University Press, 2002), esp. section 1.

40. A careful reading of Adam Smith reveals that he was clearly aware of this. It is a pity that most of his latter-day followers are not.

41. See Susan Strange, *Mad Money* (Manchester: Manchester University Press, 1998).

Suggested Readings

Block, Fred. *The Origins of International Economic Disorder*. Berkeley: University of California Press, 1977.

Burnham, Peter. *The Political Economy of Post-war Reconstruction*. London: Macmillan, 1990.

Dyson, Kenneth, ed. *European States and the Euro*. Oxford: Oxford University Press, 2002.

Gardner, Richard. *Sterling-Dollar Diplomacy in Current Perspective*. New York: Columbia University Press, 1981.

Milward, Alan S. *The Reconstruction of Western Europe 1945–1951*. London: Methuen, 1984.

Schwartz, Herman M. *States versus Markets: History, Geography, and the Development of the International Political Economy*, 2nd edn. London/New York: Macmillan/St Martin's Press, 2000.

Shonfield, Andrew G., V. Curzon, et al. *Politics and Trade*, vol. 1 of Shonfield, ed., *International Economic Relations of the Western World 1959–1971*. Oxford: Oxford University Press, 1976.

Spero, Joan, and Jeffrey Hart. *The Politics of International Economic Relations*, 6th edn. Belmont, Calif.: Wadsworth, 2003.

Stopford, John, and Susan Strange. *Rival States, Rival Firms*. Cambridge: Cambridge University Press, 1991.

Strange, Susan. *International Monetary Relations*, vol. 2 of Shonfield, ed., *International Economic Relations of the Western World 1959–1971*. Oxford: Oxford University Press, 1976.

———. *Mad Money*. Manchester: Manchester University Press, 1998.

Tsoukalis, Loukas, ed. *The Political Economy of International Money*. London: Sage, 1985.

Underhill, Geoffrey R.D. *Industrial Crisis and the Open Economy*. London: Macmillan, 1998.

———. ed. *The New World Order in International Finance*. London: Macmillan, 1997.

Chapter 7

The Political Economy of Post-9/11 Security

Brian Burgoon

The last two decades have seen enormous changes in international security that have sharpened but also complicated the connections between political violence and political economy. The interaction of economic and security relations has always been important to international politics, where interstate conflicts and power balances often had origins (at least partly) in struggles over wealth and resources. But the dispersion and diffusion of political authority of the last decades have changed and made more prominent the role of intra- and international economic interaction in shaping violence. The end of the Cold War is perhaps the most obvious, where that profound change in power relations and Great Power conflict was itself partly caused by and constituted rises in international economic interdependence—globalization. Furthermore, as state-to-state conflicts of the Cold War subsided, a wide range of civil, ethnic, and religious conflicts remained in the context of economic and political collapse, such as in the aftermath of Soviet intervention in Afghanistan or Cold War-sponsored strife in Africa. Finally, whether or not connected to the end of the Cold War, the last few decades have seen a rise in the scale and number of civil and ethnic conflicts throughout the developed and developing world, where the struggles between states and their societies, or among groups within these societies, have clear roots in economic organization, inequalities, distributional conflicts, and other faces of political economy.

One might expect, then, that the post-11 September rise to prominence of international ter-rorism and rapidly changing grand strategies to address it—among the most important security developments since the Cold War—would also be seen as an interaction between political economy and violence. Indeed, perceived oppression—glaring inequalities, poverty, or ethnic discrimination—is intuitively connected to terrorism and similar responses as the weapon of the weak. And yet, in the post-11 September debate over what causes terrorism and what can be done to stop it, there is marked uncertainty about how and whether the economy is a factor—not only about how economic conditions might explain when and why particular conflicts generate terrorism as opposed to other possible responses, such as full civil war or peaceful protest, but whether economic conditions matter at all.

On the one hand, some policy commentary and academic scholarship suggest that domestic and international economic conditions very much matter to the origins of terrorism, as in other cases of asymmetric violence and ethnic and civil wars. Many observers claim, for instance, that poverty and income inequality within countries breed hatred, religious and political extremism, and terrorism. This view finds support in survey research revealing strong correlation between poverty and Irish nationalism and Indonesian religious fundamentalism, and violent extremism.[1] This suggests we should think of terrorism as anchored in underlying socio-economic injustices and instability. In cross-country and time-series studies of international terrorist incidents, terrorism correlates negatively with wealth (per capita GDP) and positively with income inequality.[2] Also common are competing claims that globalization (openness to and flows of goods, capital, and people) worsens or diminishes poverty and inequality, or the ease of illicit political organizing, thereby worsening/reducing the likelihood of terrorist responses. Such views find support in evidence that international financial crises increase poverty and religious extremism in the crisis countries, and cutting the other way, in anecdotal evidence that terrorism happens in or emerges from the least globalized countries, such as Saudi Arabia and Lebanon.

On the other hand, both intuition and scholarship suggest that economic conditions do not much affect terrorism and who commits it. The official statement of US grand strategy emphasizes that poverty has little to do with terrorism, pointing out that the terrorist attacks on New York and Washington were perpetrated by middle-class, educated misanthropes led by a rich religious fanatic.[3] Scholarly research actually provides plenty to support this view, including surveys suggesting that hate crimes have little bearing on local economic conditions, or that Palestinian tastes for terrorism and for Hezbollah actions are independent of individual wealth and education. Cross-country evidence further suggests that the involvement of a country's citizens in terrorism correlates weakly with national wealth.[4] Some who believe that poverty or inequality make a difference accept nonetheless that economic globalization has little effect on terrorism, pointing to the poor correlation between terrorism and FDI, portfolio, and trade flows.[5] These studies point to terrorism's roots not in the economy, but in clashes of civilizations, authoritarian rule, failed states, and elsewhere.

This debate, of course, is not just about social science explanation; it is about which policies make sense to combat terrorism and other kinds of post-Cold War/post-11 September conflict. The conviction that economic and related social conditions matter inspires many to insist that the best defence against terrorism and the conditions that

generate it is to promote economic growth and combat inequality through more economic aid, to sustain welfare states and social justice, and to foster more or less or different economic globalization.[6] In turn, the alternative view is that pure politics, not economics, motivates terrorism, or this view at least rationalizes anti-terrorism campaigns that target terrorist groups and failed states with the intent to promote democratization—including the aggressive combination of preventive war and nation-building in the Bush administration's 'Wilsonianism in boots'. In short, at stake in understanding how political economy affects terrorism and its underlying conditions are the grand strategies of and basic relations between modern states and non-state political actors of all stripes.

This chapter argues that existing debate has only scratched the surface of the role of international and domestic economic development in shaping outbreaks of terrorism and identifies three ways in which we can come to a more sophisticated understanding of that role. First, the effects of the usual economic suspects, such as inequality and poverty, vary widely and depend on how one defines these economic conditions and the 'terrorism' they may influence. Second, economic globalization has offsetting effects for terrorist patterns, and in any event plays out differently depending on the institutional setting, such as the level of democracy. Third, especially underanalyzed is how the social policies and partisanship of the left may reduce the sources of conflict and thus the incidence of terrorism. These claims add up to the conclusion that economic factors *very much matter* to post-11 September security, but in ways that are often different from and more complicated than currently realized, interacting in a complex fashion with other possible causes of terrorism, from authoritarian rule to cultural clashes.

Thus the context in which terrorism emerges is more complex than much of the current literature and policy response would admit. The rest of this chapter briefly lays out the conceptual logic of and presents quantitative evidence for these claims. The arguments and evidence are far from conclusive and cast limited light on how economic factors relate to terrorism, yet they should help clarify how political economy matters for the most central questions of post-11 September—what *underlies* terrorism and what can be done about it.

Specifying Terrorism and the 'Usual' Economic Suspects

Finding a connection between terrorism and even the most commonly implicated socio-economic conditions, poverty and inequality, depends on how terrorism and these economic conditions are specified. First, the effects of economic conditions as underpinnings for terrorism may look very different if we look at the poverty or inequality position of *individuals* as opposed to the more macro-level poverty or inequality of the *settings* in which individuals live. Some studies focus only on the micro level, and thereby miss how contextual economic conditions might matter. Krueger and Maleckova's frequently cited study admits that evidence that poorer individuals are not more likely to support or commit terrorism says very little about whether poorer economic conditions inspire more conflicts likely to breed terrorism. Widespread poverty might motivate the wealthy and educated to act, and may also influence the tolerance of other (non-terrorist) citizens for extremism in their midst. Understanding the impact of poverty or inequality on individuals thus requires attention to how perceptions of injustice and national or regional incidences of terrorism interact with conditions of poverty and inequality.

Second, the influence of economic factors depends on which terrorist phenomenon (which response to what sorts of extremism) one seeks to explain. Even within the broad definition of terrorism that we shall use throughout this chapter—the use of coercive force against non-combatants for a broader audience and a political purpose—many different patterns of such terrorism need to be understood.[7] For instance, big differences exist between 'transnational' terrorism (i.e., involving perpetrators and victims of different nationalities) and 'all' terrorist incidents (i.e., both domestic and

transnational acts), or between incidents measured by *where incidents take place* or by *home country or nationality* of perpetrators of terrorist acts.

Third, the different ways in which given economic conditions such as economic inequality are specified can affect their implications for different measures of conflict expressed as terrorism. Most scholarly literature has focused on levels of domestic inequality as a variable: rising gaps between rich and poor in societies (especially if accentuated by ethnic or religious cleavages) tend to fuel feelings of unfairness and injustice that, all other things equal, can spark political extremism. Existing evidence suggests that measures of inequality correlate positively with where terrorist acts are committed. But this is incomplete. Is *transnational* terrorism (where perpetrator and victim are from different countries) inspired by within-country inequality or by inequality *between* countries—where groups (possibly wealthy individuals) in the poorest countries chafe more at the global or regional inequality gap than between rich and poor within their national economy?

To address these various issues, consider the relationship between various measures of terrorism and both cross- and intra-national inequality. First, to judge whether global inequality spurs terrorism we need also to consider how cross-national inequality relates to *trans*national incidents of terrorism. Cross-country studies will not test this, because cross-national inequality varies over time rather than space. Figure 1 tracks how cross-national inequality[8] develops along with both 'total' and 'significant' *transnational* terrorist incidents from 1968 to 2003 as measured by the US State Department.[9] The figure reveals little correlation between international inequality and *total* transnational incidents, especially after 1988 or so, when terrorist incidents fall but inequality grows.[10] Since many of the incidents in the 'total' category are trivial acts of vandalism, however, the pattern of 'significant' incidents may matter more. Here inequality between countries is positively correlated to clearly rising terrorism,[11] with 2003 having the highest incidence of significant terrorism since the State Department began keeping track in 1985.[12]

Figure 1: Transnational Terrorist Incidents and Cross-national Inequality, 1968–2003

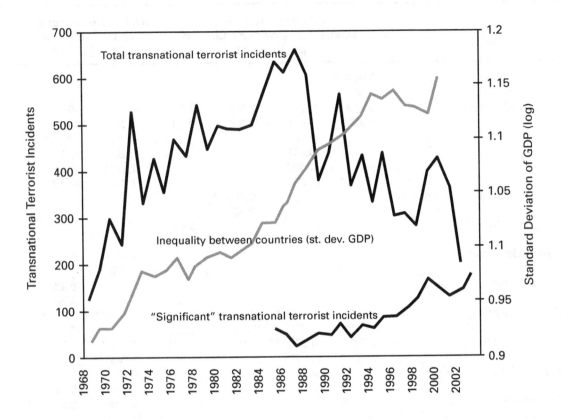

SOURCES: US State Department, *Patterns of Global Terrorism*, various years; Alan Heston, Robert Summers, and Bettina Aten, 'Penn World Table Version 6.1', Center for International Comparisons at the University of Pennsylvania (CICUP), Oct. 2002 (own calculations).

Furthermore, taking *total* incidents, both transnational *and* domestic, from 1968 to 2002,[13] a clearly rising trend positively and significantly correlates with cross-country inequality,[14] and suicide attacks since 1983 show roughly the same positive relationship.[15] Thus, whatever the origins of inequalities, we have good reasons to suspect that international inequality may fuel terrorism.

Inequality *within* countries also positively affects terrorist incidence. Li and Schaub have already found a positive and significant (though substantively small) effect of national levels of inequality on transnational terrorist incidents

within countries. The effect may be stronger if one looks at the incidence in the countries from which terrorist perpetrators come. Following Krueger and Maleckova's work, I estimate the number of 'significant' terrorist incidents from 1996 to 2001 using the State Department's annual accounting, where one can surmise the perpetrators' nationality from the State Department and other media information about each incident.[16] The first column in Table 1 shows the results of testing for possible cross-national correlation between the total number of terrorist incidents attributable to citizens of a given country between 1996 and 2001, and various eco-

Table 1: Terrorism and Inequality, Wealth, Globalization, Social Policy, and the Left

	Incidents of Terrorism Perpetrated by Nation's Citizens				Incidents of Terrorism on Nation's Soil	
	(1)	(2)	(3)	(4)	(5)	(6)
Inequality (Gini)	0.063** (2.40)					
GDP per capita (log)	-0.954** (2.45)	-0.217 (0.64)	-0.993** (2.21)	-1.392** (2.24)	-0.23*** (3.33)	-0.047 (0.64)
Trade (% GDP)		-0.720 (0.91)			-0.001 (0.53)	-0.000 (0.25)
FDI (% GDP)		0.399 (1.56)			-0.003 (0.18)	-0.002 (0.12)
Aid received (% GDP) (log)			-0.498** (2.00)			
Left party strength				-3.9*** (3.98)		
Trade x democracy					-0.000** (2.03)	
Social welfare (% GDP)						-0.21*** (3.64)
Democracy rating	-0.197 (1.15)	-0.407** (2.39)	-0.46*** (2.73)	0.017 (0.07)	0.036*** (3.00)	0.015** (2.21)
Population (log)	0.987*** (5.03)	0.929*** (3.67)	0.855*** (4.43)	0.907*** (4.80)	0.298*** (8.54)	0.272*** (7.50)
Portfolio flows (% GDP)					-0.003 (0.34)	-0.000 (0.02)
Government capacity					0.556*** (4.51)	0.503*** (3.78)
Conflict					0.026 (0.18)	0.038 (0.25)
GDP of export partners					-0.57*** (3.63)	-0.39** (2.19)
Terrorist incidents (t-1)					0.086*** (9.58)	0.079*** (9.39)
Regional dummies	Yes	Yes	Yes	Yes	Yes	Yes
Year dummies	No	No	No	No	Yes	Yes
Constant	4.499* (1.66)	1.018 (0.36)	7.166** (2.22)	10.442** (2.18)	2.363* (1.84)	-0.827 (0.53)
Observations	121	115	119	81	1996	1744
Pseudo R-squared	.07	.103	.105	.093	.307	.135
Likelihood-ratio alpha=0	879.4	737.1	996.2	654.5	4115.8	3872.3

*Significant at 10 per cent.

**Significant at 5 per cent.

***Significant at 1 per cent.

Negative binomial regression, with robust standard errors (z statistics in parentheses).

Sources: For Columns 1–4: Cross-section estimation (across countries) where dependent variable is transnational terrorist incidents by country of perpetrator(s), 1996–2001: US State Department, *Patterns of Global Terrorism*, various years; own calculations. Independent variables: Gini score 1995 (UN); GDP per capita (1995): Heston, Summers, and Aten, 'Penn World Table Version 6.1'; trade and FDI flows (logged) (1960–95 average): William Easterly and Aart Kraay, Dataset for 'Small States, Small Problems? Income, Growth and Volatility in Small States', *World Development* 28, 11 (Nov. 2000): 2013–27; aid received (logged), 1960–95 average: ibid.; left party (per cent years 1975–95 that left party controls chief executive and legislature): Thorsten Beck, George Clarke, Alberto Groff, Philip Keefer, and Patrick Walsh, 'New Tools in Comparative Political Economy: The Database of Political Institutions', *World Bank Economic Review* 15, 1 (Sept. 2001): 165–76; democracy rating, 1996–7: Freedom House, 'Freedom in the World Database', 2004, at: <www.freedomhouse.org/research/survey2005.htm>; population (log) (UN); dummies for Africa, Asia, Americas, and Europe.

For Columns 5 and 6: Time series cross-section of terrorist incidents by country where incident occurred: Quan Li and Drew Schaub, 'Economic Globalization and Transnational Terrorist Incidents', *Journal of Conflict Resolution* 48, 2 (2004). Independent variables lagged one year: Social spending, 1998–2001 (logged social security and health expenditures, per cent GDP): Jacek Kugler, Yi Feng, and Paul J.Zak, 'Politics of Fertility and Economic Development (POFED)', 2002, National Science Foundation Grant (No. SBR–9730474); democracy rating (Polity IV); GDP per capita (log); trade, FDI and portfolio flows; GDP per-capita of export partners: Li and Schaub, 'Economic Globalization'; government capacity (correlates of war measure); conflict dummy (1 = civil or international conflict in correlates of war measure); dummies for Africa, Asia, Americas, Europe.

nomic measures, including inequality and wealth.[17] The results show the significant and positive effect of national income inequality, and Figure 2 illustrates the size of this effect.[18] As we can see, a country evolving from average (fiftieth percentile, comparable to Portugal) to high inequality (the ninetieth percentile, comparable to Zimbabwe) should see an increase from one to nearly four significant terrorist incidents perpetrated by its citizens.[19] Thus, we have good reasons to suspect that both international *and* domestic inequality significantly spur not only how much terrorism takes place in general, but where it takes place and by whom. Where serious economic and social injustice is perceived, terrorism may well prove to be one of the responses.

The Complexity of Globalization and Terrorism

Existing studies also consider whether economic globalization either stimulates or discourages terrorism. Globalization, as a complex phenomenon, can be expected to influence responses to it in equally complex ways, sometimes feeding and sometimes curtailing sentiments feeding terrorist responses. Based on logical argument, standard measures of globalization can be expected to have mutually contradictory implications for both *incentives* and *capacities* to commit terrorism, and many of these implications are likely mediated by the domestic political settings where globalization is played out. Figure 3 summarizes this model.

The effects of globalization are likely to work in several directions, not least because of its likely contradictory effects on inequality and wealth. If inequality increases and wealth decreases the likelihood of terrorism, then globalization may have offsetting effects for terrorism. As Figure 3 hypothesizes, globalization can be expected to spur both inequality and growth. Whether this is true in practice is still an open question, but the balance of evidence suggests that economic globalization is likely to promote growth and per capita wealth by opening opportunities for investment and providing markets for production.[20] But the balance of the evidence is also that globalization tends to increase cross-national inequality—partly by virtue of leaving those more economically closed economies behind—and has contradictory effects on inequality within countries depending on which characteristics of globalization are considered.[21] If we oversimplify matters we can assume that globalization spurs terrorism by virtue of raising inequalities, while discouraging it by virtue of diminishing poverty levels. But these two phenomena are likely to vary over time and place.

Figure 2: Income Inequality and Terrorist Incidents Perpetrated by Nation's Citizens

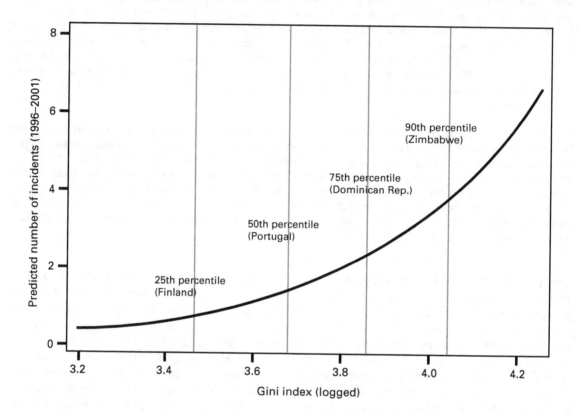

As a number of scholars of terrorism have found, globalization may also affect capacities to commit terrorism by providing more opportunities for groups to conduct their illicit activities both at home and abroad. The 11 September debacle is an extreme example of this possibility, with financial dealings made possible by extensive banking ties between countries; with terrorists coming from, working in, and moving between a slew of rich and developing countries; and with the tool of attack (commercial airlines) a key medium of globalization itself. Globalization can thus be expected to spur transnational terrorism, not just by spurring grievances but by making terrorism easier.

If we add these conditions together, economic globalization has strong yet mutually offsetting effects on terrorism. We should not be surprised, then, by the empirical results at the aggregate level:

Table 1 shows the lack of significant correlation between globalization and terrorist incidence not only in estimating terrorist incidents by perpetrator (column 2), but also in cross-sectional time-series estimation of where incidents take place (columns 5 and 6). These patterns do not so much tell us that globalization doesn't matter for terrorism as they indicate that globalization's (plausibly strong) offsetting effects may cancel each other out in aggregate correlation between globalization and terrorist incidence. Only in some places will they cancel each other out or will wealth creation overwhelm increases in inequality—local concentration of one thus may not at all be offset by the other. In any event, the intervening links between globalization and poverty and inequality, and the relationship of terrorism to poverty and inequality, suggest that the uneven benefits of globalization are a factor in terrorist activity.

Figure 3: Globalization and the Preferences and Capacities for Terrorism

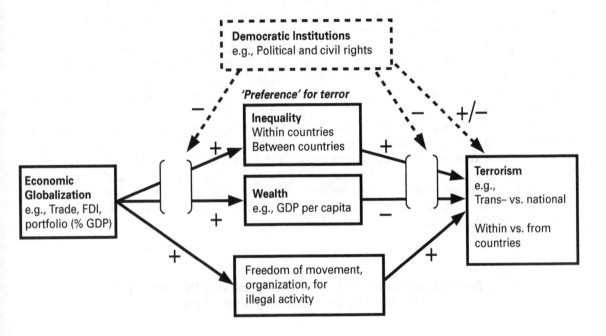

Finally, the effects of economic globalization on terrorism are mediated by domestic institutions, especially those regulating political access. In particular, a non-democratic context is likely to *intensify* globalization's incentive effects for terrorism and to weaken its discouraging effects. This is because the losers of trade or FDI in less democratic settings likely have less voice to ask for compensatory policies to address their losses. Likewise, non-democratic settings are likely to intensify globalization's spurring of terrorists' organizational capacities because a lack of political voice may imply that the technical means of illicit activity shape capacities for political action all the more. Thus in less democratic settings with underlying social tensions, economic globalization will stimulate more or constrain less the incidence of terrorism than in more democratic settings.

This can be tested by estimating how terrorist incidents relate to democracy and globalization, *and* their interaction. Rising democracy under conditions of globalization should diminish the posi-

tive effect (in the sense of positive correlation) or strengthen the negative effect (negative correlation) on incidents of terrorism. Such possible interaction can be judged by entering an interaction term for (a simple multiplication of) democracy and globalization measures. This captures what the effect of globalization on terrorism is expected to be, conditional on varying levels of democracy (and vice versa). Table 1 above shows the results of such an analysis, using the Li and Schaub dataset of 116 countries, observed annually, from 1975 to 1997. The table shows results of the interaction between democracy[22] and trade (imports plus exports as a percentage of GDP), quantitatively captured by estimating terrorist incidents as a function of democracy, trade, and an interaction term (the multiple of democracy and trade).[23] The results show, as we have seen, that globalization does not significantly spur or constrain the likelihood of terrorist incidents. But the negative and statistically significant coefficient for the interaction term of trade and democracy shows what we expect: that increased trade correlates with fewer terrorist incidents at high levels of democracy, but has a weaker or even positive effect on incidents at low levels of democracy. This effect is significant, net of variables such as conflict, government capacity, wealth, wealth of trading partners, population, past incidents, and unmeasured regional effects, and is robust to other interactions between democracy and portfolio investment or FDI.

To visualize better what this tells us, Figure 4 shows how rising trade openness affects predicted incidence of terrorism in non-democratic versus democratic countries:[24] where countries are very autocratic, increasing trade openness from roughly Haiti's to Jordan's average level will modestly increase the incidence of terrorism by a bit less than

0.5 incidents, or 30 per cent; but where countries are very democratic, increasing openness from France's to Belgium's level tends to decrease terrorism by a bit less than one incident, or about 30 per cent. It graphically captures how globalization's effects for terrorism are likely mediated by domestic political conditions. Globalization does not affect terrorism in simple and direct ways, independent of patterns of governance.[25] Simply put, grievances driven by trade or other factors exist in all societies; how they are channelled and dealt with has an important impact on whether they erupt as violent conflict such as terrorism. And democracy is certainly not the only way in which grievances get channelled, as the next section shows.

Figure 4: Interaction of Trade Openness and Democracy in Influencing Terrorism on National Soil

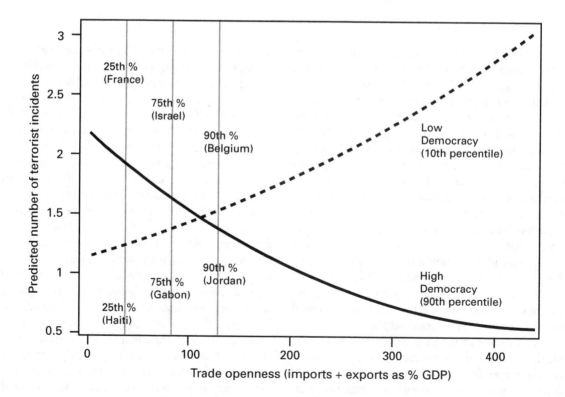

Terrorism and the Left Political Economy: Social Democracy, Welfare, and Aid

Understanding the political economy of terrorism requires understanding how particular economic policies and their associated parties affect terrorism. Surprisingly, this is an area virtually ignored in existing scholarship, and yet there are good arguments and empirical data to suggest that they are very important. In particular, there are reasons to suspect that three such factors play an important role in discouraging the incidence of terrorism 'in' and 'by' countries: (1) social welfare spending and provision; (2) aid flows to the developing world; and (3) social democratic (or leftist) political parties tending to support these and other policies.

Social policy can be expected to discourage the incidence of terrorism taking place on national soil or perpetrated by citizens. We have seen that inequality and, to some extent, poverty can be expected to encourage the incidence of terrorism at national levels. Democracy can help channel grievance and reduce the likelihood of violence emerging. If social welfare provision diminishes poverty and national inequality, it should also help reduce terrorism, with democratic conditions once again more likely to allow such policies to emerge. This cannot, however, simply be assumed. In OECD countries social policy clearly plays a strong redistributive role that fights both poverty and inequality.[26] But in the developing world, standard social policy measures such as pensions and health are often the exclusive province of relatively skilled and public employees, thereby doing little to fight and in some respects even exacerbating inequalities. Whereas in OECD countries social policy helps reduce inequality and poverty, when we look at only developing countries the opposite occurs. Clearly, it matters *how* welfare states actually operate. However, if we pool all countries in our 116-country sample, social welfare provisions tend to diminish significantly both inequality and, especially, poverty levels.

Welfare policy may also discourage terrorism by providing alternative channels to address socio-economic needs otherwise filled by extremist religious or political communities. We know that many fundamentalist religious communities provide social services and payments, which make them an imperfect substitute for social policy.[27] Hamas in the Palestinian territories is a well-known example, but the phenomenon is visible across a range of denominations and countries—such as the Koran study programs and religious groups in Indonesia (Chen, 2003). Such a pattern is important, because these groups are most likely to breed toleration, or even perpetration, of terrorism to achieve political-religious goals. If social policy and such religious extremism tend to be substitutes, albeit imperfect, we can hypothesize that countries with higher levels of *ex ante* social policy should diminish religious extremism. Higher levels of social welfare provision and spending should lead to less terrorism in and by countries.

In estimating all measurable patterns of terrorism across time and space—transnational and total, within and by countries—evidence suggests that higher levels of social spending do lead to lower incidence of terrorism. This applies both to cross-sectional estimations (including the incidents of terrorism perpetrated by citizens of different countries) and to cross-sectional time-series estimation of transnational terrorism within countries.[28] Table 1 shows in column 6 the results of the pooled cross-section time series, where we can see that higher levels of (logged) social security and health spending tend to have a statistically significant and negative effect on the incidents of terrorism, net of conflict, government capacity, wealth, wealth of trading partners, population, past incidents, and unmeasured regional effects. Figure 5 suggests the substantive size of this negative effect, which we can see is modest: increasing spending on social security and health expenditures from the twenty-fifth to the seventy-fifth percentile— equivalent to moving from Burundi's average of 1.8 per cent of GDP to Argentina's average of 18 per cent of GDP—decreases by only 0.5 the number of expected incidents (though as a simulation of such rare events, this is actually a large drop). It is important to point out, however, that this evidence generally is robust in regard to particular forms of social welfare spending taken individually, such as health, education, and pension spending, and that it has a signifi-

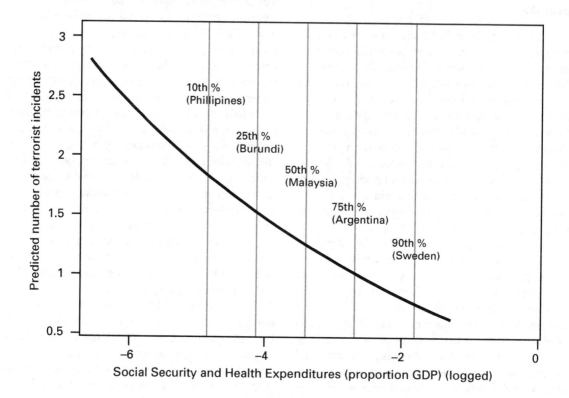

Figure 5: Effects of Social Welfare on Terrorism on Nation's Soil

cant negative relationship with all measures of terrorist incidents.[29]

Foreign aid (welfare from without) may also discourage terrorism. Generous foreign aid—overseas development assistance (ODA), IMF standby provisions, or other kinds of humanitarian and development help—may supplement or replace domestic social welfare provisions that diminish fundamentalist religious participation, and may also soften anti-Western feelings. To be sure, the opposite logic is also possible, where 'dependence' on foreign countries and institutions might breed resentment of aid-givers and foreigners generally. The more positive effects may well overwhelm the negative, however, suggesting the hitherto unexamined hypothesis that acts of and support for transnational terrorism within countries will decrease with rising aid provision. This is

hard to test, given limited data and the obviously high correlation between aid levels and GDP per capita. But within these limitations, the data generally support this expectation. Table 1 shows that the number of incidents that a country's citizens perpetrate goes down with rising levels of received ODA as a percentage of GDP, and similar results are found with respect to other measures of external assistance such as use of IMF quotas or standby provisions. In all cases, assistance significantly diminishes the likelihood of terrorists arising from a particular national society, net of GDP per capita, population, democracy, and unmodelled regional effects. Figure 6 summarizes this effect.

Figure 7 shows that *giving* more aid may also diminish the likelihood of transnational terrorism on one's own soil. The limited evidence is based on a

Figure 6: ODA Received and Terrorist Incidents Perpetrated by Nation's Citizens

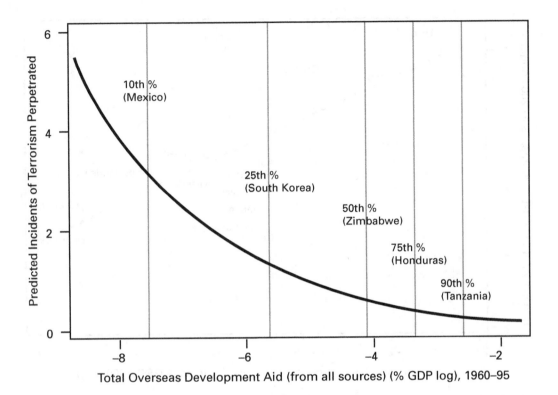

Total Overseas Development Aid (from all sources) (% GDP log), 1960–95

snapshot of the relationship between incidents of transnational terrorism to take place within 22 OECD countries and the extent of these countries' overseas development assistance. More controlled testing is difficult, given the relatively small quantity of available data, but the correlation, as expected, is strongly negative. Such a negative relationship between terrorism and aid holds up if we look at ODA adjusted for levels of genuine economic development and humanitarian aid, as opposed to 'aid' that veils support for donor exporters or other interests. Thus, we have hints that providing aid diminishes chances of being a terrorist target. It should be noted, however, that the great (former colonial) powers (US, UK, France, Germany, Italy) are all high targets for transnational terrorism despite differing levels of aid provision, showing that other factors undoubtedly play a role. However, that the US sends relatively low

levels of non-military aid as a percentage of GDP may only exacerbate the way its broader foreign policies, power, and influence might make it a more frequent target for terrorism.

Finally, left-wing partisanship in countries is another variable that could discourage the incidence of terrorism taking place on national soil or perpetrated by their citizens. Leftist parties tend to support social welfare and other policies that address poverty and inequality and therefore diminish grievances and political extremism. This partisanship indeed tends to correlate strongly and positively with social welfare expenditures and generosity.[30] Left-wing parties might also support more 'social' foreign policies that provide aid to developing countries, in turn diminishing resentments towards citizens in the 'sending' countries. Stronger leftist parties thus provide and/or *may in the future* provide

Figure 7: ODA Assistance Given (% GDP) and Transnational Terrorism on Nation's Soil

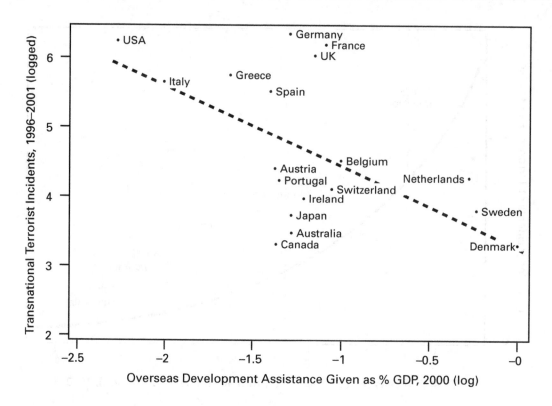

Note: Minuses included because the numbers here (and in Figures 5 and 6) are 'natural logarithm' transformations of the original numbers to make the tables more readable and the statistics more reliable.

social policies addressing the grievances of the vulnerable. In any event, compared to centrist and right-wing parties, political parties on the left tend also to disproportionately represent economically vulnerable groups in developing and developed countries and might thus help these groups feel better represented in formal political channels, in turn diminishing feelings of political exclusion that fuel extremism. One can reasonably hypothesize, thus, that stronger left-wing parties should correlate with fewer citizens being responsible for terrorist attacks *and* with fewer attacks on home soil.

There is some evidence to support these hypotheses. Table 1 shows in column 4 that as the percentage of years in which leftist parties controlled

the chief executive and legislatures rises, levels of terrorism committed by citizens from countries in which those parties are strong declines. Not shown in Table 1 is that this negative correlation also applies to estimations of total transnational or other terrorism committed within countries, as well as to alternative estimates of power on the left. Figure 8 simulates the substantive effect of left-wing partisanship on terrorism by countries.

Conclusion

This chapter demonstrates that the political economy of terrorism is complex: economic factors *do* influence terrorism, but in ways not accounted for by

Figure 8: Leftist Party Strength and Terrorist Incidents Perpetrated by Nation's Citizens

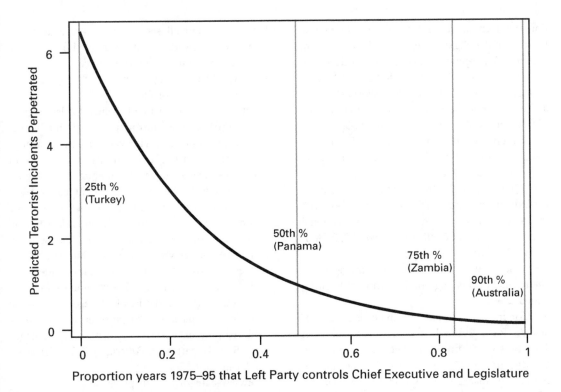

existing studies of terrorism. These conclusions, of course, only scratch the surface of the political economy of post-11 September security. There are other avenues of influence—from unstudied faces of globalization, to other interactions between economic and institutional conditions, to the economic origins of security policies in the Middle East. The evidence focusing on broad quantifiable correlations between terrorism and economic conditions needs to be supplemented by deeper tests of the claims through case studies that capture causal chains in history, demonstrating the direct links between underlying socio-economic grievances and terrorist activity as a specific political expression. In any event, it is important to recognize that inequality, poverty, globalization, social policies, and leftist political parties appear to have substantively modest effects on terrorist incidence. Indeed, other factors may well matter more—

political-ideological development of various religions, various forms of democratic and other governance, evolving ethnic relations, chafing at Western policies in the Middle East. But the findings suggest that even these may be reflexively related to economic conditions, which in general appear to be a significant part of how and why the bundles of factors that underpin socio-economic grievances might find expression in terrorism. This provides a social-scientific basis for taking seriously the hunches of many that combatting terrorism and broader post-Cold War conflicts requires not only weeding out terrorist or insurgent groups and the states that support them, but also addressing poverty, inequality, and other political-economic conditions through social policy and aid. To do otherwise, given what we are learning, would be to squander a key opportunity to foster a more humane post-9/11 security.

Notes

1. For the former, see Daniel Chen, 'Economic Distress and Religious Intensity: Evidence from Islamic Resurgence during the Indonesian Financial Crisis', Project on Religion, Political Economy, and Society (*PRPES*) Working Paper #39, 2003. For the latter, see Christina Paxson, 'Comment on Alan Krueger and Jitka Malecková, "Education, Poverty, and Terrorism: Is There a Causal Connection?"', mimeo, Princeton University, May 2002.

2. See Quan Li and Drew Schaub, 'Economic Globalization and Transnational Terrorist Incidents: A Pooled Time-Series Cross-sectional Analysis', *Journal of Conflict Resolution* 48, 2 (Apr. 2004): 230–58.

3. US White House, *National Security Strategy of the United States* (Washington: Government Printing Office, 2002).

4. See, for instance, Donald P. Green, Jack Glaser, and A. Rich, 'From Lynching to Gay-bashing: The Elusive Connection between Economic Conditions and Hate Crime', *Journal of Personality and Social Psychology* 75 (1998): 82–92; and especially Alan Krueger and Jitka Malecková, 'Education, Poverty and Terrorism: Is There a Causal Connection?', *Journal of Economic Perspectives* 17, 4 (2004): 119–44.

5. See Li and Schaub, 'Economic Globalization and Transnational Terrorist Incidents'.

6. For among the baldest statements in this direction, see James Wolfensohn, 'Fighting Terrorism and Poverty', at: <www.worldbank.org.cn/English/content/964m6286227.sthtml>.

7. There is plenty of disagreement within this broad definition of who are 'non-combatants', what 'for a political purpose' means, and whether state actors perpetrating such acts count as 'terrorists'. For the sake of the theoretical arguments below, we define all broadly, thus including non-active, non-uniformed military personnel as non-combatants; all economic, political, ethnic, or other broad audiences and goals as having political purpose; and all state and non-state actors as potential terrorists. Empirically, the definition varies according to the data source.

8. Measured as standard deviation of logged GDP per capita for 140 countries.

9. Title 22 of the United States Code, Section 2656f(d) defines terrorism as 'premeditated, politically motivated violence perpetrated against noncombatant targets by sub-national groups or clandestine agents, usually intended to influence an audience'. 'Noncombatant' includes, 'in addition to civilians, military personnel who at the time of the incident are unarmed and/or not on duty' and 'military installations or . . . armed military personnel when a state of military hostilities does not exist at the site.' 'Significant incidents' in this database meet the US government's Incident Review Panel criteria: incident 'results in loss of life or serious injury to persons, abduction or kidnapping of persons, major property damage'. US State Department, *Patterns of Global Terrorism* (Washington, 2004), at: <www.state.gov/s/ct/rls/pgtrpt/>.

10. Regressing total incidents on standard deviation of GDP_{t-1} yields an R-square of .004. For those readers without any statistics background, picture this number as suggesting that international inequality as measured here can explain a mere 0.4 per cent of the variation over time in the number of total transnational incidents. More careful estimation on the basis of more observations might allow us to introduce controls to see how much inequality can explain of variation in incidents that is not already accounted for by other conditions, such as wealth or democracy.

11. R-squared of .46, suggesting that international inequality explains 46 per cent of the variation over time in significant transnational incidents.

12. In April 2004 the Bush administration celebrated declining 'total' transnational incidents as affirmation of its policies, ignoring the much gloomier recent spike in 'significant' incidents as they themselves define it (Figure 1 shows both).

Facing strong criticism that they were fudging the numbers, administration officials later announced that they would revise their estimates. See Alan Krueger and David Laitin, 'Faulty Terror Report Card', *Washington Post*, 17 May 2004, A21.

13. Here, the data source is RAND-MIPT Terrorism Database, at:
<http://db.mipt.org/rand_tidb.cfm>.

14. R-squared of .32.

15. R-squared .28.

16. I allocate incidents to countries in proportion to the nationality of terrorist groups or individuals responsible for each attack. For instance, an ETA attack in Portugal gets coded as 1 for Spain; and, more complex, the first plane to hit the World Trade Center on 11 September 2001 counts as one incident, with four known terrorists whose respective nations of citizenship are scored with .25 of an incident. These are very rough estimates, given ambiguity about nationality of all involved terrorists, let alone upbringing. And even within this ambiguity, 19 per cent of the incidents cannot be counted due to poor information on attackers' nationality.

17. Inequality measured as post-tax, post-transfer Gini index scores, wealth as logged per capita GDP; results controlled for population size (logged), democracy (based on Polity IV scores), and regional dummies to account for fixed effects. The estimates are negative binomial regression given the enormous dispersion of counts (lots of countries with no transnational terrorist attackers in the period, with many fewer counts ranging from one to many dozens). The regressions also use robust standard errors to address possible sources of bias and inaccuracy in the estimation due to correlated differences between the countries in the sample (heteroskedasticity).

18. Using the estimation in column 1 to calculate the predicted number of incidents at varying levels of inequality, taking all the other variables at their means or, in the case of categorical variables, their medians.

19. The substantive effects of wealth are stronger in this particular estimation, but are sensitive to the inclusion of other controls, whereas inequality is much less sensitive and more robust.

20. See, for instance, Jeffrey Frankel and David Romer, 'Does Trade Cause Growth?', *American Economic Review* 89 (1999): 379–99.

21. Some find evidence that trade decreases inequality while FDI increases it (portfolio openness having little effect either way). This pattern may be underpinned by the fact that trade broadly diffuses benefits to consumers throughout the economy, while FDI concentrates its benefits (losses) on employers and workers in industries or firms where investment takes place, thereby widening inequality. See Rafael Reuveny and Quan Li, 'Democracy, Economic Openness, and Inequality: An Empirical Analysis', *Comparative Political Studies* 36, 5 (June 2003): 575–601.

22. Polity IV scale of −10 as most authoritarian to +10 most democratic.

23. The coefficients for trade and for democracy show what the marginal effect is of each, if the other is set as zero (higher levels of democracy, for instance, increase terrorist incidents if trade openness is zero), and more importantly, the interaction term ('Trade x Democracy') suggests whether rising levels of democracy make trade have a stronger negative or positive effect for the incidence of transnational terrorism in countries. If the interaction term is negative, that means rising democracy makes trade have a stronger negative effect on incidents (i.e., it lowers incidents or raises incidents less), while a positive term suggests that rising democracy makes trade have an increasingly positive effect on incidents (i.e., it raises incidents or lowers incidents less).

24. Respectively, the tenth percentile (−9 on the Polity IV scale, −10 being most authoritarian) and ninetieth percentile (9 on the Polity scale, 10 being most democratic) of the sample's distribution on democracy levels.

25. This figure does not capture the varying levels of statistical significance of the effects—insignificant on much of the scale—nor does it show what the turning point is where rising democracy might turn the terror-increasing effect of trade

to a terror-decreasing effect.

26. See, for instance, Lane Kenworthy, 'Do Social-Welfare Policies Reduce Poverty? A Cross-National Assessment', *Social Forces* 77, 3 (1999): 1119–39.

27. See Eli Berman, 'Hamas, Taliban, and the Jewish Underground: An Economist's View of Radical Religious Militias', mimeo, UCLA, 2003; and Chen, 'Economic Distress and Religious Intensity'.

28. Higher number of observations (country-years) allows for the quantitative analysis to control for more possible factors, thus more clearly revealing the 'all-other-things-equal' effects of the political-economic conditions of interest.

29. It also holds for a sample of only developing countries, though not for OECD countries alone (perhaps reflecting how the forms of terrorism in richer nations are more de-linked from economic conditions than the terrorism in the developing world). This evidence also only looks at spending levels, not measures of generosity.

30. For instance, regressing measures of welfare generosity (replacement rates, waiting periods, coverage, etc. of pensions, health, and unemployment insurance) on percentage of years between 1975 and 1995 that leftist parties controlled the chief executive and the legislature (controlling for regional dummies, population, and wealth) yields significant and positive coefficients.

Suggested Readings

Chen, Daniel. 'Economic Distress and Religious Intensity: Evidence from Islamic Resurgence during the Indonesian Financial Crisis', Project on Religion, Political Economy and Society, Weatherhead Center for International Affairs, Harvard University, Working Paper #39, 2003.

Krueger, Alan B., and Jitka Malecková. 'Education, Poverty and Terrorism: Is There a Causal Connection?', *Journal of Economic Perspectives* 17, 4 (2004): 119–44.

Li, Quan, and Drew Schaub. 'Economic Globalization and Transnational Terrorist Incidents: A Pooled Time-Series Cross-sectional Analysis', *Journal of Conflict Resolution* 48, 2 (Apr. 2004): 230–58.

Web Sites

Foreign Policy Association, Great Decisions: Guide to Terrorism:
www.fpa.org/newsletter_info2478/newsletter_info.htm

MIPT-RAND, Terrorism Incident Database, 1968–2003: http://db.mipt.org/rep_inrg_rep.cfm

Project on Defense Alternatives: www.comw.org/pda/
Social Science Research Council, After September 11th Archive: www.ssrc.org/sept11/essays/
US State Department, *Patterns of Global Terrorism*: www.state.gov/s/ct/rls/pgtrpt/

Chapter 8

Global Finance and Political Order

Louis W. Pauly

During the past few decades, short-term capital flows across borders expanded at a staggering pace. To many observers, the explosive growth and global reach of contemporary financial markets signalled the dawn of a new era. The ease with which such flows could occur certainly did represent a distinct reversal of the dominant set of national policy preferences evident during the years immediately following World War II. But the international mobility of capital was in fact not a novel development in the history of modern capitalism. In retrospect, the real aberration was the reversal occurring in the disastrous decades spanning 1914 and 1945.

The causes and consequences of the renewed cross-national mobility of finance are important topics of research. Much economic analysis begins with the assertion that freer international capital flows enhance efficiency, supplement domestic savings, and promote growth. Research informed by political and social concerns, conversely, tends to concentrate on the disruptive effects of such flows and on the difficulty of preventing and managing financial crises now routinely spanning geographic and functional borders. Wide-ranging policy debates are today framed by the assumption that the international mobility of short-term capital facilitates longer-term foreign direct investment and expanding trade in goods and services. Many of those debates rest on the assumption, however, that associated economic growth and development come with new risks for governments, societies, and individuals. In this light, academic and popular commentators draw connections between inter-national financial integration and such diverse phenomena as political and social turbulence in East Asia, wrenching structural transformations in Russia and its neighbouring states, a bold experiment in monetary union in Europe, the abandonment of failed development models in Latin America and Africa, and sweeping regulatory reforms in an evolving North American economy. In the wake of a profound systemic crisis beginning in Thailand in 1997 that would eventually spread even to Wall Street, nevertheless, at the dawn of the twenty-first century few close observers depicted the restoration of global finance as an unmitigated blessing. Instead, even the most sanguine were now mindful of the fact that the economic logic of globalization remained in deep tension with the realities of national and international politics.

A short chapter cannot fully explore that tension or survey the burgeoning research programs currently focusing on it. The aim here is simply to provide an orientation to the most obvious challenges for international political order posed by the freer movement of short-term capital. The chapter begins by placing international capital mobility into conceptual and historical context. It then examines the challenge of designing effective systems for crisis prevention and management in a world where actual regulatory authority is ever more widely dispersed. Finally, it underlines the related but more fundamental dilemma posed by the necessity of grounding that authority on stable foundations when the logic of markets suggests globalism but the logic of politics remains primarily local.

International Capital Mobility in Context

The cause of freer trade won renewed rhetorical support after the cataclysm that came to be called the Great War of 1914–18. Rhetoric was translated into successful policy, however, only after an even greater catastrophe ended in 1945. The international economic interdependence deliberately sought by the victorious allies (minus the Soviet Union) through the expansion of trade was to be underpinned by a system of stable exchange rates. Codified at the 1944 Bretton Woods Conference, such a system was designed to avoid both the perceived rigidities of the nineteenth-century gold standard and the undisciplined currency manipulations commonly deemed to have contributed to the depth and duration of the Great Depression.

During the decades following World War II, the explicit policy preference for freer trade came to be ever more widely supplemented by efforts to reduce impediments to foreign direct investment. The vast post-war expansion in trade (in both goods and service) and in cross-border investment in plant and equipment had far-reaching effects, many of which are explored in other chapters in this book. The subject of concern in this chapter, which essentially boils down to currency convertibility in the current and/or capital accounts of national payments balances, cannot be separated from that broader movement towards more liberal trade and investment regimes.

In any economy (other than one based on barter), trade, investment, and production must be financed. If financial claims are freely convertible across national currencies, liquid balances in personal or corporate accounts can be used for other purposes. In advanced economies, there exists a historical tendency for purely financial operations to grow at a rate far exceeding tangible business requirements. Much of this growth reflects speculation, which can either stabilize or destabilize other economic variables. In practical terms, it has proven impossible to draw a clear and unassailable dividing line between the prudent hedging of

financial risks and purely speculative gambling. To many observers, therefore, the economic history of the latter decades of the twentieth century was decisively marked by cross-border markets for short-term capital taking on a life of their own increasingly disconnected from real economies where goods, services, and new technologies are produced. The reality is more complex.

When national economies are open to trade, investment, and the accommodating financing for these, their interest rates, exchange rates, and internal prices (including the price of labour) become interdependent. This implies certain policy trade-offs. Those trade-offs open the conceptual terrain of open-economy macroeconomics. In the 1960s, two International Monetary Fund (IMF) economists launched a still-continuing effort to map that terrain.[1]

The Mundell-Fleming model suggested that governments and central banks overseeing open economies could not simultaneously give priority to maintaining the independence of their internal monetary policies, stabilizing their exchange rates, and permitting unrestricted inward and outward capital flows. Since interest rates, inflation rates, and exchange rates influenced one another, only two of those goals—at most—could be achieved simultaneously. If priority is given to open capital markets and stable exchange rates, domestic interest rates will reflect external developments. When the autonomy of national monetary policy and exchange rate stability are clearly preferred, capital movements must be limited. Finally, if capital mobility and monetary autonomy are defined as top policy objectives, exchange rates must be allowed to adjust.

When fiscal policy—the taxing and spending activities of governments—is brought into the model, the standard economic analysis is also straightforward. When exchange rates are flexible and capital is perfectly mobile, changes in monetary policy become the only effective tool for influencing national economic performance, and changes in fiscal policy cease to have any effect. Alternatively, when exchange rates are fixed and capital movements are controlled, fiscal policy becomes effective and monetary policy ineffective. Such trade-offs are forced by systematic and predictable changes in underlying spending, saving, and investor behaviour inside national economies.

In other words, the more open an economy becomes to inward and outward capital flows, the more difficult it is for governments to maintain stable exchange rates *and* monetary policies targeted on the task of advancing exclusively national priorities. If unilateral monetary actions are nevertheless taken—say money supplies are constricted to dampen domestic inflation—exchange rates will immediately come under pressure. If governments wish their fiscal policies to retain their capacity to reinforce the line of monetary policy, they will have to find ways to dissipate that pressure. In practice, if they are committed to exchange rate stability, this means they will have to find ways to moderate or impede the flow of capital. Such trade-offs are further complicated if high levels of external debt exist.

Refinements and modifications of this model continue to fill academic journals and textbooks, but its central message is clear. The space for effective economic stabilization policies at the national level—in other words, the space for monetary and fiscal policies to work at all or to work in complementary directions—is defined by the choice of exchange rate regime and the degree of capital market/account openness.

In the real world, perfect capital mobility or freely floating exchange rates have never existed, but they have sometimes been approached. Monetary autonomy has usually been highly prized by governments, but some have given it up in order to promote the cause of exchange rate stability and preserve the net benefits perceived to accrue from capital mobility. Economic and monetary union in Europe, for example, rests on such deliberate policy choices. The absence of similar momentum in North America indicated a different choice: the desire to preserve a maximal degree of monetary independence even at the cost of sometimes painful exchange rate fluctuations. Analogously, since the early 1970s, the world's financial leaders—the United States, Germany, the United Kingdom, and Japan—typically proved themselves willing to sacrifice exchange rate stability among themselves when their monetary independence was threatened by inward or outward capital movements. Rarely, however, were any of them completely indifferent to the external value of their currencies. The basic political reasons are not hard to locate.

Industrial sectors engaged in trade and international investment account for significant economic growth. That growth and the international interdependence associated with it are the intended consequences of the post-war foreign economic policies pursued by the leading states. The impulse to stabilize exchange rates between them arises out of the challenge of maintaining both domestic and international political coalitions of sufficient strength to keep national markets open. Although short-term fluctuations in exchange rates do not necessarily compromise the maintenance of such coalitions, longer-term misalignments between major currencies—differences between where real exchange rates actually are and where they should be to promote payments equilibrium—threaten to do exactly that.

When trade and investment across borders is unhindered, exchange rates should track underlying changes in the purchasing power of national currencies. Nominal exchange rates might fluctuate, but real (inflation-adjusted) exchange rates should be stable. In fact, that stability is often elusive. A high degree of international capital mobility may be one reason. When it exists, changes in nominal exchange rates tend to reflect events and expectations in stock, bond, and other asset markets. Much economic research focuses on this issue, but the hypothesis that these markets can and do sometimes move wildly, even irrationally, has never been convincingly dismissed. In light of the fact that the actual prices of goods and services can be sticky, unpredictable, and unstable, exchange rates can in principle hurt the real economy by encouraging a misallocation of human and financial resources.

Although such a view is commonplace, empirical support for it is not conclusive. In any event, economists have not been able to find evidence that the most easily measurable costs of exchange rate instability are very high. They have rightly noted, however, a connection between the enduring interest of governments in exchange rate stability and the challenge they face in keeping intact the political coalitions necessary to support economic openness. When exchange rates are highly volatile, protectionist pressures can escalate.

In the 1950s and 1960s, the United States and its key allies sought to combine the advantages of fixed exchange rates with the capacity to adjust them whenever warranted by underlying conditions in national economies. In theory, the 'pegged' rates of the Bretton Woods system depended on a rule-based form of international co-operation, specifically on an interstate legal agreement to collaborate through a multilateral organization—the International Monetary Fund.

The original Articles of Agreement of the IMF specified certain rules to guide the exchange rate policies of members and gave the organization the power both to sanction changes in exchange rates when required by economic fundamentals and to provide temporary financing in cases where such changes were not required. Governments did not formally have to co-ordinate their internal monetary and fiscal policies to keep their exchange rates stable. In theory, the discipline of exchange rate rules would automatically promote necessary adjustments in internal policies. In practice, the rules of the game were often honoured in the breach and the IMF was often marginalized. When the system worked, it depended in fact on a low degree of international capital mobility and on the willingness of the United States to keep its import markets open and its domestic price level reasonably stable, thereby providing to its trading partners an adequate supply of reserves at a reliable cost. Often, close co-operation among key central banks also helped.

For obverse reasons, the Bretton Woods arrangements collapsed in the early 1970s; technical innovation and policy liberalization in leading currency markets, as well as the financial effects of rapidly rising foreign direct investment, made it ever more difficult to control short-term capital movements. At the same time, inflationary macroeconomic policies in the United States, including current account deficits, lax budgetary control, and combined high social and military spending, rendered the country an unreliable monetary anchor. Since then, efforts to stabilize key exchange rates by way of negotiated policy co-ordination have been episodic. In general, the major powers have relied on the assumption that exchange rates would stabilize in the long run if anti-inflationary macroeconomic policies were pursued simultaneously but independently. In short, internal self-discipline would have salubrious external effects. A system that would force such discipline by way of pegged (fixed but adjustable when underlying conditions warranted) exchange rates was widely viewed as infeasible. Indeed, the mainstream view suggested that individual states faced a stark choice: allowing their currencies to float or fixing their exchange rates irrevocably.[2]

The Politics of Financial Integration

Is it reasonable to assert that the Mundell-Fleming trade-off reflects intentional choice by policy-makers vested with the authority to make such decisions? Do governments actually have the freedom to choose between capital mobility, exchange rate stability, and monetary autonomy? Or are their choices constrained in very practical ways?

Today, there is a widespread sense that one of those policy options—capital mobility—is no longer subject to choice, except in the most extreme circumstances. Such circumstances presented themselves in the late 1990s, and some countries, like Malaysia, did indeed defy the conventional wisdom by reimposing capital controls in a bid to calm a global panic. But even in such cases, controls were lifted as soon as possible and the global march towards financial liberalization across advanced industrial countries and much of the developing world soon resumed. Even if 'perfect' capital mobility does not exist, national markets in foreign exchange, money market instruments, bank claims, bonds, and stocks are now much more open to one another than they were when the Bretton Woods system came to an end. Markets once clearly separated along functional and national lines are much more interdependent. Given this present trend, certain truly integrated markets—where some financial assets are fully substitutable or where similar assets in different geographic locations trade at identical prices—are no longer hard to imagine. But all of this did not happen by accident, nor was it dictated by economic forces no one could resist.

Throughout the post-World War II period, albeit at different paces and with occasional backsliding, the United States, Canada, and the advanced industrial states of Europe deliberately moved to reduce direct controls and taxes on financial transactions, to loosen long-standing regulatory restrictions on financial intermediaries, to permit the expansion of lightly regulated 'offshore' financial markets (originally mislabelled the 'Euromarkets'), and to oversee the introduction of new technologies that sped up capital movements and stimulated the development of innovative financial products. In the 1970s, Japan cautiously joined the trend. Throughout the 1980s, many developing countries followed. And after the Cold War ended, Russia, many of its former satellite states, and China began to build internal markets for private capital and, at varying speeds, decisively to open them up to foreign involvement. Moments of crisis may occasionally have linked such an opening to popular feelings of unease, but when such moments passed political resistance typically dissipated.

As capital market liberalization proceeded apace, scholars proposed explanations at various levels of analysis.[3] Some studies emphasized a competitive, system-level dynamic as states are drawn to the economic stimulus, the jobs, and the raw power promised by expanding national capital markets. Others stressed the conjoined role of liberal ideology and the overwhelming influence of dominant class interests. In a complementary fashion, economic analyses tended to stress the pres-

sures towards openness that arose from technological change and financial innovation. More disaggregated studies, however, tended to argue that expanded financial openness remained rooted in unique patterns of domestic politics and in the consequences of earlier policy decisions. In truth, there was enough evidence to support and to cast doubt on any single mono-causal theory. By the turn of the century, a widespread consensus existed on the need for a dynamic model of policy change and financial market deepening.

Less consensus existed, however, on the consequences of increasing international capital mobility. Some analysts diagnosed a widening gap between the emergent structure of global finance and the dearth of authoritative regulatory institutions at the international level capable of managing that structure. Certainly, repeated financial crises around the world pointed to such a gap. Still, other analysts generally supported the view that the scale and durability of international capital movements were now constitutive of a new regime in world politics, a regime that mixed private authority and public authority to make it increasingly difficult for individual states to diverge from dominant norms of appropriate policy behaviour.

Relatively open financial markets were not, in fact, new in world politics. Conditions approximating those of today did exist before 1914 among the most advanced economies and their dependencies. The extremities of war and economic depression succeeded in disrupting an evolving system of international economic adjustment that accommodated, even necessitated, international capital flows. The system, which dated back to the 1870s, rested on a rough consensus among the principal trading nations. At the centre of that consensus was a version of the gold standard, backed by the wealth and power of Great Britain. In theory, if not always in practice, the behavioural norms embedded in the system prescribed relatively passive domestic policy responses to external economic changes. British statecraft and the pivotal role of the Bank of England provided the keys to actual practice. The situation changed completely in 1914.

Among other shifts in the tectonic plates of world politics, the tumultuous era that began with World War I witnessed the rise of the modern democratic nation-state, whose citizens expected it to ensure their military security and, increasingly, their economic security. Following the catastrophe of the Great Depression and war, those national expectations defined the terrain upon which a new intergovernmental consensus on monetary issues was defined at Bretton Woods in 1944 and, more fundamentally, upon which that consensus evolved in subsequent years. For leading states, as noted above, the initial policy mix expressing that consensus privileged exchange rate stability and limited capital mobility, thereby suppressing any challenge to the legitimacy of the state itself under conditions of interdependence.

The contemporary reconstruction of global capital markets, or more precisely the dramatic expansion in the capacity of capital to move more rapidly across national and regional markets, is intimately linked to the disruption of the Bretton Woods consensus in the 1970s and the dawn of a new era of flexible exchange rates. The expectations of citizens concerning the responsibilities of democratic nation-states, however, have not substantively changed. Witness, in this regard, the resistance apparent across the advanced industrial world when many governments during the past two decades tried to make abrupt adjustments in social safety nets. Driven by mounting national debts and deficits, as well as by a return to the orthodoxy of the early twentieth century concerning their consequences, far-reaching attempts were made to trim the sails of the welfare state, if not to cut down the masts altogether. In most if not all countries, actual results turned out to be modest.

Not yet perfected, the tendency towards a new Mundell-Fleming trade-off was quite widely observable. Except within an expanding Europe, where regional monetary authority now spanned national borders, international capital mobility was accorded a higher priority than exchange rate stability. Although, again, this was not unprecedented in modern history, it was unprecedented to combine such a policy priority with the continu-

ing acceptance of political responsibility by states for the broadly defined security of their citizens. Never before had the Mundell-Fleming preference for international capital mobility and national or regional monetary autonomy had to confront the exigencies of the welfare state. What this has meant in practice is that governments are left with exchange rate adjustment as a primary policy mechanism for buffering in a politically sustainable manner the effects of deepening international economic interdependence.

Still, economic commentators, prominent bankers, and conservative politicians now commonly underscore the 'discipline' on autonomous state action implied by international capital mobility. If that discipline implied cutting back the welfare states of the post-World War II era, they asserted, then so be it. Many of their opponents on the left may have disliked such a conclusion, but they intuitively understood its logic. Indeed, a mounting body of popular literature written both by conservatives and radicals in the 1990s envisaged the consolidation of a new global order, the borderless order of advanced capitalism.

Whether they embraced it or loathed it, such a vision tended to be evoked in the language of inevitability. Enjoining governments to yield to signals from the global market, this language implied that a profound shift in policy-making authority was necessarily taking place, a shift away from the national level. Proponents typically extolled the surrender of the retrograde idea of sovereignty to the rational economic logic of markets beyond national control. Opponents might not have liked such a conclusion, but their own research bolstered the notion that transnational coalitions beyond the nation-state now exercised determinative influence over a widening range of economic policies.

Sovereignty has, in fact, always been a contested concept.[4] But conflating it with the notion of policy autonomy is needlessly confusing. A turning away from deeper financial integration by individual states or by the collectivity of states may not be desirable, and it would be costly, but it is certainly possible. In this sense, states remain as 'sovereign' as they have ever been. In practical terms, however, there is no doubt that many states today do confront tighter economic constraints—or clearer policy trade-offs—as a consequence of a freer potential flow of capital across their borders. This is the flip side of the opportunities for accelerated growth (beyond that capable of being financed by domestic savings) that can be presented by that same flow of capital. Again, the phenomenon itself is not new. What is really new is the widespread perception that all states, all societies, and all social groups are now affected. In light of the historical record, such a perception is ironic. The losers in the process suffered as much then as they do now, and the governments of contemporary democracies arguably face the consequences more directly than their counterparts did in the nineteenth century. But the perception today of inexorable systemic adjustment pressures does blur important distinctions between and within states. Underneath the overt discourse on sovereignty and efficient capital markets, there really lies a covert discourse on power, legitimacy, and hierarchy.

If effective governing authority has been usurped by global capital markets, or if such authority has surreptitiously been devolved to those markets by states themselves, surely questions are raised about the process by which such a shift has taken place and about the obligation of citizens to comply. There remains today only one place where such questions can be directed and satisfactorily addressed. And whether we conceive of it as an arena, a structure, or a set of institutions, that place is called the state.

The Mundell-Fleming trade-off tells us a great deal about the internal choices states make when they seek mutually to harness the benefits of economic openness without incurring unacceptable costs. The sum of those choices during the past few decades has been increasingly global financial markets. But those markets were not actually built by economic happenstance. They reflect a political project that was shaped mainly by the domestic priorities and external strategies of leading states. International political institutions had an impor-

tant and often misunderstood role in that project.

International Institutions and Global Markets

From the 1970s onward, leading states in practice never made stark and irrevocable decisions to favour financial openness above all other economic objectives, but they did adjust a widening range of internal policies to promote and accommodate potentially more mobile international capital flows. They simultaneously reshaped the mandates of such international organizations as the IMF, the World Bank, the Bank for International Settlements (BIS), and the Organization for Economic Co-operation and Development (OECD) in this light, and they established new kinds of informal institutions to assist in general oversight tasks. The abandonment of exchange rate pegs and the privileging of international capital mobility opened up the possibility that unco-ordinated national policies would complicate the resolution of collective action problems. Who would supervise banks operating outside of the country where they were licensed? Who would bail out financial intermediaries that ran aground overseas? Who would track illegal financial transfers through offshore markets?

Questions like these proliferated after leading states abandoned the original post-war monetary system. Once they had abandoned their formal obligation to hold their currencies in a fixed relationship with one another and allowed their exchange rates to be determined by freer capital flows, these were the kinds of questions that could not be avoided. They encouraged such flows through direct policy actions to liberate market forces, finance budget and trade deficits, and respond to competitive threats from other states. They also often did so by not taking decisions, such as decisions to subject 'offshore' transactions to the sorts of regulatory and tax requirements routinely imposed on domestic transactions.

Having set in motion a system that now lacked a reliable mechanism for pegging currency values, states subsequently found that further capital liberalization, combined with enhanced market supervision, represented a less politically costly alternative than any other on offer. To be sure, many other states continued to rely on explicit or implicit measures to influence capital flows and to buffer national economies. In the wake of disruptive bouts of capital flight in a number of industrializing countries, for example, such policies would sometimes be acquiesced in by other states and by an IMF charged with the task of facilitating adjustment in the current accounts of its members, accounts increasingly difficult to differentiate from capital accounts. But Fund acquiescence in unilateral controls on short-term capital movements, whether formal or tacit, was almost always conditional on an understanding that they would be temporary. After the late 1970s, capital decontrol came ever more clearly to define a basic tendency in the international economy.

Let us be clear on the crucial point. Even today, capital flows continue to encounter friction at national borders. That is, there has yet to arise a truly global financial market characterized by perfect capital mobility and structural homogeneity, and there is no global regulatory authority with the mandate or the resources to ensure the smooth operation of such a market. Nevertheless, national policies, which formerly accommodated the possibility, even at times the necessity, of controls on short-term capital movements, have converged decisively in the direction of liberalization in the past few decades. Such convergent policies, and a consequent reorientation of the expectations of state and market actors, suggest a fundamental break with the original post-World War II consensus. In 1989, that convergence was recognized by the member countries of the OECD as they widened the scope of the Capital Movements Code supervised by that organization. Although escape clauses were retained, the subsequent activism of the OECD in working to minimize the reservations of member states suggests an attempt by leading members to replace the formal legal right to control capital movements with a new right. The effort paralleled continuing work on crafting new rules to govern longer-term investment, both in the OECD

and in the World Trade Organization. In the 1990s, the Fund's Articles of Agreement were almost altered to encourage members to open their capital accounts to international capital flows, a move aborted in the midst of the systemic crisis marking the end of that decade.

The reluctance of states to embrace unambiguously the capital mobility norm or clearly to designate an international organizational overseer for truly integrated capital markets, even as their own policies promote such a norm, suggests a deeper concern. The legal issue masks an issue of power and authority. The legitimacy of the new order remains in question. More fundamentally, the struggle suggests that the architects of that order cannot easily calibrate emergent market facts with enduring political realities. They cannot lodge ultimate political authority over integrating capital markets at the level where it logically belongs. Like subnational governments in a confederation trying to establish a fully integrated national market while retaining all substantive economic powers themselves, states confronting global finance have a problem.

One doesn't need to be a right-wing nationalist to sense the full dimensions of the problem. One only needs to observe market and governmental reactions to the financial crises that characterize any order that relies on private markets to allocate capital, and that have in fact been reshaping the new international order since the 1970s. Subsequently, advanced industrial states have tried to manage the proclivity of financial markets to become unstable without fundamentally compromising their otherwise efficient operation. They have also demonstrated their distinct preference for private markets to provide the bulk of financing required by developing countries. Their path has been strewn with near-disasters, but none serious enough to cause a collective policy reversal.

To be sure, in the resulting order financial crises with potentially devastating systemic effects can occur anywhere, and they have. From Mexico in 1982 to Russia, South Korea, and Indonesia in the late 1990s—real disasters for the citizens of those states threatened to become catastrophes for the great post-1970s systemic experiment in financial integration. But who was truly accountable for the necessary bailouts or subsequent regulatory reform? Could bankers and their depositors in the United States legitimately hold anyone in Mexico responsible? Could Canadian mutual fund investors perceiving themselves to have been defrauded in Indonesia seek redress anywhere? Where could the stakeholders in German banks find assurance that the risks of new types of financial involvement in Eastern Europe would not be ineptly managed? Who would actually be held responsible if the panicked reaction to financial turbulence in, say, China began to bring down large commercial and investment banks and even large private funds around the world? Some would say no one, because the authority to manage global finance has dispersed. This is doubtful. National governments, especially the governments of leading industrial states, would surely be blamed, not least by their own aggrieved citizens. And surely they would respond.

Avoiding the need for such an end-game in the new world of global finance provides the driving force behind contemporary efforts to clarify and strengthen the mandates of international financial institutions, as well as to construct less formal networks to safeguard payments systems, track illegal financial flows, and encourage private financiers adequately to monitor and manage the more complicated risks to which they are exposed.[5] The same dynamic reinforces internal pressures within many states to move towards 'independent' central banks and financial market supervisors as well as to participate in ad hoc intergovernmental committees like the Basel Committee of the BIS and the Financial Action Task Force established by the G-7 finance ministers. In the best case, such technocratic instruments can promote common standards of financial regulation and supervision around the world, design functional programs for crisis prevention, debt relief, and crisis management, and generally encourage cost-effective collaboration. In the worst case, they can take on the politically crucial role of scapegoats.

What states apparently cannot yet do is to shift substantive regulatory authority and power to the level of governance suggested by the term 'global finance'. Perhaps they do not need to do so, because the term exaggerates the reality of global financial integration in the contemporary period. But surely they also do not want to do so. Only in Western Europe, and in the context of a much larger half-century experiment in regional integration, was such a shift beyond the national level in sight. Elsewhere, as explored in other chapters in this volume, intensifying interdependence was the order of the day as states and their citizens, with varying degrees of success, sought the benefits of capital mobility without paying high political costs. Futurists were left to speculate about the final destination. Cosmopolitan liberals predicted the inevitable rise of global governing systems. Critics expected mounting resistance if capital mobility did not reliably work to the benefit of the many instead of just the few. Realists imagined a policy reversal if open markets began compromising the ability of states to provide basic security. The rest of us were left to contemplate a dilemma constructed by the conflicting logics of global economics and local politics that could not be resolved but could, with a bit of skill and a bit of luck, continue to be managed.

Notes

1. Jacob Frenkel and Assaf Razin, 'The Mundell-Fleming Model a Quarter Century Later: A Unified Exposition', *IMF Staff Papers* 34 (Dec. 1987); W.M. Corden, *Economic Policy, Exchange Rates, and the International System* (Chicago: University of Chicago Press, 1994); Peter Kenen, *The International Economy*, 3rd edn (Cambridge: Cambridge University Press, 1994), ch. 15.

2. See Barry Eichengreen, *International Monetary Arrangements for the 21st Century* (Washington:

Brookings Institution, 1994).

3. For an overview, see Benjamin J. Cohen, 'International Finance', in Walter Carlsnaes, Thomas Risse, and Beth A. Simmons, eds, *Handbook of International Relations* (New York: Sage, 2002).

4. See Hendrik Spruyt, *The Sovereign State and Its Competitors* (Princeton, NJ: Princeton University Press, 1996); Stephen D. Krasner, *Sovereignty: Organized Hypocrisy* (Princeton, NJ: Princeton University Press, 1999); Daniel Philpott, *Revolutions in Sovereignty* (Princeton, NJ:

Princeton University Press, 2001); Edgar Grande and Louis W. Pauly, eds, *Complex Sovereignty: Reconstructing Political Authority in the Twenty-First Century* (Toronto: University of Toronto Press, 2005).

5. See Tony Porter, 'Institutional Learning and International Financial Regimes', in Meric S. Gertler and David Wolfe, eds, *Innovation and Social Learning* (Basingstoke, UK: Palgrave Macmillan, 2002). Also see Anne-Marie Slaughter, *A New World Order* (Princeton, NJ: Princeton University Press, 2004).

Suggested Readings

Andrews, David M., Louis W. Pauly, and C. Randall Henning, eds. *Governing the World's Money.* Ithaca, NY: Cornell University Press, 2002.

Armijo, Leslie Elliott, ed. *Financial Globalization and Democracy in Emerging Markets.* Basingstoke, UK: Palgrave Macmillan, 2001.

Blustein, Paul. *The Chastening.* New York: Public Affairs, 2001.

Boughton, James. *Silent Revolution: The International Monetary Fund, 1979–1989.* Washington: IMF, 2001.

Bryant, Ralph. *Turbulent Waters: Cross-Border Finance and International Governance.* Washington: Brookings Institution, 2003.

Cohen, Benjamin J. *The Future of Money.* Ithaca, NY: Cornell University Press, 2004.

Eichengreen, Barry. *Capital Flows and Crises.* Cambridge, Mass.: MIT Press, 2003.

Germain, Randall C. *The International Organization of Credit.* Cambridge: Cambridge University Press, 1997.

Gill, Stephen. *Power and Resistance in the New World Order.* Basingstoke, UK: Palgrave Macmillan, 2003.

Helleiner, Eric. *States and the Reemergence of Global Finance.* Ithaca, NY: Cornell University Press, 1994.

Kirshner, Jonathan, ed. *Monetary Orders: Ambiguous Economics, Ubiquitous Politics.* Ithaca, NY: Cornell University Press, 2003.

Palan, Ronen. *The Offshore World.* Ithaca, NY: Cornell University Press, 2003.

Pauly, Louis W. *Who Elected the Bankers?* Ithaca, NY: Cornell University Press, 1998.

Sinclair, Timothy. *The New Masters of Capital.* Ithaca, NY: Cornell University Press, 2005.

Strange, Susan. *Mad Money.* Manchester: Manchester University Press, 1998.

Underhill, Geoffrey R.D., and Xiaoke Zhang, eds. *International Financial Governance under Stress.* Cambridge: Cambridge University Press, 2003.

Web Sites

Bank for International Settlements: www.bis.org
Financial Stability Forum: www.fsforum.org
Institute of International Finance: www.iif.com
International Monetary Fund: www.imf.org

Jubilee Research: www.jubilee2000uk.org
Organization for Economic Co-operation and Development: www.oecd.org
World Bank: www.worldbank.org

Chapter 9

The Emerging World Financial Order and Different Forms of Capitalism

Jonathan Story

Two views compete in the market for ideas on how to interpret the emerging world financial order. Economic optimists hold that financial markets have leaped free from government control and envisage a radiant future of 'convergence' where the world economy is at long last launched upon a voyage to integration. 'Within a generation', gasps *The Economist*, 'several [advanced industrial economies] are likely to be dwarfed by newly emerging economic giants.'[1] State-centric democrats and regulators dispute this thesis. Their main contention is that the imperfections in world markets derive from the distribution of corporate, state, and market power. World capitalism, they conclude, is in charge, and the populations even of advanced industrial states and regions are at the mercy of 'autonomised and globally uncontrollable, because global, forces'.[2]

Both views exaggerate. If capitalism were uncontrollable, determinism would reign and the future would be predictable. Neither is the case. Quite the contrary, the argument here is that global financial markets are the result of competing corporate structures, and above all of *divergent state policies and structures*, which provide significantly different sets of incentives for market participants. The dominant 'globalization vision' in the 1980s and 1990s was stamped 'made in the USA', and had One World driving towards shared prosperity, democracy, and better living conditions for all. It failed to allow for capitalist diversity and complex interactions, or for *'la longue durée'*. The 1990s version of a One World vision was an impatient program in a hurry.

States are embedded in markets, alongside corporations, and are also members of the world system or society of states. Abstractly, relations among states, corporations, and markets may be presented in triangular form: state-state, state-firm, and firm-firm.[3] Over time, political systems evolve and develop divergent structures and performances, which, in an ever more interdependent world, become a main cause of turbulence in world markets and politics. Contrasting financial systems lie at the heart of the divergent forms of corporate governance that underpin differing forms of capitalism in world markets. States are participants in, and not separate from, the financial markets they have jointly contributed to create.

From Different Systems to Global Capitalism

Sometime in the course of the 1970s, the world embarked on four simultaneous, interactive, but non-synchronized processes of transformation involving world markets, the norms of state governance, the way that corporations were managed, and the state system itself.

After World War II, none in the Bretton Woods discussions (see Introduction to this section) wanted to return to orthodox gold-standard economics. Both world wars demonstrated that governments could organize national production and consumption on a grand scale, and the interwar years of financial instability stood as a reminder of the dangers of attempts to return to the market-driven ways of the past. Not least, the Soviet Union continued to wage war on capitalism.

The central idea of the Bretton Woods accords of 1944 was that governments were inherently mercantilist in their promotion of domestic industries, their channelling of credit, and their protectionist tendencies. National economic expansion to meet citizens' demands for higher living standards was a government responsibility, for which an extensive array of policy instruments were available. But governments were also beholden to co-operate with the Bretton Woods institutions and among themselves jointly to regulate the markets of the world. Optimally, the visionaries of the post-war world economy looked forward to enlightened governance of peoples by officials of international organizations, rather than by the well-heeled denizens of world financial markets. Short-term capital movements were to be kept figuratively under lock and key, and currencies were to be fixed at a rate of $35 to an ounce of gold.

This post-war government-centred design for the world economy, inspired by the ideals of liberal internationalism but implemented within the bounds of the Western containment policy, proved an unprecedented success. Fifty years on, the rising tide of wealth had lifted most boats. Continuous expansion brought extraordinary improvement in living conditions as child death rates tumbled, along with malnutrition and illiteracy, for 3–4 billion people.[4] At the same time, the gaps in income between the richest 20 per cent and poorest 20 per cent of countries widened from a factor of 30:1 in 1960 to 60:1 by the turn of the century, with the gap between the richest 20 per cent of the world population and the poorest 20 per cent widening to a factor of 150:1 in terms of the three broad categories mentioned above.

Growing inequalities among peoples were only one major imbalance in the world economy. Another was government spending in rich countries, which jumped from an average among advanced industrialized countries of about 28 per cent of GDP in 1960 to 43 per cent in 1980. Over 20 years later, spending in the euro area was just under 50 per cent on average, while about 35 per cent in Japan and the US. The main source of the spending boom was an explosion in public transfers and subsidies, in good times as in bad. Elected politicians learned that re-election was best secured by having governments issue 'securities' to cover expenditures rather than raising taxes. Financial institutions discovered the virtues of trading this abundant volume of paper in a liquid world market, thus boosting global capital markets enormously. The share of the world financial market that was liquid and tradable grew at the expense of the market under governments' control, i.e., the domestic money supply. Bretton Woods was undermined by fiscal excess; governments often wail at the consequences but they were willing participants in this process.

Imbalances also derived from interstate disagreements about sharing the burden of adjustment to competition in world markets. These disagreements became more salient once the industrialized countries moved in the late 1950s to a partial liberalization of capital movements. Dollar and sterling balances began to build up abroad, but both Washington and London considered that international imbalances were due to trade discrimination in the EU and Japan and that continued growth in the world economy required easy money and expansionary public finances. In August 1971, President Nixon announced an end to the dollar's convertibility into gold, thereby terminating the US economy's role as anchor of the world financial system. Within two years, the major currencies had abandoned fixed exchange rates.

There followed in the 1970s the two surges in world oil prices and the recycling of funds that could not be consumed by oil-producing states on to the world dollar markets, located in London and New York. Commercial banks lent dollars to oil-importing states, especially to Central and Eastern Europe, Africa, and Latin America. Real interest rates on the international markets stayed around zero, so borrowers flocked there and banks fell over each other to lend. This was the period when Portugal, Spain, and Greece showed the way to what became a political contagion of transition towards representative forms of government around the globe. Meanwhile, the end of the cheap oil era accelerated the rise of the two champion export economies, Germany and Japan, confirmed the dollar as emperor on world financial markets, and kept the moribund Soviet economy alive for a further couple of decades.

The 1970s saw a sharpening of the 'struggle for market share'[5] among advanced industrial states. During the mid-century boom, they had all adopted the formalized idiom of Keynesian economics to explain their policies. But their very different reactions to the oil crises of the 1970s revealed the peculiarities of their domestic structures.[6] The opposite ends of the spectrum in policy were allotted to the United States as a paragon of liberal markets and to Japan as the successful practitioner of a mercantilist strategy characterized by extensive intervention by state institutions in the market. France, Germany, and Italy were somewhere in between, with the UK tilting towards the American approach. This more jaundiced view of Western economic policies pointed to differences in internal structures as the source of conflicts in international relations between states.

In October 1979 the mood in the US and Europe turned in favour of price stability, and the US Federal Reserve engineered a worldwide rise in interest rates. Debtors were figuratively strangled by the high interest rates, and in 1982 the markets responded to the debt crises in Latin America by 'securitization' of commercial bank debts. Bank debts were converted to bonds. The 1982 switch to securities opened the prolonged boom on world capital markets. The exponential development of wholesale capital markets was driven by the growth of government and corporate bond markets, as the US and European states vied for world savings and the world's corporations raised capital by the issue of shares. New York and Chicago set the pace in breaking down the inherited barriers to efficient financial markets and were followed by London, Paris, and Amsterdam, with Frankfurt and Tokyo in the rear. Poorer indebted countries were squeezed until their figurative pips squeaked. Global daily trade in foreign exchange markets shot up from $15 billion in 1973 to peak at $1.4 trillion in 1998, or 60 to 100 times the average turnover of trade in physical goods, falling back to $1.2 trillion in 2001 following the financial crisis emanating from East Asia and the introduction of the euro.

US President Ronald Reagan and British Prime Minister Margaret Thatcher set themselves the goal of strengthening the role of the market as the main co-ordinating device for the world polity. The crusade to roll back the state gathered force in the 1980s, while corporations felt their way towards operating as transnationals and the leading financial centres competed to end capital controls. The collapse of the Soviet empire transformed the world system of states.

Freeing of short-term capital flows in Europe and German unity in the pivotal year 1990 marked the end of the Cold War structure that had simultaneously contained both communism and capitalism. With savings able to go in search of the highest remuneration, the assumptions of Bretton Woods—whereby governments should manage their national economies—were undermined because unregulated markets were not to be trusted. In addition, the resolution of the 1980s Latin American debt crisis under a plan advanced by US Treasury Secretary Nicholas Brady enabled mid-income indebted countries to restructure their debt to commercial banks through officially supported debt reduction programs tied to broad policies of liberalization, stabilization, and privatization. Brady's debt relief plan spurred Mexico to negotiate the NAFTA accords with the US and Canada, while Brazil and Argentina formed the MERCOSUR customs union with Uruguay and Paraguay. This enabled one Latin American government after another to embark on policies of trade liberalization and privatization, combined with domestic institutional reforms and the introduction of more welcoming foreign direct investment (FDI) regimes. The formula was then applied to Poland, with success, and to Russia, with a redounding failure. A global financial system was emerging rapidly, dominated by short-term capital flows and promoted by widespread economic liberalization policies.

The Soviet collapse converted the world into

Western corporations' metaphorical oyster. Its most immediate effect was to propel upward of 3 billion people onto a *world* labour market—from the former Soviet Union, Central and Eastern Europe, China, and India. These 3 billion people would grow to 6 billion by 2025 due to demographic trends. The average cost of labour around the world fell correspondingly. The implication for high-wage countries was that their relative wage was bid down at home as immigration rose, or as companies disinvested and moved to cheaper wage locations. With local governments strapped for cash and eager to attract investment, Western corporations accelerated the adoption of global strategies, i.e., integrated production and marketing strategies intended to reconcile the contradictory exigencies of competition in world markets and the need to be responsive to local conditions. Whereas in the late 1980s, investment flowing to developing countries had been 15–18 per cent of the total recorded, in the 1990s these flows to developing countries leapt to 30–40 per cent. The investment flows to developing countries fell off drastically after 1997–8, but with China's entry to the WTO in 2001, corporate boards opted for China as the preferred location for investment, with China (mainland and Hong Kong) taking 70 per cent of all FDI going to *all* of Asia. New technologies facilitated the process as corporations learned to integrate their component manufacturing processes and flexible manufacturing enabled distinct markets to be serviced at low cost.

Developing countries were eager to tap global capital markets to finance the balance of payments or to accelerate the buildup of their productive capacity. This entailed reforming their financial systems to meet investors' demands for liquidity or for transparent information about local opportunities. The set of principles equated with such policy shifts came to constitute the new model of economic development, loosely referred to as the 'Washington Consensus' in favour of market liberalization, privatization, and stabilization.

Private capital in the 1990s flowed in unprecedented volumes to 'emerging markets'. The ranks of net suppliers of funds to the markets widened from the initial list of the US and UK on capital account, to the financial surplus from oil-producing states, and to Germany and Japan as chronic trade-surplus countries. Central banks, financial institutions, and corporations, all in varying form protected from bankruptcy, placed their surpluses and took their bets in the world casino.[7] The rich from Latin America and Africa, and *nomenklatura* from the Communist Party states, joined the game. World foreign exchange, government and corporate bonds, and equities formed a seamless web to span the whole risk-and-return spectrum.

Whether or not governments of developing countries were far advanced in reform, the markets often would form a favourable view. They could choose between long-term direct investment and short-term portfolio or more speculative instruments. The frequent result was a local boom fuelled by cheap credit, a surge in real estate prices, an appreciation of the exchange rate, and a widening deficit on external accounts. If the investment climate turned sour, fleet-footed financial institutions could move. In Mexico in December 1994, and again in East Asia in 1997–8, they left behind devalued currencies, governments in disrepute, bankruptcies, and rising unemployment. Against this backdrop, the mass exodus of investors from emerging markets hit the South African rand in May 1998, the Russian ruble in August 1998, and forced the Bank of Brazil to withdraw support for the real in January 1999. One of the worst episodes in the history of international financial crises then hit Argentina in 2001–2: after the government had pledged bank deposits as a currency guarantee, investors fled the peso, which was devalued nearly 400 per cent against the dollar. The government defaulted on its debt and the savings of Argentine citizens were wiped out.

The world financial markets had, in effect, become judge and jury of the world economy. National economic performances and government policies were judged in the foreign exchange and bond markets. Corporate returns were measured through integrated corporate bond and equity markets. Their verdict was recorded in the risk-assessment agencies of the major financial capitals that consigned credit ratings on currencies, bonds, or shares. A rise in the credit ratings of, say, Moody's or Standard and Poor's would lower the cost of capital, while a negative verdict would raise the cost of capital for firms as for governments. Of course, some governments, currencies, or firms were treated with more respect than others, but there was a limit. Markets could not impose policies on sovereigns who refused to comply, but they could make the cost of non-compliance very high.

National Financial Systems, Corporate Governance, and Models of Capitalism

The chapter has so far reviewed how the global financial order emerged in the post-war period. We can now turn to consider how different models of capitalism are structured and how they interact with one another in world markets. As institution-alist economists point out, how the markets are structured, what values are embedded in the prevailing rules, and which organizations develop within the range of prevailing incentives make all the difference to outcomes.[8] Economic policy within and between states is thus about different conceptions of politics and distinct patterns of policy process. Different models involve different patterns of corporate governance, underpinned by contrasting financial market systems. The muddle at the heart of the Washington Consensus was that no final choice was made by market participants about which of the many capitalist models on offer should meet with their approval. Developing countries were invited to learn from a variety of capitalist models on display after the end of the Cold War.

Corporate strategy is understood here as the link between the external capital market, populated by shareholders and financial institutions, and the internal allocation of corporate resources.[9] Given the oligopolistic nature of competition

Figure 1: Market Competition, Corporate Strategy, and National Structures

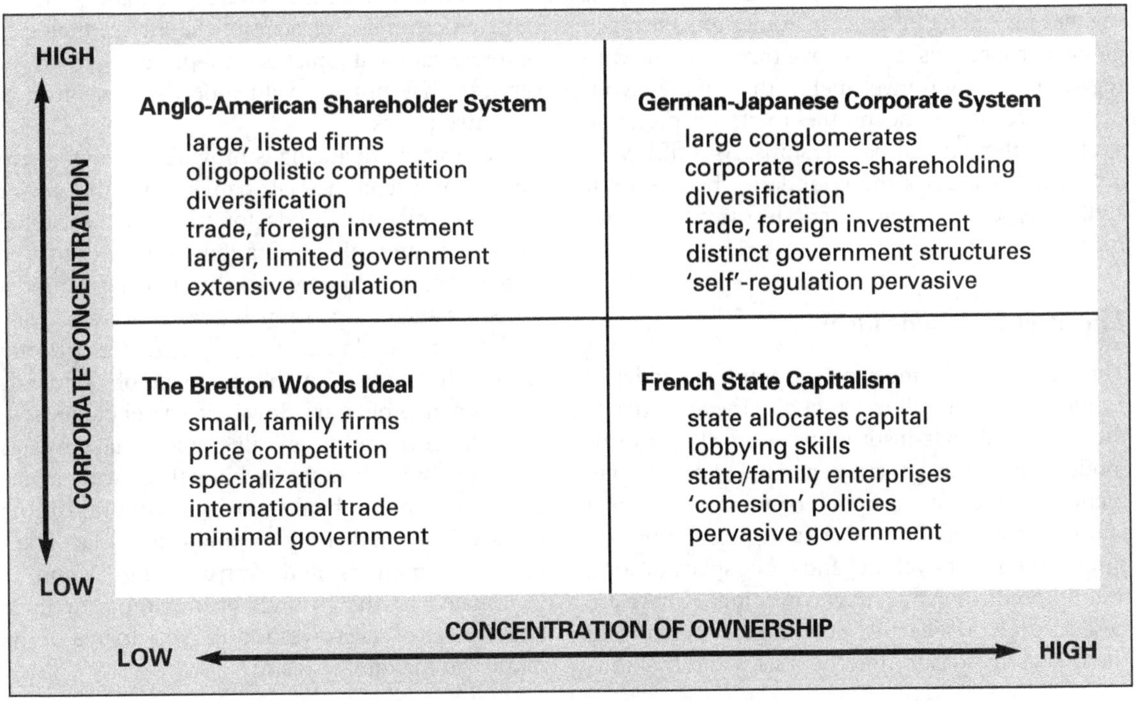

Anglo-American Shareholder System	**German-Japanese Corporate System**
large, listed firms	large conglomerates
oligopolistic competition	corporate cross-shareholding
diversification	diversification
trade, foreign investment	trade, foreign investment
larger, limited government	distinct government structures
extensive regulation	'self'-regulation pervasive
The Bretton Woods Ideal	**French State Capitalism**
small, family firms	state allocates capital
price competition	lobbying skills
specialization	state/family enterprises
international trade	'cohesion' policies
minimal government	pervasive government

CORPORATE CONCENTRATION — HIGH / LOW

CONCENTRATION OF OWNERSHIP — LOW ← → HIGH

among corporations in a sector and the variety of states in world markets, diverse incentives affect the strategies of firms.[10] The corporate population of different states may therefore be presented along two dimensions, as illustrated in a matrix (Figure 1): one dimension is the concentration of ownership, whether dispersed among a wide public or concentrated in the hands of a few institutions; the other is the degree of corporate concentration in terms of assets, sales, and numbers employed.

Figure 1 provides four models: the implicit model of the Bretton Woods institutions and three distinct types: the Anglo-American shareholder system; the German or Japanese system of cross-shareholding; and the French statist model, which has many variants around the world.[11] In effect, the Bretton Woods institutions assume that mercantilism is the norm, and that countries and companies may be induced towards an ideal of open markets and thus avoid the worst of self-centred behaviour. We shall use the matrix here to portray different corporate governance and financial market systems and to stylize the dynamics of changing regimes prevailing in states as homes or as hosts to global corporations. States have three options with regard to foreign investment: they may favour direct investment, be hostile to it, or prefer to sponsor international partnerships. As a fifth variant, which straddles the boundaries between our stylized types, we sketch some features of China's business system.

The 'Bretton Woods Ideal'

The starting point must be the implicit model of an ideal state that informs much of the activities of the Bretton Woods institutions. According to this model, minimum government is a vital complement to an open economy composed of small family farms and firms that compete sharply on price. Their survival depends on specialization and on predictable business conditions. These are best secured by effective government policing of their local markets to prevent abuses and by bind-

ing agreements on international free trade. A firm from a 'Bretton Woods ideal' country is content with exporting—until foreign governments threaten to impose duties or quotas. So our exporter decides to invest abroad to ensure continued market access. The government gets into the business of making the country an attractive target for foreign corporate investments through light taxation or education.

The Anglo-American Shareholder System

In the US and the UK, managerial hierarchies ran large, publicly quoted, and diversified corporations and predominated over shareholder interests until the sweeping changes in the tightly linked financial markets of New York, Chicago, and London in the 1970s and 1980s. The revival of shareholder capitalism in both countries drew on a legal tradition, which regards companies as a private entity set up by investors for their own benefit, who in turn hire managers to conduct business. Managers keep constant track of input costs, such as labour, raw materials, and capital, and seek the most efficient use of state-of-the-art technologies or organizational practices to produce goods or services that provide value for the consumer at attractive prices.

Corporate financing is provided by short-term funds from commercial banks, but the major source of external funds for firms is the capital market. Shares of corporations are held by the public, either directly or through institutional investors such as pension funds, and are actively traded. This Anglo-American system gives priority to the shareholder in the payment of dividends even when profits are down. If shareholders sell, then the corporation is vulnerable to takeover as predators bid to buy shares, sometimes with advice from investment banks, at a premium to the market. This market for corporate assets facilitates corporate mergers and restructurings,[12] and is legitimated on the grounds of providing the most efficient set of incentives for all participants in the market to maximize wealth.

Hence, both the US and UK governments have sought a shareholder-driven corporate economy, underpinned by a shareholder democracy, whereby the voting public participates in the performance of corporations and in the rewards. Supporters also argue that free markets are the most compatible with political democracy as a system of limited government. Free financial markets allocate savings to the most efficient investments, not politically determined investments. Labour market legislation in particular has to be supportive so that labour forces may be shrunk or shifted in task or location with the minimum of friction. The model also assumes that the government will not prove a light touch for corporate lobbies seeking to avoid restructuring or takeover through access to the public purse as a less demanding source of funds.

Government's major tasks are to provide the regulatory and legal structure within which open capital markets may function and to supply a safety net for the unemployed, the infirm, and the old. Consumer and shareholder interests are assumed to be paramount. Managers and workers must sweat to earn their keep. Domestic markets are deliberately kept open to foreign competitors and to inward investors. Government policy is predicated less on giving political advantage to national producers than on satisfying the demands of national shareholders and consumers. What the nationality of the shareholders may be is less important than the performance of the corporation. Its performance is best assured by diversifying the locations of its businesses to avoid downturns in any single national market.

Both US and UK corporations have worldwide reach but have suffered from powerful chairpersons who stuff their boards with golfing partners and conceal the true state of corporate accounts from shareholders and the markets. When these scandals (Robert Maxwell in the UK, Hollinger and Conrad Black in Canada, Enron and WorldCom in the US) were exposed, tighter statutory regulations were imposed. Some of the chiefs and golfing partners found themselves in prison, with more to go at time of writing.

The German–Japanese Cross-shareholding System

The German and Japanese cross-shareholding systems have significant institutional differences but also a few important similarities. Both countries were late industrializers and promoted universal banks taking deposits and investing shares in order to accelerate industrial growth. Both fostered the development of large corporate conglomerates in private hands and sought to reduce trade and financial dependency on foreign sources. Managers were placed in the driving seat of corporate Germany and Japan, along with bureaucracies and political parties, and their powers were legitimated by appeals to corporate or national loyalties[13] or through mechanisms to promote worker participation.[14] Labour policy and capital markets were designed to achieve a cohesive national polity, and to overcome the wounds of the wars, rather than as a means to create an 'efficient' economy.

Financial markets in both economies were highly regulated to ensure monetary stability and to protect depositors from bank failure. In both the German and Japanese financial systems of corporate control, the internal market to allocate resources *within* corporations took precedence over the demands of the external capital market. The portion of shares that float freely on the market is small, so that stock markets may be thin and volatile as investors (including foreigners) move in and out of shareholdings. Thus, many of the market disciplinary functions performed by impersonal capital markets on companies must be generated by the *insider* elites of corporations and financial institutions—the managers. Their attention is thus focused on the battlefield in product markets rather than on their share performance.

This is possible because, in both Germany and Japan, large, diversified corporations also protect themselves against takeover threats in the share markets by dispersing shares among each other and among financial institutions. Shareholders thereby enjoy institutional representation on the boards of the companies whose shares they hold and whose boards they share. In Germany, employees are also represented, and act as additional allies with roots in the labour markets against hostile takeovers. To avoid pressure from external creditors, the best condition for corporations with high fixed costs is to achieve self-financing by building market share. The bank-industrial cross-holding system complements close domestically based supplier-customer relationships, with dependability and co-operation often dominating price as transactions criteria.

Such a bank-industrial cross-holding system, because of its very 'insider' characteristics, curtails foreign market access and ownership while requiring open markets for exports and for corporate assets in other countries. The home market is the launch pad for the conquest of foreign markets, and the domestic market may be protected by all manner of corporate practices. The financial system as a whole must be prepared to deal with the consequences of large trade surpluses, which flow from joint corporate interest in market shares. Domestic inflationary pressures have to be kept down through rapid recycling of funds earned from exports. This entails the building up of portfolio investments in other markets around the world, revaluations of the currency, and foreign direct investments to avoid the high costs of domestic production. This is national mercantilism's Achilles heel. Corporations become detached from banks as their external sources of funds on world markets grow, while regulatory segmentation within the financial system breaks down as financial institutions compete across boundaries for new clients.

Both Japan and reunited Germany have failed to live up to their promise in the 1990s and beyond. Slow domestic growth saw Germany's biggest companies breaking loose from the national corporate culture and their shareholder bases often dominated by US or UK investors. They also headed into the new EU member states where wages were up to six times below average Western European levels. China's entry into the WTO saw Japanese companies, who also faced slow domestic market growth, open up to cheap imports and accelerate outward investment into China in particular. The national champion Nissan was successful-

ly turned around by *foreign* management (the French firm Renault) and others saw no alternative but to adapt to global market forces.

The State-led Financial Market System

France is the reference point for the model of top-down development through a state-led financial market system.[15] In terms of precedence, though, the title should arguably be awarded to Italy or Turkey. Typically, the state-led model of industrialization featured as some 'third way' between US capitalism and the Soviet system, and appealed to countries whose agriculture was backward, where small business enterprises predominated and larger corporations were few and often foreign-owned. In France, the Ministry of Finance regulated the capital market directly. Surplus funds of deposit-taking institutions were taken up by public-sector institutions, which lent them to specific industries, such as housing, agriculture, nuclear energy, or regional investments.

Over time, the French state-led financial system promoted a queue. Organizations with close contacts and claims on the loyalties of public officials, such as state-controlled economic enterprises or large private firms, got served first. The regular cycle of local, regional, or national elections thus also became contests between competing producer coalitions for a silver key to public finance. The whole edifice ground to a near halt when, in 1981, the new Mitterrand administration extended the public sector just as the external debt exploded and domestic savings shrank. France's financial market reforms of 1984–8 were introduced to promote Paris as an international centre, and above all to lower the cost of government financing.

The legitimacy of the state officials in the system derives from a claim to act in the public interest, but patronage, too, flows through state officials. Institutions whose resources they deploy directly or indirectly expand their stakes in business enterprises, extending further the field open to public patronage in the pursuit of private promotion. Corporate cross-shareholdings centre on state entities, and top management positions in these firms thereby remain part of the career circuit for elite state officials in what is in effect a political market for corporate control. The stench of corruption and the odour of incompetence creep under the doors and float through the windows of the most exquisitely perfumed salons, and the ruling oligarchy's legitimacy becomes more difficult to defend.

Such a system is unsustainable. State-led capitalism by definition seeks to allocate national resources for national purposes. Foreign investors seek entry and bring access to technologies, management skills, and foreign markets. Inward investors compete with national producers on their home markets, and this prompts national producers to retaliate by entering international markets through both trade and investment. But as markets open to foreign competition, government officials find themselves immersed in an ocean of corporate details, about which they know too little. The state finds itself torn between its old role and its new task of championing freer trade. As state capitalism's corporations internationalize, they seek to loosen the ties that bind them to their home state.

In the longer term, national corporations join their foreign corporate brothers and sisters as world citizens on the world market stage. But as state capitalism's corporations internationalize, so their tendency is to loosen the ties that bind them to their home state. Such was the fate of Jean-Marie Messier, who turned the water utility Compagnie Générale des Eaux into a $51 billion global media giant, Vivendi. This spree made Vivendi highly vulnerable to the meltdown in financial markets at the tail of the dot-com boom in March 2001, when Vivendi registered the largest losses in French history. But Messier's fundamental error was to have alienated the Parisian left bank, nationalist cultural establishment. He made his primary residence in New York and talked aloud, saying that France's 'exception culturelle' was an outdated idea. Without friends in Paris, and within a month, his career lay in ruins.

Squeezed by the limits of liquidity in French national capital markets, governments since the 1980s have also sought to overcome this 'global temptation' and to prevent French companies from falling under foreign ownership. The chosen method was cross-shareholdings among French institutional funds and investors while the state retained discretionary powers to preserve and promote French companies on the world market and to retain their autonomy. The state-led model adapts to globalization, but insists on its privileges to retain control in the national interest.

East Asian Business

During the latter half of the Cold War, East Asian and Southeast Asian countries rode on the coattails of the US and Japanese economies and remained aggressively pro-business and anti-Communist. They developed state capitalisms and relatively closed financial systems characterized by networks of cross-shareholdings among banks and producers. Accumulation proceeded apace as they followed Japan up the value-added chain of production and exports.

East Asia's boom was further stimulated by the dollar's devaluation against the yen in the 10 years following the September 1985 G-5 Plaza Accord on exchange rates. With their currencies tied to a low dollar and foreign investment pouring in from Japan, Taiwan, Singapore, and Hong Kong, as well as from the US and the EU, East Asian exports grew at 20 per cent per annum. East Asian shares in world manufacturing exports shot up, along with growth rates and living standards. Not surprisingly, the East Asian 'growth model' attracted widespread interest around the world in the 1990s among the many countries exiting from import substitution. As the World Bank argued (with some support from the Development Bank of Japan):

the body of East Asian evidence points to the dominant contribution of stable and competitive economic policies to the unleashing of private entrepreneurship. More often than not, the key to the policymaking process was the positive role of government in charting a development course, creating a longer-term vision shared among key participants, and fashioning an institutional framework for nonideological and effective policy implementation.[16]

The model was Taiwan and its state elite,[17] sub-ordinating their private passions to the public inter-est. This was the model that mainland China adopt-ed as its own at the 14th Party Congress in November 1993. All components of the reform, which together form the basic framework of the socialist market economy (SME), are considered by the leadership as comprising one 'interrelated and mutually conditioning' organic entity.

The World Bank's story of the Asian miracle envisaged Japan and the overseas Chinese business community as the spearhead of the Asia-Pacific's economic emancipation. The Chinese business com-munities are family-based and patrimonial net-works, where ownership is not divorced from man-agement, the leadership style is autocratic, and rela-tionships are personal.[18] Highly adaptable and pre-pared for adverse circumstances, they rode through the Asia-Pacific financial crash of 1997–8. By con-trast, Japan's failure to implement the liberalization measures announced in 1986 led to stagnation. Japan's deficiencies were the main cause of the melt-down in the Asia-Pacific economy in 1997–8. Its economy had reached the end of its mercantilist trail. Matters were made worse for Southeast Asian countries when China devalued the yuan in 1993 and entered into direct competition with exports from the Asia-Pacific region. Then, in 1995, the US Federal Reserve had the dollar rise against the yen to help the hard-pressed Mexican economy. East Asian exports slowed as their currencies rose against the yen. Savings flooded out of Japan, and a low-growth EU, in search of higher returns in the small East Asian economies at the top of their 10-year boom. Boom abruptly turned to bust as the Asian crisis began and global financial market investors turned on their erstwhile darlings. Currencies and living standards plummeted, while the region's massive production potential was discounted onto US or EU markets in a desperate bid to export or die.

In retrospect, the difficulties affecting the coun-tries of the Asia-Pacific in the late 1990s were a result of their previous successes. Japan had provided an example or model for many. The United States imported the region's cheap goods, underwrote its security and trade, and exported American 'can-do'

attitudes. Governments came to base their legitima-cy on growth, meaning the expansion of capacity and the race for market share. This transformed their societies, created aspirations, extended interdepend-ence between highly diverse societies, inflicted severe environmental damage, and prompted demands for political development. What the late 1990s revealed was that the old patterns of econom-ic growth—overdependence on the US markets, a still narrow range of export products, and an empha-sis on the simple expansion of capacity—were no longer sustainable. While Japan edged painfully towards opening its mind and economy, Asia-Pacific countries, notably Indonesia, moved further along the path to embrace representative government on which adaptable, market societies depend.

China nonetheless continued to boom, breed-ing its own brand of emerging market capitalism as it moves from state-planning to global integration. Foreign investors had to tread carefully as central and local-level state officials kept an eye on their own interests, and as the army, too, became a major player in the business world. Ailing state-owned enterprises, new private players, and foreign capital were a heady mix for an undercapitalized financial system that only survived by implicit state guaran-tees and bailouts, punctuated by the occasional offi-cially induced bankruptcy. While the particular nature of the model is unclear, there is little doubt that internal political and economic dynamics will continue to play a dominant role in the emergence of Asia's giant.

Conclusion

It is easy enough to see what happened when world history turned on its hinges in the years between 1989 and 1992. Fortified by a combination of One World thinking, the US administration, supported by the global agencies (the IMF, the World Bank, the WTO), steered financial markets towards a pro-longed roller coaster of boom overall, and bust here and there. The idea was to persuade poorer coun-tries to open to trade and to capital flows, in return for an opening of Western markets to their prod-ucts and for an encouragement of corporations to go global. Worldwide liberalization was to be accompanied by promotion of democracy, and with democracy would come a great era of peace.

The centre of the world economy was expected to slip inexorably to the Asia-Pacific. The implicit watchword of US foreign economic policy was 'no more Japans'. This went for China, too, though China has proved far less open to US persuasion. Countries with national systems of corporate mercantilism were seen as a major source of global disequilibrium. Hence the US-backed global institutions' proposals for governments to adopt what in retrospect appears overly hasty full currency convertibility and financial market liberalization. Participation in world business meant universal acceptance of adjustment to markets, which again China and others have often done selectively. Here lay the root of the world travails: governments had radically different views on bankruptcies, some emphasizing the importance of market clearance, but most more concerned to retain political support by their espousal of the Too-Big-To-Fail principle.

In retrospect, the years 1999–2001 mark the end of the post-Cold War transition to new structures in the first half of the twenty-first century. In January 1999, 11 countries in the EU had their bond markets, swollen by decades of government deficits, converted into euros. European corporations and governments could now finance their needs by recourse to a capital market the size of the US. By 2000, retail payments were made in euros. The euro will eventually develop as the other major trading currency, along with the dollar, and the world's second reserve currency for central banks on condition that its national political and economic structures adapt over time to a continental-size currency and polity.

There was still no final verdict possible concerning which type of financial system and corporate governance structures—French, German, or Anglo-American—the EU would move towards. There had been three scenarios:

1. The continental states would move rapidly to an Anglo-American type of corporate finance, given the stimulation from large, liquid capital markets populated by financial institutions searching for corporate winners. Shareholders and consumers would become the two kings of corporate strategy, to which managers would have to defer in a highly competitive US-type market.

2. The continental states would not change corporate governance structures, predicated on national cross-shareholdings and on the search for market shares over profits. Governments would still consider trade surpluses to be virtuous, and national labour market structures would remain much as before. The only change would be the greater facility afforded corporations in raising funds on the euro-capital market.

3. Some middle ground would be achieved: corporate managers would have plenty of incentives to raise capital to finance the intensive investments required to supply a market of 350 million people. Financial institutions would demand much higher returns for shareholders than in national capital markets; but the traditions acquired of shareholder patience, existing national labour laws, and taxation differences would provide the basis for an EU-wide social-liberal compromise.

The second major event, alongside the terrorist attacks on New York and Washington, DC, on 11 September 2001, was China's entry to the WTO that December. Following the Asian crisis, China's leadership, determined to ensure continued growth and continued transformation towards the market, went after full and immediate membership in the WTO. This came at Doha in December 2001, after arduous negotiations with the major trading powers of the United States and the EU. With the future path of economic policy laid down in the market-opening terms stipulated in WTO membership, foreign investors flooded into China from the advanced industrial states, accompanied also by investors from such mid- to low-income countries as South Africa, Brazil, and India. The attractions included low labour costs, heavy government investment in infrastructure, the rapid development of transport and communications, and an eager and educable workforce. Not least of the attractions was that China, like India, refused to open its capital markets along the lines of the 'Washington Consensus' proposals. Looking at China, global corporate chairpersons tended to see stability in capital controls, compared to countries that had liberalized capital movements. Another factor of stability, it was assumed, was strong leadership shown by the party-state in promoting generally market-friendly policies. As mentioned, by the early 2000s China absorbed 70 per cent of *all* foreign direct investment going to the whole of Asia. China became *the* emerging market.

By 2004, China's emergence in the global economy was creating a different dynamic in the Asia-Pacific, previously structured around US–Japan relations. China in effect became the region's manufacturing platform, importing components through MNC supply chains and re-exporting to US and EU markets. For the first time since 1945, China replaced the United States as the prime export market for Japan. Both China's and Japan's central banks intervened to maintain the value of their respective currencies against the dollar—thereby creating exchange rate stability for the rest of the Asia-Pacific, while using surplus funds to buy US Treasury bonds. In this manner they sustained growth of their exports, helped to finance the US current account and budget deficits, and fed the US consumer boom. With corporate America deeply engaged in China's

development through outsourcing operations, the main opposition to this growing dependency of the United States on the new Asia-Pacific came from US workers and professionals, fearful of losing their jobs to lower-paid workers in China or India. The expansion of the global labour market meant that average world wages were far below the levels achieved in the advanced industrial countries, while careful management of operations in China, in India, or indeed in Central Eastern Europe could ensure productivity levels at least as high as those in developed countries.

Over a decade after the Soviet Union's collapse, the two ends of the Eurasian land mass acknowledged the changes in global markets and politics through the parallel entry of China to the WTO and the enlargement of the EU to include most of the former Communist Party satellites of the Soviet empire. Which paths would these different capitalisms take—the ex-planned economies of the former Communist system and the varied capitalisms of Europe, as well as of the rest of the world? The most probable path was that the different capitalisms would retain their distinctiveness, but that that distinctiveness would be notably different from inherited forms. World financial markets would continue to absorb and retransmit the ways in which the many forms of capitalism simultaneously evolve, interact, and compete over time. Politics and finance are inseparable twins in the future, as in the past of the world's long march to integration.

Notes

1. 'The Global Economy: War of the Worlds', *The Economist*, 1 Oct. 1994.
2. Paul Hirst and Grahame Thompson, *Globalisation in Question* (London: Blackwell, 1996).
3. John Stopford and Susan Strange, *Rival States, Rival Firms* (Cambridge: Cambridge University Press, 1991).
4. Figures from UN Development Program, *Human Development Report*, 1990–2003.
5. Helmut Schmidt, 'The Struggle for the World

Product', *Foreign Affairs* 52 (Apr. 1974).
6. See Peter Katzenstein, ed., *Between Power and Plenty: Foreign Economic Policies of Advanced International States* (Madison: University of Wisconsin Press, 1978).
7. Susan Strange, *Casino Capitalism* (Oxford: Basil Blackwell, 1986); Strange, *Mad Money* (Manchester: Manchester University Press, 1998).
8. Douglas C. North, *Institutions, Institutional*

Change and Economic Performance: Political Economy of Institutions and Decisions (Cambridge: Cambridge University Press, 1991), 109.

9. See Michael Porter, 'Capital Disadvantage: America's Failing Capital Investment System', *Harvard Business Review* (Sept.–Oct. 1992).

10. C.K. Prahalad and Yves Doz, *The Multinational Mission: Balancing Local Demands and Global Vision* (New York: Free Press, 1987).

11. See Jonathan Story and Ingo Walter, *Political Economy of Financial Integration in Europe: The Battle of the Systems* (Manchester: Manchester University Press, 1998).

12. T.N. Rybczynski, 'Corporate Restructuring', *National Westminster Bank Review* (Aug. 1989).

13. James C. Abegglen and George Stalk, *Kaisha, the Japanese Corporation* (New York: Basic Books, 1985).

14. Wolfgang Streeck, 'German Capitalism: Does It Exist? Can It Survive?', in Colin Crouch and Streeck, eds, *Political Economy of Modern Capitalism: Mapping Convergence and Diversity* (London: Sage, 1997).

15. John Zysman, *Governments, Markets and Growth: Financial Systems and Policies of Industrial Change* (Oxford: Martin Robertson, 1983).

16. Danny M. Leipziger and Vinod Thomas, *The Lessons of East Asia: An Overview of Country Experience* (Washington: World Bank, 1993).

17. See Robert Wade, *Governing the Market: Economic Theory and the Role of the Government in East Asian Industrialization* (Princeton, NJ: Princeton University Press, 1990).

18. S. Gordon Redding, *The Spirit of Chinese Capitalism* (Berlin: de Gruyter, 1993).

Suggested Readings

Schmidt, Vivienne. *The Futures of European Capitalism*. Oxford: Oxford University Press, 2002.

Story, Jonathan. *The Frontiers of Fortune*. London: Pitman's, 1999.

———. *China: The Race to Market*. London: Pearson Education, 2003.

———, and Ingo Walter. *Political Economy of Financial Integration in Europe: The Battle of the Systems*. Manchester: Manchester University Press, 1998.

Zysman, John. *Governments, Markets and Growth: Financial Systems and Policies of Industrial Change*. Oxford: Martin Robertson, 1983.

Web Site

Nouriel Roubini's Global Macroeconomic and Financial Policy site:
www.stern.nyu.edu/globalmacro/

Chapter 10

The Group of Seven and Global Macroeconomic Governance

Michael C. Webb

The globalization of financial markets, begun with the emergence of the Euromarkets in the 1960s, accelerated during the last years of the twentieth century. Short-term financial capital now moves with great speed across national borders among the advanced capitalist countries (ACCs) and increasing numbers of so-called emerging market economies (EMEs). These flows generate international economic instability and pose serious problems for traditional tools of national economic policy, as well as for the achievement of broader political goals such as democratic accountability and government legitimacy. As cross-border economic links have grown, international co-operation has been widely seen as a mechanism for responding to these problems. This chapter examines the response of the Group of Seven (G-7) to the macroeconomic policy problems associated with financial globalization, assessing the character and effectiveness of G-7 policy co-ordination and the implications of G-7 action for the broader political goals of liberal and social democracy. I focus on the G-7 meetings of finance ministers and central bank governors rather than on the G-8 summits (which include Russia), since the key deliberations on macroeconomic policy and related issues occur in the ministerial meetings.[1]

Broadly speaking, political action is essential both for promoting the growth of international markets and for coping with negative consequences of that growth, especially regarding social equity and stability.[2] Post-war international trade and monetary regimes were designed to promote a kind of international liberalization that was embedded in a prior concern for domestic economic and social stability.[3] The Bretton Woods system did so by matching trade liberalization with measures to shelter national macroeconomic policies from international market pressures. These measures included capital controls, balance-of-payments lending through the IMF, and co-ordinated intervention in foreign exchange markets to maintain fixed exchange rates.

International capital mobility undermined the Bretton Woods compromise. International capital markets now react very quickly to differences in macroeconomic policies between countries, and especially to monetary policies. For example, a loosening of monetary policy in one country can cause an immediate capital outflow, as investors search for higher interest rates and lower inflation abroad. This would trigger an immediate depreciation of the national currency, a problem exacerbated by the tendency of foreign exchange markets to 'overshoot' appropriate levels. The threat of currency depreciation can encourage central banks to keep interest rates high to defend the currency, even if slow growth and high unemployment merit lower interest rates. The risk of capital flight also can force governments to pursue restrictive fiscal policies, even if domestic demand is weak and unemployment is high. Finally, international capital mobility can create or exacerbate international financial crises, as investors' herd instincts drive excessive capital flows both into and out of particular countries or regions.

Countries are not equally vulnerable to open capital markets. Larger countries and regions—especially the United States and the members of the EU's single currency area—are sheltered from global instability by their relatively low dependence on international trade and by their status as the home bases for much international capital. The United States also benefits from the dollar's status as the key international currency, allowing it to borrow from abroad in its own currency. This shifts the costs of dollar instability onto foreign lenders and investors. China is sheltered by its enormous size and tight controls over international capital flows. Emerging market economies with open capital markets are much more vulnerable to global financial instability, as are other developing countries.

Inequalities in political power in global macroeconomic policy-making reinforce the inequalities in economic vulnerability. The United States remains the most influential by virtue of its ideological leadership and dynamic economy, the key-currency status of the dollar, and broader American political power. The EU and its member states in the G-7 (Germany, Britain, France, and Italy) collectively have the economic capacity but not the political capacity to exercise leadership in the G-7. Japan's economic and political weakness has undermined its influence in the G-7. China now has a leading role in the global economy, but it is not a member of the G-7.

Returning to the issue of global macroeconomic governance, the G-7 has responded to problems created by international capital mobility primarily by supporting the expansion and efficient functioning of international financial markets. It has done little to respond to the challenges those markets pose to national macroeconomic management or the achievement of social equity and stability. Ideological convergence around orthodox norms for macroeconomic policy has been matched by convergence in economic performance around low inflation rates and, until 2001, shrinking budget deficits. But this convergence was accompanied by extended periods of slow growth outside the United States, serious economic instability, growing international imbalances, and worsening economic inequality. G-7 co-operation to ensure that the benefits of economic globalization are better distributed would require reasserting political authority over international markets. Ideology, the technical difficulty of effective action in the face of open international capital markets, and traditional political differences have all contributed to the G-7's rejection of more interventionist approaches in favour of market liberalization and macroeconomic orthodoxy, combined with modest levels of policy co-ordination to combat crises.

International policy co-ordination is not just a technical exercise for promoting international adjustment; it is also central to the resolution of broader political questions about government legitimacy and democratic accountability. Liberal democratic theory assumed a territorial state in which there was a direct correspondence between the citizens affected by a government's decisions and the citizens who exercised democratic control over that government by virtue of the vote. Economic globalization undermines that correspondence. Governments must now be responsive to non-citizens (e.g., foreign currency traders), which makes them less able to respond to the preferences of their own citizens.[4]

The legitimacy of democratic capitalist governments also rests in part on their economic performance, in particular their ability to redistribute the benefits of market outcomes through progressive taxation, social welfare programs, and full employment policies. Financial globalization makes it difficult to employ these traditional Keynesian tools, but 'citizens in democratic societies continue to hold the government of their own state—alone—responsible for widening economic prosperity.'[5] Failure to meet these expectations has undermined governmental legitimacy and contributed to the anti-government malaise affecting many ACCs since the 1990s. The G-7's legitimacy deficit was highlighted by activist protests in the late 1990s and early 2000s, a movement fuelled in part by the perception that the G-7's push for free-market economic globalization was biased in favour of transnational capital. Governments in EMEs and developing countries face even greater difficulties meeting their citizens' expectations in the face of global economic instability. These countries are not represented in the G-7, yet its decisions have an enormous impact on people and governments throughout the world. Recognizing this problem of international legitimacy, the G-7 recently created the Group of 20 (G-20) to provide an institutional framework for consultations with other important countries.

I return to arguments about democratic accountability and government legitimacy in the conclusions. The next two sections of this chapter examine the performance of the G-7 in managing the global economy in two key areas, monetary and fiscal policy co-ordination, and managing exchange rates and short-term capital flows. I then examine the G-20 as a response to the G-7's lack of international legitimacy.[6]

Monetary and Fiscal Policy Co-ordination

International capital mobility became a serious problem for macroeconomic policy-making in the mid-1960s, with the emergence of the Eurodollar market in London. Governments first tried to block capital flows that threatened fixed exchange rates and macroeconomic policy-making autonomy, but by the early 1970s this strategy was failing. Most governments then chose to let their exchange rates fluctuate, hoping that flexible exchange rates would adjust gradually to accommodate differences in macroeconomic policies in different countries. Extreme exchange rate volatility in the 1970s and 1980s showed that this faith in the automatic equilibrating tendencies of private markets was misplaced.

Macroeconomic problems since the 1970s stimulated discussion of two broad alternatives. The first would align government policies with market preferences. The second favours active policy co-ordination to address world economic problems. The G-7 moved clearly in the first of these directions in the 1990s, after experiments with more active policy co-ordination in the late 1970s (e.g., the 1978 Bonn Summit agreement) and the 1980s. Reaganomics in the early 1980s combined tight

monetary policy with enormous fiscal deficits that drove the dollar up and created a massive US trade deficit. The Plaza Accord of 1985 brought the dollar down, and by 1987 the United States had persuaded reluctant Japanese and German governments to reflate in return for US budget deficit reduction. But Japanese and German reflation actually made it easier for the United States to avoid reducing its own budget deficit and fuelled speculative excesses in Japan that caused prolonged stagnation in the 1990s after the bubble burst.

Partly as a result of this experience, the rhetorical tide turned against discretionary macroeconomic management by the early 1990s. G-7 central bankers reinforced each others' determination to maintain independence from political leaders and keep interest rates up to prevent inflation, while finance ministers encouraged their counterparts' efforts to cut spending and shrink deficits. Ideological convergence was accompanied by policy convergence as inflation rates fell, fiscal deficits shrank, and growth returned in most countries, at least until economies slowed after 2000.

Orthodox rhetoric and international market constraints did not prevent the G-7 from occasionally attempting to co-ordinate macroeconomic policies. There were some calls in the mid-1990s for a co-ordinated G-7 growth strategy to combat slow growth and high unemployment, but the G-7 explicitly rejected a macroeconomic response to these problems. Macroeconomic policy, it argued, should emphasize price stability and fiscal consolidation. High unemployment should be addressed by deregulation to make labour markets more flexible.[7] In the absence of co-ordinated macroeconomic stimulus, low American interest rates fuelled rapid economic growth in the United States, generating strong demand for imports that helped offset the global deflationary impact of Japanese recession and stagnation in continental Europe. Americans had become 'the consumers of last resort in a world of excess savings'.[8]

The international financial crises of 1997–8 forced the G-7 to consider co-ordinated reflation to avoid a global recession, discourage EMEs from tightening controls on international capital flows, and contain a crisis that threatened the stability of Western financial institutions. The United States cut interest rates to relieve pressure on East Asian economies suffering from capital flight and called on other G-7 countries to follow suit. However, many European leaders saw no reason for Europe to lower interest rates just to help troubled EMEs, and believed that the imminent introduction of the single currency had sheltered EU financial markets from global turmoil. The crisis deepened in 1998, and it was not until late fall of that year that the G-7 agreed on the need for measures 'to create or sustain the conditions for strong, domestic demand-led growth and financial stability in each of our economies'.[9] Interest rate cuts by central banks in Germany and other G-7 countries followed, stimulating growth and helping European economies prepare for the January 1999 launch of the euro. Even though policy co-ordination eventually assisted global recovery, the episode generated little optimism about the ability of the G-7 to manage the global economy.

G-7 deliberations since the late 1990s usually revolved around the contrast in policies between the United States, on the one hand, and the Eurozone and Japan on the other. American officials called on Japan and European governments to stimulate their economies, while officials from those countries called on the United States to reduce its current account deficit and (after 2001) budget deficit. Finance ministers and heads of government from Japan and the Eurozone countries often supported American calls for monetary stimulus, and were frustrated by their central banks' preoccupation with fighting the old war against inflation at a time when prices were falling in much of Europe and Japan. G-7 officials argued heatedly over the language in communiqués issued after each meeting, but the language usually was ambiguous enough to support a variety of interpretations. American officials (under both the Clinton and Bush administrations) dismissed the concerns expressed by their G-7 counterparts, having faith in the ability of capital markets to finance the twin current account and budget deficits. The Bank of Japan and the European Central Bank (ECB) often

appeared impervious to criticism from abroad and from elected political leaders in their own countries. Indeed, these central banks sometimes put the maintenance of institutional independence ahead of economically appropriate monetary policy, delaying or resisting desirable interest rate changes simply to preserve the appearance of political independence. The debates had an interesting transgovernmental dimension, with central banks jointly resisting pressure from elected leaders on any of their number, in some cases even when they agreed with the substance of politicians' critiques.

The stark dangers to the global economy posed by the 11 September 2001 terrorist attacks helped shift policy-makers' concerns. One week after the attacks, the US Federal Reserve, the Bank of Japan, the ECB, and central banks in a number of smaller ACCs joined in a co-ordinated reduction of interest rates by 0.5 per cent (in most cases) to restore confidence and offset the expected deflationary impact of the attacks. In relation to fiscal policy, there was a shift in consensus away from the strict orthodoxy of the 1990s. All G-7 governments except Canada ran large budget deficits after 2001 and justified tax cuts and spending financed by borrowing in language reminiscent of traditional Keynesianism. Indeed, so far did the consensus shift that when Canadian Prime Minister Jean Chrétien extolled the virtues of fiscal discipline at the 2003 G-8 summit in Evian, France, his comments were politely ignored by the other leaders in favour of growth-oriented macroeconomic policies.[10]

Thus, the G-7 record of macroeconomic management since the 1990s reveals an inability to co-ordinate policies on an ongoing basis, combined with effective co-ordination in crisis (1998, 2001) and important effects on dominant ideas about appropriate policies. Political dynamics—not economic constraints—are the key to the weakness of G-7 action. Governments often disagreed on the relative importance of price stability and growth, as did finance ministries and central banks within some G-7 countries. Even when governments do agree, effective global economic management is difficult because it must involve policies close to the heart of national sovereignty and domestic politics.

This is what makes policy co-ordination so much more difficult today than in the Bretton Woods era, when it focused on exchange rates and balance-of-payments lending rather than interest rates and national budgets. Finally, active policy co-ordination was impeded by the consensus in favour of price stability as the only target for monetary policy, and by the determination of central banks to assert their independence from political authorities.

The weakness of policy co-ordination in the G-7 also reflected the preoccupation of the group's continental European members with regional policy co-ordination. The governments of these countries chose to pursue political management of markets through regional economic and monetary union. As they had hoped, the introduction of the single currency did help insulate their economies from instability generated by open international capital markets and American policies. This reduced European G-7 governments' interest in policy co-ordination at the inter-regional level and focused their attention on European issues such as the ECB's monetary policy and the budgetary implications of the Stability and Growth Pact.

Obstacles to macroeconomic policy co-ordination encouraged the G-7 to pay more attention to 'structural reforms'—code for deregulation and market-oriented restructuring—at the microeconomic level, on the assumption that these would accelerate growth, reduce unemployment, and solve other economic problems.[11] American officials had been pushing their G-7 counterparts to emulate the US's market-oriented approach in labour market and financial regulations since the 1990s. The ECB and the Bank of Japan also favoured structural reforms rather than monetary expansion, to shift responsibility for slow growth onto elected governments rather than their own monetary policies. Finally, a number of G-7 governments sought G-7 support to help them overcome domestic opposition to planned policies, including bank restructuring in Japan and labour market deregulation in Germany, Italy, and France. Thus, the significance of G-7 discussions of structural reform probably lies less in the specific measures listed in communiqués than in the normative support the

discussions give to market-oriented approaches and to microeconomic rather than macroeconomic tools for encouraging growth.

As for macroeconomic policy, it is striking that the G-7 has paid so little attention to the risks posed by the buildup in US foreign indebtedness, particularly under the Bush administration. American budget and current account deficits have been financed by heavy borrowing from abroad, including massive purchases of US government bonds by central banks in Asia seeking to prevent their currencies from appreciating against the dollar. Officials from other G-7 countries criticized American deficits, but the United States was powerful enough to ignore their criticisms and keep them out of G-7 communiqués. No one knows how long the American borrowing binge can be sustained, but if foreign lenders lose confidence the consequences for the global economy will be severe. The pattern of the past is likely to be repeated; the G-7 will do little to prevent crises, but if a crisis does emerge the G-7 will be able to agree on ad hoc measures to contain it.

Managing Exchange Rates and International Capital Markets

During the Bretton Woods era, modest and restricted international short-term capital flows facilitated foreign exchange market intervention to enforce fixed exchange rates. The abandonment of fixed exchange rates in 1971–3 and subsequent growth of private international finance and of foreign exchange trading in particular make international capital market and exchange rate management much more difficult today. By 2001, the *daily* value of trades in foreign exchange markets (estimated by the BIS at $1.2 trillion) substantially exceeded the combined foreign exchange reserves of the industrialized countries (approximately $775 billion). This makes stabilization without altering interest rate policies very difficult.

Foreign exchange market volatility has generated the same two broad policy approaches that characterized debates about macroeconomic policy co-ordination: seeking stability by bringing government policies more into conformity with market preferences (combined with measures to make markets more efficient); and enhancing monetary and fiscal policy autonomy via collaborative measures to influence and control international markets directly. The G-7 has generally favoured the first approach, although international financial crises and currency misalignments generated some interest in more direct market interventions.

G-7 finance ministers have repeatedly claimed that 'the pursuit of sound domestic monetary and fiscal policies' (e.g., low inflation and deficits) is the key to achieving greater exchange rate stability,[12] demonstrating a strong faith in the efficiency of private international markets as arbiters of significant international economic relationships. But the faith is misplaced. Exchange rate volatility and misalignment persisted, with costly effects, even when macroeconomic policies converged around orthodox norms. As a result, the G-7 countries occasionally have co-ordinated intervention in foreign exchange markets, with occasional success. But intervention often came too late to prevent major misalignments, or was not sustained over enough time to have a lasting impact.

Some analysts and governments argue that co-ordinated intervention in foreign exchange markets is no longer viable, given the massive volume of trading in foreign exchange markets. But this belief in government powerlessness is exaggerated. Some co-ordinated interventions have succeeded, including efforts in 1995 to support the dollar, in 1998 to support the yen, and in 2000 to support the euro. Even the Bank of Japan's unilateral (though admittedly huge) US$316 billion intervention kept the yen from appreciating as much against the dollar as did the euro in 2003–4.[13] These examples suggest that the principal obstacles to more effective co-ordinated foreign exchange intervention are political, not technical or economic. G-7 governments often disagree about appropriate currency values, and even when they do agree they have devoted few of their combined reserves to the effort.[14] Central banks often resist calls from finance ministers for intervention in the interests of preserving

their institutional autonomy from political leaders. Ideological disagreement also blocks exchange rate co-ordination. While the German, French, and Japanese governments often favour ongoing co-operation to manage exchange rates, American officials usually argue that only markets can determine appropriate exchange rates. American disinterest in exchange rate co-operation also reflects the relatively small share of international trade in American GDP and the willingness of investors to lend to the US in its own currency, both of which mean that exchange rate volatility and misalignment cause fewer problems for the United States than for other G-7 countries.

American officials do call for exchange rate adjustments in the G-7, but they frame their remarks as criticism of excessive government intervention rather than of foreign exchange markets. The US has attacked China's policy of tying its currency to the dollar, a policy supported by strict capital controls and large-scale foreign exchange market intervention. American manufacturers and politicians complain that this policy keeps the yuan undervalued, giving China an unfair advantage in international trade and worsening the American trade deficit. Recent G-7 communiqués criticize China's exchange rate policy by calling for more flexible exchange rates based on market mechanisms.[15] Chinese leaders reject this criticism, in part because of their sensitivity to foreign criticism of any kind, but also because they believe it is illegitimate for an institution that excludes China to take such a stand on Chinese policy.

Another way to deal with market-driven exchange rate instability would be to re-establish some controls on short-term capital flows, thereby reducing the speculative pressures that can generate volatility. The idea of a Tobin tax on foreign exchange transactions to discourage currency speculation attracted interest from some G-7 heads of government,[16] but was rejected by G-7 finance ministers. The latter argued (correctly) that the tax could easily be evaded and (more controversially) would prevent countries from capturing purported welfare gains from free international capital flows.[17]

While the G-7 countries have themselves suffered some ill effects, the worst effects of unregulated capital flows have been borne by emerging market economy countries like Mexico, Argentina, and Korea. EMEs have been hit by repeated international financial crises since the mid-1990s, often even when they were pursuing policies favoured by international investors and the IMF. These crises encouraged the G-7 to take a more direct role in reforming and managing the global financial system, especially in response to interest in the reintroduction of controls on short-term capital flows. Malaysia and Russia introduced capital controls in 1998 to slow capital flight, and other EMEs examined less drastic measures such as those Chile and China had used to insulate themselves from short-term financial market volatility. These developments suggested that if the G-7 and IMF were unwilling to support systemic efforts to limit speculative short-term capital flows, EMEs might do it themselves. In response, some G-7 countries and the IMF reluctantly acknowledged that controls on short-term capital flows could be appropriate for countries with weakly developed financial systems. The United States, however, continued to insist on capital market liberalization, and denied that speculative financial flows had played a significant role in emerging market crises.

The G-7's response to financial crises therefore continued to encourage capital market liberalization and aimed instead to reduce and manage crises by strengthening prudential regulation of financial markets and by bringing government policies more in line with market preferences.[18] To achieve the latter, the G-7 put a high priority on increasing policy transparency. It claimed that 'well-informed and well-functioning financial markets are the best line of defence against financial crises',[19] although there is much evidence that market players simply fail to respond to information that runs counter to the instincts of the herd. The IMF and other international agencies have developed codes and standards for economic policy and statistics, and have encouraged adherence to these standards by making it an element of

the policy conditions attached to IMF loans and by providing technical assistance. Stricter IMF supervision and increased data publication in the context of open international capital markets expose EMEs and developing countries more fully to the disciplining effects of private investors, and are therefore best seen as measures to regulate governments, not markets.

At the same time, the role that weak domestic financial regulation and corruption played in worsening financial crises in EMEs encouraged the G-7 and international financial institutions (IFIs) to pay more attention to governance rather than straightforward deregulation. Policy advice and conditionality in the 1980s and early 1990s had been dominated by the 'Washington Consensus', which focused on removing government barriers to market-oriented economic activity. The financial crises of the mid-1990s contributed to the emergence of a post-Washington Consensus around the need for developing countries to establish appropriate regulatory mechanisms, supported by open, transparent, and impartial political institutions, and to build safety nets to protect vulnerable groups from the instability that often accompanied deregulation and market liberalization.[20] At the G-7 level, attention to these kinds of issues also reflected a perception by many leaders that their push for economic globalization needed to be accompanied by more attention to social concerns,[21] to combat the resistance to economic globalization apparent in the activist movement that grew up around meetings of the G-8, the WTO, and the World Bank-IMF in the late 1990s and early 2000s. With G-7 support, the goal of strengthening domestic governance became part of the policy conditions imposed by the IMF on governments wanting loans to cope with international financial crises after 1997. However, increased attention to positive roles for government should not obscure the underlying orientation of the post-Washington Consensus: improved public governance was intended to make markets work more efficiently and less inequitably, not to strengthen direct government intervention in markets.

The G-7 also took a larger role in overseeing prudential supervision of the global financial sector after the 1997 crises, creating in 1999 the Financial Stability Forum to encourage co-operation among the many agencies involved in supervising private international financial activity and to identify emerging problems before they became major crises. Finally, the G-7 initiated increases in the financial resources available to the IMF for lending to crisis countries following the 1997–8 Asia and Russian crises, though limits also were introduced on the size of loans to individual countries. There was much discussion in the G-7 and elsewhere about measures to facilitate the resolution of debt crises, though no clear solution has yet been agreed. Most G-7 governments and the IMF favoured something like an international bankruptcy court to oversee debt restructuring and ensure that private creditors bear fair shares of the burden of adjustment. However, the United States and private-sector lobbies blocked the idea of a sovereign debt restructuring mechanism, instead favouring market-led procedures assisted by new clauses in loan agreements to ease collective decision-making by private creditors in the wake of a crisis. Attention has since shifted to developing a voluntary code of conduct for debt reschedulings (see below). The tension between the American preference for market-oriented mechanisms and other G-7 members' interest in explicitly political mechanisms for crisis prevention and management has affected all of the G-7 debates about the international financial system. The fact that the measures intended to strengthen political supervision of international capital markets generally were rejected testifies to the continuing power of the United States in the G-7 and IFIs.

A striking feature of all of these responses to financial crises is the fact that they were designed primarily by the G-7, not by the countries in crisis. This undermines the international legitimacy and the effectiveness of G-7 proposals for reform, and encouraged G-7 countries to create a broader, more representative forum to consider these issues. It is to that forum—the Group of 20—that we now turn.

From G-7 to G-20?

As a steering committee for the global economy, the membership of the G-7 is both too narrow and too broad. It excludes all developing and emerging market countries, groups that account for the vast majority of the world's population. The exclusion of China is especially important now that it ranks as one of the largest national economies[22] and plays such a large role in relation to global macroeconomic imbalances and exchange rates. Efficiency criteria alone would favour including the smallest number of systemically important authorities—perhaps the US, the EU, Japan, and China. Legitimacy criteria suggest that this list be expanded to include more EMEs, especially since so much of the G-7's recent work involves managing the integration of EMEs into the global financial system. Canada's membership is superfluous in relation to both efficiency and legitimacy criteria, as is the current over-representation of European authorities.

The G-7 tried to address its international legitimacy deficit by creating the G-20 in 1999. The G-20 is a forum for deliberation and consensus-building among finance ministers and central bank governors from the G-7 countries, Australia, China, India, Russia, eight other EMEs, and the EU (IMF and World Bank officials also participate in G-20 meetings).[23] Membership was determined by the G-7. On paper, the mandate of the G-20 parallels the broad emphasis of the G-7 on economic policies relevant to global economic management, but its deliberations have focused on the international financial architecture and crisis management rather than macroeconomic policy.

Accounts of G-20 ministerial meetings to date suggest that the new forum has had a modest impact. While G-20 communiqués highlight the social dimension of globalization and the needs of developing countries to a greater extent than do their G-7 equivalents, G-7 countries appear to have dominated the discussions.[24] Furthermore, the G-20's own legitimacy as a forum for considering the social implications of economic globalization is limited by the fact that the finance ministers and central bank governors who meet in the G-20 are not directly responsible for social issues in their own countries and by the absence of an institutional link to heads of government.[25] The G-20's most important contribution has been to give EMEs a stronger voice in debates about international financial reform. For example, Latin American members of the G-20 strongly opposed the proposal for a sovereign debt restructuring mechanism favoured by the IMF and all G-7 countries except the United States. Brazil and Argentina argued that it would raise their borrowing costs, and the G-20 provided them with an effective forum for making their voices heard. American and Latin American opposition was sufficient to defeat the idea of a compulsory mechanism and to shift debate towards a voluntary 'code of conduct' to guide debt crisis prevention and management, with the G-20 given responsibility for developing the draft code.[26] But one should not exaggerate the centrality of the G-20 to this process, since the more exclusive G-7 has simultaneously undertaken its own strategic review of the IMF and World Bank.

On balance, the G-20 has the potential to address the G-7's international legitimacy deficit in relation to international financial issues, but it holds little potential in relation to macroeconomic issues and cannot address the G-7's democratic deficit (indeed, key G-20 countries like China, Russia, and Saudi Arabia are less democratic than the G-7 countries). The first chair of the G-20, Canadian Finance Minister (now Prime Minister) Paul Martin, hoped that the G-20 could address challenges to the G-7's democratic legitimacy by developing links with groups in civil society, but little has come of this idea. Good arguments can be made in favour of shifting responsibility for global economic management from the G-7 to the G-20,[27] but the G-7 countries currently are unwilling to move in this direction.

Conclusion

The G-7 is sometimes decried as a failure because it has done so little to tackle problems like slow growth, international payments imbalances,

exchange rate volatility, and global economic inequality. Bergsten and Henning criticized what they called the G-7's 'new consensus on inaction' in the 1990s, with G-7 countries claiming to be powerless in the face of capital mobility and tacitly accepting a 'non-aggression pact' whereby each refrains from criticizing the others' policies in return for freedom from foreign criticism of its own policies.[28] But from a perspective that celebrates the global spread of market principles, the G-7 might well be considered a success. The G-7 consensus favours reducing the role of governments in managing private market economies and submitting governments more clearly to the discipline of private market pressures. It eschews interventionist and Keynesian responses to problems like unemployment and currency instability in favour of liberalization and re-regulation to make markets work more efficiently.

What accounts for the weakness of active political management of the global economy at the G-7 level? Neo-liberal arguments against political management of the economy neglect evidence that collective political action can have positive effects. In the area of exchange rates, more active co-ordinated intervention is possible and could have a stabilizing impact. Limits on speculative capital movements are also possible, although the difficulties of implementing highly effective restrictions should not be underestimated. The ability of the United States to stimulate global demand and the modest positive impact of policy co-ordination in 1998 and 2001 both suggest that active macroeconomic policy co-ordination to stimulate growth and correct international imbalances is possible.

The obstacles to political management of the global economy therefore are political, not technical or economic. Capital mobility makes macroeconomic management more difficult, but not impossible. The neo-liberal ideology that has dominated G-7 discussions is itself one of the key obstacles to action, as it suggests that there is no alternative to orthodox macroeconomic policies and neo-liberal, market-oriented restructuring.[29] But effective interference with international capital markets generally must be co-ordinated, given the severe international market pressures that face any government that unilaterally diverges from neo-liberal norms. To date the United States has blocked co-ordinated efforts to manage directly short-term capital flows and G-7 exchange rates, while its proposals for co-ordinated macroeconomic expansion usually were resisted by monetary authorities in Europe and Japan. Another obstacle to effective political management of the global economy is the commitment of the European G-7 countries to economic and monetary union in the EU. This commitment reduces their interest in inter-regional policy co-ordination by eliminating exchange rate volatility within the single currency area and helping to insulate continental Europe from global financial crises.

While the US has faced resistance to its repeated calls for co-ordinated macroeconomic expansion, it has been remarkably successful in promoting its ideological vision of a market-oriented society with modest government intervention. The G-7's adoption of this view has been sweeping, including in its recent discussions of structural reform. This is deeply ironic. American governments have been able to pursue policies that generate huge fiscal and current account deficits only because of the unique political power of the United States, which enables Washington to escape the market constraints on economic policy that it wishes to impose on other governments.

Even though the potential for policy co-ordination remains, the G-7 has favoured only one aspect of what Karl Polanyi called the double movement of history. The G-7 has promoted the expansion of markets across national borders, but has done little to protect societies from the negative consequences of that expansion. This is perhaps most obvious in the case of exchange rates, where the G-7 has done little to tame the costly instability and economic distortion generated by private foreign exchange trading. Similarly, without co-ordination involving American fiscal restraint and stimulus in Europe and Japan, the US current account imbalance will get worse, bringing with it threats of further instability and American protectionism.

The activities of the G-7 have undermined democratic accountability in macroeconomic policy-making. The emphasis on orthodox anti-inflationary policies encouraged exaggerated concern about inflation long after it had disappeared in the G-7, and discouraged positive responses to popular concerns about stagnant incomes and persistent unemployment. The G-7's rhetoric also encouraged the trend towards central bank independence, and a transgovernmental coalition of central bankers in the G-7 resists encroachments on central bank independence by elected political leaders. Central bank independence may be functional if the goal is to ensure price stability at all costs, but the associated increase in accountability to financial markets comes with a reduction in accountability to citizens. Finally, the orthodox character of policies favoured by the G-7 in the 1990s contributed to poor economic performance in many G-7 countries, with that poor performance in turn contributing to an erosion of government legitimacy and growing popular alienation from traditional partisan politics.

The activist movement that arose to challenge international economic institutions in the late 1990s was fuelled in part by the belief that economic globalization was biased in favour of transnational capital, at the expense of other groups in society. The G-8 became a prominent target of this movement, though meetings of finance ministers and central bank governors attracted fewer protestors. Popular criticism of its pro-business approach did generate some responses by the G-7 and G-8. Meetings since the onset of violent protest have been held in isolated locations, which made it easy for security forces to keep protestors far from the leaders (e.g., Kananaskis, Alberta; Evian, France; Sea Island, Georgia), and the G-8 and G-7 paid more rhetorical attention to social issues. Communiqués now regularly identify a need to ensure that the benefits of economic globalization are widely shared, and more attention has been paid to issues like debt relief and African poverty. However, actual financial contributions usually fall far short of these rhetorical commitments.

In relation to core issues of global macroeconomic management, the G-7 has barely modified its orthodox, market-oriented approach. Instead of trying to enhance legitimacy by direct interventions to improve economic performance in areas of greatest popular concern (for example, by stimulating demand and growth), the G-7 has tried to make subordination to international market pressures legitimate. G-7 communiqués continually repeat the idea that there is no alternative to orthodox, market-oriented policies, and demonstrate an inordinately strong faith in freer international markets as the solution to most international economic problems. These claims do not correspond to the lived experiences of many people in the ACCs, for whom financial globalization has meant increased economic insecurity and growing inequality, never mind those in developing countries. The G-7's recent tentative endorsements of monetary expansion to prevent deflation and of fiscal stimulus to promote growth show some sensitivity to those concerns, but they do not herald acceptance of the desirability of active government intervention to address problems associated with market-oriented economic globalization.

Notes

1. This chapter focuses on issues relevant to global macroeconomic management. The G-7 also deals with issues like debt relief, African poverty, and combatting terrorist financing.
2. Karl Polanyi, *The Great Transformation: The Political and Economic Origins of Our Time* (Boston: Beacon Press, 1957 [1944]).
3. John Gerard Ruggie, 'International Regimes, Transactions, and Change: Embedded Liberalism in the Postwar Economic Order', in Stephen D. Krasner, ed., *International Regimes* (Ithaca, NY: Cornell University Press, 1983).
4. David Held, 'Democracy, the Nation-State, and the Global System', in Held, ed., *Political Theory Today* (Stanford, Calif.: Stanford University Press, 1991), 197–235.
5. Louis W. Pauly, *Who Elected the Bankers? Surveillance and Control in the World Economy* (Ithaca, NY: Cornell University Press, 1997), 16.
6. Information about discussions at G-7 and G-20 meetings in the 1990s and 2000s is based in part on media reports; the *Financial Times* (www.ft.com) has particularly useful coverage.
7. Group of Seven, 'Strengthening G7 Cooperation to Promote Employment and Noninflationary Growth' (Finance Ministers' Report to the Tokyo Summit), 1993.
8. Economist Rosanne Cahn, quoted in *Wall Street Journal*, 11 Aug. 1998, A1, A6.
9. 'Declaration of G7 Finance Ministers and Central Bank Governors' and 'G7 Leaders Statement on the World Economy', 30 Oct. 1998. At: <www.g8.utoronto.ca/>.
10. *Globe and Mail*, 3 June 2003, A6; 'Chair's Summary', Sommet d'Evian 2003, 3 June 2003. At: <www.g7.utoronto.ca/summit/2003evian/>.
11. See, for example, the grandly titled 'Agenda for Growth', statement of G-7 Finance Ministers and Central Bank Governors, Dubai, 20 Sept. 2003. At: <www.g7.utoronto.ca/finance/fm040207_growth.htm>
12. Group of Seven, 'The Halifax Summit Review of International Financial Institutions: Background Document', 15–17 June 1995.
13. Bank for International Settlements, *74th Annual Report 1 April 2003–31 March 2004* (Basel, 2004), 89–90.
14. Media reports indicate that approximately $7 billion was spent in support of the euro in September 2000, about 1 per cent of the combined reserves of G-7 countries.
15. 'Statement of G7 Finance Ministers and Central Bank Governors', Boca Raton, Florida, 7 Feb. 2004. At: <www.g7.utoronto.ca/finance/fm040207.htm>.
16. Nicholas Bayne, 'The G7 Summit and the Reform of Global Institutions', *Government and Opposition* 30, 4 (Autumn 1995): 502–4; *Financial Times*, 5 Sept. 2001.

17. Group of Seven, 'Halifax Summit Review'.

18. See Group of Seven, 'Halifax Summit Communiqué', 16 June 1995; Group of Seven, 'Statement of G7 Finance Ministers and Central Bank Governors', 21 Feb. 1998.

19. Group of Seven, 'Halifax Summit Review'.

20. For a key statement of the new consensus, see World Bank, *World Development Report 1997: The State in a Changing World* (Washington, 1997).

21. John J. Kirton, Joseph P. Daniels, and Andreas Freytag, 'Introduction', in Kirton, Daniels, and Freytag, eds, *Guiding Global Order: G8 Governance in the Twenty-First Century*. G8 and Global Governance Series (Aldershot: Ashgate, 2001).

22. According to World Bank data, China ranks second on a purchasing-power parity basis and seventh on the basis of current exchange rates.

23. On the origins of the G-20, see Tony Porter, 'Technical Collaboration and Political Conflict in the Emerging Regime for International Financial Regulation', *Review of International Political Economy* 10, 3 (Aug. 2003): 520–51; John J.

Kirton, 'Guiding Global Economic Governance: The G20, the G7 and the International Monetary Fund at Century's Dawn', in Kirton and George M. von Furstenberg, eds, *New Directions in Global Economic Governance: Managing Globalization in the Twenty-First Century*. G8 and Global Governance Series (Aldershot: Ashgate, 2001).

24. Kirton, 'Guiding Global Economic Governance', 160.

25. Tony Porter, *Globalization and Finance* (Cambridge: Polity Press, 2005).

26. *Financial Times*, 28 Oct. 2003; see also the G-20 website: <www.g20.org/public/>.

27. Colin I. Bradford Jr and Johannes F. Linn, 'Global Economic Governance at a Crossroads: Replacing the G-7 with the G-20', *Brookings Institution Policy Brief* No. 131 (Apr. 2004).

28. C. Fred Bergsten and C. Randall Henning, *Global Economic Leadership and the Group of Seven* (Washington: Institute for International Economics, 1996), ch. 5.

29. Ibid.

Suggested Readings

Baker, Andrew. 'The G-7 and Architecture Debates: Norms, Authority and Global Financial Governance', in Geoffrey R.D. Underhill and Xiaoke Zhang, eds, *International Financial Governance Under Stress*. Cambridge: Cambridge University Press, 2003.

Bergsten, C. Fred, and C. Randall Henning. *Global Economic Leadership and the Group of Seven*. Washington: Institute for International Economics, 1996.

Fratianni, Michele, Paolo Savona, and John Kirton, eds. *Sustaining Global Growth and Development: G7 and IMF Governance*. G8 and Global Governance Series. Aldershot: Ashgate, 2003.

Kirton, John J. 'The G20: Representativeness, Effectiveness and Leadership in Global Governance', in Kirton, Joseph P. Daniels, and Andreas Freytag, eds, *Guiding Global Order: G8 Governance in the Twenty-First Century*. G8 and Global Governance Series. Aldershot: Ashgate Publishing, 2001.

Porter, Tony. *Globalization and Finance*. Cambridge: Polity Press, 2005.

Webb, Michael C. *The Political Economy of Policy Coordination: International Adjustment Since 1945*. Ithaca, NY: Cornell University Press, 1995.

Web Site

University of Toronto, G8 Information Centre: www.g7.utoronto.ca/

Chapter 11

The WTO and the Governance of Globalization
Dismantling the Compromise of Embedded Liberalism?

Jens Ladefoged Mortensen

The World Trade Organization (WTO) is an experiment in global economic governance. It is also an institution in crisis. The breakdown of the Cancun Ministerial in 2003 was a clear manifestation of that. Not only did it reflect a structural reordering of the global economy but it also revealed differences among members regarding the future direction of the WTO. At Cancun, a critical mass of developing-country WTO members—grouped together in the G-20 under the leadership of emerging trade powers like Brazil, China, and India—rejected the transatlantic agricultural deal, rebelled against US cotton subsidies, and resisted the further inclusion of new areas into WTO governance. Yet, the WTO crisis goes deeper than the occasional diplomatic breakdown. Unlike previous crises, the current crisis is not just about efficiency and effectiveness but also about legitimacy. The aggressive use of the dispute settlement system has put the WTO itself in a dilemma. If WTO panels fail to provide market access in individual cases, the WTO may lose political support among the major trading powers. Yet, if WTO panels prove too successful in their efforts to liberalize markets, the WTO may further aggravate anti-global sentiments among many citizens. In its governance of globalization, the WTO faces the difficult task of striking a balance between effective market liberalization and public acceptance of its activities.

The Cancun crisis is only one of many diplomatic breakdowns in the history of multilateral trade governance. Indeed, the renewed effort to revitalize the Doha Development Round in July 2004 demonstrated that the WTO remains one of the principal gravity centres in the governance of globalization. At each critical juncture of its history, however, the same question has been asked: Will the multilateral trade system survive? So far, it has proven remarkably resilient, almost as if it thrives on frequent crises. The current crisis is not necessarily a fundamental one, understood as a 'norm-transforming crisis', that is, a change of the underpinning norms and principles of the trade regime itself, as opposed to a 'norm-governed crisis', or a change within the regime. Yet, something has changed. The WTO appears to have overstretched itself beyond what can be accepted by its near-global constituency. The split between power and social purpose in WTO governance can no longer be ignored. It is decoupling market-based authority from society-based authority in the governance of globalization. The compromise of embedded liberalism is being dismantled from the outside and from within.

This chapter offers an institutional interpretation of the current crisis. To understand its depth, it is necessary to look at its sources. Drawing on institutionalist thought in IPE, I argue that the legal activities of the WTO have widened the separation between the markets and politics, in particular by allowing particular corporate interests to misuse the system. Yet, the WTO itself is also updating some of the outdated aspects of embedded liberalism. Still, embedded liberalism remains one of the defining characteristics of the trading system and indeed is necessary for the governance of globalization, but its continued relevance is under threat from both inside and outside the WTO.

Perspectives on WTO Governance

'Governance' has replaced 'regimes' as the focal point for the study of international institutions. Governance is an ambiguous concept. Yet, it has served as a catalyst for an interdisciplinary debate on the transformation of power and authority in an era of globalization. It also signifies a new approach to the study of international institutions, emphasizing the multi-level structures of overlapping authorities in which new actors and ideas have come to matter in global politics. But as Susan Strange sarcastically noted, it seemed only to offer 'some alternative to the system of states, yet something subtly different from world government'.[1] The WTO presents itself as a unique case of how states have voluntarily delegated authority to a quasi-supranational institution at the global level.

Outside the IR discipline, the WTO has been hailed as a milestone in international relations, signifying a shift away from 'power-based' towards 'rule-based' diplomacy.[2] The bulk of the WTO literature focuses on its legal aspects, leaving a false impression that WTO governance is depoliticized. In contrast, realist IPE understands the WTO in terms of institutionalized power and American leadership.[3] Its current transformation is a derivative of the reconfiguration of positional power relations. By implication, if the WTO does not reflect the concerns of the US and the other major economic powers it is doomed to irrelevance. Bilateral and regional negotiations offer a more attractive route to limited liberalization among the triad economies of the United States, the European Union, and Japan and among bigger developing countries.

Liberal IPE takes the WTO institution more seriously. It portrays the WTO in terms of a 'legalization' of world politics, as a necessary update of an inefficient GATT regime and a case of 'progressive constitutionalisation'.[4] The liberal WTO debate circles around the efficiency of its organizational design. It argues that the future of the WTO depends on its ability to deliver the global common good of trade liberalization, its 'output legitimacy' so to speak. Much of liberal IPE is positive about the prospects of a dialogue between governments and civil society. Yet, it maintains that only states are capable of balancing sovereignty, democracy, and welfare in trade politics. Finally, most liberals emphasize the progressive nature of the WTO. It has become a 'rule of law' system, if not a 'proto-constitution' that ensures the freedoms of individuals to trade across borders without state interference.

In contrast, critical IPE pictures the WTO as something like a 'neo-liberal conspiracy of neo-constitutionalism' or as a segment of an emerging transnational 'mercatocracy'[5]—a system of non-state arbitration of business disputes rooted in medieval laws. The argument is that private power in the WTO has undermined public authority and democratic governance. The WTO has not been 'misused' by private power. Rather, it is intended to serve private power. The WTO is encapsulated within an ideological hegemony of global capitalism alongside the other sites of global economic governance. Embedded liberalism merely gives transnational capitalism a deceitful appearance of fairness and justice. Critical IPE, therefore, distrusts the WTO institution. It is a manifestation of transnational capitalism and its underpinning ideology. Ironically, the higher visibility of WTO governance has improved the situation. The Seattle protests of 1999 have been interpreted by critical IPE as the mobilization of counter-hegemonic forces in the governance of globalization.

Capturing the Complexities of WTO Governance

The complex nature of WTO governance makes it difficult to analyze the WTO crisis. As a discipline, IPE continues to be at odds with the possibility of supranational governance of globalization. Only critical IPE captures the transnational dynamics of WTO governance. Yet, even here the institution itself is treated as a passive transmission belt for corporate interests. Most IPE perspectives maintain a state-centric view, emphasizing domestic politics or interstate diplomacy while dismissing the power of the WTO institution itself. However, both state-centric and critical IPE oversimplify the nature of WTO governance. In actuality, WTO rules reflect a com-

plex set of norms. The WTO is not about unconditional or unrestricted trade liberalization. Rather, it
aims to contain and subsequently disarm protectionists. However, since WTO law on controversial
trade issues tends to reflect delicate and multi-layered compromises of the past, WTO governance of
such issues is based on imprecise or even inconsistent rules. By implication, WTO enforcement frequently entails difficult choices between conflicting
objectives and competing interpretations of imprecise rules. Trade lawyers and experts have consequently become important actors in WTO governance, and WTO dispute settlement has become a
distinct legal mode of decision-making in trade
politics.

WTO Governance: Towards 'Disembedded Neo-liberalism'?

The WTO is a continuation of the General
Agreement on Tariffs and Trade (GATT)—plus a lot
more. The WTO, which was established in 1995
after an agreement signed by all 125 members of
the GATT, signifies a series of important departures
from the compromise of embedded liberalism.
Before these are explored in more detail, it is
important to clarify the meaning of embedded liberalism. It lies at the interface of markets and political authority. The WTO defines the demarcation
lines between legitimate and illegitimate state intervention in the market. By implication, everything
in WTO governance is about defining the scope of
government in the market.

The Original Argument of Embedded Liberalism

The notion of embedded liberalism was developed
by the American economist, moralist, and anthro-
pologist Karl Polanyi in 1944[6] in the context of his
historical analysis of the 'dual movement' that led
to the breakdown of nineteenth-century liberal
economic order in Britain. By 'dual movement',
Polanyi meant that the move towards unregulated
market liberalization, whereby the economy was
disembedded from its social compound, was

accompanied by a political countermove towards
regulating market liberalization. He concluded that
successful market liberalization rested on its societal legitimacy. Polanyi accepted markets as important social institutions but warned against their
alienating effects on society and individuals.
Unregulated liberalization contains the seeds of its
own self-destruction. Translated into the WTO
debate, Polanyi tells us that globalization must be
regulated by legitimate forms of authority. This
duality of markets and public authority inspired
John G. Ruggie to apply the concept to the Bretton
Woods institutions.[7]

The GATT represented a fusion of international
power and domestic societal norms of the dominant states of the immediate post-war era, the
United States and the United Kingdom. Embedded
liberalism captures an essential feature of the GATT;
its substantive rules legitimize policy practices that
are intended to cushion the domestic sphere from
the destabilizing effects produced by international
market liberalization. The GATT norm was best
described as 'Smith abroad, Keynes at home'.[8]
Moreover, the compromise also dictated a state-
centred, diplomatic mode of multilateral governance. It rests on a separation of 'the domestic' and
'the international'.

The survival of embedded liberalism in WTO
governance requires rethinking among lawmakers,
the WTO members. One critique of embedded liberalism concerns its outdated social purpose. The failure to integrate agricultural trade is one manifestation
of how powerful embedded liberalism remains in the
WTO. It is important to ask whose societal interests
are cushioned against liberalization at the expense of
others. For instance, embedded liberalism permits
WTO members to enact anti-dumping measures subject to certain requirements and to restrict imports
under certain circumstances. It also permits subsidies
to uncompetitive industries in particular situations.
However, the surge in anti-dumping investigations
over the past decade cannot be understood as a societal response to global competition. Rather, firms
have realized that embedded liberalism offers quick,
reliable, and effective strategies to shield themselves
temporarily from foreign competitors.

Embedded liberalism does not equal protectionism. Rather, in order to restrict protectionism, it specifies situations and procedures whereby protectionism is permissible in the WTO. The logic is that a certain tolerance of protectionism is the price for effective markets. Embedded liberalism is about successful trade liberalization. However, that logic is seriously threatened by the rise of aggressive legalism in WTO governance.

IR Research on Embedded Liberalism

The liberal component in WTO governance clearly manifests itself in the 'most-favoured-nation' (MFN) principle (Article I), and in the 'national treatment' principle (Article III).[9] In contrast, the embedded component is not easily observable. It permits WTO members to exempt certain policies from the MFN and national treatment principles. Embedded liberalism is not listed among the official WTO principles on the organization's web site. It can only be detected through the often convoluted exceptions found throughout all WTO agreements and in the institutional practices of the WTO. Ironically, however, it is often easier to observe the demise of a norm than its existence.

Ruggie correctly detected the normative duality underpinning GATT governance and its importance for international trade liberalization. Yet, his approach is not without its weaknesses. First, in an era of globalization, the power to replace the norm of embedded liberalism is not necessarily confined to states exclusively. It is necessary to widen the focus and include non-state actors—transnational firms, international bureaucrats, and experts—as potential sources for a transformation of the WTO. Second, in its original formulation, embedded liberalism excluded from its focus the institutional design of the GATT and its decision-making procedures. It seems logical, however, to include the institutional dimension into the analysis; that is, the voluntary and sovereign-sensitive nature of GATT pragmatism, as manifested in the diplomatic mode of dispute resolution, was a part of the compromise. Thus, the fusion of international power and social purpose within the GATT was complemented by a deliberately weakened design of the GATT institution. Third, embedded liberalism presumes that governments share an implicit understanding of what is 'domestic' and what is 'international', ignoring both the widening and deepening of WTO governance. Since the WTO regulates a global liberalization of markets, the organization's non-state constituency escapes the state-centric logic of embedded liberalism. Both national business and transnational business are heavily affected by WTO governance, and, consequently, both are engaged in the politics of WTO governance at all levels. Likewise, the resistance to WTO governance can no longer be understood in terms of domestic politics. It is also a transnational phenomenon.

The essence of the embedded liberalism argument is crucial for understanding the current situation. The GATT was designed to facilitate state-controlled market liberalization within the limits of what was socially and politically acceptable within the dominant economies of the early post-war era. Its purpose was not to dismantle the state. The GATT represented the fusion of social purpose and international power. Everything in the GATT ensured that states were not forced to open up markets unwillingly. This is not the case in the WTO.

Expanded Scope: The Deepening of WTO Governance

The WTO domain is composed of three issue-areas: trade in goods, which is covered by the GATT; trade in services, which is covered by the General Agreement on Trade in Services (GATS); and intellectual property rights, which are covered by the trade-related intellectual property rights (TRIPS) accord. Overall, more than 26,000 pages spell out the WTO rules in some 60 specific agreements on issues ranging from tariff-binding and anti-dumping procedures to rules on agricultural trade and food safety, electronic commerce and telecommunications, and patents and trademarks. Its jurisdiction has grown from 23 countries in 1947 to 147 countries in 2004. Despite its near-global membership, WTO decision-making is governed by the 'one-state, one-vote' principle, unlike the weighted voting procedures of the IMF and World Bank. In addition, WTO voting is governed by a consensus norm, even if, formally speaking, majority voting is possible in certain situations. Thus, certain core elements of multilateralism are largely intact in WTO decision-making.[10]

In contrast, the deepening of WTO governance has transformed the normative core of the trading system. International trade has expanded considerably over the years, and the WTO, by implication, has redefined the 'acceptable' scope of government in numerous trade-related areas. In 1947, the GATT issue-area was easily identified as 'international trade', meaning policy instruments regulating cross-border flows of goods, including border restrictions such as tariffs and quotas, subsidies, and anti-dumping and countervailing duties. Since 1979, the scope of the trading system has expanded steadily, culminating in the inclusion of international standards, intellectual property rights, and liberalization of services in 1993. The expansion of the WTO domain is one source behind the dismantlement of embedded liberalism.

GATS and TRIPS

WTO critics have accused the TRIPS and GATS agreements of having a pro-business bias. Both agreements were concluded after intense business lobbying and against the will of the developing world.[11] Both severely limit the scope of government interference in the market and are unique in WTO governance. On balance, the GATS is perhaps the less intrusive of the two. Unlike all other WTO areas, the GATS does not operate with an unconditional MFN principle. Instead, market access is offered on the basis of concessions. For better or worse, GATS governance is more power-driven than TRIPS governance. The TRIPS agreement is distinctively more legalistic. It is about procedural harmonization of national enforcement systems in the area of intellectual property rights. This is prescriptive, and positively defines what WTO members must do rather than defining what is prohibited under WTO law. Yet, recent events indicate mounting opposition to a deepening of WTO governance in these areas, even among WTO members. For

instance, the sub-Saharan HIV/AIDS crisis translated itself into an attack against the TRIPS agreement during the Doha Ministerial meetings. Likewise, the rejection of 'the Singapore issues' in Cancun underlined the scope of the southern revolt in the WTO.[12] Time will tell whether WTO members will permit the service industry and intellectual property right (IPR) holders to use the WTO to enforce their newly acquired rights. While only a few cases have reached the dispute settlement system so far, TRIPS and the GATS have the potential to redefine the essence of WTO governance.

International Standards

The issue of global standardization has already surfaced within WTO dispute settlement. The Uruguay Round produced two domains of WTO governance: the Agreement on Technical Barriers to Trade (TBT) and the Agreement on Sanitary and Phytosanitary Measures (SPS). The agreement on TBTs governs the use of technical standards in trade in goods (including safety and labelling requirements), while the latter governs health standards in agricultural trade. It is questionable whether the TBT and SPS agreements support the norm of embedded liberalism. On the face of it, both agreements merely refine the scope of legitimate state regulation on public health and environment issues. Both build on the original 'environmental charter' of the GATT (Article XX), which remains intact in the WTO. Among other provisions, Article XX permits WTO members to violate the principle of national treatment under specified circumstances and subject to certain requirements.

The problem is that the TBT and SPS agreements contain ambiguous references to 'international standards, guidelines and recommendations'. On one hand, it is permissible for WTO members to protect their own territories and populations against trade-induced health and environmental risks. On the other hand, both aim to prevent the misuse of such standards as disguised forms of protectionism by stipulating that WTO governments provide scientific evidence of harmful environmental or public health risks if they decide to impose higher and more restrictive standards than the internationally recognized ones. In this manner, critics argue, these agreements go much further than eliminating disguised protectionism. First, none of the mentioned 'international standards' have been agreed upon in the multilateral trade system but, instead, originate from the non-binding recommendations negotiated under the auspices of the Codex Alimentarius Commission. To many, the WTO has undermined the right of the state to establish its own level of acceptable risks to public health within its own borders. Second, the WTO system is not designed to protect consumers against such risks. It is designed to protect exporters and producers against opportunistic governments. There is no equal to the WTO in global governance on food or environmental issues. By default, the WTO is the only venue for tackling food- or environment-related trade wars. But it is not designed to tackle such complex issues.

The expansion of the scope of trade governance within the WTO regime has thereby contributed to the erosion of the underpinning societal acceptance of the institution. The wording of the TBT and SPS agreements is dangerously ambiguous. However, none of these vague references to the Codex standards would have caught the attention of those outside the academic WTO community if it had not been for the spectacular trade wars on hormone-treated meat or genetically modified organisms (GMOs). Crucially, then, the legalization of WTO dispute settlement has become the most significant source of transformation in WTO governance.

The Hardening of WTO Governance: The Legalization of Dispute Settlement

An important component of embedded liberalism is its compatibility with state sovereignty. The non-binding nature of GATT transparency and enforcement procedures produced a diplomatic mode of trade governance. Everything in the GATT ensured that states were not forced to open up markets unwillingly. This is not the case in the WTO.

The impetus for redesigning the GATT came from the US. Early in the Uruguay Round, the US demanded a legalistic mode of dispute resolution in the GATT. The GATT rules were to be enforced, not ignored. To underline the point, the US threatened to act unilaterally, enacting the notorious Section 301 and Super Section 301 of the 1988 Trade and Omnibus Act, which gave it the power to retaliate against countries deemed to have unfair trade barriers. This move reshaped the entire Uruguay Round. Behind the scene, however, the US exporters and transnational business were in effect dismantling embedded liberalism by convincing the US government to push for better market access and to include intellectual property rights and services in the GATT. The demand for a harder mode of GATT governance was an inherent element in that strategy. It was a continuation of a decade-long tendency to incorporate legal strategies into US trade diplomacy.

By 1989, the basic contours of a new dispute settlement system were evident. However, in the course of the negotiations, the US preference for a legalization of GATT dispute settlement was not unconditionally supported by the other delegates. The Canadians and Europeans demanded firmer institutionalization of the entire trade system in return for a legalization of the dispute settlement system. Eventually, a compromise between 'the legalists' and 'the pragmatists' was found. The bargain ensured a legalistic dispute settlement system, which was characterized by its mandatory jurisdiction, fixed timetables, and automatic retaliation in case of non-compliance. However, it was to be supplemented with an appeal body empowered to reverse the initial rulings by expert panels. Signatories also agreed to institutionalize a legal system to administer all agreements in a uniform manner. The next logical step was then to suggest the establishment of a permanent organization to oversee the functioning of the entire system. Neither the WTO nor the Appellate Body was an American invention. It was a Canadian and European countermeasure to the American demands for unchecked legalization of GATT dispute settlement.[13] In return for more rigorous enforcement, the US reluctantly accepted a quasi-supranational WTO institution. In hindsight, the WTO was the product of not only diplomatic bargaining but also continuous reformulation of the governance process by the actors involved in the process.

Problems in WTO Dispute Settlement

The dispute settlement system has been praised for its successes. On the occasion of the three-hundredth complaint in September 2003, General Director Supachai Panitchpakdi congratulated the WTO system by emphasizing that it:

> continues to show how even the most intractable international issues can be resolved successfully under a multilaterally-agreed system. A few headline-grabbing disputes belie the fact that a large number of cases brought to the WTO are settled without litigation. However, where litigation is necessary, the WTO offers an efficient, impartial, and highly credible system within which Members can present their arguments and receive rulings to help them to resolve their differences.[14]

WTO enforcement is not without its imperfections, however. A comparison between the GATT and the WTO reveals a dramatic rise in legal activity (Table 1). The WTO has coped with more cases than the GATT did in its entire existence. The annual complaint rate peaked around 1997 with 52 cases a year, but has since then dropped to about 20 cases.

By September 2003, 130 WTO cases had reached final conclusion. Altogether 116 cases are active in the WTO. Roughly a third of them have resulted in WTO investigations. The remaining cases are 'hibernating' within the system. In spite of what WTO officials say, the diplomatic mode of dispute settlement is not the most characteristic feature in WTO governance. WTO members increasingly resort to aggressive litigation rather than prudent diplomacy.

A persistent problem in WTO dispute settlement is the panel system. The panels perform the only factual investigations of WTO complaints. Subsequent appeals are limited to the legal aspects only. What has surprised observers is the high frequency of appeals. The Appellate Body has proven more important than anticipated. In 52 out of 73 adopted rulings, the losing party has used its right to appeal the ruling. In addition, about a fifth of the final Appellate Body reports have been subject to prolonged implementation controversies. The legal system has increasingly been pushed to its outermost limits. The burden of litigation on the least resourceful members and the WTO secretariat has multiplied. Moreover, despite ample opportunities for diplomatic settlements within the WTO system, altogether seven cases have resulted in WTO authorization of retaliations so far. Much evidence suggests that the WTO is at the brink of procedural overload, suggesting that the limited resources of the WTO secretariat and of individual WTO members have become a structural problem in WTO governance.

There are positive tendencies as well. The developing WTO members account for about 40 per cent of all complaints. However, the less-developed countries (LDCs) remain marginalized in the WTO dispute settlement process. For instance, sub-Saharan Africa only launched its first complaint, against the EU sugar regime, in 2003. Overall, the system is dominated by the US

Table 1: GATT and WTO Dispute Settlement

	Total Cases	Adopted Rulings	Settled	Appeals	Arbitration	Re-examination	Retaliation
GATT (1947–94)	247	112	64	-	-	-	(1)*
WTO (1995–2003)	301	73	57	52	17	14	7

*Authority given but retaliation not implemented.

and EU, even if major developing countries like Brazil and India have become frequent participants in WTO dispute settlement.[15] While the correlation between share in global trade and participation in WTO dispute settlement is obvious, it is far from perfect. Rather, the correlation between participation and the organizational resources devoted by the individual governments to WTO governance is more striking. The possession of adequate legal expertise is a prerequisite for influence in WTO governance.

These experiences also suggest that there are limits to supranationalism in WTO governance. Unlike the EU Commission, the WTO secretariat has no independent mandate to propose new rules or initiate cases against its members. Like the GATT, the WTO remains a member-driven organization. Despite its newly acquired status as a proper international organization, the WTO bureaucracy has been kept at a minimum. Given its prominent position in the debate, it is surprising to find that the WTO is one of the smallest international organizations in existence, employing a total of about 600 people.[16] The autonomy of the WTO secretariat as a policy entrepreneur—developing and selling policy ideas to its members—is severely limited, and its analytical capability is minimal compared to the IMF, the World Bank, and the OECD. Nonetheless, the WTO is an extremely efficient organization. Almost out of necessity, its governance style is knowledge-intensive and expert-orientated. Its organizational resources, however, remain very limited. This is increasingly problematic. For instance, WTO officials are supposed to provide special advice to developing-country delegations during negotiations and to offer legal expertise to LDCs in the dispute settlement system. Yet, the secretariat is barely able to fulfill its mandate with so few resources. Despite recent efforts to provide technical assistance to developing members, the minimal size of the WTO prevents a restructuring of the governance process. Without reallocation of resources, the multilateral qualities of WTO governance are overshadowed by the unbalanced distribution of knowledge and expertise among WTO governments.

WTO Dispute Settlement: Self-sustained Polity Construction

States have not withered away in WTO governance. WTO governments are the only lawmakers in the WTO Council. The expansion of the WTO has resulted in an extension of the domain of trade diplomats to new areas of globalization. Yet, it is important to acknowledge that the WTO is engaged in a process of what can be termed 'self-sustained polity construction'.[17] One of the epicentres in this polity construction process is the dispute settlement system.

The five WTO cases listed in Table 2 were not only among the handful of 'headline-grabbing disputes' but also defining moments in the construction of a WTO polity. On each of these occasions, the WTO itself has redefined crucial aspects of WTO governance without political interference. Trade and environment disputes stand out as prominent examples of this. In the shrimp-turtle case, for instance, the WTO panel outlawed an American import ban on shrimp caught by a fishing method that minimized (but did not avoid) the accidental killing of sea turtles, which are recognized as near-extinct species by the Convention on International Trade in Endangered Species (CITES). The WTO panel repeated the notorious pro-trade logic of the 1992 tuna-dolphin case, namely that it was irrelevant whether the production method of an imported good was environmentally harmful since the GATT could not permit states to discriminate between identical end products. Moreover, it ruled that the GATT could not accept the extraterritorial reach of more stringent standards of pro-environmental governments.

This ruling provoked a public outcry. The developing world was nervous about 'green protectionism'. The Western public was concerned about the downgrading of environmental protection, a

Table 2: Important WTO Cases

Case	Period	Complainants vs Defendant	Outcome*
Shrimp-Sea Turtle (DS58)	Oct. 1996– Nov. 1998	India, Malaysia, Pakistan, Thailand vs US	US import ban on uncertified, turtle-unsafe shrimp imports overruled. Case resolved after appeal and re-examination.
Hormones (DS26, DS48)	Jan. 1996– July 1999	US & Canada vs EU	EU import ban on hormone-treated beef overruled. Case unresolved after appeals, re-examination, arbitration, and retaliations (US: $116.8 million; Canada: Can$113 million).
Asbestos (DS135)	May 1998– Apr. 2001	Canada vs EU	French import ban on white asbestos permitted. Case resolved after appeal.
Banana (DS16, DS27)	Sept. 1995– May 2000	Ecuador, Guatemala, Honduras, Mexico, Panama, US vs EU	EU banana import regime overruled. Case solved after appeals, re-examinations, arbitrations, and retaliations (US: $191.4 million; Ecuador: $201.6 million).
Foreign Sales Corporation (DS108)	Nov. 1997– May 2003	EU vs US	US tax exemptions to exporters overruled. Case currently unsolved after appeals, arbitration, and retaliations (EU: $4.01 billion).

*Figures in parentheses indicate amount of retaliation authorized.

'race to the bottom' in terms of environmental standards. The tension between market liberalization and environmental protection almost pushed the WTO to the verge of extinction. The Appellate Body was instrumental in defusing the crisis. In one of its most intelligent rulings, the Appellate Body managed to signal sympathy with the concerns of the developing world by reaffirming the illegality of the ban and at the same time indicated a 'greening' of the WTO by dismissing the legal analysis of the original panel report. Instead, the Appellate Body offered its own analysis of the meaning of Article XX. While confirming the legality of extraterritorial environmental laws, it also emphasized that the use of environmentally justified trade restrictions must meet 'the necessity test' as outlined in Article XX, which requires the use of the least restrictive policy

instruments and the conduct of 'good faith negotiations'. After a number of re-examinations and negotiations, the case was settled in November 2001. The greening of the WTO from within was confirmed in the asbestos case. For the first time the trading system dismissed a complaint against pro-environmental trade discrimination by supporting a French import ban on asbestos on the grounds that it constituted a scientifically proven health risk to workers and was necessary for effective protection of public health. The WTO clarified the meaning of its own law and offered a correct, authoritative interpretation of Article XX without consulting the 'lawmakers' in the WTO Ministerial Council.

Significantly, it was the WTO itself that tackled the contentious relationship between states and non-state actors in WTO governance. For instance, the asbestos case gave the Appellate Body an opportunity to define the scope of states' monopoly in WTO dispute settlement. It ruled that unrequested information provided by outsiders is permissible. The WTO itself—i.e., the panels and not the states—decides what information is to be included in a particular case. In the banana case, the Appellate Body permitted the smaller developing-country WTO members to be represented by hired, non-governmental lawyers and overturned the panel ruling. Despite these clarifications, the core principle is nonetheless that only states have the right to initiate cases in the WTO. Firms and NGOs must persuade governments to launch a WTO case. Supranationalism in WTO governance has not made domestic politics irrelevant. On the contrary, access to the relevant sections of governments has become even more important.

The Privatization of WTO Governance: Dysfunctional WTO Retaliations

The legal system offers new avenues for private actors to pursue their commercial interests beyond the domestic scene. Influence on WTO governance requires extensive organizational resources and legal expertise. Similar to domestic legal systems, the 'rule of law' system in the WTO tends to favour the most resourceful actors. For instance, the power of the US farm lobby in Washington explains why the hormones dispute was pushed into the WTO. To US farmers the WTO offered additional access routes into the lucrative European market. The banana case is the best example of how firms have misused the WTO. The 'Big Three'—Chiquita International, Del Monte, and Dole—persuaded the US government to launch an attack on the cumbersome EU banana regime, which gave preferential access to otherwise uncompetitive African and Caribbean banana producers. Despite the fact that few bananas were produced within the US, the WTO offered a 'legitimate' venue for the Big Three to consolidate their dominance of the global banana market. Yet, the strategy was flawed. In theory, the WTO ruling should have defused a transatlantic

trade war and enabled the European pro-traders to bypass special interests in a much needed reform of a failed policy experiment. Although the WTO outlawed the EU regime, in particular the allocation of import permissions, the process escalated the trade war and actually prolonged the EU reform of the banana regime.

Whereas GATT dispute settlement relied on diplomacy, the WTO uses sanctions. The dramatic surge in WTO retaliations is hardly surprising. The hormones and banana cases were the first to use the ultimate weapon of WTO governance. After seven cases in which retaliation was employed, its usefulness started to be called into question. Evidence suggests that WTO retaliations are dysfunctional. For example, it took more than six years to resolve the banana war. The hormones case, in which the WTO outlawed a European Union ban on imported hormone-treated beef, remains as explosive as ever. Part of the explanation is found in the 'retaliatory merger' of the hormones and banana cases. The legalist strategy of the United States made the US Trade Representative misread the political game in the European Union. The retaliatory merger prevented the Northern European pro-traders on the banana issue, led by Germany and Britain, from putting the Southern Europeans, led by France, on the defensive in terms of the reform of the regime covering banana imports. Germany and Britain were strong defenders of the precautionary EU approach on the hormones issues, especially in the wake of the outbreak of bovine spongiform encephalopathy (BSE) in Britain.

The Americans also misread the political game by inventing a new trade weapon, the 'carousel retaliations'. By rotating the list of targeted EU products on a six-month basis, the intention was to multiply the pressure on the EU but it merely escalated the trade war. The EU launched a counter-complaint on the legality of the carousel method, which the WTO later deemed 'potentially WTO inconsistent'. To make matters worse, the target list was designed to maximize political pressure on EU decision-makers. In response to the US targeting of French luxury goods like Louis Vuitton bags and bottled Evian water, the French rallied behind the flag in spectacular defiance of American bullying. As a result, the room for compromise narrowed considerably. Moreover, many US importers were contractually obliged to import the targeted EU products. The costs of WTO retaliations were therefore passed on to the American importers and consumers of European luxury goods. WTO retaliations are extremely blunt instruments of trade governance in a global economy.

Yet, darker clouds are gathering on the horizon. The foreign sales corporation (FSC) case, in which the EU successfully challenged a US tax law providing corporations tax benefits for their export earnings, is especially dangerous for the WTO. Robert Zoellick described it as 'a nuclear bomb' in the WTO. In terms of transatlantic trade, the size of the hormones and banana retaliations are barely noticeable. In the FSC case, however, the EU is permitted to retaliate to the tune of US$4 billion annually, roughly about 1 per cent of total transatlantic trade. The frequency of WTO litigation and retaliations is an alarming tendency. Given the intensity of recent trade wars, it is not unconceivable that perhaps 5–10 per cent of future transatlantic trade could be affected by WTO retaliations. This strongly suggests that the WTO should abandon its retaliatory approach and force the violators to open up their markets instead. Or perhaps offenders should pay compensation to the violated government or directly to a global development fund.

It could be argued that the speedy diffusion of the 'Steel War' of autumn 2003 indicates that the sharper teeth of WTO governance have begun to bite. Yet, the analysis of earlier WTO retaliations offered here suggests quite the opposite. Retaliations are blunt instruments that solidify defiance rather than promote conciliation. Whereas threats of WTO retaliations are generally constructive, the execution of WTO retaliations tends to be counterproductive.

Conclusions: Decoupling Society-based Authority from Market-based Authority

A deep-rooted crisis in WTO governance has become increasingly evident. The hardening of WTO governance, resulting in numerous high-profile trade disputes, seems to have ignited resistance within states, among states, and beyond states. The seeds of counter-hegemonic resistance scattered in Seattle and Cancun exemplify the potential of societal resistance to unregulated, neo-liberal globalization. The higher visibility of the WTO itself has multiplied such public discontent. It is increasingly held accountable for the evils of globalization. The legalization of WTO governance is partly responsible for this. The outbreak of WTO trade wars has mobilized political resistance across a broader segment of society so that, within societies and across boundaries, the legitimacy of WTO governance is being questioned. Still, the WTO members are ultimately responsible for this situation. Only states can ignite new trade wars. Only states can update the compromise of embedded liberalism. Only states can remedy the imperfections in WTO governance.

The WTO crisis is rooted in the decoupling of society-based authority from market-based authority. It has little to do with the expanded membership of the WTO. Rather, the WTO offers the only platform for effective multilateral trade governance. It presents itself as a realistic alternative to unregulated globalization. On its 10-year anniversary, the WTO deserves at least some credit for its contribution to more legitimate governance of globalization, regardless of its current imperfections. Yet, it has been pushed in a dangerous direction by political and private misuse of its unique powers in global economic governance.

Notes

1. Susan Strange, *The Retreat of the State* (Cambridge: Cambridge University Press, 1997), 183.

2. See John H. Jackson, *The World Trade Organization: Constitution and Jurisprudence* (London: Pinter, 1997).

3. See, e.g., Robert Gilpin, *Global Political Economy: Understanding the International Economic Order* (Princeton, NJ: Princeton University Press, 2001).

4. See Ernst-Ulrich Petersmann, *The GATT/WTO Dispute Settlement System: International Law, International Organisations and Dispute Settlement* (The Hague: Kluwer Law, 1997).

5. Stephen Gill, 'Globalisation, Market Civilisation, and Disciplinary Neoliberalism', *Millennium* 24, 3 (1993): 399–424; A. Claire Cutler, *Private Power and Global Authority: Transnational Merchant Law in Global Political Economy* (Cambridge: Cambridge University Press, 2003).

6. Karl Polanyi, *The Great Transformation: The Political and Economic Origins of Our Time* (Boston: Beacon Hill Press, 1957 [1944]).

7. John G. Ruggie, 'International Regimes, Transactions, and Change: Embedded Liberalism in the Postwar Economic Order', *International Organization* 36, 2 (1982): 195–231; John G. Ruggie, 'At Home Abroad, Abroad at Home: International Liberalisation and Domestic Stability in the New World Economy', *Millennium* 24, 3 (1995): 507–26.

8. The GATT was only one element in the broader compromise reached at the Bretton Woods conference in 1944 between economic liberalists and social-liberal interventionists. In its entirety, the Bretton Woods compromise, which also entailed the establishment of the World Bank and the IMF, was an attempt to balance international market liberalization, as advocated by the classical liberalism of Adam Smith, with the Keynesian objective of full employment following extensive government intervention in the domestic economy.

9. GATT Article I obliges WTO members not to discriminate against each other and to extend trade concessions granted to one nation (most-favoured-nation status) to all WTO members. GATT Article III obliges WTO members to treat foreign-produced imports identically to domestically produced goods.

10. Neo-liberals call for more 'realistic' and 'efficient' WTO procedures, arguing that equality and consensus in WTO decision-making endanger trade liberalization. See, e.g., Razeen Sally, 'Who Will Put the WTO Humpty Dumpty Back Together?', *The Financial Express*, 1 Dec. 2003. Pascal Lamy, the EU Trade Commissioner, echoed such criticism after Cancun by calling the WTO 'a medieval organization'. Pascal Lamy, 'Brussels Urges Shakeup of "Medieval" WTO', *The Guardian*, 16 Sept. 2003.

11. See Susan K. Sell, *Private Power, Public Law: The Globalization of Intellectual Property Rights* (Cambridge: Cambridge University Press, 2003); Peter Drahos and Ruth Mayne, *Global Intellectual Property Rights: Knowledge, Access and Development* (Basingstoke: Palgrave/Oxfam, 2002).

12. Establishing the 'Singapore issues' was an attempt to further the deepening of WTO law by including issues of investment, competition, and transparency in government procurement and trade facilitation on the Doha agenda. The framework agreement of July 2004 eliminated all of these except 'trade facilitation', that is, the streamlining of custom rules and practice, from the agenda. The other items remaining on the Doha agenda are agriculture, non-agricultural market access, development issues, and services. See 'Doha Work Programme', WTO document WT/L/579.

13. US diplomacy resisted the WTO proposals to the last minute, preferring a less sovereign-intrusive version of GATT legalism. For details, see Jens L. Mortensen, WTO, *Governance and the Limits of Law* (London: Routledge, forthcoming).

14. From 'WTO disputes overtake 300 mark', WTO

press release 353, 11 Sept. 2003.

15. By September 2003, the US had launched 75 complaints and been subject to 81 complaints. The EU had launched 62 complaints and defended itself in 58 cases. Other active WTO complainants are: Brazil (22), India (15), Japan (11), Mexico (13), Argentina (9), Turkey (9), Thailand and Korea (both 10), Philippines (8), Hungary, Guatemala, Australia (7 each), Indonesia and Peru (both 6).

16. In 2003, the World Bank employed about 10,000 people, the IMF employed about 2,900, and the OECD employed about 2,300.

17. See Alec Stone Sweet, 'Judicialization and the Construction of Governance', *Comparative Political Studies*, 32, 2 (1998): 147–84

Suggested Readings

Gilpin, Robert. *Global Political Economy: Understanding the International Economic Order*. Princeton, NJ: Princeton University Press, 2001.

Held, David, and Anthony McGrew. *Governing Globalization: Power, Authority and Global Governance*. Cambridge: Polity Press, 2002.

Hoekman, Bernard M., and Michel M. Kostecki. *The Political Economy of the World Trading System: The WTO and Beyond*, 2nd edn. Oxford: Oxford University Press, 2001.

Ruggie, John Gerard. *Constructing the World Polity: Essays on International Institutionalization*. London: Routledge, 1998.

Trebilcock, Michael J., and Robert Howse. *The Regulation of International Trade*, 2nd edn. London: Routledge, 1999.

Wallach, Lori, and Patrick Woodall. *Whose Trade Organization? A Comprehensive Guide to the WTO*. New York: New Press, 2004.

Web Sites

European Union:
  europa.eu.int/pol/comm/index_en.htm
International Centre for Trade and Sustainable Development: www.ictsd.org

Third World Network: www.twnside.org.sg
United States Trade Representative: www.ustr.gov
World trade law: www.worldtradelaw.net

Chapter 12

Big Business, the WTO, and Development
Uruguay and Beyond

Susan K. Sell

The establishment of the World Trade Organization has altered the global trading regime in profound and interesting ways.[1] The Uruguay Round of multilateral trade negotiations (1986–93) led to the creation of the WTO. This round ushered in a new era in multilateral trade policy by dramatically expanding the scope of disciplines covered and strengthening the dispute resolution mechanisms. For the first time, the multilateral agreements explicitly incorporated intellectual property, investment, and services (such as financial services, insurance, and accounting). The dispute settlement mechanisms of the WTO altered the multilateral global trading regime from a power-based bargaining system to a more rule-based system.[2] This chapter examines the driving forces behind the new issues, and developments in the wake of the Uruguay Round that have challenged the most powerful actors in unexpected ways.

The failure of the 1999 Seattle WTO Ministerial meeting, the promise of the launching of a new trade round at Doha in November 2001, and the acrimonious conclusion to the September 2003 Cancun Ministerial meeting underscore an important and irreversible trend. As first provocatively demonstrated in Seattle, the WTO is under extensive pressure from non-governmental organizations (NGOs) and civil society. Developing countries also have emerged as a force to be reckoned with. Their 'insistence on meaningful participation—and willingness to block progress until this demand is satisfied—marks a sea change from earlier periods of GATT history.'[3] Trade policy-making is no longer the cosy prerogative of policy elites and trade ministers

from the OECD, but has become 'a high-profile enterprise'.[4] Finally, while powerful multinational corporations pushed hard for an effective dispute settlement system, the rules-based and enforceable WTO system has provided developing countries with new options. For example, Brazil successfully has challenged US cotton subsidy policies as being inconsistent with WTO obligations.[5]

However, like a beginner paddling a canoe, the trade regime's post-Uruguay Round trajectory has veered back and forth in wildly conflicting directions. Analytically, this pattern may be understood through the concept of structured agency. Structured agency underscores the fact that agents act in circumstances not of their own making. For instance, the private-sector agents who lobbied for the new issues in the Uruguay Round were embedded in a broader set of structures such as global capitalism and the distribution of power across nations. In simple terms, structures may be seen as material and social 'hard facts' that provide constraints and opportunities for action. While agency, i.e., voluntary choice to pursue a certain course of action, is an important driver of change it is 'ever trammelled by past structural and cultural constraints and by the current politics of the possible'.[6] While structures may well be socially constructed, what at one time is a social construction later becomes a structure that agents confront and may seek to preserve or change.

The notion of structured agency assumes that structure and ideas, like tectonic plates, can move in independent rhythms. They need not, but they can. Rather than positing some necessary relation-

ship between the two, stressing the inherent predominance of one over the other, this perspective
encourages analysts to examine, *not assume*, the
relationship between material factors and ideas
(structures and agents). Both neo-Gramscian
scholars and constructivists in various ways seek
to integrate the two. Invariably, the former emphasize the predominance of material factors (while
acknowledging the centrality of ideas)[7] or 'the
material structure of ideas'.[8] The latter emphasize
the importance of norms (while acknowledging
the broader context).[9] A neo-Gramscian account
of the global trade regime would emphasize structural factors, the power of transnational capital in
leading sectors. It would analyze those challenging the WTO for their potential to be 'organic intellectuals' to launch a counter-hegemonic movement. By contrast, the approach presented here
incorporates agency and the difference it makes
rather more. An examination of the variation in
outcomes in the new issues in the WTO and the
chequered post-Uruguay trajectory reveals that
agency matters.

A constructivist account of these same events
would emphasize the activities of 'norm entrepreneurs' and the skill of the agents in deploying
norms and discourse to effect change. The constructivist assessment of changes in the global trade
regime would focus on the transnational mobilization of NGOs and developing countries to bring
moral pressure to bear on the United States to
change its policies and practices.[10] Constructivist
accounts tend to leave out structural power and
minimize the role of material, structural constraints
and opportunities. Skills of agents are embedded in
broader and deeper structures. By overemphasizing
voluntarism and efficacy, many constructivists
obscure the fact that successful agents are those
who take advantage of contingent structural constraints and opportunities.

This chapter first compares the variable success of private-sector actors in incorporating new
subject matter into the global trade regime in the
Uruguay Round and further explores the concept
of structured agency by examining tensions
between development needs and the preferences of

big business. It highlights the efforts of NGOs and
developing countries to promote social goals, most
notably public health, through the trade regime.
The resolution of the tensions between commercial
and social agendas, between the more powerful
and the weaker parties, has not uniformly favoured
powerful states and commercial interests at the
expense of the weak. While a focus on structure
inspires caution, agency can make a difference.

The Difference That Agency Makes: Big Business and the Uruguay Agreements

US private-sector actors were the driving forces
behind the Agreement on Trade-Related Aspects of
Intellectual Property Rights (TRIPS), the financial
services agreement, the General Agreement on
Trade in Services (GATS), and trade-related investment measures (TRIMS). Structural changes in the
global political economy, changes in technology
and markets, have empowered a new set of actors
pushing for greater liberalization in investment and
services and stronger intellectual property protection. These actors represent the most globally competitive industries and the strongest transnational
corporate players. In services and intellectual property protection, the US government responded to a
sustained, decades-long effort of private-sector
actors to link these issues to trade. These actors
succeeded in getting recognition for this linkage in
amendments to US trade laws in the 1970s and
1980s, and the United States Trade Representative
(USTR) pursued their goals by threatening trade
sanctions against countries whose policies the US
did not like. These agreements would not exist
without the private-sector efforts. However, despite
these common origins, the outcomes of their multilateral quests were varied.

Agreements are authoritative if parties regard
them as binding and the agreements alter outcomes
for others.[11] Placing these agreements—TRIPS, the
agreement on financial services, GATS, and TRIMS—
on a spectrum, the TRIPS and the financial services
agreements are the most authoritative, the GATS is
in the middle, and the TRIMS agreement is the least

authoritative. Decisive factors leading to the TRIPS and financial services agreements were transnational private-sector mobilization of an OECD consensus, along with the absence of sustained opposition. By contrast, in the weaker agreements, GATS and TRIMS, there was considerable transnational private-sector mobilization but no OECD consensus, and sustained opposition. The TRIMS agreement was further stymied by two additional factors—substantial host-country bargaining power and US government opposition to the private sector's goals on the grounds of national security.

These agreements are a product of structured agency. Changes in technologies and markets have empowered actors who are pushing for greater liberalization in investment and services and greater protection of intellectual property (such as patents, trademarks, and copyright). While the old General Agreement on Tariffs and Trade (GATT) traditionally focused on trade in goods, today services and investment have become among the most dynamic areas of the global economy. During the Uruguay Round negotiations (1986–93) services trade grew at an annual average rate of 8.3 per cent.[12] Throughout the 1980s services trade grew faster than trade in goods. By 1993 global services trade amounted to US$930 billion, equalling 22 per cent of global trade (goods plus services).[13] Similarly in investment, between 1985 and 1995 the annual global flow of foreign direct investment rose from $60 billion to $315 billion; in 1993 sales by foreign affiliates were estimated at $6 trillion, well above the total world trade in goods and services ($4.7 trillion).[14]

The GATT's success in cutting tariffs and reducing border impediments over successive negotiating rounds has led negotiators to address inside-the-border, or structural, impediments and non-tariff measures that distort free trade. These measures implicate domestic regulatory policy, fundamentally challenging states' policy-making discretion. Issues such as market access, rights of establishment for foreign enterprises, and the protection of intellectual property rights reach much deeper into state policies than previous GATT issues. The United States pushed hardest for the inclusion of services, intellectual property protection, and a revamped dispute settlement mechanism.

Intellectual Property Protection

As technological prowess has become diffused throughout the global economy, certain technologies have become relatively easy and cheap to appropriate. Computer software and digital audio and visual recordings are just three of the more glaring examples. American-based firms have comparative advantage in these products, but felt that they would lose that advantage without government help in prompting other countries to protect US-held intellectual property.

First, acting through industry associations, American firms urged the government to pressure foreign governments to adopt and enforce more stringent intellectual property protection. They sought and won changes in US domestic laws, most notably Sections 301 and 337 of the US trade laws, to facilitate the use of US economic leverage to secure desired results. A handful of US-based transnational corporations formed the Intellectual Property Committee[15] in March 1986 and spearheaded the effort to secure a multilateral instrument codifying their interest in stricter intellectual property protection. The IPC lobbied the US government to support and promote a multilateral intellectual property instrument through GATT. Transnationally, the IPC member executives directly engaged their European and Japanese counterparts to press for TRIPS in the GATT. The IPC succeeded in forging an industry consensus with its European and Japanese counterparts. By the launch of the Uruguay Round, the US, Europe, and Japan all favoured an intellectual property code in the GATT. The transnational leadership of the IPC was crucial for the achievement of TRIPS.

Industry representatives met in October and November 1986 to prepare a consensus document. By June 1988 this trilateral group released its 'Basic Framework of GATT Provisions on Intellectual Property'. The IPC and its European and Japanese private-sector counterparts went home to sell this proposal to other companies and industries. The

US government requested 100–50 copies of the June 1988 proposal and sent it out as reflecting its views.[16] By 1994 the IPC had achieved 95 per cent of what it wanted.[17]

The 1994 TRIPS agreement codifies a trade-based approach to intellectual property rights. It requires signatory states to enact implementing legislation, adopt enforcement measures, provide intellectual property owners with a 20-year monopoly right, and face the threat of trade sanctions if they fail to comply with TRIPS provisions. This approach privileges property creation over diffusion, raises the price of information and technology by extending monopoly privileges of rights holders, and requires states to play an active role in defending them. While the long-term redistributive implications of TRIPS are not yet fully understood, the short-term impact undoubtedly will be a significant transfer of resources from developing-country consumers and firms to firms based in industrialized countries.[18] The World Bank has estimated that TRIPS should yield an annual $19 billion for the United States, whereas South Korea would sustain the largest loss—$15 billion.[19] In short, it represents a decisive triumph for private-sector interests.

Initially, developing countries resisted the inclusion of intellectual property in the negotiations, but by April 1989 they had dropped their opposition. Having faced escalating US aggressive unilateralism, they hoped that co-operation on TRIPS would ease this pressure. Further, they were willing to go along with TRIPS in exchange for concessions on issues such as agriculture and the phasing out of the Multifibre Arrangements.

General Agreement on Trade in Services

The spectacular growth of global trade in services and intensified competition in large markets have sharpened concerns over differences in domestic regulatory policy. Activist private-sector service providers sought expanded market access and the elimination of domestic regulations and practices that interfere with free trade. Unlike trade in goods, many services depend on the proximity of the provider and consumer; services trade often requires international direct investment to establish offices in host countries. Accounting for 60 per cent of world consumption, services make up only 20 per cent of world trade;[20] this discrepancy highlights the pervasiveness of domestic impediments facing foreign services providers.

US private-sector actors sought significant liberalization of foreign services markets. Beginning in the 1970s, the financial services sector, led by American Express and American International Group, 'invented the term "trade in services" with the intention of bringing investment within the framework of multilateral trade rules'[21] and to remove barriers to market access. Like the intellectual property lobby, private-sector services activists convinced the US government to incorporate services in revisions to its trade laws, and the United States pursued Section 301 actions against Europe and Japan for barriers to services trade. US private-sector lobbyists touted US services surpluses as part of the solution to the trade deficit problem, and the USTR and Treasury came to champion their cause. Over time additional support came from the Coalition of Service Industries. Its primary targets were highly regulated Asian service markets. Developing countries, led by India and Brazil, protested the inclusion of services in the Uruguay Round but agreed to negotiate a separate services agreement.

To the extent that GATS exists at all, the private sector won an important victory, but the private sector was disappointed with the results. First, the US private-sector lobbyists favoured, yet failed to achieve, an ambitiously liberalizing agreement, meeting with opposition from both developing countries and the Europeans. Second, GATS is weak, and codifies significant derogations from the GATT treatment of trade in goods. For example, GATS dilutes the twin pillars of non-discrimination—the GATT principles of most-favoured-nation status (MFN) and national treatment. GATS signatories are free to include a list of sectors in an Annex, to which MFN will not apply (the 'negative list' approach). Service providers in relatively open markets pressed for the MFN exemption out of concern that competitors based in sheltered markets would be able to free-ride on the agreements.[22] In a perfect world, US service providers preferred extensive market access; short of that, their fallback position was to reserve the right to deny insufficiently open countries MFN treatment. Since GATS failed to open foreign markets to their satisfaction, US private-sector interests sought to maintain negotiating leverage by invoking sectoral (or mirror-image) reciprocity—withholding MFN privileges from those competitors in restricted markets. Third, the national treatment commitment was also watered down through a 'positive list' approach in which national treatment applies only to those sectors listed in a member's schedule of commitments.[23] As Low and Subramanian point out, 'national treatment has been transformed from a principle into negotiating currency under GATS.'[24] Thus, GATS only partly reflects the goals of the private sector; it is 'second best', and is a substantially weaker agreement than TRIPS. It is essentially a standstill on existing restrictions in various services sectors—there was no significant rolling back of barriers to services trade.

Financial Services Agreement

Throughout the course of the GATS negotiations, negotiators realized that the financial services sector was proving to be exceptionally contentious, and participants agreed to negotiate basic principles plus a separate agreement after the conclusion of the Uruguay Round. Asian countries' reluctance to open their financial services markets became a major sticking point. Frustrated by the lack of progress at the end of 1995, the US delegation, prompted by its domestic industry, walked out. Two significant developments between 1995 and December 1997 turned the tide in favour of a strong multilateral agreement on financial services. The first factor was the leadership of the EU; second, the Asian currency crisis pushed countries towards an agreement.

In 1995 the EU 'rallied other WTO members' and negotiated an interim agreement without the United States.[25] Between 1995 and 1997 the EU assumed

leadership within the deliberations and worked hard to secure improvements in member states' commitments and to get the United States back on board. At the Global Economic Forum in Davos, Switzerland, in early 1996, transnational private-sector mobilization began in earnest. After the Davos meeting, US, UK, and European financial services industry representatives met at the office of British Invisibles and formed the Financial Leaders Group (FLG) to present a unified business view of objectives in the financial services deliberations. The FLG largely reflected UK and US views, but substantially broadened its base of support and made significant progress in identifying common ground.

Back in 1995 the US was particularly frustrated with the lack of market access commitments from East Asian and Southeast Asian countries. However, the currency crisis that erupted in Asia in July 1997 provided an unexpected boost to open Asian financial services markets that were recalcitrant targets of Uruguay Round talks. OECD governments and the International Monetary Fund urged affected countries to adopt market-opening measures to inspire 'investor confidence', and the crisis spurred a conclusion to the financial services negotiations. US negotiators were sufficiently satisfied with the improved market-opening commitments and withdrew broad MFN exemptions based on reciprocity. American private-sector representatives of Citicorp, Goldman Sachs, Merrill Lynch, and insurance industries set up command posts near the WTO and conferred with American negotiators throughout this last round of talks.[26] Negotiators reached an eleventh-hour agreement in Geneva on 13 December 1997. The vice-chairman of Salomon Brothers International said the agreement 'will go some way to lock in a trend that was already in effect in the world toward liberalization. . . . It's like an insurance policy for the structure of the world.'[27]

Trade-Related Investment Measures

Foreign direct investment (FDI) grew dramatically in the 1980s and 1990s. US private-sector activists also spearheaded the TRIMS effort, but in this instance they were stymied by a complex array of factors: developing countries' opposition; host-country market power; disagreements between OECD member states; and within the United States, disagreements between business and government. First, developing countries' opposition to the inclusion of investment issues led negotiators to address TRIMS on a separate track. Second, countries such as India and Brazil, with their large, relatively protected markets, possess considerable negotiating leverage vis-à-vis foreign investors. Third, fundamental disagreements among OECD members meant that the ultimate provisions were likely to be weak. The negotiating committee was committed to producing an agreement to which all nations could unanimously subscribe, so that only the 'most egregious of practices in clear violation of existing GATT articles'[28] were ultimately included. And fourth, the US private-sector activists found themselves at odds with the US government on security issues.

The US private sector lobbied on investment issues through the US Council for International Business (the American affiliate of the International Chamber of Commerce), the Coalition of Services Industries, and the Securities Industry Association.[29] TRIMS advocates sought non-discrimination, especially for rights of establishment, national treatment, and the elimination of trade-distorting investment measures (e.g., requirements mandating local content and subsidies for export performance). They sought to open the Japanese and East and Southeast Asian markets to foreign investment. European and Latin American markets already were comparatively liberal. At the outset of the negotiations, the US produced an ambitious agenda to create a GATT for investment. The United States, faced with stiff opposition from developing countries, 'conceded—for the sake of keeping TRIPS and services on the agenda—to a narrow mandate for the TRIPS negotiations'.[30]

Furthermore, many OECD states were reluctant to lock in liberalizing reforms under a multilateral instrument on investment. As Low and Subramanian suggest, 'doubts linger about how monopolistic MNE [multinational enterprise] behaviour might become in some circumstances,

and worries about sovereign control of resources also continue to cut political ice.'[31] The TRIMS agreement protects only the 'trade flows of investor-enterprises',[32] and affirms two GATT disciplines, national treatment and the prohibition of quantitative restrictions, for investment policies that directly affect trade flows. Signatories must notify the WTO secretariat of performance requirements such as local content and trade-balancing policies that are in violation of these GATT disciplines. Members are then bound to eliminate such measures within the grace periods (ranging from two to seven years depending on the country's level of development). Rather than representing a strong instrument for investment liberalization, in legal terms the TRIMS is 'retrograde, since it recognize[s] that countries were in violation of their GATT obligations, and then [gives] them time . . . within which to establish conformity'.[33] Significantly, the TRIMS agreement guarantees neither rights of establishment nor full national treatment for foreign investors. In addition, much to the dismay of the private-sector activists, export performance requirements were left untouched by the TRIMS agreement. Countries such as India have successfully reserved the right to require export performance of investors seeking entry into their large, sheltered markets. Host-country market power is an important factor militating against a strong investment agreement.[34]

The TRIMS negotiations revealed deep and intractable differences even among allegedly 'like-minded' states. While the UK, Germany, the Netherlands, and Japan were generally supportive of US aims, other OECD countries (France, Canada, Australia, New Zealand, and new members such as Mexico, South Korea, Poland, and the Czech Republic) were not. Furthermore, the US government opposed certain US business interests in the name of national security. The government defended its right to uphold the Helms-Burton Act prohibiting investment in Cuba, and the Iran-Libya Sanctions Act. The business community was deeply disappointed in the TRIMS negotiations; its initial enthusiasm waned as the process unfolded. It soon became apparent that the best they could

Table 1: Summary of the Cases: Private Power in Comparative Perspective

	Transnational Private-Sector Mobilization	Sustained Southern Opposition	OECD Consensus	US Firms/US State Consensus	Authoritative Outcome
TRIPS	Yes (IPC)	No	Yes	Yes	Yes
Financial Services	Yes (FLG)	No	Yes	Yes	Yes
GATS	Yes (IAS*)	Yes	No	Yes	Mixed
TRIMS	Yes (IAS)	Yes	No	No	No

*Industry associations.

hope for in the multilateral context was a 'lowest common denominator'[35] approach, which is exactly what they got.

TRIPS and the financial services agreement, as shown in Table 1, provide the strongest evidence that private-sector activists achieved their objectives. GATS presents a mixed picture: the private sector achieved some of its aims, but the final agreement fell well short of its liberalizing intentions by reserving a broad scope for state discretion. The TRIMS agreement is the weakest; the private sector failed to achieve its objectives and the weakness of the agreement does little in terms of redefining options for others.

Private-sector success in TRIPS was largely due to transnational mobilization, led by the IPC, to produce an OECD consensus on specific negotiating proposals and the lack of persistent opposition among OECD states. Similarly in financial services, transnational private-sector mobilization—this time led by British and European service providers—and the Asian financial crisis, which prompted eleventh-hour improved market access commitments, led to private-sector triumph. In the other cases the mobilization was pursued through more traditional channels, such as industry associations. Both the GATS and TRIMS deliberations revealed sharp differences among OECD countries in addition to differences between the OECD and developing countries. In the investment area, host-country market power and differences between the US private sector and

the US government on national security issues further reduced the prospects that the private sector would achieve its goals.

Overall, these comparisons should inspire caution about structural determinism. Broad claims about globalization, whether derived from economic liberalism or variants of Marxism, appear to be somewhat suspect in light of these findings. The variation in these cases points to the difference that agency makes. Structure played an important part in the negotiations as well. For example, in the TRIMS case, political debate within the US reflected conflicting imperatives between the security structure, on the one hand, and the production and finance structure, on the other. This reduced US government support for TRIMS. The most important structural feature in the TRIMS negotiations was the distribution of host-country market power. Those resisting TRIMS had significant leverage. Agency must be analyzed in its structured context.

Compliance, Legitimacy, the Quid Pro Quo, and the Backlash

The process of public law-making reverberates far beyond the final agreement. Many scholars assume that states sign treaties because they are mutually beneficial. Some compliance scholars of international law emphasize this perspective.[36] Examining international agreements as 'contracts' embodying reciprocal exchange implies that they leave 'everyone better off' and suggests that such agreements are substantively valid and based on consent.[37] The 'contract' story implies that consent begets legitimacy. However, states may co-operate based on shared interests, reciprocal exchange, or coercion.[38] States also may co-operate because they see no better choice when powerful states have unilaterally altered the status quo.[39] Indeed, in regard to intellectual property, developing countries realized that their choice was not between two multilateral venues, the World Intellectual Property Organization and GATT (the old status quo), but rather between GATT and aggressive unilateralism (US economic coercion). In the TRIPS case, the OECD countries and the developing countries did not share interests and make serious trade-offs. While issues were linked, the negotiations took place in a broader context of economic coercion and asymmetrical power.

This fact has become increasingly evident in the wake of the Uruguay Round. Several noteworthy trends reveal this imbalance. First, the OECD countries have pursued actions aggressively against developing countries in the WTO—particularly under the TRIPS agreement. Second, this aggressive approach has motivated an important backlash, particularly in the context of the HIV/AIDS pandemic and pharmaceuticals. Third, the failed promises of the quid pro quo have animated subsequent multilateral trade negotiations. There is no evidence that developed countries are making good on their commitments to open their markets more widely to developing countries' agricultural and textile exports. Fourth, developing countries have begun to challenge this failed bargain through the WTO. I will discuss each of these in turn.

TRIPS and Public Health

In the past, many countries chose not to offer patents for pharmaceuticals, in the interests of keeping down the costs of necessary medicines. The TRIPS agreement removed this option by requiring states to offer patent protection for pharmaceuticals and by sharply restricting the conditions under which compulsory licences could be grant-

ed. Many developing countries previously had adopted regulations stipulating that patents had to be 'worked' in their countries, and mere importation of a patented item did not satisfy the working requirement. The TRIPS agreement changed this as well, stipulating that importation 'counts' as working the patent. All these changes redounded to the benefit of the patent holder and reflected the interests of the powerful lobby of US-based global corporations that had worked so hard for TRIPS.

After the Uruguay Round, the corporations that had supported TRIPS pursued an aggressive campaign, with the help of the USTR, to ensure compliance with TRIPS, to speed its implementation prior to the negotiated deadlines, and in many cases to negotiate higher levels of property protection (known as 'TRIPS-Plus'). TRIPS-Plus refers to standards that either are more extensive than TRIPS standards or that eliminate options under TRIPS standards.[40] US bilateral investment treaties, bilateral intellectual property treaties, and regional trade agreements invariably are TRIPS-Plus. Economic coercion remains a viable tool for US policy-makers. The United States also has filed more WTO complaints involving intellectual property than all other member countries combined.

This aggressive campaign made headlines when the US pressured South Africa, ravaged by the HIV/AIDS pandemic, to revise its 1997 Medicines Act. This Act allowed revocation of patents on medicines to manufacture generic versions of HIV/AIDS drugs. Article 15c permitted parallel importing so that South Africa could import the cheapest available patented medicines. The US non-generic pharmaceutical industry was outraged and complained to the USTR, denouncing the South African Act. Subsequently, 39 members of the Pharmaceutical Manufacturers of South Africa (mainly local licensees of global pharmaceutical firms) filed a lawsuit challenging the Act's legality in Pretoria High Court.

Despite relentless pressure, South Africa refused to repeal its law and gained many health activist supporters in the process. A civil society 'access to medicines' campaign, spearheaded by consumer advocate Ralph Nader's Consumer

Project on Technology, Médecins Sans Frontières, Health Action International, and the AIDS Coalition to Unleash Power (ACT UP) mobilized protest against US government policy. ACT UP members targeted then Vice-President Al Gore's fledgling presidential campaign in the summer of 1999 and disrupted his early campaign appearances with noisemakers and banners that read 'Gore's Greed Kills'. Within one week of ACT UP's activities on the Gore campaign trail, the Clinton administration withdrew two years' worth of objections to the South African Medicines Act.[41] While the US government dropped its objections the American non-generic drug lobby, the Pharmaceutical Research and Manufacturers of America (PhRMA), continued to pursue legal action. After a barrage of extensive negative publicity, PhRMA ultimately dropped its legal case against South Africa in March 2001.

Brazil also exercised leadership in the access to medicines campaign. Brazil has provided anti-retroviral therapy free to HIV/AIDS patients as a matter of public policy. By producing and distributing generic HIV/AIDS drugs, Brazil has dramatically cut the rates of infection and death from HIV/AIDS. Brazil retained a 'working' requirement in its 1996 patent law that permits it to issue compulsory licences for goods that are not manufactured locally within three years of receiving patent protection. The threat of compulsory licensing has helped Brazil to negotiate steep discounts on patented HIV/AIDS drugs to keep these medicines affordable. The Brazilian government has stood firm in the face of US challenges. In February 2000, the USTR petitioned the opening of a WTO panel against Brazil for alleged violations of TRIPS. The Brazilian government mobilized extensive NGO support in defence of its policies and gained significant media attention.[42] Brazil's refusal to back down and the groundswell of support led the US ultimately to withdraw its case in June 2001.

The successes of the public health campaign catalyzed the formation of a developing-country bargaining coalition in the WTO to seek gains at the November 2001 Doha Ministerial.[43] The African Group, Brazil, and India were particularly active in this coalition. Throughout the summer of 2001, leading up to the launch of the Doha Round in Qatar, developing countries worked together to develop a consensus on a Declaration on TRIPS and Public Health. US actions against South Africa and Brazil had underscored the urgency of obtaining clarification about the scope of permissible measures to protect public health under TRIPS. The coalition maintained its unity, and agreed that its main goal was to achieve a declaration underscoring that TRIPS shall not prevent member states from taking steps to protect public health. The coalition made it clear that without such a declaration there would be nothing to discuss at Doha.

Just before the Doha meeting, the US was rocked by terrorist attacks on 11 September 2001 and an anthrax episode in October. Several postal and media workers had died from exposure to powdered anthrax spores sent through the mail. Not knowing the full scale of the anthrax threat, some US and Canadian leaders threatened to issue compulsory licences for Bayer's ciprofloxacine (Cipro) to ensure adequate supplies of the drug for treatment of anthrax. Ironically, the US was threatening to take the very steps for which it sought to punish Brazil and South Africa. The irony was lost on no one and it helped buttress support for the developing countries' public health coalition at Doha.

On the third day of the Doha Ministerial meeting, negotiators reached consensus on the Doha Declaration on TRIPS and Public Health affirming members' rights to issue compulsory licences and the freedom to determine grounds for such licences.[44] While the Declaration constitutes 'soft law', public health advocates are hopeful that it will guide panels in dispute settlement proceedings on TRIPS and public health.[45]

Public law is ultimately constructed. Law does not exist 'out there' or come down from on high. Further, by 'pigging out at the IP trough'[46] in the wake of TRIPS, the triumphant private-sector activists spawned social and political backlash. The truly important resisters of the TRIPS regime are those who see the grotesque nature of aspects of TRIPS and the heavy-handed TRIPS-Plus demands of the United States 'on the ground' in the HIV/AIDS pandemic. For them, resisting these demands truly is a matter of life and death.

Big Business versus the Development Agenda: The Singapore Issues and the Unfinished Business of the Uruguay Round

As discussed above, the Uruguay Round introduced a number of new disciplines that big business favoured. Pushed by the EU, the 1996 Singapore Ministerial Declaration mandated the creation of working groups to analyze four additional issues that big business promoted. The so-called Singapore issues are: investment, competition policy, transparency in government procurement, and trade facilitation. Developing countries have not been enthusiastic supporters of the Singapore issues for three main reasons. First of all, these issues seem to be of primary interest and importance to developed countries. Second, new issues require new implementation capacities that many countries lack. Third, and more importantly, developing countries resist an expanded negotiating agenda as long as the Uruguay promises remain unmet. Post-Uruguay trends have revealed a one-sided bargain in which developing countries are pressured to uphold their commitments in the new issue-areas while developed countries fail to fulfill their side of the bargain. Developing countries are 'apprehensive over the "intrusiveness" of new rules'.[47] Until developed countries make good on their agriculture and textile market access commitments—the quid pro quo of the contract story—developing countries will not support WTO incorporation of the Singapore issues.

The unfulfilled promises of the Uruguay deal have led the developing countries to press hard for market access in agriculture. The developing countries' concerns about retaining policy-making flexibility also animate their negotiating stance. While some elements of the Singapore issues may be substantively acceptable, developing countries 'have queried the appropriateness of the WTO as a forum because of power asymmetries among Members,

including with regard to enforcement obligations.'[48] At the end of the Doha Ministerial meeting negotiators struck a new bargain. 'In return for agreeing to a stronger mandate for post-Doha agricultural negotiations, the EU (European Union) and others managed to secure a conditional—but only conditional—negotiating track for the "Singapore issues".'[49]

The Cancun Ministerial Conference in September 2003 was to advance the Doha Development Agenda. Instead, it fell apart in an acrimonious stalemate. As Pascal Lamy, the EU Trade Commissioner, stated, 'I do not want to beat around the bush: Cancun has failed.'[50] Inspired by the negotiating tactics of the public health advocates, developing countries negotiated as the G-21 group. This coalition of mid-sized and small developing countries acted as a veto coalition to block consensus on a framework to conclude negotiations by 2005. Speaking on behalf of the G-21, Brazilian Foreign Minister Celso Amorim, who had been active in the public health coalition in Doha, declared the Cancun conference to be a '"political victory" for developing countries that showed unity in pressing their demands'.[51] The G-21 opposed OECD agricultural subsidies and singled out developed-country cotton policies as particularly egregious and damaging to West African cotton growers. The Europeans and Japanese insisted on including the Singapore issues despite G-21 protests. Less-developed countries refused to pledge to lower their tariffs, much to the chagrin of US negotiators. There was plenty of blame to go around and much angry finger pointing.

While the USTR predictably criticized the G-21 tactics, and it certainly is true that developing countries tend to do better in the multilateral WTO setting than in bilateral and regional negotiations, it is not clear that the G-21 has hurt itself by playing hardball at Cancun. Post-Cancun developments suggest that there may be opportunities to advance developing countries' interests in efforts to keep the Doha Round alive. In May 2004, Pascal Lamy and Franz Fischler[52] wrote a letter to all WTO members pledging the EU's willingness to drop the most contentious Singapore issues (investment, competition policy, and transparency in government procurement).[53] Their letter reflected a widespread consensus that without forward movement on agriculture there will be little to discuss. Negotiators are taking developing countries' demands for agricultural market access seriously. Does this trend vindicate the G-21's tactics at Cancun? It clearly is too soon to tell whether its negotiating strategy has backfired, as suggested by critics.[54] In the contest between big business and development agendas, however, this progress on the European front suggests at least a temporary retreat from the business agenda.

Using the Rules: Brazil and US Cotton Subsidies

When the WTO was established, many praised it as ushering in a new era of rules-based (versus bargaining-based) multilateral trade governance. The rules were there for everyone to use. Ten years after the establishment of the WTO, it appears that a developing country has used the rules to its advantage in a very consequential decision. Brazil requested the opening of a WTO panel to investigate US cotton subsidies, arguing that the subsidies were a barrier to fair trade competition and market access. In an April 2004 preliminary panel report, the WTO ruled in Brazil's favour.[55] The report supported the view that in the case of cotton, northern subsidies cause low international prices and unfair competition. 'In its victorious claim against US cotton subsidies, Brazil showed that eliminating subsidies would reduce US production 29 per cent, US exports 41 per cent, and this would lead to a rise in international prices of 13 per cent.'[56] 'The panel found that US payments had indeed caused serious prejudice to the interests of Brazilian producers by suppressing cotton prices.'[57] Brazil's Foreign Minister, Celso Amorim, underscored that the ruling would be 'very important for the future of the Doha Round'.[58] The WTO panel report is a significant example of the promise of a rules-based system for traditionally weaker

actors. Brazil's leadership in pressing its case and winning may inspire other developing countries to pursue their interests through the WTO dispute settlement mechanism.[59]

Conclusion

This first decade of the WTO has revealed escalating tension between big business and development agendas. While the business agenda dominated the Uruguay Round and Singapore Ministerial, subsequent negotiations have challenged that agenda. Developing countries and NGOs have publicized the perceived shortcomings of the WTO in negotiations, in the media, and in public protests such as in Seattle. To the extent that this challenge has been effective, and the jury is still out, it highlights the importance of agency in shaping the politics of the global trade regime. However, this agency is embedded in broader and deeper structures characterized by glaring power asymmetries. The complexity of contemporary multi-level governance privileges the structurally powerful in important ways. For example, the business agenda is alive and well and proceeding apace through US bilateral and regional trade agreements.[60] Developing countries' gains at the multilateral level quickly can be undone at regional and bilateral levels. The transactions costs are high for resource-poor developing countries to keep abreast of the barrage of trade policy rule-making at multiple levels.

Structured agency recognizes the way that structural factors condition agency, by examining the way that structure identifies and creates agents and distributes resources of 'vested interests and bargaining power'.[61] Social interaction—the role of agency—may result in structural change, depending on 'how (or whether) bargaining power is converted into negotiating strength between . . . agents'.[62] Change or stasis arises from social interaction, i.e., bargaining, but is not reducible to it because all agency is structured.[63]

Power alone does not determine outcomes. Structural power and agency are not logically dependent on one another; their relationship is contingent.[64] For example, contingency and unintended consequences played a role in the TRIPS and public health debate. Immediately after TRIPS, an unintended consequence of the TRIPS architects' success and vigorous prosecution of perceived wrongdoing was the emergence of a robust opposition campaign. The HIV/AIDS pandemic was a contingency that sped up the revelation of the negative consequences of TRIPS. The battle over TRIPS and public health is a good test case of effective advoca-cy without obvious economic (structural) power.

Politics lies at the heart of this analysis of the global trade regime. Who gets what, why, when, and where? The chequered course of the post-Uruguay trade regime demonstrates that a much broader range of stakeholders is shaping trade policy. The contest between the business and development agendas will continue to animate the evolution of the global trade regime.

Notes

1. I would like to thank Christopher May, John Odell, James McCall Smith, Geoffrey Underhill, Andrew Walter, and Stephen Woolcock for helpful comments and insights.

2. See 'Legalization and World Politics', special issue of *International Organization* 55, 2 (Spring 2001).

3. Jeffrey Dunoff, 'The WTO in Transition: Of Constituents, Competence and Coherence', *George Washington International Law Review* 33, 3 and 4 (2001): 983.

4. Ibid., 1007.

5. International Centre for Trade and Sustainable Development, *Bridges* 8, 5 (May 2004): 7.

6. Margaret Archer, 'Morphogenesis versus Structuration: On Combining Structure and Action', *British Journal of Sociology* 33, 4 (Dec. 1982): 470

7. Andreas Bieler and Andrew Morton, 'The Gordian Knot of Agency-Structure in International Relations: A Neo-Gramscian Perspective', *European Journal of International Relations* 7, 1 (2001): 24–5.

8. Andreas Bieler, 'Questioning Cognitivism and Constructivism in International Relations Theory: Reflections on the Material Structure of Ideas', *Politics* 21, 2 (2001): 94.

9. Audie Klotz, *Norms in International Relations: The Struggle Against Apartheid* (Ithaca, NY: Cornell University Press, 1995), 167–8.

10. Margaret Keck and Kathryn Sikkink, *Activists Beyond Borders* (Ithaca, NY: Cornell University Press, 1998).

11. Susan Strange, *The Retreat of the State* (Cambridge: Cambridge University Press, 1996), 184.

12. Bernard Hoekman, 'Assessing the General Agreement on Trade in Services', in Will Martin and L. Alan Winters, eds, *The Uruguay Round and the Developing Economies* (Washington: World Bank, 1995), 329.

13. Bernard Hoekman and Michel Kostecki, *The Political Economy of the World Trading System: From GATT to WTO* (Oxford: Oxford University Press, 1995), 127.

14. Andrew Walter, 'Globalization and Corporate Power: Who Is Setting the Rules on International Direct Investment?', paper prepared for the conference on Non-State Actors and Authority in the Global System, 31 Oct.–1 Nov. 1997, 1.

15. In 1986 the IPC represented: Bristol-Myers Squibb; Digital Equipment Corporation; FCM; General Electric; Hewlett-Packard; IBM; Johnson & Johnson; Merck; Pfizer; Procter & Gamble; Rockwell International; and Time-Warner.

16. Author's interview with Jacques Gorlin, adviser to the IPC, 22 Jan. 1996, Washington, DC.

17. Ibid.

18. Dani Rodrik, 'Comments on Maskus and Eby-Konan', in A. Deardorff and R. Stern, eds, *Analytic and Negotiating Issues in the Global Trading System* (Ann Arbor: University of Michigan Press, 1994), 449.

19. World Bank, *Global Economic Prospects and Developing Countries 2002: Making Trade Work for*

the *World's Poor* (Washington, 2001), 133. At: <www.worldbank.org/prospects/gep2002/>.

20. DeAnne Julius, 'International Direct Investment: Strengthening the Policy Regime', in Peter Kenen, ed., *Managing the World Economy: Fifty Years after Bretton Woods* (Washington: Institute for International Economics, 1994), 277.

21. Dunoff, 'The WTO in Transition', 1003.

22. Hoekman and Kostecki, *Political Economy of the World Trading System*, 132.

23. Ibid., 131.

24. Patrick Low and Arvind Subramanian, 'TRIMS in the Uruguay Round: An Unfinished Business?', in Martin and Winters, eds, *The Uruguay Round*, 423.

25. This discussion of the EU's role is based on Stephen Woolcock, 'Liberalisation of Financial Services', *European Policy Forum* (London) (Oct. 1997).

26. 'Accord is Reached to Lower Barriers in Global Finance', *New York Times*, 13 Dec. 1997, A1, B2.

27. 'Nations Reach Agreement on Financial Services Pact', *Washington Post,* 13 Dec. 1997, A17.

28. Edward M. Graham, 'Investment and the New Multilateral Context', in OECD, *Market Access after the Uruguay Round* (Paris: OECD, 1996), 50.

29. Walter, 'Globalization and Corporate Power', 17.

30. Low and Subramanian, 'TRIMS in the Uruguay Round', 416.

31. Ibid., 421.

32. Daniel M. Price, 'Investment Rules and High Technology: Towards a Multilateral Agreement on Investment', in *Market Access after the Uruguay Round: Investment, Competition and Technology Perspectives* (Paris: OECD, 1996), 182.

33. Low and Subramanian, 'TRIMS in the Uruguay Round', 418.

34. Walter, 'Globalization and Corporate Power', 19.

35. Based on ibid., 28, 38.

36. For a survey, see Kal Raustiala, 'Compliance and Effectiveness in International Regulatory Co-operation', *Case Western Reserve Journal of International Law* 32, 3 (Summer 2000): 387–440.

37. Peter Gerhart, 'Reflections: Beyond Compliance Theory—TRIPS as a Substantive Issue', *Case Western Reserve Journal of International Law* 32, 3 (Summer 2000): 371.

38. Margaret Archer, *Realist Social Theory: A Morphogenetic Approach* (Cambridge: Cambridge University Press, 1995), 296; emphasis added.

39. Lloyd Gruber, *Ruling the World: Power Politics and the Rise of Supranational Institutions* (Princeton, NJ: Princeton University Press, 2001).

40. Peter Drahos, 'BITS and BIPS: Bilateralism in Intellectual Property', *Journal of World Intellectual Property Law* 4, 6 (Nov. 2001): 793.

41. Barton Gellman, 'Gore in Conflict for Health and Profit', *Washington Post*, 21 May 2000, A1. At: <www.washingtonpost.c...rticle&nodecontentID =A41297-2000May20>.

42. Tina Rosenberg, 'Look at Brazil', *New York Times*, 28 Jan 2001. At: <www.nytimes.com/library/magazine/home/ 20010128mag.aids.html>.

43. This discussion is based on John S. Odell and Susan K. Sell, 'Reframing the Issue: The WTO Coalition on Intellectual Property and Public Health, 2001', paper prepared for a conference on Developing Countries and the Trade Negotiation Process, 6–7 Nov. 2003, UNCTAD, Geneva.

44. World Trade Organization, 'Declaration on the TRIPS Agreement and Public Health', WT/MIN(01)/DEC/2, 20 Nov. 2001. At: <www.wto.org/english.thewto_minist_e/min01_ e/mindecl_TRIPS_e.htm>.

45. Just before the Cancun Ministerial negotiators finally agreed on a provision that would make it easier for developing countries to import generic drugs manufactured under compulsory licensing if they are unable to manufacture the drugs themselves. See World Trade Organization, 'The General Council Chairperson's Statement', *WTO News,* 30 Aug. 2003. At: <www.wto.org/english/news_e/news03_e/ TRIPS_stat_28aug03_e.htm>.

46. Robert Merges, 'One Hundred Years of Solicitude: Intellectual Property Law 1900–2000', *California Law Review* 88 (Dec. 2000): 2233.

47. ICTSD and IISS, 'The Singapore Issues', *Doha Round*

Briefing Series 1, 6 (Feb. 2003): 3. At: <www.ictsd.org>.

48. Ibid., 2, 6 (Aug. 2003): 3.

49. Ibid., 1.

50. Pascal Lamy, Speeches and Articles by Pascal Lamy: 'Press Conference Closing the World Trade Organisation 5th Ministerial Conference', 14 Sept. 2003. At: <http://europa.eu.int/comm/commissioners/lamy/speeches_articles/spla190_en.htm>.

51. Christina R. Sevilla, 'The WTO's North–South Conflict: A Dangerous New (Old) International Economic Order?', *The National Interest* (Winter 2003–4): 121.

52. Member of the European Commission responsible for Agriculture, Rural Development and Fisheries.

53. Pascal Lamy and Franz Fischler, letter dated 9 May 2004. At: <www.ictsd.org>.

54. Sevilla, 'The WTO's North–South Conflict'.

55. ICTSD, . 'Brazil Wins Landmark Cotton Dispute', *Bridges* 8, 5 (May 2004): 7.

56. Timothy A. Wise, 'Barking up the Wrong Tree: Agricultural Subsidies, Dumping and Policy Reform', *Bridges* 8, 5 (May 2004): 3.

57. ICTSD, 'Brazil Wins Landmark Cotton Dispute', *Bridges* 8, 5 (May 2004): 7.

58. Ibid.

59. For another example, see James McCall Smith, 'Compliance Bargaining in the WTO: Ecuador and the Bananas Case', paper prepared for a conference on Developing Countries and the Trade Negotiation Process, 6–7 Nov. 2003, UNCTAD, Geneva.

60. For a comprehensive overview, see <www.ustr.gov>.

61. Archer, *Realist Social Theory*, 327.

62. Ibid.

63. Ibid., 295–6.

64. Margaret Archer, 'Human Agency and Social Structure: A Critique of Giddens', in J. Clark and C. Modgil, eds, *Anthony Giddens: Consensus and Critique* (London: Falmer Press, 1990), 81.

Suggested Readings

Cutler, A. Claire. *Private Power and Global Authority: Transnational Merchant Law in the Global Political Economy.* Cambridge: Cambridge University Press, 2003.

————, Virginia Haufler, and Tony Porter. *Private Authority and International Affairs.* Albany, NY: State University of New York Press, 1999.

Drahos, Peter, and John Braithwaite. *Global Business Regulation.* Cambridge: Cambridge University Press, 2000.

Sell, Susan K. *Private Power, Public Law: The Globalization of Intellectual Property Rights.* Cambridge: Cambridge University Press, 2003.

Shaffer, Gregory. *Defending Interests: Public-Private Partnerships in W.T.O. Litigation* Washington: Brookings Institution, 2003.

Strange, Susan. *The Retreat of the State.* Cambridge: Cambridge University Press, 1996.

Trebilcock, Michael, and Robert Howse. *The Regulation of International Trade.* New York: Taylor & Francis, 1998.

Web Sites

Consumer Project on Technology: www.cptech.org

International Centre for Trade and Sustainable Development: www.ictsd.org

International Institute for Sustainable Development: www.iisd.org

Médecins Sans Frontières: www.msf.org

Office of the United States Trade Representative: www.ustr.gov

Pharmaceutical Research and Manufacturers of America: www.PhRMA.org

Quaker United Nations Offices: www.quno.org

World Trade Organization: www.wto.org

Chapter 13

Multinational Corporations in the Global Economy

Winfried Ruigrok

Multinational corporations (MNCs) have become prominent actors both in the world economy and in world politics. They account for a large part of the world's production and innovation capacity, provide employment to a disproportioned share of well-educated people, and provide goods to fill our fridges, living rooms, streets, factories, and offices. MNCs occasionally attempt to influence domestic and international policy-making, and the chief executive officers (CEOs) of some MNCs have become well-known public figures commenting on business developments and sometimes even featuring in TV shows. At the same time, MNCs have been the object of fears or anger in many countries because of their ability to relocate production and jobs, the accounting scandals that some have produced, or the way certain MNCs have disrespected human rights or social and environmental standards.

In this chapter I attempt to move beyond a discussion of whether MNCs should be regarded as positive or negative actors. Rather, I discuss the interplay of MNCs and domestic and international institutional arenas. I review trends in company internationalization, discuss the role of MNCs' home countries, and look at the way MNC internationalization may affect firm performance. Finally, I evaluate recent changes in corporate governance arrangements and the role MNCs have played in this process.

The Significance of MNCs

A multinational company controls operations or income-generating assets in more than one country.[1] A simple way to categorize MNC challenges is provided in Figure 1. The horizontal axis refers to the geographical boundaries of countries: home vs abroad. The vertical axis refers to the boundaries inside or outside the MNC. Put together, four sets of MNC management challenges emerge. An MNC's influence is highest in the first quadrant, and lowest in the fourth.

Firms may have a host of reasons to set up foreign activities (i.e., to move to the second quadrant in Figure 1), for instance, to gain market share abroad (the main motive for consumer-oriented firms such as Unilever or Procter & Gamble) or to tap into specialized knowledge (which explains why many European pharmaceutical corporations have moved a large part of their R&D [research and development] activities to the United States). However, as will be argued below, another motive for firms to internationalize may be to 'escape' from domestic institutional arrangements (i.e., the third quadrant).

MNCs as a phenomenon have a very long history. The oldest documented MNCs date back to 2,000 BC, when in the Assyrian kingdom an organization had evolved that in every respect would qualify for the term MNC, with clear 'command and control' structures, market-seeking behaviour, and the king acting as a de facto chief executive officer.[2] Throughout human civilization, firms have employed multinational activities, whether in the Greek and Roman empires, during the Middle Ages and the Renaissance period, or during the early days of modern capitalism. Some of these companies have had strong ties with political authorities, such as in the case of the Dutch and later the

Figure 1: Four Types of MNC Management Challenges

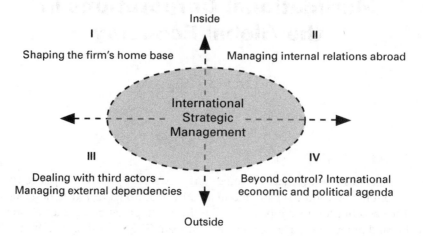

British East India Companies. The 'modern' MNC only evolved in the second half of the nineteenth century, when new management techniques (such as the rise of functional specialization) and organizational structures (such as divisional structures), as well as modern transportation and communication techniques, enabled companies to manage activities further away from home.

The periods 1880–1914 and 1965–80 saw a rapid increase in the number of MNCs and in the scope of their international activities. By definition, every MNC has engaged in foreign direct investment (FDI) through which it either built new facilities or acquired a majority or minority share in existing activities. Between the second half of the 1990s and the beginning of this century, foreign direct investments have grown dramatically, reflecting a growing importance of MNCs. After 2001, FDI flows diminished, largely due to a marked decline in mergers and acquisition activity (Figure 2).

According to the United Nations Conference on Trade and Development (UNCTAD) there were some 61,000 MNCs in 2004, which in turn owned over 900,000 foreign affiliates.[3] MNCs are not spread evenly over the globe, but are concentrat-

ed in certain countries and industries. About 90 per cent of the world's largest MNCs are headquartered in North America, Western Europe, or Japan. MNCs can be found especially in the electrical and electronic equipment, transportation vehicles, petroleum exploration, and distribution industries. All of these are capital-intensive industries, where economies of scale (i.e., cost advantages that originate from producing large volumes) play an important role. These have also been industries traditionally characterized by relatively high degrees of vertical integration (i.e., firms also manufacture key inputs or components they need in their production process) and by large numbers of employees. In 2004, the world's 100 largest MNCs (less than 0.2 per cent of all MNCs in the world!) controlled approximately 14 per cent of total worldwide sales, 12 per cent of global assets, and 13 per cent of all employment worldwide.[4] Many MNCs have played a central role in their home country's (but often also in host countries') defence industries. Therefore, MNCs wield considerable political power, and at the same time are the object of struggles to protect or upgrade employment, to foster industrial innovation, or to safeguard nations' defence activities.

Figure 2: Trends in Mergers and Acquisitions

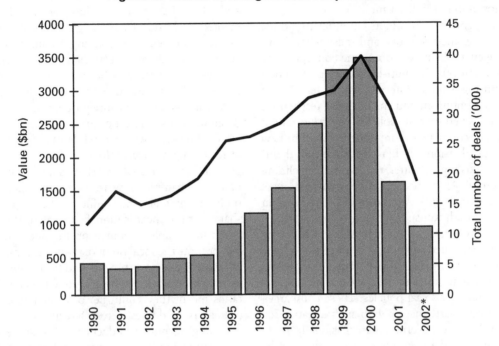

*To 25 Oct. 2002
Source: *Financial Times.*

The Embedded MNC: 1970 to the Early 1980s

The first 30 years after World War II witnessed the rise and subsequent diffusion from the US to Europe and to a lesser extent Asia of the vertically integrated, multi-divisional corporation, which by the late 1970s was the dominant form of economic organization across the most advanced Western economies. Oliver Williamson argued that vertically integrated structures had diffused over the period 1935–75 because their transaction costs were lower than those of firms with lower degrees of vertical integration.[5] Put simply, during this period manufacturers tended to aim for vertically integrated structures if they:

- were active in capital- or technology-intensive industries (i.e., industries with high asset specificity);

- were producing very large volumes and therefore needed high volumes of specific parts or components (i.e., faced a high frequency of transactions);
- depended on a timely delivery of reliable quality parts or components because supply interruptions would lead to high costs later on in the production process (i.e., faced a high degree of uncertainty).

In North America and Europe, the rise of the vertically integrated firm and the multi-divisional structure went hand in hand. A chief advantage of the multi-divisional firm was the efficiency of the internal capital market, which enabled the firm's corporate centre to allocate capital to promising business ideas more efficiently than the capital market could at a time of relatively little financial transparency.[6] The multi-divisional structure was a hierarchical organization adopted by most MNCs and replaced earlier market relationships among smaller units.

Management consultants, politicians, trade unionists, business schools, and mass media have each played a role in developing the concept of the vertically integrated, multi-divisional corporation and diffusing it on an international scale.[7] Due to managerial optimism and institutional restrictions (such as governmental policies or trade union opposition) companies more often invested in new businesses (divisions) rather than divesting themselves of existing activities representing declining profitability. As a result, large conglomerates emerged across North America and Europe and in Japan and South Korea.

In many European economies these took the shape of so-called 'national champions'—large diversified conglomerates that became ideal objects for national authorities to develop industrial, competition, trade, or social policies. These companies were not necessarily happy with such a status, for instance, because governments occasionally pressured them to take over ailing firms and co-ordinate national industrial restructuring.[8] As a result of their political status and high visibility, national champions also became logical targets for actors in the third quadrant of Figure 1. Thus trade unions targeted national champions such as Philips, Renault, Olivetti, and Volkswagen to negotiate wage deals that could subsequently serve as a 'model' to be diffused to other companies. National champions also attracted the attention of domestic industrial banks, which saw national champions as potential investment objects, and small and medium-sized enterprises (SMEs), which attempted to secure long-term business with high-profile clients. Thus, in many European countries in the 1960s and 1970s corporate expansion and the development of national systems of production and innovation[9] went hand in hand, even if this was a marriage of reason, not of love.

The rise of large diversified conglomerates and the intervention by governments to save domestic firms and restructure national industries were not isolated European phenomena. Japanese and South Korean companies were, if anything, even more subject to government intervention over the 1960s and 1970s. For instance, it has been widely documented how the Japanese government has frequently intervened in shaping an internationally competitive auto and electronics industry and how it helped Japanese producers through a range of protectionist and industrial policies to shield their domestic market from foreign entrants.[10] A major difference between European and Asian MNCs in the 1970s, however, was that while many Asian MNCs were willing to accept lower profit margins and gained international market share, European national champions were faced with shrinking profit margins and had difficulty keeping market share. For European national champions this created an unsolvable dilemma: on the one hand they had become the focal point of domestic aspirations, especially from governments and trade unions, but on the other hand declining productivity and profit ratios meant they could perform their role as co-ordinators of domestic restructuring and as milk cows of government budgets ever less successfully.

National industrial systems in Europe did offer some refuge to national champions during the 1970s recession. However, those national champions that could escape their stifling domestic systems began to invest more actively abroad. Those that could not break out became absorbed in the last attempts to formulate national industrial policies (such as in France during the beginning of the Mitterrand administration) and typically had to carry out more painful and expensive restructuring activities afterwards, and/or became the target of further consolidation or acquisitions.

The Emancipated MNC: Late 1980s–2000

The period up to the late 1970s saw the diffusion of vertically integrated multi-divisional organizations, largely operating within the confines of their national systems, but the 1980s and 1990s saw the opposite trend towards less diversified, less vertically integrated, and more network-like structures, operating increasingly on an international scale. In terms of Figure 1, firms attempted to restructure operations (first quadrant), increase their foreign presence (second quadrant), and reduce their dependency on domestic institutions and bargaining partners (third quadrant).

A major cause of restructuring was the rise of global competition. European and US firms, including national champions, from the late 1970s on became increasingly confronted with other, especially Japanese, exports and, later on, inward investments in key industries such as autos, consumer electronics, and microelectronics—the previous domain of many European national champions or traditional US producers. Unlike their Western competitors, Japanese manufacturers had expanded using a production model of much lower degrees of vertical integration, i.e., making more extensive use of suppliers not owned by the end producer. This model of vertical *de-integration* made it more difficult for trade unions and SMEs to target and bargain with core MNCs .[11]

Leveraging their growing international presence and initially accepting lower profit margins, Japanese firms successfully circumvented national institutions in Europe and the US, highlighting reduced effectiveness of these institutions. Ultimately, the creation of the North American Free Trade Arrangement (NAFTA, 1994) and the European Union (EU, 1993), with its single market and later on its single currency (1999), were the US and European responses to the Japanese challenge. Both of these regional trade arrangements provided former national champions with scale and strengthened governments' bargaining power vis-à-vis foreign entrants. This process of international institution-building has obviously made most progress in the EU. While initially most European institutions supplemented rather than supplanted national institutions, the EU effectively diminished the relative importance of pre-existing national institutions in Europe.

Over the 1980s and 1990s, US, European, and Asian MNCs all stepped up their international exposure, though their motives differed widely. Japanese internationalization had been motivated largely by the creation of NAFTA and the EU. Since the mid-1980s, US and European trade authorities had imposed so-called voluntary export restraints

(VERS) in industries such as autos and electronics—which were anything but voluntary to Japanese (and to a lesser extent South Korean) exporters. By the early 1990s, VERS affected more than 33 per cent of all Japanese exports to the United States and the EU.[12] Japanese producers therefore feared that they could be the object of additional regional trade restrictions if they had not transferred substantial parts of their production process to North America and Europe before the creation of NAFTA and the EU. After this objective had been achieved by the mid-1990s, Japanese FDI flows diminished considerably and in the course of the 1990s shifted towards the Asian mainland due to increasing domestic cost pressures and the relative strength of the yen.

American MNCs in this period could benefit from a depreciating dollar, and especially sought to open up new markets and achieve economies of scale. After 1995, the emerging dot-com and stock market boom also made it much easier for US firms to take over foreign firms and finance deals through equity.

The emergence of new markets and production locations in Central and Eastern European countries, after the fall of the Berlin Wall, led to a rush of FDI by European national champions, which in the process became less 'national'. Ironically, this FDI was often supported by European governments concerned about political and economic stability in these neighbouring transition economies. To European MNCs, internationalization promised emancipation from institutional constraints and thus more of a level playing field with their US and Japanese competitors.

Technological developments played an important role for MNCs of all nationalities. New information and communication technologies enabled companies to manage information more efficiently (e.g., through enterprise resource planning systems); to outsource activities that were previously performed in-house and to better manage supply chains (e.g., through electronic data interchange systems); and to communicate directly across unit and divisional boundaries, as well as across managerial hierarchies and national boundaries.

Political changes such as the creation of the EU also affected MNCs' corporate structures. Research has suggested that restructuring patterns over the 1990s were remarkably similar across Europe, a phenomenon unlike the previous situation dominated by distinct national systems. Over the 1992–6 period, for instance, companies across Europe reported notable changes in corporate structures (such as 'delayering' and a decentralization of decision-making), processes/organization (such as a relative increase of communication across units and divisions), and boundaries (such as the increased use of outsourcing and alliances, and de-diversification).[13]

How have MNC internationalization strategies developed more recently? The next sections of this chapter will look at which home countries have been the home base of large MNCs, examine recent developments in firms' international exposure, and discuss the link between internationalization and performance. Subsequently, we will conclude by assessing the current nature of MNCs' relations with their home countries and other external bargaining partners.

What Home Countries Generate MNCs?

An interesting way to understand MNCs is to compare the fate of particular MNCs over time to that of competitors and firms from other industries and countries. There are numerous methods for doing so—total sales, employment, market value, reputation, etc. Several periodicals, including *Fortune* and *Business Week*, provide lists that receive wide attention in the business world. For instance, the *Fortune* Global 500 lists firms by total sales, whereas the *Business Week* 1,000 ranks firms by total market value (number of outstanding shares multiplied by share price). These methods lead to different results: in the *Fortune* 500 list traditional manufacturing firms feature more prominently than in the *Business Week* list, where technology firms take a more prominent place. Other factors, such as exchange rate shifts and the development of countries' financial markets, obviously influence these rankings.

Table 1 therefore takes both the *Fortune* Global

500 and the *Business Week* Global 1,000 lists and looks at the home countries in which the firms listed were headquartered in 1983, 1988, 1993, 1998, and 2003. This overview enables one to identify longer-term patterns in the success of specific home countries in generating large companies (not just MNCs), and shows the ebb and flow of national economies.

Table 1 shows that while the *Fortune* and *Business Week* ranking methods suggest slightly different trends, both methods indicate that US companies saw their global position erode during the 1980s and then return to prominence in the late 1990s. These data help to understand the 1980s US-based view that the US economy had lost its hegemony[14] and industrial and trade union pressures to raise trade barriers to emerging Japanese and Asian competition. While US companies faced difficult times over the late 1980s and early 1990s, this period was the heyday of Japanese companies. The second theme of the IPE literature 15 years ago was therefore the rise of the Japanese industrial model and the challenge this posed to Western companies' ability to sustain employment, innovation, and ultimately the welfare state that many European countries had developed.[15] As Japanese companies have been coping with adjustment problems after the post-bubble recession (1992), the attraction of the Japanese model has subsided. Today, much attention is diverted to US companies again competing successfully on an international basis, and it may appear difficult to believe that scholars 20 years ago really anticipated the end of US hegemony. In addition, a lot of Western business people follow with great interest the formidable progress in emerging countries such as China and India, which are also becoming attractive locations for Western firms to outsource activities.

As Table 1 shows, European economies have largely maintained their position as a home base for large firms. France has even produced many more large firms according to the *Business Week* ranking, reflecting not just ongoing efforts to create national and European 'champions', but also a growing significance of financial markets in France—as in some other countries in continental Europe.

Table 1: Frequency of Firms' Home Countries Appearing in International Rankings, 1983–2003

	Fortune Global 500					*Business Week* Global 1,000				
	*1983**	*1988**	*1993*	*1998*	*2003*	*1983*	*1988*	*1993*	*1998*	*2003*
Australia	5	5	9	7	6	10	21	14	12	27
Austria	1	1	2	0	0	0	0	2	1	2
Belgium	4	5	4	4	4	7	11	9	15	9
Brazil	0	5	1	5	4	3	0	0	0	0
Canada	17	14	8	8	14	62	35	22	31	41
China	n.a.	n.a.	n.a.	4	11	0	0	0	0	0
Denmark	0	0	0	0	0	1	1	5	8	6
Finland	1	2	4	2	3	4	5	0	3	5
France	34	44	30	39	40	7	25	45	51	48
Germany	48	55	32	42	35	33	35	32	46	35
Hong Kong	n.a.	n.a.	n.a.	n.a.	n.a.	7	13	21	13	18
India	0	0	3	1	1	2	0	0	0	0
Italy	12	15	6	13	9	11	17	11	24	24
Japan	79	107	128	112	88	97	310	281	116	129
Netherlands	9	10	8	13	14	14	11	14	24	19
Norway	1	2	5	2	2	1	1	1	2	5
Russia	n.a.	n.a.	n.a.	1	3	0	0	0	0	0
Singapore	0	0	0	0	1	7	4	5	4	6
South Africa	1	1	4	0	0	30	7	4	0	0
South Korea	3	2	12	12	13	3	0	0	0	0
Spain	2	2	4	5	5	4	16	11	11	18
Sweden	4	8	14	4	6	25	16	10	22	17
Switzerland	9	13	9	12	11	14	16	13	20	17
Taiwan	0	0	1	2	1	10	0	0	0	0
UK	40	44	42	37	36	53	112	93	115	77
US	226	160	161	175	192	494	345	403	480	488

*Based on 1982 and 1987 USD sales figures obtained from Worldscope.
SOURCES: *Business Week, Fortune,* and Worldscope.

Neighbouring economies with similar cultures, languages, and wealth levels may nevertheless show different patterns, as indicated in Table 1. Thus, small countries such as Sweden, Switzerland, and the Netherlands have traditionally been the cradle of many successful MNCs, while neighbouring small countries Norway, Austria, and Belgium have consistently produced fewer large firms. The answer to this pattern lies in different histories, different banking systems, and different domestic political networks.

How International Are MNCs?

A firm's internationalization can be measured in various ways. As a result, companies may be quite international by some indicators but much less so according to other indicators. A company like Nestlé is a case in point. Based in Switzerland, the company sells about 99 per cent of its products abroad and employs about 97 per cent of its workforce outside its home country. Today it has a variety of nationals on its top management team (TMT), but Nestlé is listed on stock exchanges only in Switzerland, Germany, and Austria.

Table 2 lists the average percentages of foreign sales, foreign employment, foreign TMT, and foreign board members for the 100 largest companies in the US, Japan, Germany, France, the UK, the Netherlands, Switzerland, and four Nordic countries. This list includes MNCs as well as large domestically oriented firms. The discussion below is based on ongoing research activities at the author's Research Institute for International Management, University of St Gallen (Switzerland).

Table 2 tells a number of stories. First, it illustrates the emancipation of the MNC: over the recent period, the overriding trend for the 100 largest companies in each of the listed economies has been to become more international by almost every measure. Only in the UK has the ratio of foreign sales to total sales decreased between 1995 and 2000, partly reflecting exchange rate shifts over this period.[16]

Second, firms may pursue host-country-specific internationalization strategies. Thus, on average US and UK firms have sought not just to generate foreign revenues, but also to shift production and employment abroad. By contrast, Swiss, German, and Scandinavian companies have traditionally been more export-oriented and more cautious in relocating production, although the trend here has also been to increase international production activities significantly.

Third, when it comes to the composition of their top echelons, most MNCs remain remarkably 'national'. While the percentage of firms taking on a foreign TMT or board member has increased considerably, many firms have nevertheless been hesitant to open up decision-making circles to non-nationals. Indeed, firms that hire a foreign TMT or board member tend to gain experiences with this one person first before deciding to accelerate the process of internationalizing their TMTs or boards. Obviously there are many cultural, language, and political barriers to the creation of truly multinational TMTs or boards. Some countries have had legal rules restricting the share of foreigners

allowed on a company's board (such as in Switzerland until 2003). Most Japanese and South Korean firms still have close to zero per cent foreign TMT and board members.

Those companies that hire a foreign TMT or board member tend to recruit these individuals from culturally similar countries. For instance, in 2003 over a third of Swiss top executives at the top 100 largest firms originated from abroad, yet over 15 per cent in fact came from neighbouring Germany, where language and cultural differences are relatively small. Likewise, while almost 25 per cent of executives of the 100 largest UK firms came from abroad, almost 15 per cent originated from other English-speaking countries. Thus the creation of an international labour market for executive and non-executive (outside) directors is taking shape, but this is a slow process—with international political implications. Since British firms tend to recruit foreign executives from other English-speaking economies rather than from nearby continental Europe—where many potential executives these days speak acceptable English—UK economic elites will be exposed less to individuals and forces speaking up in favour of further UK integration in the EU.

Fourth and finally, Table 2 illustrates that MNCs have not become the model of global footloose companies that some predicted. While research suggests that firms have definitely become more international (including variables not listed in Table 2, such as percentage of R&D abroad), for many MNCs today the home market or home region (i.e., Europe, North America, and Asia-Pacific) remains the most important point of reference. Even the interest of North American and European MNCs in China and India as potential markets *and* production locations via *offshoring* (relocating *in-house* activities to other countries) and *outsourcing* (farming out activities to other companies not legally controlled) is unlikely to change this pattern dramatically over the next years.

The fact that many MNCs' boards and top management teams are still dominated by domestic nationals shapes economic elites' horizons and institutional preferences. In fact, there have been

Table 2: Degree of Internationalization among Top 100 Firms in Selected Countries, 1995 and 2000

	% foreign sales 1995	% foreign sales 2000	% foreign employment 1995	% foreign employment 2000	% foreign TMT members 1995	% foreign TMT members 2000	% foreign board members 1995	% foreign board members 2000
US	27.3	31.0	25.0	38.6	3.7	10.3	4.6	7.6
Japan	20.6	25.8	15.6	(n.c.)	0.5	(n.c.)	(n.a.)	(n.a.)
Germany	39.3	47.3	27.6	37.4	7.2	9.3	5.4	7.3
UK	50.0	45.8	42.5	49.6	15.1	22.8	18.0	25.6
Netherlands	45.4	55.4	37.5	57.3	17.7	15.6	19.9	20.0
Switzerland	55.5	71.4	48.8	56.1	22.4	34.9	14.4	22.1
Nordic countries	61.6	62.3	(n.c.)	45.9	9.1	18.0	6.4	14.6

Notes:
1. Percentages are averages of largest 100 companies per country.
2. Foreign sales are revenues generated outside the firm's home country; foreign employment refers to the number of employees outside the firm's home country; foreign TMT members refers to top executives with a different nationality than that of the firm's home country; foreign board members refers to board members with a different nationality than that of the firm's home country. In countries with a one-tier board structure (such as the UK or the US), board data only include outside/non-executive members.
3. Nordic countries are Norway, Sweden, Denmark, and Finland (Iceland has not been included).
4. n.c. = not collected; n.a. = not available (Japanese firms only have [very large] TMTS, no boards).
Source: Research Institute for International Management, University of St Gallen (FIM-HSG).

important barriers to further internationalization even when one looks at the link between internationalization and performance.

The Link between Internationalization and Performance

Ultimately, the decision regarding the extent to which firms will internationalize activities depends heavily on the performance implications of internationalization. This has been one of the most contested areas of international management research over the past decade. In Figure 3 the horizontal axis shows firms' degree of internationalization, from low (left-hand side) to high (right-hand side), the vertical axis shows firms' performance, again from low (bottom) to high (top). Degrees of internationalization may be measured by percentage of sales, assets, or employment abroad, by the number of foreign countries in which the MNC has subsidiaries, or by an index based on a number of

these indicators.

Until the late 1980s, thinking about the link between internationalization and performance was simple: it was assumed that as firms increased their degree of internationalization, their performance would improve (Figure 3, line 1). This may seem logical, since if there are no performance incentives for firms to step up internationalization, why would they do so? However, from the late 1980s thinking has become more sophisticated. Scholars have since agreed that there are costs and benefits to internationalizing activities. Benefits include the possibility for firms to reap economies of scale; to exploit national differences in factor prices, tax levels, and capital sources; to export superior technologies, organizational structures, and management techniques to new markets; and the ability to exploit cultural diversity. Costs, on the other hand, emerge from political uncertainty. These include tax rates and regulation; financial risks such as exchange rate shifts and inflation rates; consumer boycotts of foreign products; cross-border transportation and communication costs; and difficulties of leading and motivating culturally diverse workforces.

Since 1989, two schools of thought have emerged in the internationalization-performance debate. One group of scholars argues that firms internationalize along an inverted J- or S-curve (Figure 3, line 2). Their argument is that firms expand abroad up to a 'threshold of internationalization', beyond which internationalization costs outweigh the benefits. This argument has found support from research on US and UK firms.[17] The other group of scholars argues that in some cases internationalizing firms may follow a (non-inverse) J- or U-shaped trajectory (Figure 3, line 3). This argument suggests that firms go through a long and painful process of 'organizational learning' before performance picks up again.[18] Research on the link between internationalization and performance of German and Japanese firms has supported this latter view.

This evidence suggests two things. First, ultimately the internationalization-performance link is probably not universal but is rather context-dependent. On the one hand, firms with large home markets and large institutionally and cultur-

ally related host markets (a starting point faced by US and UK firms) may internationalize along an inverted J- or S-curve (Figure 3, line 2). At early stages, when firms enter easier and more related markets, there will only be minor pressures to overhaul existing organizational structures, since these will fit to some extent also in the newly accessed countries. Only at higher degrees of internationalization, when firms move into highly dissimilar countries and become confronted with unfamiliar market structures, modes of regulation, and cultures, will firms face much higher pressures to restructure—and learn from foreign subsidiaries. On the other hand, firms with large home markets yet *without* large institutionally and culturally related host markets may internationalize along a J- or U-shaped trajectory (Figure 3, line 3). German and Japanese companies face such a situation in which they are forced to learn from day 1. The different internationalization-performance link also explains why German and Japanese firms have found it more difficult to internationalize than US or UK firms.

Second, and irrespective of the exact shape of the internationalization-performance link, interna-

Figure 3: The Link between Internationalization and Performance

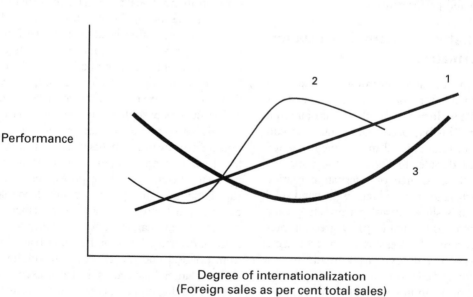

Performance

Degree of internationalization
(Foreign sales as per cent total sales)

tional management researchers agree that the graph line is not straight and that there are performance barriers to internationalization irrespective of the company's home country. This explains why very few MNCs have become truly 'footloose'. It also suggests that corporate internationalization trajectories will tend to be incremental rather than revolutionary.

Corporate Governance: MNC Checks and Balances

Although MNCs have increased their degrees of internationalization even more recently, the days of almost unrestrained internationalization appear to have passed. Apart from the performance restraints internationalization presents to companies, checks and balances are also re-emerging in a less expected way. In the favourable 1990s investment climate, many MNCs entered the international financial market to attract cheaper capital and foreign investors' interest. In 2000, 20 per cent of German shares were owned by foreign investors (as opposed to only 12 per cent of UK shares).[19]

While the booming stock market and limited shareholder emancipation increased MNCs' financial freedom in the 1990s, the rules of the game have changed since 2000. First, continental European and Asian MNCs have learned that international investor expectations often differ dramatically from those of domestic investors.[20] Second, the various accounting scandals have reinforced the drive for more effective corporate governance. Corporate governance refers to the ways companies are directed and controlled, and to how senior management is made accountable—primarily to shareholders as the owners of a company, but in a wider sense also to other stakeholders such as employees, suppliers, governments, and consumers. While on a global level the Enron and WorldCom scandals have received most attention, many economies have had to deal with similar incidents.

The aims of key corporate governance reforms are transparency and the monitoring of standards. Two responses have emerged in reforming corporate governance standards. First, the UK in 1993 set out to develop specific yet voluntary codes of conduct, which recommend effective practices that firms should consider implementing. However, rather than aiming for binding legislation, the critical words were 'comply or explain'. The advantage of codes of conduct has been that firms and governments have been able to gain experience with newly introduced corporate governance arrangements, to identify new areas of improvement, and even to allow firms to deviate from the recommended practices—provided they offer good reasons for this. Here the thought has been that firms that do not implement recommended practices will face negative responses from investors, which research indicates has indeed been the case.

The second approach to corporate governance reform has been through legislation. In the aftermath of the big Enron-type accounting scandals and a deep investor trust crisis, the US government made it clear to investors and managers alike that a breach of trust would be prosecuted. The resulting Sarbanes-Oxley Act provides a highly detailed set of binding rules stating how companies need to disclose information to outside stakeholders.

MNCs have played a notable role in the process of institutionalizing corporate governance standards. Since MNCs are more exposed to innovative practices in different markets and especially to international investor demands than domestically oriented firms, MNCs have been more likely to implement corporate governance reforms and have played an active role in diffusing stricter corporate governance standards to other markets. In many countries, CEOs of leading MNCs have led or have participated in committees drafting codes of conduct or legislation.

Why do MNCs co-operate in refining corporate governance codes and laws, if this will only reduce their operational and strategic independence? The explanation points to some fundamental demographic shifts. Over the next decades, the percentage of retired people will increase dramatically in North America, Europe, and Asia, and state institutions will be unable to provide for these people's pensions. Most employees today are therefore saving funds and investing in pension schemes, managed by institutional investors such as banks, insurance companies, and private pension funds. Paradoxically, this can make a person both the co-owner and employee of a company, with potentially diverging interests. The leading proponents of corporate governance reforms in many countries have been the institutional investors owning ever larger parts of MNC stock. In the UK, some 85 per cent of stocks traded at the London Stock Exchange are owned and traded by institutional investors who usually invest with a long-term perspective.

Finally, the concepts of corporate governance and corporate social responsibility are not identical. Corporate governance primarily refers to the financial and strategic monitoring of a firm by its shareholders and stakeholders and the quality of information this firm provides to its shareholders. Firms may score high in terms of corporate governance mechanisms and low in terms of corporate social responsibility, and vice versa. However, the drive to reform corporate governance in North America, Europe, and Asia may ultimately strengthen the hand of stakeholders such as government institutions, employees, and consumers vis-à-vis MNCs and enable them to influence MNC strategies and behaviours. Numerous institutional investors today offer funds consisting of socially responsible firms, and there are influential indices of socially and environmentally responsible firms. Indeed, one could speculate that in the future 'shareholder value' may not necessarily be equated anymore with a narrow financial orientation of directors and investors but will give way to a more socially responsible view of the needs of large and vulnerable sections of society and of less-developed countries. This would be the ultimate 'industrial democracy' that trade unions have aspired to for the past century.

Conclusion: The Taming of the MNC?

In this chapter, I argued that MNCs over the past 40 years have gone through a cycle of close institutional embeddedness, followed by a process of internationalization and MNC emancipation, only for MNCs to be confronted with—and indeed to be architects themselves of—new checks and balances. Despite opportunities in emerging markets such as China and India, the times of rapid international expansion and unbridled hubris have given way to a more incremental approach towards firm internationalization. A number of internal company reasons account for this, such as the fact that the link between internationalization and performance is not a positive linear one, which suggests that for MNCs the internationalization process is extremely difficult to manage. Also, the slow process of admitting foreign nationals to MNCs' top decision-making structures suggests there are limits to internationalization. One could even identify other checks on MNC autonomy, such as the rise of international institutions, but these have been beyond the scope of this chapter.[21]

Looking at corporate and institutional restructuring patterns over the last 40 years, one may argue that domestic institutional contexts in Europe and Asia have served as incubators helping economically viable actors (such as domestic firms or 'organized pensioners') to grow stronger in a relatively protected environment and eventually face international competition. Optimists would argue that internationalizing institutional environments may play a similar role to that previously played by domestic institutions, serving as emancipation vehicles for 'infant industries' and SMEs while attempting to uplift political rights and social justice.

Notes

1. G. Jones, *The Evolution of International Business* (London/New York: Routledge, 1996), 4. Other authors have used terms such as 'global' and 'transnational', which refer either to the geographical scope or to supposedly high degrees of coordination within MNCs. As argued in this chapter, neither of these claims really holds for the bulk of today's MNCs.

2. K. Moore, and D. Lewis, *Birth of the Multinational: 2000 Years of Ancient Business History—from Ashur to Augustus* (Copenhagen: Copenhagen Business School Press, 2000).

3. UNCTAD, *World Investment Report 2004: The Shift towards Services* (New York and Geneva: UN, 2004), xvii.

4. Ibid.

5. O. Williamson, *Markets and Hierarchies: Analysis and Antitrust Implications* (New York: Free Press, 1975).

6. H.O. Armour and D.J. Teece, 'Organizational Structure and Economic Performance: A Test of the Multi-Divisional Hypothesis', *Rand Journal of Economics* 76, 5 (1978): 971–83.

7. E. Abrahamson, 'Management Fashion', *Academy of Management Review* 21, 1 (1996): 254–85; A. Lipietz, 'Towards Global Fordism?', *New Left Review* no. 133 (1982): 33–47.

8. For a detailed historical overview of how national governments had influenced the strategies and structures of the world's 100 largest corporations in 1993, see W. Ruigrok and R. Van Tulder, *The Logic of International Restructuring* (London/New York: Routledge, 1995), 239–68.

9. For this term, see B.Å. Lundvall, ed., *National Systems of Innovation: Towards a Theory of Innovation and Interactive Learning* (London: Pinter, 1992); R. Nelson, *National Innovation Systems: A Comparative Analysis* (Oxford: Oxford University Press, 1993). For the somewhat related term of 'business system', see R. Whitley, 'Competing Logics and Units of Analysis in the Comparative Study of Economic Organizations', *International Studies of Management and Organization* 29, 2 (1999): 113–26.

10. C. Johnson, *MITI and the Japanese Miracle: The Growth of Japanese Industrial Policy (1925–1975)* (Tokyo: Tuttle, 1982); B. Cumings, 'The Origins and Development of the Northeast Asian Political Economy: Industrial Sectors, Product Cycles, and Political Consequences', *International Organization* 38, 1 (1984): 1–40; H.J. Chang, *The Political Economy of Industrial Policy* (New York: St Martin's Press, 1994).

11. Ruigrok and Van Tulder, *The Logic of International Restructuring*.

12. OECD, *Obstacles to Trade and Competition* (Paris: OECD, 1993), 9.

13. W. Ruigrok, A. Pettigrew, S. Peck, and R. Whittington, 'Corporate Restructuring and New Forms of Organizing: Evidence from Europe', *Management International Review* 39, 2 (1999): 41–64. See also A. Lewin, S. Massini, W. Ruigrok, and T. Numagami, 'Convergence and Divergence of Organizing: Moderating Effect of the Nation State', in A. Pettigrew et al., eds, *Innovative Forms of Organizing: International Perspective* (Thousand Oaks, Calif.: Sage, 2003), 277–300.

14. R.O. Keohane, *After Hegemony: Cooperation and Discord in the World Political Economy* (Princeton, NJ: Princeton University Press, 1984).

15. Ruigrok and Van Tulder, *The Logic of International Restructuring*.

16. At the Research Institute for International Management, University of St Gallen (Switzerland), complete data are collected every five years. Post-2000 data for a number of countries suggest that the trend of rising degrees of internationalization has continued, albeit at a slower rate.

17. For this view, see F.J. Contractor, S.K. Kundu, and C. Hsu, 'A Three-Stage Theory of International Expansion: The Link between Multinationality and Performance in the Service Sector', *Journal of International Business Studies* 34 (2003): 5–18.

18. For this view, see, e.g., W. Ruigrok and H. Wagner, 'Internationalization and Performance: An Organizational Learning Perspective', *Management International Review* 43 (2003): 63–83.

19. R.A.G. Monks and N. Minow, eds, *Corporate Governance* (Oxford: Blackwell, 2001), 276.

20. S.I. Peck and W. Ruigrok, 'Hiding behind the Flag? Prospects for Change in German Corporate Governance', *European Management Journal* 18, 4 (2000): 420–30.

21. K.W. Abbott and D. Snidal, 'Why States Act through Formal International Organizations', *Journal of Conflict Resolution* 42, 1 (1998): 3–32; J. Braithwaite and P. Drahos, *Global Business Regulation* (Cambridge: Cambridge University Press, 2000).

Suggested Readings

De Wit, B., and R. Meyer, eds. *Strategy: Process, Content, Context: An International Perspective*, 3rd edn. London: Thomson Business Press, 2004.

Laserre, P. *Global Strategic Management*. New York: Palgrave Macmillan, 2003.

Pettigrew, A., H. Thomas, and R. Whittington, eds. *Handbook of Strategy and Management*. Thousand Oaks, Calif.: Sage, 2001.

UNCTAD. *World Investment Report 2004: The Shift towards Services*. New York and Geneva: UN, 2004.

Web Sites

Columbia University Library, Internet Resources for International Business:
www.columbia.edu/cu/lweb/indiv/business/ir/intlbs.html

European Corporate Governance Institute:
www.ecgi.org/

Gateway to the European Union: www.eu.int

Journal of International Business Studies:
www.palgrave-journals.com/jibs/

Management International Review:
www.uni-hohenheim.de/~mir/

Research Institute for International Management, University of St Gallen (Switzerland):
www.fim.unisg.ch

Socially Responsible Investing: www.socialfunds.com

UNCTAD : www.unctad.org

Chapter 14

The Political Economy of the Internet and E-Commerce

Henry Farrell

How have new information technologies affected international political economy? In the heady years of the dot-com bubble, many academics and commentators predicted that the Internet and e-commerce would empower private actors and weaken states. Indeed, some libertarians hoped that the Internet would lead to a collapse in state authority. However, these predictions have not come to pass. Although private actors have come to play an important role in some areas of Internet and e-commerce regulation, they hardly predominate. Indeed, in many instances, private actors play an important role only because states have pushed them into doing so.

In this chapter, I examine the changing relationship between states and private actors in the governance of the Internet and e-commerce. This is a significant test case for more general international relations theories about how states and private actors interact with each other. International relations scholars are increasingly interested in how private actors are creating their own 'islands of transnational governance' without much regard to international or national law.[1] Initially, it appeared that the Internet and e-commerce would be governed primarily by private authority, with states playing only a peripheral role.[2] Yet, despite the efforts of private actors to create their own independent governance regimes (and of prominent states such as the US to encourage them in these efforts), this has not transpired. Indeed, private actors, far from displacing states as sources of authority, are increasingly becoming vectors of state influence. States are using private actors to achieve their regulatory goals, sometimes in co-operation with other states, sometimes in conflict with them.

The Nature of the Internet

What precisely is the Internet? The answer to this question is by no means as simple as it seems at first. Definitions of the Internet vary from Milton Mueller's succinct definition of the Internet as effectively identical with the TCP/IP (Transmission Control Protocol/Internet Protocol), through Lawrence Lessig's distinction between three different layers of the Internet, to Lawrence Solum and Minn Chung's invocation of no less than six different layers of Internet architecture. In this chapter, I simplify Solum and Chung's account, distinguishing between (1) the physical infrastructure of the Internet, (2) TCP/IP and domain name system (DNS), and (3) the various applications that run on top of the TCP/IP protocol and DNS.

It is easy to forget that the Internet requires a physical basis if it is to work at all—a complicated material infrastructure intervenes between the source of a piece of information (for example, a Web page at www.amazon.com) and its destination (someone downloading Amazon's Web page on her home computer). Information will be carried across cables and/or other communications links (satellite links, wireless links) on its journey from source to destination. In this journey, it will be passed along between different routers (specialized computers for data transfer). The physical infrastructure of the Internet has important political consequences. Those parts of the world in which the physical infrastructure is underdeveloped or is difficult for citizens to access (because of decisions made by the government or perhaps by other actors) will not experience the same opportunities—or vexing political issues—as regions or countries where the Internet is easily accessible. Second, it may be possible for providers of physical infrastructure (such as cable operators in many advanced industrialized democracies) to limit their subscribers' access to certain kinds of content. This may be at the behest of government or, alternatively, may be driven by the providers' own economic interests. For example, one can easily imagine cable operators trying in the future to limit their customers' access to pirated movies, which cut into their own profits, or perhaps even limiting access to services provided by their competitors.

Second is TCP/IP, which is the cornerstone of the Internet. A protocol is a set of technical specifications that permits communication between different systems. TCP/IP is the basis for 'packet switching'—the fundamental basis for all Internet communications. The two elements of the protocol, TCP and IP, play different roles. TCP disassembles a coherent item of information (such as a Web page or an e-mail) into a series of discrete 'packets', each of which contains some of the original information, as well as a header, which contains key information about the packet's origin, destination, and contents. Once TCP has disassembled the information into a number of packets, IP allows the information to be routed through the network. When the packets are sent out onto the Internet, IP allows routers to try to figure out the best way to get each data packet to its destination, one step at a time, moving the packet from router to router until it reaches its final destination. Routers do this by examining the IP address (a unique numerical address with up to twelve digits in its current form) for the destination computer and then consulting tables to tell them which router in their neighbourhood is likely to be 'closest' to the final

destination. Each packet may travel a separate route from the originating computer to the destination computer, which then uses TCP to reassemble the packets into a whole again. If blockages prevent some packets from reaching their destination, the originating computer may resend them through alternative routes.

As stated, TCP/IP uses numerical IP addresses (such as 128.57.224.53) in order to move packets from their origin to their destination. This system, while technically efficient, is hardly very user-friendly—human beings have difficulty in remembering long numbers. Thus, in addition to TCP/IP, there is a secondary system for translating IP addresses into more human-friendly domain names, such as www.amazon.com. A master file (the so-called 'root' file) of the domain names associated with various IP addresses is maintained under the Internet Corporation for Assigned Names and Numbers (ICANN) and propagated through various specialized computers (domain name servers). Thus, each time an Internet user requests a Web page from www.boingboing.net or sends an e-mail to an address at oxford.ac.uk, a name server will translate the name (oxford.ac.uk) into a numerical IP address so that the information can be expeditiously routed across the Internet.

While the details of this system are rather technical, they have important political consequences. First, TCP/IP is *content neutral*. It does not distinguish between different kinds of information, nor does it try to prioritize the delivery of certain kinds of information over others. Second, TCP/IP greatly facilitates *distributed communication*. Internet communication is not centralized—there is no central server through which all information flows. This allows the system to adapt quickly to breakdowns in communication. If, for example, a major router stops working, other routers will quickly begin to send their information through alternative routes. Third, the existence of the domain name system and a root file allows for some degree of centralized power over the Internet. As long as most people use domain names rather than IP addresses to send and receive information, the organization in control of the root file will have considerable power over everyday users' access to the Internet.

Finally, various applications run on top of TCP/IP. At the most basic level these include e-mail, the File Transfer Protocol (which allows files to be sent to or received by remote computers), the Hyper Text Transfer Protocol (HTTP), which allows for the transmission of Web pages, and Telnet and SSL (Secure Sockets Layer), which allow remote access to computers. A host of other services and applications also invoke the Internet, and specialized software packages (Web browsers, e-mail clients) allow users to view Web pages and send and receive e-mail without having to struggle themselves with technical protocols. Indeed, very few users have direct contact with the basic protocols of the Internet; instead, they use software and applications that effectively shield them from the (rather complex) technical underpinnings that permit communication. This has important political consequences, as we shall see.

Early Debates on Internet Policy

The Internet is not a new phenomenon—its ancestor network, ARPANET, was created to foster academic and military research collaboration in the late 1960s, and the first version of TCP/IP was described in 1974.[3] However, it was not until the mid-1990s that the Internet began to broaden its appeal beyond the research community and attract serious political attention. The development of the World Wide Web (WWW) played a key role in popularizing the Internet and e-commerce.

When the Internet became a mass phenomenon, controversies arose as to how or whether it should be regulated. Even though the Internet's development had been funded by the US government, it was actually run by an ad hoc process of consensual decision-making among its users. The original universe of Internet users was both small and technically sophisticated—the relevant individuals could discuss standards and necessary

changes to them through e-mail (one of the first major Internet applications), the Internet Engineering Task Force (IETF), and other forums. Even if arguments were sometimes hard-fought, there was sufficient *ex post* consensus that the Internet could function without hierarchical guidance. Many believed that IETF-style processes could be extended to new areas of Internet governance as necessary, so that there was little need for direct government regulation.

Furthermore, the Internet seemed to be directly relevant to two major debates on the governance of 'cyberspace'.[4] First, there was an intra-US dispute over the proper scope of government authority in cyberspace. Prior to the popularization of the Internet, US law enforcement authorities had gone to counterproductive extremes in their efforts to stamp out certain forms of computer use (hacking, software piracy).[5] This provoked a backlash from many prominent computer users and the creation of an organization—the Electronic Frontiers Foundation (EFF)—that sought to defend individual freedom in the sphere of electronic communication. While the EFF represented a variety of political viewpoints, the libertarians in its ranks were especially vociferous—they perceived government efforts to regulate cyberspace as a fundamental assault on free speech and other liberties. This characterization of politics was to have substantial consequences for Internet policy, both within the US and abroad.

The second major debate involved a disagreement between the United States and other Organization for Economic Co-operation and Development (OECD) countries over proposed international instruments to regulate electronic communications. As multinational corporations began to engage in early forms of e-commerce and information exchange, some OECD countries worried that 'transborder data flows' would undermine their citizens' privacy and other human rights. They proposed binding international agreements as a solution, but met strong opposition from the United States, which was guided by the interests of its large firms.[6] This led to a stalemate, in which many OECD countries wished to create strong and comprehensive international instruments but found it difficult to do so without US agreement. They were forced either to reach agreement on new institutions among themselves, accepting that the United States would opt out (and thus perhaps undercut the effectiveness of the institution in question), or to negotiate non-binding agreements (such as the OECD Privacy Guidelines), which had little substantive force.

The Internet affected both of these disputes in important ways. First, it initially seemed to provide a technology that, by its very nature, would protect individual liberty against government intrusion. Because TCP/IP was designed to allow communication to flow around blockages in the network, many believed that it was effectively invulnerable to censorship. In John Gilmore's famous formulation, 'the Net interprets censorship as damage, and routes around it.'[7] This led libertarians to hope that the Internet would be impossible for governments to control.[8] Some even anticipated that the combination of the Internet and the use of powerful cryptographic techniques ('public key' encryption) to conceal information might undermine the power of states to tax their citizens (who could hide their money beyond the reach of the state) and thus reshape national and international politics.

These libertarians found allies in the burgeoning e-commerce sector, which in turn was able to influence the US administration towards an emphasis on self-regulation. E-commerce firms were strongly opposed to government regulation—they argued that it was likely to strangle an economic sector in the throes of rapid change. They found a ready audience in Ira Magaziner, the Clinton administration's e-commerce 'czar', who indeed drafted industry figures to write large portions of the administration's e-commerce and Internet policy.[9] E-commerce firms, like libertarians and privacy advocates, wanted strong cryptography to be readily available; it was a critical component of secure payment systems across the Internet. When the US security establishment sought to use existing laws to restrict the availability of cryptography to the general public, Magaziner, together

with a coalition of businesses and privacy advocates, succeeded in changing administration policy towards a more 'hands-off' stance.

The increased salience of the Internet also had important consequences for international disagreements over data flows. The US administration could point to the success of the IETF and similar bodies as evidence in favour of self-regulatory solutions. In 1997, the White House issued its main policy document, the 'Framework for Global Electronic Commerce', which attributed the 'genius and explosive success of the Internet . . . in part to its decentralized nature and to its tradition of bottom-up governance'.[10] It recommended that governments should refrain from regulating the Internet and e-commerce except where absolutely necessary. Instead, it proposed that industry should be allowed to take the lead in regulating itself where at all possible. In other words, firms would sign up to self-regulation—they would voluntarily commit themselves to adhere to market-driven standards without any need for government intervention. This accorded well both with the existing US regime and with the express wishes of large e-commerce firms with deep pockets and a commensurate influence on administration policy. The US further sought to create a series of bilateral agreements with its important trading partners, encouraging them to favour self-regulation instead of government-mandated rules.[11] Many other states, including some member states of the European Union (EU), were at least temporarily impressed. The US administration advocated the widespread use of self-regulation at least in part because it believed that self-regulation would undermine other states' efforts to push for comprehensive regulation of cyberspace. Self-regulation would not only prevent the creation of binding interstate institutions, it would create a *fait accompli* that would forestall external demands for regulatory changes within the US.[12]

Thus, in the mid-1990s there was a strong tendency towards self-regulation of the Internet as a means of promoting policy goals. Because the Internet was for the most part a US creation, internal US politics played a crucial formative role in shaping the politics of the Internet. This led to a strong bias towards self-regulatory solutions and against government regulation, which satisfied vocal groups that had succeeded in politicizing previous efforts by US authorities to impose law on electronic communications. Perhaps more importantly, it accorded with the interests of wealthy and influential firms, which did not want their freedom of action to be stymied by strong regulations. Finally, it helped protect the United States against pressures from other states, which had previously pressed for regulation of transborder data flows that might have had substantial repercussions for the regulation of the US economy.

Promoting Self-Regulation on the Internet

The early US proponents of self-regulation on the Internet assumed that the key to encouraging self-regulation was to keep government out. In the absence of government interference, firms and individuals would be willing to regulate themselves; indeed, they would have little choice. As Debora Spar described it, in the absence of an effective state, 'firms [would] have to write and enforce their own rules, creating private networks to facilitate and protect electronic commerce.'[13] To the surprise of many, firms showed no such willingness. Indeed, they only appeared willing to set up meaningful systems of self-regulation when it was the only viable alternative to direct state intervention. Paradoxically, US government actors found that after they had tried to forswear direct government involvement in the regulation of cyberspace, they had to intervene, if only to press private actors to regulate themselves (and thus remove any future excuse for government intervention). Two examples of this may serve to illustrate a more general trend.

The first of these was in the realm of privacy regulation. As previously mentioned, the right to privacy was a source of contention between the United States (which opposed comprehensive privacy agreements) and other industrialized democracies (which wanted such agreements). These ten-

sions came to a head in the late 1990s, when the European Union began to demand that the American government introduce formal privacy laws. EU decision-makers were worried that the privacy of EU citizens could be compromised by US firms that could acquire personal information (or gather it on the WWW) and process it in the US, outside the grip of European authorities. They thus demanded that the US introduce legislation along European lines to protect individual privacy. The US response was to argue that privacy should be protected through self-regulation rather than through law. Unfortunately, this argument was not very credible: there was little evidence that US firms had any interest in signing up to self-regulatory schemes if they could avoid it. Although one self-regulatory scheme for privacy protection, TrustE, had been set up, businesses had shown little interest in signing up to its (not very demanding) principles. European negotiators, not surprisingly, were unconvinced that self-regulation of individual privacy had any merits.

The response of the US administration was twofold. First, it pushed the Better Business Bureau to set up a self-regulatory program for privacy protection. The Better Business Bureau had no experience or prior interest in privacy protection, but was a well-established organization that might help convince the Europeans that self-regulation was a possible solution. Second, the US administration began to threaten to introduce legislation unless firms began to show their commitment to self-regulation. This had immediate results; in the words of TrustE's chairman, firms began to sign up to TrustE in large numbers, 'strangely coincidental to about the time when the government started really putting down their heavy hand'.[14]

The US administration had a somewhat similar experience in the area of domain name assignment. Through a series of developments, the US government found itself in control of the process for assigning top-level domain names, that is, of deciding who had authority to issue domain names like 'http://www.amazon.com'.[15] As the Internet took off, this became a potential source of political controversy. There was a land rush for potentially valuable domain names, and conflicting pressures existed to expand the supply of top-level domain names (which would favour those who had not already gotten valuable domain names) or, alternatively, to continue to restrict it (which would favour those who had property rights in valuable names). Top-level domain (TLD) names identify the most general part of the domain name and refer either to the purpose of the entity (e.g., .com for a commercial enterprise or .edu for an educational organization) or to the country in which the entity is located (e.g., .fr for France). TLDs are therefore limited in number. In response to the pressures associated with allocating TLDs, the US government sought to privatize the domain allocation process and hand over responsibility and authority to a private-sector actor. The US administration issued a policy paper calling for the 'spontaneous' formation of a private-sector body and committed to co-operating with such a body if it came into being and fulfilled certain conditions. Unsurprisingly, just such a body, ICANN, was created by Jon Postel, a principal figure in the debate, and was duly assigned control of key aspects of domain name management. In Michael Froomkin's words, 'ICANN exists because the [US] Department of Commerce called for it to exist. Once ICANN was formed, it owed its power, purpose and relevance to the Department of Commerce.'[16] ICANN is nominally an independent, self-regulatory body, which only has a contractual relationship with the US government, for which it has agreed to undertake certain duties. This has led over time to an ever-growing role for the US and other states in ICANN's decision-making processes. Increasingly, government actors set the rules for ICANN, excluding other actors, such as Internet activists, from the process.

Thus, the second wave of self-regulation differed in important ways from the first. The IETF and other early examples of Internet self-regulation may genuinely be described as spontaneous examples of bottom-up self-organization, in which actors came together to meet specific technical needs. However, the success of this mode of self-regulation depended to a great extent on the relatively limited set of issues involved and the willingness of the relevant actors to engage in reasoned debate over technical standards. The second wave of self-regulation was not spontaneous; rather, it was the direct result of US administration policy. The US sought, for its own political purposes, to ensure that self-regulation predominated in the Internet and e-commerce. The move to self-regulation thus did not represent a fundamental challenge by private actors to state authority. Instead, self-regulation flowed from a set of choices made by the most powerful state in the international system. However, these choices have had consequences that the US did not expect.

Self-Regulation and the International System

The move towards self-regulation in e-commerce and the Internet was in large part the result of choices made by US authorities. These choices had an important international dimension—the US believed that it could forestall other states' demands for formal regulation by creating an effective international lowest common denominator of self-regulation. This would mean that the American domestic regulatory preferences would effectively become the international default.

In retrospect, it is clear that this policy was based on a false assumption. Key policy-makers in the US administration advocated a 'pure' form of self-regulation, in which private actors would set the rules for the Internet and e-commerce, independent of states. Even though private actors came to play an important role in governance, this did not transpire. Instead, private actors are increasingly serving as channels of influence, or proxies for states. In other words, private actors are *not* creating self-regulatory realms beyond the reach of states. Rather, they are increasingly coming to serve as vectors of state influence. They are able to do this in large part because few individuals access the Internet directly; most employ intermediaries of some sort—ISPs, e-commerce companies, Web browsers supplied by firms, etc. Insofar as these intermediaries are gatekeepers through which most Internet users go, they provide states with a potential means of influencing a large number of individuals at low cost, through persuading or compelling the intermediary to do their will.

This has important consequences for the regulation of the Internet and, more generally, for areas of policy affected by the Internet. Just as in earlier eras, states continue to disagree about fundamental issues of governance. However, they now have new tools at their disposal. Those states that are able to exert influence on the relevant private actors may be able to insulate themselves from aspects of the Internet that they consider to be undesirable. In some cases, they may even be able to use their influence over private actors to shape the effective international lowest common denominator so that it reflects their preferences rather than the preferences of other states.

Consider each of these possibilities in turn. First, states are increasingly using their influence over Internet service providers (ISPs) and other actors to insulate their societies from aspects of the Internet they dislike. Most obviously, many non-democratic regimes limit their citizens' access to Web sites, e-mail, and other forms of communication that advocate democracy or are critical in other ways. Contrary to the prediction that governments would not be able to censor the spread of information on the Internet, governments can and do censor the spread of information with a reasonable degree of success. Shanthi Kalathil and Taylor C. Boas argue that 'the Internet is not necessarily a threat to authoritarian regimes', and examine how various repressive regimes have limited their citizens' access to the Internet.[17] Many authoritarian states require ISPs to route all access to the Internet through proxy servers, which allow them to filter access to content that criticizes the regime, advocates democracy, or is objectionable to them in some other way (e.g., pornography). Frequently, access to non-local news sites is limited as well. It is extremely difficult for these states fully to block access to this content, and as they develop new technologies of censorship, democracy activists and others develop new ways of circumventing these blockages. Even so, authoritarian regimes have shown themselves far better able to cope with the

challenge of open communication on the Internet than might have been expected. Indeed, some authoritarian states have shown themselves adept at using the Internet to disseminate their views (or even hack the Web sites of regime opponents).

Nor has this behaviour been confined to authoritarian regimes. Many democracies impose limits on the Web sites that their citizens can reach. Many Western European democracies maintain blacklists of Web sites that their ISPs are asked—or required—to block access to. Many of these sites advocate political positions (neo-Nazi party platforms, racist hate) that are not legally protected by freedom of speech legislation in the countries in question. Continental European states such as France and Germany are especially concerned with neo-Nazism, for historical reasons, and have taken a very proactive stance.

Second, and perhaps most interesting from the point of view of international relations theory, states are using private actors not only to insulate themselves but to extend their international influence. France, Germany, and other countries have taken steps to prevent their citizens from accessing neo-Nazi material that go beyond the forms of domestic censorship already described. They have induced important international e-commerce firms such as eBay (a specialized Internet auction house) and Yahoo! to implement their preferences, by banning all users of their services from distributing objectionable materials. France, for example, has acted to prevent Yahoo!'s customers from buying or selling neo-Nazi paraphernalia through Yahoo!'s auction Web site. Such material is illegal in France, yet French customers of Yahoo! could buy it relatively easily from people who lived in other jurisdictions such as the US, where it is perfectly legal to own it. After activists launched a court case in France, French courts ruled that Yahoo! had a legal responsibility to prevent French citizens from accessing this material through Yahoo!'s Web site, although it allowed Yahoo! some discretion in deciding how to implement this policy. Yahoo!'s immediate response was to declare that it was not bound by the French ruling and to seek a ruling in a US court that the French judgement was unenforceable. After going through the motions of declaring that it had no need to comply with French courts, Yahoo! nonetheless banned all its customers, whether they were French citizens or not, from buying or selling this material. Simultaneously, it claimed, rather implausibly, that this new policy had nothing to do with France's legal threats. On the other hand, eBay has been more forthright—in the wake of pressure from Germany, it, too, acted to ban the sale of Nazi-related paraphernalia through its Web site, noting that many eBay users were banned by their own home country from buying or selling such material. Both Yahoo! and eBay complied with European authorities because they stood to lose more than they could gain if they did not comply. Both firms had a strong interest in developing their presence in European markets, through European subsidiaries that might very possibly have been subject to substantial fines and other legal penalties. If eBay and Yahoo! had not had these important economic interests, it is doubtful that France and Germany could have done anything to persuade them to comply. Certainly, US-based ISPs that host neo-Nazi sites have shown no particular desire to comply with German demands that they shut down or otherwise limit access to these sites.

In addition, the US has tried to prevent its citizens from accessing offshore gambling sites by pressuring financial intermediaries. The regulation of gambling in the US is a complex topic—federal law is murky in important respects, and regulations vary from state to state. Some US states ban gambling completely, while others allow it (and, indeed, prosper greatly from it). As the WWW became more easily accessible, operators began to set up gambling operations in offshore locations that were effectively beyond the reach of US jurisdiction. These sites allowed US citizens living in states where gambling was banned to evade the law with ease—by gambling on-line, they could flout the law. The small Caribbean state of Antigua and Barbuda was an especially popular base for offshore operations—at the end of the 1990s, a substantial portion of its GDP flowed directly from

Internet gambling operations aimed at the US. Because these activities were offshore and because previous US regulatory decisions made it difficult for US authorities to force ISPs to block access to these offshore sites, it appeared that the US had little choice but to acquiesce to the unravelling of its domestic gambling regime.

However, lawyers working for the New York Attorney General's office hit upon an unorthodox solution—holding financial institutions such as banks and credit card agencies responsible for facilitating illegal transactions between New York citizens and offshore gambling operations. Through fines and the threat of fines, the state of New York succeeded in forcing financial institutions to stop these transactions from taking place. Other authorities—including those at the federal level—appear to be following suit. The results have been striking: the size of the Antiguan on-line gambling industry halved over a few years, in large part because of the US crackdown. Antigua's response was to take an action against the US at the World Trade Organization. While Antigua won an initial judgement in November 2004 that the US action was illegal under world trade law, this was effectively overturned at appeal. As matters stand, it appears that the US is entitled to prevent on-line gambling, as long as its law applies with equal force to domestic and offshore gambling services.

In both of these cases, states have used their influence over certain private actors (Internet auction houses, financial institutions) to exert extraterritorial control over other private actors' activities on the Internet. Nor are these the only cases of this phenomenon. States are increasingly using influence over private actors to achieve their political goals for Internet regulation, even in the absence of agreement from other states. This is an unexpected development. Contrary to the predictions of some, private actors are not replacing states as the chief sources of Internet governance. Nor, for that matter, are states reasserting control through traditional instruments (international agreements, direct action) in many important areas of Internet policy. Instead, what we are seeing is the creation of a new set of relationships between states and private actors, as states begin to use private actors as proxies to achieve policy goals that they otherwise could not achieve. This has important implications for the international regulation of the Internet.

Conclusion

In this chapter, I have argued that the Internet's consequences for international politics and the international political economy are not at all what might have been expected. Private actors, rather than replacing states and transforming the international system, are becoming proxies for states in many instances. This is not unique to the Internet. States have used private actors (standard-setting organizations, for example) to achieve their aims in areas of politics other than Internet regulation. This said, theories of international relations and international political economy have had very little to say about the sources and consequences of these state-private actor arrangements to date. Thus, these emerging forms of Internet regulation may have interesting lessons not only for Internet policy more generally but also for other emerging actors, both from the state and within the private sector.

Most prominently, it is clear that the ability of states to persuade private actors to do their bidding varies. In particular, where states have few bargaining tools vis-à-vis private actors (they cannot make credible threats or credible promises to sway these actors) they will have little success in making these actors do their bidding. Thus, for example, France and Germany succeeded in persuading Yahoo! and eBay to implement their preferences for the censorship of certain material rather than the US preference for the free dissemination of even offensive political material. They were able to threaten adverse consequences (fines, effective legal sanctions) if Yahoo! and eBay did not comply. In contrast, however, Germany did not succeed in persuading US-based ISPs to take down neo-Nazi material—because it could not threaten effective punishments (these ISPs were beyond its reach), its influence over the relevant actors was negligible.

This has interesting implications for US bargaining power. Because of the early choices made in regard to Internet structure and governance, the United States has tied its hands behind its back in important areas of Internet policy. It has voluntarily forsworn Internet regulation, and thus has few effective ways of threatening many private actors who do not do its bidding. For example, it is highly difficult for US authorities to make ISPs block access to certain kinds of content—even when they would prefer this—or share certain kinds of content with government enforcement authorities. It is important not to exaggerate this problem. The US has managed in many instances to exert control, either by using actors not directly involved with the Internet (financial institutions) to extend its extraterritorial grip, or by invoking urgent security needs to make private actors comply. Still, the US now enjoys less influence over many aspects of Internet policy than one might reasonably have expected five years ago, or even today, if one looks at the enormous importance of the US market.

The diminution of US influence over the Internet also is likely to have important implications for the existing international structures governing international exchange, even if these implications are still rather difficult to discern. Existing international institutions such as the WTO rely on definitions of goods and services that are increasingly adrift from reality and fail explicitly to regulate categories of activity (such as the kinds of influence through private actors that I have discussed) that are demonstrably important to the world economy. It is difficult to predict how well such institutions will adapt. If the last five years of discussion on the international regulation of the Internet have focused on broad questions about the role of states and private actors, the next five are likely to be much more closely concerned with the particular impact of the Internet—and the state-private actor relationships associated with it—on a variety of issues in international politics and international political economy.

Notes

1. Alec Stone-Sweet, 'Islands of Transnational Governance', in Christopher Ansell and Giuseppe di Palma, eds, *On Restructuring Territoriality* (Cambridge: Cambridge University Press, 2004).

2. For examples, see David R. Johnson and David Post, 'Law and Borders: The Rise of Law in Cyberspace', *Stanford Law Review* 48 (1996): 1367–76; Leslie David Simon, *NetPolicy.Com: Public Agenda for a Digital World* (Washington: Woodrow Wilson Center Press, 2000); Debora L. Spar, 'Lost in (Cyber)space: The Private Rules of Online Commerce', in A. Claire Cutler, Virginia Haufler, and Tony Porter, eds, *Private Authority and International Affairs* (Albany: SUNY Press, 1999), although for an account with important revisions, see Debora L. Spar, *Ruling the Waves* (New York: Harcourt and Brace, 2001).

3. For a good history of the Internet, see Kaite Hafner and Matthew Lyon, *Where Wizards Stay Up Late: The Origins of the Internet* (New York: Touchstone, 1998).

4. The term, which has its origins in William Gibson's science fiction novel *Neuromancer*, has come to serve as a catch-all for the social environment created by the Internet and e-commerce.

5. See Bruce Sterling's *The Hacker Crackdown*, at: <www.eff.org/Misc/Publications/Bruce_Sterling/Hacker_Crackdown/Hacker_Crackdown_HTML/>.

6. William J. Drake, 'Territoriality and Intangibility: Transborder Data Flows and National Sovereignty', in Kaarle Nordenstreng and Herbert I. Schiller, eds, *Beyond National Sovereignty: International Communications in the 1990s* (Norwood: Ablex, 1993).

7. The precise moment at which Gilmore came up with this pithy formulation of libertarian ideas about the Internet is uncertain.

8. See John Perry Barlow, *A Declaration of the Independence of Cyberspace* (1996), at: <www.eff.org/~barlow/Declaration-Final.html>.

9. Simon, *NetPolicy.com*.

10. White House, 'Framework for Global Electronic Commerce', at: <www.technology.gov/digeconomy/framewrk.htm>

11. Henry Farrell, 'Constructing the International Foundations of E-Commerce: The EU–US Safe Harbor Arrangement', *International Organization* 57, 2 (Spring 2003): 277–306.

12. Ibid.

13. Spar, 'Lost in (Cyber)space', 32.

14. Susan Scott, Chairman of TrustE; remarks available at: <www.research.ibm.com/iac/transcripts/internet-privacy-symp/johnpatrick.html>.

15. For histories, see Michael Froomkin, 'Wrong Turn in Cyberspace: Using ICANN to Route Around the APA and the Constitution', *Duke Law Journal* 50 (2000): 17–184; Milton L. Mueller, *Ruling the Root: Internet Governance and the Taming of Cyberspace* (Cambridge, Mass.: MIT Press, 2002).

16. Froomkin, 'Wrong Turn in Cyberspace', 70.

17. Shanthi Kalathil and Taylor C. Boas, *Open Networks, Closed Regimes: The Impact of the Internet on Authoritarian Rule* (Washington: Carnegie Endowment for International Peace, 2003), 3.

Suggested Readings

Drezner, Daniel H. 'The Global Governance of the Internet: Bringing the State Back In', *Political Science Quarterly* (forthcoming). Also available at: <www.danieldrezner.com/research/egovernance.pdf>.

Farrell, Henry. 'Constructing the International Foundations of E-Commerce: The EU–US Safe Harbor Arrangement', *International Organization* 57, 2 (Spring 2003): 277–306.

Kalathil, Shanthi, and Taylor C. Boas. *Open Networks, Closed Regimes: The Impact of the Internet on Authoritarian Rule.* Washington: Carnegie Endowment for International Peace, 2003.

Spar, Debora L. *Ruling the Waves.* New York: Harcourt and Brace, 2001.

Web Sites

The Berkman Center for Internet and Society at Harvard Law School:
http://cyber.law.harvard.edu/home/

The Information Economy:
www.sims.berkeley.edu/resources/infoecon/

Chapter 15

The Agency of Labour in a Changing Global Order

Robert O'Brien

Students of international political economy, whether beginners or veterans, face a difficult task in identifying the sources of change in global order. As outlined in the introductory chapter to Part I of this book, some approaches emphasize anarchical competition between states. An alternative approach has outlined how the transformation of production from Fordism to post-Fordism influences the global political economy. Some have suggested that the international arrangements in particular issue-areas (regimes) are central. Others have focused on the agency of multinational corporations. Another strategy has identified domestic institutions and interest groups as crucial to understanding international change and co-operation. This chapter argues that one of the prime factors in helping us understand the direction of global change involves how labour shapes global order.

The division of labour and the manner in which work is organized are central to understanding the structure of the global economy. People play a role in this global economy based on their position in the division of labour. Some people are fortunate enough to be knowledge workers making impressive salaries in the financial markets, some are manufacturing workers engaged in intense competition with their counterparts around the world, and many others are subsistence farmers trying to survive in a system moving towards the increased commercialization of agricultural production. The division of labour is also gendered and racialized, which means that people are concentrated in particular activities based on their gender, race, or ethnicity. For example, about 80

per cent of the workforce in export processing zones is female. These differing positions in the production process lead to different sets of interests and political action among various groups of workers. Their attempts to influence the trajectory of the global economy is a neglected, but significant, factor in understanding the basis and possibilities of global order.

Labour groups play a significant role in shaping global order through four mechanisms. First, they attempt to influence state policies. A change in labour support for international policies can challenge the basis of global order and the plans of other significant actors. Second, labour engages directly with international organizations to influence the rules of the game that govern international economic activity. Third, labour attempts to influence the structure of the market by engaging directly with the most powerful market actors—transnational corporations (TNCs). Fourth, labour plays a significant role in the development of 'new internationalisms' by linking up with other social movements to challenge global governance norms and practices. The remainder of this chapter illustrates these points with specific examples.

Before moving on, it is necessary to clarify that 'labour' refers to a wide range of people acting in their capacity as workers. It includes workers organized in unions and engaged in bargaining with firms and states. In some states such unions may be autonomous, acting on the instructions of their members. In other states the unions may be penetrated by state or party officials and adopt a relatively passive role. Most students of IPE will be familiar with the existence of organized workers in the form of unions. However, unionized workers make up only a small percentage of the labour force. Labour also refers to the majority of people who can be classified as 'unprotected workers'.[1] These vulnerable workers receive little union, political party, or state protection from power holders. Examples of such workers are people engaged in subsistence agriculture, peasants working for landholders, those in the informal sector forced to scavenge employment on the streets or work within the household (usually women and children). Their role in the shaping of global order is important even if it is usually indirect and neglected.

Although it is a lifestyle far removed from the reality of most of the readers of this volume, we should not forget that the vast majority of the world's population are subsistence farmers, fishers, or day labourers. The constant liberalization of economic activity since the end of World War II has implications for these people as well. More importantly, their response to the further encroachment of the liberal system upon their lives will have serious implications for the direction of globalization. This is what McMichael calls the 'agrarian question'.[2] Put somewhat crudely, the agrarian question concerns the implications of replacing peasant-based agriculture with capitalist agriculture. Although this was a subject of grave concern in Western states in the nineteenth century and attention to peasant affairs was also raised during social revolutions in China, Cuba, and Vietnam in the middle of the twentieth century, the agrarian question has not been posed again until very recently. It has re-emerged in response to the threat that liberalization of agriculture poses to billions of peasants around the world.

The State

As a great deal of IR and IPE literature argues, the state is a pivotal actor in creating and maintaining governance in the global system because of the connection between law and political authority. The state is the central legal actor and primary representative of individuals in the international system.

Agreements binding the population of a country can only be made by a state. While its representative function is often imperfect, the state is the only institution that can make a legitimate claim to represent all of the people within its territory.

Labour groups often influence state policy, which in turn shapes global order. However, the nature and influence of labour organizations on the state vary widely across the globe. While trade unions are independent in some countries, in others they are dominated by the state or are agents of political parties. In countries where labour is directly controlled by the state or a political party (the majority of states) the influence of unions on policy will be limited. In states where labour organizations are autonomous and have a sufficient membership density or occupy key industries, unions can be expected to influence state policy. These modified state policies can then influence international relations.

Several attempts have been made to link the nature of the post-1945 global economy to the strength of domestic labour groups in key states. John Ruggie argues that the post-war era of embedded liberalism reflected a compromise between those social forces seeking liberalization of economic activity and those groups desiring protection for domestic welfare.[3] Thus, the trade and monetary regimes from the 1950s until the 1970s liberalized economic activity, but within limits set by national coalitions defending full employment. Andrew Martin argues that the eventual undermining of this system is due to the weakness of US labour compared to the social democratic or corporatist states of Western Europe. Since the 1970s successive US governments pursued trade liberalization and capital mobility in a form that ran against the interests of US labour and the welfare state. In this view the degree of compatibility between international economic order and Keynesian welfare states is partially a function of the relative strength of labour in the most powerful states.[4]

The experience of the United States can be used as an example of how labour activity can shape international order. Labour was a significant supporter of the global expansion of US capitalism during the height of embedded liberalism because unionized workers participated in the politics of productivity.[5] This arrangement involved subsuming class conflict by ensuring that growth and productivity gains were distributed between corporate profits and the unionized workforce. It was a method of neutralizing labour opposition by integrating unionized workers into a division of economic spoils. For its part, US labour supported the extension of US capitalism by marginalizing radical workers' organizations in Latin America, Asia, and Western Europe. However, as international competition increased for the US workforce, organized labour shifted from offering strong support for a global economy to being a growing obstacle to further liberalization and internationalization. Co-operation with state elites was further undermined as neo-liberal governments in the United States and Britain, accompanied by a business offensive against workers, led to the ejection of labour from the governing coalition.

A turning point for US labour and its view of international economic relations was the North American Free Trade Agreement. US organized labour reacted differently to this liberalizing agreement than it had to earlier initiatives (e.g., GATT). First, it acknowledged that the unfettered expansion of US-based MNCs was not in the interest of US workers. This was in contrast to its previous supportive stance towards the expansion of American capitalism to other parts of the world. Second, labour rejected the political leadership of the Democratic Party and opposed the initiative of a sitting Democratic President. Third, it sought out other social movement allies such as environmentalists to build a broad-based political coalition capable of slowing the neo-liberal agenda. Fourth, labour worked with autonomous unions (rather than those tied to right-wing governments) in other countries. In dealing with Mexico the ALF-CIO was forced to cultivate relations with the emerging independent Mexican unions rather than rely on the Mexican government-sponsored CTM

(Confederación de Trabajadores de México) union. The CTM was an adequate ally for US workers during the Cold War, when the fight was against Communism, but allies in the fight against transnational exploitation would have to be found in unions controlled by their members. In summary, the US NAFTA debate is likely to prove to have been a watershed in organized labour's acceptance of the dominant brand of liberalism.[6]

While large corporations retain a stranglehold on the US political system through the financing of election campaigns, changes in the position of US labour have weakened the social base for an open liberal economic system. Efforts by labour to protect itself in the face of an increasingly competitive economy and a state less committed to economic redistribution may raise obstacles to US leadership of the global economy. For example, labour opposition to NAFTA forced the negotiating parties to include in the agreement a side accord on labour rights.

Another significant example of labour's role in shaping global order through influencing state power is provided by Brazil. In October 2002 the labour backed Workers' Party (PT) won the presidential election and began to challenge the previous administration's acceptance of neo-liberal economic policies. One element of this challenge was to attack forcefully the trade policies of developed countries by demanding the end of agricultural subsidies before agreeing to further trade liberalization. This stance resulted in a much watered down Free Trade Agreement of the Americas and a deadlock at the World Trade Organization's 2003 Ministerial Meeting in Cancun, Mexico. Brazil has taken the lead in reviving a developing-world coalition in trade matters by forming a G-3 alliance of Brazil, India, and South Africa. Brazil's President Lula Da Silva, a former trade union official, has initiated intensified economic relations with China in an attempt to balance US influence. The hope is that China and perhaps Russia will join the G-3 to counteract US and European dominance in international economic relations.

Workers' organizations have also played a crucial role in changing state policy and elements of international order in states where their activities were often curbed. Two excellent examples are in Poland and South Africa. The collapse of the Soviet Empire and the end of the Cold War had several important causes, including the exhaustion of the Soviet economic model and intense competition from Western states and economies. However, the activities of workers' organizations (Solidarity in Poland) in the early 1980s opened the first cracks in the Soviet system of control that would eventually lead to a wider disintegration of East European Communist states in 1989. In South Africa, workers' groups, in alliance with other social activists and the African National Congress, waged a long and ultimately successful campaign to overturn the apartheid system of racial oppression. The labour movement was central to 'creating the conditions for transition, in shaping its character and indeed in legitimating the process itself'.[7] Labour played a significant role in both of these democratization processes and, as a result, helped to change the political economies in these regions and in the broader international system.

Agricultural workers have also had an influence on state policy in recent years. Perhaps the most dramatic case has been the peasant and Aboriginal rebellion in the southern Mexican state of Chiapas.[8] Although the rebellion draws on a historical legacy of oppression, it was clearly linked to steps taken by the Mexican government to liberalize agricultural landholdings in the run-up to NAFTA. Local concerns were linked to broader developments in IPE. The Zapatista rebels have been quick to exploit modern technology to broadcast their cause worldwide and have begun the task of forging links with like-minded groups in other parts of the world (www.ezln.org). The rebellion soon moved from a local protest to challenging the power structures of the Mexican state, its economic policies, and insertion of Mexico into the global economy. The potential for other peasant-based challenges to state policy exist in a large number of developing states, including China, India, Indonesia, and the Philippines.

International Organizations

The proliferation of international organizations is one of the most striking developments in the international relations of the twentieth century. They have increased both in number and in importance. Their growth has been a product of industrial change and facilitated the growth of an international and a global economy.[9] Regional organizations have joined multilateral organizations to provide a web of coverage across issues and between states. International organizations shape the global economy by providing a venue for interstate co-operation, providing advice to governments and citizens, and compelling states to abide by treaties and agreements.

Labour groups have a complex relationship with international economic organizations, ranging from support for their objectives to determined opposition. They have caused the creation of at least one major institution, influenced the policies of others, and provided firm resistance to the activities of many international economic institutions.

Worker dissatisfaction with the destructive nature of capitalism led to the creation of the oldest element of the United Nations system—the International Labour Organization (ILO). The ILO originates with the League of Nations, the predecessor of the UN. Fearing the mass mobilization of the working class in World War I and operating under the shadow of the Communist victory in the Russian Revolution, the victorious allied capitalist states created an international institution to address and pacify the concerns of the workers. As one former ILO official has put it, 'The ILO was Versailles' answer to Bolshevism.'[10] The ILO constitution recognized that peace could only be based on social justice and that the conditions of workers were central to social justice.

A distinctive element of the ILO is that voting rights are split on a 2:1:1 ratio between state, employer, and labour representatives. Recent union activity in the field of international organizations is aimed at extending some element of the tripartite ILO structure so that labour has a voice in a wide range of policy issues. The goal is to force major international organizations to address worker and social issues. We will consider this attempt at the World Trade Organization (WTO) and the International Monetary Fund (IMF).

The WTO is a product of the Uruguay Round negotiations of the General Agreement on Tariffs and Trade (GATT). It established a permanent international trade organization with enhanced regulatory powers and a mandate to spearhead further liberalization initiatives. Many elements of the international labour movement, such as the International Confederation of Free Trade Unions (ICFTU), viewed the establishment of the WTO as one of a series of international regulatory regimes created to protect the interests of capital and undermine labour in the 1980s and 1990s. For example, the WTO had provisions to protect the intellectual property rights of corporations, but was silent about labour rights.

The goal of the international labour movement (as represented by the main international confederations of trade unions) is for the WTO to have core labour standards (a social clause) brought into its purview. The social clause would commit states to respect seven crucial conventions of the ILO (Conventions 87, 98, 29, 105, 100, 111, 138). Among other rights, these conventions provide for: freedom of association, the right to collective bargaining, abolition of forced labour, prevention of discrimination in employment, and a minimum age for employment. The key to having the conventions built into the WTO structure is that for the first time they would become enforceable rather than be dependent on the whims of individual states. In contrast to the ILO's reliance on moral argument, the WTO has the ability to enforce compliance. In order to achieve their goal, groups such as the ICFTU and affiliates, including the ALF-CIO have pressured the United States and the European Union into raising the issue of core labour standards at the WTO. They argued that continued support for trade liberalization in developed states required a minimum floor for workers' rights.

Other elements of the labour movement have opposed both the idea that core labour standards should be part of the WTO and the existence of the WTO itself. For example, the linkage between labour standards and the WTO was rejected in two national conferences of independent Indian unions in March and October 1995. Delegates expressed fears that the social clause initiative was driven by protectionist desires in northern countries. The Indian unions' suggestion was that rather than working through the WTO, workers should push for a United Nations Labour Rights Convention and the establishment of National Labour Rights Commissions.[11] The issue was not whether all workers should be entitled to basic rights, but whether the WTO was the appropriate institution for such a task. The conclusion among many grassroots Indian activists was that the WTO, along with the IMF and World Bank, was irrevocably tied to exploitative northern interests.

A similar, oppositional stance towards the WTO has been adopted by an alliance of peasant groups reacting against the liberalization of agriculture—the Peoples' Global Action against 'Free' Trade and the World Trade Organization (PGA). The PGA is an instrument for co-ordination that brings together peoples' movements to oppose trade liberalization.[12] The PGA organizes conferences approximately three months before the biannual Ministerial Meetings of the World Trade Organization. Conferences are used to update the PGA manifesto and to co-ordinate global and local action against free trade. The conference committee for the February 1998 event included groups such as the Frente Zapatista de Liberación Nacional (FZLN) from Mexico, Karnataka State Farmers' Association (KRRS) from India, Movemento sem Terra (MST) from Brazil, and the Peasant Movement of the Philippines (KMP). The PGA is committed to non-violent civil disobedience and a confrontational stance in pursuit of its opposition to free trade. It represents a constituency firmly in opposition to dominant trends in the global political economy.

Labour and peasant resistance to the neo-liberal tenets of the WTO have been part of a broad debate about the role of the trade institution. While organized labour did not succeed in having labour standards included in the WTO purview, its agitation did result in movement on labour rights in other forums. For example, the ILO responded by bundling its core labour rights into a new declaration that commits all members of the institution to respect basic labour rights. The Secretary-General of the United Nations responded by initiating the Global Compact, which brings together selected TNCs and civic associations to highlight best practices in corporate activity respecting human rights and environmental standards. Peasant resistance has highlighted the dangers of agricultural liberalization and complicated the task of trade negotiators at the regional and national levels.

The IMF is another institution of concern to labour groups. In developing countries its policy guidelines of privatization, deregulation, and liberalization are seen to be the cause of enormous suffering, savage decreases in living standards, and a justification for anti-union campaigns.[13] IMF policies are interpreted as imposing a neo-liberal economic model on the weakest countries and tolerating, if not encouraging, authoritarian forms of industrial relations.

In response to these criticisms, in the mid-1990s the IMF tried to work with labour groups to formulate and implement revised structural adjustment programs. The IMF director called on organized labour to help hold governments accountable for financial mismanagement and the content of structural adjustment programs.[14] His view was that labour could be a strategic partner in ensuring that money is properly spent by national governments. The leadership of the ICFTU has responded positively to these overtures, seeing them as an opportunity to influence policy. Other parts of the union movement are much more reluctant to co-operate because they see IMF policies as the cause of exclusion. Potential interaction between the IMF and the ICFTU is limited by widely conflicting goals. The IMF is seeking the help of unions to limit government corruption and contribute to good governance, whereas the unions desire a rethinking of the core assumptions underlying structural adjustment programs.

The importance of organized labour to the IMF and its main funders and supporters (such as the US Treasury) increases dramatically in times of economic crisis. During the 1997 East Asian financial crisis the activity of labour organizations was viewed as crucial to the success of IMF financial packages. One example occurred during the December 1997 discussion between a US Treasury official and incoming South Korean President Kim Dae Jung about IMF rescue packages and economic reform. David Lipton, the Undersecretary for International Affairs at the Treasury, indicated to the Korean president-elect that labour and labour flexibility were key to Korea's situation. Other evidence can be seen in the willingness of the former IMF first deputy managing director, Stanley Fischer, to meet with legal and (at the time) illegal union leaders in Indonesia in 1998.

Unprotected workers also have a role in influencing international organizations by setting limits to what types of programs are accepted by recipient countries. For example, 'IMF riots'—spontaneous demonstrations that break out in response to government cutbacks that are part of an IMF-negotiated structural adjustment program—can slow or turn back neo-liberal projects by making them politically unfeasible. Demonstrators express public anger, but usually do not have a coherent strategy for economic reform. Despite this lack of strategic direction, unprotected works can still raise obstacles to global governance initiatives.

Labour relations with the WTO, IMF, and World Bank face ideological and interest-based opposition. Although the Bretton Woods institutions are re-evaluating their economic management approaches, neo-liberal ideology opposes political interference in the market, such as international labour standards or social dimensions to structural adjustment programs. Financial interests oppose curbs on speculation, while employers in most countries and entrenched authoritarian governments resist the introduction of meaningful international labour standards.

The Corporation

Corporations are significant global actors, with some TNCs commanding more resources than many states. They shape the global economy through their investment decisions, business practices, and influences on state and interstate actors. Because of this influence, unions and groups concerned about labour issues are trying to shape global order by influencing the activity of corporations. Where state or international organization regulatory efforts are non-existent or inadequate to protect workers' interests, corporations are directly targeted for reform.

Worker response to the globalization of production has taken place inside and outside of firms. Within firms, workers have continued to mobilize and agitate for worker rights. In some industries, corporations and labour have played a global game of hide and seek, with investors shifting production away from areas populated by organized labour. However, labour militancy tends to follow corporate relocation so that the conflict between labour and capital continues unabated. Beverly Silver's study of the auto industry provides a good example as she traces the transfer of production and labour militancy from the US in the 1930s to Western Europe in the 1960s and 1970s to Brazil and South Korea in the 1980s and 1990s.[15] Corporations attempt to institute new technology and relocate production in an effort to escape labour militancy, but respite from labour unrest is only temporary.

One of labour's greatest challenges is the shift of manufacturing production to China. Western and Asian companies have invested heavily in Chinese economic zones and are exporting products around the globe. The Chinese state does not allow independent labour organizations and TNCs are provided with a cheap and compliant labour force. The lower cost of production resulting from this coerced form of labour threatens the economic development of numerous states and workers. Workers in advanced industrialized economies can feel threatened because they cannot match Chinese wages. An additional problem is that manufacturers can locate plants in China and export key components to their Western operations in the event of strikes in the US or Europe. This might, for example, make it much more difficult for US auto workers to launch a successful strike against their employers because components would just be imported from China. Chinese labour conditions also pose a problem for many developing countries. For example, since the debt crisis of 1982, Mexico has based it economic strategy on serving as a low-wage platform for US TNCs. However, even Mexican wages are too high when compared to China, and Mexico faces the possibility of investors shifting money across the Pacific.

In addition to organizing within firms, workers have shown an interest in building a system of multinational collective bargaining. Such a step would bring organized labour closer to the social democratic form of industrial relations because it would legitimate its role in the economy. The aim is to establish a form of global industrial relations where unions are able to bargain with multinational companies unhindered by geographic dispersal. The global union federations and the ICFTU have taken a number of initiatives. One step is to put all the collective agreements of a particular firm into a single database so that union negotiators will be aware of arrangements at sister plants. Another initiative is to host world congresses of workers from the same company, such as Nissan. A third initiative has been to reach framework agreements with multinational corporations that provide for basic worker rights in all subsidiaries.

Caution should be exercised in anticipating the growth of multinational collective bargaining. In its most fertile ground, Western Europe, progress has been extremely slow.[16] Despite high levels of economic integration, geographic proximity, and an overreaching institutional structure in the European Community and European Union, the obstacles are immense. Unions remain weak and dominated by national structures, employer organizations and firms are reluctant to engage in such activity, and EU institutions lack the structure and desire to become active in the industrial relations domain. Given such difficulty in a region of economic and political convergence, the possibilities in more diverse arenas appear remote.

Outside the corporation, concern about corporate activity has led to increasing pressure for ethical trade. In its broadest sense ethical trade encompasses two elements.[17] The first element is a concern with how companies make their product. This involves pressuring companies to ensure that the production process respects basic human rights and environmental standards. Examples include companies that adopt codes of conduct guaranteeing respect for workers' rights or banning child labour. The second element is the fair trade movement, which seeks to increase the financial return to poor-country producers as a method of improving sustainable development. Major fair trade initiatives have taken place in products such as coffee and chocolate.

In response to the demand for more ethical trade many corporations have implemented codes of conduct governing their operations and a number of labelling schemes have been created to signal to consumers that products have been made in particular ways or that profits flow back to developing-country producers. The results of this activity have been mixed. Many corporations have changed their rhetoric about socially and environmentally responsible production and have joined public schemes to improve behaviour, such as the UN's Global Compact. On the other hand, there have been doubts about whether TNCs actually adhere to guidelines or only use them as a public relations exercise. Moreover, many businesses are invulnerable to consumer campaigns because they are subcontractors or do not rely on brand names for sales. They have little incentive to participate in ethical trade. The proliferation of codes of conduct and labelling schemes has led to an uneven set of guidelines and regulations and thus has created some expense for industry and confusion for consumers. Doubts have also been raised about the degree to which ethical trade actually benefits southern producers or is designed to satisfy the conscience of northern consumers.

Ethical trade is an evolving and growing aspect of global political economy. Existing mechanisms have many shortcomings and numerous difficult issues remain to be resolved. Nevertheless, workers and consumers have had considerable success in forcing many corporations to at least acknowledge a set of social and environmental norms that had previously been ignored. It is no longer legitimate for major corporations to argue that their only business is business and that social and environmental aspects of production are not their responsibility. While practice falls short of desired outcomes, this represents a significant change in the global order.

Labour and the New Multilateralism

The labour movement is in a process of transition where international labour activity is moving beyond the preserve of international union organizations such as the ICFTU and the global union federations to encompass the activities of grassroots union locals and social groups with an interest in labour issues. Capitalizing on the development of information technology, labour activism is now feasible via networks of concerned people rather than reliant on hierarchical, bureaucratic internationals. Consequently, groups are starting to reinvent their practice of internationalism.

Labour groups are beginning to take their place in efforts at building a 'new multilateralism'. This is a form of internationalism that seeks to 'reconstitute civil societies and political authorities on a global scale, building a system of global governance from the bottom up'.[18] In contrast to traditional notions of multilateralism as 'an institutional form that coordinates relations among three or more states on the basis of generalized principles of conduct',[19] the new multilateralism starts with social organizations independent of the state. In terms of policy, the desire is to create sustainable development shielded from the ravages of neo-liberal competition.

This shift to transnational civic activity on the part of a wide range of actors has led to discussion about the development of global civil society. Focusing on the activity of environmental, women's, and human rights groups, scholars have pointed to the development of a global citizen politics because of the growing importance of transnational advocacy networks.[20] This is a form of politics that includes the state, but goes beyond it to influence market behaviour and societal norms.

What is the significance of this transnational social movement activity? Were it to fulfill its potential, such activity could lay the basis for a counter-hegemonic bloc.[21] It could be the core of an alliance of social forces that would work through states and international organizations to change the principles at the heart of international order. These groups are in the process of articulating a vision of the future counter to the dominant views of how society and global order should operate. Rather than stressing the virtues of a market-based society, they pose other values such as environmental sustainability, human dignity, equality, and justice. They are engaged in a long process of changing social norms and influencing power holders. They have the potential to be the source of structural change.

Labour's contact with the new multilateralism is significant for two reasons. First, the collision of old unionism and new social movements is having a transformative effect on workers' organizations. In an attempt to survive the anti-union environment, unions are turning to new members, especially women. This has forced them to take on a new series of issues, such as gender equity and child care. Thus, unions are increasingly looking beyond basic issues of pay to broader questions of social and economic organization. They are also reaching out to unprotected workers and other social movements to form broader coalitions. This is tipping the balance away from conservative business unionism to an activist social unionism. Social unionism takes a more aggressive and antagonistic approach to corporations and governments that favour business over other interests.

Second, organized labour remains a principal strategic actor in any process of political economy. Its relatively high degree of institutionalization has benefits, as well as costs. Labour has firmer claims to represent identifiable constituencies than many NGOs because of its institutionalized structure and mechanisms for accountability (elections and dues

payments). Unions can also negotiate agreements with governments or corporations knowing that they can usually deliver their members' compliance. This makes labour a serious and important negotiating partner. Finally, through industrial action unions can impose direct costs on those driving the globalization process—corporate and state elites.

Although it will not be easy, organized labour, social organizations with labour interests, and the new social movements may be capable of working together to influence the evolution of global order. A good example is provided by the World Social Forums that are usually held in Porto Alegre, Brazil. These forums bring together thousands of social activists challenging the neo-liberal basis of global order. Brazilian labour groups have been instrumental in providing logistical and intellectual support, although the majority of activity is not directly concerned with organized labour. After a slow start, many of the traditional union organizations have also been pulled into this process and have developed links with a wide variety of social forces. Drawing on their distinct strengths and compensating for each others weaknesses, they offer a challenge to governing corporate and political elites. Their intention is to transform the structure of global order and reorient the principles of political and economic organization. They are not united and they may not succeed, but labour and the new multilateralism will have a significant role to play.

Conclusion

This chapter has argued that labour is not simply a passive actor at the receiving end of the dictates of global order, but that it is a crucial actor or agent in the creation of that order.[22] Clearly, it is in a subordinate power relationship with government and business elites. However, as a critical agent of resistance to neo-liberal globalization, labour has an impact on state policies, international organizations, and corporate behaviour. Furthermore, by participating in a broad-ranging society-based internationalism or new multilateralism, labour groups are finding allies and increasing their effectiveness in influencing corporate and state policy.

Theories created to assist our understanding of the changing global order that ignore the agency of labour risk overlooking a crucial source of change in the global political economy. Attention to the agency of labour as illustrated in this chapter highlights two main points about the changing global order. First, changes in the nature of work, the distribution of wealth, and life chances mobilize social forces that impact on political and economic entities such as states and corporations. Second, inequality and injustice remain significant concerns for many actors attempting to shape the global political economy.

Notes

1. Jeffrey Harrod, *Power, Production and the Unprotected Worker* (New York: Columbia University Press, 1987).

2. Philip McMichael, 'Rethinking Globalization: the Agrarian Question Revisited', *Review of International Political Economy* 4, 4 (Winter 1997): 630–62.

3. John Ruggie, 'Embedded Liberalism and Postwar Economic Regimes', in Ruggie, *Constructing the World Polity: Essays on International Institutionalization* (London: Routledge, 1999), 62–84.

4. Andrew Martin, 'Labour, the Keynesian Welfare State, and the Changing International Political Economy', in Richard Stubbs and Geoffrey R.D. Underhill, eds, *Political Economy and the Changing Global Order* (Toronto: McClelland & Stewart, 1994), 60–74.

5. Charles S. Maier, 'The Politics of Productivity: Foundations of American International Economic Policy after World War II', *International Organization* 31 (1977): 607–33.

6. Mark Rupert, '(Re) Politicizing the Global Economy: Liberal Common Sense and Ideological Struggle in the US NAFTA Debate', *Review of International Political Economy* 2: 658–92.

7. Glen Adler and Eddie Webster, 'Challenging Transition Theory: The Labour Movement, Radical Reform, and Transition to Democracy in South Africa', *Politics and Society* 23, 1 (Mar. 1995): 75–106.

8. Andrew Reding, 'Chiapas Is Mexico', *World Policy Journal* 11, 1 (Spring 1994): 11–25.

9. Craig Murphy, *International Organization and Industrial Change: Global Governance Since 1850* (Cambridge: Polity Press, 1994).

10. Robert W. Cox, 'ILO: Limited Monarchy', in Cox and Harold Jacobson, eds, *The Anatomy of Influence* (New Haven: Yale University Press, 1974), 101.

11. 'Towards a UN Labour Rights Convention' and 'Conclusions of the National Consultation Concerning the Social Clause in World Trade Agreements', *Asian Labour Update* 20 (Nov. 1995–Mar. 1996): 11–12, 17.

12. PGA, 'First Conference of the Peoples' Global Action Against 'Free' Trade and the World Trade Organisation', Manila, Philippines, PGA Secretariat, 1997.

13. Jeffrey Harrod, *Labour and Third World Debt* (Brussels: International Federation of Chemical, Energy and General Workers' Union, 1992).

14. Michel Camdessus, 'The Impacts of Globalization and Regional Integration on Workers and Their Trade Unions', speech delivered to the ICFTU 16th World Congress, Brussels, 26 June 1996.

15. Beverly J. Silver, *Forces of Labour: Workers' Movements and Globalization Since 1870* (Cambridge: Cambridge University Press, 2003).

16. Bernhard Ebbinghaus and Jelle Visser, 'European Labor and Transnational Solidarity: Challenges, Pathways, and Barriers', in Jytte Klausen and Louise A. Tilly, eds, *European Integration in Social and Historical Perspective from 1850 to the Present* (Lanham, Md: Rowman & Littlefield, 1997), 195–221.

17. Mick Blowfield, 'Ethical Trade: A Review of Developments and Issues', *Third World Quarterly* 20, 4 (1999): 753–70.

18. Robert W. Cox, 'Introduction', in Cox, ed., *The New Realism: Perspectives on Multilateralism and*

World Order (Basingstoke: Macmillan/United Nations University Press, 1997), xxvii.

19. John Gerard Ruggie, 'Multilateralism: The Anatomy of an Institution', in Ruggie, ed., *Multilateralism Matters: The Theory and Praxis of an Institutional Form* (New York: Columbia University Press, 1993), 11.

20. Margaret Keck and Katherine Sikkink, *Activists beyond Borders: Advocacy Networks in International Politics* (Ithaca, NY: Cornell University Press, 1988).

21. On notions of hegemony and counter-hegemony in international relations, see Robert W. Cox, 'Gramsci, Hegemony, and International Relations: An Essay in Method', *Millennium* 12 (1983): 162–75.

22. For a similar argument in the US context, see Andrew Herod, 'Labor as an Agent of Globalization and as a Global Agent', in Kevin Cox, ed., *Spaces of Globalization* (New York: Guilford Press, 1997), 167–200.

Suggested Readings

Harrod, Jeffrey, and Robert O'Brien, eds. *Global Unions? Theory and Strategy of Organised Labour in the Global Political Economy*. London: Routledge, 2002.

McMichael, Philip. 'Rethinking Globalization: The Agrarian Question Revisited', *Review of International Political Economy* 4 (1997): 630–62.

Munck, Ronaldo, ed. *Labour and Globalization: Results and Prospects*. Liverpool: Liverpool University Press, 2003.

———. *Globalisation and Labour: The New Great Transformation*. London: Zed Press 2002.

O'Brien, Robert, and Marc Williams. *Global Political Economy: Evolution and Dynamics*. New York: Palgrave, 2004.

Silver, Beverly J. *Forces of Labour: Workers' Movements and Globalization Since 1870*. Cambridge: Cambridge University Press, 2003.

Waterman, Peter, and Jane Wills. *Place, Space and the New Labour Internationalisms*. Oxford: Blackwell, 2001.

Web Sites

Global Compact: www.unglobalcompact.org/Portal/
Global unions: www.global-unions.org/
International Labour Organization: www.ilo.org/

People's Global Action:
    www.nadir.org/nadir/initiativ/agp/en/
Via Campesina:www.viacampesina.org

Chapter 16

Post-Colonial Readings of Child Labour in a Globalized Economy

Geeta Chowdhry

Although the participation of child labour in the global economy is an accepted fact, estimates of the number of working children range from 200 million to 500 million. According to the International Labour Organization (ILO), over 250 million children in the world, or just under one-fifth of all children in the 5–14 age group, work today: 120 million are employed full-time and 130 million combine work with non-economic activities.[1] Asia is estimated to have 153 million, Africa 32 million, and Latin America 17.5 million economically active children between the ages of 10 and 14.[2] These estimates are an important reminder of the magnitude of the child labour problem, which has been at the centre of the global movement to eradicate child labour. Although staggering statistics and heart-rending stories of child labour have captured international attention and spurred international abolitionist efforts, they have also obfuscated the discourses of geo-economic and identity politics that are engendered through the telling of the child labour story.

Child labour is not only about the 'production and circulation of commodities' in the international political economy; it is also about the 'production and circulation of meanings' through which geopolitical identities and hierarchies are (re)produced.[3] Thus, examining child labour requires that at the very least we situate child labour 'in the current conjuncture of global capital'[4] in which commodities are produced and circulated, and surplus value is produced and realized. In addition, to comprehend fully the global politics of child labour also requires an examination of how the 'production and circulation of meanings', including meanings surrounding identities and rights, are produced in this exchange of commodities. Consequently, debates surrounding child labour not only uncover global labour practices and the human rights struggles of a 'globalized civil society', but also underscore the geopolitical dimensions of these struggles and the 'human rights internationalism and the nationalisms that are sustained by it'.[5]

Human rights and labour discourses on children have become important symbols of transnational geopolitics and offer important insights into the exercise of power in a post-colonial world. Focusing on child labour in the global political economy, this chapter explores these discourses by focusing on the production and circulation of commodities and meanings at the international and national levels. International discourses on child labour, heavily influenced by the language of universal human rights and/or by national discourses generally premised on a culturally relativist human rights position, are situated within the global capitalism and provide similar and unhelpful arguments about human rights and child labour. A post-colonial reading of child labour, human rights, and international political economy—one that unveils the 'cultural politics' of the human rights regime and makes visible the hierarchies of power within international relations—better explains the complexity of child labour in a globalized and post-colonial world.[6]

Child Labour and Human Rights in International Relations

Although the literature on international relations (IR), including that of international political economy (IPE), provides us with several theoretical frameworks with which to consider child labour, this chapter focuses exclusively on the debates in the human rights literature that seek to frame the discussion of child labour. For example, the 'norms' school of human rights suggests that the human rights regime enumerates norms that should be implemented universally. These human rights norms are internationalized through the advocacy of transnational activist networks.[7] While the norms school has brought attention to the role of transnational advocacy in 'international relations scholarship, long preoccupied with anarchy and order, sovereignty and security', it has been limited by its own normative biases.[8] Since the norms school focuses mostly on political rights, its 'liberal' understanding of human rights often does not address the complicity of capital and Western hegemonic regimes in human rights violations. In addition, since the liberal arguments about human rights originated within the discourse of the Enlightenment and are juxtaposed against the practices of colonization, slavery, the theft of land, and genocide, there is deep suspicion about these moral claims among the critics of the norms school.

In many ways, the liberal assumptions of the norms school regarding human rights overlap with the traditional 'universalist' position that gained prominence in the human rights literature with the universalist versus cultural relativist debate. Despite the differences between them, both the universalist and cultural relativist positions use cultural arguments to pursue their cause and are equally embedded in global capital. The universalists make rights-based universal claims regarding 'human nature, universal human dignity, and conceptions such as "crimes against humanity"'.[9] Critics argue their claims are ensconced in the Enlightenment project, the imperial juncture, and colonial readings of 'native' culture. According to Talal Asad, the export of European understandings of human rights began with Europe's colonial projects, when European claims of bringing their supposedly more highly evolved civilization to local populations played a central role in their justifications of imperialism.[10] For example, as part of their 'civilizing mission', colonizers routinely outlawed cultural practices they considered 'barbaric' and 'inhumane'. Women and gender were critical to the racialized constructions of 'native' cultures; 'oppressive' practices like veiling and dowry were opposed, and in general 'native' women were to be rescued from indigenous culture and 'native' men were used to legitimize imperial incursions.[11] These racialized and gendered images of the European colonies served as identity markers, and were critical to the cultural, political, and economic struggles that marked the colonial project. It is not surprising, then, that human rights claims of the universalists continue to be received with a great deal of scepticism in the developing world. To many, 'these highly abstracted formulations of humanity and morality' are still regarded as the 'products of an international order dominated by western institutions and as far removed from the basic cultural conceptions of justice and morality found in non-western locales'.[12]

The cultural relativist position, influenced by the emphasis on cultural difference and identity politics, has been supported by, among others, many cultural anthropologists and non-Western governments. Many of these governments have suggested that the concept of universal human rights basically reflects Western understandings and is not compatible with other cultural understandings. In addition, relativists argue that Western countries use human rights to pursue their own national interests through the effective use of trade sanctions, denial of development assistance, and pressure to liberalize the economies of countries in the global South. Although it is possible that Western countries use human rights to protect Western hegemonic status, it is also apparent that the cultural relativist position of Asian states is shaped by the global capitalist system. Nations using the cultural relativist argument suggest that their preoccupation with economic development forces them to give low priority to political and civil liberties. This justification is also known as the first generation of human rights. In these cultural arguments, political and civil rights are positioned as inimical to economic rights and non-Western values. In contrast, non-governmental organizations (NGOs) and scholars from non-Western countries have not only argued that many 'traditional' values are consistent with human rights, but have also suggested that this type of rhetoric is used by some leaders to legitimize their authoritarian rule and to obfuscate their complicity with global capital.

Post-Colonial Analyses of Human Rights and Child Labour

Despite the presence of post-colonial studies in other disciplines for almost three decades, post-colonial analysis has only recently made incursions into the field of international relations. Influenced by the work of Frantz Fanon, Albert Memmi, Aime Cesaire, and other anti-colonial and nationalist thinkers, post-colonial studies gained momentum in the 1970s with the publication of *Orientalism*, one of the most influential works of Edward Said.[13] While the influence of subaltern scholarship (predominantly focused on the retelling of South Asian history from subaltern perspectives) on post-colonial studies is worth noting, it is also important to emphasize that post-colonial critiques of the French empire from West Africa 'originate from a longstanding anticolonialism that owes its character to its ambivalence toward Enlightenment ideas, associated modes of inquiry, and the political project of colonial assimilation.'[14] In addition, post-colonial feminists' emphasis on gender as central to the mapping of power has been critical in deepening post-colonial analysis.[15] While it is not desirable to collapse the contributions of post-colonial inquiry into a singular, overarching, and cohesive theory, Sheila Nair and I have suggested elsewhere that there are certain broad identifiable assumptions within which post-colonial theorizing occurs.[16] The focus of post-colonial analysis on several factors provides us with a unique vantage point from which to examine power in a post-colonial world. These factors include: (1) the colonial project

as foundational in shaping the modern world; (2) the salience of representation to power and the underwriting of representation through narratives of race, gender, class, and nation; (3) the silences and erasures of IR around race (and its intersections) despite its foundational presence in global politics; (4) the centrality of global capital in the construction of the modern world; and (5) the importance of resistance and agency.

A post-colonial approach to human rights and child labour shifts the terrain of inquiry from the universal versus cultural relativism debate to one premised on an inquiry into 'the operations of power in relation to knowledge formation'.[17] Thus, the importance of the imperial project to knowledge production about colonized cultures is noteworthy. Equally important to note are the continuities and disjunctures in knowledge production that came about as the result of decolonization and that are emerging in the context of globalization today. In other words, narratives of human rights must be situated within the colonial and post-colonial discursive economy of hierarchy and representation, and post-colonial analyses of child labour must come to terms with the discourses of human rights, child labour, identity production, and power by asking how the ideas about human rights circulate. What representations and identities do they enable? What are the cultural contests over human rights? How is global and local capital implicated in the discourses on human rights?

As suggested earlier, my analysis of child labour is not seeking to address whether human rights are important or not. Instead, I explore how power gets constructed around child labour and human rights by focusing on (1) the universal rights arguments that suggest that child labour is a pathology of traditional culture; (2) cultural relativism and the script of nation and nationalism that it deploys; and (3) the voices of working children and their efforts to redefine their own struggles. In addition, the discussion is attentive to how various standpoints on child labour are imbricated on global capital and to how these views circulate meanings and inscribe identities, particularly those that are mediated by race, class, gender, and nation.

Universal Rights, Child Labour, and Global Capital: Scripting North–South Identities

The discourse of universal rights circulates meanings and a certain common sense about child labour by focusing on two areas in which the rights-based discourse has been influential. An examination of the human rights regimes and international legislation on child labour, as well as of the presentations of child labour in US mainstream media and 'expert' statements, helps us to see how their 'scripts' underwrite identity, particularly North–South identities.

Human Rights Regimes

Rights-based discourses of child labour are premised on the image of childhood developed in the modern age. The modern conception of childhood as an innocent and carefree period of life before responsibility and adulthood is a fairly recent construction. According to Aries, this notion of childhood did not exist in medieval society. The idea of children as separate from adults emerged in bourgeois society from the fifteenth to eighteenth centuries in Europe.[18] Children in agricultural and early modern societies provided essential and valued labour for the family, and as a consequence of their contribution to family sustenance their opinions were 'sought and respected'. As the idea of a modern childhood evolved, children gradually gained rights to be protected from work, but this resulted in the loss of their power within the family and society.[19]

The European and bourgeois idea of childhood was exported around the world through the colonial project of modernity. Stephens observes that the export of European values and European domestic life was critical to the production of empire and its 'uncivilized' colonial subjects; indeed, modern abstractions about childhood, family, and gender roles serviced the empire. For example, racialized, gendered, and infantalized constructions of Africans, Asians, and Native

Americans served as a counterfoil to the 'moral manhood' of the European male. Native men were constructed as uncivilized, inferior, feminine or hypermasculine, and cunning or childlike. Thus, it is important to note that in the late nineteenth and twentieth centuries, childhood became a racialized and gendered site for the construction of civilized Europe and its barbaric colonies.

The universal rights-based discourse on child labour reflected in the juridical pronouncements of international human rights regimes, the work of some human rights NGOs, and human rights scholars is deeply embedded in the European image of childhood discussed above. The globalization and acceptance of this image have provided support for the development of global human rights laws and norms to protect children from work. These have been enumerated in the 1959 Declaration on the Rights of the Child, the 1989 Convention on the Rights of the Child, and various pieces of child labour legislation from the International Labour Organization (ILO). Of particular importance is the ILO Convention 138, which states that formal education, not work, is the basis for a child's development. Thus, according to this convention, a child's right to work begins at age 15 (age 14 in developing countries) when mandatory schooling ends. Child labour before age 15 is criminalized by this convention. However, as discussed later in the chapter, many working children, NGOs, and developing nations make a distinction between work and exploitation and oppose the criminalization of child labour.

Recent literature on empire and the new imperialism has referred to human rights as the 'swords of empire', as the 'official moral ideology of Empire', and as 'the ark of the liberties of the world'. Perry Anderson calls human rights not just a 'jemmy in the door of national sovereignty', but also sees them as reflective of the 'arrogance of the international community'. For him, human rights provide the foundation for hegemony and empire.[20] For many other critical thinkers as well, empire is sustained not only through brute force, but also by a discourse of human rights that produces consent. Thus, the discourse of human rights regimes embodied in the United Nations (the UN and the ILO) is critical in providing legitimacy for the actions of powerful Western countries. The point here is that the discourse of child rights is based on the construction of an ideal childhood in which child labour is seen as deviant. It is arguable that within the human rights regime, the 'deviant childhoods' of working children in less-developed countries are used as tropes to demarcate cultural boundaries of civilized and backward, modern and traditional.

Mainstream Media, Experts, and Human Rights

The role of mainstream media in the circulation of meanings is critical.[21] Since the mainstream US media are widely disseminated, they are able to naturalize certain understandings of child labour. The role of the media in forging a certain common sense around identity and foreign policy has been explored by scholars like Herman and Chomsky, Edward Said, and others.[22] Said suggests that daily newspapers, 'mass-circulation news magazines', and television and radio networks 'constitute a communal core of interpretations providing a certain picture of Islam' to the United States. Further, the coverage of foreign countries by the US media not only forges their identity but also forges US identity and 'intensifies interests we already have there.'[23]

Until recently, Western media discourses have provided rather simplistic and reductive accounts of child labour. In general, the coverage of child labour by mainstream media reinforces the image of 'child labour' as deviant and as a social disease. Since the image of ideal childhood has been accepted as the global norm by groups that circulate meanings, child labour is regarded as deviant. In addition, representations of child labour in mainstream media are often clustered around the binaries of Western/non-Western, developed/developing, First World/Third World, rich/poor, and importing/exporting nations, with only the latter usually being implicated in child labour. However, 'since a labour activist revealed that daytime TV host Kathy Lee Gifford's line of

sportswear was produced by youngsters working long hours in a Honduran workshop' some media sources have began to pay attention to the involvement of Western countries, capital, and consumers in child labour.[24] Nevertheless, media coverage and political rhetoric still portray Western consumers as innocent recipients of goods made from child labour, rather than as being directly implicated in its practice. Take, for example, the address by Robert Reich, Labour Secretary under President Clinton, to Christian Century Foundation Leaders in 1996. Reich said he wanted the religious leaders of Christian and Jewish faith to spread the anti-sweatshop word to their congregations because this 'is not just an economic issue; it is also a moral issue. . . . Sweatshops are wrong—wrong not only for our country's economic future but wrong simply because the exploitation of working people is antithetical to America's values—our family values, our community values and our moral and religious values.'[25] Contrast Reich's articulation about sweatshops and American values with Myron Weiner's analysis of child labour in India. According to Weiner:

> there is historical and comparative evidence to suggest that the major obstacles to the achievement of primary education and abolition of child labour are not the level of industrialization, per capita income and the socio-economic conditions of families, the level of government expenditures in education, nor the demographic consequences of a rapid expansion in the number of school age children, four widely suggested explanations. India has made less of an effort . . . than many other countries not for economic or demographic reasons but because of its attitude of government officials, politicians, trade union leaders, workers in voluntary agencies, religious figures, intellectuals, and the influential middle class towards child labour and compulsory primary education.[26]

In Reich's statement, the mythology of American family, community, and religious values is used as a spatial metaphor to demarcate the distinctive identity of America as one that is opposed to exploitation of labour. Weiner, on the other hand, argues there is an essential and pervasive Indian attitude supportive of child labour that cuts across different professional, class, ideological, religious, and other categories. This attitude results from a cultural and religious acceptance of child labour—'that some people are born to rule and to work with their minds while others are born to work with their bodies.'[27] In the former instance, the location of America, where there is alleged foundational opposition to exploitation, is not merely informative; rather, it is used to distance the United States from those countries, religions, and communities where child labour is allegedly culturally sanctioned and practised. Here, the mythologies about American values are maintained. In the second instance, Weiner's mythology about Indian culture provides a homogenized and undifferentiated view of India and Indians. Further, he suggests that child labour is the excrescence of 'Indianness', not a function of poverty or the pathology of modernity. Pharis Harvey, a child labour activist, who generally provides a sophisticated analysis of child labour, also falls victim to an easy Orientalism[28] when he suggests that Indian religions support a social and economic hierarchy (read 'child labour') in contrast to Christianity, where the 'gospel does not allow us to assign a higher value to some of God's people than others.'[29] While it may be true that Hinduism condones some hierarchies and injustices, the responsibility of Christianity in the imperialist project, the spread of capitalism, and global injustice have also been rather acute. The links to knowledge production and the circulation of meanings are thus evident in this discourse. India and Indians have been represented as deeply embedded in the irrational and unequal tradition of Hinduism. In contrast, American values and the West emerge as Christian, fair, and basically moral. The complicity of the West and Western capital in child labour is easily obfuscated and the responsibility of child labour is placed squarely in the hands of the developing world.

The dissimulation around child labour practices can also be noted in the following statements by US Senator Tom Harkin when he introduced his bill, the Child Labour Deterrence Act. Here he resorts to the 'plea of innocence' to displace responsibility from US consumers and corporations to foreign countries and companies:

> I do not believe that American consumers knowingly would buy products made with child labour, but most often they don't know. Moreover, no respectable importer, company or department store willingly would promote the exploitation of children.
>
> . . . [The bill] prohibits the importation of any product made in whole or in part by youngsters under 15. In addition, the bill directs the US Secretary of Labor to compile and maintain a list of foreign industries and their respective countries of origin that use child labor in the production of exports to the US. Once such a foreign industry has been identified, the Secretary of Treasury is instructed to prohibit the entry of any of its goods.[30]

Typically, blame is placed on foreign countries and their practices, not on US corporate practices. When global capital is implicated, US corporations are once again excused from any culpability in child labour; irresponsible subcontractors from the developing world and the difficulty of monitoring decentralized global commodity production are blamed for the continued existence of child labour.

Finally, the relationship between the universalist position and capital has been highlighted by Pheng Cheah. Cheah does not imply that a conspiracy exists; rather, he suggests that human rights arguments are deployed in neo-mercantilist ways to further US and Western business interests. An example of this imbrication is the global campaign to link labour standards and trade by Western countries (with the exception of Germany and Britain), human rights NGOs, and trade unions in the West. According to this view, the 'illicit protectionism' engendered through child labour practices provides an unfair advantage to the non-Western world. In contrast, the Forum of Indian Leftists (FOIL) has argued that the Child Labour Deterrence Act, which seeks to link labour standards to trade, is an effort by the US Congress to help the US textile industry 'equal input costs' so that it does not lose its share of the US market.[31]

Cultural Relativism and Peripheral Capitalism: Scripting Nation and Nationalism

If the universalist discourse fosters an Orientalism and dissimulates the workings of capital with child labour, the counter-discourse of cultural relativism uses the scripts of nation, nationalism, development, and modernity to blur its complicity with child labour and its embeddedness in the workings of global capital. Cultural relativist discourses generally use the following arguments to make their case. First, the economically disadvantaged position of industrializing nations in the global arena creates conditions of penury within these countries. Uneven development, both within the global arena and within the nation, encourages the state and families to sanction the participation of children in work. They further suggest that, in poor families, the contributions of children to family income are significant and their labour makes the difference between survival and extinction of the family. Thus, child labour is the economic response of families who have been unable to participate in development and modernity.

A second and related cultural argument suggests that the perception of child work among the poor in many cultures is significantly different from Western ideas of childhood. In a 1960s study of working-class Mexican children, Lomnitz found that cultural norms of reciprocity, where resources were pooled to ensure survival of the extended family, better explained children's participation in work. The argument made here is that families living on the margins realize that the integration of children in a larger social community will more likely ensure survival than can a nuclear family. The norms of this integration demand that children do their share of work and contribute to the welfare of the community.[32] These arguments are based on understanding the role that different cultural and economic perceptions of childhood play in

child labour. In a similar vein, the 1993 Bangkok Declaration to the United Nations Conference on Human Rights held in Vienna, issued by 30 Asian countries, stated that despite their support of universal human rights, these countries were opposed to the 'imposition of incompatible values'. For them, 'Asian values' were more appropriate guides for the pursuit of human rights in Asian societies.[33]

A third argument, based on the insights of the first two, can be gleaned from the All India Carpet Manufacturers Association (AICMA) and the Carpet Export Promotion Council (CEPC), a parastatal of the government of India. AICMA and CEPC claim that the demands of Western countries and human rights NGOs to ban and regulate child labour in the carpet industry advantage the economic interests of the Western nations in a competitive global economy. The comment by Butterflies, an NGO working with street children, is telling in this regard:

> The campaign for the use of trade sanctions against child labour in developing countries is another variant of the same abolitionism (foreclosing the option of labour as a tool of survival) . . . . Such a campaign would contribute to extending the power of developed countries over the supply chain to the Western market, thereby dominating the terms of international trade.[34]

Although many of the Third World-based NGOs, such as the South Asian Coalition on Child Servitude (SACCS), work to abolish child labour, they are usually not in favour of protectionism. Kailash Satyarthi, for example, a prominent child labour activist in India, has said that while he supported the Child Labour Deterrence Act proposed by Senator Tom Harkin, he opposed its protectionist clause.[35] Satyarthi has been a prominent critic of child labour in the carpet industry and has worked tirelessly to expose child labour. He has also been responsible, along with German and US activists, in establishing Rugmark, a label that declares that the carpet was not made with child labour. Not surprisingly, because of his activism, he has been the target of much mud-slinging by AICMA, CEPC, and others. For example, charges of anti-nationalism have been levelled against him and he has also been called a Western agent. Commenting on the 'adverse' publicity that anti-child labour activists generate about the carpet industry in India, CEPC commented that 'the adverse publicity as such can be termed as an act which is anti-Indian and the government should take immediate action against such acts before it is too late.'[36] Responding to the Child Labour Act of 1986 in India, AICMA attacked the Indian government and child labour activists. In a 1991 edition of *Carpet-e-World*, the journal of the carpet industry, manufacturers suggested that the government and activists wanted to keep children poor. While the government has been accused of creating laws that prevent children from escaping poverty, activists have been accused of wanting increases in poverty so that service to the poor will always be in demand![37]

Here, appeals to the nationalist project of modernity and development from businesses like the carpet manufacturers resonate well with the declarations of Asian leaders signing the Bangkok Declaration, discussed above. Although claims to include children in the long-term project of modernity are made, it is clear that the poverty of these children is a function of nationalist exclusions. The promise of governments that development will 'trickle down' to the poor—if they wait patiently— barely hides the class bias of the state. For many of the poor, development and modernity are ephemeral, and no rhetoric of nationalism hides the exclusions of the nationalist project.

Voices of Children: Scripting Agency and Resistance

While the universal and relativist discourses have advanced the correctness of their positions regarding child labour, neither of them have made the effort to listen to children who work. The recovery of children's voices is critical for challenging the dominant discourses discussed above. Although children can be exploited through waged or bonded work, it is important to note that they also

resist their condition and act as agents of change.

This view that children who work should have the right to be part of the decision-making process about child labour is based on several concerns about the legal and moral interventions in the child labour debate. First, there is serious concern about the implications of a ban on child labour for children who work in order to survive. An intervention strategy that bans child labour without actually making alternative arrangements to ensure improvement and security in the lives of children is problematic to say the least. The 'tragedy' of children working in Bangladesh's textile sector is informative in this regard. According to a UNICEF report, the mere threat of sanctions against the textile industry induced panic among the textile manufacturers and 'forced' them to dismiss child workers from their industries or subcontracting units. In lieu of any other arrangements for their security, some of these children ended up in more hazardous industries like prostitution.[38]

A related and second concern focuses on the rights of children to participate in deliberations about their rights. It is indeed ironic that efforts to create universal rights to protect children from hazardous work ignore the rights of working children to have a voice in their own destiny. This marginalization of working children from the right to speak about their own conditions and desires is analogous to a third concern about the 'images of childhood, discussed above, that underpin the child labour debate'.[39] As already noted, this image of childhood is historically, culturally, and class specific. That the globalization of this culturally and historically specific form of childhood is problematic has not deterred global rights regimes from pursuing this agenda without much consideration for the wishes of the children they may want to save.

A Radda Bamen (Swedish Save the Children) study, *Children's Perspectives on their Working Lives*, based on the participation of 300 children from Bangladesh, Ethiopia, the Philippines, and Central America, explores the feelings of working children about work, school, and other private and public institutions that may promote or hinder their welfare. The Children's Perspectives Protocol, as this activity-based study was called, invited children not directly involved with NGOs or other child-based organizations to participate in several activities. Woodhead reports that many children evaluated their own work positively and felt pride in their work despite the difficult conditions and nature of it. For example, Bangladeshi girls emphasized the vulnerability of domestic work and brick chipping. In three out of four cases they ranked flower selling and garment manufacturing as the most desirable work:

> A person who knows how to sew gets Tk 1200. When it is time for us to marry and people ask us what we do, it will feel good to tell them we work in a garment factory instead of as a domestic helper.[40]

As stated earlier, the garment industry in Bangladesh was targeted for a boycott. The failure of an intervention designed without any input from Bangladeshi girls is evidence enough to argue for the involvement of children in decisions about their own lives.

Many of the children in the Radda Bamen study noted that they disliked hazardous conditions of work, injury risk, humiliation and abuse, economic exploitation, and the feeling of general insecurity in that order. They did, however, like earning money, supporting their families, acquiring skills and training, earning pride and respect, and making friends and having fun (rank ordered). Overall, 77 per cent of the children preferred combining work and school, although more girls tended to favour 'only school' and more boys favoured 'more work'. The study concludes that an overwhelming majority of the children across all countries sought the regulation of their working conditions so that they could 'survive' and have self-esteem and respect, as well as learn and play. It is important to note that they did not seek the prohibition of work.

The conclusions of the Radda Bamen study are reflected in the demands of several organizations of working children across Latin America, Africa, and Asia. In December 1994, the Campaign Against Child Labour organized a con-

ference in Chennai attended by 1,000 child workers. The youth demanded access to education 'near our houses', 'free books and uniforms . . . and jobs for their parents (who struggle with debt), and daycare for their siblings. In the meantime, they hoped for some rights in the workplace—some form of unionization as an interim measure.'[41] At the first world meeting of working children in Kundapur, India, in 1996, working children declared 'we want respect and security for ourselves and the work that we do. We are against exploitation at work; but we are in favor of work with dignity and appropriate hours, so that we have time for education and leisure.' This sentiment was also expressed at the fifth meeting of Latin American Working Children: 'YES to work—NO to exploitation! YES to work in DIGNITY—NO to conditions without dignity! YES to work—NO to marginalisation! YES to work—NO to discrimination.'[42] The demands of working children's organizations like Programa Muchacha Trabajador (PMT) in Peru, Niños y Adoloscentes Trabajadores (NATS), and Movimiento de Adoloscentes y Niños Trabajadores Hijos de Obreros Cristianos (MANTHOC) resonate well with the statements above. Arguing for a distinction between exploitation and child labour, they suggest that dehumanized categories of labour, such as slavery, prostitution, drug trafficking, and work that is harmful to health, should be regarded as exploitation, not work. In addition, these organizations ask child labour activists and rights regimes to disavow their efforts to ban child labour; rather, they suggest that working for better pay and safe working conditions and unionization might be much more to their benefit.

It would be remiss not to acknowledge that many working children also seek an end to child labour. Many working children across the globe participated in the Global March Against Child Labour and asked for the rights and privileges of a safe childhood. Working children have collaborated in the Bachpan Bachao Andolan (Save Childhood Movement) in India. Many of the children that I interviewed at Balashraya during my research on child labour in the carpet industry of Mirzapur and Badohi supported the ban on child labour and universal access to education. However, they also agreed that better and safe working conditions and pay are also desirable.

Conclusion

Child workers appear to be caught in what Pheng Cheah calls 'the aporetic embrace between a predatory [international] capitalism and an indigenous capitalism' seeking to compete. Those who are committed to an intrepid implementation of universal human rights are often unwilling to see the complexity of child labour in a diverse world. Further, they are often unwilling or unable to address the structural (global and national) reason for poverty and thus child labour. Culturally relativist discourses of child labour are also unable and unwilling to provide a way out of poverty. The promise of development and modernity does not lessen the harsh realities of child labour. Meanwhile the cruelty of poverty continues to affect children who work.

Further, the rights of children to have a say in their own destiny continue to be marginalized in these debates. Thus the debate on human rights, with all its binaries, remains polemical. It serves to dissimulate the international politics of power and the role of global capital that underwrite the issue of child labour. A post-colonial analysis, this chapter argues, reveals the workings of power in these discourses.

So what should readers make of all this? By claiming that universal rights discourses about children who work serve Western interests, I am not in any way suggesting that child labour does not exist or that abuse of child labour does not occur in Africa, Asia, and Latin America. Indeed, child labour statistics for these regions are much higher than such statistics in Western countries. Rather, I suggest that the failure of both the universalist and relativist discourses to address the fact that child labour lives in the 'aporetic embrace' of global and national capital, and that rights discourses are used to service national and capital interests, demonstrates the limitations of their claims. In contrast, the chapter suggests that a post-colonial analysis of child labour better situates child labour in global and national hierarchies, and is attentive to both the production and consumption of commodities as well as meanings.

Notes

This chapter is a revised and updated version of my earlier work in 'Postcolonial Interrogations of Child Labour: Human Rights, Rugmark and the Carpet Trade in India', in Geeta Chowdhry and Sheila Nair, eds, *Power, Postcolonialism and International Relations: Reading Race, Gender and Class* (London and New York: Routledge, 2004 [2002]), 225–53. Many quotes and material that I have used here are taken from this work.

1. International Labour Organization, 'Statistical Information and Monitoring Programme on Child Labour (SIMPOC): Overview and Strategic Plan 2000–2002', available at: <www.ilo.org/public/english/standards/ipec/publ/simpoc/others/globalest.pdf>.

2. A. Kebebew, 'Statistics on Working Children and Hazardous Child Labour in Brief', International Labour Organization, 1998. Available at: <www.ilo.org/public/english/standards/ipec/publ/clrep96.htm>.

3. For the argument that international political economy is 'not only about the production and circulation of "things" . . . political economy is also about the circulation of meanings', see Craig N. Murphy and Christina De Ferro, 'The Power of Representation in International Political Economy', *Review of International Political Economy* 2 (1995): 63–83.

4. Pheng Cheah, 'Posit(ion)ing Global Human Rights in the Current Global Conjuncture', in S. Geok-Lin Lim, W. Dissanayake, and L. Smith, eds, *Transnational Asia Pacific: Gender, Culture and the Public Sphere* (Urbana: University of Illinois

Press, 1999), 13. Cheah also suggests that the cultural relativist argument is equally embedded in the workings of capital.

5. Inderpal Grewal, '"Women's Rights as Human Rights": Feminist Practices, Global Feminism, and Human Rights Regimes in Transnationality', *Citizenship Studies* (Nov. 1999): 337.

6. By cultural politics I mean the ways in which cultural and political issues about identity, meaning, and geopolitics are embedded in material exchange and vice versa. For an elaboration, see Sonia E. Alvarez, Evelina Dagnino, and Arturo Escobar, eds, *Culture of Politics, Politics of Cultures: Re-visioning Latin American Social Movements* (Boulder, Colo.: Westview Press, 1998).

7. M. Keck and K. Sikkink, *Activists Beyond Borders: Advocacy Networks in International Politics* (Ithaca, NY: Cornell University Press, 1998); J. Donnelly, 'The Social Construction of Human Rights', in T. Dunne and N.J. Wheeler, eds, *Human Rights in Global Politics* (Cambridge: Cambridge University Press, 1999); T. Risse, S.C. Ropp, and K. Sikkink, *The Power of Human Rights: International Norms and Domestic Change* (Cambridge: Cambridge University Press, 1999).

8. Sheila Nair, 'Human Rights and Postcoloniality: Representing Burma', in Chowdhry and Nair, eds, *Power, Postcolonialism and International Relations*, 257.

9. Richard Ashby Wilson and Jon P. Mitchell, 'Introduction: The Social Life of Rights', in Wilson and Mitchell, eds, *Human Rights in Global Perspective: Anthropological Studies of Rights, Claims and Entitlements* (London: Routledge, 2003), 1.

10. Talal Asad, 'On Torture, or Cruel, Inhuman and Degrading Treatment', in R. Wilson, ed., *Human Rights, Culture and Context: Anthropological Perspectives* (London: Pluto Press, 1997).

11. See, e.g., Gayatri Spivak, 'Three Women Texts and a Critique of Imperialism', *Critical Inquiry* 12, 1 (1985): 243–61; Leila Abu-Lughod, *Veiled Sentiments: Honor and Poetry in a Bedouin Society* (Berkeley: University of California Press, 1986); Lata Mani, 'Contentious Traditions: The Debate on Sati in Colonial India', in K. Sangari and S.

Vaid, eds, *Recasting Women* (New Delhi: Kali for Women, 1989); Leila Ahmed, *Women and Gender in Islam: Historical Roots of a Modern Debate* (New Haven: Yale University Press, 1992); Uma Narayan, *Dislocating Cultures: Identities, Traditions and Third World Feminism* (London: Routledge, 1997).

12. Wilson and Mitchell, 'Introduction', 1.

13. Frantz Fanon, *The Wretched of the Earth*, trans. Constance Farrington (New York: Grove Press, 1965); Fanon, *Black Skin, White Masks*, trans. C.L. Markmann (New York: Grove Press, 1967); Albert Memmi, *The Colonizer and the Colonized* (Boston: Beacon Press, 1965); Edward Said, *Orientalism* (New York: Pantheon Books, 1978); Said, *Culture and Imperialism* (New York: Vintage Books, 1993).

14. Siba Grovogui, 'Postcolonial Criticism: International Reality and Modes of Inquiry', in Chowdhry and Nair, eds, *Power, Postcolonialism and International Relations*, 36.

15. See Chandra Mohanty, 'Under Western Eyes: Feminist Scholarship and Colonial Discourses', in Mohanty, A. Russo, and L. Torres, eds, *Third World Women and the Politics of Feminism* (Bloomington: Indiana University Press, 1991).

16. Geeta Chowdhry and Sheila Nair, 'Introduction: Power in a Postcolonial World: Race, Gender and Class in International Relations', in Chowdhry and Nair, eds, *Power, Postcolonialism and International Relations*.

17. Grewal, '"Women's Rights as Human Rights"', 338.

18. Philippe Aries, *Centuries of Childhood*, trans. Robert Baldick (London: Jonathan Cape, 1962).

19. Nancy Scheper-Hughes and Carolyn Sargent, eds, *Small Wars: The Cultural Politics of Childhood* (Berkeley: University of California Press, 1998).

20. Amy Bartholomew and Jennifer Breakspear, 'Human Rights as Swords of Empire', in Leo Panitch and Colin Leys, eds, *The New Imperial Challenge, Socialist Register* (London: Monthly Review Press, 2003), 125–45.

21. I analyzed articles from mainstream media sources including the *New York Times, USA Today, US News and World Report, Time Magazine*, and

Newsweek over the period 1994–2000. I have tabulated findings for anyone who is interested. Jessica Urban assisted me in this analysis.

22. See, e.g., Edward Said, *Covering Islam: How the Media and the Experts Determine How We See the Rest of the World* (New York: Vintage Books, 1997); Edward Herman and Noam Chomsky, *Manufacturing Consent: The Political Economy of Mass Media* (New York: Pantheon Books, 1998).

23. Said, *Covering Islam*, 52.

24. J. Berlau, 'The Paradox of Child Labour Reform', *Insight on the News* (Nov. 1997): 20.

25. 'Religious Groups Target Sweatshops', *The Christian Century* (6 Nov. 1996): 1066–8. Available at: <http://web2.searchbank.com/infotrac/session/854/687/2018324wl/56!xrn_l&bkm>.

26. Myron Weiner, *The Child and the State in India: Child Labour and Education Policy in Comparative Perspective* (Princeton, NJ: Princeton University Press, 1996), 287–9.

27. Ibid., 31.

28. Edward Said suggests that Orientalism is based on an 'ontological' and 'epistemological' distinction between the 'Orient' and the 'Occident', which fosters a relationship of 'power and domination'. This discursive relationship is structured in such a way that the West retains cultural superiority and the upper hand. See Said, *Orientalism*. Ronald Inden, *Imagining India* (Oxford: Blackwell, 1990), has used the 'Orientalism' of Said to examine how 'imperial formation and imperial knowledge' have structured understandings of India. According to him, the production of knowledge about India by the West is privileged by the West's historical colonial relationship and its economic power.

29. Pharis J. Harvey, 'Iqbal's Death', *The Christian Century* 112, 18 (1995): 2. Available at: <http://web2.searchbank.com/infotrac/session/854/687/2018324wl/41lxrn1&bkm>.

30. Tom Harkin, 'Put an End to the Exploitation of Child Labor', *USA Today Magazine* 124, 2608

(1996): 74; emphasis added.

31. Forum of Indian Leftists, 'Those That Be in Bondage: Child Labour and IMF Strategy in India', FOIL, Pamphlet 1 (1996): 2. Available at: <www.proxsa.org/economy/labour/chldbr.html>.

32. Larissa Adler de Lomnitz, *Networks and Marginality: Life in a Mexican Shantytown* (New York: Academic Press, 1977), and Anne Bar Din, *Los niños marginados rurales: estudio de caso en Morales* (Cuernevaca, Mexico: Centro regional de Investigaciones Multidisciplinarias, 1998), discussed in David Post, *Children's Work, Schooling and Welfare in Latin America* (Boulder, Colo.: Westview Press, 2001).

33. See <www.unhchr.ch/html/menu5/wcbangkok.htm#l>.

34. Butterflies, *The Convention on the Rights of the Child: The Alternate Report* (New Delhi: Rainbow Publishers, 1998), 51.

35. I interviewed Kailash Satyarthi in the summers of 1999 and 2000 in New Delhi.

36. CEPC in B.N. Juyal, *Child Labour in the Carpet Industry in Mirzapur-Badohi* (New Delhi: International Labour Organization, 1993), 28.

37. AICMA in Juyal, *Child Labour in the Carpet Industry in Mirzapur-Badohi*, 27.

38. G. Fairclough, 'It Isn't Black and White', *Far Eastern Economic Review* (Mar. 1996): 54–8.

39. Martin Woodhead, 'Combatting Child Labour: Listen To What the Children Say', *Childhood* 6, 1 (1999): 27–49.

40. Quoted ibid., 35.

41. Vijay Prashad, 'Calloused Consciences: The Limited Challenge to Child Labour', *Dollars and Sense* (Sept. 1999): 4. Available at: <http://web5.infotrac.galegroup.com...rn_33_0_A56027400?sw_aep>.

42. Manfred Liebel, 'Child Labour and the Contribution of Working Children's Organisations in the Third World', *International Review of Education* 48, 3/4 (2002): 265–70.

Suggested Readings

Chowdhry, G., and S. Nair, eds. *Power, Postcolonialism and International Relations: Reading Race, Gender and Class*. London: Routledge, 2002.

Liebel, M. 'Child Labour and the Contribution of Working Children's Organisations in the Third World', *International Review of Education* 48, 3/4 (2002): 265–70.

Post, D. *Children's Work, Schooling and Welfare in Latin America*. Boulder, Colo.: Westview Press, 2001.

Wilson, R.A., and J.P. Mitchell, eds. *Human Rights in Global Perspective: Anthropological Studies of Rights, Claims and Entitlements*. London: Routledge, 2003.

Woodhead, M. 'Combatting Child Labour: Listen To What the Children Say', *Childhood* 6, 1 (1999): 27–49.

Web Sites

Global March Against Child Labour: www.globalmarch.org

International Labour Organization, Statistical Information and Monitoring Program on Child Labour: www.ilo.org/public/english/standards/ipec/publ/simpoco/page2.htm#2

PRONATS group in Germany on working children's movements: www.pronats.de

Rugmark: www. rugmark.org

UNICEF, The State of the World's Children: www.unicef.org/sowc

Chapter 17

Environment, Economy, and Global Environmental Governance

Steven Bernstein

The rise of environmentalism as an international issue in the early 1970s coincided with a recognition of its intimate connection to the economy. Although it took some 15 years, 'sustainable development' emerged from those beginnings as the breakthrough idea to cement that linkage. But that was not the end of the story. What advocates of 'sustainability' did not anticipate was the triumph of 'liberal environmentalism'. This concept, I argue, captures the fundamental content and purposes of actual policies and programs to address environmental problems in the name of sustainable development. Liberal environmentalism legitimates the primacy of the global marketplace—by either putting it to work in an instrumental fashion or favouring it when trade-offs are required—rather than adapting the marketplace to operate in sympathy with requirements of ecological integrity and sustainability. Global environmental governance has not been the same since.

The linkage of environment and economy was not a coincidence. Development intellectuals and officials from the global South pushed for this connection, most notably prior to the 1972 United Nations Conference on the Human Environment in Stockholm, the first major international gathering of states from the North and South to deal with a full spectrum of the world's environmental problems.[1] They did so out of fear of planetary 'lifeboat ethics' and the imposition by the North of a no-growth philosophy, which was implied in high-profile though controversial studies such as *Limits to Growth*. This Club of Rome study used an MIT computer-generated simulation of rising population and declining resource stocks to predict a collapse of social and economic systems within 100 years if trends continued.[2] Officials also voiced concerns that industrial and chemical pollution and disasters making headlines in the late 1960s would overshadow links between environment, culture, and economics or the fight against poverty. They especially worried that trade barriers would be erected under the guise of environmental protection, a concern that continues today.

This is not to say that officials in the North had never before looked at their own environmental policies through the lens of economic implications. But when policy elites articulated the need for *international* action, they followed the framing of the largely Western-based environmental movement that generated popular pressures to 'save the planet'. Thus, the philosophical statement of planetary concern commissioned for the Stockholm Conference included calls for a 'loyalty to the Earth' that recognized planetary interdependence of all life and massive changes in over-consumptive lifestyles of the wealthy. The environmental *problématique* it reflected centred on the negative consequences of unregulated industrial development, conservation of natural and biological resources, and suspicion of economic growth. It also treated problems such as population growth and causes and effects of physical pollution largely in isolation from socio-economic structures. Aided by the conference secretariat, officials and development economists from the South countered with new thinking that brought development onto the environmental agenda.[3]

It is worth emphasizing that the particular environment/economy linkage that subsequently evolved resulted from a combination of political, social, and economic forces, not because it provided the most rational or effective response to environmental problems or a deep consensus among economic and environmental experts about how to reconceptualize the economy along ecological lines.

Indeed, despite valiant attempts by a handful of academics to mine political and economic thought in order to identify intellectual foundations for a 'green' global political economy,[4] the environment continues to be treated by global policy-makers, and most scholars, as an issue that politics or the marketplace affects, but not one in which they are embedded. This is arguably the biggest failure of sustainable development thinking.

Here I analyze the consequences of this disembedding and how forces in the international political economy shaped and subordinated global environmentalism to them. Environmental governance can only be understood in the wider context of the historical evolution of these forces. The remainder of the chapter examines current trends and prospects for addressing some of the most serious global environmental problems, given the resulting configuration of global environmental governance.

Liberal Environmentalism: History and Context

The concept of liberal environmentalism predicates global environmental protection on the promotion and maintenance of a liberal economic order. Liberal environmentalism is neither a grand bargain among states, although it reflects important elements of North–South compromise, nor is it simply a reflection of the triumph of neo-classical economics or disciplinary neo-liberalism.[5] Rather, it arose through a conscious effort on the part of international policy elites to develop a set of ideas that changed the issue from one of preserving the environment to one that promoted economic growth, but of a sustainable kind given natural support systems required for the economy. These elites worked through institutions such as the

Organization of Economic Co-operation and Development (OECD) and the United Nations environment and development organizations, their efforts culminating in the 1987 World Commission on Environment and Development led by Gro Harlem Brundtland.[6] The Brundtland Commission's formulation of 'sustainable development'— by resonating with broader trends in the international economy, appealing to the core concern in the developing world with economic growth, and mobilizing public and political support with the backing of the UN General Assembly—legitimated the connection between environmental protection and economic growth. Notably, this was not the only way to combine environment and economy to achieve sustainability. Prominent ecological economists have defined sustainable development as 'development without growth in throughput [of raw materials and energy] beyond environmental carrying-capacity'.[7] This conception places a much greater emphasis on reducing consumption, stabilizing population, and incorporating accounting of natural capital into economic models. Whereas both visions share a concern with development and redistribution, the Brundtland report is more sanguine that an expanding economic pie could achieve these goals while simultaneously reducing throughput.

The 1992 United Nations Conference on Environment and Development in Rio de Janeiro went even further down the path of economic liberalism, mirroring a shift in economic policy in many domestic economies in the 1980s. Thus, in contrast to the promotion of a loose international Keynesianism by the Brundtland Commission, Rio institutionalized the view that trade and finance liberalization and corporate freedom are consistent with, even necessary for, international environmental protection and sustained economic growth. Thus, the Earth Summit embraced, and perhaps even catalyzed, the new economic orthodoxy then sweeping through the developing world.

Space limitations prevent a full exploration of how and why liberal environmentalism became institutionalized,[8] but the shifting international political, social, and economic context at the end of the Cold War played a major role. In North and South alike, the late 1980s ushered in the general acceptance, by will or submission, of the retreat of the state from the economy, open financial markets, free trade, and market forces as the main engine of economic growth. The reasons for this historical shift are important in their own right, but its significance here is simply that it and the framing of the environment *problématique* agreed to in Rio were mutually legitimating.

The main elements of the specific compromise institutionalized at Rio include, on the political side, state sovereignty over resources (and environment and development policies) within a particular state's borders; the promotion of global free trade and open markets on the economic side; and the polluter pays principle (and its implicit support of market and voluntary instruments over strict regulatory mechanisms) and the precautionary principle on the environmental management side.

For example, Principle 12 of the Rio Declaration on Environment and Development, the consensual statement of norms agreed to in Rio, proclaims free trade and environmental protection perfectly compatible: 'States should cooperate to promote a supportive and open international economic system that would lead to economic growth and sustainable development in all countries, to better address the problems of environmental degradation.' The polluter pays principle—and by extension the user pays principle—refers to the idea that the polluting firm ought to shoulder the costs of pollution or environmental damage by including it in the price of a product. Ideally, price signals would reflect the real costs of pollution. This principle favours market mechanisms (such as tradable pollution permits or privatization of the commons and public lands) since they operate via the incorporation of environmental costs into prices. It also promotes an end to market-distorting subsidies. The precautionary principle essentially says that under conditions of risk of serious environmental harm, a precautionary stance is warranted under conditions of uncertainty. Nowhere does the declaration state how these values are to be combined when they conflict.

The 2002 World Summit on Sustainable Development (WSSD) in Johannesburg—referred to by some as Rio + 10—further reinforced liberal trends. For example, a number of northern delegations went to great lengths to ensure that the Johannesburg Declaration and Plan of Implementation, the two negotiated texts produced by the conference, did not contradict or undermine existing trade agreements.[9] Such arguments reinforced Rio Principle 12, as well as that of subsequent trade agreements that refer to Principle 12 for legitimation. For example, trade ministers negotiating the World Trade Organization (WTO) agreed, citing Principle 12, 'that there should not be, nor need be, any policy contradiction between upholding and safeguarding an open, non-discriminatory and equitable multilateral trading system on the one hand, and acting for the protection of the environment, and the promotion of sustainable development on the other.'[10]

The WSSD also heralded the legitimation of another trend consistent with the pattern of working with the market and private sector: public-private partnerships for sustainable development (discussed further below). Indeed, most analyses identify partnerships as one of two things most notable about the Johannesburg Summit, the other being its recognition of the dismal progress since 1992 on implementing the Rio agreements, combined with its failure to generate any significant new commitments or financing.

The consequences of liberal environmentalism are thus double-edged. On one hand, it has enabled environmental concerns to rise to a much more prominent place on the international agenda than would otherwise have been possible, even if the original goals and transformative hopes of global environmentalism have been altered in the process. On the other hand, critics assert that these linkages have 'constrained efforts to develop an alternative paradigm' by co-opting the goals of both environment and development organizations, while 'adjusting the language of the environment and developmental movements to other purposes . . . [and thereby] exacerbating divisions between moderate reformists and radical environmentalists'.[11] This criticism highlights the power of the discourse surrounding liberal environmentalism to frame policies and inform understandings of the environment-economy relationship, with potentially destructive effects on the environmental movement.

Liberal environmentalism also has institutional implications. Rules are written and policies formulated in a context where institutions designed for other purposes limit and direct the types of practices deemed appropriate or acceptable for the environment. For example, institutions such as the World Bank, United Nations Development Program, OECD, United Nations Conference on Trade and Development, and WTO have become lead organizations on global environmental issues, along with traditional leaders such as the United Nations Environment Program. Moreover, the goals of environmental agreements and organizations increasingly intermingle with economic goals. While this has the potential to contribute to global equity and development, the practical effect is often to weaken environmental priorities, either owing to the institutional power and dominance of economic concerns within these institutions or because existing rules in the international political economy more broadly favour corporate and investor rights and freedom. Thus, the fate of environmental quality is not unlike other non-economic goals increasingly being addressed under a neo-liberal framework, where the rosy 'win-win' scenarios painted by institutions such as the World Bank, IMF, and advocates of globalization generally have often failed to materialize. In the environmental case, one sees the tension most directly in the trade-environment debate, but also in the fragmentation of global environmental governance itself where new initiatives must not run afoul of international trade rules and increasingly attempt to work with market forces.

Adaptation and Use of the Market in Environmental Governance

Three prominent examples illustrate the institutional effects of liberal environmentalism: (1) in the realm of intergovernmental co-operation, the compromise linking action on climate change to market mechanisms in the Kyoto Protocol; (2) the proliferation of non-state governance schemes that work through the marketplace; (3) the rise in voluntary agreements and public-private partnerships.

Kyoto Protocol

The 1997 Kyoto Protocol to combat global climate change was designed to deliver concrete targets, timetables, and mechanisms to implement and further develop the goals of the 1992 Framework Convention on Climate Change (UNFCCO). While other intergovernmental examples illustrate similar trends, I focus here on climate change because of its scope and significance, plus the sheer magnitude of scientific, political, and economic resources devoted to this problem compared to other prominent global environmental issues. The institutionalization of liberal environmentalism began with the parent UNFCCO, which rests on the link between developed countries 'modifying' greenhouse gas emissions while recognizing *inter alia* 'the need to maintain strong and sustainable economic growth'.[12]

The key political compromise of the Kyoto Protocol negotiated to achieve this goal was to link quantitative reductions or limits in greenhouse gas emissions in developed countries to three main market mechanisms that involve transferring 'credits' for emissions to help countries meet their targets:

- emission trading among developed countries;
- joint implementation among developed countries, where emission reductions financed by foreign investments would be credited to the source country;
- a clean development mechanism (CDM) to finance projects in developing countries, where the investor, from a developed country, would receive 'certified emissions credits' for emission reductions produced by the project in the developing country.

The Kyoto mechanisms all work on the same basic principle: that assigning property rights to emissions and creating a market that allows them to be transferred will enable reductions to be achieved where it is most efficient to do so. They rely on the establishment of a market for emission credits to create price signals, and thus incentives for buyers, sellers, and investors, as long as abatement costs vary across countries. As negotiations progressed to try to secure the necessary ratifications for entry into force, states agreed to permit greater and greater reliance on these market mechanisms. The latest concession, agreed to in July 2001, allows credits for carbon sequestration or 'sinks' to be eligible under the CDM.

The Protocol came into effect on 16 February 2005, 90 days after Russian ratification brought adherent countries to the required 55 per cent level of 1990 greenhouse gas emissions from developed countries. The trajectory of climate policy by parties that have ratified, and even some that have not, clearly embraces 'liberal environmental' logic. Indeed, the eventual support for Kyoto from Russia's President Putin was tied to EU support for Russia to join the World Trade Organization.[13] National and regional implementation plans have evolved to rely heavily on domestic corollaries to the Kyoto mechanisms. A notable case is the European decision to launch a greenhouse gas emission trading scheme in 2005 that will link with the international mechanism. At 10 times larger than the United States' acid rain trading program, its size and scope will be unprecedented.[14] The EU directive marks a reversal for many member states that opposed market mechanisms in Kyoto negotiations and subsequently tried to limit their scope. Canada's national plan to combat climate change calls for a similar scheme.[15] Internationally, the number of projects in the pilot phase of Activities to be Implemented Jointly (the precursor to joint implementation launched prior to Kyoto's signing) increased by almost 50 per cent, to 150 projects, following Kyoto's signing in 1997.[16] In addition, many states have embraced voluntary policies and measures, incentive-based policies, and investments in new technology over regulatory policies that imply trade-offs between environmental and economic goals.

Whereas the Kyoto example suggests that liberal environmentalism enables international environmental agreements that otherwise might have been more difficult to achieve, the irony may be that the kind of agreement created may be vastly inadequate to significantly forestall, let alone stop or reverse, current trends in greenhouse gas emissions. Critics charge that even should market mechanisms work to reduce emissions efficiently, their logic is counterproductive to the large-scale global transformation in consumption patterns required to seriously check or reverse human-induced climate change. Especially problematic is the use of mechanisms such as the CDM, which allow developed countries to 'offset' their own emissions by reducing emissions in developing countries. As explained by one critic, offsets do 'nothing to redirect the trajectory of technological development or consumption patterns that originate in the world's high-throughput societies and then emanate globally through processes of technology transfer, foreign investment and cultural diffusion.' Instead, developed countries and corporations effectively diffuse 'dominant technological and consuming templates', the very practices that cause the problem.[17] The real issue is whether market mechanisms can be designed to address such criticisms or, combined with other measures, are likely to produce the necessary individual and societal-level transformations. Whether those measures in turn can be compatible with liberal environmentalism is an open question.

Non-State Governance

In many cases—and the jury is still out on climate change—interstate co-operation has failed to effectively address known environmental problems. Whether or not the constraints of liberal environmentalism contributed to this failure, it has opened up the alternative of non-state global governance schemes to fill the void. Non-state governance schemes do not focus on states as their starting point or seek state authority to promote compliance. Rather, they target firms in the global marketplace. In effect, they create their own source of authority through a combination of market pressure and strategies to gain legitimacy from consumers and producers of goods and services in the economic sectors they target. Their most remarkable feature is that they are generally NGO-led, although they usually engage the private sector in decision-making to gain legitimacy. A small but accelerating number of such schemes have started to operate at the transnational level over the last 10–15 years as demands for governance of the global marketplace increase. They currently cover aspects of forestry, food security and production, labour standards, tourism, fisheries, and human rights. For example, after consumer and NGO pressure, Ikea and Home Depot have both agreed to sell wood products derived only from certified sustainable forestry practices. Other such schemes are in development, including in the energy and mining sectors. Many include specific performance criteria and employ systems of third-party verification and regular auditing and monitoring of compliance in which firms must participate to maintain 'certified' status. Most importantly, they qualify as governance because what they do rests on the acceptance of shared rule. Those that do not meet these criteria, such as some industry-led self-regulators, would not qualify as governance in the same sense.

Their rationale is as follows. Global liberalism effectively frees mobile multinational firms from inconvenient national regulation. Countries, desperate for foreign investment and income from trade, are thereby discouraged from raising environmental or social standards. The practices of these firms directly, or indirectly through perverse incentives to keep standards and costs low in their supply chains, are a primary culprit in the social dislocation and negative environmental consequences that accompany globalization. Since states and intergovernmental institutions have shown a limited ability or willingness to regulate firm activity in the global marketplace, direct governance *through* the marketplace is necessary. In effect, non-state governance schemes aim to reverse the pressure in the supply chain by targeting large multinational companies, which in turn will put pressure further up their supply chains in local settings.

The pressure they exert is usually through a system of certification that verifies a firm is in compliance with the standards established by the scheme. A label may be used so consumers can identify products from certified companies. While other forms of direct pressure such as boycotts similarly use market leverage, certification formalizes and legitimizes a process whereby firms can show they follow the environmental practices covered by the scheme. In both cases, firms whose markets derive in large part from their brand are especially vulnerable to the publicity—positive or negative—this kind of market pressure provides.[18]

Public-Private Partnerships

Somewhere in between intergovernmental and non-state governance are public-private partnerships for sustainable development. They differ from non-state governance, which operates wholly in the marketplace, because partnerships ultimately derive their authority from the state. They involve joint participation of governments and non-governmental groups—firms, civil society groups, individuals, or groups of experts. They work under the assumption that combining the resources, skills, and commitment of non-state actors with the authority of states will succeed where state action has not. Partnerships are now commonplace at the domestic level, where governments increasingly turn to the private sector to deliver services and programs, provide expertise, and even perform management functions formerly monopolized by the state.[19] But the trend towards privatization is still relatively novel beyond the nation-state.

Almost 300 such partnerships were identified before or at the Johannesburg Summit, giving this mechanism of global environmental governance a huge boost in legitimacy.[20] They range from links between medical schools in the North with physicians and social programs in the South to establish public health programs, to a partnership between Shell and the Philippine government for the multi-billion dollar Malampaya Deep Water Gas to Power Project. The latter includes partnerships with a local university, the World Wide Fund for Nature (WWF), and local NGOs, as well as community involvement to take into account environmental and social impacts.[21] While such projects appear to be the pinnacle of sustainable development—combining economic, environmental, and social goals—sceptics worry that their success depends on the goodwill and voluntary participation of the private sector.

The engagement of the corporate sector at the WSSD can be viewed as part of the general response to globalization within the UN system. The ultimate aim is to embed the marketplace in broader social and environmental goals. Ideally, such partnerships are meant to put in practice demands for greater corporate responsibility and accountability. Yet, the summit made much less progress in these areas than expected. Moreover, as Paul Wapner has pointed out, 'notwithstanding their promise, so far the number and magnitude of the partnerships proposed seem minuscule to the tasks at hand. . . . Indeed, the WSSD's embrace of the private sector to spearhead partnerships has led many critics to refer to the Summit as "Rio-minus-10".'[22]

But the most damning critique comes not from those suspicious of turning to the marketplace to solve social and environmental problems, but from those who simply acknowledge, as delegates did at the WSSD, that for all the rhetoric, agreements, promises of action, and international efforts, institutions and processes established to address the world's most serious environmental issues have fallen woefully short of addressing the problems for which they were established.[23] To be fair, this is not necessarily an indictment of sustainable development or liberal environmentalism—after all, without them matters might have been worse. But it does suggest a rethinking of policy directions is in order, especially in an institutional context where economic institutions are gaining power and influence.

All of these trends point to an overarching effect of liberal environmentalism: its contribution to the fragmentation of global environmental governance as international agreements have failed to live up to their promise. Whereas I have focused on a few specific examples, one sees fragmentation consistent with the trend towards engaging the corporate sector in the proliferation of self-regulation schemes, codes of corporate responsibility, and reliance on standard-setting bodies such as the International Standards Organization (ISO), which function in co-operation with industries for which standards are being developed.

Even the United Nations, an organization established by and for states, has launched a voluntary 'Global Compact' for corporations through the Secretariat. To join, corporations commit to a set of 10 human rights, labour, anti-corruption and environmental principles drawn from existing international agreements. The compact does not enforce specific standards but attempts to create a learning process whereby practices gradually improve over time. In the long run, the hope is that best practices will develop consistent with the compact's broad principles. Corporations may even begin to demand that governments step in to ensure fairness in the marketplace for environmentally and socially responsible companies. The success of the Global Compact depends on the extent to which learning networks develop, corporations engage, and NGOs hold them to account. While the UN edifice provides added legitimacy, profile, and transparency compared to pure self-regulation, the Global Compact is subject to limitations of all voluntary schemes.

In sum, the wide variation in the degree and location of authority granted, in the stringency of standards and enforcement, and in acceptance of relevant actors (whether firms or states) in these different types of governance suggests the continued fragmentation of environmental governance, barring catastrophic environmental events that produce irresistible pressures for consolidation.

Environment, Trade, and Resistance

Nowhere are the limitations of liberal environmentalism to achieve ecological goals more visible than in the trade realm. Whereas liberal environmentalism assumes that the wealth-creating effects of free trade help efforts to protect the environment in principle, this is an untestable proposition since few (if any) examples of truly free trade exist. Moreover, the hegemony of neo-classical economics means no policy proposal is taken seriously that attacks the *goal* of liberalizing markets. Given the largely academic character of the trade theory debate, I focus below on whether liberalized trade in practice, and the institutions that enable it, are benefiting or undermining environmental goals. Three developments since the early 1990s suggest how the trade/environment tension is playing out.

The first development is the advent of liberal environmentalism. Its promise of the compatibility of free trade and environmental protection has proven double-edged. On one hand, it opened the door to environmental demands that trade agreements—traditionally understood as strictly economic agreements and of no concern to environmentalists—take into account the consequences of trade and trade rules on the natural environment and on environmental regulations. On the other hand, the institutionalization of the linkage subordinates environmentalism by posing potential conflicts as challenges to free trade instead of to the environment. For example, Rio Principle 12, based on the trade norm of non-discrimination, reinforces a binary view of all trade-related measures as either liberalizing or protectionist by imposing the burden of proof on national environmental regulations to show they are not discriminatory. It concludes, 'Trade policy measures for environmental purposes should not constitute a means of arbitrary or unjustifiable discrimination or a disguised restriction on international trade.' Nowhere does it say non-discrimination or open markets should not constitute an unjustifiable restriction on environmental protection or ecosystem health.

The normative power of Principle 12 is evidenced by its citation in WTO political decisions and trade disputes, as well as in the WTO Committee on Trade and Environment (CTE) created along with the WTO in 1994. Official discussions to reconcile trade and environment repeatedly stress internalization of environmental costs,

reduction of subsidies, and clarification of intellectual and other property rights, and emphasize that unilateral measures or protectionism should be resisted.[24] Within the CTE specifically, discussions reflect the subordination of environmental protection to trade and development rather than a balance or integration of the three goals. For example, the report to the Cancun WTO Ministerial Meeting in 2003 stated:

> It was generally recognized that *improved market access* for developing countries' products was key to the goal of achieving sustainable development. It was recalled that, in line with Rio Principle 11, environmental standards, objectives and priorities needed to reflect the particular environmental and developmental context to which they applied and that standards applied by some countries could be inappropriate and of unwarranted economic and social cost to others, particularly developing countries.[25]

Together, Rio Principles 11 and 12 leave little room to write environmental measures into trade rules. Indeed, many southern governments view any such attempts as aimed at their exports, especially those of economically vulnerable communities dependent on the natural resources or agricultural sectors. This fear is not unfounded since two of the most significant environmental disputes— tuna/dolphin and shrimp/turtle (discussed below)—were launched in response to US unilateral trade action targeting developing countries. Thus, southern demands for 'special and differential treatment' in the current Doha Round of trade negotiations extend to treatment on rules related to environmental measures, following the logic of 'common but differentiated responsibility' to protect the environment, a principle agreed to in Rio.

Sympathetic supporters of sustainable development thus face a conundrum: how to reconcile the goal of equity with their fear that allowable deviations from non-discrimination will be to prevent environmental measures, not to allow them. Unfortunately, the CTE to date has made virtually no progress on addressing this dilemma or other core issues, such as the relationship of the WTO and multilateral environmental agreements. North–South divisions also remain powerfully in place, although the South is beginning to move away from a strictly oppositional stance to include environmental concerns, given uncertainty as to how deviations from non-discrimination will play out in the absence of multilateral consensus on the way forward.[26]

The second historical development was the mobilization during negotiation of the Canada–US Free Trade Agreement of environmental groups that feared liberalized trade rules would lead to downward pressure on environmental standards.[27] Environmental activism has since become a primary source of the popular challenge to the legitimacy of the WTO. Following the pattern already noted, however, environmental activists are split on whether international trade agreements ought to be opposed outright as inevitably causing a regulatory 'race to the bottom' as countries compete to attract investment and keep costs of exports low, or whether trade agreements might be a vehicle to 'harmonize up' environmental standards.[28] The experience of the North American Free Trade Agreement, where environmental concerns were relegated to a side agreement, and of subsequent efforts to 'green' the WTO have militated against the latter view.[29]

Proposals for reform from environmental groups still willing to engage the WTO now generally call for scaling back its scope, particularly its ability to rule on domestic environmental policies.[30] The problem is that trade rules do no such thing explicitly, but they have that effect when interpreted by dispute panels, newly empowered under the WTO. Critics thus complain that the sum effect of new trade rules and their interpretation by international panels of trade experts, which have limited accountability to governments or populations directly affected by their rulings, gives the WTO undue power to rule on domestic regulations at the same time as its enforcement capacity has increased. These trends mark a shift in the understanding of the trade regime under the General Agreement on Tariffs and Trade (GATT), which ensured adequate room for domestic intervention in order to maintain economic and social stability.[31]

The third development is a series of trade rulings that have sent these signals. Beginning with tuna/dolphin in 1991, they seemed to confirm the institutional bias in favour of trade over environmental goals, although some evidence suggests this bias is diminishing.[32] In tuna/dolphin, a dispute launched by Mexico, a GATT panel ruled that US regulations outlawing imported tuna caught in nets that endangered dolphins violated GATT rules that protected sovereignty. Ironically, liberalized trade and the market integration it fostered opened the door to US environmentalists and environmental legislation influencing Mexican regulations at the same time as specific GATT rules protected Mexico from the extraterritorial application of US law.

The shrimp/turtle dispute followed a similar pattern, although successive rulings began to shift the terrain. In the first ruling, India, Malaysia, Pakistan, and Thailand successfully challenged a US measure that prohibited imports of shrimp caught with nets that threatened endangered sea turtles. Although a second ruling, of the appellate body in 1998, found that the US measure could not be justified under Article XX of the GATT, which covers environmental and health exceptions, it acknowledged that Article XX had to be interpreted in line with current understandings of sustainable development, which had since been recognized in the WTO. In 2001, a third decision upheld a new version of the US law that allowed more flexibility in the methods used for protecting sea turtles and acknowledged US 'good faith' negotiations towards a multilateral solution.[33]

The 1998 decision was also notable for allowing, for the first time, an NGO to submit a brief as amicus curiae to a dispute resolution process. This signalled a new access point for environmental advocacy in an organization notorious for closed-door negotiations and for privileging commercial interests and rights. Still, institutional biases are in evidence since business groups also have NGO status. The net result may therefore be to reinforce rather than diminish corporate influence.[34]

Underlying these and many other environmental trade disputes is the problem of how to treat product and processing methods (PPMs). They come into play because, from an environmental perspective, the issue is not only the end product, but also its content, the processes through which they were produced, and how their use might affect local and global ecosystems. Taking exports of forest products as an example, the problem is not necessarily that trees get chopped down to produce wood, but whether producers followed principles of sustainable forest management or protected biodiversity in doing so. But international trade rules operate on the basis of national sovereignty under which PPMs are considered an internal matter to be regulated in any way the state party to a trade agreement sees fit. One possible exception is if there is an internationally accepted standard that the WTO recognizes, such as of the International Standards Organization (ISO). Even then, it would probably need to be shown to be non-discriminatory, transparent, effective, and least trade-restrictive.

The issue of PPMs also arises in cases of eco-labelling, because they frequently target processes, life-cycle analysis, and externalities. Non-state governance schemes, owing to their operation in the marketplace rather than through border controls (unless a state adopted one as a mandatory requirement for entry), are largely immune from trade action under the WTO. While CTE discussions suggest openness to voluntary eco-labelling in principle because it does not deny market access, developing countries continue to express concern that they could restrict sales. Given the poor CTE record to address such tensions, increased conflict is likely as such schemes proliferate and the lines between public and private schemes blur.

Taken together, these trends suggest some movement on acceptance of environmental measures, but little willingness on the part of dispute panels or the CTE to diverge from strict interpretations of core WTO norms such as that measures be non-discriminatory, least trade-restrictive, or demonstrably effective. Although it could be argued that environmentalists should applaud such an approach for being fair and promoting multilateral rather than unilateral measures,[35] the practical effect has been that domestic environmental regulations with trade implications must adapt to international rules, not vice versa.

Thus, even among environmental groups willing to engage the WTO, most remain highly critical of what they view as a systemic bias against upholding domestic environmental regulations in trade disputes.[36] These groups can be faulted, however, for publicizing only rulings that found environmental and health regulations violated WTO rules, while ignoring or dismissing decisions that protected these regulations, such as the third shrimp/turtle decision, in 2001, and the 2000 and 2001 asbestos decisions. In the asbestos case, panel and appellate body rulings rejected Canada's challenge to France's import ban on asbestos and on products containing asbestos. Critics dismissed the decision as driven only by defensive politics to counteract the damaged reputation of the WTO from earlier rulings. They said the resultant 'legal sophistry' to avoid a straight reading of the Technical Barriers to Trade Agreement, which would have led to a ruling against the ban, created jurisprudence that will make it even harder to invoke the WTO's health exception.[37]

Assessing the veracity of such claims and WTO counterclaims is extremely difficult given the highly technical legal language in which decisions are couched. In addition, decisions have generally avoided passing judgement on environmental and health regulations directly, ruling instead on the basis of trade rules such as whether the regulation was applied differentially (shrimp/turtle case) or whether risk assessments were properly undertaken to justify a trade restriction. For example, the lack of a proper risk assessment led a WTO panel and the appellate body to rule against an EU ban on hormone-fed beef. Such assessments had to bear a 'rational' and 'objective' relationship to the ban under the 1994 WTO Agreement on Sanitary and Phytosanitary Measures (SPS), which applied in this case. Significantly, however, the appellate body also ruled that under the SPS agreement, risk assessments need not be based exclusively on laboratory science under controlled conditions, but also on assessments of risks in human societies as they actually exist, which is more consistent with the precautionary principle. This ruling occurred in the context of ongoing political disagreements on the application of the precautionary principle, which are likely to play out in future conflicts over genetically modified organisms.

Focusing on rulings also says nothing about how WTO rules and institutional biases can create a 'chill' on domestic regulations when they diverge from those of dominant trade powers. It is difficult to imagine, in the absence of multilateral agreements, how standards would ratchet up in this institutional environment.

Conclusion

To overcome institutional biases towards neo-liberal policies, some have proposed a global environmental organization that would include a dispute mechanism to counteract the power of the WTO.[38] However, liberal environmentalism militates against any move to centralize environmental governance under a super-organization to counteract the WTO for two reasons. First, it supports tendencies towards fragmentation, not centralization, as the experience of environmental governance to date has shown. Second, under liberal environmentalism the goals of trade, development, and economic growth are not an either/or proposition with environmental protection. Rather, conflicts ought to be resolved working with the goals that

the relevant economic organizations pursue, just as environmental agreements ought to consider economic goals.[39] Unfortunately, the record to date is not encouraging in this regard, which suggests a radical restructuring of institutions is in order.

However, if liberal environmentalism marks the boundaries of politically acceptable policy, working within such constraints offers a more viable alternative. Liberal environmentalism may even offer potentially subversive avenues of political action. For example, it opens up trade regimes to environmental critiques, thus erasing the firewall that formerly divided the two issues—especially if the reality of trade regimes belies the promise of being compatible with environmental protection. Similarly, it opens up potential avenues for direct action to address environmental problems through the marketplace, and thus can bypass lowest-common-denominator agreements among states that jealously protect their sovereignty and interests. Moreover, an underlying liberal ideology in the political rather than economic sense can be read into the discourse of liberal environmentalism that suggests a democratic normative basis on which to counter the elevation of corporate rights and freedom above individual and community rights.

Nonetheless, if the effects of liberal environmentalism are as divisive on the environment movement as critics maintain, and institutional and structural power favours economic over environmental interests, generating sufficient political action to take advantage of those subversive elements will be difficult, at best.

Notes

i. Miguel Ozorio de Almeida, 'The Confrontation between Problems of Development and Environment', *Founex Report* (New York: Carnegie Endowment for Peace, 1972), 37–56; *Founex Report* (1972): 12–13, 27.

2. Donella H. Meadows et al., *The Limits to Growth*, 2nd edn (New York: Signet, 1972).

3. See Steven Bernstein, *The Compromise of Liberal*

Environmentalism (New York: Columbia University Press, 2001), ch. 2, for the story of this effort, which was central to securing developing-country participation in Stockholm.

4. Eric Helleiner, 'International Political Economy and the Greens', *New Political Economy* 1 (1996): 59–77; Eric Laferrière, 'International Political Economy and the Environment: A Radical

Ecological Perspective', in D. Stevis and V.J. Assetto, eds, *The International Political Economy of the Environment* (Boulder, Colo.: Lynne Rienner, 2001). Helleiner presents the fullest picture of such a paradigm, in which the world political economy ought to resemble a neo-medieval structure wherein self-regulating local communities run their own economies, regulated by decentralized institutional arrangements, and a global civil society controls the worst global environmental problems.

5. Stephen Gill, 'The Constitution of Global Capitalism', paper presented to the 41st Annual International Studies Association Conference, Los Angeles, 14–18 Mar. 2000.

6. World Commission on Environment and Development, *Our Common Future* (Oxford: Oxford University Press, 1987).

7. Robert J.A. Goodland, Herman E. Daly, and Salah El Serafy, 'The Urgent Need for a Rapid Transition to Global Environmental Sustainability', *Environmental Conservation* 20, 4 (1993): 299. Carrying capacity, in the authors' view, refers to sink capacity to assimilate wastes and source capacities to regenerate raw materials, such as clean air. Ibid., 297, 305.

8. See Bernstein, *The Compromise of Liberal Environmentalism.*

9. Paul Wapner, 'World Summit on Sustainable Development: Toward a Post-Jo'burg Environmentalism', *Global Environmental Politics* 3, 1 (2003): 6; James Gustave Speth, 'Perspectives on the Johannesburg Summit', *Environment* 45, 1 (2003): 27.

10. 'Decision on Trade and Environment', adopted by ministers at the meeting of the Uruguay Round Trade Negotiations Committee in Marrakesh, 14 Apr. 1994. The preamble to the Agreement Establishing the WTO includes a similar understanding of the trade/environment relationship.

11. Marc Williams, 'In Search of Global Standards: The Political Economy of Trade and the Environment', in Stevis and Assetto, eds, *The International Political Economy of the Environment*, 43.

12. United Nations Framework Convention on Climate Change, 1992, Article 4(2) (a and b).

13. Entry into force required ratification by 55 parties that account for 55 per cent of developed-country emissions in 1990. As of the summer of 2004, 122 states had ratified, accounting for 44.2 per cent of developed-country emissions. Since the United States announced its withdrawal from the treaty, the ratification by the Russian Federation, which accounts for 17.4 per cent of 1990 developed-country emissions, was necessary to bring the total above the 55 per cent threshold. See Erin E. Arvedlund, 'Europe Backs Russian Entry into WTO', *New York Times* 22 May 2004, C1–C3.

14. Directive 2003/87/EC of the European Parliament and of the Council of 13 Oct. 2003 establishing a scheme for greenhouse gas emission allowance trading within the Community and amending Council Directive 96/61/EC. Available at: <http://europa.eu.int/comm/environment/climat/emission.htm>.

15. Government of Canada, *Climate Change Plan for Canada* (Ottawa: Government of Canada, 2002).

16. UNFCCC Secretariat, 'Issues in the Negotiating Process: Activities Implemented Jointly Under the Pilot Phase', 2002. Available at: <http://unfccc.int/issues/aij.html>.

17. Ken Conca, 'The WTO and the Undermining of Global Environmental Governance', *Review of International Political Economy* 7, 3 (2000): 491.

18. For a broader discussion of such schemes, see Steven Bernstein and Benjamin Cashore, 'The Two-Level Logic of Non-State Global Governance', paper presented at the International Studies Association Conference, Montreal, 17–20 Mar. 2004; Benjamin Cashore, 'Legitimacy and the Privatization of Environmental Governance: How Non-State Market-Driven (NSMD) Governance Systems Gain Rule-Making Authority', *Governance* 14, 4 (2002): 502–29; Gary Gereffi, Ronie Garcia-Johnson, and Erika Sasser, 'The NGO-Industrial Complex', *Foreign Policy* 125 (July–Aug. 2001): 56–65.

19. Pauline Vaillancourt Rosenau, ed., *Public-Private Policy Partnerships* (Cambridge, Mass.: MIT Press, 2000); Kathryn Harrison, 'Talking with the Donkey: Cooperative Approaches to Environmental Protection', *Journal of Industrial Ecology* 2, 3 (1999): 51–72.

20. Peter Doran, 'World Summit on Sustainable Development: An Assessment of IISD', Briefing Paper (Winnipeg: International Institute for Sustainable Development, 3 Oct. 2002).

21. Wapner, 'World Summit on Sustainable Development', 3; Speth, 'Perspectives on the Johanessburg Summit', 28. On the project, see: <www.malampaya.com/web/index.html>.

22. Wapner, 'World Summit on Sustainable Development', 4.

23. Speth, 'Perspectives on the Johanessburg Summit'.

24. Michael Reiterer, 'Trade and Environment: Reflections on the Impact of the OECD Joint Session', *International Environmental Affairs* 9 (1997): 69–81; Committee on Trade and Environment (CTE) Report to the 5th Session of the WTO Ministerial Conference in Cancún, WT/CTE/8 11 (July 2003) (03–3739).

25. CTE, Report to the 5th Session of the WTO Ministerial Conference in Cancún.

26. Pedro da Motta Veiga, 'Trade and Environment Negotiations: A Southern View', paper prepared for South American Agenda for Trade and Environment Regional Consultation, Santa Cruz, Chile, 10–11 Oct. 2003. Available at: <www.ictsd.org/issarea/environment/partner ships/sagenda>.

27. Williams 'In Search of Global Standards', 39.

28. Conca, 'The WTO and the Undermining of Global Environmental Governance', 485; Steven Bernstein and Benjamin Cashore, 'Globalization, Four Paths of Internationalization and Domestic Policy Change: The Case of Ecoforestry in British Columbia, Canada', *Canadian Journal of Political Science* 33, 1 (2000): 78–81.

29. Conca, 'The WTO and the Undermining of Global Environmental Governance', 485.

30. Lori Wallach and Patrick Woodall, *Whose Trade Organization? A Comprehensive Guide to the WTO* (New York: New Press, 2004).

31. John Gerard Ruggie, 'International Regimes, Transactions, and Change: Embedded Liberalism in the Postwar Economic Order', *International Organization* 36, 2 (1982): 379–415.

32. Carrie Wofford, 'A Greener Future at the WTO: The Refinement of WTO Jurisprudence on Environment Exceptions to GATT', *Harvard Environmental Law Review* 24, 2 (2000): 563–92.

33. Elizabeth R. DeSombre and J. Samuel Barkin, 'Turtles and Trade: The WTO's Acceptance of Environmental Trade Restrictions', *Global Environmental Politics* 12, 1 (2002): 12–18.

34. Williams, 'In Search of Global Standards', 46.

35. DeSombre and Barkin, 'Turtles and Trade'.

36. Wallach and Woodall, *Whose Trade Organization?*; Friends of the Earth, *Environmental Scorecard* (2004), available at: <www.foe.org/camps/intl/ greentrade/scorecard.pdf>.

37. Wallach and Woodall, *Whose Trade Organization?*, 102–7.

38. Frank Bierman, 'The Emerging Debate on the Need for a World Environment Organization', *Global Environmental Politics* 1, 1 (2001): 45–55. For an opposing view, see Konrad von Moltke, 'The Organization of the Impossible', *Global Environmental Politics* 1, 1 (2001): 23–8.

39. Sanford E. Gaines, 'International Trade, Environmental Protection and Development as a Sustainable Development Triangle', *RECIEL* 11, 3 (2003): 259–74.

Suggested Readings

Bernstein, Steven. *The Compromise of Liberal Environmentalism.* New York: Columbia University Press, 2001.

Clapp, Jennifer, and Peter Dauvergne. *Paths to a Green World: The Political Economy of the Global Environment.* Cambridge, Mass.: MIT Press, 2005.

Conca, Ken, Thomas Princen, and Michael F. Maniates. *Confronting Consumption.* Cambridge, Mass.: MIT Press, 2002.

Gallagher, Kevin P., and Jacob Werksman, eds. *The Earthscan Reader on International Trade and Sustainable Development.* London: Earthscan, 2002.

Stevis, Dimitris, and Valerie J. Assetto, eds. *The International Political Economy of the Environment.* Boulder, Colo.: Lynne Rienner, 2001.

World Commission on Environment and Development. 1987. *Our Common Future.* Oxford: Oxford University Press.

Web Sites

Greenpeace: www.greenpeace.org/international_en/

International Centre for Trade and Sustainable Development: www.ictsd.org

International Institute for Sustainable Developement: www.iisd.org

UN, sustainable development: www.un.org/esa/sustdev/index.html

World Wildlife Fund (WWF): www.panda.org

Chapter 18

Gendered Representations of the 'Global'
Reading/Writing Globalization

Marianne Marchand

These days much has already been said about globalization.[1] And, although many disagreements exist about the effects, impact, scope, and future of globalization, there is a general sense that we are living in times of profound change. Whenever such change occurs, it tends to produce feelings of uncertainty and being adrift. Moreover, as social and political analysis has taught us, major changes or transformations never take place on a level playing field. Instead, such changes involve the exercise of power and are superimposed on, as well as mediated through, already existing unequal relations of class, ethnicity, gender, race, and so forth. There is no reason to believe that this should be different in the case of globalization or global restructuring.

As I argued in the second edition of this volume, feminist and other critical approaches to IPE have already done much to identify some of the power dimensions of globalization.[2] A first step in revealing these power dimensions has been to dispense with a number of the persistent myths surrounding globalization. This is an important strategy because the language in which globalization is often couched tends to depoliticize public discussions. As one author remarks on the replacement of earlier developmentalist ideologies by the new ideology of globalism:

> The agenda of globalism shows its continuities with earlier discourses of development. If globalism is more efficient as a developmentalist ideology, it is because it seeks to *conceal*, with some success, that this agenda is set still within the old locations of power. But now it is

with the complicity of Third World states, corporations, intellectuals and experts, who are allowed increasingly to participate in the discourse and processes of development.[3]

These efforts to reveal globalization's power dimensions have been mirrored by the activities and analyses of the anti-globalization movement, or critical globalization movement (CGM).[4] The latter, in particular, has been very succesful in exploding existing myths about globalization.

A second step in the process of revealing the power dimensions of globalization has been to develop a gender analysis of the current transformations. In this context it is important to note that gender operates on at least three interconnected levels: the individual, the collective, and the ideational/ideological.[5] As a consequence, developing a gender analysis allows us not only to introduce subjects or 'people' and subjectivity into an otherwise rather abstract discussion about processes, structures, markets, states, and so forth; it also sensitizes us to the specifically gendered representations and valorizations of global restructuning: for instance, is the market becoming increasingly masculinized and (civil) society feminized (and what are the consequences of this)?

In the remainder of this chapter I will, first of all, explore how feminist and other critical IPE analyses, as well as the CGM, have been able to explode some of the myths surrounding globalization. Based on these insights I will further address the issue of globalization's inherent 'genderedness' through which certain inequalities are, on the one hand, being fostered, reified, and perpetuated, while, on the other, they may be challenged, eroded, and reversed. For the second part of the analysis I will look primarily at how gender operates ideationally. This is not to say that the individual and collective dimensions are less important; rather, this vantage point will allow us to explore whether certain new or dominant spheres and practices of globalization are discursively constructed and associated with 'masculine' values as opposed to other more 'feminized domains'.[6] What this means is that particular processes, spheres, and practices of globalization tend to produce differential constraints and opportunities for men and women. Yet, this is not as straightforward or banal as it may seem at first sight, because notions of masculinity and femininity are embedded in other social practices and subject to change over time and across space. Moreover, although highly masculinized spheres of the global economy may be predominantly occupied by men, women are not entirely absent in these spheres. The spaces and practices associated with so-called masculine values, however, not only may be more easily accessible to certain types of men, but they are also likely to project a certain image of power and to be associated with the exercise of power.

Alternatively, feminized spaces and practices may provide relatively easy access for women and subordinated groups of men, including working-class, minority, and migrant men; the association with these spaces and practices is mostly one of lack of power and disempowerment. Interestingly, however, these same feminized spaces on occasion can become an alternative source of power: it is often within these spaces that alternatives, oppositional strategies, challenges, and resistances are being articulated, thus undermining dominant forces of globalization.

Globalization and Its Myths

At least three persistent myths can be identified and challenged by the CGM and critical IPE analyses.[7] Most of them stem from the rather indiscriminate use of the term 'globalization' in the media

and by policy-makers. Often, 'globalization' is used as a blanket statement, covering a variety of changes and transformations. At other times the term is used to legitimize certain painful socio-economic policies, such as budget cuts or a more general reorientation of the foundations of the (European) welfare state.[8] Over the last decade or so, there have been various efforts to define and even to distinguish different forms of globalization. While some analysts provide a very narrow economic definition of globalization, others emphasize its more comprehensive nature and reach rather different conclusions about its repercussions. Trying to distinguish between its positive and negative aspects has been another way of approaching globalization: neo-liberal globalization or 'globalization from above' is seen as negative while 'globalization from below' is positively associated with such efforts as improving human rights, the environment, and labour conditions. Finally, it is possible to discern various distinct 'global' discourses with each emphasizing a particular dimension, ranging from a process (globalization), to an ideology (globalism), to a state of being (globality). Despite these efforts, a few persistent myths about globalization still linger. Some of the most pervasive include the following.

Myth 1: Globalization Is First and Foremost an Economic Process

Many analyses still assume that globalization almost exclusively concerns economics and the economy. They tend to discuss globalization in terms of the market, trade, and finance. However, a fuller understanding of globalization should recognize that, although economic processes play an important role, they are part of a larger complex set of processes encompassing the market, state, and civil society.[9] Exponents of the CGM are presenting this view and have been rather successful in disseminating it among a wider public.[10] This does not mean, however, that the myth has entirely disappeared. The contributions made by authors such as Hardt and Negri, Hertz, and Klein[11] do not so much discard the importance of the economy and economics but emphasize the negative ripple effects. Going beyond their analyses, a useful starting point is the notion that the market, state, and civil society are interdependent or contingent spheres of interaction and that all three are undergoing profound restructuring. These restructuring processes are complex and tend sometimes to reinforce and sometimes to contradict each other. In short, the entire process of global restructuring involves a reassessment of the relations among the state, the market, and civil society

Myth 2: Globalization Is a Process Generated Outside Our Own (Immediate) Environment

Often, globalization is portrayed as a 'major league' game, designed for such players as large international banks and transnational corporations. Some exponents of the CGM are no exception in accepting this portrayal. This image of globalization sometimes leads to a situation where people at the grassroots as well as within NGOs feel alienated, overwhelmed, and disempowered. However, if there is one myth that we need to dispense with, it is this one. Fortunately, Hertz and Klein have been able to do just this—by becoming interlocutors, on the one hand, with the CGM, and, on the other, with corporate representatives. They have also been successful in giving globalization a human face and explaining how it affects ordinary people's lives.

In other words, we are all involved in the globalization process, although obviously not in the same ways. For instance, subsistence farmers in sub-Saharan Africa may be affected by the decision of large-scale agro-businesses to expand their production in the region or to introduce a new seed variety. As a consequence, some of the local women farmers may lose their land or experience a dramatic change in their access to seeds, while other local people may find work with one of these agro-business companies and thus be involved in producing directly for the world market. Although research on cash-crop agriculture in sub-Saharan Africa has shown that many of these changes are negatively affecting local farming communities, it is

important to recognize that even among these communities there are differences among individuals in terms of their involvement in globalization. Moreover, these farmers' future survival will also depend on their (personal) perceptions of the changing situation.

Likewise, teenagers in Western Europe are influenced by globalized marketing strategies and the globalization of the media to buy a certain type of jeans, watch particular videos and television programs, and buy a specific kind of music—all of which means that they are also participants in globalization. While local youth subcultures define what is cool and what isn't, European teenagers are also heavily influenced by the global advertising campaigns of, for example, shoe companies and clothing manufacturers.

Needless to say, there are considerable differences among the CEOs in the boardrooms of the agro-businesses, the subsistence farmers, and the Western European teenagers in terms of their capacity to structure the direction of globalization processes. However, it is important to recognize that they are all involved in, and affected by, globalization. Hertz's and Klein's significant contribution is their demonstration, through their analysis and personal intervention, that being affected by the globalization process does not necessarily mean that one is disempowered.

Myth 3: Globalization Is a Universalizing Process and Has a Similar Effect on Everyone

One of the fears often voiced is that globalization will lead to the 'McDonaldization' of the world, leaving little room for distinct local cultural expressions. It is true that the universalizing force of globalization should not be underestimated, especially since many large companies are involved in global marketing strategies for their products. However, the mistake often made is to assume that this universalizing force will affect everyone in much the same way. To recognize certain commonalities in processes of globalization does not imply that their effects are the same. Processes of globalization are mediated through local economic, political, and social structures and, consequently, the outcomes vary considerably, resulting in specific local or regional expressions of globalization.

Gendered Representations of Globalization/Global Restructuring

I prefer the term 'global restructuring' over 'globalization' since 'it explicitly refers to a process of (partially) breaking down an old order and attempting to construct a new one.'[12] In addition, the concept of global restructuring allows us to analyze how the market, the state, and civil society are simultaneously undergoing some kind of global restructuring. In Janine Brodie's words:

> The current round of restructuring represents a fundamental shift in regimes of accumulation and with it a change in institutional practices, regulatory regimes, norms and behaviours—in other words, the simultaneous realignment of the economic, social and political. A feminist analysis must begin with the premise that restructuring represents a struggle over the appropriate boundaries of the public and private, the constitution of gendered subjects within these spheres and, ultimately, the object of feminist political struggles.[13]

For Brodie, the boundaries that need to be renegotiated are primarily those between the public and private, the state and market, as well as the national and international spheres. I would argue that these are not the only 'shifting' boundaries and that globalization involves renegotiating an intricate complex of boundaries including those pertaining to the state/market/civil society complex, the global/local, global/regional, and so forth.[14] Despite this difference with Brodie over which spheres and boundaries are the subject of restructuring, her insights are very helpful. For instance, she recognizes that global restructuring simultaneously involves the economic, social, and political. In other words, changing gender relations, such as the backlash against feminism and the neo-conservative agenda on family

values, are, for her, clearly part of this restructuring process. She also notes that the 'gendered subjects' inhabiting the spheres under transformation are being reconstituted in the process.

Although Brodie's analysis is helpful in understanding the inherent gendered nature of globalization, it does not directly address our concern with the gendered representations of globalization. For this, we need to turn to recent scholarship on the social construction of gender and gender identities in the context of the global political economy.[15] In his work on masculinity, Bob Connell identifies and traces a hegemonic (Western) masculinity being articulated, through various social practices, in relation to other masculinities as well as femininities.[16] According to Connell it is important to recognize that the construction of gender is dynamic and historical. In other words, he agrees with Brodie that periods of transformation are also characterized by changes in the social organization of gender.

Connell's notion of hegemonic masculinity brings us one step closer to understanding the connections between gendered representations of globalization and its dynamics of power. In Connell's words:

> The concept of 'hegemony', deriving from Antonio Gramsci's analysis of class relations, refers to the cultural dynamic by which a group claims and sustains a leading position in social life. At any given time, one form of masculinity rather than others is culturally exalted. Hegemonic masculinity can be defined as the configuration of gender practice which embodies the currently accepted answer to the problem of legitimacy of patriarchy, which guarantees (or is taken to guarantee) the dominant position of men and the subordinate position of women. . . .
>
> Nevertheless, hegemony is likely to be established only if there is some correspondence between cultural ideal and institutional power, collective if not individual. So, the top levels of business, the military and government provide a fairly convincing cor-

porate display of masculinity, still very little shaken by feminist women or dissenting men. It is the successful claim to authority, more than direct violence, that is the mark of hegemony (though violence often underpins or supports authority).[17]

Brodie's and Connell's observations lead us to two related questions. What characteristics make up contemporary hegemonic masculinity (and are these changing)? What spheres of the global political economy are associated with this hegemonic masculinity (and are these changing)? Connell himself only provides a partial answer to the first question. For him, the foundation of contemporary hegemonic masculinity was laid by the accumulation and concentration of wealth during colonial times. This accumulation and concentration of wealth—and its continuation today—have been beneficial to men in core countries because wealth bestows power over natural resources and other people's labour and services. In addition, the use of technology, especially in the context of the rationalization of the production process and the emergence of a knowledge-based society, has modified contemporary hegemonic masculinity's claim to authority based on 'direct' domination to include claims based on expertise.[18]

Connell does not really address whether hegemonic masculinity is also undergoing changes as part of the larger process of global restructuring. Charlotte Hooper suggests that this is precisely what is happening. Based on her analysis of *The Economist*, she suggests that globalization is evoking images of a new 'entrepreneurial frontier masculinity' combining science, technology, and business.[19] In other words, the global arena is still relatively uncharted terrain that needs to be explored and discovered, not on horseback this time but through the use of new means of communication and information technologies. The most interesting feature of this new global arena, where markets are waiting to be discovered and conquered,[20] is that it is both real and virtual. In fact, to discover the virtual global arena one does not

need to move physically; a laptop with Internet connection, mobile phone, fax, and a thermos of coffee are all the gear the explorer needs.

Hooper's analysis also enables us to address our second question about which spaces and practices are associated with contemporary hegemonic masculinity. From her account it is clear that contemporary hegemonic masculinity is being redefined in conjunction with those sectors that have become of central importance to the new global economy. Two examples provide support for this claim. The first shows the primacy of the international or global economy over domestic economic concerns. The example is taken from an article in a prominent Dutch newspaper by Rick van der Ploeg, who used to be professor of economics at the University of Amsterdam as well as undersecretary of cultural affairs in the Dutch government. In the article he argues that the Dutch economy (and by extension, other national economies) can be divided into 'hard' and 'soft' sectors. According to van der Ploeg, the 'hard' sector is exposed to international competition and encompasses horticulture, agriculture, mining, heavy industry, international transportation, business and commercial services, trade, and communication. In contrast, the 'soft' sector is relatively insulated from the vagaries of the global economy and is made up of areas dealing with social security and 'welfare'—public health care, culture, education, safety, fighting crime, housing, and the domestic service sector.[21] Van der Ploeg notes that the gap between the 'hard' and 'soft' sectors is increasing, whereby the former is characterized by export orientation, self-sufficiency (receiving few state subsidies), high growth rates of labour productivity, and pollution of the environment. The 'soft' sector, in contrast, displays the opposite characteristics. Van der Ploeg's conclusion is that the gap between these two sectors needs to be closed by exposing the 'soft' sector to market forces, while the state remains in charge of providing a (reduced) safety net.[22]

This account is an almost classic example of the construction of gendered representations and dichotomies. First, it clearly prioritizes the internationally oriented sectors of the economy over more 'domestic' concerns. Second, statistics tell us that these internationally oriented sectors generally tend to attract more men than women, while the reverse is true for the domestic sectors. Third, the description of the 'hard' sector evokes elements associated with contemporary hegemonic masculinity: facing tough competition, taking on responsibilities, and the use of new technologies. The sector's masculinity is further stressed by the frequent use of the term 'hard'. In other words, van der Ploeg's message is not only that the Dutch economy needs to be restructured, but also that this is the new frontier of the Dutch economy and one needs to be a participant in order to gain the authority and power associated with it.

For the second example of entrepreneurial new frontier masculinity at work we need to turn to the financial community. In the aftermath of the collapse of the Bretton Woods system in the early 1970s, the international financial sector took on a much larger role in international economic affairs than before. As some authors have suggested, a gravitational shift took place through which sectors associated with financial capital assumed a central position in the global political economy and gained a certain degree of structural power previously identified with sectors linked to productive capital.[23] Aided by new communication and information technologies, the international financial sector became truly 'globalized' by the mid-1980s. This makes it one of the true new frontiers of the global economy.

Concurrent with these changes, the image of the international (now global) financial sector has also changed dramatically. Nowadays the image of the 'global financial community', inhabited by the likes of George Soros and Nick Leeson, is a far cry from the stuffy, reliable, almost boring, long-gone world of banking symbolized by middle-aged bankers dressed in pinstriped suits and sporting bowler hats and umbrellas. As Susan Strange put it so eloquently:

The Western financial system is rapidly coming to resemble nothing as much as a vast casino. Every day games are played in this casino that involve sums of money so large that they cannot be imagined. At night the games go on at the other side of the world. In the towering blocks that dominate all the great cities of the world, rooms are full of chain-smoking young men all playing these games. Their eyes are fixed on computer screens flickering with changing prices. They play by intercontinental telephone or by tapping electronic machines. They are just like gamblers in casinos watching the clicking spin of a silver ball on a roulette wheel and putting their chips on red or black, odd numbers or even ones.[24]

From this depiction it is clear that contemporary hegemonic masculinity at the new frontier of the global financial community is (re)constructed on the basis of risk-taking (i.e., gambling), expertise as exemplified by the use of new information technologies, the idea that one needs to communicate 24 hours a day about the latest developments in the market, the idea that one is able to survive in a fast-paced environment, and, finally, age—being young is virtually a prerequisite. This brief description illustrates that the global financial community is much more than a network of integrated computer systems and worldwide financial flows; it is inhabited by real people. Yet, the kind of people associated with the sphere of global finance evokes images of adventurous, risk-taking, fast-paced, globe-trotting young men. Collectively, they are one of the groups embodying contemporary hegemonic masculinity.

What happens, then, when (young) women try to find a place in such an environment and are even looking to promote their careers? As a recent article in the British newspaper *The Observer* suggests, women have encountered a quite hostile work environment in financial firms located within the Square Mile of the City. As a result, there has been a wave of court cases brought by women. Most of the litigation concerns unfair dismissal claims, sex discrimination (especially in terms of salary and bonuses), and sexual harassment. One of the conclusions one may draw from this is that for women to enter an environment associated with hegemonic masculinity is difficult because they are likely to face obstacles or barriers to their careers resulting from the implicit notion that these women are 'out of place'. Interestingly, the court battles have resulted in financial firms making changes to their codes of conduct and discriminatory practices. Ideally, this means the construction of a more inclusive work environment and adaptations in associated hegemonic masculinity. However, there are also signs that another strategy (implicitly or subsconsciously) employed by these firms is to hire fewer women—thus partially closing the arena of global finance for women.[25]

In addition, another side to the global financial community is often overlooked—this same global financial community cannot function without the existence of an internationalized service economy in both the private and public spheres. For instance, large groups of migrant women (and men) are employed in the global financial centres of London, New York, and Hong Kong as domestic help, nannies, gardeners, etc.; alternatively, migrant women (and men) may find themselves cleaning the offices of Chase Manhattan and similar banks at night; and increasingly, it is also possible for women to find work in the Philippines or India as data-entry clerks for large companies abroad.[26] This suggests that the activities of the global financial community encompass much more than trading in stocks, options, and futures; they also involve the emergence of a feminized 'internationalized' service economy in which male and female migrant labour plays a significant role. Yet these groups are notoriously absent in representations of the masculinized sphere of global finance. In other words, representations of the global economy tap into and help to structure existing power inequalities based on class, ethnicity, gender, race, and so forth.

In addition to the export-oriented sectors of the domestic economy and the global financial community, many other spheres and practices of global restructuring can be analyzed from a gender perspective. For instance, national and international labour markets have been restructured in such a way that they are increasingly segmented and hierarchically organized along the lines of class, race, ethnicity, gender, and age. The increasing flexibility of labour policies in the OECD countries is leading to a shrinking group of masculinized core labour with relative job security and a growing group of feminized flexible labour[27] with little job security. In the South we find increasingly a feminization and casualization of labour in the rapidly expanding export industries.

Likewise, the changing role and makeup of the state can also be read in terms of gendered representations. Within the state apparatus the balance of power has shifted towards those sectors whose functions are directly related to the growing economy (finance, economic affairs, etc.) at the expense of the bureaucracies dealing with such issues as health, education, and social welfare. In other words, patterns of gender representation in the market are being replicated within the state apparatus. The state sectors involved with the global economy are associated with notions of contemporary hegemonic masculinity while departments dealing with, in van der Ploeg's terms, the 'soft' sector of the economy are linked to notions of femininity. Obviously, there are always local exceptions. For instance, in Mongolia the ministry of finance and the banking sector were until recently run by women. The apparent reason is that in Mongolian nomad society women were traditionally responsible for taking care of the money, left in their care by the men who were out herding cattle.

Globalization from Below

It would go beyond the scope of this analysis to discuss global transformations in depth. However, I would like to turn to one other example to illustrate how gendered representations work and how global restructuring also involves the reconstruction of masculinity and femininity. As we have focused thus far on 'globalization from above', I would like to turn now to 'globalization from below'.[28] Loosely defined, globalization from below refers to the mounting opposition to and resistance against neo-liberal global restructuring. What is significant and new about this resistance is that it can take many forms, that it tends to be grounded locally but almost always has a transnational dimension, and that it tries to combine knowledge with politics.[29] As such, globalization from below constitutes an important part of the emerging civil society.[30] Because of its more diffuse and unstructured character, associating globalization from below with certain gendered representations is challenging. One thing is clear, though: it is not a high-powered space inhabited by chain-smoking, risk-taking, and globe-trotting young men. And, whereas it would be difficult to come up with names of women who are key players in globalization from above, it is much easier to devise a list of prominent women who have entered the global arena in opposition to this globalization from above. The names of Hannah Asrawi, Cory Aquino, Gro Harlem Brundtland, Aung San Suu Kyi, Rigoberta Menchú, Jody Williams, Wangari Maathai, Noreena Hertz, and Naomi Klein come to mind. And their names are associated with such social causes as justice, democracy, human rights, peace, the ban on anti-personnel landmines, the environment, and the CGM. Why is this? Is it just a coincidence that women in leadership positions are more clearly identified with globalization from below than from above? Does this have anything to do with the different rendered representations of globalization from above and globalization from below?

One plausible answer to these questions builds on Connell's notion that hegemonic masculinity is being constructed in opposition to all femininities and subordinate masculinities.[31] Following this line of reasoning, globalization from above, being associated with contemporary hegemonic masculinity, is constructed in opposition to globalization from below, which then almost automatically comes to be linked to notions of reconstructed contemporary femininity and alternative masculinities. At first

sight this appears to be a familiar replay of a gendered division of labour: the more powerful spheres and practices are linked to a new-frontier hegemonic masculinity while the 'soft' spheres of the global arena are the terrain of feminized subjects.

Yet, this interpretation hides the fact that global civil society is a somewhat ambiguous and unstructured space, which is not entirely devoid of power or authority. For one, the fact that four of the women mentioned above have received the Nobel Peace Prize based on their activities within the context of globalization from below forces us to take this part of the global arena seriously, as it is hard to deny the (moral) authority and power attached to the Nobel Prize. Moreover, some scholars go so far as to argue that this global civil society actually provides the site and starting point for the construction of a new world order.[32] This view is shared by the Commission on Global Governance, which was created as a follow-up to the Willie Brandt, Olaf Palme, and Gro Harlem Brundtland commissions to report on the challenges facing the world community at the end of the Cold War in terms of global security and global governance.[33] In its report the Commission on Global Governance likens global civil society to a global neighbourhood. The image of a neighbourhood is used to underscore the interconnectedness of the world today: whether we like it or not, we are all neighbours and have to adjust to this new reality and learn to live together. In the Commission's opinion, this can only be done by strengthening certain neighbourhood values (respect for life, liberty, justice and equity, mutual respect, caring, and integrity) and developing a global civic ethic.[34] In other words, global civil society is being actively promoted and upgraded by dominant actors in the global political economy in terms of its projection of (moral) power and authority. Moreover, it is perceived as the site where 'people-centred' alternatives to ongoing neo-liberal global restructuring are being articulated and developed.

This positive reinforcement of globalization from below has an interesting parallel in the fact that dominant notions of femininity have been undergoing some changes as well. As a result of several factors—the emergence of second-wave feminism, the United Nations Decade for Women (including the four UN women's conferences)—women have entered the public sphere of politics and work in large numbers. This transformation has been accompanied by a reconstruction of middle-class, Western femininity, which is now based on the pursuit of such ideals as autonomy, independence, and a career.[35] More generally, it is clear that women's movements worldwide have been actively pursuing a rearticulation of various forms of femininity in their struggle for empowerment. The message conveyed is that empowerment is now part of contemporary, reconstructed expressions of femininity. Yet, this same contemporary, empowered femininity is regularly juxtaposed with hegemonic masculinity, whereby the latter stands for ruthless, individualistic, risk-taking, and competitive behaviour and the former is associated with teamwork, social concerns, and co-operation. Needless to say, individual men and women rarely, if ever, fit any of these stereotypical categories and most often combine characteristics from both, some of which may become more pronounced depending on the environment in which an individual happens to be active.

We can tentatively infer from the previous discussion that the sectors attached to globalization from below appear to be more receptive to women's leadership aspirations than, for instance, the global financial community. For one, in the higher echelons of the corporate world the glass ceiling is still very much present and creates a barrier for many women to further their careers and assume leadership positions in their professions. In addition, there still may be an implicit assumption, based on constructed stereotypes of femininity, that women are better suited to deal with social issues than men (self-selection may also be the result of this assumption). Finally, over the years women have collectively built up a large expertise not only in social causes, but also in oppositional politics. The experiences gained from participating in the women's movement and other social movements in challenging the estab-lished order from the margins have created an important legacy. They have shown that power and authority are not only to be found in the boardrooms and halls of government, but that other sites need to be empowered in order to effect the necessary changes. Therefore, the activities connected to globalization from below are familiar terrain to women, as well as among the most interesting if women want to be involved and try to effect changes. However, as I have argued elsewhere, this does not mean that women's involvement in opposition to globalization automatically leads to either 'feminist' or 'feminized' politics.[36]

Conclusion

This chapter has presented a brief glimpse into the gendered nature of globalization. As gender operates at the individual, collective, and ideational levels it is important to dissect globalization with these three levels in mind. In this particular instance I have focused primarily on the ideational and collective levels. As such, the chapter should, therefore, be read in the context of other significant work on gender and globalization or global restructuring. An important starting point for developing a feminist analysis of globalization is to reveal how processes of global restructuring are gendered. This can be done by explicitly bringing subject and subjectivity (that is, people) into the analysis of global restructuring and by focusing on its gendered representations.

To accomplish this, various myths need to be dispelled before we can look at the gendered representations of globalization. The overview of such gendered representations illustrates that a rather paradoxical situation is being created. On the one hand, there are clear signs that contemporary hegemonic masculinity is being rearticulated and linked to the high-powered spheres of global finance and the export sector of the domestic economy. On the other hand, a more diffuse and unstructured part of the global arena, global civil society, has been constructed in such a way that it seems to be associated with notions of reconstructed femininity and subordinate masculinities. This gender division of

labour between globalization from above and globalization from below loosely reflects the structural
inequalities between women and men. Yet, the
feminized part of the global arena is not to be interpreted as a space entirely devoid of power and
authority. Rather, it appears that it is increasingly
perceived as a site open to alternative expressions
of power and authority as well as a site where
people-centred alternatives and strategies to counter neo-liberal globalization are being formulated.

In sum, students of international political economy are very much interested in analyzing its materialist underpinnings in the form of production and
circulation of goods. This chapter argues that IPE's
relative neglect of the circulation of meaning and the
power of representation prevents us from establishing a fuller understanding of the global political
economy. Through using gendered images and
assigning meanings to spheres of the global economy, existing inequalities may be reinforced or new
ones created. Yet, these meanings and representations are also subject to change, thus creating
opportunities for counteracting these inequalities.

Notes

This chapter is based on some of my earlier work, in
particular: 'The New Challenge: The Gender and
Development Community Goes "Global"', *Connections*
1, 3 (Sept. 1996): 16–19; 'Reconceptualising "Gender
and Development" in an Era of Globalization',
Millennium 25, 3 (1996): 566–604; 'Globalization
versus Global Restructuring', *Connections* 2, 7 (Sept.
1997): 25–8. In addition, I am relying on some of the
insights in Marianne H. Marchand and Anne Sisson
Runyan, eds, *Gender and Global Restructuring:
Sightings, Sites, and Resistances* (London: Routledge,
2000).

1. See, for example, Underhill's Introduction to Part
   I and Chapters 2–4 in this volume, by Cox,
   Schwartz, and Mittelman.
2. See Robert Cox, 'Making Sense of the Changing
   International Political Economy', in Richard
   Stubbs and Geoffrey R.D. Underhill, eds, *Political
   Economy and the Changing Global Order* (Toronto:
   McClelland & Stewart, 1994), 45–59; Stephen
   Gill, 'The Global Panopticon? The Neoliberal
   State, Economic Life and Democratic
   Surveillance', *Alternatives* 2 (1995): 1–49; Susan
   Strange, *The Retreat of the State: The Diffusion of
   Power in the World Economy* (Cambridge:
   Cambridge University Press, 1996); Timothy J.
   Sinclair, 'Passing Judgement: Credit Rating
   Processes as Regulatory Mechanisms of
   Governance in the Emerging World Order',
   Review of International Political Economy 1, 1

(Spring 1994): 133–60; Sandra Whitworth,
'Theory as Exclusion: Gender and International
Political Economy', in Stubbs and Underhill, eds,
Political Economy and the Changing Global Order,
116–29; Jill Steans, *Gender and International
Relations* (Cambridge: Polity Press, 1998);
Marchand and Runyan, eds, *Gender and Global
Restructuring*.

3. Arif Dirlik, 'Globalism and the Politics of Place',
   Development 41, 2 (June 1998): 11; emphasis
   added.
4. The term 'critical globalization movement' is
   technically correct—most groups that make up
   the so-called anti-globalization movement are
   not against any kind of globalization but oppose
   globalization along neo-liberal lines.
5. At the individual level, gender operates through
   the social construction of (physical) male and
   female bodies; at the (collective) level of social
   relations gender structures the interactions
   among men and women in terms of (gender)
   roles and expectations; the ideational or ideological dimension involves the gendered representations and valorizations of social spheres, processes, and practices. See Marianne H. Marchand and
   Anne Sisson Runyan, 'Introduction: Feminist
   Sightings of Globalization: Conceptualizations
   and Reconceptualizations', in Marchand and
   Runyan, eds, *Gender and Global Restructuring*.
6. On the power of representation and internation-

al political economy, see Craig N. Murphy and Crisitina Rojas de Ferro, special eds, Theme Section: 'The Power of Representation in International Political Economy', *Review of International Political Economy* 2, 1 (Winter 1995): 63–183.

7. This section is taken from Marchand, 'Globalisation versus Global Restructuring'. For other accounts about globalization myths, see Marchand and Runyan, 'Introduction'; James H. Mittelman, 'How Does Globalization Really Work?', in Mittelman, ed., *Globalization: Critical Reflections*, International Political Economy Yearbook, vol. 9 (Boulder, Colo.: Lynne Rienner, 1997), 229–41.

8. A case in point is the current effort by EU governments to meet the Economic and Monetary Union (EMU) criteria of fiscal restraint: low inflation and low foreign debt.

9. For more details, see Marchand, 'The New Challenge'; Marchand, 'Reconceptualising "Gender and Development"'.

10. Michael Hardt and Antonio Negri, *Empire* (Boston, Mass.: Harvard University Press, 2000); Noreena Hertz, *The Silent Takeover: Global Capitalism and the Death of Democracy* (London: Arrow Books, 2001); Naomi Klein, *No Logo* (London: Flamingo, 2001).

11. Ibid.

12. Marchand, 'Reconceptualising "Gender and Development"', 577.

13. Janine Brodie, 'Shifting Boundaries: Gender and the Politics of Restructuring', in Isabella Bakker, ed., *The Strategic Silence: Gender and Economic Policy* (London: Zed Books, in association with The North-South Institute, Ottawa, 1994), 51–2.

14. Marchand, 'Reconceptualising "Gender and Development"', 577.

15. See R.W. Connell, *Masculinities* (Berkeley: University of California Press, 1995); Kimberly Chang and Lily Ling, 'Globalization and Its Intimate Other: Filipino Domestic Workers in Hong Kong', in Marchand and Runyan, eds, *Gender and Global Restructuring*; Charlotte Hooper, 'Masculinities in Transition: The Case of Globalization', ibid.

16. Connell argues that the dominant (and possibly hegemonic) position for Western masculinity finds its roots in colonialism and has more recently been sustained by the spread of 'Western values' through cinema, pop culture, mass media, etc. Obviously, Western masculinity's hegemonic position is being challenged by Asian constructions of masculinity (as embedded in the 'Asian values' debate) and by various religious fundamentalist notions of masculinity. See Connell, *Masculinities*, 185–203.

17. Ibid., 77.

18. Ibid., 164–5, 201.

19. Hooper, 'Masculinities in Transition'.

20. In a distasteful choice of language, *The Economist* referred to this conquering of new 'virgin territories' or markets in an article on Myanmar (Burma), which it titled 'Ripe for Rape', *The Economist*, 15 Jan. 1994, 65. For a further analysis of this article, see Hooper, 'Masculinities in Transition'.

21. Rick van der Ploeg, 'Zachte Sector van de Economie Moet naar Markt Worden Overgeheveld', *NRC Handelsblad*, 9 Apr. 1994. It is important to realize that the Dutch agricultural and horticultural sectors are very export-oriented and high-tech.

22. Ibid.

23. See Cox, 'Making Sense'; Gill, 'The Global Panopticon?'; Mittelman, 'How Does Globalization Really Work?'.

24. Susan Strange, *Casino Capitalism* (Oxford: Basil Blackwell, 1986), 1.

25. Conal Walsh, 'Pick your Suit', *The Observer*, 18 July 2004, Business Section, 3.

26. Chang and Ling, 'Globalization and Its Intimate Other'.

27. This includes contract work, part-time work, subcontracted work, homework, and so forth.

28. Richard Falk uses this terminology in 'Resisting "Globalisation-from-above" Through "Globalisation-from-below"', *New Political Economy* 2, 1 (Mar. 1997): 17–24.

29. Ibid., 19. See also Marchand and Runyan, 'Introduction'.

30. Paul Ekins, *A New World Order: Grassroots*

Movements for Global Change (London: Routledge, 1992).

31. Connell, *Masculinities.*

32. Ekins, *A New World Order.* See also the discussion on cosmopolitan democracy in David Held, *Democracy and the Global Order* (Cambridge: Polity Press, 1995).

33. Commission on Global Governance, *Our Global Neighbourhood* (Oxford: Oxford University Press, 1995).

34. Ibid., 41–75.

35. For an account of the backlash against this new notion of femininity, see Susan Faludi, *Backlash: The Undeclared War Against American Women* (New York: Crown Publishers, 1991). More recently there have been some suggestions that neo-liberal ideas have influenced feminist thought and that so-called 'power feminism' and 'girl power' are expressions of this.

36. Marianne H. Marchand, 'Challenging Globalisation: Toward a Feminist Understanding of Resistance', *Review of International Studies* 29, S1 (Dec. 2003): 145–60.

Suggested Readings

Enloe, Cynthia. *The Curious Feminist: Searching for Women in a New Age of Empire.* Berkeley: University of California Press, 2004.

Klein, Naomi. *No Logo.* London: Flamingo, 2001.

Marchand, Marianne H., and Anne Sisson Runyan, eds. *Gender and Global Restructuring: Sightings, Sites, and Resistances.* London: Routledge, 2000.

Peterson, V. Spike. *A Critical Rewriting of Global Political Economy: Reproductive, Productive and Virtual Economies.* London: Routledge, 2003.

Web Sites

ATTAC: http://attac.org/

Corporate Watch: http://corpwatch.org.uk

World Bank Group, Gender and Developement: www.worldbank.org/html/extdr/thematic.htm

Women Watch: www.un.org/womenwatch/

Chapter 19

Crime in the Global Economy

H. Richard Friman

Governments and scholars alike argue that the criminal underside of globalization is expanding at an alarming rate. Media headlines repeat warnings of transnational drug cartels and terrorist groups flooding markets with illegal drugs ranging from cocaine and heroin to methamphetamines and ecstasy. National borders appear to be overrun by criminal organizations smuggling migrant workers into fields and factories, and horror stories abound concerning the brutal trafficking of men, women, and children into prostitution and sweatshops. Each day new revelations emerge about the complex networks of banks, non-bank financial institutions, and underground banking networks that launder the profits of criminal activities and challenge the integrity of the world's financial systems.[1]

Though a criminal underside of globalization clearly exists, scholars also have revealed that politicians, law enforcement and security agencies, and the media have benefited from overstating its nature and challenges.[2] This chapter briefly explores the extent to which transnational criminal activities and criminal actors have flourished in the global economy and the primary causes of this criminal underside of globalization. I argue that the criminal underside of globalization is an expanding and important challenge, but one whose scale relative to the broader global economy has been overstated by an absence of conceptual clarity and methodological caution. The sources of the expansion of crime in the global economy stem primarily from the ways in which states have *nested* prohibition regimes in increasingly liberal international economic systems and *embedded* them in consider-

ations of the domestic stability of advanced industrial countries. The implication of this argument is that co-ordinated multilateral enforcement efforts, often advocated as essential for eliminating the criminal underside of globalization, always will fall short. Multilateral steps can help to address the inherent problems of co-ordination in an international system of sovereign states faced with transnational actors and practices. But criminal activities and actors thrive in the space that exists between state prohibitions and the inability and unwillingness of states to enforce fully their own laws.[3] A focus on nested and embedded prohibition reveals that the criminal underside of globalization is in large part an extension of societies and social practices in the developed world that multilateral enforcement is doing little to address.

Shedding Light on the Dark Side

At a basic level, transnational criminal activities are practices that extend across national borders and are designated as illegal by states. Criminal activities include 'predatory' actions involving elements of fraud or force, as well as more 'market-based' activities entailing 'mutually agreeable exchanges in which there is value offered for money'. Market-based activities include exchanges discussed in traditional definitions of *criminal economies* involving the production and distribution of illegal goods and services, as well as exchanges discussed in traditional definitions of *informal economies* involving the illegal production or distribution of otherwise legal goods and services. Criminal activities become transnational when the 'perpetrators, their victims, the goods and services being transacted, or the orders directing such transactions' extend beyond national borders.[4]

Transnational Criminal Activities

The United Nations Convention against Transnational Organized Crime (CTOC) has emerged as a centrepiece of multilateral efforts against transnational crime and as such helps to illustrate the difficulties of conceptual clarity. The CTOC and its protocols focus on 'serious' crimes—offences punishable by maximum imprisonment of 'at least four years or more serious penalty'—especially those involving drug trafficking, firearms and component and ammunition trafficking, migrant smuggling, trafficking of women and children, and money laundering. In early deliberations over drafts of the CTOC, national delegates defined transnational criminal activity in terms of serious crime 'committed in more than one State' or 'committed in one State but a substantial part of its preparation, planning, direction, or control, takes place in a different State.' By the final version, the definition had been broadened to include crime 'committed in one State but [that] involves an organized criminal group that engages in criminal activity in more than one State; or is committed in one state but has substantial effects in another State.'[5] In effect, the CTOC reveals how governments have narrowed the concept of transnational crime to serious offences, turned to protocols to expand the activities requiring national designation as serious, and broadened the concept of transnational criminal activity to include both national activities associated with groups that are otherwise transnational and national activities whose impact, broadly defined, is ultimately transnational.

In this context of contracting and expanding definitions of transnational criminal activity, policy practitioners and scholars have tended to focus on the evasion of state regulations, prohibitions against the cross-border movements of goods and persons, and the laundering of profits from such activities.[6] The figures used to illustrate these trends suggest staggering patterns of transnational criminal activity. Trafficking in drugs, small and light arms, and persons are three major sectors in the global criminal economy. The drug trade comprises the largest area of activity, supplying an estimated 234 million illicit drug users and generating annual revenue estimated as large as $400 to $500 billion. The United States alone consumes an estimated 250 metric tonnes of cocaine, 13 to 18 metric tonnes of heroin, and 8,500 metric tonnes of cannabis each year. Estimated production of pure cocaine, based on trends in Latin American coca leaf cultivation, reveals amounts surging from under 300 metric tonnes in 1985 to over 950 metric tonnes in 1996 and declining to roughly 800 metric tonnes in 2002. Global production of opium, the raw material for heroin, increased from an estimated 3,700 metric tonnes in 1990 to 5,700 metric tonnes in 1999 before falling to 1,600 metric tonnes in 2001 due to disruptions in Afghanistan. By 2002, and the resurgence of the Afghan drug trade, global opium production had recovered to an estimated 4,500 metric tonnes with the potential to manufacture 450 metric tonnes of heroin. By 2003, Afghanistan alone had the potential to generate 337 metric tonnes of heroin destined primarily for European markets and easily overshadowing the potential heroin production of Myanmar (Burma), Colombia, and Mexico combined.[7]

The illicit trade in small arms and light weapons includes goods ranging from handguns and rifles to grenade launchers and hand-held rocket launchers. The trade draws on illegal production, diverted legal production and sales, and the clandestine movement of stockpiles of recycled/used weapons, generating an estimated $1 billion in revenue or roughly 10–20 per cent of the legal small arms trade. According to the United Nations, 40–60 per cent of the estimated 500 million small and light arms in the world are illicit.[8] Trafficking in persons annually victimizes between 600,000 and 800,000 persons, generating an estimated $9.5 billion in illegal revenue. An estimated 70 per cent of those trafficked are women; furthermore, 'over half' of all persons and the 'majority of women and girls' trafficked are exploited in the sex trade.[9] As observed by Paula J. Dobriansky, US Undersecretary of State for Global Affairs, 'unofficial estimates' place the number of victims of transnational trafficking at close to four million persons, suggesting that trafficking 'could grow to exceed the illegal trade in drugs within a decade.'[10]

Estimates of the overall annual revenue generated by the criminal underside of globalization, the gross criminal product, range from $1.0 to $1.5 trillion a year.[11] Money laundering seeks to hide the origins of this revenue by moving it through the world's financial systems. The process is threefold: placement of funds into the financial system; layering the funds through multiple transactions and a series of conversions to disguise their source; and integration of the funds into the legal economy. Launderers work through banks using cash and electronic wire transfers, as well as through non-bank financial institutions such as brokerage houses and informal financial networks, the latter consisting of havalah and fei chien networks used by South Asian and Chinese migrants, respectively, to send remittances back to their home countries.[12] International Monetary Fund (IMF) estimates commonly cited by experts posit annual levels of money laundering at 'between two and five percent of the world's gross domestic product', or between $590 billion and $1.5 trillion in 1996 US dollars.[13]

Although the criminal underside of globalization clearly exists, the methodological limitations of accurately capturing the scale of transnational criminal activity require caution in claims concerning its expansion. The United Nations has been the source of the commonly cited high-end estimates of $400 to $500 billion in annual illegal drug revenue, but even the officials who worked on these estimates have acknowledged that the figures have served more as a means to attract public attention than as an accurate portrayal of the drug trade.[14] The UN's more specific estimates of drug production, trafficking, consumption, percentage of drugs seized, and revenue rely on national estimates that are in turn based on regional and local estimates. The US Department of State, one such source, acknowledges that while it is confident in statistics regarding hectares of coca and opium poppies under cul-

tivation, it is much less certain on estimates of crop yields and drug processing and production.[15]

The figures for arms trafficking, trafficking in persons, and money laundering also need to be read with caution. Statistics on illegal small and light arms sales suffer from the absence of clear data on the legal arms industry, let alone accurate data on used arms stockpiles and recycling patterns, as well as price differentials for the array of new and used weapons. Statistics on the trafficking of persons, especially concerning women and children trafficked into the commercial sex industry, face problems with victim under-reporting and selective state enforcement.[16] Statistics on money laundering have been more problematic, in large part due to the reliance on revenue estimates for specific sectors of the criminal economy, various assumptions on the extent of estimated criminal revenues that are laundered, and flaws in constructed measures of gross criminal product. As R.T. Naylor observes, 'the reality is that no one has a clue about how much illegal money is earned, saved, or laundered or moved around the world.'[17]

Statistics on the scale of transnational criminal activity relative to the broader global economy are also problematic. Since 1995, experts have posited that the annual drug trade is equivalent to roughly 8 per cent of total world trade. This figure not only draws on the flawed UN revenue estimates but inflates the relative size of the drug trade by comparing total illegal drug revenue, rather than just export revenue, with world *export* data.[18] Similarly, experts often cite the IMF estimate of global money laundering at between 2.0 and 5.0 per cent of global GDP. The lower figure has been in circulation since 1994, attributed by the *Financial Times* to US and UK officials, and, at the time, disturbingly equivalent to the questionable drug trade figure of $500 billion. The upper figure appears to stem from a passing statement by former IMF Managing Director Michel Camdessus at the February 1998 Financial Action Task Force Plenary session in Paris that '2 to 5 per cent of global GDP would probably be a consensus range' for the 'present scale of money laundering transactions'.

Applying this range to rising global GDP levels has led in turn to expanding estimates of the level of money laundering.[19]

Even though describing the massive scale of transnational criminal flows, experts still commonly use the image of a needle in a haystack to describe the difficulty in finding these flows in the broader transnational movement of legal goods and services and financial transactions. In effect, transnational criminal activities remain relatively small when compared to a global GDP of $32.3 trillion, exports and imports of $6.5 and $6.7 trillion, and daily international financial flows of $1.5 trillion. Moreover, given the expansion of the global economy, it remains difficult to say with any degree of precision that the relative size of the criminal economy has reached unprecedented levels.[20] Ultimately, transnational criminal activities have greater meaning when explored in specific contexts. In Afghanistan, for example, the opium and heroin trade appears to account for between 40 and 60 per cent of GDP, providing farmers with approximately $1 billion a year and generating another $1.3 billion to processors and traffickers. Such estimates are more useful than the all-too-common claims that worldwide money laundering is greater than the GDP of Spain.[21]

Criminal Actors

Organized criminal groups, left- and right-wing insurgencies, government intelligence agencies, corporations, and individual entrepreneurs are among the many actors with a long history of engaging in transnational criminal activity. As argued by Susan Strange, 'what is new and of importance' in the global economy are the networks of transnational linkages among organized crime groups. Strange posits the existence of an 'anarchical "international society" of mafias' linking crime groups together in 'formal organization or just as a loose network of bilateral deals'.[22] The proliferation of organized crime groups appears to be widespread—Italian and Sicilian crime groups, Colombian and Mexican drug trafficking organizations, Chinese Triads, Japanese Yakuza, Balkan

drug and migrant smuggling/trafficking networks, Nigerian drug and financial scam operations—and all of these are overshadowed by warnings of an explosion of criminal organizations from the former Soviet Union. However, organized crime remains a contested concept among scholars, illustrated by long-standing debates over the extent of formal organization of criminal enterprises as well as the broader organization of markets for goods and services in criminal economies.[23]

The prominent image of organized crime emphasizes hierarchical criminal groups exerting formal and brutal control over their own organizations and linked to other criminal groups through treaties and standing commissions, and co-ordinating operations over multiple sectors of the criminal economy. This image vies with evidence of extensive variation in patterns of criminal organization, internal hierarchy and the formality of external linkages, and the durability of co-operative endeavours across sectoral operations and countries.[24] Although often described by law enforcement agencies as tightly organized drug cartels, the classic examples of the Colombia-based Medellin and Cali trafficking organizations instead relied on 'layers of subcontractors and freelancers' at all stages of the trade and expanded into US and European drug markets through 'co-operative relationships' with multiple foreign crime groups. Arms trafficking networks, including those moving arms into the Balkans, Afghanistan, and Africa, have relied on multiple tiers of government agencies, arms brokers, banks, and shippers to link buyers and sellers. Networks trafficking women and children range from 'small crime rings and loosely connected criminal networks' to more vertically integrated operations, linking local recruiters and kidnapping operations to brothels in Europe, Asia, and the United States.[25]

The United Nations CTOC broadly defines an organized criminal group as 'a structured group of three or more persons, existing for a period of time and acting in concert with the aim of committing one or more serious crimes or offenses established in accordance with this Convention, in order to obtain, directly or indirectly, a financial or other material benefit.' 'Structured' in this context refers to 'a group that is not randomly formed for the immediate commission of an offence and that does not need to have formally defined roles for its members, continuity of its membership, or a developed structure.'[26] The considerable grey area in this definition increases the size of statistical estimates on the number of organized crime groups and the extent of organized criminal activity well beyond major criminal organizations. The definition also does little to capture the variation in group size, organization, or scale of operations, which is central to understanding the extent and nature of the challenges posed by organized crime.

Terrorism has always been a contested concept, with international disputes over the identification of states, governmental agencies, and societal groups as terrorists and their actions as terrorist activity. In the aftermath of 11 September 2001, the United States has pressed for a broad international consensus on terrorism focusing on non-state actors with global reach who engage in 'premeditated, politically-motivated violence perpetrated against non-combatants', as well as on those who provide direct and indirect logistical, financial, or other forms of support.[27] In this context, the intersection of terrorists and the criminal economy can be a multi-faceted one, especially in the areas of drug trafficking and money laundering.

In contrast to organized criminal groups, terrorists have turned to transnational criminal activities less for the sake of profit and more to generate revenue to finance violent operations for political ends. The drug trade offers terrorists multiple opportunities for revenue, ranging from taxation on cultivation, production, and transport networks to direct terrorist participation in all levels of the trade.[28] During the 1980s, the Reagan administration used the term 'narcoterrorism' to describe the relationship between leftist insurgency movements, such as the Revolutionary Armed Forces of Colombia (FARC) and Shining Path in Peru, and drug trafficking cartels, while downplaying drug trafficking by US-backed, right-wing Colombian paramilitaries and Central American and Afghan

freedom fighters.[29] Hyphenated now as 'narco-terrorism' or 'narco-terror', the term broadly refers to the use of drug trafficking 'to further, or fund, politically motivated violence'.[30]

FARC continues to be the primary example, followed by the paramilitary United Self-Defence Forces of Colombia (AUC) and the National Liberation Army (ELN) in Colombia. As argued by a Congressional Research Service report, FARC generates an estimated '$500 million to $1.0 billion annually from criminal activities, mostly from taxing or participating in the narcotics trade'.[31] Narco-terrorism arguments also have pointed to Al-Qaeda's reliance on drug trafficking as one of many sources of terrorist financing and as part of a broader strategy of spreading drugs into the Western world. However, the nature of this reliance appears to be indirect at best. Prior to the American-led invasion of Afghanistan, Al-Qaeda benefited from a percentage of Taliban taxation policies on opium cultivation, production, and transport. Estimates of total Taliban revenue from the drug trade (thus, not by any means the share that Al-Qaeda received), prior to a ban on opium production in 2000, range from $20 to $40 million. This figure pales relative to estimates of drug revenue generated by Afghan warlords in the US-backed Northern Alliance.[32]

Terrorist financing stems from multiple sources, ranging from contributions from governments, non-profit/charitable organizations, and underground banking networks to the multiple paths of laundering funds from transnational criminal activities.[33] During the height of the Cold War, governments from the contending blocs were the primary sources of funding for terrorist operations; but as the war ended, terrorist groups turned to other sources. By 2004, US assessments of terrorism noted Cuba, Iran, Syria, and North Korea as the primary 'state-sponsors of terrorism' and that the greater challenges were posed by non-state sources of terrorist financing.[34] Investigations into the Al-Qaeda financial network point to the extensive role of charitable organizations, underground banking networks, and electronic wire transfers in terrorist funding. But patterns of funding tend to vary by terrorist organization, with Latin American insurgency movements relying more on funds generated by the drug trade and other groups relying on the proceeds of smuggling of products, ranging from cigarettes to diamonds, as well as trafficking in persons.[35]

Much like monetary figures on transnational criminal activities, estimates of terrorist financing have been a source of considerable speculation and escalation. Loretta Napoleoni, for example, posits a 'New Economy of Terror' that 'amounts to nearly $1.5 trillion.' She bases the figure on the $1.0 trillion 'illegal economy'—based, in turn, on an estimated $400 billion in narcotics revenue and $100 billion in the smuggling of other goods and people, all entering money laundering networks, plus an additional $500 billion in 'illegal capital flight'— combined with an estimated $500 billion in legitimate business profits, private donations, and collections by 'Muslim charities and mosques'.[36] There is here no account of how much goes specifically to terrorists. Such methodological problems aside, terrorists clearly participate in the global economy and its criminal underside. Estimates of the funds used to carry out the 11 September attacks range from $500,000 to $2 million, underscoring that only limited funds are necessary to do 'enormous damage'.[37]

Prohibition: Nested and Embedded

Governments introduce prohibitions against specific activities for diverse reasons, including pressure from domestic interests and religious groups, non-governmental organizations, and other states as well as considerations of harm. Occasionally, and usually due to the influence of a powerful state, national prohibitions can develop into international prohibition regimes distinguished by international conventions and institutions co-ordinating 'criminal laws and police action throughout much of the world'.[38] As is the case of national prohibitions, however, gaps continue to exist between laws that criminalize activities and the actual patterns of enforcement. The more activities governments criminalize and the less they are able or willing to enforce these prohibitions, the more extensive the criminal economy can become.[39] The criminal underside of globalization reflects such a gap, distinguished by prohibitions *nested* in increasingly liberal international economic regimes and *embedded* in the domestic stability of advanced industrial countries.

Nested Prohibition

Prohibitions against transnational activities have been 'nested' within broader systems of trade, finance, and migration that have ramifications for the ability and willingness of governments to engage in enforcement. The concept of nesting was developed by Vinod Aggarwal, who explored how sectoral trade is nested in an overall trade system and, in turn, in a larger security system.[40] Early twentieth-century steps towards prohibition regimes against drug trafficking were nested within trade and financial systems in transition from multilateral liberalism to more economic nationalist treatment of transnational flows. Governments monitored the movement of goods and services across borders primarily to identify the smuggling of legal goods seeking to evade trade duties as well as to curtail the movement of prohibited goods and illegal entry by unwanted migrants.[41] Though border controls were far from complete, by the 1920s and 1930s monitoring was facilitated by an overall focus on limiting rather than facilitating transnational economic flows. This pattern began to change with economic policy shifts following World War II, and since the 1960s efforts towards prohibition regimes have been nested within broader patterns of multilateral economic liberalization, making the task of enforcement more difficult.

As other chapters in this volume have explored, negotiated reductions in tariff and nontariff barriers to trade, under the General Agreement on Tariffs and Trade (GATT) and the World Trade Organization, as well as regional integration efforts such as the European Union and NAFTA, have increased opportunities for the transnational flow of goods and services. Negotiated and unilateral reductions in capital and exchange controls have moved away from the post-war stabilization efforts of the Bretton Woods monetary regime and, facilitated by regional integration efforts, have increased opportunities for transnational flows of short- and long-term capital. Immigration restrictions have remained relatively extensive when compared with trends in trade and finance, and, with the primary exception of the European Union, have been the focus of national regulations rather than international migration regimes. Advanced industrial countries have differed in their acceptance of immigration and in the introduction of selective front doors to migration to allow legal entry to migrants with specialized skills, familial ties, or from specific countries/regions. National variations exist, as well, in regard to side doors for migrant workers and asylum seekers.[42]

Nested in expanding dynamics of economic liberalism, the enforcement of prohibition becomes a more difficult task. Government treatment of transnational flows has shifted to facilitating rather than impeding movement across borders, in effect sacrificing effective prohibition enforcement for the sake of ensuring liberal economic flows. As the image of needles and haystacks suggests, economic liberalization also has increased the overall flow of goods, services, and people across borders and has made it more difficult for law enforcement agencies to discover transnational criminal activities hidden within these flows.[43] These difficulties have been intensified by technological innovation.[44] Advances in cellular phones, personal computers, the Internet, satellites, and fibre optic networks have increased opportunities and the speed of transnational communication and co-ordination for legal and illegal transactions alike. Advances in air cargo networks, commercial airlines, and container shipping by sea, truck, and rail have increased the opportunities and speed of transnational transportation of both legal and illegal goods and migrants. In short, the intersection of economic liberalization and

technological innovation has increased opportunities for transnational criminal activity and lowered barriers to entry for criminal actors seeking to link local operations with global markets.[45]

This intersection has increased the challenges to the successful enforcement of prohibitions in more fundamental ways. Economic liberalization leads to flows of goods and services that can threaten less-competitive manufacturing and agricultural sectors and marginalized populations in developed and developing countries alike. Accelerated by technological innovation, the impact of economic liberalization is intensified, which in turn leads to more rapid transnational flows and less time for adjustment. As social safety nets become overwhelmed, the informal and criminal economies emerge as alternatives for the expanding marginalized population. Thus, an unintended effect of the intersection of economic liberalization and technological innovation is the potential displacement of individuals into the criminal economy, some as new producers of illegal goods and services and others as more likely to consume illegal goods and services out of necessity or despair. An ever-expanding pool of new drug consumers, migrants seeking assistance from smugglers to move across borders, and women recruited into trafficking networks with deceptive promises of employment helps to explain the vitality of the criminal underside of globalization.[46]

Embedded Prohibition

Multinational prohibitions against transnational activities also have been 'embedded' in assumptions of domestic stability, especially the stability of advanced industrial countries. Ruggie's concept of 'embedded liberalism' argues that the political compromise among developed countries over postwar international economic relations accepted multilateral liberalism but was 'predicated upon domestic interventionism' that would 'minimize socially disruptive adjustment costs.' The purpose was to 'devise a form of multilateralism that is compatible with the requirements of domestic stability.' The compromise in embedded prohibition regimes has been the rule, or more precisely, considerations of domestic stability of advanced industrial countries have determined patterns of enforcement.[47]

The assumptions referred to here are counterintuitive. Clearly, prohibitions address illicit transnational practices that might challenge domestic stability in important ways. Drug trafficking feeds abuse and addiction; arms trafficking provides weapons to criminals and insurgencies; migrant smuggling undermines legal immigration and inclusion; trafficking of persons facilitates modern-day slavery; money laundering erodes the integrity of financial systems—and all of these practices can lead to widespread corruption. However, the *enforcement* of prohibitions also challenges domestic political, economic, and social practices, which if not always desirable are certainly tolerated. The successful enforcement of prohibitions also can run counter to vested political and economic interests that either have a stake in the continuation of the prohibited activity, as discussed below in regard to prostitution and money laundering, or are opposed to structural shifts that may be necessary for its elimination.

These challenges call into question the norm of domestic stability that distinguishes embedded prohibition. For example, responding to the challenge of trafficking in women requires more than steps against organized trafficking networks. The successful enforcement of prohibitions against trafficking requires steps against prostitution, pornography, and sweatshops, as well as against the broader policies and practices of legislated and informal discrimination that close off economic alternatives and legitimize the exploitation of women in sending and receiving countries.[48] In this context, enforcement limited solely to action against foreign trafficking organizations imposes relatively small costs of adjustment to the domestic status quo. Another example is money laundering. Responding to the challenge of money laundering requires financial institutions to identify financial flows for illicit practices despite the inevitable profit they make from ignoring illicit flows. In practice, this has led to client identification procedures, thresholds for mandatory reporting for

financial transactions (usually US$10,000 for deposits and withdrawals and US$5,000 for cash exports and imports), and provisions requiring financial institutions to report suspicious financial transactions, primarily suspected drug, organized crime, or terrorist-related movements of money. More vigorous enforcement of prohibitions against money laundering, requiring detailed client identification and monitoring, much lower threshold levels for mandatory reporting, and a broader conceptualization of suspicious financial transactions, would cut much deeper into the profits of banks and non-bank financial institutions.[49] In both trafficking in persons and money laundering, the enforcement of prohibition is to an extent sacrificed in favour of vested interests.

Advanced industrial countries have played an integral role in prohibition regimes in determining both the activities to be criminalized and the appropriate methods of enforcement. In general, embedded prohibition has sought to minimize the costs of *domestic* adjustment by placing greater emphasis on controlling *foreign* sources of supply and transnational trafficking networks rather than on curtailing domestic sources of demand. The exception has usually been when developed countries are the primary sources of supply and developing countries are the primary locus of demand. Examples here include small arms and the toxic waste trade, where developing countries have been expected to adapt but less has been expected of the practices of developed countries.[50]

Externalizing the burden of adjustment has increased pressures on developing countries to adopt policies of prohibition that often are beyond their capacity or interest to implement fully. The result of embedded prohibition is an increasing gap between the criminalization of transnational activities and domestic adjustment and enforcement for developing countries, or between criminalization and preventative measures in developed countries. This gap is a primary *cause* of the expansion of transnational crime. Governments and experts rightly point to enforcement successes against trafficking networks and source countries. But these successes have only temporary effects, as new and often even better organized criminal networks, as well as alternative sources of supply, emerge to meet the lucrative pull of demand deeply entrenched in the domestic societies of developed countries.

A brief overview of drug prohibition helps to illustrate this pattern. The criminalization of the drug trade has evolved from an initial focus on reducing the legal trade in and smuggling of legally produced narcotics to an emphasis since the 1960s on enforcing prohibitions against the illegal production and trafficking of illegal drugs. Advanced industrial countries have played the central role in this evolution, and the enforcement agenda embraced by the United States dominates the modern prohibition regime. The 1988 Convention against the Illicit Traffic in Narcotic Drugs and Psychotropic Substances was a triumph for the Reagan administration. The Convention requires signatories: to criminalize drug production, trafficking, purchase, and possession, as well as the 'organization, management, or financing' of such offences; to criminalize money laundering; to criminalize trade in chemicals used to produce illegal drugs; and to introduce enforcement methods ranging from asset seizures to extradition.[51]

In practice, however, advanced industrial countries have been more willing to pressure developing countries to implement these provisions fully rather than to take steps that would undermine their own domestic stability. The United States has a long history of emphasizing drugs as a foreign threat despite the impact of widespread domestic consumption on the world drug trade. US enforcement strategies have focused domestically on immigrants and ethnic minorities more than on the country's white majority, despite the greater presence of this white majority in final demand for drugs. Enforcement strategies have tended towards specialized drug task forces and federal mandatory drug sentencing guidelines that in practice have affected marginalized populations less able to raise civil liberty concerns. Broader policy shifts to address socio-economic causes of drug consumption or participation in the drug trade have proven to be politically difficult to dis-

cuss, let alone implement.[52] The 2004 US *National Drug Control Strategy* report is the latest in a trend towards emphasizing health and education measures to curtail demand and the disruption of drug markets to reduce supply. Enforcement as a demand-side strategy as opposed to a supply-side strategy receives little mention in the report. The $7.1 billion slated for enforcement, out of a total $12.1 billion budget, is largely earmarked for Department of State, Department of Defence, Homeland Security, and Drug Enforcement Agency programs to disrupt foreign trafficking organizations.[53]

The US practice of externalizing the adjustment costs of drug prohibition onto Latin America has intensified challenges of corruption and internal political violence faced by the region. During the late 1800s and early 1900s, US and European pharmaceutical companies had encouraged a shift in Latin America from traditional to large-scale coca farming and to semi-manufactured cocaine production, but the pharmaceutical companies and their home countries later abandoned the industry, with early steps towards prohibition by the 1920s.[54] During the 1970s, demand for illicit cocaine in advanced industrial countries began to increase, reflecting a combination of criminalization of over-the-counter amphetamine sales and cocaine's reputation as a non-addictive and upper-class drug. Consequently, supplies increased to meet domestic demand. By the 1980s, Colombian traffickers had moved extensively into the trade. Demand surges facilitated linkages between trafficking organizations that became known as the Medellin and Cali 'cartels'. Pressure by the United States on Peru and Bolivia to curtail coca growing during the 1980s and 1990s shifted large-scale drug cultivation into Colombia. Long torn by political violence and corruption, Colombia faced extensive US pressure to devote scarce resources to curtailing the cartels. The much-heralded successes against the Medellin and Cali organizations by the mid-1990s ironically removed them as a check on the expanding movement of the FARC and right-wing paramilitaries into the cocaine trade. In this context, US initiatives against FARC such as Plan

Colombia and the Andean Counterdrug Initiative, the latter including a $731 million State Department budget for 2004 as well as sales of US military equipment and deployments of military advisers, are merely the latest chapters in the dynamics of embedded prohibition.[55]

Conclusion

Experts have noted that the inability to curtail the dramatic increase in the criminal underside of globalization lies in the very nature of an international system of individual sovereign states seeking to respond to transnational organized criminal actors in an increasingly global economy. Thus, the answer to the challenge posed by the global criminal economy lies in greater multilateral co-operation, especially multilateral law enforcement.[56] Multilateral co-operation is improving, through measures such as the expansion of Mutual Legal Assistance Treaties, an expanding network of Financial Intelligence Units to implement recommendations of the Financial Action Task Force, a growing role for the European Police Organization (Europol) in the European Union, and the broader impetus to multilateral law enforcement as a response to terrorism in the aftermath of 11 September 2001.

Despite the importance of co-operation, multilateral approaches will be little served by the absence of conceptual clarity and of methodological caution that has distinguished much of the debate over transnational crime. A criminal side of globalization clearly exists and is growing, and the path to more effective responses rests in better understanding the criminal actors and their scale of transnational activities. Attributing the expansion of transnational criminal activities and actors to the opportunities provided by globalization also risks downplaying the role of states in setting the parameters of criminal activity and the gap between criminalization and enforcement. Efforts towards prohibition regimes have been nested in broader patterns of multilateral economic liberalization intensified by technological innovation, and are embedded in considerations of domestic

stability that export the adjustment costs of prohibition to developing countries. The criminal underside of globalization ultimately is an *extension* of the societies and social practices in the developed world. Demand patterns in advanced industrial countries help to fuel the global drug trade and trafficking in persons. Entrenched interests in these countries benefit from the trafficking in drugs, persons, small and light arms, and toxic waste. The criminal underside of globalization will continue to expand unless these practices and interests are directly challenged.

In the aftermath of 9/11 and in the context of a war on terror, considerations of domestic stability appear to be changing. Societies in advanced industrial countries appear to be more willing to sacrifice civil liberties in the name of security and to tolerate intrusive enforcement efforts. However, prohibitions remain nested in multilateral economic liberalization. Rather than dramatically curtailing trade and capital flows, advanced industrial countries have embraced 'smart border' technologies, ranging from biometric and x-ray scans to sophisticated software programs, to try to identify unwanted transnational activities and actors. The United States has also turned to expanding its virtual borders by dispatching customs officials abroad and increasing pressure on trading partners to inspect goods destined for the American market before they leave foreign shores. Such steps have been justified as protecting 'the entire international supply chain' and would allow goods to enter the US market without 'special delays for inspection'.[57] Of course, such steps are less effective than screening all goods upon entry, and here, too, the burdens of enforcement are placed on foreign governments. Prohibitions also remain embedded in considerations of domestic stability. Foreigners and ethnic minorities are the primary targets of new enforcement efforts officially directed against terrorism but that have seen greater application against transnational criminal activities. In contrast, enforcement steps with broader domestic societal reach and impact, such as the data-mining provisions in the proposed US Total Information Awareness program, have faced strong public resistance, derailing their introduction.[58] Meanwhile, as illustrated by the Andean Counterdrug Initiative noted above, developed countries continue to externalize the costs of prohibition onto developing countries.

Notes

1. For example, see Susan Strange, *The Retreat of the State: The Diffusion of Power in the World Economy* (Cambridge: Cambridge University Press, 1996); James Mittelman, *The Globalization Syndrome: Transformation and Resistance* (Princeton, NJ: Princeton University Press, 2000), 203–22; Moses Naim, 'Five Wars of Globalization', *Foreign Policy* no. 134 (Jan.–Feb. 2003): 28–38.

2. For example, see Didier Bigo, 'Migration and Security', in V. Guiraudon and C. Joppke, eds, *Controlling a New Migration World* (London: Routledge, 2001), 121–49; R.T. Naylor, *Wages of Crime: Black Markets, Illegal Finance and the Underworld Economy* (Ithaca, NY: Cornell University Press, 2002).

3. H. Richard Friman and Peter Andreas, 'Introduction: International Relations and the Illicit Global Economy', in Friman and Andreas, eds, *The Illicit Global Economy and State Power* (Lanham, Md: Rowman & Littlefield, 1999), 8–10.

4. The distinction between predatory and market-based is drawn from Naylor, *Wages of Crime*, 11. The distinction between criminal and informal economies is from Manuel Castells and Alejandro Portes, 'World Underneath: The Origins, Dynamics and Effects of the Informal Economy', in Portes, Castells, and L. Benton, eds, *The Informal Economy: Studies in Advanced and Less Developed Countries* (Baltimore: Johns Hopkins University Press, 1989), 14–15. The definition of transnational is from William F. McDonald, 'The Globalization of Criminology: The New Frontier is the Frontier', *Transnational Organized Crime* 1, 1 (Spring 1995): 11.

5. To trace this development, see United Nations, General Assembly, *Report of the Ad hoc Committee on the Elaboration of a Convention against Transnational Organized Crime*, 2 Nov. 2000 (A/55/383), and session reports of 1999–2000 (A/AC.254/4–36).

6. Peter Andreas, 'Transnational Crime and Economic Globalization', in M. Berdal and M. Serrano, eds, *Transnational Organized Crime and International Security: Business as Usual?* (Boulder, Colo.: Lynne Rienner, 2002), 39.

7. Paul Stares, *Global Habit: The Drug Problem in a Borderless World* (Washington: Brookings Institution, 1996), 123–4; Naim, 'Five Wars of Globalization'; United Nations, Office on Drugs and Crime, *Global Illicit Drug Trends 2003: Executive Summary* (New York: UN, 2004), 7; Office of National Drug Control Policy, *The President's National Drug Control Strategy: Part III Disrupting the Market*, 2004.

8. Nicholas Marsh, 'Two Sides of the Same Coin? The Legal and Illegal Trade in Small Arms', *Brown Journal of World Affairs* 9, 1 (Spring 2002): 217–28; Naim, 'Five Wars of Globalization'; United Nations, *Press Kit: UN Conference on the Illicit Trade in Small Arms and Light Weapons in all its Aspects*, 9–20 July 2001.

9. See 'People Smuggling, Trafficking Generate Nearly $10 Billion Annually as Core Businesses of International Criminal Networks, Third Committee Told', *UN Information Service*, 14 Oct. 2003; Department of State, *Trafficking in Persons Report*, June 2004.

10. Paula Dobriansky, 'Bugs, Drugs and Thugs: Dealing with Transnational Threats', remarks to Women in International Security, Washington, 12 May 2004.

11. United Nations, *Human Development Report 1999: Globalization with a Human Face*; Jean-François Thony, *Money Laundering and Terrorism Financing* (Washington: IMF, 2002).

12. Financial Action Task Force (FATF), *Basic Facts About Money Laundering*; Naylor, *Wages of Crime*, 137–65. Naylor (p. 137) posits 'disassociation, obfuscation, and legitimation' as more useful terminology to describe the money-laundering process.

13. For example, see United Nations, *Human Development Report*; Financial Action Task Force, *Basic Facts*. Naim, 'Five Wars of Globalization', appears to extend the figures to current dollars to arrive at a range of $800 billion to $2 trillion.

14. See discussion in Naylor, *Wages of Crime*, x, 6, 301–2. Kleiman observes that $200 billion may be a more accurate figure. See Mark A.R. Kleiman, *Illicit Drugs and the Terrorist Threat: Causal Links and Implications for Domestic Drug Control Policy*, CRS Report for Congress, Congressional Research Service, Library of Congress, 20 Apr. 2004.

15. United Nations, Economic and Social Council, Commission on Narcotic Drugs, *World Situation with Regard to Drug Trafficking: Report of the Secretariat*, 7 Jan. 2004 (E/CN.7/2004/4); Department of State, *International Narcotics Control Strategy Report 2003*, 1 Mar. 2004. See Naylor, *Wages of Crime*, 7–8, for a discussion of flaws in acreage estimates.

16. See Marsh, 'Two Sides of the Same Coin?'; Naylor, *Wages of Crime*; Institute on Migration, 'Working Group D: Data on Trafficking of Human Beings', IOM Data Workshop, 8–9 Sept. 2003.

17. Naylor, *Wages of Crime*, 8, 138–42, 248–66; see also Thony, *Money Laundering and Terrorism Financing*.

18. For examples using this estimate, see United Nations, *Human Development Report*; Naim, 'Five Wars of Globalization'. Dividing $500 billion by $6.5 trillion, World Trade Organization export data for 2002 reveal the same 8 per cent figure.

19. Peter J. Quirk, *Money Laundering: Muddying the Macroeconomy* (Washington: World Bank, 1997); Michel Camdessus, 'Money Laundering: The Importance of International Countermeasures', speech to Plenary Meeting of the Financial Action Task Force on Money Laundering, Washington, IMF, 1998.

20. Figures are from the World Trade Organization, World Bank, and International Monetary Fund Web sites. See Naylor, *Wages of Crime*, 5, for an overview of the debate on relative historical scale.

21. On Afghanistan, see State Department, *International Narcotics Control Strategy Report* (hereafter *INCSR*), 2004. For examples of the Spain comparison, see FATF, *Basic Facts about Money Laundering*; Naim, 'Five Wars of Globalization'.

22. Strange, *Retreat of the State*, 111–13.

23. See, e.g., Phil Williams, 'Transnational Criminal Organizations and International Security', in M. Klare and Y. Chandrani, *World Security: Challenges for a New Century* (New York: St Martin's Press, 1998), 249–72; Mats Berdal and Monica Serrano, eds, *Transnational Organized Crime and International Security: Business as Usual?* (Boulder, Colo.: Lynne Rienner, 2002).

24. For overviews, see Naylor, *Wages of Crime*, 15–22; Phil Williams, 'Cooperation Among Criminal Organizations', in Berdal and Serrano, eds, *Transnational Organized Crime*, 67–80.

25. Patrick L. Clawson and Rensselaer W. Lee III, *The Andean Cocaine Industry* (New York: St Martin's Press, 1996), 40–1; Marsh, 'Two Sides of the Same Coin'?; Naylor, *Wages of Crime*, 88–132; Amy O'Neill Richard, 'International Trafficking in Women to the United States: A Contemporary Manifestation of Slavery and Organized Crime', Center for the Study of Intelligence, 1999; Department of State, *Trafficking in Persons*.

26. United Nations, General Assembly, Resolution Adopted by the General Assembly: United Nations Convention against Transnational Organized Crime, 2001 (A/Res/55/25), 4.

27. Department of State, Office of the Coordinator for Counter Terrorism, *Patterns of Global Terrorism: 2003*, Apr. and June 2004.

28. Naylor, *Wages of Crime*, 45; Berdal and Serrano, 'Introduction', in Berdal and Serrano, eds, *Transnational Organized Crime*, 7–8; Department of State, Bureau for International Narcotics and Law Enforcement Affairs, *Fact Sheet: The Nexus Between Drug Trafficking and Terrorism*, 10 Apr. 2002.

29. See Clawson and Lee, *The Andean Cocaine*

Industry, 178–91; Naylor, *Wages of Crime*, 70–5.

30. Rand Beers and Francis Taylor, 'Narco-Terror: The Worldwide Connection between Drugs and Terror', testimony before the Senate Committee on the Judiciary, Subcommittee on Technology, Terrorism and Government Information, 13 Mar. 2002; Steven Casteel, 'Narco-Terrorism: International Drug Trafficking and Terrorism—A Dangerous Mix', statement before the Senate Committee on the Judiciary, 20 May 2003.

31. Department of State, *Patterns of Global Terrorism*; Department of State, *INCSR*; Rensselaer Lee and Raphael Perl, 'Terrorism, the Future, and US Foreign Policy', Issue Brief for Congress, Congressional Research Services, Library of Congress, 2002.

32. Raphael Perl, *Taliban and the Drug Trade*, CRS Report for Congress, Congressional Research Service, Library of Congress, 5 Oct. 2001; Beers and Taylor, 'Narco-Terror'; Department of State, *INCSR*; Naylor, *Wages of Crime*, 294–5.

33. Naylor, *Wages of Crime*, 287–8; Kleiman, *Illicit Drugs and the Terrorist Threat*, 8–9.

34. Thony, *Money Laundering and Terrorist Financing*, 4–5; Department of State, *Patterns of Global Terrorism*.

35. Naylor, *Wages of Crime*, 249–73, 287–97; FATF, *Basic Facts about Money Laundering*; Department of State, *Patterns of Global Terrorism*.

36. Loretta Napoleoni, *Modern Jihad: Tracing the Dollars Behind the Terror Networks* (London: Pluto Press, 2003), 198–201, 260.

37. Kleiman, *Illicit Drugs and the Terrorist Threat*, 3.

38. Ethan A. Nadelmann, 'Global Prohibition Regimes: The Evolution of Norms in International Society', *International Organization* 44, 4 (Autumn 1990): 485.

39. Friman and Andreas, 'Introduction: International Relations and the Illicit Global Economy', 8–10.

40. See Vinod K. Aggarwal, *Liberal Protectionism: The International Politics of Organized Textile Trade* (Berkeley: University of California Press, 1985), 27.

41. John Gerard Ruggie, 'International Regimes, Transactions, and Change: Embedded Liberalism in the Postwar Economic Order', in S. Krasner, ed., *International Regimes* (Ithaca, NY: Cornell University Press, 1983), 195–231; Andreas, 'Transnational Crime and Economic Globalization', 39.

42. The literature on immigration is extensive. Useful overviews include Wayne A. Cornelius, Philip L. Martin, and James F. Hollifield, eds, *Controlling Immigration: A Global Perspective* (Stanford, Calif.: Stanford University Press, 1994); Caroline B. Brettell and James F. Hollifield, eds, *Immigration Theory: Talking Across Disciplines* (London: Routledge, 2000).

43. Mittelman, *The Globalization Syndrome*, 201; Andreas, 'Transnational Crime and Economic Globalization', 39–43.

44. The broader balance sheet as to whether technological innovations have benefited law enforcement agencies more than criminals and terrorists, or large-scale criminal/terrorist organizations more than smaller groups, remains contested by scholars. For example, see Naylor, *Wages of Crime*, 6.

45. Mittelman, *The Globalization Syndrome*, 213; Andreas, 'Transnational Crime and Economic Globalization', 39–46.

46. See, e.g., Mittelman, *The Globalization Syndrome*, 203–22; Andreas, 'Transnational Crime and Economic Globalization', 43–6; Monica Serrano, 'Transnational Organized Crime and International Security: Business as Usual?', in Berdal and Serrano, eds, *Transnational Organized Crime*, 25–6.

47. See Ruggie, 'International Regimes, Transactions, and Change', 209, 215.

48. See, e.g., Siriporn Skrobanek, Nataya Boonpakdee, and Chutima Jantateero, *The Traffic in Women: Human Realities of the International Sex Trade* (London: Zed Books, 1997).

49. Naylor, *Wages of Crime*, 270–3.

50. On the latter, see Jennifer Clapp, 'The Illicit Trade in Hazardous Wastes and CFCs: International Responses to Environmental "Bads"', in Friman and Andreas, eds, *The Illicit Global Economy and State Power*, 91–123.

51. The Convention is available at: <www.unodc.org /pdf/convention_1988_en.pdf>.

52. See, e.g., David Musto, *The American Disease:*

Origins of Narcotic Control (New York: Oxford University Press, 1987); H. Richard Friman, 'The Great Escape? Globalization, Immigrant Entrepreneurship and the Criminal Economy', *Review of International Political Economy* 11, 1 (Feb. 2004): 98–131.

53. Office of National Drug Control Policy, *The President's National Drug Control Strategy.*

54. See Paul Gootenberg, ed., *Cocaine: Global Histories* (London: Routledge, 1999).

55. Rensselaer W. Lee III, *The White Labyrinth: Cocaine and Political Power* (New Brunswick, NJ: Transaction Publishers, 1989); Clawson and Lee, *The Andean Cocaine Industry*; Office of National Drug Control Policy, *The President's National Drug Control Strategy.*

56. See, e.g., Strange, *Retreat of the State*, 120–1; Williams, 'Transnational Criminal Organizations and International Security', 268–9; Monica den Boer, 'Law-Enforcement Cooperation and Transnational Organized Crime in Europe', in Berdal and Serrano, eds, *Transnational Organized Crime*, 102–16.

57. White House press release, 'U.S.–Canada Smart Border/30 Point Action Plan Update', 6 Dec. 2002; Philip Shenon, 'U.S. Expands Plan for Cargo Inspections at Foreign Ports', *New York Times*, 12 June 2003.

58. See, e.g., David Cole, *Enemy Aliens: Double Standards and Constitutional Freedoms in the War on Terrorism* (New York: New Press, 2003).

Suggested Readings

Andreas, Peter. *Border Games: Policing the U.S.–Mexico Divide*. Ithaca, NY: Cornell University Press, 2001.

Bales, Kevin. *Disposable People: New Slavery in the Global Economy*. Berkeley: University of California Press, 1999.

Findlay, Mark. *The Globalization of Crime: Understanding Transnational Relationships in Context*. Cambridge: Cambridge University Press, 2000.

Friman, H. Richard. *NarcoDiplomacy: Exporting the U.S. War on Drugs*. Ithaca, NY: Cornell University Press, 1996.

Gambetta, Diego. *The Sicilian Mafia: The Business of Private Protection*. Cambridge, Mass.: Harvard University Press, 1993.

Kyle, David, and Rey Koslowski, eds. *Global Human Smuggling: Comparative Perspectives*. Baltimore: Johns Hopkins University Press, 2001.

Lee, Rensselaer W. *Smuggling Armageddon: The Nuclear Black Market in the Former Soviet Union and Europe*. New York: St Martin's Press, 1998.

Lumpe, Lora, ed. *Running Guns: The Global Black Market in Small Arms*. London: Zed Books, 2000.

Naylor, R.T. *Hot Money and the Politics of Debt*. Montreal: Black Rose Books, 1994.

Woodiwiss, Michael. *Organized Crime and American Power*. Toronto: University of Toronto Press, 2001.

Web Sites

International Action Network on Small Arms: www.iansa.org

International Organization for Migration: www.iom.int

European Police Office (Europol): www.europol.eu.int

United States Department of State: www.state.gov

United Nations Office on Drugs and Crime: www.unodc.org/unodc

Part III

Regional

Dynamics

Introduction

Regionalization and Globalization

Richard Stubbs and Austina J. Reed

Part III examines the increasing regionalization of the international political economy and explores some of the main theoretical and empirical questions prompted by the rise of a number of identifiable economic regions, including those surrounding the relationship between regionalization and globalization. The more pressing of these questions draw students of international political economy into debates within the literature concerning (1) pivotal developments in the historical evolution of regionalism; (2) material, institutional, and/or ideational factors that define regionalization and shape the boundaries of its relationship to globalization; and (3) the principal tools for measuring economic co-operation and integration across time. Each of these themes is briefly identified here.

The study of regionalism has waxed and waned over the years since World War II. Analyses flourished in the 1950s and 1960s with the growth of European regional organizations but then faded in the 1970s as European integration slowed markedly. Indeed, with the publication in 1975 of *The Obsolescence of Regional Integration Theory* by Ernst Haas, analyses of regional integration and regionalism virtually dried up.[1] From the mid-1980s onward, however, regionalism once again became the subject of increasing interest. There were at least three reasons for the discernible shift back towards regionalization and the study of its dynamism. First, with the end of the Cold War and the breakdown of the overarching Cold War structure that underpinned and ordered international relations, each state became aware of its need to re-evaluate its place in the international system.

Stripped of the predictability that the Cold War brought to the conduct of international relations, individual states sought out new relations with the emerging constellation of major powers and with their own immediate neighbours. Many states quickly appreciated how much their own welfare depended on the stability and well-being of the region in which they were located.

Second, regionalization was seen by governments both as a defence against globalization and as a way of taking advantage of some of the forces set in train by the process of globalization (see Chapter 20 by Hveem). Of particular significance was the need to deal with the new non-state sources of global capital, the pressures from the globalization of production, and the influence of intergovernmental organizations such as the IMF and the GATT/WTO.[2] Regional organizations could help to attract foreign direct investment and at the same time ensure that a group of states had a voice in the increasing number of international negotiations over the future of the international political economy.

Finally, when the European Community (EC), later to become the European Union (EU), started to expand its activities in the 1980s other regional organizations emerged, some in response to the demonstration effect of the EU, others as a way of countering what was perceived to be the increasing collective economic power of the Western European states. For example, since the 1990s exports from the European Union have accounted for approximately 40 per cent of total world trade, whereas North America and East Asia each contributed a little over 20 per cent to the total.³ With more than 80 per cent of trade concentrated in East Asia, North America, and Western Europe, many observers have pointed to the tripolar structure of trade flows as evidence of the force of regionalization to influence the ordering of the world economy. The wide variety of regional organizations formed from the mid-1980s onward belong to what has been termed the 'new regionalism'.⁴ What distinguishes this new regionalism from the regionalism of the 1950s and 1960s is that, rather than stressing regional self-sufficiency and independence from the global economy, the emphasis has been on positioning a region so as to strengthen its participation in the global economy in terms of both trade and capital flows.⁵ Other distinguishing characteristics include (1) the growing number of regions containing countries from both the North and the South; (2) the rise of regional consciousness or even regional identities, in various parts of the world; (3) the fact that any one country may belong to a number of regional organizations at any one time; and (4) the many different institutional forms that have been developed within which regional co-operation has been organized.⁶ Significantly, the proliferation of regional integration arrangements has made overlapping membership a common feature of the regional trading regimes. For example, the World Trade Organization (WTO) notes that if regional trade agreements (RTAs) 'reportedly planned or already under negotiation are concluded, the total number of RTAs in force might well approach 300.'⁷

Regionalism is most usefully thought of as having three dimensions. The first concerns the extent to which countries in a definable geographic area have significant historical experiences in common and find themselves facing the same general problems. For much of the Cold War, with the world divided into two camps dominated by the United States and the Soviet Union, common regional experiences and problems tended to be masked by the need to confront the common enemy. However, as the Cold War ended and the old international order began to break down, each state had to work towards new sets of relationships both with the emerging global

powers and with surrounding states. Common historical experiences and problems—for instance, in Western Europe the need to rebuild after World War II and the perceived threat from Soviet Communism—became increasingly important as states began to re-evaluate their places in the international system. Moreover, as the globalization process gathered speed, states quickly realized that their neighbours, who often had similar economies to their own, faced many of the same economic problems. Regional economic co-operation became one way of attempting to come to grips with these common problems.

The second dimension emphasizes the extent to which countries in a definable geographic area have developed socio-cultural, political, and/or economic linkages that distinguish them from the rest of the global community. Clearly the EU is most advanced in this respect. In East Asia the flood of Japanese FDI into Southeast Asia—especially Thailand, Malaysia, Singapore, and Indonesia—following the appreciation of the yen in the wake of the Plaza Accord of 1985, and the subsequent flow of investment from the newly industrialized economies of Hong Kong, Singapore, South Korea, and Taiwan into all parts of East and Southeast Asia, as well as the increased trade linkages, have combined to produce a growing sense of regional identity. Certainly, what Anwar Ibrahim has labelled as 'an Asian renaissance' and Singapore's Simon Tay has referred to as a 'rising sense of East Asian identity' has taken over the region in recent years.⁸ Significantly, contrary to some expectations in the West, the common experience of having to deal with the fallout from the Asian economic crisis reinforced this growing East Asian regional consciousness. And, in North America, arguably a crucial factor in providing the support necessary to hold together the occasionally fractious North American Free Trade Agreement (NAFTA) has been the long-standing socio-cultural ties fostered between the US and Canada and the US and Mexico and the common political, economic, and security interests that are specific to the region.

The third dimension focuses on the extent to which relations among particular groupings of geographically proximate countries have led to the development of organizations charged with the management of crucial aspects of the region's collective affairs. The degree of formal institutionalization among regional organizations varies considerably. Obviously, the EU is the most advanced, with the North American Free Trade Agreement (NAFTA) much less institutionalized and the Association of Southeast Asian Nations (ASEAN) Plus Three—the 10 ASEAN members and China, Japan, and South Korea—still working out the kind of institutional structure it wants to develop.[9] The degree and form of institutionalization tend to be influenced both by state interests and by regional norms regarding the willingness of states to cede power to a central secretariat or other form of organization.

Regions, then, may be relatively well developed along all three dimensions, as is the case with the EU, or they may be experiencing a more limited development along one or more of the three dimensions, as is the case with MERCOSUR. Moreover, the three dimensions are interrelated. Common historical experiences and increased socio-cultural, political, and economic links can lead to the development of organizations to manage the region's collective affairs. In turn, of course, the creation of a regional organization can further multiply the linkages that bind the region together. It is also important to note that while the core countries of any particular region may be easily identified, the actual boundaries often are fluid and contested. For example, there is ongoing debate about whether Turkey should be included within the European Union or whether Australia and New Zealand should be part of the emerging ASEAN Plus Three process.

However regions are defined, the one major question that appears to preoccupy students of international political economy is the extent to which regionalization promotes or obstructs globalization. Can regional patterns of market integration be considered a step down the road towards the rapid globalization of an open international economy, or will the major economic powers and the increasingly economically and politically integrated regions they lead compete with one another

in an unprecedented battle of economic giants?

Analysts have attempted to answer this question in a number of ways. A good many studies have been undertaken of the changing patterns of intraregional as opposed to interregional trade to determine the rate of regionalization of economic relations. Measured in these terms, intraregional trade indicators show just how much these economies have become dependent on each other. Among the countries of Western Europe, for example, intraregional trade reached as high as 70 per cent in the early 1970s and has since levelled off at approximately 65 per cent of total European trade. The economies of East Asia (ASEAN+3) have experienced one of the largest increases in intraregional trade in the last two decades—so much so that the region now rivals North America at over 40 per cent.[10] Analysts have also examined flows of foreign direct investment, portfolio investment, and short-term loans in order to map out the degrees of economic cohesion in various regional groupings. The increased use of the yen and the introduction of the euro have prompted discussions of competing currency blocs. Similarly, the rise of production networks in Asia has meant that regional economic integration has been viewed from the perspective of competing production arrangements in the three major economic regions—Western Europe, North America, and East Asia. Other analysts have reviewed the activities of multinational corporations and assessed the extent to which they operate regionally as opposed to globally. Finally, studies have been undertaken that examine the role of labour in the processes that influence the regionalization of economic ties between countries. The lack of labour market integration, especially in Europe, has been one such source of interest among researchers, in particular the impact that national variation in labour market structures might have on regionalization. Analysts have also explored the question of labour migration and its corollary in remittance flows: indicators of potentially deeper regional integration and the emergence of transnational diaspora communities between sending and receiving countries in the same region.[11]

Although these measurements of regional economic co-operation and integration into the global economy can be illuminating, a fundamental point should not be missed. Regional economic activity is heavily influenced by increasingly regionalized forms of capitalism. In some instances, these forms of capitalism, which are essentially rooted in regional cultures as well as in common economic, social, and political institutions and similar recent historical experiences, are underwritten by regional agreements. For example, the Economic and Monetary Union, the Single European Act, and the Maastricht Treaty provide the foundations for capitalism in Europe, and the North American Free Trade Agreement provides the blueprint for capitalism in North America. Although there are still important differences among EU members and NAFTA members in the way that they conduct economic activities, there are even greater differences between the economic policies and practices of the two regions. In Western Europe, labour still has a role to play in many aspects of economic policy-making, government intervention in the economy to redress problems created by the market is sanctioned, and the social dimension of economic activities, although under attack, is still important. In North America, NAFTA discourages government intervention in the economy, encourages the unfettered operation of rule-based markets, and underwrites Anglo-American individualistic consumer economics that stresses the importance of the maximization of short-term profits and a return for shareholders.

By contrast, economic policies and practices in East Asia are based on a third form of capitalism. The emphasis here is on economic relations reflecting a harmonious social order and stressing production rather than consumption. Economic transactions are seen as part of the general social intercourse rather than governed by the rule of law. For both Chinese and Japanese businessmen, the emphasis is on social obligations rather than legal contracts.[12] East Asian 'collective capitalism' also highlights the synergy of business networks; government intervention to produce a competitive advantage for certain sectors and industries or to

strengthen vital industries, such as machine tool suppliers and semiconductor chip manufacturers, which helps to build up other industrial sectors; and capturing market share even at the expense of profits.[13] Some see the Asian economic crisis as a consequence of this Asian form of capitalism and expect to see it change quite radically as the region works its way back to economic health. Others, however, argue that changes to this form of capitalism will be slow and may not automatically be in the direction of North American neo-liberalism because capitalism is rooted in a combination of regional culture, recent historical experiences, and unique institutions.[14] Accordingly, then, the current trajectory of economic co-operation and integration should be considered in light of the specific values, norms, institutions, and practices that not only might be unique to each region but also may vary over time.[15]

Of course, the continuing growth of regionalism is not inevitable. Indeed, a number of developments have raised questions about the future of economic regionalism. First, as regions have expanded, internal divisions have risen to the surface. Issues concerning which states in the regional arrangement should have the leadership role, how open to globalization the region should be, and what should be the speed and scope of economic liberalization have come to preoccupy nearly every regional grouping. Second, as WTO trade talks have run into difficulties, more and more states have resorted to bilateral trade agreements (BTAs).

Often these BTAs link economies already in an emerging regional structure. However, an increasing number of these agreements are connecting economies within a region to economies far outside the region. These extra-regional linkages may have the effect of undermining regional economic co-operation. Finally, within many regions, differences in the speed with which economic growth is taking place can put strains on regional co-operation. Differences in the rates of economic growth can lead to a two- or even three-tier region, which creates tensions that these regional institutions cannot properly manage. In many ways, then, the success of regional development creates its own problems, which may go some way in undermining the growth of regionalism as a response to the changing global order.

Each of the following chapters looks at a different aspect of regionalism and regionalization. Overall, the aim here is to give the reader an appreciation for the emerging political economies of important regions of the world. The analyses can then be set alongside the global changes highlighted in the first two parts of the book. These chapters also give readers a chance to decide for themselves how the relationship between regionalization and globalization might unfold. Will the emergence of regional economic organizations give a boost to globalization or do they indicate the rise of mercantilist blocs that will frustrate the drive to a truly global economy?

Notes

1. Ernst B. Haas, *The Obsolescence of Regional Integration Theory* (Berkeley, Calif.: Institute for International Studies, 1975).
2. See Anthony Payne and Andrew Gamble, 'Introduction: The Political Economy of Regionalism and World Order', in Gamble and Payne, eds, *Regionalism and World Order* (Basingstoke: Macmillan, 1996), 15–18; Stephan Haggard, 'Regionalism in Asia and the Americas', in Edward D. Mansfield and Helen Milner, eds, *The Political Economy of Regionalism* (New York: Columbia University Press, 1997), 25–31.
3. See World Trade Organization, *International Trade Statistics* 2002 (Washington: WTO, 2003).
4. See Norman D. Palmer, *The New Regionalism in Asia and the Pacific* (Lexington, Mass.: Lexington Books, 1991); J. de Melo and A. Panagariya, 'The New Regionalism', *Finance and Development* 29, 4 (1992): 37–40.
5. See Paul Bowles, 'ASEAN, AFTA, and the "New Regionalism"', *Pacific Affairs* 70 (Summer 1997): 224–5.
6. See Andrew Hurrell, 'Explaining the Resurgence of Regionalism in World Politics', *Review of International Studies* 21 (Oct. 1995): 331–2; Palmer, *The New Regionalism in Asia and the Pacific*, 1–6.
7. World Trade Organization, 'Regional Trade Agreements Gateway', available at: <www.wto.org/english/tratop_e/region_e/region_e.htm>.
8. See Anwar Ibrahim, *The Asian Renaissance* (Singapore: Times Books, 1997); Simon Tay, 'ASEAN Plus Three: Challenges and Cautions about a New Regionalism', paper presented to the 15th Annual Asia-Pacific Roundtable, Kuala Lumpur, June 2001.
9. Richard Stubbs, 'ASEAN Plus Three: Emerging East Asian Regionalism', *Asian Survey* 42 (May–June 2002): 440–55.
10. See World Trade Organization, *International Trade Statistics 2002.*
11. See Devesh Kapur and John McHale, 'Migration's New Payoff', *Foreign Policy* (Nov.–Dec. 2003): 49–57.
12. See Richard Stubbs, 'Asia-Pacific Regionalism versus Globalization: Competing Forms of Capitalism', in William D. Coleman and Geoffrey Underhill, eds, *Regionalism and Global Economic Integration: Europe, Asia and the Americas* (London: Routledge, 1998).
13. Stephen Bell, 'The Collective Capitalism of Northeast Asia and the Limits of Orthodox Economics', *Australian Journal of Political Science* 30 (July 1995): 264–87.
14. G. Hamilton, 'Asian Business Networks in Transition: Or, What Alan Greenspan Does Not Know About the Asian Business Crisis', in T.J. Pempel, ed., *The Politics of the Asian Economic Crisis* (Ithaca, NY: Cornell University Press, 1999), 45–61; Richard Stubbs, *Rethinking Asia's Economic Miracle: The Political Economy of War, Prosperity and Crisis* (Basingstoke: Palgrave, 2005).
15. See Louise Fawcett, 'Exploring Regional Domains: A Comparative History of Regionalism, *International Affairs* 80, 3 (2004): 429–46

Chapter 20

Explaining the Regional Phenomenon in an Era of Globalization

Helge Hveem

Regional integration projects are a growing phenomenon and paradoxically are occurring in tandem with what is loosely called 'globalization'. About half of all regional trade agreements established since World War II have been made since the mid-1990s. The two trends are by no means unconnected. This chapter will conceptualize the connection and suggest causes of regionalization. In so doing it will discuss the implications of these parallel developments for the contrasting regional cultures of capitalism and corporate governance, which compete in the context of globalization.

Geopolitics constituted a major factor behind even economically motivated regional projects during the early post-World War II period. Later, the factors and forces behind the regional phenomenon become more varied and the causal relationship more complex. At the beginning of the new millennium, the main factor pushing and shaping regional action is believed by many observers to be globalization. The role of this factor is usually explained in terms of the rational maximization of utility on the part of the state or corporate actors involved. These observers thus see regional integration as part of the effort of states to cope with a pervasive globalization, and they see the regional as a platform for corporate actors on their way to the global stage.

This chapter takes up, but reformulates, this argument to include theories emphasizing ideational and institutional factors as well. As a result of this reformulation, perceptions about the deepening and spread of globalization processes are revealed as exaggerated. The political, social,

and cultural barriers that these processes confront, but also problems inherent in the processes themselves, may cause them to halt, recede, or collapse. Although signs of such outcomes were visible long before the financial crisis in East and Southeast Asia in 1997, that crisis left no doubt about them. The crisis led many, including the IMF chief, to ask if another 1929 will soon be upon us. It vindicated Polanyi's analysis of systemic transformation as a 'double movement': as radical economic liberalization dissociates the economy from society, the response is social protest that may turn into radical political change. The protest movement that mobilized against the World Economic Forum and the World Trade Organization meetings and that now assembles in ATTAC (Association pour une Taxation des Transactions financières pour l'Aide aux Citoyens) and the World Social Forum are indications that the story repeats itself. The present chapter will look more specifically at another Polanyi thesis: that regional collective action is not only necessary, but the only possible international response to globalization.[1] Conditional support is offered for the thesis.

From the end of World War II, the 'first generation' of regional projects achieved the goals of security and political stability, an example of what may be termed 'doubly embedded regionalization'. First, regional projects had to take the geopolitical and ideological context of the Cold War as a primary ordering principle. Second, they were premised on the 'embedded liberalism' of Bretton Woods: liberalizing international economic transactions (within the Western world) would be done (only) along with social stabilization and state-building. The 'second generation' regional integration episode started with decolonization in the 1960s and faded out early in the 1970s. It was also strongly premised on the limits of the Cold War. Practically all the regional projects of these two generations of regional action are thus built on the Westphalian state system and were to serve economic growth as well as security motives in their assistance to state-building goals. This doubly embedded liberalism allowed them considerable freedom to impose barriers vis-à-vis non-members. Customs unions were acceptable and GATT provided legitimation of regional projects by allowing them considerable freedom.

The advance of globalization processes and the end of the Cold War have changed that context. Not only have they given more weight to regional powers;[2] they have also reordered the relative salience of economic growth and socio-political stabilization goals, but with different effects on different parts of the world. While Western nations may have put Westphalia behind them, 'transition' economies are trying to complete state-building processes while integrating with the developed market economies. The expansion of the EU in 2004 is the first vital test of this project.

The contextual changes have also allowed other motivations and types of agency to come to fruition. These are *trans*national and *trans*-state regional efforts, which reflect the emergence of *society* at the regional level and which sometimes co-ordinate with but often are in conflict with the 'inter'-national state *system*. These efforts are not primarily for *efficiency* in terms of economic growth and globalization, but for political *legitimacy* and *identity*.

The primary institution of globalization, the self-regulating market, is held to be legitimate because it creates equal opportunities to compete. But individuals, groups, or classes are differently endowed with capabilities to exploit the process. Thus, trends towards greater socio-economic inequity and systemic instability result along with—sometimes instead of—greater efficiency and growth, while legitimacy is guaranteed through equitable outcomes, not equal opportunity. This gives rise to contentious agency by those who perceive, or de facto realize, that they lose in the process. To the extent that agents who are affected associate deepening social crisis with economic globalization, they will turn against it. These agents may accept losing in relative terms. But when they lose in absolute terms as well, peoples, and even governments, voice protest or may attempt to exit from the process.

A neo-utilitarian perspective assumes that globalization is driving or dominating regional processes. This is one way to explain the 'third generation' regional projects, such as the resurgence of the European single-market project—as an attempt to maintain or improve competitiveness in more globalized markets, using regional action to ride on globalization. Yet these theories err by interpreting the apparent dominance of the riding motive as a lasting tendency. This is wrong because it over-represents rationality and assumes that agents are driven by utilitarian motives only or mostly, neglecting the possibility that humankind is driven by ideas or norms rather than utility considerations. It also risks ignoring that agents are subject to bounded rationality and that individual rationality may create collective irrationality. Cognitive, reflectivist, and social constructivist conceptions should thus complement utilitarian theories.

The regional phenomenon may be a rational strategy by governments to maximize their utility, but there are also collective action problems. Governments certainly are no longer able to act individually with authority the way they used to. The critical problem at the beginning of the twenty-first century has become one of disputed authority and insufficient governance. The hegemony of the only remaining political and military superpower is contested because of its perceived arrogant unilateralism and the war it waged in Iraq. Neither global markets nor national government suffice, nor do they provide the necessary normative underlay of legitimacy. I argue, in this chapter, that this creates a wider opening for the regional project and makes unlikely a global convergence of different forms of capitalism.

Conceptualizing the Regional Phenomenon

Regional projects differ considerably with respect to how they relate to globalization. A regional project may represent globalization or may attempt to ride on it, to regulate it, or to resist it. Under which conditions are any of these outcomes likely to happen? Relatively little consensus over definitions is to be found in the literature; theorizing must start by clarifying concepts.[3]

'Globalization' is often defined too broadly and imprecisely. Vagueness propels people towards determinism, to perceive globalization as inevitable, as destiny.[4] In the economic sphere globalization consists in the setting up of production organizations under a global strategy, world capital markets, and/or globally competitive markets for goods and services with a distinctly global reach, and in the convergence of state economic policies. It is assumed to advance through technological innovations, cultural assimilation, and adoption of the ideology of liberalization and deregulation worldwide. That advance normally also presupposes negotiation of multilateral institutions with some limited degree of worldwide authority and legitimacy. The fall of the Berlin Wall led to an exponential growth in the number of McDonald's restaurants in previously closed economies, to convergence of consumer expectations. But convergence of policies and implementation of common rules and principles, although advancing, were not close to representing a de facto globalized world system except in the important case of capital markets. National and regional variation in economic-political culture remained important when the crisis of the financial system broke out in 1997 (see Chapter 9 by Story).

To understand the relationship between globalization and the regional phenomenon it is also necessary to define the latter precisely. A 'region' may be defined (1) by geographical spatial indicators, (2) by existing networks or structures of transaction and communication, (3) and by way of cognitive maps and collective identities. Delimitation by geography is a long tradition that characterizes many or most utilitarian theorists. The 'social networks' tradition is still indebted to Deutsch's classical study of the North Atlantic area,[5] but it has been complemented by the sociological 'actor network theory'.[6] As we shall see below, the Deutsch variant is paralleled but not necessarily copied by contemporary regional networks in Asian and African contexts. Finally, representing the third class of definitions, 'cognitive regions' are a possibility.[7] In this case the 'region' exists in the minds of people, but is not necessarily an objective, institutionalized community.

Regionalism and Regionalization

Regionalism is the body of *ideas* that promote an identified geographical or social space as a regional project. Or, it is a conscious construction of an identity that represents *one specific* region. It is usually associated with a policy program (goals to be achieved) and strategy (means and mechanisms by which goals may be reached), and it normally leads to institution-building. Regionalism ties agents to a specific regional project that is clearly limited spatially or socially, but not limited in time. A historical example of a truly regionalist project is the European Coal and Steel Community. Its founders, motivated by the need to build a security community among previous enemies by means of economic co-operation, constructed political integration top-down, prior to making important economic transactions.

Regionalization, on the other hand, refers to the *process* that actually builds concrete patterns of transaction within an identified regional space. It may be caused by regionalism. But it may also emerge irrespective of whether or not there is a regionalist project. For those agents who are *not* directed by regionalism, the boundaries of the 'region' are rather pragmatically defined and regional action is temporary. As an example, a number of Finnish and Norwegian firms set up affiliates in Sweden in the 1960s and 1970s not primarily motivated by Nordic identity, but as a stepping stone to an even wider regional level and then to the global.

Conceptualizing regionalism is further complicated by what is referred to as the 'new regionalism',[8] which reflects a rather varied set of perspectives. One tendency is to emphasize subregions within nation-states and give priority to building a network of transactions and collaboration across national boundaries between such subregions, an example being the Rhine border region. This tendency is a reaction, perhaps a postmodernist one, either to globalization or to the regional projects of the state system, or to both. It appears to be strong in Europe, but may also be found in the Chinese diaspora and in some regions of Africa.

Internationalization and Transnationalization

In order to account for these two phenomena—the example of the Nordic firms and the 'new regionalism'—the distinction between internationalization and transnationalization is useful. They roughly correspond to top-down and bottom-up agency. *Internationalization* is a process initiated and managed by public authorities. It opens up national political economies to transactions with customers abroad, for example, by tariff cuts. The defining criterion is that it is state-managed, at least *de jure*. Transactions are seen as interaction between sovereign political entities.

Transnationalization results in the same outcome—an opening of economic transactions. But private, non-state agents initiate and manage this process. It transcends national boundaries as a flow, not of diplomatic exchanges, but of corporate business, social groups, or individual behaviour. At least in principle it is not dependent on the state system for initiation and management. It depends, rather, on the strategy, resources, and management of transnational corporations (TNCs) or other economic agents, *or* those of civil society, transnational NGOs, networks, and communities. These sources of action grew exponentially in the 1990s. Their actions appeared to favour regionalization as much as globalization.

We should think of these categories as ideal types. Often the processes of internationalization and transnationalization are related, one conditioning the other, sometimes even initiating it. Transnationalization thus depends entirely on internationalization in those cases where foreign investments are barred or restricted and the state is needed in order to remove barriers. In other cases internationalization is a policy that results from prior transnationalization; economic interdependence that results from a growing trade or investment exchange is one example, the opening up of national financial markets after the emergence of offshore finance markets is another illustration. The example of the Nordic firms reflects both processes. On the one hand their foreign investments reflected a transnationalization strategy. But at the same time it was facilitated, to some extent even stimulated, by the conscious internationalization conducted by the states of the national economies in the Western European region.

Since options are affected by changing contexts, the agents may also choose a flexible approach. They may keep options open, in other words, they may *hedge*.[9] If or when the regional effort becomes institutionalized or particular contextual factors demand that a definite choice is made, however, flexibility is reduced and the effort tends towards choosing one particular option. Hedging was not possible during the Cold War, and it may not be possible against the will of hegemonic authority even after it has ended. It is, therefore, possible only under particular conditions and as a temporary strategy.

Explaining the Contemporary Regional Phenomenon

The regional projects of the third generation were, to a large extent, a number of responses to global competitive pressures, thus representing regionalization. Yet there is a close relationship between this regionalization process and the more state-led process of regionalism through the negotiation of formal regional trade agreements. States have responded to the pressures of corporate actors for more transnationalization on a regional basis, providing corporate actors with the framework they needed through further internationalization.

Third-generation projects emerged for two reasons. First, they were spearheaded in the mid-1980s by the then European Community where significant institutional development and political leadership contributed to reinforcement of the European project. A number of regional projects beginning around 1990 were demanded by private transnationalizing agents as a response to the European initiative for a single market and monetary union.[10] The wave of projects was, second, also greatly accelerated by the end of the Cold War and the breakup of the Soviet Union as these events reduced the impact of global political factors.[11]

Most of the projects of the 1990s are free trade arrangements. Few aimed at the rather mercantilist type that was organized as customs unions in the 1960s and that led neo-classical economic theorists to see regional trade projects as 'trade diversion' rather than 'trade creation' and many of them to take a principled stand against regionalization. Some of the third-generation projects did, however, have elements of neo-mercantilism, or they were so perceived by third parties.

As the third generation of regional projects matures and (as a result of destabilizing financial crises) globalization fragments into contradictory tendencies, the regional phenomenon also becomes more complex—and more complicated to explain. The outcome of the various processes appears to be the result of a convergence of several factors and of an alliance of agents with rather different motives. *Transnationalization* becomes relatively less associated with *globalization* and becomes more likely to result in *regionalization*. There are also compelling reasons for believing that *internationalization* will become relatively more influenced by *regionalism* and thus more opposed to *globalization*. The reasons why this is likely are found in growing problems with the efficacy of patterns of governance and with legitimacy and identity in the face of globalization. The perception that efficacy is at stake is probably one motivating factor behind the resurgence of bilateral agreements in investments and trade seen at the turn of the century.

Transnationalization and Regionalization

Received wisdom is that transnational capital represents the most consistent protagonist of globalization and of a multilateral system[12] and that if these agents accept regional projects, it is only to further globalization, with the intention to *represent* the region only temporarily. In fact, the motive towards globalization applies for large investment banks and funds, but it is not necessarily true for transnational corporations investing with a long-term stake in production and services. These agents may rather take a pragmatic view of the choice between globalization and regionalization. Many of them have indeed been actively pushing regionalization, a fact indicated by the increase in intraregional as compared to interregional transactions, both in investments and in trade, over the last decades. If these agents follow a *sequential* strategy, regionalization is a transition to a global market arrangement and may represent the *riding* or hedge options. But corporate management differs in style along broad national and regional divisions[13] partly because business-society relations continue to differ widely[14] and significant political and cultural barriers to global strategies continue in many sectors.

The greater emphasis on flexible production conditions after Fordist production peaked meant that the location of production also became less confined. Production de-integrated, 'international production networks' replaced Fordist assembly plants, and managers are pursuing the so-called 'outward processing traffic' strategy.[15] These new tendencies do not necessarily lead corporate managers to de-emphasize the regional level. EU enlargement has probably helped firms in the 15 pre-expansion members to develop extended production agreements with firms in the 10 new members. This development has been stimulated by transformations in global competition, but may also have been helped by cultural ties that enhance trust. The regionalization of the greater European space thus is a result of political, institutional, and cultural factors as well as those related to transformations in corporate organization. This may be most visible in Europe, but there is no reason why it should not also become a growing tendency in Asia and other continents as well. In various ways geography still matters. For small and medium-sized firms the regional option is often the only option consistent with the resources they have at their disposal to reach out to external markets.

In West Africa *trans-state regionalism* illustrates a contradiction between transnationalization and internationalization. In this case, the state border is a major source of profit. A relatively undeveloped, non-diversified economy offers few alternative sources of accumulation. Thus, small firms, artisans, and traders also represent agency in favour of regional economic circuits across borders, but in opposition to tariff-hostile globalization. Transnational flows of goods and individuals are stimulated, not discouraged, by the discrepancies between neighbouring tariff and trade systems. Extra-regional sources of transnationalization are present as investors and traders, but their accumulation is mainly related to traditional colonial types of investments in raw materials extraction and trade where they are still dominant. The continent receives only a small fraction of direct investment flows despite its radical shift to a more welcoming policy.[16] Africa internationalizes because of global pressures and processes, but it is not transnationalized by them. The phenomenon referred to as trans-state regionalism transcends the state, but is not necessarily opposing it. Rather, this type of regionalism opposes internationalization (the building down of tariffs and other formal barriers) because the latter destroys an important source of income from intraregional transactions.

If private agents have been taking the initiative in most of the 'third-generation' cases, political actors often have picked up the process and institutionalized the initiatives. Governments endorsed regional projects partly for fear of a deadlock in the Uruguay Round negotiations, or for fear of a 'fortress Europe', or for both reasons. In one case,

that of Central America, governments initiated a very ambitious institutionalization project, no doubt modelled on the EU, and the Southern African Development Co-ordination Conference (SADCC) changed to the South African Development Community (SADC) by strengthening (although almost from scratch) its central institutions. A scramble for regional support contributed to the North American Free Trade Agreement (NAFTA) and MERCOSUR, and to reinvigoration of several 'second-generation' projects such as the Association of Southeast Asian Nations (ASEAN). At the same time, the end of the Cold War and the coming of globalized markets coincided with a paradigmatic shift in large parts of the South. State-centred economic policy and 'delinking' from the North were replaced by an acceptance and invitation of market-based policies. This coincidence of trends led to less contentious behaviour within the ACP (Africa, Caribbean, Pacific)–Lomé agreement, to the integration of Mexico with the United States and Canada in NAFTA, and to the setting up of the Asia-Pacific Economic Co-operation (APEC) forum.

Internationalization and Regionalization

When and how does internationalization turn into regionalization as more than just a temporary stage, as more than simply an exercise in riding on globalization? And under what conditions do transnationalization and internationalization converge to initiate, defend, or strengthen regionalism? The answer may be found by introducing a simple analytical scheme that addresses the agency-structure issue dynamically.

Above, it was argued that second-generation regionalization was shaped more by structure than by agency, whereas agency has had greater influence on the third-generation and contemporary regional projects. Our understanding of the motivations for action may *begin* with the perceived utility and efficacy of action; this corresponds to March and Olsen's 'logic of expected consequences', wherein agents ask which institutional solutions offer maximum profit, growth, welfare, and security. But to link action only to a logic of consequences is to ignore the role of identity, rules, and institutions—or 'the logic of appropriateness'—in shaping behaviour.[17] These 'appropriateness' factors represent important motivations, and it is quite possible they eventually will dominate the regional phenomenon.

Structural factors include: *level of development; market structure and industrial organization* (oligopoly and oligopsony, i.e., oligarchy of purchasers, corporate structures where there is little incentive to co-operate); and power balances and the existence (or not) of *hegemony* (the presence of a dominant power may boost a weakly institutionalized project).

Radical change in any one or several of these structural factors may affect the relationship between globalization and regional action quite strongly. The effect may be seen in the structure of *authority*, in perceptions about problems of governance, and in preferences with respect to how they should be resolved. This raises the issue of how economic efficiency relates to legitimacy in the context of regional projects.

Efficiency, Efficacy, and Legitimacy

Explanations focusing on legitimacy in relation to regionalization mainly take domestic political institutions and processes into account, such as the character of state institutions, civil society's strength, and state–civil society relations. While efficiency in terms of security or growth is a major concern at the initiating stage of regional integration, legitimating becomes more important after the momentum of regionalization has been established.

There are two ways of legitimizing: the rules-oriented and the results-oriented approaches. The core of the globalization ideology is the self-regulating market, which, its advocates claim, offers both economic efficiency and legitimacy. If all agents enjoy the same competitive conditions (rules), then they see the arrangement as legitimate.

Liberal democracy and market economy are considered by many to be twins. Even if this were

so, it is also true that democracy consists of more than market rules and property rights. Democracy may also be associated with popular resistance to the inequalities that the market generates. Both Polanyi and Hirsch, from somewhat different perspectives, have argued that since the Industrial Revolution the advances of the market economy and of democracy have occurred together, but that both *cannot* coexist with an increasingly uneven distribution of welfare.[18] This incompatibility, according to Polanyi, led to totalitarian political regimes and eventually to war in the 1930s. While a precise repetition of events is unlikely, some trends have been repeated over the last 15 years or so. The self-regulating market is advancing and democratization of national polities is a global trend, yet inequality in the distribution of welfare between and within nation-states and regions is, with a few exceptions, increasing. The self-regulating market may certainly produce more efficient allocation of resources. But if there is insufficient redistribution of the result, and there is at the same time democratization, the discrepancy becomes not only more transparent, it also is contested. And when the self-regulating market produces systemic instability, as has happened in the financial system, democratic governance is threatened.[19] The authority of the system loses legitimacy; it is challenged and may eventually break down.

But why and how would such a process lead to regionalization of the *regionalist* kind? Postmodernist critics notwithstanding, the nation-state is the level of authority still most vested with collective identity (perhaps less so in the EU where the link between the regional project and identity is most advanced). From the point of view of most citizens the nation-state is also, but probably to a lesser extent, the level of authority most vested with legitimacy. The problem of the nation-state in the era of globalization is that it is found to be less effective than it once was in delivering security, welfare, and a secure sense of identity. Evans is correct in pointing out that the 'eclipse of the state' thesis is grossly exaggerated and that there are good reasons to argue that states are still viable.[20] Still, if legitimacy and collective identity combine, they represent a strong challenge to the logic of efficiency if or when the two former collide with the latter. Therefore, the authority of global markets, being based on equal opportunity, is challenged if or when globalization is associated with marginalization.

At that point, the legitimacy of institutions tends to be associated with welfare creation and distributional outcomes. Legitimizing becomes result-based, not rules-based. Thus, *the comparative advantage of the regional project is that it may be more effective in governing globalization than the nation-state, while at the same time potentially offering more legitimacy and collective identity than globalization itself.*[21]

When the regional project attempts to *regulate* or *resist* globalization, it is often a response to problems related to legitimizing distributive implications of the latter. The response also results from several agents with coinciding, but sometimes even different, motives, combining in alliance across nation-states. As a result, authority relationships in regional action are both more complex and more unpredictable at the end of the third-generation projects than was previously the case. Rather than searching through contrasting theories such as functionalist, neo-functionalist/federalist, or intergovernmentalist approaches, it is better to look for combinations of theories focusing on the efficacy (in terms of governance), legitimacy, and identity triangle as causes of behaviour.

Identity and Regionalization

Great powers may ride effectively on globalization, but even these powers may experience problems in so doing. Whereas many regional projects in the first generation were *hegemonic* projects led by the great powers basing their authority on the geopolitics of the Cold War, hegemony is contested in the contemporary period. Examples are resistance in East Asia towards Japanese leadership and scepticism in Latin America with respect to US hegemony in organizing free trade in the hemisphere. If states attempt to regulate bilaterally, which was the US trend in the 1980s, this tends to increase the level of conflict. If they attempt to do it on a global level, the numbers of

participants—and thus collective action problems—become too large. There will still be efforts to sustain global multilateral institutions. But even the United States has been active in developing regional projects on its own doorstep, demonstrating that a regional institution may thus be an optimal solution to collective action problems.

The financial crisis in Asia led to a weakening of the work on projects in Southeast Asia, including ASEAN itself. But the weakening appears to have been temporary. Governments and corporations in that region still pursue both the regional and the global options. In 1997 leaders in the region floated the idea of creating a regional fund for handling any short-term stabilization problems that might recur. The idea was shelved due to strong opposition from the United States and the IMF. They apparently saw the idea as a potential threat not only to global multilateral rules, but to US power.[22] However, initiatives to retrieve it have arisen, partly as a response to widespread criticism of the IMF's role in the Asian crisis, and with China shifting to a favourable attitude in 2002 it has become more politically viable.

There are basically three reasons why Asian regionalism may grow. First, several of the countries in the East Asian region have a legacy of opposing tight links with global trends in culture and the political economy. Although references to an 'Asian identity' are wrong and to a 'Southeast Asian' identity mostly exaggerated, there are indications of a growing awareness of the latter. It may be partly security-driven, as the expansion of ASEAN may indicate. This tentative and still unsettled expression of identity represents a defence of a policy of emphasizing sovereignty over globalization. Second, the suggested regional financial fund is also an illustration of a new tendency. Japan's problems with its own domestic finance system and continued political and cultural strains between Japan and several of the subregional states make the odds for such ideas to materialize not particularly high. But while old political animosities remain, mere pragmatism may come to dominate them. If the global financial system, despite the post-1997 reforms and stabilization measures, should again develop a major and contagious financial crisis, the opportunity costs of failing to develop the proposed regional alternative may be high. The countries of the region have become economically so interdependent over the past decade of rapidly growing intraregional investments and trade that they may simply have to let economic reality prevail over history.[23]

The third reason is an extension of the two mentioned and may be referred to for the sake of brevity as geopolitics and the logic of inter-regional power relations. The more the United States pursues geopolitical ideas in Eurasia, and the more Europe and other regions integrate, the more will East Asia, not the least China, turn from its traditional bilateralism towards increased emphasis on regional co-opertain as a political instrument.

Regional Action as Global Governance

Thus the region may be preferred for reasons having to do with a need for authority, with the lack of appropriate governance. This applies to subregions as well; in several parts of the world they are preferred as a response to the perceived weakening of the nation-state. But it also applies to the phenomenon dealt with here—the international region.

Rationalist accounts of regional action refer to it as an element of 'layered governance'. A liberal institutionalist variant thus views regionalization as a *delegation of power* from a liberal global order. Because of the complexity and variety of issues that this order has to deal with, some governance tasks have to be referred to a lower level of governance. This perspective is represented both by those who emphasize the interstate system[24] and those who argue that international society is of growing importance.[25]

While these perspectives may have some value, they miss the vital need for agency—for somebody to have the *idea* or a pressing *interest* in choosing the regional level of governance before other solutions. To the extent that these perspectives have agency in mind, top-down solutions are generally emphasized over bottom-up initiatives.

In neo-functionalist and particularly in intergovernmentalist accounts, the agent is a state bureaucrat or national politician, respectively.

But, as we have indicated above, private agency and bottom-up initiatives are highly potent sources of regional action. For firms under the pressure of globalization, the regional level may represent collateral in helping to sustain particular capitalist cultures. Regional institutions may contribute to competitiveness by helping fund R&D and organize industrial policy supports in several ways. They may even protect firms with long-term investments and high asset exposure against the volatility of the financial system.

If the 'layered governance' perspective is valid, it is because it helps us view regionalization as part of transnational and international *alliance-building*. Besides being a means of organizing collective action to support competitiveness or represent a sense of identity, regional action may also be a means to achieve national domestic political reordering and convergence towards the dominant regional culture. Domestic interest groups thus may build alliances at the regional level to strengthen their own relative power at the expense of other domestic groups. Business groups in several of the democratic-corporatist Western European countries that applied for membership in the EU at the beginning of the 1990s sought membership, *inter alia*, in order to weaken domestic corporatist structures and procedures. Mexican industrial elites also appear to have wanted NAFTA as a means to deregulate and liberalize the domestic economy, including agriculture.[26] Regional decision-making may be used thus to level the playing field nationally. But it is also true that in several countries with a strong social democratic and corporatist tradition, such as Norway and Sweden, regional institutions were defined by leading proponents of this tradition as an optimal level of governance by which global capital may be regulated.[27]

Environmentalists may, on the other hand, use the regional level to pressure business to adopt more environment-friendly policies and practices. Even labour may pursue this strategy. Liberalizing regional projects may be perceived as a zero-sum game by labour if they are facilitating the free movement of capital. Again, NAFTA illustrates both tendencies from the perspective of US interest groups: environmentalists found it legitimate only after having the environmental side agreement passed, whereas US labour opposed it for the reason indicated. But the 'Eurostrike' in 1997 illustrates that national labour unions may use the regional level to their own advantage. Workers in a Renault plant in Belgium mobilized unions all over the EU because they could point to Renault's decision to close the plant as a breach of EU policy, namely, that the interests of the totality of the corporations's workforce at the regional level must be taken into account.[28]

Operating at a global level may mean considerable transaction costs for even the most efficient firms. There are several reasons why a bilateral arrangement of market transactions may be more cost-efficient than multilateral options, particularly global ones. However, if a large number of bilateral arrangements were to be initiated, implemented, and controlled, this would represent a significant cost factor. But since for most actors markets are concentrated, a limited number of such deals are sufficient for coping with most transactions, a fact that made this option so attractive in the 1980s. The optimal way of reducing transaction costs, and at the same time to have a trade regime that is also more legitimate than bilateralism, is a regional solution.

Is this governance scenario in fact what is developing? The call of the International Commission on Global Governance to resolve the inadequacies of the Westphalian system in managing the world by exploiting the 'potential of regional cooperation' went mostly unnoticed.[29] The call resurfaced in a statement made by Guy de Verhofstadt, the President of the European Council right after 9/11, when he advocated that 'the G-8 of rich countries be replaced . . . by a G-8 of existing regional partnerships . . . where the South is given an important and deserved place at the table to ensure that the globalization of the economy is headed in the right direction'.[30] Leaving aside the question of what motivated the proposal and how

it was met by G-8 members inside the EU, the issue is whether in fact the scenario contained in the proposal is not coming true. One of the obvious tendencies in current internationalization is that the growth in regional agreements is accompanied by a growth in the number of interregional agreements, such as that between the EU and MERCOSUR. And both the United States and Japan have openly stated their intent to negotiate bilateral agreements, as the US Trade Representative put it, in order to catch up with the EU, which, according to the official, had gained a competitive advantage in the field of political agreement on market access in other regions.

Conclusion

There will still be strong agency in favour of globalization, chiefly by internationalizing governments whose countries stand to gain from it, from transnationalizing big corporations and financiers, and from neo-liberal economists. The need for conflict resolution, standardization, and other aspects of co-ordination among regional projects will also represent a strong globalizing argument.

The argument developed above is that three main sources of agency will make regional projects more than just episodes or steps towards the global. The first is that, despite years of globalizing efforts, considerable political and cultural diversity remains among the various national and regional capitalisms. Second, there are strong and apparently growing tendencies for top-down internationalizing and bottom-up transnationalizing forces to work in parallel or even to converge over a policy that favours regional action. The third source of regional action is the apparent or likely trend towards emphasizing collective identity and legitimacy in addition to, sometimes even before, efficiency. The declining efficacy of nation-states in organizing action that links efficiency (growth and security) with identity and legitimacy combines with pressures from globalizing tendencies, in particular destabilizing and marginalizing patterns, to open up greater room for regional projects as alternative governance structures.

This means that neo-utilitarian theories are necessary, but they are insufficient for understanding the regional phenomenon and need to be modified and supplemented by alternative accounts drawing on reflectivist and social constructivist perspectives. If security is the utilitarian motive that leads agency and it calls for a regional project, economic efficiency motivations may be subordinated to it. And if security is defined broadly, there are even stronger reasons to argue that security may join with collective identity and legitimacy to construct a strong basis for regionalism.

Notes

1. Karl Polanyi, *The Great Transformation* (Boston: Beacon Press, 1957 [1944]); Karl Polanyi, 'Universal Capitalism or Regional Planning', *London Quarterly of World Affairs* (Jan. 1945).

2. Peter Katzenstein, 'Regionalism in Comparative Perspective', *Cooperation and Conflict* 31, 2 (1996): 123–59.

3. This section is based on critical reading of several different sources, including Louise Fawcett and Andrew Hurrell, *Regionalism in World Politics: Regional Organization and International Order* (Oxford: Oxford University Press, 1995); Peter Katzenstein and Takashi Shiraishi, eds, *Network Power: Japan and Asia* (Ithaca, NY: Cornell University Press, 1997); Jeffrey A. Frankel and Miles Kahler, eds, *Regionalism and Rivalry: Japan and the United States in Pacific Asia* (Chicago: University of Chicago Press, 1993); Andrew Gamble and Anthony Payne, eds, *Regionalism and World Order* (London: Macmillan, 1996).

4. For a broad definition, see Philip Cerny, 'Globalization and the Changing Logic of Collective Action', *International Organization* 49, 4 (1995): 595–625.

5. Karl W. Deutsch et al., *Political Community and the North Atlantic Area* (Princeton, NJ: Princeton University Press, 1957).

6. Michel Callon, 'The Embeddedness of Economic Markets in Economics', in M. Callon, ed., *The Laws of the Markets* (Oxford: Blackwell, 1998).

7. Emmanuel Adler, 'Imagined (Security) Communities', paper presented at the annual meeting of the American Political Science Association, New York, Sept. 1994, 1–4.

8. See Bjørn Hettne and Andras Inotai, *The New Regionalism* (Helsinki: WIDER, 1994).

9. Davis B. Bobrow and Robert T. Kudrle, 'Regionalism as Accelerator, Brake, Ratchet and Hedge: FDI and Competition Policies', paper presented at the Third Pan-European Conference of the ECPR Standing Group on International Relations, organized jointly with the International Studies Association, Vienna, 16–20 Sept. 1998.

10. Gerard Lafay and Deniz Unal-Kesenci, 'Les trois pôles géographiques des échanges internationaux', *Economie prospective internationale* 45, 1 (1991).

11. See Peter Katzenstein, 'Asian Regionalism in Comparative Perspective', in Katzenstein and Shiraishi, eds, *Network Power*.

12. Helen Milner, *Resisting Protectionism* (Princeton, NJ: Princeton University Press, 1988).

13. Louis Pauly and Simon Reich, 'Enduring MNC Differences Despite Globalization', *International Organization* 51, 1 (Winter 1997): 1–30.

14. David Soskice, 'Divergent Production Regimes', in Herbert Kitschelt et al., eds, *Continuity and Change in Contemporary Capitalism* (Cambridge: Cambridge University Press, 1999).

15. John Zysman and Andrew Schwartz, eds, *Enlarging Europe: The Industrial Foundations of a New Political Reality* (Berkeley, Calif.: IAS Publications, 1998); Julie Pellegrin, *The Political Economy of Competitiveness in an Enlarged Europe* (London: Palgrave, 2001).

16. Daniel Bach, 'Institutional Crisis and the Search for New Models', in Réal Lavergne, ed., *Regional Integration and Cooperation in West Africa: A Multidimensional Perspective* (Ottawa

and Trenton, NJ: IDRC and Africa World Press, 1997), 77–02; *World Investment Report* (Geneva: United Nations, various years).

17. James G. March and Johan P. Olsen, 'The Institutional Dynamics of International Political Orders', *International Organization* 52, 4 (1998): 943–69.

18. Polanyi, *The Great Transformation*; Fred Hirsch, *Social Limits to Growth* (London: Routledge and Kegan Paul, 1977).

19. Eric Helleiner, 'Democratic Governance in an Era of Global Finance', in Maxwell A. Cameron and Maureen Molot, eds, *Canada Among Nations 1995: Democracy and Foreign Policy* (Ottawa: Carleton University Press, 1995).

20. Peter Evans, 'The Eclipse of the State? Reflections on Stateness in an Era of Globalization', *World Politics* 50 (Oct. 1997): 62–87.

21. The argument has been more extensively developed in H. Hveem, 'Global Governance and the Comparative Political Advantage of Regional Cooperation', in D. Tussie, ed., *The Environment and International Trade Negotiations: Developing Country Stakes* (Basingstoke: Macmillan, 2000).

22. Paul Krugman, interview on CNBC, reported on Internet in Dow Jones Newswires (28 Aug. 1998).

23. Richard Higgott, 'Globalization, Regionalism and Identity in East Asia', in Peter Dicken et al., eds, *The Logics of Globalization in the Asia Pacific* (London: Routledge, 1998).

24. Beth V. Yarbrough and Robert M. Yarbrough, 'Regionalism and Layered Governance', *Journal of International Affairs* 48, 1 (1994): 95–118.

25. James N. Rosenau, 'Governance in the Twenty-First Century', *Global Governance* 1, 1 (Winter 1995): 13–43.

26. Jose Luis Calva, *La Disputa por la Terra* (Mexico City: Fontamara, 1992).

27. Jacob Gustavsson, 'The Politics of Foreign Policy Change', Ph.D. dissertation (University of Lund, 1998).

28. *The European*, 13–19 Mar. 1997.

29. ICCG, *Our Global Neighbourhood* (Oxford: Oxford University Press, 1995), 285.

30. Guy de Verhofstadt, text available at: <www.eu2001.be/VE_adv_Press>.

Suggested Readings

Coleman, William D., and Geoffrey R.D. Underhill, eds. *Regionalism and Global Economic Integration: Europe, Asia, and the Americas.* London: Routledge, 1998.

Fawcett, Louise. 'Exploring Regional Domains: A Comparative History of Regionalism', *International Affairs* 80, 3 (May 2004): 429–46.

Hettne, Bjorn, Andreas Inotai, and Osvaldo Sunkel, eds. *Comparing Regionalisms: Implications for Global Development.* Basingstoke: Palgrave Macmillan, 2001.

Spindler, Manuela. *New Regionalism and the Construction of Global Order.* CSGR Working Paper No. 93/02. Coventry: Centre for the Study of Globalisation and Regionalisation, University of Warwick, March 2002.

Web Sites

Asia-Pacific Economic Co-operation: www.apecsec.org.sg/apec.html

ATTAC International: www.attac.org/indexfla.htm
European Commission: europa.eu.int/index.en.htm

Chapter 21

The Transnational Political Economy of European Integration
The Future of Socio-economic Governance in the Enlarged Union

Bastiaan van Apeldoorn

While the process of globalization has been going on unabated, Europe has continued to witness its own regional project of both economic and political integration within this changing global context. This regional project, partly under the influence of global developments, has seen a major transformation over the past two decades. Since the mid-1980s the European project has undergone both an ongoing deepening as well as successive rounds of widening, with the latest expanding the European Union (EU) from 15 to 25 members. The EU now has a single market as well as a single currency, and a set of associated socio-economic policies increasingly affecting the domestic political economies of its member states. In addition, the so called European Constitution—on which, after much haggling, Europe's leaders finally agreed in June 2004 but which still has to be ratified—has been hailed as a significant step on the road to political union. In spite of these achievements, Europe seems rather unsure of itself as it sails into the uncharted waters of post-enlargement: Euro-skepticism is on the rise while the European economy is still struggling to get out of the prolonged post 9/11 recession. In fact, given the dismal performance with regard to both growth and employment, the EU's own ambition—as proclaimed at the so-called Lisbon summit in 2000—to become the most competitive economy in the world by 2010 seems further away than ever.

In terms of socio-economic governance, the direction the European project has been taking in recent years has been rather clear. After the successful implementation of the internal market pro-

gram, the thrust of the integration process has more than ever become one of market liberalization. What is viewed by some as a process of neo-liberal globalization on a world scale has in this respect largely been mirrored by the European integration process. The result has been a fundamental restructuring of the prevailing European socio-economic order, involving a tendency towards 'disembedding' the market from the institutions that made up the post-war 'Keynesian welfare state', shifting the balance between the public and the private (that is, of private market forces) in favour of the latter. The question to be raised now is to what extent this trend can be sustained in the foreseeable future given that the success of this restructuring is, even by its own standards, far from guaranteed.

With this critical question regarding the future of European (socio-economic) governance in mind, I examine the changing political economy of European integration, mainly to analyze the social forces involved in the current transformation of the European socio-economic order. My critical analysis of the dynamics of European integration seeks to identify and explain what can be called its underlying 'social purpose'. Moreover, unlike conventional integration theories, which tend to take the EU as a self-contained entity, this analysis squarely places Europe within the context of the changing global political economy. Emphasizing the deepening transnationalization of economic, social, and political forces within that economy, I take the European integration process to be a specific and in some respects amplified manifestation of that global transnationalization process. The EU is seen in this context as an arena in which *transnational* social forces struggle to redefine the social purpose of European governance.

Transnational Social Forces in the European Integration Process: Structures and Actors

From the early days of the European Coal and Steel Community (1952) and the European Economic Community (1958), scholars have been preoccupied with the question of what drives the historically unprecedented process of European integration.[1] At least until the early 1990s the dominant theoretical debate pitted so-called supranationalist against intergovernmentalist approaches. Supranationalism—still the earliest and the most significant variety of neo-functionalism—emphasizes the autonomous dynamics of the integration process. Taking European integration as a *sui generis* phenomenon, supranationalism argues that the functional needs of the (no longer purely national) economy necessitate common policies beyond the nation-state, in turn provoking the need for more (related) common policies. Once common policies and common, so-called supranational institutions have been established, interest groups benefiting from integration also tend to organize at the new European level and become important levers of a self-expanding integration process. Finally, in supranationalist approaches, a key role is being played by the supranational institutions themselves, above all the European Commission, the bureaucracy and quasi-executive of the Union, whose 25 commissioners are supposedly independent from any national political pressures. The Commission is regarded as an important agenda-setter and policy entrepreneur because of its sole right to propose European legislation.

On the other hand, the intergovernmentalist tradition, which has its intellectual roots in realism, stresses the continuing primacy of the nation-state and of national interests in the integration process. Whereas early neo-functionalists predicted a gradual evolution into a federal Euro-state, intergovernmentalists claimed that states would never permit a transfer of sovereignty. States want to and do make sure that their national interests are well protected, and it is only when it serves their interests that they agree to co-operate, posing clear limits to the integration process. European integration is thus seen as primarily an intergovernmental bargaining process in which the outcome is determined by the relative bargaining power of the states, and supranational institutions such as the European Commission, the European Parliament (EP) or the European Court of Justice (ECJ) play a much less important role. It is the Council of Ministers—representing the member states—that adopts or rejects the Commission's proposed laws (although for an increasing number of areas the EP now has so-called co-decision power). More important still is the regular European Council summit, the meetings of which often set out the direction that the EU is to take on important issues.

Although each perspective emphasizes aspects of the reality, an important drawback of this classical debate is that it almost exclusively focuses on the institutional *form* of the integration process. While form is an important dimension of the political economy of European integration, it misses the equally important question of the socio-economic *content* of the integration process: which social purpose is served by the European project?[2] More contemporary approaches to European integration tend to agree that the EU is in fact neither a mere international organization nor a full-blown supranational state, but rather a new type of polity in which authority is shared between different and partially overlapping layers of governance (hence the term 'multi-level governance'): from the regional to the European, but with the national level far from being redundant.[3] The new literature on European governance also contends that intergovernmentalism versus supranationalism is not the only significant dimension of EU politics. Much of it is also about 'traditional' left-right issues or the socio-economic substance of European policies. Building on these insights, this chapter will add a specific focus on the *transnational* nature of this multi-dimensional and multi-level politics. It will do so from a critical IPE perspective that argues that we cannot study the process of European integration in isolation (as especially the neo-functionalists tended to do) but only within the context of a changing global order.[4] The European order as constructed through the integration process and the global order are seen as fundamentally linked by transnational *social forces* engendered by the transnationalization of capitalism.

Since the 1970s, and accelerating in the 1990s, the global economy has witnessed a restructuring process driven by a deepening transnationalization of capital. This has produced a qualitative shift in the world economy marked by a steep rise of foreign direct investment (FDI) by the world's growing number of transnational corporations (TNCs) over the past two decades.[5] Being central actors that both drive and are driven by this transnationalization process, these TNCs developed more transnational strategies during the 1990s. In fact, European capitalism has become more transnational both *within* the borders of the EU, bolstering the integration of Europe's national economies, and *beyond* the EU (Asia, the United States, Eastern Europe), thereby locking Europe into global networks of capitalist production and finance. It is within this structural context that we have to understand the rise of a transnational business elite as a principal actor within the European arena. Operating simultaneously in the global and the European arenas—responding to the pressures of globalization that they help to create—these transnational agents seek to shape the socio-economic content of European governance.[6]

Transnational Business in European Integration

The transnationalization of European capital, and the rise of a transnational business elite as a political actor in its own right, coincided with the revitalization of the integration process in the mid-1980s. When integration was at its low point and growing global competition threatened the position of large sections of European industry, leading members of Europe's big business elite perceived the need for a *political* initiative not yet seen among

Europe's politicians. Thus, in 1983 the European Round Table of Industrialists (ERT) was founded 'to revitalise European industry and make it competitive again, and to speed up the process of unification of the European market'.[7] Today, the ERT consists of about 45 heads of Europe's largest and most transnational industrial corporations (such as Bayer, BP, Philips, Nestlé, Nokia, and Total).[8] Membership of the ERT is personal and by invitation only. Thus, the ERT is not a traditional business lobby or an interest association but rather an elite forum from within which its leaders can work out a common and cohesive strategy that is then propagated through the European institutions, in particular the European Commission.[9] The ERT is generally recognized to be one of the most powerful business groups in Europe, and is acknowledged to have played a major agenda-setting role with regard to the relaunching of Europe, in particular by bringing the completion of the internal market back onto the agenda.[10]

The transnational business elite increasingly dominates the landscape of European interest representation. Next to the ERT, a number of other less formal business groups are modelled on the Round Table, with the CEOs themselves being directly involved and exercising leadership based on their experience and prestige. The most prominent among these groups in fact have been largely the outcome of initiatives by (former) ERT members. An early example was the Association for Monetary Union in Europe (AMUE), which from 1987 onward has lobbied for a European single currency. Another major initiative was taken in 1995 with the start of the Transatlantic Business Dialogue (TABD), bringing together CEOs of leading TNCs from both sides of the Atlantic. They mainly discuss transatlantic trade relations so as to promote further liberalization, and the TABD has been credited with breaking the deadlock in negotiations over several difficult issues.[11] The most recent addition to the growing number of Round Table-inspired forums is the European Round Table of Financial Services, comprising the heads of 13 of Europe's largest banks and insurance companies (among them Allianz, AXA, Deutsche Bank, and ING) and headed by the founding

Chairman of the ERT, Pehr Gyllenhammar. The rise of the transnational business elite is thus a reflection of the growing structural power—which has both an economic and an ideological dimension—of transnational firms within the European economy and the global political economy.

In contrast to the power of transnational business, the power of organized labour and of other societal groups remains relatively weak, despite a proliferation of all kinds of interest and lobbying groups within Brussels. The establishment of an effective European working-class movement continues to be hampered by national fragmentation. This does not mean that there is no opposition or resistance to the agenda of big business. The opposition, however, comes less from interest associations (even if they do play some role of significance in EU policy-making) than from NGOs and transnational social movements, in particular the so-called anti-globalization movement. Thus, the European Social Forum (ESF) has been formed as a regional spinoff of the World Social Forum, attracting a large number of activists from diverse backgrounds to their annual gatherings.[12] Thus far, however, it is hard to find any evidence of a direct influence on European governance on the part of these loosely defined groups. However, this is probably also not what one would expect from a movement that works towards a much more radical transformation of the existing European (and global) order. What we can conclude is that the transnationalization process is no longer restricted to business interests only, and that the EU in fact forms an arena for the struggle between diverse and contending transnational social forces.

The Transnational Struggle over European Integration: From the Single Market to the Single Currency and Beyond

Until the mid-1980s the integration process appeared moribund (the era of 'Euro-pessimism' and 'Euro-sclerosis'). In 1985 Europe was 'relaunched' through the Commission's 'Europe 1992' single-market program, which became the Single European Act of 1987. This relaunch and the subsequent struggle over the content of the revived integration process is understood here as the outcome of a struggle between contending 'strategic' projects and their corresponding social constituencies. Three such rival projects can be identified: 'neo-mercantilism', 'neo-liberalism', and 'supranational social democracy'. Within this configuration the primary struggle was initially between neo-liberalism and neo-mercantilism, representing the contending strategies of rival groups or 'fractions' within the ranks of Europe's emergent transnational business elite. Throughout the 1980s and into the 1990s, the main dividing line within this elite was between a 'globalist' fraction consisting of Europe's most globalized firms (including global financial institutions) and, on the other hand, a 'Europeanist' fraction made up of large industrial enterprises primarily serving the national/European markets and competing against the often cheaper imports from outside Europe (East Asia in particular).[13] The perspective of the former has tended towards neo-liberalism, whereas the latter came to promote the neo-mercantilist project. The social democratic project, on the other hand, came to be supported not only by major social democratic parties but also by parts of the European trade union movement.

Rival Projects for the Relaunching of Europe

All three projects favoured a relaunching of Europe through a completion of the internal market, but they fundamentally differed on what kind of European market it was to be. In the *neo-mercantilist* conception, the project of European integration was first of all conceived as one of creating a big home market in which 'European champions'—profiting from the larger economies of scale—would be able to confront successfully the American and Japanese competition. The neo-mercantilist project in fact constituted a defensive regionalization strategy oriented towards the creation of a strong regional bloc, with an internal market supported by an active industrial policy if necessary protected by European tariff walls.

The *neo-liberal project,* on the other hand, emphasized the free-market aspects of the internal market, a free market that should also be free for non-European firms and hence open to and fully integrated into the emerging global economy. In the neo-liberal conception of European integration, then, the process should be restricted to *negative* integration (the removal of barriers to trade), resulting in more market and less state at all levels of governance. In short, the 'aim [was] to make Europe by the year 2000 a model of what free trade and open markets can achieve'.[14] In contrast to the neo-liberals, the *social democratic project* sought to protect and consolidate in a supranational framework what is referred to as the 'European social model' in a discourse that was particularly promoted by the then Commission President Jacques Delors.[15]

Within the European Round Table the struggle in the 1980s and early 1990s was between a neo-liberal and a neo-mercantilist conception of the single market. The latter was at first dominant. Most of Europe's large firms were still effectively *regional* TNCs aspiring to become global by creating a European market shielded against global competition. It was from this defensive perspective that the ERT successfully set the agenda for what later became the Europe 1992 program, taking the initiative before politicians were willing or able to do so. But the internal market program as actually *implemented* (by treating non-EU-owned subsidiaries the same as EU firms) led to a further opening up of Europe's national economies to the global economy. It is thus that the regionalization of the European economy, in the sense of the further integration of its national economic systems, went hand in hand with a further globalization of the European region. The external liberalization of the new European market was later completed by the signing of the GATT Uruguay Round in 1994, which effectively sealed the fate of the neo-mercantilist project. In the transnational struggle over Europe's relaunching, neo-liberal social forces, strengthened by the ongoing and deepening globalization process, were thus gaining the upper

hand over those who had favoured a neo-mercantilist conception of the 'New Europe'. This shift—which also became manifest in a changing membership and outlook of the ERT—must be understood in the context of the deepening globalization of European industry in this period and the concomitant rise of neo-liberal ideology within the European political economy.[16] As the globalist fraction rose to dominance, the new ERT that emerged in the early 1990s thus became a staunch supporter of both internal and external market liberalization, i.e., global free trade.

The neo-liberal reorientation of Europe's transnational business elite also occurred in a context in which the old world order experienced a major upheaval with the collapse of the Communist bloc. What was widely celebrated as a triumph of liberal capitalism created a whole new set of challenges and market opportunities for West European business and allowed for a reintegration of Central and Eastern Europe into a globalizing capitalist world economy. In this context of both global and European upheaval, intergovernmental bargaining led to the Maastricht Treaty, which created the European Union. The focus of the treaty negotiations, however, was rather on the intended creation of an Economic and Monetary Union (EMU), a project whose design was neo-liberal.[17] The move towards a single currency has been strongly supported by large sections of European transnational business, in particular as represented by AMUE and the ERT, with transnational capital clearly set to gain from the removal of this particular 'non-tariff barrier' to trade.

Next to neo-liberal social forces, however, transnational social democratic forces under the leadership of Commission President Delors also aimed to shape the Maastricht process by seeking to complement monetary union with a strong political and social union, or a federal Europe capable of reasserting the primacy of politics over the European market. The social democratic interpretation of Maastricht, however, largely failed to materialize. While much of the federalist plans met with the opposition of several of the bigger member states, the lobbying efforts of big business ensured that the social chapter did not go much beyond symbolic politics. In fact, Maastricht marked the defeat of the Delorist project that at the end of the 1980s had come to challenge neo-liberalism.

Yet the treaty on European Union concluded at Maastricht was not a triumph for undiluted neo-liberalism, as chapters on 'Trans-European [infrastructure] Networks' and 'Research and Technological Development' did provide a basis for some form of European industrial policy speaking to the interests of the former neo-mercantilist wing of European transnational capital. Moreover, the watered-down 'social chapter' nevertheless succeeded in incorporating European social democracy and the trade union movement into the 'New Europe'.

The New European Socio-economic Order: The Rise of Embedded Neo-Liberalism

In retrospect, the Maastricht compromise reflected the gradual emergence of what can be identified as an 'embedded neo-liberal' synthesis. On the one hand, the primacy lies with freedom of capital and markets, implying that the post-war 'European model' needs to be fundamentally restructured. On the other hand, this restructuring will have to be a gradual process in which a high degree of social consensus is maintained. Finally, and crucially, a pure neo-liberal strategy would also undermine the long-term prospects of industrial capital, which still needs the state to educate the workforce, to provide the infrastructure, to pursue policies that favour growth and investment, to maintain social stability, etc. Thus, Europe's transnational business elite has moved away from neo-mercantilism and towards neo-liberalism, but without adopting a pure laissez-faire perspective.

In the construction of an embedded neo-liberal European order we can once more observe the political and ideological agency of this transnational business elite in shaping European governance. With the input of the ERT and other business groups, the transnational policy discourse has come to centre on the word 'competitiveness', appealing to neo-liberals, neo-mercantilists, and social democrats alike. But what competitiveness actually means, and how it has to be achieved, is an open question decided in political struggle. Here we can observe that competitiveness has increasingly been defined in neo-liberal terms. In the articulation of the new neo-liberal competitiveness discourse, the concept of 'benchmarking'—which, again, the ERT has been the first to promote through the Commission—also plays a critical role. Invoking the concept, the industrialists of the Round Table leave no doubt as to how competitiveness must be measured: the most competitive country or (macro-) region is the most successful in attracting mobile capital: 'Governments must recognize today that every economic and social system in the world is competing with all the others to attract the footloose businesses.'[18]

In sum, embedded neo-liberalism defines the social purpose of European integration primarily in terms of interests bound up with transnational capital, with the concepts of competitiveness and benchmarking being mobilized to promote a neo-liberal restructuring of the European political economy. However, ideologically and to a limited extent materially as well, the interests of other groups are also taken into account. In fact, these interests and identities are appealed to through the new competitiveness discourse. It is through this discourse that formerly contending social forces have been incorporated into what in Gramscian terms we may call a hegemonic project.[19] The rise to hegemony of this project within European governance can be most clearly read in the socio-economic agenda that the EU adopted at the Lisbon summit of March 2000 in which the government leaders proclaimed the 'new strategic goal . . . to become the most competitive and dynamic knowledge-based economy in the world, capable of sustainable economic growth with more and better jobs and greater social cohesion.'[20]

This ambitious agenda for socio-economic reform has been very much welcomed by the ERT, which in fact saw many of its ideas reflected in it. Subsequently—and in light of the noticeable lack of progress—the ERT has devoted much energy to call for the implementation of the Lisbon agenda, prioritizing (among others) innovation, the creation of an integrated European capital market, full liberalization of services and public utilities, deregulation, pension reform, and labour market reform.[21] Apart from its plea for increased public spending on R&D—reflecting the specific needs of industrial capital—this clearly advances a neo-liberal agenda. Failing to implement this agenda, the Round Table warns, will result in falling levels of investment and employment in a Europe suffering from 'high labour costs, excessive regulation and gaps in completing the internal market'.[22]

The neo-liberal competitiveness agenda underpinning Lisbon seems to contradict its aim to enhance social cohesion at the same time. Yet, the combination of both goals—the 'magic formula' of competitiveness and cohesion—is critical to the hegemonic project of embedded neo-liberalism. In fact, what it implies is a new social policy agenda that moves away from the 'old' idea of supranational market-correcting regulation (as advanced by the Delorist social democratic project) and towards promoting a market-enabling strategy. At the national level, while welfare states will not disappear, they will be adapted, and social cohesion is to be achieved by letting the labour market work better. Thus is social cohesion made compatible with, but at the same time also subordinated to, the goal of neo-liberal competitiveness. The European Employment Strategy (EES), first launched in 1994, is a case in point. Given the constraints imposed by the internal market and by EMU and the rules of the 1997 Stability and Growth Pact, the EES is limited to a supply-side strategy in which labour market flexibility is seen as the main policy instrument.[23]

Towards 2010: The Dilemmas and Contradictions of European Governance

The outcome of embedded neo-liberalism rather than a pure or orthodox neo-liberalism was necessary inasmuch as the latter could never have generated sufficient consent on the part of competing (if weaker) social groups. It was particularly within the European context that the neo-liberal offensive had to overcome the resistance of the institutionalized traditions of corporatist labour relations, social and industrial protection offered by an often interventionist state, and other elements of 'embeddedness'. However, this incorporation is done in such a way that these concerns are in the end subordinated to the overriding objective of 'competitiveness', defined in neo-liberal terms of market liberalization and market discipline. This is first of all manifested through the neo-liberal character of the internal market, which remains at the core of the EU's governance regime. The activism in this area of both the Commission and the ECJ has led to an ever more far-reaching extension of market competition to an increasing number of sectors—from telecommunications to transport and the energy market—hitherto shielded from the discipline of the market.[24] Second, it transpires from the failure of the social dimension as well as from the new European employment flexibility strategies that focus on market-making. Third, it is manifested in the openness of Europe's regionalism, as the strong commitment to free trade and freedom of foreign investment (despite occasional flare-ups of trade conflict in limited areas such as agriculture) has allowed the full integration of the European region into the globalizing world economy. Finally, it is apparent from the neo-liberal character of EMU, with the fiscal discipline of the Stability Pact and the monetary discipline exercised by the highly independent European Central Bank, which sets interest rates primarily to achieve price stability (i.e., as opposed primarily to promote growth and employment).

To understand fully the socio-economic content of the present European order, we also have to take into account that the EU is a *multi-level* system. Much of the embeddedness still present in the European political economy is to be found at the national level, and indeed business groups like the ERT would like to keep it at that level. In fact, this *national* nature of much of the institutional embeddedness posits the main problem from a perspective favouring what Karl Polanyi called the 'principle of social protection' over the 'principle of economic liberalism'.[25] The logic of the internal market, that is, an area without national border control, implies the threat of regulatory or regime competition in those areas of socio-economic policy that remain at the national level, such as policies bound up with the national welfare state.

To what extent, then, can embedded neo-liberalism, as a project for European integration and in particular European socio-economic governance, be sustained in the longer run? A first point is that the project of embedded neo-liberalism rests, above all, on the active consent of transnational elites, and this consent tends to be much more passive among the European populations in general. There are clear signs that this passive consent is weakening in recent years, especially since the post-9/11 economic downturn. We are in fact witnessing a deepening of an already existing legitimacy deficit faced by an EU that never has been known for its democratic credentials.[26] The looming legitimacy crisis of the EU may be related in particular to two central recent developments within the integration process—the enlargement to the East, on the one hand, and the project of monetary union in combination with the ongoing liberalization of the European economy, on the other.

Like other grand integration projects, such as the single market and the single currency, the big-bang enlargement of 1 May 2004 has been perceived as a highly elitist project and as such has generated much more scepticism than enthusiastic support on both sides of the former Iron Curtain. The enlargement is also likely to undermine further the limited embeddedness of Europe's current socio-economic order. Thus, the complete underdevelopment of the 'social cohesion' dimension of the enlargement process tends to turn this historic unification of pan-Europe into in a mere geographical extension and deepening of neo-liberal restructuring.[27] As such, this project has also been consistently supported by Europe's transnational business elite, especially through the ERT.[28] Indeed, the benefits for Europe's TNCs, which have already invested heavily in the countries of Central and Eastern Europe, were clear: restructuring would provide them with a continuing guaranteed access to new markets reformed on the basis of the neo-liberal policy paradigm reigning in the EU.

With regard to European socio-economic governance, the neo-liberal discipline of EMU, in combination with the EU's current drive for further market liberalization and in the context of an economic recession, threatens to undermine the cohesion of social forces underpinning embedded neo-liberalism. We are already witnessing as much with the recent crisis around the Stability Pact, with France and Germany, in particular, seeking—with some success—to evade the Pact's fiscal discipline in a time of stagnant growth. As EMU may increasingly be perceived as endangering the European social model, it becomes doubtful whether the support of trade unions, as well as some sections of social democratic and centrist parties, will be sustained. Monetary union should also be understood in the broader context of the creation of a single European financial area—a core part of the Lisbon strategy. In a related area, the Commission has also taken a number of initiatives—some of them, as yet, more successful than others—to push Europe towards a more capital market-driven form of corporate governance. Whether or not this may lead to a backlash of social forces, for instance, as organized around parts of industrial capital that do not necessarily stand to benefit from this finance-led model, remains to be seen.

Finally, the current commitment to global free trade on the part of European transnational capital and of the EU is not necessarily irreversible. For now, there is still a considerable pro-free trade consensus, both among Europe's politicians and among the ranks of European transnational business. Hence, the ERT's clear support for the current Doha (development) Round of the World Trade Organization.[29] Yet, a profound global economic crisis may see the resurgence of European protectionism on the part of some sections of European industry. This partly depends on how successfully the new members can be absorbed and how their electorates react. It also depends on the global context, and in particular evolving transatlantic relations. The openness of European regionalism is premised first and foremost on the bonds of the transatlantic economy. Ongoing US unilateralism under the Bush administration may continue to undermine Atlantic unity. Moreover, spillover from the sphere of security and military relations may yet seriously affect the management of the global economy itself. A new era of protectionism may well be around the corner. In other words, whether the project of European integration will continue to be part and parcel of a neo-liberal globalization process is not decided in Europe alone, either on the part of its political elite or its business elite, but will depend also on the geopolitical and geo-economic developments within the global system.

Conclusion

The transnational struggle over European governance will continue. It will continue in the context of an unfolding legitimacy crisis of the European Union, putting the long-term viability of the

European neo-liberal governance regime in doubt. As its hegemonic appeal may start to unravel, this project may in fact aggravate rather than alleviate the EU's evolving legitimacy crisis. This is indeed likely sooner or later to produce a backlash calling for a much deeper form of social embeddedness. However, there is as yet no coherent and politically viable alternative to neo-liberalism, at least not on a pan-European level. What might occur instead is a prolonged crisis of European governance. Whatever the outcome, I have argued that it is to a large extent shaped by the agency of *transnational* social forces located in a changing structural context of the global political economy. For now these transnational forces have constructed a European socio-economic order that integrates the European region into the global economy and in line with the interests of global transnational capital. The future may yet witness an EU premised on a different social purpose, but that future is a history yet to be made.

Notes

1. For a critique from a critical IPE perspective of established integration theories, see Bastiaan Van Apeldoorn, Henk Overbeek, and Magnus Ryner, 'Theories of European Integration: A Critique', in Alan W. Cafruny and Magnus Ryner, eds, *A Ruined Fortress? Neoliberal Hegemony and Transformation in Europe* (Lanham, Md: Rowman & Littlefield, 2003), 17–45. For a good general introduction to the politics of the EU, see, e.g., Stephen George and Ian Bache, *Politics in the European Union* (Oxford: Oxford University Press, 2001).

2. Here I borrow the words of John Ruggie, 'International Regimes, Transactions and Change: Embedded Liberalism in the Postwar Economic Order', *International Organization* 36, 2 (1982): 379–416, esp. 382.

3. On multi-level governance, see Liesbet Hooghe and Gary Marks, *Multi-Level Governance and European Integration* (Lanham, Md: Rowman &

Littlefield, 2001).

4. For a more elaborate account of this perspective on European integration, see Bastiaan van Apeldoorn, *Transnational Capitalism and the Struggle over European Integration* (London: Routledge, 2002), ch. 1.

5. In spite of a downturn since 2000 (mainly due to the global recession), the world stock of FDI in 2002 still stood at US$7.1 trillion, that is, a tenfold increase since 1980. See United Nations Conference on Trade and Development, *World Investment Report 2003: FDI Policies for Development: National and International Perspectives* (New York and Geneva: United Nations, 2003), 23.

6. See Bastiaan van Apeldoorn, ed., 'Transnational Historical Materialism: The Amsterdam International Political Economy Project', *Journal of International Relations and Development* Special Issue, 7, 2 (2004).

7. In the words of co-founder Wisse Dekker, quoted in 'Industrialists Drive for a Stronger Europe. Interview with Prof. Dr. Wisse Dekker', *Europe 2000* 2, 2 (1990): 17–19.

8. For a complete list of current ERT members as well as all of ERT's publications, see <www.ert.be>.

9. For this interpretation of the nature and role of the ERT, see van Apeldoorn, *Transnational Capitalism*, esp. ch. 3; see also Bastiaan van Apeldoorn, 'Transnational Class Agency and European Governance: The Case of the European Round Table of Industrialists', *New Political Economy* 5, 2 (2000): 157–81; Otto Holman, 'Transnational Class Strategy and the New Europe', *International Journal of Political Economy* 22, 1 (1992): 2–22.

10. See especially Maria Green Cowles, 'Setting the Agenda for a New Europe: The ERT and EC 1992', *Journal of Common Market Studies* 33, 4 (1995): 501–26; Nicola Fielder, 'The Origins of the Single Market', in Volker Bornschier, ed., *State-building in Europe: The Revitalization of Western European Integration* (Cambridge: Cambridge University Press, 2000), 75–92; van Apeldoorn, *Transnational Capitalism*, 127–30.

11. Maria Green Cowles, 'The Transatlantic Business Dialogue: Transforming the New Transatlantic Dialogue', in Mark A. Pollack and Gregory Schaffer, eds, *Transatlantic Governance in the Global Economy* (Lanham, Md: Rowman & Littlefield, 2001).

12. On the ESF, see <www.fse-esf.org/>.

13. See Holman, 'Transnational Class Strategy', 3–22.

14. Former British Prime Minister Margaret Thatcher quoted in Alex Krause, *Inside the New Europe* (New York: HarperCollins, 1991).

15. See, e.g., George Ross, *Jacques Delors and European Integration* (Cambridge: Polity Press, 1995).

16. For an account of this shift and its underlying causes, see van Apeldoorn, *Transnational Capitalism*, 130–42.

17. See Lloy Wylie, 'EMU: A Neoliberal Construction', in Amy Verdun, ed., *The Euro: European Integration Theory and Economic and Monetary Union* (Lanham, Md: Rowman & Littlefield, 2002), 69–89.

18. ERT, *Benchmarking for Policy-Makers* (Brussels: European Round Table of Industrialists, 1996), 15. Many of the ideas contained in this report also are included in a Commission report published shortly after the ERT publication. See European Commission, *Benchmarking the Competitiveness of European Industry* (Brussels, Com [96] 436 final, 9 Oct. 1996).

19. The term 'hegemonic project' is taken from Bob Jessop, 'Accumulation Strategies, State Forms, and Hegemonic Projects', *Kapitalistate* 10, 11 (1983): 89–111.

20. Presidency Conclusions Lisbon European Council, 23 and 24 Mar. 2000, at: <http://ue.eu.int/en/Info/eurocouncil/index.htm>.

21. See ERT, *Will European Governments in Barcelona Keep Their Lisbon Promises?* (Brussels: European Round Table of Industrialists, 2002).

22. As the ERT stated in a letter to the Prime Minister of Ireland, then President of the EU, letter dated 17 Feb. 2004, published on-line at: <www.ert.be>.

23. On the EES, see also Stefan Tidow, 'The Emergence of a European Employment Policy as a Transnational Political Arena', in Henk Overbeek, ed., *The Political Economy of European Employment: European Integration and the Transnationalization of the (Un)employment Question* (London: Routledge, 2003), 77–98.

24. See Fritz W. Scharpf, *Governing in Europe: Effective and Democratic?* (Oxford: Oxford University Press, 1999).

25. Karl Polanyi, *The Great Transformation. The Political and Economic Origins of Our Time* (Boston: Beacon Press, 1957 [1944]), 132.

26. Cf. Scharpf, *Governing in Europe*.

27. See Otto Holman, 'Integrating Peripheral Europe: The Different Roads to "Security and Stability" in Southern and Central Europe', *Journal of International Relations and Development* 7, 2 (2004): 208–36.

28. It was not long after the fall of the Berlin Wall

that the ERT already emphatically pleaded for eastern enlargement. See European Round Table, *Reshaping Europe* (Brussels: ERT, 1991). Several reports specifically on enlargement followed in 1999 and 2001. Most recently the ERT has expressed its support for a continuing enlargement process to create a yet bigger single market.

See ERT, *ERT's Vision of a Bigger Single Market* (Brussels: ERT, 2004).

29. See ERT, 'European Business Leaders Stress Continued Support for Multilateral Trade Negotiations and Urge Progress', press release, available at: <www.ert.be>.

Suggested Readings

Bornschier, Volker, ed. *State-building in Europe: The Revitalization of Western European Integration.* Cambridge: Cambridge University Press, 2000.

Bieler, Andreas, and Adam David Morton, eds. *Social Forces in the Making of the New Europe.* Basingstoke: Palgrave, 2001.

Cafruny, Alan W., and Magnus Ryner, eds. *A Ruined Fortress? Neoliberal Hegemony and Transformation in Europe.* Lanham, Md: Rowman & Littlefield, 2003.

Overbeek, Henk, ed. *The Political Economy of European Employment: European Integration and the Transnationalization of the (Un)employment Question.* London: Routledge, 2003.

Rhodes, Martin, and Bastiaan van Apeldoorn. 'Capital Unbound? The Transformation of European Corporate Governance', *Journal of European Public Policy* 5, 3 (1998): 406–27.

Scharpf, Fritz W. *Governing in Europe: Effective and Democratic?* Oxford: Oxford University Press, 1999.

Van Apeldoorn, Bastiaan. *Transnational Capitalism and the Struggle over European Integration.* London: Routledge, 2002.

Websites

Gateway to the European Union: http://europa.eu.int/index_en.htm
The European Roundtable of Industrialists: www.ert.be/

History of European Integration, Leiden University: www.eu-history.leidenuniv.nl/

Chapter 22

The North American Free Trade Agreement

Tony Porter

In 1994, amid much controversy, Mexico, the US, and Canada joined together in the North American Free Trade Agreement (NAFTA), a dramatic change from their wary relationships in earlier periods. By 2004 NAFTA included 430 million people and US$11.4 trillion in economic activity, constituting a formidable economic bloc. This chapter will discuss, in turn, the reasons for NAFTA, its key features, its effects, and its significance.[1] Although NAFTA is often seen primarily as an economic arrangement, this chapter stresses, consistent with one of this book's overall themes, that politics has played a key role in its negotiation and implementation. I argue that political initiatives are needed in response to the failure of NAFTA to improve the well-being of citizens in its three member countries in the way that its supporters claimed it would.

Why Was NAFTA Created?

For much of the post-World War II period few people would have imagined that Canada, Mexico, and the US would sign an agreement such as NAFTA.[2] A growing Canadian nationalism, associated with fears about the negative consequences of Canada's increasing dependence on US investment and trade, reached a high point during the 1970s with new government initiatives, such as the Foreign Investment Review Agency, which sought to shape incoming investment in ways that were more beneficial to Canadians, and efforts to establish closer economic links with Europe and Japan. The Canada–US Free Trade Agreement (CUFTA), which came into effect in 1989, and NAFTA, which

went beyond that agreement by including Mexico and by adding new issues, marked a remarkable turn away from the earlier, more nationalist period.

In Mexico nationalism had even stronger roots than in Canada. Anger at foreign influence had helped fuel the Mexican Revolution of 1910 and had contributed to the strongly nationalist Constitution of 1917. In the post-World War II period Mexico had been a leading advocate of the right and duty of governments to build economic sovereignty through such measures as controls over cross-border capital and trade flows and the nationalization of important industries.[3] Government spending as a share of GNP increased from 13.1 per cent in 1970 to 39.6 per cent in 1976. In 1973 Mexico enacted two major laws to regulate foreign investment and the transfer of technology.[4] Even in 1982 the Mexican government's response to the debt crisis was to take over the privately owned banks, adding them to more than a thousand other state-run enterprises.[5] Yet by 1986 Mexico had signalled its commitment to free trade by joining the General Agreement on Tariffs and Trade, and then, in 1990 by initiating talks with the United States on NAFTA.

While the turn towards regional free trade could be traced through domestic political factors that were specific to each of the three countries, the simultaneous upsurge in enthusiasm for it in all three countries suggests that systemic factors were at work, and it is these that this chapter will stress.

One systemic factor, which is frequently cited, especially by supporters of NAFTA, is the worldwide expansion of markets and the opportunities and constraints this expansion presents to policy-makers. Opportunities reside in the capacity of market exchanges to generate growth through allowing people to specialize in the economic activities they can do best, in allowing capital to flow to the activity in which it is most productive as measured by the highest rate of return, and in forcing uncompetitive firms and individuals to modify their behaviour if they wish to survive, a point that also highlights the constraints imposed by markets. These considerations might suggest that NAFTA is simply an expression of the recognition by governments and citizens of these opportunities and constraints, perhaps stimulated by technological advances that have increased the fluidity of international trade and capital flows.

There are three clues, however, that such an explanation is inadequate. First, these countries' earlier policies, for most of the post-World War II period, were associated not with stagnation but rather with unprecedented growth—indeed, with higher growth rates than those that have followed NAFTA. Second, the advantages of market exchange cannot alone explain the regional character of NAFTA. Third, the timing of NAFTA is difficult to explain on the basis of an ongoing expansion of market exchanges alone.

An explanation that accounts for these issues must highlight the impact of historically specific international political structures on the three countries, and most particularly the changing fortunes of the United States as the hegemonic leader of the West during the Cold War. In the aftermath of World War II, the United States was unrivalled, in part due to the damage inflicted on its major competitors, including the division of Europe, as a result of the war and in part due to the superiority of its productive capacity. In constructing a post-war order with itself at the centre, the United States found it was willing and able to support the arrangements within which international markets flourished, including the trade and monetary regimes, as well as bilateral arrangements with key allies in which political and ideological allegiance was exchanged for relatively free access to US markets. These political arrangements were accompanied by a particular set of production arrangements: the rapidly expanding manufacturing industries upon which the United States had built its ascendancy were organized by US-based multinational corporations and spread to other countries through those corporations' branch plants and subsidiaries.

Canada's and Mexico's integration into these arrangements was, given their proximity to the Unites States, a particularly distinctive feature of their post-war political economies. US direct foreign investment poured into Canada in the 1950s and 1960s, dominating both the extraction of natural resources destined for the US market and manufacturing industries catering to the Canadian market. These economic ties were facilitated by close and informal political ties, symbolized by phrases such as 'special relationship' and 'quiet diplomacy': as a trusted ally Canada had privileged access for its diplomats in Washington, allowing it to manage tensions and promote integration in the economic relationship. Close economic ties also were associated with a strengthening of the Canadian state, allowing it to cushion its citizens from the negative effects of economic dependence through tariffs and social welfare spending. Similarly, Mexico experienced huge inflows of US capital during the 1960s, and, by the end of the 1970s, 70 per cent of direct foreign investment and foreign debt originated from the United States and 70 per cent of Mexican exports were to the United States.[6] Beginning in World War II, in which hundreds of thousands of Mexicans were recruited into the US army and brought into the country to replace mobilized US workers, migration from Mexico to the United States strengthened economic ties.[7] Like Canada, Mexico tried to offset the negative effects of its close economic relationship to the United States by strengthening state intervention in the Mexican economy.

During the 1970s these arrangements began to change. In response to US fears about its diminishing economic lead over the rest of the world, US indulgence began to be replaced by a more aggressive unilateralism, evident for instance in the United States ending its support of the Bretton

Woods monetary regime and its unexpected imposition of a new duty on imports in August 1971. There were direct negative effects for Canada and Mexico, such as increased trade frictions, but indirect effects as well. For instance, the United States took measures with regard to global finance that, due to the size and centrality of its financial markets, enhanced its own position but left smaller countries, including Canada and Mexico, vulnerable. This was evident in the early 1980s in the contribution to the Mexican crisis of high US interest rates, government deficits, and massive inflows of capital to the United States, and the related contribution of the overvalued US dollar to raising the Canadian dollar and making Canadian exports to the rest of the world less competitive.

Given the constraints facing Canada and Mexico during the 1980s the political balance in both countries began to shift towards support for free trade with the United States. Washington was in favour of negotiations on free trade as well, but this was far from a passive recognition of the mutual benefits that could be obtained by allowing markets freer play. The United States had key goals related to its competitive position in the world as a whole and it saw the creation of strong new rules with Canada and Mexico as part of this larger campaign. These included establishing extensive rights for investors, strong intellectual property provisions, and rules compelling Canada and Mexico to open their financial sectors to US firms. Improved access to Mexican and Canadian oil was a way to offset the negative effects on the United States of the high oil prices of the 1970s and to alleviate US anxiety about the long-run implications for its economic strength and political power of its dependence on oil imported from outside North America.[8] There were, in addition, goals specific to Mexico. The United States aimed to obtain a nearby low-wage location in which the labour costs of US corporations could be reduced (and their competitiveness thereby enhanced) by shifting parts of production to Mexico. Low-wage export-oriented manufacturing in Mexico was more likely to use US inputs and be controlled by US firms than would similar manufacturing in Asia. Allowing freer access for products made in Mexico to US markets was also seen as a way to stem the tide of illegal immigration from Mexico as the work done by these immigrants could be shifted back south of the border.

While economic arguments can be made for strengthening rules governing investment, intellectual property, and financial services, these arguments lack decisive empirical confirmation and tend to obscure the political factors contributing to the US enthusiasm for them. In each case such rules facilitated internationalization in areas in which the US saw itself as having a competitive advantage that would offset its diminished lead in manufacturing. This would be accomplished by establishing new rights that were traceable more directly to the political process of threat and negotiation than to a generalized recognition of their economic or ethical merits. In the case of investment many countries, including Canada and Mexico, had, at various times, argued that the state had a legitimate and useful role to play in seeking to offset the economic and organizational capacity of multinational corporations and that the state should monitor and regulate incoming investment in an effort to enhance benefits and minimize costs for their own citizens. Intellectual property rights establish a temporary monopoly in knowledge, and it is far from clear that the resulting benefits of the increased incentives to produce new knowledge outweigh the costs from the barriers to the free flow of knowledge that this monopoly creates.[9] The financial sector, because of its centrality to the economy as a whole and the intangible and interdependent nature of the transactions on which it is based, is filled with externalities—social costs and benefits not captured by the prices of particular transactions, which have traditionally been a reason for strong state regulation—and it is not clear that the efficiency gains from greater international competition in financial services outweigh the losses from a diminished capacity for regulation. These three areas were ones for which Washington had been campaigning in bilateral negotiations and at the

Uruguay Round of trade negotiations and their inclusion in NAFTA would enshrine previous efforts more comprehensively and boldly in a major trade agreement, as well as prodding the global negotiations with an implicit US threat to withdraw into a hemispheric alternative.

In short, NAFTA did not simply come about as a result of a sudden recognition by the three governments of the mutual benefits they would enjoy from a generalized expansion of market exchange. Each government came to the table influenced by constraints and power associated with their particular role in the evolving structure of the international political economy. For the United States, NAFTA was merely one element in a larger effort to promote, in a restructured form, the continuation of the leadership role it had played since World War II, and to promote the interests of powerful US firms. Canada and Mexico, by contrast, constrained by the restructuring of the international political economy, had to focus more narrowly on obtaining more secure access to the US market, and to substitute negotiated rules governing their relationship with the United States for previous informal understandings and independent deployment of their states' capacity.

Key Features of NAFTA

While the final text of NAFTA runs to more than 2,000 pages and is impossible to review comprehensively here, it is useful to discuss its most significant provisions. The agreement is striking in its blending of an unprecedented level of legal detail on international trade obligations with very weak collaborative institutions, as compared, for instance, to the European Union. Politically, this is consistent with the great disparities in power between the United States and the other two NAFTA partners.[10] The United States wanted to preserve its traditional independence from international institutions, and Canada and Mexico were wary of creating a set of US-dominated continental political arrangements that would go too far in weakening their decision-making autonomy.[11]

The NAFTA rules include greater market access in a variety of sectors, investment rules, intellectual property rights, dispute settlement, and side agreements on environmental and labour rights. These will be examined in turn, emphasizing especially the political significance of the Agreement's provisions.

On energy, NAFTA reproduced the controversial measures agreed between Canada and the United States in CUFTA—a prohibition, except under specified unusual circumstances such as national security reasons, on restrictions on energy trade, foreclosing export taxes and other measures that had been used in the past to support nationalist economic policies. The Mexican government did not go that far, but did agree to open up procurement by Pemex, its oil company, to foreign participation, although it retained control of Pemex in Mexican hands.

On automobiles, NAFTA included provisions for the elimination, over a 10-year period, of tariffs between the three countries for vehicles meeting requirements for substantial regional content. The regional content rules, which deviate from pure free trade principles, highlight the degree to which these provisions were designed to improve the prospects of firms engaged in North American-based auto manufacturing by allowing them to produce at a more efficient scale, shifting key manufacturing processes to low-wage locations in Mexico, while protecting these firms from competitors from other regions. NAFTA provisions on textiles and clothing, which also eliminated tariffs over 10 years for products that satisfied strict regional content rules, displayed a similar logic. Mexico agreed to phase out its rules that had been designed to get US auto firms to produce in Mexico rather than just export to it, such as restrictions on imports of new vehicles or requirements for certain levels of local content in auto parts.

On agriculture, the provisions called for the immediate elimination of tariffs on 57 per cent of US–Mexican agricultural trade and the phasing out of other tariffs and quotas over 15 years. While NAFTA supporters have argued that this has benefited

Mexico by providing Mexicans cheap US corn for tortillas and creating new export opportunities for Mexican growers of other vegetables, fruits, and flowers, critics have argued that the cheap US corn, which benefits from US government subsidies, has created severe dislocations for poor Mexican corn farmers, forcing many to abandon their land and move in search of work, threatening the unique genetic diversity and distinctive ecologically appropriate practices of traditional Mexican corn-growing.

One of the main goals of US and Canadian negotiators was to get access to the Mexican market for their financial firms. Mexico made important concessions while seeking to retain control over the pace at which foreign financial services firms were allowed to expand their activities in Mexico. However, the near-catastrophic Mexican financial crisis that began soon after NAFTA was signed (discussed below) led Mexican authorities, desperate to rescue their teetering financial system, to throw open their financial sector much more quickly than intended, including allowing 100 per cent foreign ownership of banks in 1999. In 1995 only 6.2 per cent of Mexican banks were majority foreign-owned, a number that had increased to 85 per cent in 2002.[12] US access to Canadian financial services markets had already been expanded under CUFTA, although this earlier agreement had had little effect given the traditional size, strength, and competitiveness of Canadian banks.[13]

The NAFTA investment rules in Chapter 11 have been the most controversial aspect of the Agreement. For NAFTA supporters they promote productive foreign investment by assuring investors that they will be protected from discriminatory or arbitrary treatment. For critics the ability of investors to seek judgements against states in secret, binding arbitration processes provides excessive rights to investors and undermines democracy, especially since some firms have used the process to claim that environmental regulations are a form of expropriation for which they should be compensated by governments. Chapter 11 provisions apply to both long-term direct foreign investments and portfolio investments (where there is no direct control by the investor of the enterprise) and prohibit interference, except under certain restricted circumstances, with investors' transfer of capital or profits across borders. Many governments have been reluctant to eliminate controls on portfolio investments because they are more likely to be short-term and speculative. Arguably these rules, by stimulating volatile inflows and outflows before adequate prudential financial regulations were established in Mexico, contributed to the 1994 peso crisis. Overall, the investment provisions of NAFTA went well beyond any other multilateral agreements, including those being negotiated through the GATT.

The intellectual property provisions are also striking. Governments are obligated to protect copyrights on computer programs, to prosecute decoding of encrypted satellite transmissions (such as television programs), and to protect new sound recordings for 50 years, new trademarks for 10 years, and new patents for 20 years. Such levels of protection, as noted previously, are controversial because critics see them as giving producers of new technologies excessive profits as a result of the monopoly they are given and because this protection is seen as interfering with the flow of knowledge to places where it is needed. Supporters argue that the increased profits are a justifiably necessary incentive if new knowledge is to be produced. Canada, in a political process that generated a great deal of domestic political conflict, reworked its patent regulations for pharmaceuticals to bring them in line with NAFTA obligations. A thriving Canadian generic drug industry had developed as a result of compulsory licensing provisions that were prohibited by NAFTA, despite the support of many Canadians for generic producers on public policy and economic grounds. Multinational pharmaceutical companies, however, were determined in NAFTA to overturn these provisions, in part due to the increased revenues that could be obtained from the Canadian market, and in part to eliminate Canada as a negative example for other countries. NAFTA's consolidation of previous efforts by the United States to strengthen Mexico's rules on intellectual property was also seen by the United States as an important precedent for future negotiations with developing countries.

Canada and Mexico hoped that NAFTA would reduce what they saw as the frequent arbitrary use by Washington of two types of trade measures, anti-dumping and countervailing duties, which are supposed to be used only when an exporter engages in predatory flooding of a foreign market with products sold below their real cost. CUFTA had put in place a dispute resolution mechanism that, in its first five years, had led to two-thirds of Canadian appeals of US decisions being successful, twice the success rate of appeals by other countries using the non-CUFTA procedures provided by the United States, perhaps creating a deterrent to the initiation of trade actions by the United States against its partners. While the reduced rate of US trade actions against its NAFTA partners relative to trade actions against other countries could be taken as evidence that this deterrent was at work with the NAFTA panel mechanism, it may also be due to other factors, such as the contrasts between robust North American growth and the East Asian crisis in the late 1990s.[14] Indeed, a World Bank study found that the overall number of trade actions taken by the United States against its NAFTA partners does not appear to have been affected by NAFTA.[15] Overall the process 'yields leeway to the reality of the Parties' power asymmetry' by its reliance on self-help in enforcement, and by the fact that it is restricted to reviews of the implementation of each country's own laws.[16] This deficiency would become glaringly apparent in the softwood lumber dispute in which, despite favourable panel decisions, Canada was successfully pressured by threats from Washington to impose restrictions on its exports to the United States and then was subjected to punitive US duties.

Faced with strong concerns on the part of US citizens that NAFTA would allow US firms to avoid US standards by moving production to a lightly regulated location in Mexico, and then to freely export manufactured goods back into the United States, US President Bill Clinton decided to negotiate two side accords, one on environmental standards and one on labour standards. These established a Commission for Environmental Co-operation and a Commission for Labour Co-operation, each with a council composed of the relevant ministers from the respective countries, who would meet once a year, and a secretariat, the members of which are expected to remain independent of their governments and which is responsible for ongoing administrative and technical support for the commission. The Commission for Environmental Co-operation, reflecting the greater participation of non-governmental organizations in its negotiation, has in addition a 15-member Joint Public Advisory Committee, which can be composed of scientific experts or others active on environmental issues.[17] The labour agreement establishes national administrative offices in each country that play an important role in receiving and initially considering complaints lodged by either individuals or NGOs.

The agreements both focus on monitoring and enforcing national standards rather than establishing and enforcing common international standards. There are, however, general statements regarding the desirability of standards, the making of joint recommendations, and in the case of the labour agreement all of the parties commit themselves to promoting 10 'labour principles', including, for example, the right to organize and to be compensated for injury. Most complaints are envisioned as being resolved by consultation and arbitration without the use of sanctions. Opinion was sharply divided on the significance of the environmental and labour side agreements. Some felt they were precedent-setting in being the first significant attempt to integrate environmental and labour issues into a trade agreement. Others, especially the labour movement, dismissed them as unenforceable window-dressing.

The provisions of NAFTA, in sum, were very significant, not just because three countries that might otherwise not have been expected to conclude a trade agreement did so, but also because the commitments went well beyond other trade agreements in the range of activities covered and in the strictness of the procedures for enforcement. The US goals concerning investment, intellectual property rights, and financial services were met or exceeded. Canada and Mexico received improved access to the US market for a variety of products. However, the letter of trade agreements, as with any law, is sometimes not as important as their implementation and broader significance. We turn to assess these in the next section.

The Effects and Significance of NAFTA

Anyone seeking to evaluate NAFTA faces serious challenges both in separating the economic effects of unrelated factors and in developing criteria for success that are not contested. Supporters and opponents of NAFTA often selectively use some facts and ignore others in making their arguments. Nevertheless, it is useful to review some of the main points of debate.

One obvious effect of NAFTA has been to increase trade and direct investment among the three partners. Between 1993 and 2000, trade in the NAFTA region grew annually at 12.5 per cent, higher than the 8 per cent annual growth rate of world trade, and foreign direct investment flows between the NAFTA partners tripled between the 1989–94 period and the 1995–2000 period.[18]Some NAFTA supporters assume this must prove that NAFTA was beneficial, because they believe that free trade and investment always lead to economic growth.[19] Most people, however, rather than assuming that growth in trade and investment is an end in itself or will automatically raise living standards, want some evidence that the well-being of citizens has improved.

For most people, a key factor in their well-being is the number and quality of jobs available. NAFTA supporters in all three countries argued that it would have a major positive impact on employment through the exports it would generate. However, it is misleading only to count jobs created from exports, as for instance the US President did in his 1997 report to Congress on NAFTA, without subtracting jobs lost from imports. The US Department of Labor's NAFTA–Transitional Adjustment Assistance Program had recorded, by the end of 2001, 415,371 workers certified to

receive adjustment benefits, a rough estimate of US job losses.[20] The Economic Policy Institute has considered the impact of both imports and exports on US employment and has estimated that NAFTA resulted in a loss of 879,280 US jobs between 1993 and 2002.[21] Others have been sceptical of the ability of this method of separating the effect of NAFTA on US jobs from other factors, such as technological change, cycles of expansion and recession, or world trade. During the late 1990s, a vigorous expansion added millions of jobs to the US economy, suggesting at a minimum that NAFTA did not have the disastrous effect on jobs that US presidential candidate Ross Perot had ominously labelled the 'great sucking sound', even if more than two million jobs were subsequently lost between 2001 and 2004.[22] A Carnegie Foundation study concludes that the effect of NAFTA on US unemployment was probably minimal relative to other factors shaping the huge US economy.[23]

Supporters of NAFTA claimed that it would lead to an expansion of higher-quality jobs as the United States specialized in the high-value-added industries in which it had comparative advantage. Critics suggested instead that there would be downward pressure on the quality of jobs as US workers were forced to compete with Mexican workers. A 2004 report from CIBC World Markets found a dramatic decline in US job quality between 2001 and 2004 as high-pay jobs were replaced by low-pay ones and permanent jobs by temporary ones,[24] a development that could be taken as lending support to the critics' contentions. Critics point also to the toll taken on individuals of having their factory threaten to move to Mexico, as has been the case with a large number of unionized firms, or actually close down. A post-NAFTA study by Bronfenbrenner found that half of US firms facing unionization drives countered with the threat to relocate to Mexico, and when forced to negotiate with a union, 15 per cent actually did close all or part of a plant (three times the rate before NAFTA), confirming the fears of NAFTA critics.[25] Combined with similar problems in Canada and the anti-union environment in the *maquiladora* region in Mexico, the NAFTA-related weakness of North

American labour plays an important part in the widening gap between productivity and wages and in growing inequality in all three countries,[26] as fewer workers produce more without benefiting from that improved effort.

For Canada, like the United States, separating non-trade factors, such as the decline in the value of the Canadian dollar over the 1990s, from NAFTA is difficult. One plausible assessment is that Canada experienced significant employment difficulties in the first decade after CUFTA and then modest improvements.[27] A growing productivity gap with the US—from 17 per cent in 1995 to 33 per cent in 2001—and persistently higher unemployment rates in Canada as compared to the United States, however, might suggest that Canada's relative position in the continent had been weakened rather than strengthened by NAFTA, contrary to what liberal economic theory had predicted.[28]

Of the three countries, Mexico's experience in the post-NAFTA period was the most negative: the real minimum wage lost over 23 per cent of its value between 1993 and 1999 and labour income as a share of GDP fell from over 40 per cent in the 1980s to 18.7 per cent in 2000, while profits as a share of gdp jumped from 31 per cent to 68 per cent over the same period. Employment fell drastically after the peso crisis, grew strongly for several years, but then stagnated.[29] In the decade after NAFTA's signing, annual per capita growth in Mexico averaged 1 per cent, as compared to 3.2 per cent from 1948 to 1973, or to the South Korean growth over the same period of 4.3 per cent, despite the East Asian crisis.[30] There is, however, sharp disagreement about the relationship of this performance to NAFTA. Some argue that Mexico's problems were due to the 1994 peso crisis and that NAFTA was important in helping Mexico recover from that crisis. Yet, as noted above, NAFTA should also share some blame for the peso crisis, since it encouraged volatile cross-border flows of capital without ensuring that the prudential regulations and other policy tools needed to avoid and manage financial crises were in place.[31]

A major problem in Mexico has been massive agricultural unemployment created by huge NAFTA-related inflows of heavily subsidized corn and other US agricultural products, destroying an estimated 1.5 million livelihoods as prices paid to Mexican farmers dropped by 70 per cent.[32] (Ironically, this has occurred in the land where corn was first domesticated several thousand years ago.) The connection of many Mexican workers to their land was further weakened by the replacement of redistributive communal land-holding policies dating back to the Mexican Revolution with private landownership as part of the neo-liberal economic restructuring with which NAFTA was associated.

Liberal economic theory might lead one to expect that these workers have been absorbed into rapidly expanding NAFTA-related export-oriented employment. Unfortunately, such increases in employment did not keep pace with job losses. Employment generated in the *maquiladora* region failed to lead to linkages or lasting transformations of the Mexican economy more generally. This failure was due in part to the degree to which the foreign firms manufacturing in Mexico were treating their operations as merely one dispensable link in a processing chain starting and ending elsewhere and in part due to the Mexican government not investing sufficiently in infrastructure, legal reform, or the upgrading of the skills of their population through education. As a Federal Reserve economist noted, 'Mexico's old role as a low-skill, low-wage producer is now played by other countries, and Mexico has been slow to move on to the next step in the production process.'[33] The inability of poorly represented Mexican workers to demand their share of the wealth generated by productivity increases further inhibited their ability to upgrade their own human capital. An estimated half-million manufacturing jobs were lost from Mexico to lower-wage countries from 2000 to 2003, including, for instance, 1,200 jobs at a $250 million Mitsubishi computer monitor plant, created in 1998 and closed a few years later when it could not compete with flat-screen monitors produced in East Asia.[34] China has been particularly worrisome for Mexico, after the former increased its connection with the US market by joining the World Trade Organization in 2001.

Contrary to the expectations of its supporters, NAFTA did not reduce immigration to the United States by creating employment in Mexico. On the contrary, the number of Mexican-born residents in the United States increased by more than 80 per cent between 1990 and 2000, and the pace of illegal border crossings grew despite huge American investment in border controls, with the greater danger of the crossings reflected in the 1,600 deaths of migrants between 1999 and 2004.[35] A decade after NAFTA's launch it was estimated that one in five Mexicans lived in the United States.[36]

In assessing NAFTA's performance it is also important not to rely only on aggregate figures that obscure important differences. In all three countries social inequality has increased significantly since NAFTA and the growth of a relatively small number of very high incomes at the upper levels can hide growing poverty and distress among the population more generally. The differences across industries are also an important part of the NAFTA story. One study found substantial variation across the 39 sectors it examined. For instance, the experience of electronics has been positive while the experience of apparel and textiles has been negative.[37] A study of NAFTA lobbying patterns similarly found that its strongest supporters were in those industries for which economies of scale and high amounts of intra-firm trade would allow firms to reap considerable competitive advantages from being able to operate on a continental basis.[38]

NAFTA's effects on the environment have been a major concern. While some of these effects have been positive they appear to be outweighed by the negative effects. The positive environmental effects are primarily related to the North American Agreement on Environmental Co-operation (NAAEC), the environmental side agreement, and the Commission for Environmental Co-operation (CEC), which it created. NAFTA itself is path-breaking in the way in which it went beyond previous trade agreements in acknowledging and seeking to address institutionally the links between trade and environment. The structure of the institutions, in which the Secretariat and the Joint Policy Advisory Committee have been able to operate with substantial autonomy from the member states and with a significant degree of participation from non-state actors, has contributed to the strengthening of a continent-wide environmental policy network. The NAAEC can take credit for some important accomplishments, including its initiation of a yearly, high-profile ranking of polluting jurisdictions and firms in its *Taking Stock* reports; its contribution to Mexico's adoption of new procedures for tracking the emissions by firms of pollutants; agreements to restrict the use of persistent and toxic pollutants, including getting Mexico to agree to phase out the use of DDT, and actions taken to protect habitats of migratory birds.[39] The North American Development Bank, which was supposed to play a large role in cleaning up severe environmental problems around the US–Mexican border, has played a disappointingly small role, with only $15 million in funding of its $3 billion total lending capacity dispersed by 2001.[40]

Critics of NAFTA feared that it would lead Mexico to become a pollution haven for firms wishing to escape environmental regulation in the United States and Canada, and that the ability of these firms to export back into the United States and Canada would put downward pressure on those countries' regulatory standards. One study found no evidence that dirtier industries shifted to Mexico in higher proportions than clean industries, a shift one might expect if these fears were realized.[41] However, this may be because some of the dirtier industries, including steel and chemicals, are highly capital-intensive, with massive fixed investments in plants and infrastructure, and are not easily moved, and it is possible that the cleaner industries may still produce serious pollution problems. The environmental degradation of the *maquiladora* area and the growth of infection and cancers have been horrifying.[42] Studies have estimated that in 1997 only 12 per cent of 8 million tons of hazardous wastes generated in that area were treated and that the average annual cost in Mexico of environmental damage of US$36 billion exceeds the growth from trade and the economy as a whole.[43] This suggests that many of the measurements of the benefits of economic growth from NAFTA are overstated because they do not take into account the associated environmental and social costs.

The CEC's citizen submission process by 2004 had involved 43 complaints, of which nine resulted in 'factual records' (CEC reports), 10 remained active, two were dropped because they were being pursued elsewhere, and 22 were rejected or dropped because they did not, in the CEC's judgement, meet its criteria.[44] The procedure is innovative in allowing citizens to engage in whistle-blowing and in providing a means of spotlighting violations, but the CEC has been careful to restrict the scope of the process, and its outcomes remain very modest relative to the severity of the environmental problems in the continent.

One of the most troubling environmental effects of NAFTA has been the use of the Chapter 11 investor dispute mechanism by firms seeking compensation from governments for restrictions imposed on them by environmental regulations. Critics have pointed to the similarity between this mechanism and an earlier failed proposal of the right wing of the Republican Party to have the US government provide such compensation to US firms.[45] The Chapter 11 mechanism has raised concerns in general because its deliberations are secret, and it is not clear that its panellists, many of whom have been trade lawyers, are as independent from industry as they should be. There are also no mechanisms for ensuring that environmental expertise will be brought to bear in the judgements made by the panel. Sometimes critics overstate the dangers. For instance, the panels have rejected some of the claims of the firms, and governments may be able to avoid future complaints by being more careful to devise regulations that are strong but not vulnerable to charges that they are really designed to discriminate against foreign firms and support domestic firms, a problem associated with the Canadian government's effort to prohibit the export of toxic PCBs from Canada by a US-owned firm while allowing similar activities by a

Canadian-owned firm. The NAFTA governments also agreed in 2001 to narrow somewhat the conditions under which investors can claim damages.[46]

Nevertheless, serious concerns remain. The award to Metalclad of $16 million when it was not allowed to open a toxic chemical processing operation in Mexico, for example, is portrayed in superficial accounts as a case in which a local authority acted arbitrarily to undermine a commitment made by the Mexican government to Metalclad, and thus a case of Chapter 11 working as it should. More careful and detailed examination reveals, however, that Metalclad must have been aware of a history of intense local opposition to the illegal burial at the dump site in question of 20,000 tons of toxic materials, which resulted in extensive contamination of the local environment and suspected links with birth defects; that Metalclad made questionable payments to government officials in its efforts to get permission to operate; and that it would seem reasonable that those in the neighbourhood of the prospective toxic processing operation should have some say over whether it should be permitted to proceed.[47] All this suggests that the critics are correct in seeing Chapter 11 as providing for a secret process that is biased towards giving foreign firms the ability to pre-empt local democratic rights.

The North American Agreement on Labor Co-operation, the labour side agreement, has been less effective than the environmental side agreement. As of 2004, 28 submissions had been filed, 13 of which led to ministerial consultations. Supporters note dramatically increased Mexican spending on the enforcement of labour standards since NAFTA.[48] The Commission has had some modest positive impact in publicizing complaints about violations, promoting cross-border co-operation among labour rights advocates, and affecting the treatment of some of the workers concerned.[49] In a 2001 article Compa lists nine cases brought to the Commission that resulted in concrete, positive outcomes for labour.[50]

A development that starkly reveals the importance of politics for NAFTA is the fallout from the terrorist attacks of 11 September 2001. The immediate response of the US government was to sharply restrict entry at its land borders with its NAFTA partners, a clear reminder of the secondary importance to the United States of the economic and legal provisions of NAFTA when its national security interests were threatened. Trucks were lined up for miles at the Canada–US border, and auto firms that had retooled their production processes to be dependent on just-in-time cross-border parts delivery were losing Cdn$1 million to $1.5 million per hour.[51] While this problem was subsequently addressed and new technologies were explored for facilitating the fast but secure cross-border transit of goods (the 'smart border'),[52] it provoked discussions in both Mexico and Canada of how best to respond to US anxieties about the security of its own and North America's borders. Although the Mexican government and some prominent Canadian commentators and politicians called for using this as an occasion to further strengthen North American integration,[53] the differences between the government of US President George W. Bush and the Mexican and Canadian governments over the conduct of the war against terrorism, especially evident in the latter two countries' lack of support for the invasion of Iraq, make such integration appear unlikely. Interestingly, despite NAFTA and many previous decades of heavy inflows of US cultural influences into Canada, survey research revealed that Canadian and American values in the new millennium were diverging rather than converging, suggesting that moves towards closer political integration would meet resistance.[54]

The stalling of the Free Trade Area of the Americas negotiations, which once had seemed like a logical and inexorable outgrowth of the successful negotiation of NAFTA, provides a further indication of the political problems that have developed in the years since the launch of NAFTA. Initiated in 1994, the FTAA languished in the late 1990s when US Presidents Clinton and Bush were denied fast-track negotiating authority by a US Congress concerned about the political fallout from free trade dislocations. Fast track had restricted congressional involvement to acceptance or rejection of any trade deal negotiated by the executive branch and without it US trading partners were reluctant to negotiate because they feared Congress would make modifications in the legislation implementing the agreement. Bush was able to obtain fast-track authority, renamed 'Trade Promotion Authority', in 2002, but only a small number of aggressive actions to protect US domestic economic interests, such as protection and financial support for steel and agriculture, were undertaken. With the Bush administration distracted from the FTAA by the war on terror and displaying aggressively unilateralist and protectionist economic policies, it is not surprising that by 2004 the FTAA negotiations had lost their momentum, with expectations reduced to, at most, an 'FTAA lite' in which the most important issues would be set aside and a series of bilateral agreements would be made between the United States and other countries, the first of which was Chile. Indeed, it was not clear that the negotiators would be successful in concluding any FTAA agreement at all.

Conclusion

The political character of NAFTA is evident in both the process leading to its negotiation and in its effects and evolution since it was established. The provisions of most concern to important interests in the United States and to the long-range strategy of the US government—the investment, intellectual property rights, and financial services provisions—are the ones that were most innovatively and strongly developed. The dispute resolution mechanism for investment, with the role it permits for private parties, is unprecedented in addressing this new issue and in its strengthening of international legal constraints on sovereignty. The dispute resolution mechanism for other matters, by contrast, remains subject to power politics and the mechanisms in the labour and environmental agreements are especially weak.

NAFTA helps consolidate a strongly market-oriented regime for North America, weakening pre-existing national political instruments that had been developed to offset the negative effects of markets, without developing alternative international instruments. In contrast to the European

Union, for instance, where a great deal of effort has been devoted to developing an institutional solution to regional inequality and exchange rate problems, such issues in North America are dealt with by individual government initiatives on an ad hoc basis. This market-oriented regime poses more challenges for Canada and Mexico than for the United States, in part because of the latter's size and in part because it matches more closely the traditional relationship between state and market in the United States than it does in the other countries. Mexico's failure to translate NAFTA-related rapid export growth of the mid-1990s into long-range development, its vulnerability to lower-wage juris-

dictions such as China, and the growing inequality across the continent all reinforce the importance of government initiatives in promoting the capacities of their citizens, in fostering innovation, in helping those harmed by trade-related dislocations, and in ensuring that the costs and benefits of trade are fairly distributed. Without such initiatives the negative effects of trade agreements can outweigh the benefits, and political opposition will prevent further trade agreements. In short, NAFTA, as with other issues in international political economy, reveals the intensely political nature of the evolving international economy.

Notes

1. Research assistance by Diana Cucuz is gratefully acknowledged.
2. Stephanie R. Golob, 'Beyond the Policy Frontier: Canada, Mexico and the Ideological Origins of NAFTA', *World Politics* 55, 3, (Apr. 2003): 361–98.
3. Mexico originated the initiative that culminated in the Charter of the Economic Rights and Duties of States, approved by the UN General Assembly in 1974. Bernardo Sepúlveda Amor, 'International Law and National Sovereignty: The NAFTA and the Claims of Mexico Jurisdiction', *Houston Journal of International Law* 19 (1997): 565–93, esp. 568.
4. Richard S. Weinert, 'Foreign Capital in Mexico', in Susan Kaufman Purcell, ed., *Mexico–United States Relations,* Proceedings of the Academy of Political Science, 34, 1 (New York, 1981), 115–24.
5. The figures in this and the previous sentence are from George W. Grayson, *The North American Free Trade Agreement: Regional Community and the New World Order* (Lanham Md: University Press of America, 1995), 36.
6. Maria Del Rosario Green, 'Mexico's Economic Dependence', in Purcell, ed., *Mexico–United States Relations,* 104–14, esp. 110.
7. See George W. Grayson, *The United States and*

Mexico: Patterns of Influence (New York: Praegar, 1984), 27–31. Mexico's criticisms of excessive US influence in Latin America were tolerated by the United States, which was grateful for its anti-communism, evident for instance in Mexico's support of the US blockade during the Cuban Missile Crisis.
8. Stephen J. Randall, 'NAFTA in Transition: The United States and Mexico', *Canadian Review of American Studies* 27, 3 (1997): 1–18; Paul Ciccantell, 'NAFTA and the Reconstruction of US Hegemony: The Raw Materials Foundations of Economic Competitiveness', *Canadian Journal of Sociology* 26, 1 (2001): 57–87.
9. Bhagwati, a leading economist in favour of free trade, has commented with regard to intellectual property: 'As is now widely conceded among economists . . . there is no presumption of mutual gain, world welfare itself may be reduced by any or more IP protection, and there is little empirical support for the view that "inadequate" IP protection impedes the creation of new technical knowledge significantly.' Jagdish Bhagwati, 'Regionalism versus Multilateralism', *World Economy* 15, 5 (September 1992): 553.
10. Frederick M. Abbott, 'NAFTA and the Legalization of World Politics: A Case Study', *International*

Organization 54, 3 (2000): 519–47.

11. Although many critics feel that NAFTA went too far and in effect created a new constitution for the rights of foreign corporations. See, for instance, Stephen Clarkson, 'Canada's Secret Constitution: NAFTA, WTO and the End of Sovereignty?' (Ottawa: Canadian Centre for Policy Alternatives, Oct. 2002). Available at: <www.policyalternatives.ca>.

12. *OECD Report on Mexico* (Paris: OECD, 2002), 94, 112; Paul Day, 'And Now?', *Business Mexico* (Sept. 2001): 30.

13. For a useful summary of NAFTA provisions, from which this summary has drawn, see Gary Clyde Hufbauer and Jeffrey J. Schott, *NAFTA: An Assessment,* rev. edn (Washington: Institute for International Economics, 1993). On the financial services provisions, see Tony Porter, 'NAFTA, North American Financial Integration, and Regulatory Cooperation in Banking and Securities', in Geoffrey Underhill, ed., *Making Markets: The New World Order in International Finance* (Basingstoke: Macmillan, 1997), 174–92.

14. Alan M. Rugman and Andrew D.M. Anderson, 'NAFTA and the Dispute Settlement Mechanisms: A Transaction Costs Approach', *Journal of World Trade* 20, 7 (Nov. 1997): 935–50, esp. 942; Gilbert Gagné, 'North American Free Trade, Canada and US Trade Remedies: An Assessment after Ten Years', *World Economy* 23, 1 (Jan. 2000): 77–91

15. Daniel Lederman, William F. Maloney, and Luis Servén, 'Lessons from NAFTA for Latin American and Caribbean (LAC) Countries: A Summary of Research Findings', at: <www.worldbank.org>.

16. Michael Reisman and Mark Wiedman, 'Contextual Imperatives of Dispute Resolution Mechanisms', *Journal of World Trade* 29, 3 (June 1995): 34.

17. NAFTA also set up the Border Environmental Co-operation Commission, designed to address problems along the US–Mexico border, and the North American Development Bank, designed to fund environmental infrastructure and cleanup projects. For a critical account, see Andrew Wheat, 'Troubled NAFTA Waters', *Multinational Monitor* (Apr. 1996): 23–5.

18. Gary Clyde Hufbauer and Gustavo Vega-Cánovas, 'Whither NAFTA: A Common Frontier?', in Peter Andreas and Thomas J. Biersteker, eds, *The Rebordering of North America: Integration and Exclusion in a New Security Context* (New York: Routledge, 2003): 128–52, esp. 130–1.

19. For instance, a 10-year assessment by the partners' three trade ministers has a full page of data about trade and investment but only a sentence on standards of living: 'lower tariffs mean that families pay less for the products they buy and they have a greater selection of goods and services, which increases their standards of living.' NAFTA: *A Decade of Strengthening a Dynamic Relationship,* at: <www.dfait-maeci.gc.ca/nafta-alena/nafta10-en.asp>.

20. The number may underestimate total losses because of the stringency of the criteria for receiving such assistance and because they do not account for jobs lost because of imports, but they may also overestimate losses because not all certified workers actually lose their jobs. M. Angeles Villareal, *Industry Trade Effects Related to NAFTA,* Report for Congress (Washington: Congressional Research Service, 3 Feb. 2003), Table 7, 15. See also Earl H. Fry and Jared Bybee, 'NAFTA 2002: A Cost/Benefit Analysis for the United States, Canada and Mexico', *Canadian–American Public Policy* 49 (Jan. 2002): 1. The NAFTA adjustment assistance program was folded into a more general one in which it is not possible to distinguish job loss specific to NAFTA, and thus more recent figures are not available.

21. Robert E. Scott, 'The High Price of "Free Trade": NAFTA's Failure Has Cost the United States Jobs Across the Nation', Economic Policy Institute Briefing Paper 147, 17 Nov. 2003.

22. Bureau of Labor Statistics, total non-farm employment data at stats.bls.gov, Series CES0000000001.

23. John J. Audley, Demetrios G. Papademetriou, Sandra Polaski, and Scott Vaughan, *NAFTA's Promise and Reality: Lessons from Mexico for the Hemisphere* (New York: Carnegie Endowment for

International Peace, 2003), available at: <www.ceip.org/pubs>.

24. Reported in Terry Weber, 'US Market Sees Major Decline in Job Quality', *Globe and Mail*, 22 June 2004, B11.

25. Kate Bronfenbrenner, 'We'll Close! Plant Closings, Plant Closing Threats, Union Organizing, and NAFTA', *Multinational Monitor* (Mar. 1997): 8. A more recent and more extensive study confirmed these conclusions: Kate Bronfenbrenner, 'Uneasy Terrain: The Impact of Capital Mobility on Workers, Wages and Union Organizing', Report Submitted to the US Trade Deficit Review Commission, 6 Sept. 2000. Available at: <www.ustdrc.gov/research/research .html>.

26. Audley et al., *NAFTA's Promise and Reality*.

27. Ibid.

28. Standing Committee on Foreign Affairs and International Trade, *Partners in North America: Advancing Canada's Relations with the United States and Mexico* (Ottawa: House of Commons, 2002).

29. Miguel D. Ramirez, 'Mexico Under NAFTA: A Critical Assessment', *Quarterly Review of Economics and Finance* 43 (2003): 863–92.

30. Joseph E. Stiglitz, 'The Broken Promise of NAFTA', *New York Times*, 6 Jan. 2004, A23.

31. Porter, 'NAFTA, North American Financial Integration, and Regulatory Cooperation'.

32. 'Ten Year Track Record of the North American Free Trade Agreement: The Mexican Economy, Agriculture and Environment', Public Citizen NAFTA at Ten Series, at: <www.citizen.org/docu-ments/NAFTA_10_mexico.pdf>.

33. William C. Gruben, 'Americas: Mexico Is Frittering Away Its NAFTA Gains', *Wall Street Journal*, 19 Dec. 2003, A15; John Authers and Sara Silver, 'Free Trade with Canada and the US Did Not Spur Wider Economic Reform, and Limited Progress Toward Creating Prosperity Is in Danger of Stalling', *Financial Times,* 1 July 2003, 19. For a more detailed analysis, see Daniel Lederman and William F. Maloney, 'Innovation in Mexico: NAFTA Is Not Enough', part of the World Bank 'Lessons from NAFTA' research project, available at: <www.worldbank.org>.

34. Chris Kraul, 'NAFTA 10 Years Later: After Initial Boom Mexico's Economy Goes Bust', *Los Angeles Times*, 2 Jan. 2004, 1.

35. Jeff Faux, 'How NAFTA Failed Mexico: Immigration Is Not a Development Policy', *American Prospect* 14, 7 (3 July 2003), at: <www.prospect.org>. In NAFTA's first decade the budget of the US Immigration and Naturalization Service more than tripled and more INS agents were authorized to carry guns than were those of any other federal law enforcement agency. See Peter Andreas, 'A Tale of Two Borders: The US–Canada and US–Mexico Lines after 9-11', in Andreas and Biersteker, eds, *The Rebordering of North America*, 1–24.

36. Stephen Handelman, 'Rough Trade for North America', *Time* (Canadian edn) 162, 17 (27 Oct. 2003): 38.

37. Raúl Hinojosa-Ojeda and Robert K. McCleery, 'NAFTA as Metaphor: The Search for Regional and Global Lessons for the United States', in Edward J. Chambers and Peter H. Smith, eds, *NAFTA in the New Millennium* (San Diego and Edmonton: Center for US–Mexican Studies and University of Alberta Press, 2002), 61–82.

38. Kerry A. Chase, 'Economic Interests and Regional Trading Agreements: The Case of NAFTA', *International Organization* 57 (Winter 2003) 137–74.

39. See David L. Markell and John H. Knox, eds, *Greening NAFTA: The North American Commission for Environmental Cooperation* (Stanford, Calif.: Stanford University Press, 2003).

40. 'Ten Year Track Record'.

41. Claudia Schatan, 'The Environmental Impact of Mexican Manufacturing Exports Under NAFTA', in Markell and Knox, eds, *Greening NAFTA*, 133–51.

42. Letta Tayler, 'A Free Trade Boom or an Environmental Bust? NAFTA Missteps Harm Mexico Critics Say', *Newsday,* 29 Dec. 2003, A12.

43. 'Ten Year Track Record'; Audley et al., *NAFTA's Promise and Reality*, 6.

44. Calculated from list at <www.cec.org/citizen/status/index.cfm>.

45. The Republican initiative, pursued in the mid-

1990s, was the 'Contract with America'. See John D. Echeverria, 'The Real Contract on America', *Environmental Forum* (July–Aug. 2003): 28–9, 31.

46. Edward Alden, 'NAFTA Deal Changed to Curb Companies', *Financial Times*, 1 Aug. 2001, 3.

47. Fernando Bejarano González, 'Investment, Sovereignty, and the Environment: The Metalclad Case and NAFTA's Chapter 11', in Timothy A. Wise, Hilda Salazar, and Laura Carlsen, eds, *Confronting Globalization: Economic Integration and Popular Resistance in Mexico* (Bloomfield, Conn.: Kumarian Press, 2003), 17–41.

48. US President Bill Clinton, *Study on the Operation and Effects of the North American Free Trade Agreement*, Report to Congress, July 1997. Available at: <www.ustr.gov>.

49. Roy J. Adams and Parbudyal Singh, 'Early Experience with NAFTA's Labour Side Accord', *Comparative Labor Law Journal* 18, 2 (Winter 1997): 161–81. Information on the side accords is available from the commissions' Web sites, at: <www.cec.org> and <www.naalc.org>.

50. Lance Compa, 'NAFTA's Labor Side Agreement and International Labor Solidarity', *Antipode* 33, 1 (July 2001): 451–67.

51. Andreas, 'A Tale of Two Borders', 10.

52. John R. Shuman, 'Preserving and Expanding Our Important NAFTA Trading Relationship in Light of September 11', *Business Credit* 104, 8 (Sept. 2002): 53–61.

53. See, for instance, Thomas J. Courchene, 'FTA at 15, NAFTA at 10: A Canadian Perspective on North American Integration', *North American Journal of Economics and Finance* 14 (2003): 263–85; Wendy Dobson, 'Shaping the Future of the North American Economic Space: A Framework for Action', C.D. Howe Institute Commentary, *The Border Papers* 162 (Apr. 2002).

54. Michael Adams, *Fire and Ice: The United States, Canada and the Myth of Converging Values* (Toronto: Penguin, 2003).

Suggested Readings

Audley, John J., Demetrios G. Papademetriou, Sandra Polaski, and Scott Vaughan. NAFTA's *Promise and Reality: Lessons from Mexico for the Hemisphere.* New York: Carnegie Endowment for International Peace, 2003. Available at: <www.ceip.org/pubs>.

Chambers, Edward J., and Peter H. Smith. *NAFTA in the New Millennium.* San Diego and Edmonton: Center for US–Mexican Studies and University of Alberta Press, 2002.

Kirton, John J., and Virginia Maclaren. *Linking Trade, Environment and Social Cohesion: NAFTA Experiences, Global Challenges.* Aldershot: Ashgate, 2002.

'Happily Ever NAFTA?', a debate pitting critics John Cavanagh and Sarah Anderson against NAFTA negotiators Jaime Serra and J. Enrique Espinosa, in *Foreign Policy* 132 (Sept.– Oct. 2002): 58–65.

Web Sites

Free Trade Area of the Americas: www.ftaa-alca.org

NAFTA, Chapter 11 cases: www.naftalaw.org

NAFTA Secretariat: www.nafta-sec-alena.org

North American Agreement on Environmental Co-operation: www.cec.org

North American Agreement on Labour Co-operation: www.naalc.org

Stop the FTAA: stopftaa.org

US Government Office of NAFTA and Inter-American Affairs: www.mac.doc.gov/nafta/index.html

Chapter 23

Latin America in the Global Political Economy

Nicola Phillips

Philip McMichael's recent observation that development in the contemporary era has 'more to do with global positioning than with the management of the "national household"'[1] invites two key arguments about the political economy of Latin America. The first is that which McMichael himself aims to advance, namely that a significant shift in thinking about development and development strategies has occurred, such that these now rest on integration into the global political economy and the achievement of greater competitiveness within it. It is, of course, important to remember that development always was conditioned by the manner of countries' insertion into the international political economy: dependency theory and its offshoots taught us at least that much. Yet the contemporary era has indeed featured a new and distinctive emphasis on engagement in the global political economy as the source of development and strong economic performance, rather than the structural brake on them that was perceived by dependency theory. Latin American development strategies over the 1980s and 1990s came thus to emphasize these goals of global 'positioning' and the pursuit of advantageous modes of insertion into the global political economy—the prospects for 'successful' development being seen to be conditioned fundamentally by the *form* of positioning pursued and achieved. The Washington Consensus, as is well known, constituted the particular policy manifesto associated with these strategies; its familiar tenets of trade liberalization, financial deregulation, privatization, fiscal discipline, tax reform, and the maintenance of 'compet-

itive' exchange and interest rates were disseminated across Latin America by neo-liberal policy elites, in conjunction with the international financial institutions (IFIS) and the other agents of the international financial community.

Yet the second argument prompted by McMichael's observation is that one of the striking anomalies of neo-liberal understandings of development lies in their conceptualization of the roots of development *failures*. While the determinants of good economic performance are deemed to lie in the global economy and prospects for development deemed to rest on the achievement of effective insertion into it, development remains conceptualized within the neo-liberal orthodoxy as an inherently national process. By extension, development failures are understood to stem purely from endogenous, or internal, factors. For much of the 1980s and 1990s, these were depicted as arising in the main from 'incorrect' government policies (read: failure to implement fully the Washington Consensus agenda) or from excessive state intervention in economic affairs, and consequently were deemed amenable to remedy by the implementation of 'appropriate' policies and the retrenchment of the state.[2]

There are two problems with this understanding, both of which provide useful starting points for our analysis of Latin America. In the first place, it pays little or no attention to the characteristics of the contemporary global political economy that are crucial to explanations of development failures and the myriad obstacles to successful development encountered by the majority of the world's societies, countries, and regions. In the second place, it pays insufficient attention to the deficiencies of the Washington Consensus prescriptions themselves in fostering stability and development. These deficiencies include, on the one hand, the ways in which many of these policies have heightened the vulnerability of Latin American economies to internal and external shocks and have exacerbated inequality and social dislocations, and, on the other, the ways in which key questions of governance and institutions in development processes were largely excluded from the Washington Consensus agenda in favour of an emphasis on macroeconomic 'fundamentals'. In a nutshell, the Washington Consensus was an agenda of internal policy reform that left untouched the issues of the global environment within which these policies were articulated and the institutional foundations necessary for their successful implementation and developmental performance.

The result of over a decade of neo-liberal reform in Latin America has been a pattern of disappointing economic performance and increasing political tensions across the region, leading many to speak of the second part of the 1990s as another 'lost half-decade'.[3] By 2003, per capita GDP was 1.5 per cent lower than in 1997; unemployment had reached a regional level of 10.7 per cent—with much higher levels in countries such as Argentina (21 per cent in 2002)—along with significant, concomitant rises in underemployment, informal economic activity, and overall poverty levels, the latter reaching 44 per cent of the region's total population by 2003. The devastating collapse of the Argentine economy in 2001 infected neighbouring countries in the Southern Cone, which occasioned a devaluation of the Uruguayan currency and recession in Brazil. Political instability remained in the Andean region—especially in Colombia and Venezuela. The economic costs of the ongoing Colombian civil war have been estimated now to account for around 25 per cent of GDP.[4] Recent Venezuelan politics have been dominated by devastating levels of political violence and opposition and—in a manner reminiscent of a

political era in Latin America supposed by many to have been consigned to history—by a short-lived coup against President Hugo Chávez in 2002. The resulting and prevalent disillusion with neo-liberalism has found expression in the election of a rash of leftist presidents in such countries as, notably, Brazil, Venezuela, Argentina, and Chile. By no means has there been a rejection of market economics, even by presidents like 'Lula' da Silva in Brazil; nevertheless, the political trend has been towards the rejection of the neo-liberal orthodoxy embedded in the Washington consensus. Even President Ricardo Lagos of Chile—supposedly the neo-liberal success story—has claimed recently that the key to his country's relatively stronger economic performance is that its development strategies have not conformed closely to Washington Consensus prescriptions.

My purpose in this chapter is to analyze in this light the positioning—or modes of insertion—of the Latin American region in the global political economy, and to assess how the development aspirations and prospects of the region have been, and are being, conditioned by the global and regional contexts within which development strategies are formulated and enacted. I emphasize not only the structural environments within which Latin American development processes are taking place, but equally the *politics* prevailing within these environments—what Anthony Payne has called a 'global politics of unequal development'[5]—that are of pivotal importance in explaining the trajectory and outcomes of these processes. In this spirit, we will look in turn at the arenas of trade, finance, and production.

Global and Regional Trade

As one of the centrepieces of the Washington Consensus agenda adopted over the 1990s, trade reform across Latin America was premised on a wide-ranging and, crucially, *unilateral* process of tariff liberalization. Average tariff levels were reduced precipitously, almost uniformly to under 15 per cent, from the strikingly high levels associated with the inward-looking and protectionist post-war development model. This process of trade liberalization in Latin America both reflected and was buttressed by two shifts.

The first shift was towards a much greater and more active participation in the multilateral trading system. The prevailing development model and the salience of nationalist and 'Third-Worldist' ideologies in the post-war period had meant that Latin American countries were both marginalized from the mainstream of multilateral trade and reluctant to participate fully in the multilateral system, despite widespread and often early membership of the General Agreement on Tariffs and Trade (GATT).[6] With neo-liberal reform, greater engagement in multilateral trade and the political processes surrounding it became logical and necessary, both as one of the principal means by which Latin American governments sought to advance their commercial interests, in the new context of a more 'outward-looking' development orientation, and as a mechanism by which domestic liberalization processes could be 'locked in' and lent international and domestic credibility.

This enhanced participation in the multilateral system was especially important for the countries of the largest subregional grouping in Latin America, the Southern Common Market (MERCOSUR) in the Southern Cone. This subregion (consisting of Argentina, Brazil, Paraguay, and Uruguay, with Chile and Bolivia as associate members of the MERCOSUR) remains less open than many of the other blocs in the Americas when measured by the ratio of trade to GDP. But the region is characterized by a much greater degree of diversification in its patterns of export destination than those economies and subregions in Latin America that are most dependent on the US market (Mexico and the Central American and Caribbean economies). Brazil, in addition, is one of only four economies in the Americas (the others being the United States, Canada, and Mexico) with genuinely diversified export economies and trade profiles. In Chile, while the trade/GDP ratio, at around 52 per cent, is high (and considerably higher than in neighbouring Southern Cone countries), government strategies over the 1990s focused on positioning Chile as

a 'global trader' rather than one oriented solely to the western hemisphere. Collectively, then, the large Southern Cone countries have more at stake in the multilateral system than many other countries of the region; consequently, they have consistently sought an active and visible role in multilateral trade negotiations.[7]

The second supporting shift, across Latin America, was towards regionalism. MERCOSUR was created in 1991 and existing but stagnant regionalist projects in the Andean, Central American, and Caribbean subregions were 'relaunched' around the same time. This coincided with the abandonment by the United States of its traditional reticence towards regionalism and the creation of the North American Free Trade Agreement (NAFTA). Latin American regionalist projects were conceived uniformly as a strategic response to the pressures of globalization and as a means of achieving the forms of 'global positioning' on which national development strategies had come to be premised. For this reason, the new regionalism in Latin America rested on a strategy of 'open regionalism', which conceived of unilateral trade liberalization as the best means to achieving more effective participation in the global economy and multilateral trade, and sought to buttress domestic reform efforts by placing trade liberalization at the core of new regionalist projects.

It was in this context of open regionalism that efforts first emerged to formulate and secure an extension of regionalism to a hemispheric level. These efforts were instigated by the US administration of George H.W. Bush with the announcement of its Enterprise for the Americas Initiative in 1990. The agenda was propelled forward from that time largely under Latin American and Caribbean steam, assuming the form of negotiations for a Free Trade Area of the Americas (FTAA) by the time of the 1994 Summit of the Americas held in Miami. In part, Latin American pressure for an FTAA emerged from the same logic as that which catalyzed the various subregionalist projects. This logic related to the projection of the region into the mainstream of global economic activity and the reinforcement of domestic reforms. At the same time, Latin

American participation in an FTAA project was also motivated by a concern to secure enhanced market access to the United States, primarily for trade in goods. While the particular incentives for individual countries varied widely, along with the degree of commitment to the process, for all of the participants market access was the prime reason for their engagement in the process and their negotiating priority within it.

In both the global and regional trading arenas, however, Latin American countries have encountered myriad obstacles to their effective participation and the realization of their commercial interests. During the Uruguay Round of GATT negotiations (1986–94), Latin American countries played a visibly active role and secured some reasonably significant gains, such as the inclusion on the negotiating agenda of agriculture, the elimination of tariffs on textiles, and the establishment of more encompassing dispute settlement mechanisms. Yet, in a pattern that endured for the next decade of multilateral trade politics, these gains were offset by the array of disadvantageous concessions demanded of Latin American and other developing countries. The principle of reciprocity, which had always underpinned both the multilateral trading system and US trade strategies, was entrenched—to the detriment of a notion of special and differential treatment for smaller and poorer economies; the concessions achieved by Latin American and developing countries on market access came only at the price of stringent agreements on investment, intellectual property, services, and so on.[8] And in any case, as demonstrated by the unfolding of multilateral trade politics from the time of the 1999 Seattle ministerial meetings onward, many of the concessions secured during the Uruguay Round failed either to be implemented by the most powerful trading nations or to generate meaningful changes in the substance or conduct of their trade policies.

Consequently, although some tariff and non-tariff barriers to trade flows to Latin America remained by the end of the 1990s, these were both fewer in number and less varied in character than those that Latin American exports encountered in the markets of the most powerful trading nations, the United States being naturally the most significant of these for the region. Average tariff levels have remained fairly low in the United States (at around 4.5 per cent); nevertheless, access to the US market for Latin American goods has remained impeded by both tariff barriers (in the form of the highest sectoral peaks in the region, notably in sectors of significant importance in the export profiles of Latin American economies) and, more problematically, by a raft of non-tariff barriers ranging from prolific agricultural subsidies to an armoury of trade remedies (anti-dumping measures, countervailing duties, and safeguards), ad hoc compensatory mechanisms, and discretionary measures such as quotas on steel imports.[9] The multilateral trading system remains characterized by significant tariff and non-tariff barriers to trade in sectors of particular importance to Latin America (such as agriculture, textiles, and steel) and by only slight progress in establishing binding multilateral agreements on the use of trade remedies, negotiation in this latter area being especially hampered by reticence on the part of successive US administrations.

Widespread Latin American opposition to the 'post-Doha' WTO agenda in the early 2000s thus rested on perceptions of the prejudicial terms on which participation in the multilateral system was, and remains, conducted. Latin American countries became pivotal in the post-Uruguay Round political movements to inject a greater presence for developing countries in the WTO process, most obviously in the Brazilian leadership of the 'G-20+' coalition that emerged at the Cancún ministerial meetings of 2002. Yet, the insertion of the Latin American region into the global politics of trade has been hampered not only by the unevenness of the playing field on which the negotiations have been conducted and the exclusionary nature of much of the negotiating process, but also by a generalized ineffectiveness of national negotiating strategies arising from a lack of technical expertise and bargaining power. The comparative efficacy of the Brazilian negotiating team, as demonstrated by its collaboration with Indian and other negotiators over such issues as intellectual property and pharmaceuticals, contrasts noticeably with the relatively ineffectual participation of most other Latin American countries, particularly the smaller and poorer ones clustered in Central America and the Caribbean. Almost without exception, attempts to bolster the bargaining power of Latin American countries by means of subregional 'bloc bargaining' strategies have been limited in cohesion and impact by divergences in the interests and positions of the member countries of the blocs, and by the absence of institutional vehicles through which effective participation might be pursued.

The politics of regional trade have been in many ways similar to the politics of multilateral trade, and many of the major sticking points in the latter have been mirrored in the regional setting. The original vision of the FTAA espoused by the United States was one essentially of NAFTA enlargement—a form of 'NAFTA on steroids', as it came to be dubbed. Adoption of a NAFTA template augured a hemispheric agreement peculiarly in line with a US (and, to an extent, Canadian) agenda, marginalizing many of the main concerns of Latin American participants in the structures of the negotiations. This dominant agenda has consisted of an emphasis on the entrenchment of regional rules in a range of trade-related areas such as investment, intellectual property, government procurement, and competition policy, along with the liberalization of service sectors in the region, reflecting the negotiating priorities that the United States Trade Representative (USTR) has pressed in the multilateral arena. US negotiating positions in these areas have been based on a strategy of bringing the rest of the region into line with existing US legislation and/or the provisions set out in NAFTA. This has been most notably the case in US attempts to replicate the NAFTA investment chapter in an FTAA, which gained notoriety for its entrenchment of investor rights on a par with the sovereign rights of states. As in the multilateral arena, as well, any (fairly minimal) concessions on market access for (some) Latin American exports to the United States have been made conditional on the acceptance of US demands in the various 'trade-related' areas with which it is primarily concerned.

Conversely, negotiation in those areas of most strategic interest to Latin American participants in the FTAA negotiations—agriculture, subsidies, and trade remedies—has been effectively vetoed by the US government.[10]

The resulting perceptions of systematic disadvantage to Latin American interests in an FTAA have generated a set of political reactions akin to those in evidence in the multilateral system. First, the commitment to bloc bargaining has also been brought to bear on the hemispheric negotiations. In this arena, too, its effectiveness was hampered in all cases by the problems of divergent interests and an array of institutional and political weaknesses. Second, a sharp polarization has emerged in the region between those countries most in favour of a comprehensive agreement along the lines proposed by the United States and those opposed to it, the latter led again by Brazil. Brazilian positions, supported in particular by a range of countries in the Southern Cone and Caribbean, have rested primarily on an insistence that, if an FTAA is to be 'comprehensive', as the US government prefers, it must be *genuinely* comprehensive and include meaningful negotiation on agriculture and trade remedies.[11] The Brazil–US relationship in the FTAA context has been consistently tense and at times hostile. The divergent visions represented by these two protagonists led to the abandonment, in late 2003, of the 'single undertaking'—the principle of a single agreement encompassing all the areas under negotiation—that had underpinned the FTAA process until that time. In its place, the Brazilian and US governments joined forces to defend a new format based on a 'buffet-style' approach to an FTAA, which stipulated a relatively minimal raft of basic commitments and left countries free to choose the type and extent of other commitments it wished to assume under an agreement. Most, but not all, Latin American governments saw this ' FTAA-lite' as preferable, *faute de mieux*, to an encompassing hemispheric agreement that would be very peculiarly in line with US preferences and of significantly negative developmental prospects for much of the region.

The responses, both to this drastic scaling back of the level of ambition in the FTAA project and to the collapse of WTO negotiations at Cancún, were further injections of vigour into bilateral trade negotiations. These had been becoming increasingly the fulcrum of US trade strategies in any case, but were animated as a political response to the inability of the United States to realize its particular vision of the multilateral and hemispheric trading systems. The strategy of 'competitive liberalization', to be pursued primarily by bilateral negotiation, came to represent the 'credo' of US approaches in both arenas.[12] Yet the shift to bilateralism also found fertile ground in the trade strategies of a range of Latin American countries, particularly vis-à-vis the United States. Chile–US negotiations were concluded in December 2002; negotiations for an agreement between four Central American countries and the United States were concluded exactly a year later, with Costa Rica and the Dominican Republic following suit in early 2004. Around that time the United States also announced its intention to negotiate bilaterally with a range of Latin American countries, including Bolivia, Colombia, Ecuador, Peru, and Panama. Crucially, both the Chile–US and the Central America–US agreements reflected the distinctively US-driven trade agenda and US preferences concerning such issues as investment and intellectual property that had proved to be sticking points in the wider hemispheric negotiations. Similarly, the other intractable points of tension—agricultural subsidies, trade remedies, and trade in certain goods such as textiles and steel—were excluded from these two agreements and thus largely circumvented by the shift to bilateral negotiation. The new bilateralist emphasis thus facilitates the construction of precisely the hub-spoke regional arrangements and the uneven playing field that have limited the effectiveness and developmental potential of Latin American trade strategies.

Global Finance and the Politics of Crisis

The region's insertion into the structures of contemporary global finance was occasioned by the widespread processes of financial deregulation that accelerated across the region in the 1990s. In the vast majority of cases, such as in Argentina and Mexico, this deregulation process was conducted in a precipitous and thoroughgoing fashion; in a couple of cases, notably Chile, the process was more gradual. In fact, the Chilean case has frequently been held up as the example of how controls on financial flows, contrary to the neo-liberal orthodoxy, can enhance stability and contribute positively to growth in an open economy. Continued regulation in the Chilean financial sector from 1991 onward, by means of various controls on the entry and exit of capital,[13] proved entirely compatible for a time with the explosion of capital flows to emerging markets. Latin America and the Caribbean accounted for 29 per cent of the total flows to emerging markets in 1995 and for 37 per cent of this total by 2000, the latter representing a tripling of the average annual flows for the 1990–4 period.[14] Together, Brazil and Mexico consistently accounted for around half of the total flows to the region.

The composition of these financial flows also was restructured over the 1980s and 1990s in line with the evolution of global financial markets. First, private capital became much more significant than public capital in the investment profiles of Latin American economies; second, financial capital became considerably more important relative to long-term productive capital than in preceding decades; and third, private-sector destinations for investment came to be favoured over public-sector ones, privatization processes being central to the surges of inward investment experienced by Latin American economies and, by extension, the slowing of these flows towards the end of the decade as the targets proffered by privatization were gradually exhausted.[15] It is important to note, however, that the profile of investment in Latin America remained dominated by foreign direct investment (FDI) as opposed to the more volatile portfolio investment, despite the enormous increases in the volume of the latter: in the late 1990s, around two-thirds of the total flows to the region still consisted of long-term, direct productive investment.

The combination of these trends—particularly

of precipitous and blanket financial liberalization, along with the explosion of private and speculative capital flows—has exacerbated and sharpened the structural dependence on foreign financial and investment capital already characteristic of the region's economies. While vulnerability to movements in international markets is clearly not a new feature of late industrializing economies, the characteristics of the current phase of financial globalization have heightened the extent of vulnerability of most emerging markets and occasioned degrees of financial and economic instability that were forcefully in evidence in the three major Latin American crises: Mexico in 1994–5, Brazil in 1999, and Argentina in 2001–2.

Undoubtedly, explanations for all of these crises lie in part in the domestic arena, and particularly in the nature of domestic financial reform processes underpinned by the Washington Consensus. It has become generally accepted that financial reform, in many cases, was conducted in simply too rapid a manner, without due regard to the institutional conditions necessary to manage the impact of the explosion of capital inflows on the fabric of national political economies, and certainly those necessary to deal with sudden and massive episodes of capital flight such as occurred in Brazil, Argentina, and elsewhere. In all but a few cases—Chile, possibly Uruguay, and Mexico as a result of measures taken in the aftermath of its 'tequila' crisis—financial and banking sectors in the 1990s were underdeveloped, inadequately supervised, and largely unable to perform the regulatory functions necessitated by these impacts of financial liberalization.

In addition, the recent crises were unleashed by the unfolding of domestic political battles. Indeed, they less represented instances of speculative attacks against currencies (such as those seen in East Asia) than episodes of large-scale capital flight occasioned by moments of essentially domestic political crisis and economic instability. The Brazilian devaluation of January 1999 was associated with concern in financial markets over the scale of the fiscal deficit and the overvaluation

of the *real*, and was sparked directly by the political conflict between the federal government and the state of Minas Gerais over internal debt payments.[16]The devaluation of the Argentine peso and the default on external debt payments in December 2001, in turn, represented a full-scale collapse both of the economy and of the political system. The striking levels of external vulnerability of the Argentine economy arose from the maintenance of the policy of convertibility established in 1991, under which the currency was pegged at 1:1 parity with the US dollar and all new issues of money were required to be backed by available reserves of gold and foreign exchange in the Central Bank. While successfully anti-inflationary in outcome, convertibility introduced a disabling rigidity into the Argentine economy, sharpened its dependence on inflows of foreign capital, and provoked a steady and significant process of currency appreciation; this in turn eroded the competitiveness of the external sector and consequently exacerbated the increasingly serious debt situation. In 1998, the ratio of total debt to foreign exchange revenues from export reached 500 per cent and its ratio to GDP reached 41.4 per cent, the latter figure increasing further to around 50 per cent by 2000.[17]

Apart from these macroeconomic disequilibria and specific, probably ill-advised, economic policy decisions in the run-up to the devaluation and default, the Argentine collapse was occasioned by a set of intrinsically political and institutional factors. Among the most important of these factors were the extent of corruption and clientelism that permeated the structures of Argentine politics, the political tensions occasioned by burgeoning unemployment, and perceptions of the failure of neo-liberal reform to produce sustained growth, significantly reduce inequality, or address the characteristics of the political class—including corruption and incompetence—that were seen to hamper the prospects for achieving these goals.[18]

Domestic political, economic, and institutional factors are thus clearly to be given weight in any account of the financial instabilities and crises experienced by Latin American economies. Yet they provide only a partial explanation, and the key to understanding their significance lies in their interaction with the specific characteristics of global finance. In a nutshell, as Moisés Naím has put it, 'the Washington Consensus overlooked globalization.'[19] Thoroughgoing deregulation has undoubtedly allowed for a certain harnessing of the benefits of financial globalization in the attraction of capital flows; probably in much greater part, it has generated a dangerous exposure of fragile domestic financial and banking sectors, given the intrinsic volatility of new forms of capital flows and, especially, the amplified and disproportionate scale of capital flight that occurs once economic crises are sparked. In other words, financial deregulation was designed and advanced in Latin American economies without regard to the nature and behaviour of globalized financial markets. Thus, economies were left largely unable to deal with such associated phenomena as contagion, speculation, panics, moral hazard, or crises of financial 'confidence'.

These issues also are associated in important ways with the agendas and strategies of the IFIS, particularly the International Monetary Fund (IMF). The shortcomings of their prescriptions have received considerable attention in the context of the Asian crises[20] and are equally evident in Latin America, particularly in the management of the Argentine crisis. The IMF's ideological adherence to Washington Consensus principles, as well as concerns about electoral politics in recipient countries, meant that few concrete strategies emerged for addressing either growing Brazilian difficulties or, perhaps more crucially, the gradual implosion of the Argentine economy. Rather, economic problems arising across the region—whether associated simply with severely disappointing economic performance or with impending or actual crisis—were deemed, as noted earlier, to be of internal provenance and effectively the result of the insufficient implementation of Washington Consensus policies. Such was the diagnosis even in the case of the IMF's 'star pupils'

of the 1990s, such as Argentina, where one of the most orthodox versions of the neo-liberal agenda had been elaborated by the government of Carlos Menem and his Economy Minister, Domingo Cavallo. The result was that IMF policies towards Argentina were limited to a series of packages that carried conditions stipulating further liberalization and further austerity, and eventually a striking reluctance (working in tandem with the George W. Bush administration and US Treasury) to offer assistance once the economy 'officially' collapsed at the end of 2001.

From 2000, the sharp contraction of capital flows to Latin America and the Caribbean—by 33 per cent in 2002—was due in large part to the deterioration of investor confidence in the region in the light of these economic and financial crises, together with the gradual exhaustion of privatization targets noted earlier and the effects of slower economic growth across the region.[21] The contraction was felt most sharply in Mexico and the Caribbean, due in large part to the additional impact, in evidence across the region', of the recession in the US economy. The highly significant dimension of management of the crisis-ridden regional environment, however, was the Chilean government's abandonment of the system of capital controls at the time of the Asian financial crises in order to shore up investor confidence and offset the contraction of capital flows. Strikingly, the free trade agreement negotiated with the US in 2002 included further provisions that placed severe constraints on the ability of the Chilean government to enact similar controls in the future. The upshot was the removal, both by market dynamics and by direct political intervention by the United States, of some of the flagship mechanisms by which countries had sought to mitigate many of the deleterious trends that recently beset the region, indicating a policy direction that augurs an entrenchment rather than amelioration of the region's vulnerability to global finance. Put together, these trends reveal clearly that 'international competitiveness based on efficiency seeking FDI can be lost just as fast as it is gained',[22] highlighting again the intrinsically precarious nature of the set of contemporary development strategies predicated on the pursuit of 'global positioning' and the adoption of a Washington Consensus policy framework for this purpose.

Global Production Structures

The restructuring of global production wrought by the current phase of globalization has three principal facets: (1) the elaboration of 'transnationalized' production chains; (2) the growing importance of intra-firm, as opposed to inter-firm, trade; and (3) the marked 'tertiarization' of global economic activity, featuring an emphasis on the production and trade of services as opposed to goods and, as such, an increasingly sharp divergence between those national and regional economies that are competitive in the services sector and those that still depend on the production of more traditional goods for export. All of these trends have found clear expression in the contemporary political economy of production in Latin America. The first two of these relate primarily to the participation of transnational corporations (TNCs). While post-war development strategies led to (and indeed rested on) a heavy participation of TNCs in Latin American economies, the level of their penetration in the region and domination of production activities were sharpened during the 1990s by the investment opportunities offered by privatization. The consequence was a significant redefinition of the structures of ownership across the region, with foreign ownership representing by the end of the decade some 63 per cent of the largest manufacturing firms and 41 per cent of the largest exporters.[23] The most striking trend in this broad picture, however, has been towards the acquisition of formerly state-owned enterprises by consortia of both foreign and domestic capital, and thus the creation of a progressively more solid and politically powerful business 'oligarchy'.

The trend towards trade in services, not surprisingly, has been one in which few Latin American economies have been able to find a toe-hold. Across Latin America and the Caribbean in 2002, the share of services in total trade remained under 15 per cent, a level inferior to the world average of around 19 per cent.[24] The Caribbean economies (particularly in the eastern Caribbean) and a number of Central American economies are the only ones in which services represent an important part of the structures of production.[25] The loss, as a result of NAFTA, of competitive advantage to Mexico in traditional sectors such as textiles, apparel, and export assembly precipitated the emergence of 'service economies' based largely on the supply of cheap labour and specializing in such sectors as tourism and entertainment and commercial and financial services, both legal and illegal. Southern Cone economies also feature important service sectors: non-financial services have accounted for around 40 per cent of total FDI to Brazil from the mid-1990s onward; energy, telecommunications, tourism, and financial services represent the bulk of Uruguayan GDP and an increasingly significant proportion of exports; around 64 per cent of total FDI to Chile in 1996–2000 was directed to the service sector, especially to utilities and financial services.

However, the Southern Cone fits into a wider South American model that is inserted into global production and trade primarily on the basis of natural resources. A significant degree of export diversification has taken place in many South American economies—notably Chile—and, as mentioned earlier, the Brazilian economy is exceptional in Latin America for the extent of its industrial base and a high proportion of manufactured exports. Yet, the overall South American profile is one of capital-intensive industry associated with the processing of natural resources, these activities being characterized by low levels of domestic value-added goods. Within this model, countries such as Argentina and Paraguay remain largely dependent on agriculture; Chile and most of the Andean countries remain dependent on natural resources and higher value-added, natural resource-based products in sectors such as copper, minerals, and fishing.

Finally, Mexico, some Caribbean, and some Central American countries are inserted into global production structures by means of their progressive integration into the production structures of the US economy as its 'offshore' arms, generating an increasingly valid notion of a wider 'North American' political economy of production. This model rests on their integration into 'vertical' flows of trade in manufactured goods associated with export assembly (*maquiladora*) industries, particularly in Mexico, and export-processing zones in a number of Caribbean economies, especially in sectors such as textiles and apparel. Crucially, however, these non-resource-based exports that have come to constitute the mainstay of these economies are uniformly at the low value-added ends of the production chain, the added value accruing only once the goods are exported to the United States and onward from there.[26]

From the foregoing analysis it is obvious that these patterns of insertion into global production structures have been both fostered and entrenched by the global restructuring of production and that, on the whole, few Latin American economies have managed to find and occupy competitive market niches at the high value-added ends of production chains. However, there are also salient domestic mechanisms by which these patterns have been reinforced, relating to the generalized paucity in Latin America of effective promotion or support for domestic productive activity. With again a few exceptions—notably Chile, Brazil, and, to an extent, Mexico—fiscal and institutional weaknesses, along with ideological inclinations towards highly orthodox versions of neo-liberalism, have meant that few effective industrial or export promotion activities have been undertaken by Latin American states. The prevalent weaknesses of banking systems—weaknesses exacerbated by the levels of vulnerability and instability identified earlier in the chapter—have meant that credit systems have been largely ineffective and that solid foundations for business and financial entrepreneurship have been generally lacking in Latin American economies.

Conclusion

What emerges forcefully is that contemporary Latin American development is conditioned and shaped by the complex interaction of domestic economic, institutional, and political factors and by the manner of the region's insertion into the global political economy. This interaction, in turn, was articulated over the 1990s within a neo-liberal ideological framework, which has now widely been deemed in Latin America to have failed to achieve sustained growth, development, and stability. In part these failures arose from the neglect of questions of institutions and broader notions of governance within the central precepts of the Washington Consensus. As is well known, a growing recognition of the importance of administrative, legal, and institutional structures in economic reform processes translated into a 'post-Washington Consensus' agenda, encapsulated in notions of 'good governance' and 'second-generation reform', again adopted across Latin America. Yet the post-Washington Consensus agenda focuses in essence on putting in place the conditions in which the Consensus itself might be made to work better. It continues to understand the 'lost half-decade' of development in Latin America as lying in the incomplete implementation of its policy prescriptions,[27] and thus constitutes more an agenda of 'Washington Consensus-plus' than any meaningful new direction in the ways development is conceived or development strategies are designed.

Moreover, it leaves untouched both the 'endogenist' understandings of development and the emphasis on global positioning without attention to the impact of the global environment in which these positioning strategies are articulated. This chapter has demonstrated the ways in which Latin American development is not only shaped but also, in important respects, constrained by the structures of the global political economy and the politics that prevail within it. What is clear, however, is that these global politics and the ideological frameworks that underpin the contemporary world order currently are subject to vigorous challenge and contestation, both within Latin America and outside it. The recent evolution of Latin American politics reveals a sustained debate about development strategies that do not rely on orthodox neoliberalism and, in a variety of arenas, about the sorts of reforms that need to be instigated in the global arenas of trade, finance, and production in order to achieve a more equitable global environ-ment. While severely constrained in many cases by dependence on the United States, and indeed by the fact that the Americas is probably the only region of the world in which the United States can be said to be truly hegemonic, these trends point to the possible opening of a new, genuinely post-Washington Consensus phase in Latin American political economy.

Notes

1. Philip McMichael, *Development and Social Change: A Global Perspective*, 2nd edn (Thousand Oaks, Calif.: Pine Forge, 2000), 150.

2. See John Toye, *Dilemmas of Development* (Oxford: Blackwell, 1987), 70.

3. United Nations Economic Commission for Latin America and the Caribbean (ECLAC), *Preliminary Overview of the Economies of Latin America and the Caribbean, 2002* (Santiago: United Nations, 2002).

4. Gabriel Marcella, 'The United States and Colombia: The Journey from Ambiguity to Strategic Clarity', North-South Center Working Paper Series 13 (2003), 13.

5. Anthony Payne, *The Global Politics of Unequal Development* (Basingstoke: Palgrave, 2005).

6. Diana Tussie, 'On Shifting Ground: The Crossroads of Regional and Sectoral Associations', in Tussie, ed., *Trade Negotiations in Latin America: Problems and Prospects* (Basingstoke: Palgrave, 2003), 4.

7. Nicola Phillips, *The Southern Cone Model: The Political Economy of Regional Capitalist Development in Latin America* (London: Routledge, 2004), 117; Marcelo de Paiva Abreu, 'Latin American and Caribbean Interests in the WTO', in Tussie, ed., *Trade Negotiations in Latin America*, 23–4.

8. Tussie, 'On Shifting Ground', 5.

9. See Nicola Phillips, 'The Americas', in Anthony Payne, ed., *The New Regional Politics of Development* (Basingstoke: Palgrave, 2004), 29–58.

10. Nicola Phillips, 'Hemispheric Integration and Subregionalism in the Americas', *International Affairs* 79, 2 (2003): 334.

11. See, e.g., Rubens Barbosa, 'A View from Brazil', *Washington Quarterly* (Spring 2001): 149–57.

12. Robert B. Zoellick, 'Our Credo: Free Trade and Competition', *Wall Street Journal,* 10 July 2003.

13. For details, see Susanne Soederberg, 'A Historical Materialist Account of Chilean Capital Controls: Prototype Policy for Whom?', *Review of International Studies* 9, 3 (2002): 490–512.

14. ECLAC, *Foreign Investment in Latin America and the Caribbean, 2000* (Santiago: United Nations, 2001), 35–6.

15. Phillips, *The Southern Cone Model*, 183. Also Javier Santiso, *The Political Economy of Emerging Markets: Actors, Institutions and Financial Crises in Latin America* (New York: Palgrave, 2003).

16. For an account, see Victor Bulmer-Thomas, 'The Brazilian Devaluation: National Responses and International Consequences', *International Affairs* 74, 4 (1999): 729–41.

17. Michael Mussa, 'Argentina and the Fund: From Triumph to Tragedy', Institute of International Economics, 25 Mar. 2002. Available at: <www.iie.com>.

18. For an analysis along these lines, see Luigi Manzetti, 'The Argentine Implosion', North-South Agenda Papers 59, North-South Center, Nov. 2002.

19. 'Washington Consensus or Washington Confusion?', *Foreign Policy* 118 (2000): 94.

20. Joseph Stiglitz, *Globalization and Its Discontents*

(London: Penguin, 2002).

21. ECLAC, *Foreign Investment in Latin America and the Caribbean, 2002* (Santiago: United Nations, 2003), 12–13.

22. Ibid., 13.

23. ECLAC, *Foreign Investment, 2000*.

24. ECLAC, *Panorama de la Inserción Internacional de América Latina y el Caribe, 2001–2* (Santiago: United Nations, 2003), summary, 8.

25. This elaboration of the various models of pro-duction draws on material in ECLAC, *Panorama*, 12

26. Phillips, 'The Americas'.

27. For a prime example, see John Williamson, 'Overview: An Agenda for Restarting Growth and Reform', in Williamson and Pedro-Pablo Kuczynski, eds, *After the Washington Consensus: Restarting Growth and Reform in Latin America* (Washington: Institute for International Economics, 2003), 1–19.

Suggested Readings

Payne, Anthony. *The Global Politics of Unequal Development*. Basingstoke: Palgrave, 2005.

Phillips, Nicola. *The Southern Cone Model: The Political Economy of Regional Capitalist Development in Latin America*. London: Routledge, 2004.

Tussie, Diana, ed. *Trade Negotiations in Latin America: Problems and Prospects*. Basingstoke: Palgrave, 2003.

Web Sites

Institute for International Economics: www.iie.com

Free Trade Area of the Americas: www.ftaa-alca.org

Stop the FTAA: www.stopftaa.org

World Trade Organization: www.wto.org

Chapter 24

Economic Regionalism in East Asia
Consolidation with Centrifugal Tendencies

Richard Higgott

In the last edition of *Political Economy and the Changing Global Order*, this chapter focused on the financial crises of the late twentieth century and considered regionalism in the *Asia-Pacific*. This version focuses on the early twenty-first century and examines economic regionalism in *East Asia*. This change reflects the consolidation of three trends in the late twentieth and early twenty-first centuries:

- a concentration on East Asia, as opposed to the Asia-Pacific, as the voice of region;
- a growing interest in multilateral *regional monetary* co-operation at the expense of *regional trade* co-operation in the wake of the crises;
- a growing interest in *bilateral* regional trading arrangements within the region on the one hand, and between the states of the region and extra-regional actors on the other.

As I wrote in the last edition:

> new forms of co-ordination may . . . give rise to a more solidly 'East Asian' [as opposed to Asia-Pacific] orientation in regional policy interaction and co-operation. . . . Regionalism will continue to be an important level of activity, probably less as an arena of dramatic initiative and more as a meso-level expression of the desire to optimize sovereign decision-making within states in the face of globalization. . . . The economic crisis will continue to ensure reform of a market-opening nature in the trade arena. But there will be a different regional spin towards these global issues in East Asia

that . . . may lead to enhanced Asian policy responses to the major global economic questions of our time.[1]

Put as a question, I asked: 'Is it more or less likely that there will be further initiatives to provide some kind of regional economic co-operation in general and financial policy co-ordination in particular?' The answer offered was twofold. In the short run, no grand regional strategies were likely to be proposed. In the longer run, however, the international responses to the Asian financial crises would make the prospect of the greater management of *East Asian* (as opposed to Asia-Pacific) economic affairs all the more likely. And, indeed, this is what has happened. This chapter details how these trends have consolidated within a global context in which actors now respond to military-strategic, rather than economic, crises—9/11 and the onset of the war on terrorism in the early twenty-first century as opposed to the financial crises of the late twentieth century.

The first section of this chapter locates East Asian regionalism within the wider context of the evolving global political economy. Inasmuch as regionalism in the early 1990s exhibited considerable optimism, it mirrored the state of neo-liberal economic globalization more generally. For policy-making elites in the East Asian region their principal task was to maximize economic opportunities offering abundant supplies of capital and to accept willingly a belief in the benefits of enhanced economic interdependence of a de facto, market-led kind, supported by evolving institutional co-operation, largely state-led and de jure in nature. Indeed, the international relations of the region saw a proliferation of initiatives, in both the economic and security domains, meant to enhance collaborative policy co-ordination.

The second half of this chapter eschews detailed discussion of the Asian financial crisis that undercut this optimism. Instead, it identifies two significant trends—the gradual, but real, movement towards enhanced monetary co-operation in East Asia and the growing interest in bilateral trading arrangements. Both are wrapped up in the wider recognition of the importance of 'East Asia', as opposed to the 'Asia-Pacific', as the voice of region. It is an assumed argument of the chapter that while the United States remains the dominant presence in the region defined as the Asia-Pacific (in both economic and military terms), it is also an unwitting exogenous catalyst to the 'East Asianization' of the Western Pacific seaboard.

Regionalism in Asia at the End of the Twentieth Century

The early 1990s were a period of exciting, if now seemingly naive, optimism for regional co-operation. This was especially the case in the scholarly economics and policy-oriented community that saw the evolution of the APEC (Asia-Pacific Economic Co-operation) forum and its agenda for securing regional free trade by 2020— through concerted unilateral liberalization following the 1994 Bogor Summit—as the only serious game in the region. However, accompanying the theoretical interest in the development of 'open regionalism' was the emergence of 'East Asia' as an actor in global affairs. This was often accompanied by what came to be known as the 'Asian Way', a distinctive approach to regional diplomacy. The principal manifestations of this process were the development of a regional security dialogue via the introduction of the ASEAN (Association of Southeast Asian Nations) Regional Forum and the development of the Asia–Europe dialogue process (ASEM) following the first Asia–Europe Summit in Bangkok in 1996. The

Asian membership of ASEM exactly mirrored those states that constituted the East Asian Economic Caucus within the APEC process.

But in 1997, the economic crisis[2] hit East Asia. This crisis called forth an explanatory and accusatory industry in both the scholarly and the popular press. Analyses of a realist persuasion, argued that the short-term effects of the crisis have been to expose the limitations of Asian regional institutions. Nowhere was this better illustrated than in the inability of ASEAN and APEC to make any serious input into the policy process in the wake of the crisis.[3] But by way of longer-term contrast, the crisis proved to be a spur to new forms of regional dialogue and policy co-ordination. These new forms of co-ordination differ to the extent that they have given rise to a more solidly 'East Asian' orientation in regional policy interaction and co-operation. They offer what we might call a hybrid combination of liberal institutionalism fused with some constructivist insights into the manner in which region-building in East Asia may, or may not, represent a new, if gradual and limited, exercise in inter-subjective identity building.[4]

Such an analysis provides a set of lenses—different from those in much of the mainstream literature—through which to look at regionalism in Asia. Most mainstream literature all too often fails to see events in the region in their necessary wider context—as but one line of response to the crisis of post-Cold War globalization. This crisis is twofold in its manifestations. At an obvious first level, a series of economic crises altered the economic and socio-political fortunes of several hitherto rapidly developing East Asian states. At a more general but no less significant level, the East Asian economic crises represented one key element in a wider setback for the inexorable process of international economic liberalization that came to be known throughout the 1990s as 'globalization'.

Starting with the financial crises of the 1990s we have experienced an emerging set of challenges to the hegemony of neo-liberal globalization. This resistance has not been uniform, nor has it been restricted to one site or group of actors.[5] Moreover, in many instances, resistance has been to the practice as much as to the principles of neo-liberalism. As we now understand, the Asian financial crises of the late 1990s did not represent the final ideological triumph of Anglo-American economic liberalism over Asian developmentalism. Rather, the crisis provided the context for rethinking aspects of the neo-liberal project in the developing world more generally[6] and East Asia specifically.

Since the last years of the twentieth century Asian governments have been caught between protagonists of continued global economic liberalization and advocates of some form of international capital re-regulation. As a result, tensions have arisen between dominant Anglo-American understandings of global liberalization and the emergence of East Asian sites of resistance to some aspects of the globalization process. Notably, at a Pacific regional level, Asian interests have tested the viability of the 'APEC consensus' as a means of driving the wider neo-liberal enterprise forward in the early twenty-first century.

We have seen a hardening, at times nationalist, resistance to neo-liberalism. The financial crises in the late twentieth century challenged the very model on which some Asian states had built their success. The long-standing critique of Asian developmental statism, inherent in the neo-classical economic literature and language of the established policy community, was thought to be vindicated by the crises. The speeches of senior US policy-makers and opinion-makers were peppered with references to the need to jettison the remaining vestiges of the Asian developmental model. This has not played well in East Asia in either the short or the long run.

The Asian model was destined to change after the end of the Cold War anyway. US willingness to supply official capital and to open its markets for an initial one-way flow of exports was predicated heavily on the security consideration of containing Communism. In the more benign security environment between the end of the Cold War and prior to the terrorist attacks on the United States of 11 September 2001, regional economic trade liberalization and financial deregulation were the payoff for a continued US security presence in the region. Those socio-political practices of the so-called Asian

model that were acceptable for security reasons during the Cold War—exclusionary politics, nepotism, and the blurred lines of authority between political and economic power—began to clash more violently with the interests of private capital—particularly American capital—in search of greater market share and profits in an era of deregulation.

At a more specific regional level, a major implication of the experience of Asian states in the crisis, and especially at the hands of the IMF, has been a growing interest in an enhanced East Asian, as opposed to an Asia-Pacific, understanding of region. The desire for national decision-making autonomy in the face of the Asian economic crisis and the enhancement of a greater collective regional understanding in the wake of the crisis are not incompatible. Regional social learning from the crisis appears to consolidate the trend towards enhanced policy coordination in a number of economic areas.

Into the Twenty-first Century: Turning Points for Regionalism in Asia

From the Financial Crisis to 9/11

The initial response to the crisis—the abortive Japanese proposal for an Asian Monetary Fund—was opposed by the United States, which consequently sowed seeds of polarization in the relationship between the Asian and Caucasian members of APEC. The alternative offer—the exhortatory liberalization rhetoric of the 1997 Vancouver APEC—only superficially concealed a deeper schism between the two edges of the Pacific. The economic turmoil reinforced the notion that the Asia-Pacific was an artificial construction of region. Faith in the longer-term salience of APEC was adversely affected by the regional resentment toward the IMF-led, and by implication the US-led, responses to the financial crisis of the late nineties.

The euphoric expectations of the 1993–6 period—that APEC would provide firm institutional ties to mitigate inter-regional tensions between Asia and the United States—clearly reflected wishful thinking of a high order. Advocates of APEC championed 'open liberalism' in the region, assuming that it was benign and its enhancement uncontested. Much of the discussion on APEC throughout the first half of the 1990s saw only the benefits of free trade and none of the pitfalls of dramatic increases in deregulated, unrestricted capital mobility. APEC always found its strongest intellectual and political support among the American, Australian, and Canadian members of APEC. During the heyday of Asia-Pacific growth, the Asian members were willing to go along with its emerging program, although not necessarily at the pace the Caucasian members wished.

In the post-crisis era, things changed. APEC, rather than being a potential instrument for trade liberalization at the Asia-Pacific level, came to be seen in large sectors of the policy communities of East Asia as but an additional site at which the United States could advance its own agendas, such as for further capital market liberalization. After 9/11 the US agenda changed. Its principal goal for APEC was for it to adapt to a US security agenda. Indeed, as I have argued at length elsewhere, US economic relations with East Asia have been 'securitized'. This process could be seen not only within institutions like APEC, but also in bilateral economic relations.[7]

Even prior to 9/11, Asian observers had increasingly evaluated APEC as a tool of American foreign policy. APEC 's failure to provide any meaningful response to the biggest economic crisis in the Asia-Pacific region since 1945 (the financial crises of the second half of the 1990s) made it, if not irrelevant, then less important for many Asian members. Resistance of Asian policy-makers to a strengthened APEC after the financial crisis was caused not only by the lack of tangible benefits but also by a fear of American dominance within the organization.[8] APEC has always struggled to reconcile its regional focus with the wider agendas of the United States. APEC 's concentration on facilitating contacts in the corporate and private sector, accompanied by an almost total neglect of developing an intra-regional network at the wider civil society level, has resulted in a weak or non-exis-

tent sense of community. As a consequence, it has failed to provide much political legitimacy for the wider regional neo-liberal economic project.

Most immediately, the manner in which the United States has treated APEC in the wake of 9/11 has confirmed Asian perceptions. Throughout the 1990s, the Asia-Pacific had been a major focus of attention for US foreign economic policy. It was an important part of the American neo-liberal global economic agenda, evinced by the (failed) US attempt to use APEC to secure early voluntary sectoral liberalization.[9] Following 9/11, US interests in regions of the world other than the Middle East and the war on terrorism were placed on the back burner. Policy began to reflect a declining American concern for the viability of an issue-specific organization such as APEC if it did not contribute to US policy on the privileged issue of the containment of terrorism.

Nothing illustrated the point better than the 2001 Shanghai, 2002 Mexico, and 2003 Bangkok APEC summits, at which most Asian leaders felt the agenda had been hijacked by President Bush to galvanize support against the war on terrorism in general and support for the military coalition against Iraq in particular. To be sure, few if any Asian leaders doubted Bush's contention that terrorism and economic development were linked, but most felt that the balance, with its overriding focus on security, was wrong for APEC.

Rivalry between an Asian integration project and APEC was, of course, not new, and not all questioning of APEC 's continued utility stemmed from American policy post-9/11. Independent of the US position towards APEC, policy elites in Asia had been reconsidering the benefits of regionalism without the Pacific Caucasian members. As noted, American opposition to an Asian Monetary Fund in, and since, 1997 sowed the seeds for further polarization and bolstered the development of a dialogue between Southeast and Northeast Asia on this and other issues. Since the late 1990s, regular ASEAN summits have been expanded by the participation of Japan, China, and South Korea in ASEAN + 3 (or APT) meetings. Steps in the search for a new monetary regionalism have been numerous.[10]

Does this represent a 'new regionalism' in East Asia without a central role for the United States? It is too early to tell. If not a new regionalism, then it may at least reflect a 'new realism' on the part of Asian leaders in the wake of the financial crises of the 1990s and other contemporaneous changes in regional mood. Irrespective of the explanations of the Asian financial crises, the closing years of the twentieth century convinced Asian regional policy elites, as Fred Bergsten noted, that 'they no longer want to be in thrall to Washington or the West when trouble hits.'[11] Bergsten was rare among American observers in recognizing the degree to which East Asian states felt that they were 'both let down and put upon by the West' in the crisis and that a more purpose-designed, specifically East Asian response to certain policy issues was neither uninteresting nor unreasonable in the circumstances.

Trade, Bilateralism, and Regionalism

Growing Asian concerns were also a reflection of the destabilizing effect on the international trade agenda of the enhanced unilateral character of US policy that accompanied the assumption of office in January 2001 of the Bush administration. While the rhetoric of the market remains strong, the impact of politics on markets is never far away. Nowhere was this better seen in US policy than in the relationships between the US government's rhetorical support for the multilateral trade regime, on the one hand, and its practice towards trade policy, on the other. The imposition of emergency tariffs in 'sensitive US sectors'—on steel imports and increased agricultural subsidies in the Farm Bill in 2001—when accompanied by the constant American hectoring of Japan, Korea, and Europe to end protection and subsidies to their sensitive sectors, highlighted for Asians the marked disconnect between rhetoric and practice in US trade policy. So, too, did the growing US interest in bilateral trading relationships, now a key element of American trade policy in Asia.

For sure, the growing interest in bilateral trade arrangements is determined by a number of factors other than US policy. The WTO had not fared well

since its inception and the unbalanced diet that is the Doha Round has proved particularly indigestible in many parts of the world. But there can be little doubt about the influence of the growth of US interest in bilateral preferential trade agreements (PTAs). Again, this interest was (and is) not simply a US phenomenon. But if the Europeans started it and other, smaller and weaker states also began to explore it, the role of the United States, as the strongest partner in any bilateral relationship, has been disproportionately influential.

For students of political economy it is interesting to note that the proliferation of bilateral PTAs is the issue on which the biggest divide between settled economic theory and short-term political behaviour can be seen in the global economy. On few things are economists and political scientists so agreed than that bilateral trade deals are suboptimal and pose major threats to the multilateral trading system. This is especially so when trade agreements are used to advance non-trade-specific issues, such as security policy. Actions, rather than rhetoric, suggest that the United States since 9/11 has attached more importance to its bilateral deals with a range of countries, including Chile, Australia, Singapore, and Morocco, than it does to the conclusion of an acceptable WTO round. In its defence the US administration argued that is was merely using its bilateral strategy to build what US Trade Representative Robert Zoellick called a 'coalition of liberalizers, placing the US at the heart of a network of initiatives to open markets'. But the decidedly political element to the choice of partners in this process was in little doubt. As Zoellick, speaking at the Institute for International Economics in Washington, noted: 'A free trade agreement is not something that one has a right to. It's a privilege. But it is a privilege that must be earned via the support of US policy goals. . . . [The Bush administration] . . . expects cooperation—or better—on foreign policy and security issues.'[12]

By way of illustration, Zoellick indicated that a free trade deal with New Zealand—given its historical ban on nuclear ship visits and a failure to support the war in Iraq—was unlikely. By contrast, the free trade agreement (FTA) with Australia was 'fast-tracked' and, symbolically, so, too, was the agreement with Singapore, a strong coalition supporter in the overthrow of Saddam Hussein. This has had important follow-up policy implications for the regional dialogue in East Asia. The signing of trade agreements is defended by Asian governments, where they are proving to be increasingly popular. Former Singapore Prime Minister Goh Chok Tong, for example, saw his country's agreement with the United States as having a strategic significance, as a way of 'embedding the US in East Asian regionalism'.[13] The Singapore–US pact also had the happy coincidence of reflecting both countries' desire to manage the role of China in the East Asian region.

The Asian interest in bilateral agreements reflects a general disillusionment with APEC and concern over the agenda of the Doha Round. More specifically, bilateral trade arrangements—in many ways a defining feature of the regional political economy in the early twenty-first century—are felt to give regional policy elites greater control over national trade policies. This reflects the fear of Asian states that their influence on deliberations within the WTO is not always as great as they would wish. As such, bilateral free trade agreements are statements of sovereignty. While the United States may see bilateral agreements as a way of bolstering or rewarding good partners in the fight against terrorism, East Asian leaders also see them as a useful policy tool with both extra-regional and inter-regional payoffs for the states concerned. The effects of this trend can be, at one and the same time, to enhance regional economic convergence and to exacerbate regional economic divergence. At the end of 2003, East Asian states were involved in 41 state-to-state bilateral free trade projects (actual and putative), with Singapore and Thailand the most active, and 23 states were involved in region-to-state agreements such as the ASEAN–China FTA.[14]

The degree to which bilateral free trade agreements or other forms of preferential trade agreements are suboptimal in comparison to the multilateral freeing of trade may be well explained in the theoretical economic literature, but the important question is why sound economic theory does not automatically lead to good public policy? The answer, which most economic theorists ignore, is that good economic theory is often bad politics. Policy-makers are prepared to engage in unco-ordinated bilateral decision-making—often leading to inferior outcomes (especially asymmetrical bargains for weaker states)—*to create an illusion of control over one's own policy processes and policy choices.* It is no coincidence that the ASEAN Free Trade Area was the only FTA project initiated in the region prior to the financial crises of 1997–8. The crisis of that period exposed the inadequacy of the existing institutions of regional economic diplomacy (notably ASEAN and APEC) and the perceived faltering of the Doha Round.

Bilateral economic co-operation in the trade domain is a fact of life in East Asia in the early years of the twenty-first century. The critical issue is the degree to which it might enhance the regional project overall or detract from greater regional economic policy co-ordination and integration. Yet this is clearly not an either/or situation. Elements of both enhanced co-operation and increased competition are present in the contemporary regional policy process. In what is essentially a 'structural argument', bilateralism is seen to bolster the economic foundations of the region with the prospect of enhanced co-operation at the regional level. It can provide a regional 'lattice' of technical and institutional arrangements to reinforce the regional project. This is an argument frequently advanced in the region by states active in the FTA game.[15]

By contrast, a 'process-led argument' in favour of the recourse to bilateralism would suggest that it has the effect of enhancing the broader discourse on regional economic co-operation and integration. No state, it is argued, pursues just a bilateral or multilateral trade policy. The two arms can surely be reinforcing. Bilateral activity should be seen as a complement to other initiatives such as the development of an ASEAN Economic Community (AEC) and the APT, both of which have different but complementary agendas and functions. Again, this is a position advanced by Singapore and Thailand as part of their trade strategies.

The jury will remain out on the strength of these arguments for the foreseeable future and opponents argue that, in fact, the increasing recourse to bilateral initiatives has the effect of undermining the wider regional projects in East Asia. Intellectual and technical capability and political will are finite resources that cannot be indefinitely subdivided without diminishing their utility and effectiveness. At the ASEAN level, bilateral activities must inevitably be in competition for attention with attempts to upgrade the ASEAN Free Trade Area to the AEC by 2020.[16] A longer-term outcome of this competition in the trade domain could be increased consolidation of existing asymmetries, enhanced interstate rivalry among regional neighbours at a more general level, and a diminution of the region's ability to present a united front to other global actors in a range of other policy domains.

In sum, support for enhanced economic co-operation and integration at the regional level is a possible outcome of the trend towards bilateralism in East Asia, but it is not inevitable and strong countervailing tendencies and outcomes are equally possible.[17] The risks may outweigh the opportunities. The degree to which the positive outcome might prevail will be determined in part by the success or failure of activities in other areas of the policy domain and with other putative economic initiatives, such as monetary co-operation, where the collective regional urge is stronger.

Towards an East Asian Economic Community

I have argued that the nascent nature of regional co-operation, when accompanied by the fear of being on the receiving end of asymmetrical agreements in times of low trust in the multilateral trading system, has seen governments developing bilateral strategies. More generally, East Asian economic co-operation (and, indeed, co-operation in the security domain) and the search for a new voice of Asian regionalism remain problematic. However, the regional dialogue has moved on dramatically since the time of the financial crises of 1997–8. The central issue here is how one defines region. The dialogue at the Asia-Pacific level has faltered. APEC's identity crisis persists, as it has become unable to decide if it is an economic or a security body. But the debate about enhanced co-operation at the level of East Asia, writ small to mean ASEAN, continues with discussions about the development of an AEC as a hosting body to integrate the activities of the ASEAN FTA, the ASEAN Framework Agreement on Services, and the ASEAN Investment Agreement. But it is at the level of East Asia—writ large to include ASEAN, China, Japan, and South Korea—that the regional dialogue on how best to mitigate the kind of volatility experienced during the financial crises of 1997–8 has developed most rapidly.

Notwithstanding the failed attempt to establish an Asian Monetary Fund in 1998, the principle behind the proposal did not die. Evidence of an emergence of monetary regionalism is indeed to be found in East Asia. By the end of 1999, the worst impact of the Asian crisis was over and East Asian policy circles once again addressed the topic of more intensive regional co-operation. The regular ASEAN summits were expanded by the participation of China, Japan, and South Korea, the new body being called ASEAN + 3 with the first East Asian summit taking place in Kuala Lumpur in December 1997. Since then, steps in the search for a new monetary regionalism have been frequent and numerous.[18] The most important of these have been:

- In May 2000, Japan suggested a network of currency swaps, in effect a regional liquidity fund, at the annual meeting of Asian Development Bank (ADB) member finance ministers. The idea was that Asian countries should be able to borrow from each other via short-term swaps of currency reserves.
- In September 2000 Thailand's then Deputy Prime Minister and now WTO Secretary-General, Supachai Panitchpakdi, underlined the need for an Asian liquidity fund.
- During the 2000 APT meeting in Singapore, the Chiang Mai initiative, which provides for currency swap agreements to assist govern-

ments faced with future crises, was reaffirmed. At the same time, the Chinese Prime Minister, Zhu Rongji, made a proposal for a free trade area between China and ASEAN. As Il Sakong, chairman of the Korean Institute for Global Economics, noted at the meeting: 'We need some kind of defence mechanism. Since not much is expected to be done at the global level, something should be done at the regional level.'[19]

- At the May 2001 ADB meeting, the Chiang Mai initiative was clarified. The network of bilateral swap agreements was more precisely defined.
- In April 2004 it was proposed that the bilateral nature of the Chiang Mai initiative should be turned into a regional common fund arrangement of some $100 billion on which any state might draw in the event of a financial crisis.

This approach to monetary regionalism only makes sense in practice if a sufficient level of funding is available to underwrite such an enterprise. It could not be countenanced in the absence of a sufficient level of foreign reserves. But funds to meet it are available in East Asia, where reserves are not only high but well distributed. The two largest economies, Japan and China, have the largest reserves. In the event of a crisis, those two economies would make the highest contribution. Also, considering the high level of reserves, a regional liquidity fund is plausible even without using too high a percentage of the reserves of participating central banks. Asia has more foreign reserves than any other region. By late 2004 reserves in the APT countries had climbed to around US$1.9 trillion. This contrasts with total EU reserves of US$260 billion.

The emerging regional (Manila) framework will offer a process of enhanced mutual, IMF-style surveillance and Asian-style 'peer pressure'. In short, it represents a contribution to the regional institutional economic architecture that departs from previous models of regional co-operation in Asia. It is very much part of the wider exercise of soul-searching that has been taking place both within ASEAN and between ASEAN and its other East Asian partners since the turn of the century. At a more exploratory and conceptual level, the idea of an Asian Monetary Fund continues to resurface as regional states seek ways to stabilize their currencies.[20] Other important twenty-first-century initiatives emanating from this mode of thinking include the Asian Bond Fund (ABF) initiative, proposed in June 2003, and the suggestion of a regional stock exchange, both of which have the aim of reducing the distances between the individual national markets and exchanges. One clear benefit of this process would be the raising of standards and regulatory norms and practices across the board in the region. The Chiang Mai initiative and the ABF collectively enhance, although they do not guarantee, the regional capability of resisting financial volatility.

The crucial point of these avenues of exploration is not their immediate significance, nor is it to underestimate the difficulties of such policy co-ordination in the region. Rather, the point is to suggest we would be naive to think that Asians will not continue to develop greater regional institutional mechanisms for the common management of financial questions. To see APT as but an exercise in extended conference diplomacy, reflecting weakness rather than strength, would be misleading. True, it is too early to see what kinds of institutional structures will inevitably be embedded in the region, but the range of interactions developing are unprecedented. APT has moved on from initial leadership meetings. Considerable deepening has taken place with regular ministerial meetings across most policy domains (economics and finance, agriculture, forestry, tourism, etc.).[21]

When looked at collectively the processes set in motion actually represent a more systematic package of activities than would at first sight appear to be the case. The whole will be greater than the mere sum of its parts. The APT process is being institutionalized through the evolution of an overlapping multi-dimensional process of regional conference diplomacy that strengthens, and indeed creates, links between the states of Northeast Asia and Southeast Asia. Whether or not the Asians will be successful in their endeavours, there can be little doubt that the continued exploration of co-operation as a way to combat vulnerability is an established item on the regional policy agenda in the early twenty-first century.

Conclusion

The financial crises at the end of the twentieth century, and Western responses to them, demonstrated the dangers of interpreting Asian political and economic practice based on Western elite assumptions. The often wholesale generalized assumption of Western policy elites that a convergence embodying universal interests would, in the wake of the financial crises, create an Asia more like the liberal stereotypes—that is, more rational, more individualist, more democratic and secular, and concerned with human rights—lacked sound foundations in political practice.[22] The Asian crises did not substantiate the economic convergence hypothesis that most neo-classical economic analyses assumed it would. Rather, the crises of the late twentieth century, and events since then, have confirmed the differences in systemic capitalist organization rather than refute them.

Asian leaders may continue to talk the language of neo-liberalism within the context of APEC gatherings, but much of it is still opposed in practice. The feeling that there was a strongly instrumental element in the Pacific economic relationships of the United States was never eradicated from APEC throughout the 1990s, and US policy in APEC since 9/11 in particular has confirmed that judgement. The financial crisis reform packages, and the overt 'power politics' manner in which they were imposed, followed by changing US policy within APEC in the wake of 9/11, have brought a North–South divide back into the open in the relationship between the Caucasian and East Asian members of APEC. Both the financial crisis and 9/11 demonstrated that APEC was paralyzed by the financial crises.

What the Asian crisis told us was that there was no consensus on how to manage international capitalism. The major financial institutions were

caught between nationalists and liberals with competing views of how the world should work. These institutions had proved to be lead-footed by comparison with the speed at which markets operate. The international financial institutions have been found wanting in both theory and practice by the events in East Asia. Nothing since then has shaken the view—held in many Asian capitals—that the market's punishment of the weaknesses in Asia's financial systems, real as they were and remain, far exceeded the crimes of the times. But the economic crisis also provided a positive learning experience at the multilateral level. That is, that globalization requires the development of institutional capability for prudential regulation at a range of different levels. While most regional policy analysts continue to recognize that regulation is best pursued at the global level, regional initiatives of the type outlined in the Manila framework and in the discussion of an Asian Monetary Fund will continue to evolve.

Thus the events of 1997–8—the most traumatic experienced in Asia since decolonization and the Cold War confrontations of the 1950s and 1960s—have had important lessons for Asian regionalism. The crises sidetracked policy elites from the regional dialogue on trade liberalization and security of the first half of the 1990s. The events of 9/11 and their aftermath exacerbated the first trend. Trade discussions became increasingly bilateral and the security dialogue came to be shaped by the new agenda of the war on global terrorism.

We can expect these multi-dimensional developments in regionalism to continue. But there is a major difference between the early 1990s and the early twenty-first century. In addition to the role of the United States, still the key player but with a different agenda, the future of the region after the crisis is also now more firmly tied to the role of the two Asian regional superpowers than at any time in the past. In a curious but telling fashion, this was seen in the Japanese desire to ensure that its aid response to the devastating Asian tsunami at the end of December 2004 was greater than that of China. Specifically, the future of the region depends not only on Japanese economic reform, but also on a willingness of the People's Republic of China to continue its new-found regional co-operative economic role that it has consolidated since 1997. Regionalism will continue to be an important level of activity, probably less as an arena of dramatic initiative and more as a meso-level expression of the desire to optimize sovereign decision-making within states in the face of globalization. Thus:

> a strikingly contradictory view of the East Asian region emerges. . . . [D]espite the overwhelming structural impediments to integration, East Asia has in recent years become considerably more interdependent, connected and cohesive. [It is] . . . a region that has developed an increasingly dense network of cross-border cooperation, collaboration, interdependence and even formalized institutional integration.[23]

In opposition to Freidberg's oft-cited suggestion that Asia is 'ripe for rivalry',[24] T.J. Pempel suggests instead that it may well be 'ripe for cooperation'. The kind of great power rivalry that Freidberg saw looming on the horizon has not yet come to pass. Regionalism in the Asia-Pacific in the early twenty-first century is different from regionalism in the 1990s. The role of major actors is important in explaining this. Especially important is the increased salience of the views of Japan and China at the expense of those of the United States. To make this assertion is not to deny the residual strength of US opinion. Rather, it is to recognize the growth in influence of the two regional powers, and of China in particular.

If we consider APEC as the dominant regional initiative of the early 1990s, then during this period we saw the US strongly proactive; Japan as a passive, reactive actor in the organization; and China giving its support to the East Asian Economic Caucus initiative of the Malaysians rather than to APEC. The AMF initiative of the late 1990s was initiated by the Japanese and met with resistance (albeit low-key) from the Chinese and outright hostile rejection by the United States. If we

take the attempts to develop enhanced regional monetary co-operation, especially since the Chiang Mai initiative, as the major exercise in regional co-operation in the last few years, we have, for the first time, a position where the United States is opposed, although not of a mind to develop strong countermeasures, and, importantly, both the Japanese and the Chinese are strongly supportive of this regional project. These two major players, it should be stressed, are not engaged in a concerted co-ordination of their foreign policies. Rather, we see a happy coincidence where it is recognized by both major powers that the regional agenda for enhanced monetary policy co-ordination is something that can be supported and advanced comfortable in the knowledge that it is a positive-sum, not a zero-sum, game.

But this is not the kind of regional co-operation with antecedents of a necessarily European intellectual pedigree. Rather, it is what we might call the rise of a regulatory regionalism that links national and global understandings of regulation via the intermediate regional level. Effectively, regionalism is a transmission belt for global disciplines to the national level through the depoliticizing and softening process of the region in which regional policy co-ordination—evolving regional governance—has become the link between the national and the global. It is emerging as a genuinely multi-level exercise and reflects several trends:

1. Regional policy co-ordination to mitigate risk is delegated to the state in order to have the cake of sovereignty and eat it. Indeed, there is a strong relationship between state form, the global economic and political orders, and the nature of regional governance emerging at the meso level. This compromise is inevitable if the continuing tension between nationalism and regionalism in East Asia is not to jeopardize the co-operative endeavour.

2. The meshing of the multi-level process of regulation reinforces the connections between international institutions (e.g., the IMF and World Bank) and regional institutions, such as the ADB, and the emerging instruments of regulation develop-

ing in the context of monetary regionalism at the level of ASEAN + 3, especially the ASEAN regional surveillance process.

3. A way of transmitting internationally agreed codes enforces market standards that tend to emanate, much more than sceptics would wish to claim, from the perceived best practice of international institutions such as the IMF.[25]

A significant point about contemporary regionalism in Asia is that the growing regulatory urge is not simply restricted to trade. Indeed, monetary regionalism is advancing most rapidly. The key to monetary regionalism is closer integration through common national 'regulation' rather than regional institution-building. In discursive terms,

'regional regulation' carries fewer negative connotations for sovereignty and regime autonomy than 'regional institution-building'. Institution-building throughout the pre-crisis days in East Asia carried with it the implications of a European-style pooling of sovereignty. The development of a corpus of regulatory governance at the regional level, rhetorically at least, carries none of the sovereignty-shedding baggage. Notwithstanding changes in Asian regionalism over the past decade, the Achilles heel of regionalism is still to be found in the fact that it remains an elite-driven activity. Despite the aspirations of bodies such as the ASEAN Peoples Forum to enhance the role of civil society in regional activity, what we might call 'a consciousness of region' does not extend deeply into East Asian societies.

Notes

1. Richard Higgott, 'Regionalism in the Asia-Pacific: Two Steps Forward, One Step Back?', in Richard Stubbs and Geoffrey R.D. Underhill, eds, *Political Economy and the Changing Global Order*, 2nd edn (Toronto: Oxford University Press, 2000), 255, 262.

2. 'Crisis' is used here as a generic term to cover a range of currency and financial crises that began in Thailand and spread to other Asian countries throughout 1997 and 1998.

3. Michael Leifer, *The ASEAN Regional Forum: Extending ASEAN's Model of Regional Security* (Oxford: Oxford University Press for the International Institute of Strategic Studies, 1998).

4. Amitav Acharya, *Constructing a Security Community in Southeast Asia: ASEAN and the Problem of Regional Order* (London: Routledge, 2001).

5. Richard Higgott, 'Contested Globalisation: The Changing Context and Normative Challenges', *Review of International Studies* 26 (2000): 131–54.

6. John Williamson, 'The Washington Consensus as a Policy Prescription for Development', Lecture Series, Practitioners of Development,

Washington, DC, 13 Jan. 2004.

7. Richard Higgott, 'The "Securitisation" of U.S. Foreign Economic Policy in East Asia', *Critical Asian Studies* 36, 3 (2004): 425–44.

8. Miles Kahler, 'Legalization as a Strategy: The Asia Pacific Case', *International Organization* 54, 3 (2000): 549–71.

9. Vinod K. Aggarwal and John Ravenhill, 'Undermining the WTO: The Case against "Open Sectoralism"', *Asia Pacific Issues* (Feb. 2001): 1–12.

10. Richard Stubbs, 'ASEAN Plus Three: Emerging East Asian Regionalism', *Asian Survey* 42, 3 (2002): 440–55.

11. Fred Bergsten, 'East Asian Regionalism: Towards a Tripartite World', *The Economist*, 15 July 2000, 20.

12. *New Statesman,* 23 June 2003, 17.

13. *Asia Inc* (Aug. 2003): 10.

14. See Christopher Dent, *The New Economic Bilateralism and Southeast Asia: Convergent or Region Divergent,* British International Studies Association, IPEG Papers in Global Political Economy No. 7, Apr. 2004.

15. See Barry Desker, 'In Defence of FTAS: From Purity to Pragmatism in East Asia', *Pacific Review* 17, 1 (2004): 3–26.

16. See Denis Hew and Hadi Soesastro, 'Realising the ASEAN Economic Community by 2020: ISEAS and ASEAN ISI Approaches', *ASEAN Economic Bulletin* 20, 3 (2003): 292–7.

17. The most trenchant criticism of bilateral PTAs is to be found in the work of Jagdish Bhagwati. See, e.g., Bhagwati, *Free Trade Today* (Princeton, NJ: Princeton University Press, 2002).

18. Heribert Dieter and Richard Higgott, 'Exploring Alternative Theories of Economic Regionalism: From Trade to Finance in Asian Cooperation', *Review of International Political Economy* 10, 3 (2003): 430–54.

19. *Financial Times*, 6–7 May 2000, 9.

20. For detailed chronologies of the development of this process, see Sanae Suzuki, *East Asian Cooperation through Conference Diplomacy: Institutional Aspects of the ASEAN Plus Three (APT) Framework* (Tokyo: Institute for Developing Economies, APEC Study Center, JETRO Working Paper 03–04, No. 7, 2004).

21. Nick Thomas, 'An East Asian Economic Community: Multilateralism Beyond APEC', Conference on Asia Pacific Economies: Multilateral versus Bilateral Relationships, Hong Kong, City University, 19–21 May 2004.

22. See Richard Higgott, 'The Asian Financial Crisis: A Study in the Politics of Resentment', *New Political Economy* 3, 3 (1998): 33–56.

23. T.J. Pempel, 'Emerging Webs of Regional Connectedness', in Pempel, ed., *Remapping East Asia: The Construction of a Region* (Ithaca, NY: Cornell University Press, 2004), 2.

24. Aaron Freidberg, 'Ripe for Rivalry: Prospects for Peace in a Multipolar Asia', *International Security* 18, 3 (1993): 5–33.

25. W. Manupipatpong, 'The ASEAN Surveillance Process and the East Asian Monetary Fund', *ASEAN Economic Bulletin* 19, 1 (2002): 114–15.

Suggested Readings

Acharya, Amitav. *Constructing a Security Community in Southeast Asia: ASEAN and the Problem of Regional Order*. London: Routledge, 2001.

Higgott, Richard. 'The "Securitisation" of U.S. Foreign Economic Policy in East Asia', *Critical Asian Studies* 36, 3 (2004): 425–44.

Jayasuria, Kanishka, ed. *Asian Regional Governance: Crisis and Change*. London: Routledge, 2004.

Pempel, T.J., ed. *Remapping East Asia: The Construction of a Region*. Ithaca, NY: Cornell University Press, 2004.

Ravenhill, John. *APEC and the Construction of Pacific Rim Regionalism*. Cambridge: Cambridge University Press, 2001.

Stubbs, Richard. *Rethinking Asia's Economic Miracle: The Political Economy of War, Prosperity and Crisis*. Basingstoke: Palgrave, 2005.

Web Sites

ASEAN Secretariat: www.aseansec.org
Asia Development Bank: www.adb.org

Asia-Pacific Economic Co-operation Secretariat: www.apecsec.org.sg

Chapter 25

Political Economies of Africa(s) at the Start of the Twenty-first Century

Timothy M. Shaw and Pamela K. Mbabazi

The year 2001 was one of marked changes in the world economy and in Africa itself . . . Africa remains the only region in the world where poverty is rising, with 70 per cent of the poor living in rural areas . . . the majority of African countries are unlikely to meet the Millennium Development Goals of reducing poverty in half by the year 2015.[1]

African countries lag behind other developing country regions in terms of attracting FDI inflows.[2]

In 2001, the global economy experienced the worst economic conditions in over a decade. . . . In marked contrast to the experience during most earlier global recessions, Africa actually outperformed all regions of the world—with the exception of Asian developing countries.[3]

Sustainable development remains elusive in much of Africa, but a minority of 'African democratic developmental states'[4] stand apart from the majority of political economies, which are not growing. Indeed, some African political economies are hardly organized into states. To get beyond the stereotypical image of a continent in chaos, we suggest that there are several Africas rather than one: the continent includes several different political economies at the start of the century. A few of these will realize most of the Millennium Development Goals (MDGs) established by the African Development Bank by 2015, but the majority of

countries and peoples will not. Thus, this analysis offers a somewhat less optimistic overview of the continent than the Africa chapter that appeared in the second edition of this volume. In that chapter it was suggested that a renaissance was possible for at least some of the countries, communities, and economic sectors of the continent.[5]

Globalization may be defined in terms of ideology and policy as well as technology and practice, and it is a process that creates both opportunities and constraints in Africa as elsewhere at the start of the twenty-first century. Given the continent's place at the global periphery, these constraints may outweigh the opportunities. Nevertheless, in terms of economic prospects, niches do exist for competitive African companies and sectors at the start of a new century and for 'new' industries like mobile telephones, fresh fruits, flowers, and vegetables. And politically, opportunities do exist for democratic developmental states like Botswana, Mauritius, and Uganda. In terms of global integration, by some measures, including formal as well as informal trade and the economic roles of diasporas and mafias, the continent appears less peripheral and less distant.

In macroeconomic terms Africa may be the most marginal of the continents. Yet it is not uniformly so. The continent contains a range of economies and polities, companies, and civil societies as well as a cornucopia of raw materials. Nonetheless, the existence of certain commonalities suggests that there may be an 'African' variant of capitalism, just as there are 'liberal' Anglo-

American, 'developmental' Asian, and European 'corporatist' varieties. For the first time, in early 2003, the annual 'Globalization Index' produced by the journal *Foreign Policy* included some African states. The top eight African countries were: Botswana (33), Uganda (36), Nigeria (37), South Africa (38), Tunisia (39), Senegal (41), Kenya (43), and Egypt (46).[6] Interestingly, this list includes the trio of countries (South Africa, Nigeria, and Senegal) that initiated the New Partnership for Africa's Development (NEPAD). This suggests that Africa can, via the G-8, take advantage of globalization, a view that echoes earlier, optimistic evaluation at century's end.[7]

And yet here, too, we are reminded of the fact of many Africas. Traditional aggregate measures of the continent's economic performance are misleading given its distinctive and uneven characteristics. For example, although half a dozen African economies have annual GNPs greater than US$30 billion, apart from South Africa they are all oil producers or are located in North Africa (Egypt, Algeria, Nigeria, Morocco, and Libya). And analysis of the continent's 'real' economy also presents a varied picture. A 'political economy of conflict' perspective reveals that part of this unevenness is attributable to those African wars fought over economic survival and gain. These conflicts, in turn, have an impact on the terms and contents of the internal and external trade of the continent.[8]

Africa's Economies at the Start of a New Millennium

Africa has become a much more interesting and challenging continent in terms of the possibilities for development in recent years. In economic terms, two trends stand out as particularly important. First is the dramatic spread of South African companies and franchises throughout the continent since the beginnings of majority rule in South Africa in the early 1990s. Second, and more recently, a trio of African leaders—Olesesegun Obasanjo from Nigeria, Thabo Mbeki of South Africa, and Abdoulaye Wade from Senegal—have defined and promoted the New Partnership for Africa's

Development that was launched in mid-2001 around the framework of the new African Union (AU). NEPAD constitutes the latest attempt by leading states and presidents to articulate an indigenous direction for the continent at the start of a new century as the overconfidence of neo-liberalism at the global level is yielding to a somewhat less triumphalist version of 'development'. While this vision of an 'African Renaissance' may be less creative or critical than Samir Amin would wish, he notes that at least it does possess some authenticity and possibility.[9]

At the end of the last century, Africa already had a distinctive—albeit marginal—place in a world of globalization(s). This has been reinforced by the intense impacts of 9/11 and the war in Iraq. To be sure, multicultural relations have become more problematic in and around the continent as a result of these events, but at the same time African oil and gas reserves, as well as UN votes, become ever more valuable in the process. In a world of some 200 states, the more than 50 countries in Africa together have some credibility, even if they constituted a smaller proportion of the world total of countries in 2000 (25 per cent) than they did in 1990 (33 per cent). Moreover, some of the 50 are not insignificant global economic players although sub-Saharan Africa, chiefly South Africa, produces only 0.4 per cent of the world's manufactured exports.

The continent includes a wide variety of states at various levels of economic prosperity. There are some 'Fourth World' countries, such as Liberia and Somalia, which control very little. There are also some aspiring 'Second World' economies, such as Botswana, Mauritius, and South Africa, which are not (yet?) in the privileged minority of the Organization for Economic Co-operation and Development (OECD). As well, there is a large middle ground of states that are relatively impoverished but not hopeless, such as Kenya, Morocco, and Senegal, a few of which—for example, Ghana and Uganda—may yet become 'democratic developmental states'. Africa also can boast a few regimes, such as Angola, that have the dubious distinction of having excelled in replicating Mobutustyle avarice. And as some established economies—e.g., Côte d'Ivoire and Zimbabwe—are in decline at the start of the century, so the fortunes of other countries—e.g., Ghana and Tanzania—are on the rise. Indeed, among the world's fastest-growing economies in 2003 were Equatorial Guinea, Chad, and Lesotho, as well as Botswana and Uganda. Such diversity on the continent means that there is significant potential for inter- as well as extra-continental trade in the twenty-first century if 'competition states', entrepreneurial companies, and flexible labour are sufficiently agile and ready to take risks.[10]

In terms of civil society, the proliferation of NGOs, along with other civic groups and social movements that champion issues ranging from ecology and feminism to governance and peace-keeping, serve to balance oppressive regimes and corrosive corporations. The proliferation of focused campaigns against particular companies, such as Shell, along with the popularization of anti-corporate demands and claims on the government from the HIV/AIDS lobby in South Africa, should have an impact on the future policy choices of states and companies alike.

Such antagonism may moderate enthusiasm for 'partnerships' between civil society, on the one hand, and governments and business, on the other, yet the popularity of these alliances in the North, as epitomized by the UN's Global Compact, suggests that they may play a more prominent role on the continent in the coming years. Indeed, partnerships with multinational corporations (MNCs) constitute something of a growth industry as major global companies seek to polish their image and protect their reputations to keep pace with the plethora of corporate codes of conduct, social responsibility, and best-practice guidelines that have developed in recent years. In South Africa, as in other major economies, reports are now published annually on which companies make the best employers (in 2003 these were, among others: BAT, Cell C, Dell, EDS, Ericsson, Ford, Microsoft, M-Web, Nissan, Volkswagen).[11] And in 'visible' or 'vulnerable' sectors, corpora-

tions rush for cover in coalitions like the Framework Convention on Tobacco Control and the International Cocoa Initiative.

After Structural Adjustment: What Prospects for an African Renaissance?

> Despite the modest performance of the African economy as a whole, it is encouraging to note that seventeen African countries achieved rates of growth in excess of 5 per cent, with sixteen others registering growth rates of between 3 and 5 per cent. The number of countries recording negative growth also declined from nine to five.[12]

At the start of a new century change is in the wind. Two decades of somewhat lacklustre structural adjustment programs (SAPs) in combination with anti-globalization forces and continuing economic difficulties have spurred a global shift (however overdue) back to greater concern for sustainable social development rather than just short-term efficiency and profitability.[13] Given the rather mixed record of 20 years of neo-liberalism, development policies may now be starting to evolve, ever so slowly, towards a post-SAP era in the first decade of the twenty-first century. This policy shift has been stimulated in part by fears that global inequality will contribute to terrorism and in part by the related challenge of trying to meet the Millennium Development Goals. These aims are also evident in the North–South 'consensus' around Doha, Monterrey, NEPAD, and the like, which have collectively rendered the notion of a future 'African Renaissance' at least possible.

The promise of long-term prosperity in exchange for short-term hardship held out by the SAPs has in many cases not been realized. Indeed, despite the efforts of heavily indebted poor countries (HIPCs) to meet the myriad SAP conditionalities, still only 1 per cent of global FDI flows reach Africa. Such inflows towards the continent averaged some US$10 billion per annum in the late 1990s, rising to $11.8 billion in 2001.[14] But this FDI was concentrated in a minority of economies, primarily South Africa, Angola, and Nigeria (oil), Botswana (diamonds), and Côte d'Ivoire. In general, surveys of the continent conducted by the UN Conference on Trade and Development (UNCTAD) show that African economies and sectors that are attractive to FDI coincide with the African Competitive Index of the World Economic Forum (WEF). According to an UNCTAD opinion survey, the most attractive African states in terms of a business-friendly environment are Botswana, South Africa, Namibia, Uganda, and Côte d'Ivoire.[15] In general, of course, these are the more liberal states, which are naturally more likely to open themselves to evaluations of their economic and political governance under any NEPAD peer review mechanism. Formal, recorded foreign direct investment outflows (i.e., excluding capital flight, often by presidential regimes!) from the continent were similarly concentrated. The primary source was South Africa, which reflects efforts to internationalize its industries, invest in listings on the London Stock Exchange, and purchase companies in the EU/UK (e.g., AAF, Digidata, OM, SABMiller) and the United States (e.g., Sasol) as well as franchises in the rest of the continent.

Five current developments indicate that at least some parts of the continent may be able to turn 'globalizations' to their advantage. First, in a few countries, companies and sectors have been expanding. One major example is the minerals sector in Tanzania. In particular, new gold mines and technologies have led to a gold rush in the boom town of Mwanza on Lake Victoria, where Anglo American, in association with Ashanti Goldfields of Ghana, is a key player. These two African giants agreed to a merger in 2003, leading to the world's second largest gold conglomerate. Large-scale mining commenced at Geita in mid-2000, where 720,000 ounces were produced by early 2003. Ashanti already operates in Ghana, Guinea, and Zimbabwe as well as Tanzania, and is now conducting explorations in seven African states.

Second, at century's turn, Africa had begun to develop some innovative development partnerships that have grouped together a range of functionally disparate actors. These have involved local and city governments and communities, as well as large and small companies responding to globalization. The most advanced of these partnership developments is the Maputo corridor in Mozambique with its toll road, electricity, and oil and water pipelines. The corridor lies between Maputo and Gauteng and has the Mozal aluminum refinery as its centrepiece. Similarly, in the Eastern Cape, the Coega Industrial Development Zone outside Port Elizabeth involves major infrastructural developments, such as a town and port to facilitate Alcan's new aluminum smelter and proposed platinum mining and refining further along the 'Wild Coast'.

Third, tourism has become the continent's second largest formal-sector industry after oil and gas. South Africa in particular benefits from the diversion of up-market travellers from places such as the Middle East and Zimbabwe. In addition, South Africa aims to attract long-term retirees to its shores by offering optional medical procedures to complement its tourist industry, which centres on golf and wine. As well, despite the two sets of terrorist attacks in Nairobi and Mombasa, Kenya, in the early 2000s and earlier strikes in Dar es Salaam, Tanzania, and Nairobi in the late 1990s, Kenya's tourism sector has proven remarkably resilient.

Fourth has been the exploitation of new technologies as well as markets. Important examples are the supply chains linking Africa to Europe, and sometimes Asia, for fresh fruit, flowers, and vegetables. Refrigerated trucks, warehouses, and air freight, all typically linked by computers, are used to supply major supermarket chains and other outlets with fresh, often organic, produce on a just-in-time basis. The primary producers with the necessary infrastructure and connections have traditionally been Kenya, South Africa, and Zimbabwe (which is now in decline), while Uganda appears to be an up-and-comer in this category. Some produce also reaches Europe from Gambia and Senegal.

Finally, in addition but not unrelated to the above developments, three leading airlines have emerged on the continent. Importantly, each facilitates global and regional connections through air freight and commercial passenger services. The continent's primary airline is South African Airways (SAA), which connects Southern Africa to the rest of the continent, Europe, Asia, and the United States all through Africa's hub, Johannesburg. Second, Kenya Airways is part of the KLM/Northwest alliance and uses Nairobi as its hub. Third is Ethiopian Airlines, which is smaller than SAA but also connects the African Union and the UN Economic Commission for Africa (ECA) to the continent and the world. Alongside these three major regional carriers, British Airways now has two major regional carriers operating under its franchise in Southern and Eastern Africa. As well, Egyptian Airlines links Africa to the Middle East.

NEPAD as Africa's Response to Globalization(s)?

> Africa's gross continental product is about $540 billion, more or less the same as that of Spain, and only fives times the size of Exxon Mobil.[16]

At the beginning of the 1980s, African leaders responded to growing disappointment with the meagre fruits of independence with a development blueprint that contradicted the emerging 'Washington Consensus'. This blueprint was called the Lagos Plan of Action. Two decades later, a new generation of more democratic leaders is concerned not to make the same mistakes as their post-independence predecessors. A trio of 'modern' presidents—from South Africa, Nigeria, and Senegal—have formulated NEPAD as the continent's attempt to accept and take advantage of globalization rather than to resist it. At least eight dimensions of the 'new' Africa's quest for more rapid growth and development through globalization can be identified.

First, in the 1990s, some African regimes had already achieved a greater degree of ownership as SAPs yielded to the HIPC initiative. These newer policies have aimed at integrating macroeconomic policy with the aims of nationally agreed poverty reduction strategy programs or papers (PRSPs).

These PRSPs were generated through distinctive national discussions and negotiations, typically involving major stakeholders from civil society and the private sector. Such 'triangular' (government, civil society, and private sector) talks led to enhanced debt reduction and official development assistance (ODA) provisions. The former has been encouraged by global campaigns such as Jubilee 2000 and the latter by growing ODA budgets, at least among many OECD donors, if not the United States.

Second, following the HIPC experiment after the end of the post-Cold War 'honeymoon' of the early 1990s and in recognition of the continent's continuing conflicts and development deficit, the G-8 became increasingly concerned about the deteriorating situation in Africa and invited leading presidents from the continent to its Genoa summit in mid-2001. This novel dialogue led to NEPAD's formation and to the G-8's response, in terms of the promise of increased aid, in mid-2002 at Kananaskis in Canada. Given the particular commitment of G-8 leaders Tony Blair of the UK and Canada's Jean Chrétien, new programming for the continent has been provided by at least some of the G-8 countries, notably Britain, Canada, and France. As well, Japan has continued its Tokyo International Conference on African Development initiative and USAID has pledged US$500 million to health care. Furthermore, the EU has replaced its Lomé agreement with the ACP countries with the Cotonou Convention and has included an 'everything but arms' trade policy. As well, the EU has now finalized a bilateral free trade agreement with South Africa. In addition, the Global Coalition for Africa, 'an intergovernmental forum for African development' until recently headed by Hage Geingob, continues to network among states and NGOs on and off the continent on topics that include corruption, governance, private-sector development, and security. Meanwhile, the WEF draws attention to the continent in both annual Davos meetings and regular conferences in and on Africa.

Third, the US African Growth and Opportunity Act announced by the Clinton administration in the late 1990s has provided significant opportunities for new manufacturing in African countries that meet its criteria. Some success has been achieved. For example, investments so far produced some US$3 billion in annual exports to the United States in 2001. To date, the primary sources of beneficiaries from such exports have been Lesotho, Nigeria, Kenya, South Africa, Swaziland, and Uganda.[17]

Fourth, some larger South African companies, reaching out to the rest of the continent in a post-apartheid world, are increasing their investments both in Africa and in other parts of the world. For example, SABMiller is now the second largest global beer corporation with activities concentrated in emerging markets in Eastern Europe, China, and recently the United States, as well as in Africa. And de Beers is active in new diamond mines and explorations in Canada. Moreover, Digidata, Investec, and Old Mutual, as well as AAC and de Beers, are now all London-based as well as operating in South Africa.

Fifth, major global MNCs are increasingly active on the continent, especially in its higher-growth countries and regions. For example, Bata (Canada) operates its shoe business in eight African states, mainly in the South African Development Community (SADC) of Botswana, Congo, Malawi, South Africa, Zambia, and Zimbabwe as well as in Commonwealth members like Kenya and Uganda. The now-notorious Parmalat (Italy) has had a major presence in South Africa with milk and yogurt outlets also in Botswana, Mozambique, Swaziland, and Zambia. And Danone (France) manufactures and sells food products in both South and North Africa. After 50 years, Volkswagen in Uitenhage now produces one in five of the cars sold in South Africa and by 2001 had exported 100,000 units. Similarly, having advanced from the assembly of completely knocked-down imported parts to full manufacture, BMW invested a billion rand in the mid-1990s and now exports 60,000 units a year, with another 2 billion rand investment in its plant in Gauteng-Rosslyn expected before the end of the first decade of the new century. Indeed, South Africa's automotive sector has grown—in terms of values of exports—from 20 billion to 40 billion rand since 2000, partly because Volkswagen, BMW, and Daimler-Benz began integrating South African operations into their global supply chains in 1996.

Sixth, regional organizations have been one familiar means by which African states have sought to achieve growth. At least at a formal level, however, such arrangements have rarely realized their targets, even if more informal regionalisms—ecological, ethnic, social, etc.—have provided more creative and resilient sources of integration. While the East African Community has risen phoenix-like from the ashes, the Economic Community of West African States (ECOWAS) is still largely moribund and the SADC has become overstretched by admitting new members, notably the non- or multi-state Congo. In other words, the SADC has suffered from expanding from a meso- to a macro-level grouping. In turn, the Common Market for Eastern and Southern Africa (COMESA) and the Cross-Border Initiative in Eastern and Southern Africa compete with the SADC. The micro-level Southern Africa Customs Union (SACU) and the Rand Common Monetary Area, however, look more promising. In effect, the strains that have attended the SADC's expansion to the 'state' of Congo are being offset by the successes of more micro-level arrangements. These relatively more attractive and manageable achievements include a renegotiated SADC (finally agreed to in mid-2003), corridors and triangles, the Highland water scheme, and the Maputo corridor.[18]

Seventh, NEPAD has begun to develop ambitious sectoral plans, including ones for agriculture, transportation, industry, and telecommunications. And the African Development Bank has committed some US$200 million in 2003 for 17 projects. These infrastructural developments are also not unconnected to the expansion of South African capital into the rest of the continent, which has been triggered by pressures for market expansion by erstwhile state-owned monopolies to privatize. Of these, electricity supplier Eskom and Vodacom, the telecom supplier, are the most salient. Given the current inability of supply to match demand, Eskom's ambitions extend well beyond the Southern African region and include investment plans for 2000–5 comprising $240 million in Southern African projects, $445 million dedicated to West Africa, $86 million to North and Central Africa, and $245 million destined for East Africa. Eskom is also expected to generate 20 per cent of Nigerian capacity by 2004 through a joint venture with Shell. Likewise, Sasol, the formerly state-owned oil company, will supply oil to Gauteng, from the Pande en Temane fields in Mozambique, along a 865-km pipeline estimated to boost Mozambique's GDP by 20 per cent! In fact, South African capital has invested a total of 25 billion rand in Mozambique over the past five years.

Finally, despite endless reassuring noises about good governance and the 'African Peer Review Mechanism', doubts remain about how stringent and effective such a process will be, given African governments' reluctance to speak out against human rights and constitutional abuses in Zimbabwe. Yet, in mid-2003, ahead of the G-8 meeting in France, the first set of eminent Africans was selected to implement the process. They are: Adebayo Adedeji (Nigeria), Bethuel Kiplagat (Kenya), Graca Machel (Mozambique), Mourad Medelci, Dorothy Njeuma, Marie Angelique Savane (Senegal) (Chair), and Chris Stahls (South Africa). As well, 16 countries have so far acceded to the Review Mechanism, signalling their willingness to open themselves up to evaluation.

Political Economy of Conflicts: Economies without States

> The illegal trade in drugs, arms, intellectual property, people and money is booming. Like the war on terrorism, the fight to control these illicit markets pits governments against agile, stateless and resourceful networks empowered by globalization.[19]

Africa is not marginal in terms of its role in illegal networks. Neither is it marginal in the number of its conflicts that have their roots in the political economy of human insecurity. While it is recognized that some of the continent's contemporary wars are functions of

'national security' imperatives, most are rooted in the lack of human security. A considerable amount of violence is associated with very basic economies that function outside of the formal state-bounded exchange relations. The human, economic, and ecological costs of such regional conflicts—from Central to West Africa—are incalculable. They certainly pose fundamental challenges to 'new' civil–military relations that incorporate the privatization of security personnel and to the claims and ideals of NEPAD.[20]

At the turn of the century, a new genre of analysis began to emerge from scholars and development agencies on the economic causes of conflict on the continent. These have been characterized by Mark Duffield as the 'merging of development and security'. He argues that this is a function of new insecurities associated with growing inequalities in the global political economy alongside changes in the character of war itself. Duffield makes the point that 'the focus of the new security concerns is not the threat of traditional interstate wars but the fear of underdevelopment as a source of conflict, criminalized activity and international instability.'[21] Interestingly, such a perspective has been articulated by both conservative and radical political economists. The former include macroeconomists from the World Bank, while the latter group features scholars such as William Reno and Duffield as well as a range of NGOs, especially Partnership Africa Canada.[22]

Nevertheless, in some cases, such as the 'Kimberley Process', African governments have successfully collaborated with non-state interests over conflict reduction. In the case of 'blood' or 'conflict' diamonds, de Beers, a South African MNC, helped to organize a partial response. Of course, the action of de Beers was in response to a potential consumer boycott, partly shaped by NGO activism. Indeed, in collaboration with the Open Society Foundation and Global Witness, 130 NGOs in an Extractive Industries Transparency Initiative are now clamouring for resource multinationals to disclose how their funds—taxes, royalties, fees, and the like—paid to African regimes are distributed. Such an initiative reveals the potential for consumer activism to emulate the Kimberley Process in relation to oil, gas, and mining.

The political economy of war and conflict is also related to the significance of African diasporas, both as a conduit for trade and as a source of remittances. The ubiquity of the yellow and black Western Union sign on the continent is but one indication of the economic importance of diasporas. Despite difficulties in estimating total flows, for societies like Cape Verde, Eritrea, Sudan, and Uganda remittances can be estimated to account for around 10–25 per cent of GDP. Similarly, Ghanaians in the United States returned between US$250 million and $350 million per annum throughout the 1990s, more than the country received in FDI.

Furthermore, the continent has to deal with the threat from the trade in human organs, endangered species, and toxic waste, all informal and illegal niche markets. Finally, looking beyond the present circumstances, a set of longer-term resource wars around the continent can be anticipated involving a range of actors. Potential future conflicts over such issues as oil and gas, fresh water, river valleys, and biodiversity suggest that, even if the causes of warfare change, Africa will likely remain a site of human and environmental toll.

Partnerships for Millennium Development Goals

Africa is now host to an array of think-tanks and networks as well as companies and organized crime rings. All of these groups affect development debates and prospects. The optimistic aura of the turn of the century led to the articulation, at the UN General Assembly, of the Millennium Development Goals (MDGs). The MDGs laid out a set of basic human development targets that would be of particular relevance to the poorest countries and communities of the continent. These goals have been espoused in NEPAD, which has set a target of 7 per cent annual growth in order to reach these aims. Given the elusiveness of many if not most MDGs for Africa, it is worth taking note of four international

political economy issues that bring together state (national and international) and non-state actors in forms of limited yet targeted 'global governance'.

First, the HIV/AIDS epidemic poses major economic and development challenges throughout the continent and has global implications. The infection rate is still rising in Southern Africa even if it has peaked further north, most notably in Uganda. The post-apartheid South African state has been the most reluctant to prescribe anti-retroviral drugs despite some 4 million HIV-positive citizens. But such reticence incited an activist NGO treatment action campaign in the late 1990s that was reminiscent of the anti-apartheid movement. Meanwhile, mining companies like Anglo American and de Beers, which are central to national and global efforts to combat HIV/AIDS, are actively pursuing HIV/AIDS campaigns that stress the importance of access to anti-retrovirals. Furthermore, encouraged by the support of the Gates Foundation, financed by Microsoft, and the US regime of George W. Bush, novel and generous partnerships have developed around the Global Fund to Fight AIDS, tuberculosis, and malaria.

Second, global anti-tobacco campaigns have profound implications for African producers and consumers, let alone tax collectors. Campaigns against ubiquitous tobacco-producing MNCs like Altria (a.k.a. Philip Morris) and British American Tobacco have continued even as manufacturers have begun to target the South rather than the litigious North. The resulting standoffs have led to a World Health Organization (WHO) Framework Convention on Tobacco Control agreed to by states and non-state actors in early 2003. The Convention has been cautiously welcomed by the tobacco industry, which has crucial African connections. Tobacco leaves have been grown in Southern Africa for a long time. Indeed, tobacco is the biggest non-food agricultural crop and British American is the largest tobacco company on the continent, especially active in Côte d'Ivoire, Kenya, and South Africa. The International Tobacco Growers Association, which includes Nigeria, South Africa, Tanzania,

Zambia, and Zimbabwe, claims to welcome the WHO process and Convention, but many outstanding legal and health issues remain.

Third, a parallel International Cocoa Initiative is intended to head off any negative fallout from 'child slavery' allegations surrounding the global chocolate industry. Like the Kimberley Process and the Tobacco Framework, this is another example of a mixed-actor 'governance' initiative involving consumers, international organizations like the ILO, organized labour, MNCs, and NGOs that aims to preempt any potential boycott campaigns like that which Nestlé endured over baby food.

Finally, the Extractive Industries Transparency Initiative, mentioned above, is a campaign to shame mining, oil, and gas companies into revealing the full details of all their payments. The initiative, which is aimed at the full disclosure of tax information along with any possible below-board payments made to regimes (e.g., those made by oil producers in Angola to the government), is an indication of the degree to which informal and illegal economic activities intermingle with the formal and legal economies. It is also a sign of the salience of good governance agendas on the continent.

Alongside these efforts, a trio of innovative academic and think-tank initiatives are bringing change to the intellectual climate of the continent. First, the African Economic Research Consortium, a novel graduate and research program supported by Western bilateral and foundation donors, has facilitated 15 years of graduate training and research, albeit of a somewhat neo-classical, World Bank-compatible orientation. Second, the World Bank and OECD donor-financed African Capacity Building Foundation has established a series of research networks and advocacy institutions throughout the continent to pursue work in development, economics, ecology, and the like. The Foundation has used these funds to help finance major think-tanks in several African capitals. Altogether 48 have been established, with more than one in a few major states. The Botswana Institute of Development Policy Analysis and the Economic Policy Research Centre (Uganda) are two good exam-

ples. And finally, the World Bank-initiated Global Development Network has a considerable African as well as Asian presence. Its networks and conferences are increasingly separated from those of the international financial institutions, yet its orientation remains excessively economic and positivist.

The 'New' South Africa in Africa

The South African business sector is becoming a force on the continent. Indeed, at the dawn of the twenty-first century there was more FDI in the rest of the continent from South Africa than from anywhere else. States and companies north of the Limpopo River now have a choice when searching out FDI. Not only can they look to capital from old sources such as the EU, the UK, and the US or from newer sources like Japan and the rest of Asia, but now South Africa, which is both closer and more familiar, is also a potential source of FDI.

South African franchises in the retail sector, notably food, clothing, and related industries, have 'invaded' the continent. For example, by the early twenty-first century Shoprite had become the continent's largest retailer, with 92 supermarkets in 13 countries in addition to South Africa. This has helped South Africa increase exports. For the emerging upper-middle classes, Woolworth franchises are now found in Botswana, Kenya, Lesotho, Mauritius, Namibia, Nigeria, Swaziland, Tanzania, Uganda, Zambia, and Zimbabwe. Interestingly, with the exception of Tanzania and Zambia, all of these fall well within the United Nations Development Program's *Human Development Report 2002* medium human development category. This suggests that not unlike the 'Big Mac index', the number of Woolworth stores may be suggestive of the size and presence of a middle class!

Meanwhile, the service sectors, from finance to communications, are also expanding. Stanbic Bank operates in Botswana, Congo, Ghana, Tanzania, Uganda, Zambia, and Zimbabwe and is considering openings in Angola and Kenya. As well, two financial companies of South African origin are becoming both continental and global. Investec operates in the SADC, especially Botswana, Mozambique, and Namibia, as well as in the United Kingdom, United States, Australia, Ireland, and Israel. And Old Mutual is already in Kenya, Namibia, and Zimbabwe as well as the UK. Two major South African-based hotel companies are increasingly active in the SADC and COMESA. Protea prides itself in being the largest hotel company on the continent. It is in a dozen African states from Egypt to South Africa, including a half-dozen hotels in Tanzania. The other, Sun International, occupies a more exclusive segment centred on casinos and golf in the SADC. In the communications sector, MTN has mobile phone licences in Cameroon, Rwanda, Swaziland, Uganda, and Nigeria. And MNet/DStv operates satellite TV facilities throughout the continent via a series of concentric circles emanating out from its South African hub.

Africa in 2020: Beyond the Fringe?

This study presents challenges to prevailing international political economy approaches and debates and has relevance beyond Africa. In particular, we suggest that informal and illegal sectors need to be juxtaposed with the formal and legal sectors[23] and that even African developmental states require energetic private sectors, such as diamonds in Botswana and gold in Tanzania. 'Success stories' in Africa, as elsewhere, require innovative coalitions or partnerships that incorporate non-state actors. Furthermore, this perspective challenges estab-

lished notions in a number of social science disciplines that have the state, society, and market as their focus. Even more than before, governance of the international political economy in the new century requires creative networking among a range of actors, as found in some franchise agreements and supply chains. Globalization necessitates adaptation at regional, national, and local levels in Africa, as elsewhere, by a wide diversity of actors.

Policy responses from state and non-state actors at all levels need to be creative in a world of 200 states and competing companies, regions, and sectors. This argument has been underscored by myriad national and regional human development reports, most recently the 460-page report of the commission for Africa, chaired by Tony Blair, which was published in March 2005 prior to the G-8 meeting at Gleneagles, Scotland, in July 2005.[24]

The very diversity found in today's Africa(s) should be cause for some optimism, a point that NEPAD tries to capture. But whether the African Economic Community, the African Union, the UN Economic Commission for Africa, and/or NEPAD are either compatible or sustainable remains an open question. Nevertheless, the dynamism of civil society in and around Africa should provide some reassurance that, despite Amin's scepticism,[25] human development and human security indicators may improve rather than worsen for some of the continent's countries, communities, and companies in the new millennium.

Notes

The first draft of this chapter, which has since been extensively revised, owed much to Timothy M. Shaw and Janis van der Westhuizen, 'Trading Africa: Transforming Fringe into Franchise', in Brian Hocking and Steven McGuire, eds, *Trade Politics*, 2nd edn (London: Routledge, 2004)

1. African Development Bank, *African Development Report, 2002: Rural Development for Poverty Reduction in Africa* (Oxford: Oxford University

Press for the African Development Bank, 2002), i.

2. UNCTAD, *World Investment Report, 1999: Foreign Direct Investment and the Challenge of Development* (New York and Geneva: UNCTAD, 1999), 52.

3. African Development Bank, *African Development Report, 2002*, 4–5.

4. Thandika Mkandawire, 'Thinking about Developmental States in Africa', *Cambridge Journal of Economics* 25 (2001): 289–313.

5. Timothy M. Shaw and Julius E. Nyang'oro,

'African Renaissance in the New Millennium? From Anarchy to Emerging Markets?', in Richard Stubbs and Geoffrey R.D. Underhill, eds, *Political Economy and the Changing Global Order*, 2nd edn (Toronto: Oxford University Press, 2000), 274–83.

6. 'Measuring Globalization: Who's Up, Who's Down?', *Foreign Policy* (Jan.–Feb. 2003): 65. The index lists countries in terms of their global links. Botswana is the highest ranked of the African countries at 33 on the list.

7. Shaw and Nyang'oro, 'African Renaissance in the New Millennium?'

8. Mark Duffield, *Global Governance and the New Wars: The Merging of Development and Security* (London: Zed Books, 2001).

9. Samir Amin, 'Africa: Living on the Fringe', *Monthly Review* 53 (Mar. 2000): 50.

10. Philip Cerny, 'Globalization and Other Stories', in Axel Hulsemeyer, ed., *Globalization in the Twenty-first Century: Convergence or Divergence?* (London: Palgrave, 2003), 51–66; Timothy M. Shaw, 'Regional Dimensions of Conflict and Peace-building in Contemporary Africa', *Journal of International Development* 15, 4 (May 2003): 487–98.

11. See <www.researchfoundation.com>.

12. African Development Bank, *African Development Report, 2002*, i.

13. Rita Abrahamsen, *Disciplining Democracy: Development Discourse and Good Governance in Africa* (London: Zed Books, 2000); Ian Taylor, 'Globalization and Regionalization in Africa: Reactions to Attempts at Neo-liberal Regionalism', *Review of International Political Economy* 10 (May 2003): 310–30; Thandika Mkandawire and Charles C. Soludo, eds, *Our Continent, Our Future: African Perspectives on Structural Adjustment* (Dakar: CODESRIA, 2001).

14. Vijay Makhan, *Economic Recovery in Africa: The Paradox of Financial Flows* (London: Palgrave Macmillan, 2002).

15. UNCTAD, *World Investment Report 1999: Foreign Direct Investment and the Challenge of Development* (New York and Geneva, 1999), 49.

16. Phoebe Griffith, *Unbinding Africa: Making Globalization Work for Good Governance* (London: Foreign Policy Centre, May 2003).

17. See <www.agoa.gov>; Additya Mattro, Devesh Roy, and Arvind Subramanian, 'The AGOA and Rules of Origin: Generosity Undermined?', *World Economy* 26, 6 (June 2003): 829–51.

18. Fredrik Soderbaum and Ian C. Taylor, eds, *Regionalism and Uneven Development in Southern Africa: The Case of the Maputo Development Corridor* (Aldershot: Ashgate, 2003).

19. Moises Naim, 'Five Wars of Globalization', *Foreign Policy* (Jan.–Feb. 2003): 29.

20. Gavin Cawthra and Robin Luckham, eds, *Governing Insecurity: Democratic Control of Military and Security Establishments in Transitional Democracies* (London: Zed Books, 2003); Sandra J. MacLean, H. John Harker, and Timothy M. Shaw, eds, *Advancing Human Security and Development in Africa: Reflections on NEPAD* (Halifax: CFPS, 2002).

21. Duffield, *Global Governance and the New Wars*, 7.

22. See William Reno, *Warlord Politics and African States* (Boulder, Colo.: Lynne Rienner, 1998); Ian Smillie et al., *The Heart of the Matter: Sierra Leone, Diamonds and Human Security* (Ottawa: Partnership Africa Canada, 2000).

23. Patrick Chabal and Jean-Pascal Daloz, *Africa Works: Disorder as Political Instrument* (London: James Currey, 1999).

24. Commission for Africa, *Our Common Interest: Report of the Commission for Africa* (London, Mar. 2005).

25. Amin, 'Africa'.

Suggested Readings

Bond, Patrick, ed. *Fanon's Warning: A Civil Society Reader on the New Partnership for Africa's Development*. Trenton, NJ: Africa World Press, 2002.

Dunn, Kevin C., and Timothy M. Shaw, eds. *Africa's Challenge to International Relations Theory*. London: Palgrave, 2001.

Grant, J. Andrew, and Fredrik Soderbaum, eds. *The New Regionalism in Africa*. Aldershot: Ashgate, 2003.

Harrison, Graham. *Issues in the Contemporary Politics of Sub-Saharan Africa: The Dynamics of Struggle and Resistance*. London: Palgrave Macmillan, 2002.

MacLean, Sandra J., H. John Harker, and Timothy M. Shaw, eds. *Advancing Human Security and Development in Africa: Reflections on NEPAD*. Halifax: CFPS, 2002.

Parpart, Jane L., and Timothy M. Shaw. 'African Development Debates and Prospects at the Turn of the Century', in Patrick J. McGowan and Philip Nel, eds, *Power, Wealth and Global Equity: An International Relations Textbook for Africa*, 2nd edn. Cape Town: UCT Press for IGD, 2002, 296–307.

Shaw, Timothy M. 'Africa', in Mary Hawkesworth and Maurice Kogan, eds, *Routledge Encyclopedia of Government and Politics*, 2nd edn. London: Routledge, 2004, 1184–97

Vale, Peter, Larry A. Swatuk, and Bertil Oden, eds. *Theory, Change and Southern Africa's Future*. London: Palgrave, 2001.

Web Sites

Africa Institute of South Africa: www.ai.org.za
African Union: www.africa-union.org
All Africa Global Media: www.allafrica.com
Business Day: www.bday.co.za
Commission for Africa: www.commissionforafrica.org

Mbendi Information for Africa: www.mbendi.co.za
New Partnership for Africa's Development: www.nepad.org
UN Economic Commission for Africa: www.uneca.org
Weekly Mail and Guardian: www.mg.co.za

Responses to Globalization

Introduction

State Responses to Globalization

Richard Stubbs and Sarah Eaton

The chapters in Part IV complement those in previous sections by examining states' responses to globalization and the effect of these responses on the changing global order. In particular, the chapters pick up some of the themes suggested in Geoffrey Underhill's Introduction to Part I of this volume and examine a number of key states and the European Union in terms of how they have reacted to the forces generated by globalization. It is important to review how states have responded to globalization because the state has long been considered the primary actor in international affairs and, therefore, pivotal to the study of international relations and the international political economy. Even though interest in the state has waxed and waned among students of international relations in recent years, it is still crucial to our understanding of the workings of the international political economy.

Despite its centrality to the discipline, however, there has been some confusion over how the 'state' should be defined. The traditional view of the state, found in realist and neo-realist international relations texts, emphasizes the state's comprehensive control, through coercive and administrative means, over its territory and population, as well as its capacity to operate as a unitary, autonomous actor in an anarchic international system. The assumption is that the state pursues policies in the international arena in the name of its people and territory. There is much to be said for this approach; it is central to international law and, moreover, nearly everyone uses it as convenient shorthand for talking about various actions in the international arena. For example, we are accustomed to media references to the 'American policy' on trade liberalization or the 'Japanese position' at deliberations of the World Bank.

But scholars who approach the study of IPE with a background in comparative politics view the state in a slightly different way. They see the state in domestic institutional, or Weberian, terms as 'a set of administrative, policing and military organizations headed, and more or less well coordinated by, an executive authority'.[1] Such a view of the state paves the way for analyses of the impact of competing domestic pressures on the state and recognition that the state itself may be divided on a particular foreign economic policy issue. These two views of the state, while not the only ones used in analyzing the international political economy, demonstrate the lack of agreement over how this core concept should be defined.

Not only is the very definition of the state in doubt, but its role in the global economy is also hotly debated. One set of analysts argues that the state's power is in decline or, as Susan Strange asserts, that what we are experiencing is the 'retreat of the state'.[2] The power of the state, so this argument goes, is being undermined by an array of factors, including the rapid mobility of capital and the increasing integration of capital markets, the rising power of the major multinational corporations, the revolution in communications, and the expanding authority of international organizations. Globalization is thus depicted as a process that subverts the state's capacity to act in the interest of its citizens.

However, there are those who would refute this view of the role of the state. Some argue that globalization and, therefore, its effects have been greatly exaggerated.[3] As a consequence, of course, this approach suggests that globalization should be viewed as not nearly as detrimental to the power of the state as the 'retreatists' would have us believe. Others argue that the state is not so much in decline as in the process of being transformed.[4] Globalization, it is argued, has required that the institutional state must reconcile the domestic interests it represents and the pressures that emanate from the international political economy. In mediating between domestic interests and the international political economy, states are being forced to transform themselves and the economies they regulate in such a way as to ride out, or even take advantage of, the changes to the international political economy brought about by globalization. Hence, the point needs to be made that arguments about the transformation of the state should not be confused with those about the decline of the state.

It should also be noted that the debate about the role of the state in the face of globalization has taken place at a time when other factors must also be taken into account. Importantly, of course, a central reason for the development of states over the last few centuries was to mobilize resources in order to fight wars. Indeed, Charles Tilly's aphorism, that 'wars make states',[5] strongly suggests that the relative peace of the post-Cold War years of the 1990s meant that some of the rationale for state intervention in the economy was eroded and, therefore, tended to reinforce the 'retreatist' position. Certainly, citizens appeared much less willing to cede power to state institutions in order to increase their security against military threats that they perceived to be receding. This lack of a perceived military threat had other consequences. For example, the calls by subnational groups for an increased role in social and economic decision-making could no longer be kept in check by the fear of an external enemy. These subnational groups began to gain in political power. In Britain, for example, this meant the devolution of powers to Scotland and Wales. During the 1990s, then,

states were depicted as either distracted by internal problems or incapable of wielding the economic power they once held. States were viewed as being increasingly marginalized as other actors were thought to be directing the global economy.

But all this changed with two major global developments. First, a series of financial crises in Mexico, Asia, and Russia during the second half of the 1990s underscored the problems created by unfettered economic liberalization. There was an increasing awareness that state intervention was necessary to provide a properly regulated environment in which economic development could take place. Gradually, during the first years of the new millennium, the institutional states began to increase their control over their economies in places such as South Korea, Thailand, and Russia.[6] Second, the 11 September 2001 attacks on the World Trade Center in New York and the Pentagon in Washington, as well as the 12 October 2002 bombings in Bali, brought security issues back onto centre stage. Many institutional states that feared a recurrence of these attacks reasserted their authority over both social and economic policy areas. Rather than the retreat of the state, therefore, it can be argued that there has been a steady advance of state power spurred on by the new security threat. Certainly, both domestic and foreign economic policies have been caught up in this renewed assertion of state authority as security concerns have come to trump economic interests and goals in particular circumstances.

Intriguingly, the Asian tsunamis of December 2004 initially underscored the role of supra-state organizations, such as the United Nations, and non-state actors, such as aid organizations and diaspora communities. However, once governments grasped the enormity of the crisis and the strength of their populations' commitment to aiding those who were suffering, many states, most notably Japan, Australia, Germany, and Sweden, made substantial contributions to dealing with the recovery process. In many ways the response of world public opinion to the Asian tsunamis was a reflection of the rapid increase in globalization that has taken place in the last decade or so. Yet, despite the major contribution made by non-state aid organizations, such as Oxfam, state aid was seen as absolutely vital to overcome the massive resource gap faced by those countries hardest hit by the tsunamis, such as Indonesia and Sri Lanka.

The chapters in this section examine how states have responded to globalization. One of the primary questions raised in analyses of state responses to globalization is the extent to which there has been convergence in economic structures and economic policies. In terms of economic structures it is clear that the central economic agencies of the state, such as finance departments and central banks, have become increasingly important in state decision-making. Moreover, these central economic agencies have also developed greater links not just with each other but with international financial institutions such as the IMF and World Bank. A constant round of meetings ensures that key finance ministers and central bankers are well informed as to the current thinking of international experts on how to resolve any particular problem, for example, inflation or unemployment. As a consequence, governments around the world have been encouraged, and in some cases forced, to adopt policies that reflect international rather than domestic imperatives. Some analysts would also see the growing links between international capital, particularly banks and other financial institutions, and governments as indicative of the changes that globalization has brought to economic structures within states.

At the same time, there has been a great deal of discussion of the way globalization has produced policy convergence among states. It is argued that this policy convergence has been brought about by a number of factors.[7] These include direct intervention by external authorities, such as the IMF and WTO; the influence of epistemic communities or transnational groups that share information and expertise about how to solve common problems; copying what are seen as 'best practices' of other states in particular policy areas and emulating the policies of those states that are competitors for foreign direct investment or even international portfolio capital; and harmonizing policies with trading

partners so that there is as little 'friction' or conflict over policies as possible. Each of these approaches, it is argued, produces some degree of policy convergence among states. In combination they are said to have created a situation in which there is a good deal of convergence in a number of policy areas, especially in economic policies.

But just as there are analysts who question the extent to which the state has been undermined by the advance of globalization, so, too, others question the degree to which state policies have converged. While it is accepted that some minimal level of convergence has taken place, policies are said to be the product of particular sets of governing institutions that have arisen out of the unique cultures and the different recent historical experiences of individual states. As one analysis of public policy in Canada and the United States argues, 'the primary forces that contribute to distinctive national choices are rooted in the culture and political traditions' of the two countries.[8] As a result, then, of the wide variety of political cultures and the very diverse political institutions to be found around the world, responses to globalization vary quite significantly.[9] Moreover, because current policies are often heavily influenced by past policies, previous differences in the way governments have responded to crises have an effect on how the current wave of globalization is managed. States, which may appear on the surface to be similar and to be in similar situations, can, therefore, enact very different policies as they attempt to deal with comparable pressures produced by the forces of globalization.[10] For example, the very different ways that Thailand, which accepted the IMF's advice, and Malaysia, which adopted policies exactly contrary to the IMF's prescription, responded to pressure in attempting to recover from the Asian economic crisis of 1997–8 provide clear evidence that the convergence thesis has its limitations.

A final area of concern for analysts is the extent to which states can be said to be autonomous in terms of both domestic social actors and the international structure. Over the years analysts have differed markedly as to whether various institutional states have been excessively influenced by particular social groups or classes within society or have maintained their autonomy and acted independently of the influences exerted by the dominant interests in a society. The argument generally is that the degree of autonomy of an institutional state will have an effect on the type of domestic and international economic policies that the state follows.

A debate has also emerged around the extent to which states can shape the international system as opposed to being creatures of the international structure.[11] The state-as-an-agent argument clearly has some force. Major players in the international political economy, such as the United States or more recently China, do have the power to determine aspects of global economic development. The United States has used access to its massive domestic market as well as its influence over key international financial institutions to further its economic interests. And China has started to use its rapidly growing market and production capabilities to expand its capacity to shape the regional East Asian political economy.

Smaller, less economically powerful states have employed a number of different strategies in an attempt to preserve their autonomy within the global economic system. Some states have found that they can band together to exert some influence over global developments. As the chapters in Part III of this book show, insofar as the processes of globalization can be thought to impinge on the autonomy of state governments, one response has been, paradoxically, to attempt the recovery of national autonomy in particular policy areas through participation in regional groupings. The EU and the slowly developing ASEAN Plus Three are excellent examples of this approach to maintaining a degree of autonomy in the international system.

However, it needs to be emphasized that it is almost impossible for smaller states to exert the kind of power that a major player like the United States can. These smaller economies must, therefore, seek to preserve their autonomy in other ways. As Berenice Carroll argues in a seminal article subtitled 'The Cult of Power', autonomy is 'an objective or product of power but of power conceived as competence or ability, rather than power conceived as influence in interpersonal or intergroup relations'.[12] She suggests that the 'powers of the powerless' include, among others, 'integrative power', 'socializing power', and 'norm-creating power'.[13] Obviously these powers are most effective when employed in concert with other, smaller economies. In other words, then, states outside the club of major economic powers have a range of strategies they can call on to maintain their autonomy in the face of the persistent forces of globalization.

The following chapters give an indication of how a number of states from different parts of the world have attempted to deal with the globalization process and the consequences of the policies they have adopted. Readers will be able to judge for themselves the validity of the various views of the role of the state in the international political economy, the extent to which globalization has affected state policies, and the success of states in attempting to preserve their autonomy within the rapidly changing global order

Notes

1. Theda Skocpol, *States and Social Revolutions* (Cambridge: Cambridge University Press, 1979), 29.
2. Susan Strange, *The Retreat of the State: The Diffusion of Power in the World Economy* (Cambridge: Cambridge University Press, 1996). One of the first to make this argument was Kenichi Ohmae in *The Borderless World* (New York: Collins, 1990).
3. Paul Hirst and Grahame Thompson, *Globalization in Question* (Cambridge: Polity Press, 1996); Paul Hirst, 'The Global Economy— Myths and Realities', *International Affairs* 73 (July 1997): 409–25.

4. See, e.g., Linda Weiss, *The Myth of the Powerless State: Governing the Economy in a Global Era* (Cambridge: Polity Press, 1998).

5. Charles Tilly, 'War Making and State Making as Organized Crime', in Peter B. Evans, Dietrich Rueschemeyer, and Theda Skocpol, eds, *Bringing the State Back In* (Cambridge: Cambridge University Press, 1985), 170.

6. See, e.g., Linda Weiss, 'Guiding Globalization in East Asia: New Roles for Old Developmental States', in Weiss, ed., *States in the Global Economy: Bringing Domestic Institutions Back In* (Cambridge: Cambridge University Press, 2003).

7. See, e.g., Colin J. Bennett, 'Review Article: What Is Policy Convergence and What Causes It?', *British Journal of Political Science* 21 (1991): 215–34; Suzanne Berger, 'Introduction', in Berger and Ronald Dore, eds, *National Diversity and Global Capitalism* (Ithaca, NY: Cornell University Press, 1996).

8. Richard Simeon, George Hoberg, and Keith Banting, 'Globalization, Fragmentation and the Social Contract', in Banting, Hoberg, and Simeon, eds, *Degrees of Freedom: Canada and the United States in a Changing World* (Montreal and Kingston: McGill-Queen's University Press, 1997), 400.

9. See, e.g., Mark Beeson, 'Conclusion: The More Things Change . . . ? Path Dependency and Convergence in East Asia', in Beeson, ed., *Reconfiguring East Asia: Regional Institutions and Organisations after the Crisis* (London: RoutledgeCurzon, 2002).

10. See Weiss, *The Myth of the Powerless State,* 194–6.

11. See the discussion in John M. Hobson, *The State and International Relations* (Cambridge: Cambridge University Press, 2000).

12. Berenice Carroll, 'Peace Research: The Cult of Power', *Journal of Conflict Resolution* 16, 4 (1972): 592.

13. Ibid., 608–14

Chapter 26

Political Globalization and the Competition State

Philip G. Cerny

Economic globalization does not translate automatically into political globalization.[1] The latter requires a transformation of politics itself, i.e., the metamorphosis of the nation-state into what is called here a 'competition state'. This process is profoundly paradoxical in at least three ways. In the first place, globalization can *both* undermine the domestic autonomy and political effectiveness of the state *and* at the same time lead to the actual expansion of de facto state intervention and regulation in the name of competitiveness and marketization. Second, states are among the greatest promoters of further globalization as they attempt to cope more effectively with 'global realities'. State actors in effect undermine the autonomy of their own 'national models'—embedded state forms, contrasting modes of state interventionism, and differing state/society arrangements—through chasing international competitiveness. In this process, the kinds of things states do well (and do badly) change significantly. And finally, states seem to be getting less socially cohesive and more cut across from outside and from below by transnational social forces, which further undermines the capacity of domestic actors to resist globalization. This political globalization, in turn, forces the pace of the wider globalization process itself, feeding back into economic, social, and cultural spheres as well.

The development of the competition state is something both old and new. The way modern capitalist society works, and how the state interacts with the economy, is generally analyzed and explained by contrasting two fundamental concepts. On the one hand, both Marxists and other critical analysts of capitalism argue that in the long run, capitalist economies and the firms and sectors that make them up become more and more characterized by a centralization of economic power—the development of *monopoly* and *oligopoly*. Fewer firms control more processes in their drive to 'accumulate capital'; markets are merely the mechanism by which monopolization proceeds. On the other hand, most 'mainstream' theorists, following Adam Smith, see the central driving force of *successful* capitalism as *competition*, i.e., the ability of well-constructed and 'efficient' markets to *prevent* too much monopolization or oligopolization. Markets act as a check on too much centralized capital accumulation—attracting new entrants to markets, keeping prices down through competition, forcing companies to continually innovate, etc. And some theorists, in turn, see the ongoing tension between monopoly and competition as what makes capitalism work. The state plays a key role in this process and this role is being expanded and transformed in the twenty-first century.

Even laissez-faire economic theorists agree that the main role of the state in this process is that of preventing or counteracting 'market failure'. There are, however, two fundamental modes of counteracting market failure. The first of these is to take certain economic activities 'out of the market', i.e., to make sure that certain basic public goods and social welfare are not neglected or 'underprovided' simply because they are not profitable. This, in social science jargon, is often called 'decommodification', supplying these goods through the state or sometimes through charity. This requires a state with the capacity to redistribute resources authoritatively among different groups of people, whether for promoting industrial development or supporting vulnerable social groups—the industrial welfare state of the late nineteenth century and most of the twentieth century. The second, in contrast, requires the state to intervene directly in economic activities to promote competition by creating and enforcing rules for how markets work, whether through anti-monopoly legislation, the prevention of fraud, support for new entrants in particular markets, regulating stock markets and accountants, ensuring price transparency, or attempting to create what is often called a 'level playing field' for different market actors. This requires a very different kind of state, one that promotes rather than limits markets, pursues effective 'commodification' rather than decommodification, and focuses on regulation rather than redistribution.

Globalization is essentially about lowering economic borders among countries. In this more open world, it becomes more difficult for states to prioritize decommodifying strategies. Domestic markets cannot be protected as they once were. Firms and sectors face increasing outside competition—except that it is no longer simply from outside, as most firms and sectors are increasingly transnationalized. In this context, traditional forms of state intervention—decommodification—often become inefficient, a hindrance on the capacity of firms based in a particular geographical area (the nation-state) to compete. Therefore, political and bureaucratic actors attempt to put together strategies for making those firms and economic activities more competitive. Developing economic policies that will be successful in a globalizing world is a complex matter, but the promotion of competitiveness and of competition in general has become a political priority. As with any capitalist political economy, however, competitiveness does not emerge automatically. There is no 'invisible hand' in international markets. In states as different as the United States, the archetypical classical liberal state, and China, supposedly still under some form of Communist rule, political actors increasingly believe (or think they know)

that the only alternative in today's world is to strive for international competitiveness in a globalizing capitalist marketplace, pursuing liberalization and commodification as the crucial road to economic growth and to the satisfaction of domestic social, economic, and political groups.

Globalization as a Political Process

So how does this process work? Economic explanations of globalization are well known. The first is the interpenetration of national markets for various goods and assets, from money to industrial products to labour, across borders. The second is the advent of new technology that, in contrast to the hierarchical technological forms of the industrial state and the welfare state, is structurally amorphous and rapidly diffused. The third involves private and public economic institutions, from multinational enterprises to strategic alliances to private and even public regulatory regimes. Sociological explanations focus on two levels. On the one hand, people's perceptions of themselves as subjects or citizens of a particular nation-state are challenged from above by the crystallization and dissemination of global images and identities from above—the 'global village'. At another level, however, for postmodernists, an intensely speeded-up world is emerging where cultural fragmentation is seen as undermining all grand narratives and socio-political projects from underneath rather than from above. But from both economic and sociological perspectives, political institutions and practices are seen as epiphenomenal, dependent variables.

In contrast, globalization as a *political* phenomenon basically means that the shape of the playing field of politics itself—the possibilities of effective collective action internally and the capacity of states to make credible commitments externally—is increasingly determined not within insulated, relatively autonomous, and hierarchically organized structures called states. Rather, it derives from a complex aggregation of multi-level games played on multi-layered institutional playing fields, *above* and *across*, as well as *within*, state boundaries. These three-level games are played out by state actors and other political forces, as well as market actors and cultural actors. Political globalization derives first and foremost from a reshaping of political practices and institutional structures in order to adjust and adapt to the growing deficiencies of nation-states as perceived and *experienced* by such actors. The very idea of what constitutes a society—and therefore a political community—in the modern world has crystallized in the idea of the territorial nation-state, looking both outward to the system of states and inward to those ties of justice and friendship that Aristotle saw as distinguishing the *politeia* from the external other. It has involved attributing to the state a holistic character, a sense of organic solidarity that is more than any simple social contract or set of pragmatic affiliations. If there is an increasingly paradigmatic crisis of the state today, it concerns the erosion of this posited underlying bond.

Globalization itself has all too frequently been assumed to be an automatic process of convergence, a homogenizing force; increasingly, however, analysts are arguing that globalization is fundamentally complex and 'heterogenizing'—even polarizing—in its nature and consequences. Complexity means the presence of many intricate component parts. It can mean a sophisticated and elegantly co-ordinated structure, but it can also mean that the different parts mesh poorly, leading to friction and even entropy. A globalizing world is intricately structured at many levels, developing within an already complex social, economic, and political context.[2] As a consequence, the globalization process does not involve some sort of linear withering away of the state as a bureaucratic power structure. In a globalizing world, states play a crucial role as stabilizers and enforcers of the rules and practices of *global* society. Indeed, state actors are the primary source of the state's own transformation into a competition state.

The Slow Erosion of the Industrial Welfare State

The essence of the post-war national industrial and welfare state (IWS) lay in the capacity state actors and institutions had gained, especially since the Great Depression, to insulate certain key elements of economic life from market forces while promoting other aspects of the market.[3] These mechanisms did not merely mean protecting the poor and helpless from poverty and pursuing welfare goals like full employment or public health, but also regulating business in the public interest, 'fine-tuning' business cycles to promote economic growth, nurturing 'strategic industries' and 'national champions', integrating labour movements into corporatist processes to promote wage stability and labour discipline, reducing barriers to international trade, and imposing controls on 'speculative' international movements of capital. The notion of national citizenship widened to include such issues, too. Following World War II, the expansion of these economic and social functions of the state came to be seen as crucial for the 'modernization' and 'development' of any country, rich or poor.[4]

But this compromise of domestic regulation and international opening was eroded by increasing domestic structural costs (the 'fiscal crisis of the state'[5]) as well as the structural consequences of growing external trade and, perhaps most importantly, of international financial transactions.[6] The crisis of the IWS was in its decreasing capacity to insulate national economies from the global economy—and from the combination of stagnation and inflation that resulted when they tried. Today, rather than attempt to take certain economic activities *out* of the market—to decommodify them as the welfare state was organized to do—the competition state has pursued *increased* marketization in order to make economic activities located within the national territory, or that otherwise contribute to national wealth, more competitive in international and transnational terms.[7]

The modern industrial welfare state was seen by neo-classical economists to combine a series of specific types of economic intervention to prevent 'market failure', such as welfare spending, macroeconomic fine-tuning, market-enforcing regulation such as anti-monopoly legislation or stock market regulation, and labour market regulation; even indicative planning was rationalized as a market-clearing exercise.[8] More direct, non-market control or regulation was legitimized by reference to the need to organize production by natural monopolies, the provision of public goods and services, or the need to maintain basic or strategic industries. In this view, then, the industrial welfare state was based on a paradox. It might save the market from its own dysfunctional tendencies, but it had the potential to undermine the market in turn.

From a market perspective, then, the IWS had to be both (a) restrained in its application and (b) regularly *deconstructed*—deregulated and privatized—to avoid the 'ratchet effect' that leads to stagflation, fiscal crisis, and the declining effectiveness of each new increment of demand reflation and functional expansion. Failure to do this would result in a lumbering, muddling, 'overloaded' state. The international recession of the 1970s and early 1980s was widely perceived in this light; as a result, political decision-makers have undergone a fundamental learning process that has altered the norms according to which they operate. The result was the rise of what has been called *neo-liberalism*, or a revival of purist versions of neo-classical economic policy nostrums associated primarily with the Thatcher government in the United Kingdom and the Reagan administration in the United States. Nevertheless, the resulting competition state took on a variety of forms.

Forms of the Competition State

The key to making the state more efficient, in the neo-liberal view, is to open it up-in terms of both its internal organizational structure and the regulatory and policy constraints it imposes on the market—to wider, or global, market forces. The challenge for state actors today, as viewed through the contemporary neo-liberal discourse of globalization (in both its economic and political versions), is mainly to juggle four kinds of policy approaches: (1) a shift from macroeconomic to microeconomic interventionism, as reflected in both deregulation and industrial policy; (2) a shift in the focus of that interventionism from the devel-

opment and maintenance of a range of 'strategic' or 'basic' economic activities in order to retain minimal economic self-sufficiency in key sectors to one of flexible response to competitive conditions in a range of diversified and rapidly evolving international marketplaces, i.e., the pursuit of 'competitive advantage' as distinct from 'comparative advantage';[9] (3) an emphasis on the control of inflation and general neo-liberal monetarism—supposedly translating into non-inflationary growth—as the touchstone of state economic management and interventionism; and (4) a shift in the focal point of party and governmental politics away from the general maximization of welfare within a nation (full employment, redistributive transfer payments, and social service provision) to the promotion of enterprise, innovation, and profitability in both private and public sectors.

In this context, there have been some striking similarities as well as major differences among leading capitalist countries. Within the competition state model, national policy-makers have a range of potential responses, old and new, with which to work. The challenge is said to be one of getting the state to do both *more* and *less* at the same time. Getting more for less has been the core concept, for example, of the so-called 'reinventing government' or 'New Public Management' movement, itself a major manifestation and dimension of the competition state approach.[10] The competition state involves a transformation of the policy roles of the state and a multiplication of specific responses to change. The essence of these changes lies in the differential capacity of the state to promote distinct types of economic development.

On the one hand, traditional kinds of strong state intervention have often been extremely effective at promoting what is called *extensive development*. Extensive development means finding and bringing in new *exogenous* resources and factors of capital (land, labour, physical capital like factories and infrastructure, and financial capital) to new (and old) economic activities. Governments can help undermine feudal and peasant structures and use taxes, spending, regulation—and physical force—to channel investment (and other factors of production such as labour) away from non- or pre-industrial uses into capitalist industry and finance. That's how Germany developed at the end of the nineteenth century and how Russia developed under both Czarist and Communist regimes. But the potential drawbacks are the increasing tendency to produce costly and technologically outdated goods produced more cheaply elsewhere, featherbedding of labour and management, and corruption and overbureaucratization—leading to a vicious circle of inefficiency, hyperinflation, and state authoritarianism to keep the system going.

On the other hand, state intervention has been notably poor at promoting *intensive development.* Intensive development occurs mainly *after* extensive development (although they can occur simultaneously), and it means improving the *endogenous* efficiency of production, investment, and market structures and processes. As Adam Smith wrote, 'to improve land, like all other commercial projects, requires exact attention to small savings and small gains'. Intensive development means continually improving the microeconomic efficiency, competitiveness, and profitability of industry—even to the extent of regularly engaging in what Joseph Schumpeter called 'creative destruction' of old capital and technology to make way for the latest cutting-edge production, financing, and marketing methods. It means giving individual owners, managers, and workers market-based incentives to involve themselves in a day-to-day process of improvement of the competitiveness of the firm. In today's world of the competition state, fundamental changes in how states and economies interact have forced several types of policy change to the top of the political agenda—changes intended to shift economic development from its extensive to its intensive form.

Among more traditional policy issue areas is, of course, trade policy, including a wider range of non-tariff barriers and targeted strategic trade policies. The core issue in trade policy is to avoid reinforcing through protection the existing rigidity of the industrial sector or sectors in question, while fostering or even imposing adaptation to global competi-tive conditions in return for temporary protection. Transnational constraints are growing rapidly in trade policy, however, as can be seen in the establishment of the North American Free Trade Agreement, the Asia-Pacific Economic Co-operation forum, and the World Trade Organization. Two other traditional categories, monetary and fiscal policy, are perhaps even more crucial today, and the key change is that relative priorities between the two have been reversed; tighter monetary policy is pursued alongside looser fiscal policy through tax cuts. And exchange rate policy, difficult to manage in the era of floating exchange rates and massive international capital flows, is nonetheless still essential; however, it is increasingly intertwined with monetary and fiscal policy.[11]

Potentially more innovative, combining old and new measures, is the area of industrial policy and related strategic trade policy. By targeting particular sectors, supporting the development of both more flexible manufacturing systems and transnationally viable economies of scale, and assuming certain costs of adjustment, governments can alter some of the conditions that determine competitive advantage, for example, by: encouraging mergers and restructuring; promoting research and development; encouraging private investment and venture capital, while providing or guaranteeing credit-based investment where capital markets fail, often through joint public/private ventures; developing new forms of infrastructure; and pursuing a more active labour market policy while removing barriers to mobility. The examples of Japanese, Swedish, and Austrian industrial policy have been widely analyzed in this context.

A third category of measures, and potentially the most explosive, is, of course, deregulation. The deregulation approach is based partly on the assumption that national regulations, especially the traditional sort of regulations designed to protect national market actors from market failure, are insufficiently flexible to take into account the rapid shifts in transnational competitive conditions characteristic of the interpenetrated world economy of the early twenty-first century. However, deregulation must not be seen just as the lifting of old regulations, but also as the formulation of new regulatory structures designed to cope with, and even to anticipate, shifts in competitive advantage. Furthermore, these new regulatory structures are often designed to *enforce* global market-rational economic and political behaviour on rigid and inflexible private-sector actors as well as on state actors and agencies. The institutions and practices of the state itself are increasingly marketized or commodified, and the state becomes the spearhead of structural transformation to international market norms both at home and abroad.[12]

Although each of these processes can be observed across a wide range of states, there are significant variations in how different competition states cope with the pressures of adaptation and transformation. There is a dialectic of divergence and convergence at work, rather than a single road to competitiveness. The original model of the competition state was the strategic or *developmental state*, which writers like John Zysman and Chalmers Johnson associated with France and Japan.[13] This perspective, which identifies the competition state with strong-state technocratic *dirigisme*, lives on in the analysis of newly industrializing countries (NICs) in Asia and other parts of the developing world. However, the difficulty with this approach has been that the scope of control that the technocratic patron-state and its client firms can exercise over market outcomes diminishes as the integration of these economies into global markets—and the resulting challenges this interdependence poses to policy-makers in different countries—proceeds.

Essentially, the developmental state, like traditional forms of state intervention, works best when it pursues extensive development. It can play a crucial role in nurturing new industries and reorienting economic structures and actors to the world marketplace, but beyond a certain threshold even the most tightly bound firms and sectors will act in a more autonomous fashion when presented with the exogenous opportunities and constraints of international markets. And as more firms and sectors become linked into new patterns of production, financing, and market access, often moving operations offshore, their willingness to follow the

script declines. However, there are distinctions even here. Within this category, for example, Japanese administrative guidance and the ties of the *keiretsu* system have remained relatively strong despite a certain amount of liberalization, deregulation, and privatization, whereas in France the forces of neo-liberalism have penetrated a range of significant bastions, from the main political parties to major sectors of the bureaucracy itself.[14] The recent Asian economic crisis, however, is essentially a crisis of the developmental state.

In contrast, the orthodox model of the competition state today is not the developmental state but the neo-liberal state (in the European sense of the word 'liberal', i.e., orthodox free-market economic liberalism, or what is called 'nineteenth-century liberalism' in the United States). Thatcherism and Reaganism in the 1980s provided both a political rationale and a power base for the revival of free-market ideology generally—not just in the United Kingdom and the United States but throughout the world. The flexibility and openness of Anglo-Saxon capital markets, the experience of Anglo-American elites with international and transnational business and their willingness to go multinational, the corporate structure of American and British firms and their (relative) concern with profitability and shareholder returns rather than traditional relationships and market share, the enthusiasm with which American managers have embraced lean management and downsizing, and the relative flexibility of the US and UK labour forces, combined with an arm's-length state tradition in both countries, are widely thought to have fought off the strategic state challenge and eventually to have emerged more competitive today.

Nevertheless, liberalization, deregulation, and privatization have not reduced the role of state intervention overall, just shifted it from decommodifying bureaucracies to marketizing ones. 'Reinventing government', for example, means the replacement of bureaucracies that directly produce public services by ones that monitor and supervise contracted-out and privatized services according to complex financial criteria and performance indicators.[15] And industrial policy is alive and well, too, secreted in the interstices of a decentralized, patchwork bureaucracy—often called 'agencification', i.e., the proliferation of specialized agencies to promote the marketization and regulation of particular economic activities—that is the American tradition and the new British obsession.

Throughout the debate between the Japanese model and the Anglo-American model, however, another model was widely canvassed. The European neo-corporatist model, rooted in the post-war settlement and given another dimension through the consolidation of the European Union, has been presented by many European commentators as a middle way (although Britain has always been on its margins). In bringing labour into institutionalized settings, not only for wage bargaining but for other aspects of the social market, in doggedly pursuing conservative monetary policies, in promoting extensive training policies, and in possessing a universal banking system that nurtured and stabilized industry without strategic state interventionism, the European neo-corporatist approach (as practised in varying ways in Germany, Austria, and Sweden in particular) has seemed to its proponents to embody the best aspects of both the Japanese and the Anglo-American models. However, despite the completion of the Single European Market and the signing of the Maastricht Treaty, the signs of what in the early 1980s was called 'Eurosclerosis' have reappeared; the European Monetary Union project is widely regarded as deflationary in a context where costs are unevenly spread; and the liberalizing, deregulatory option is increasingly on the political cards again (as it was, for a while, in the 1980s), especially in the context of high French and German unemployment.

On one level, then, the competition *among* different kinds of putative 'competition states' has been central to political globalization. 'National developments'—i.e., differences in models of state/economy relations or state/societal arrangements—as Zysman writes, have 'driven changes in the global economy'.[16] At another level, however, states and state actors seek to convince, or pressure, other states—and transnational actors such as multinational corporations or international institutions—to adopt measures that shift the balance of competitive advantage. The search for competitive advantage adds further layers and cross-cutting cleavages to the world economy that increase the complexity and density of networks of interdependence and interpenetration. Finally, genuinely transnational pressures can develop for the establishment or expansion of transnational regimes, transnational neo-corporatist structures of policy bargaining, and transgovernmental linkages among bureaucrats, policy-makers, and policy communities. These pressures can originate from multinational corporations or from nationally or locally based firms and other interests, such as trade unions, caught in the crossfire of the search for international competitiveness. In this context, the neo-liberal, Anglo-American variant of the competition state appears dominant in the early twenty-first century, paradoxically even in China.

In all of these settings, then, the state is no longer able to act as a decommodifying hierarchy (i.e., taking economic activities out of the market). It must act more and more as a collective commodifying agent (i.e., putting activities *into* the market) and even as a *market actor itself*. It is financier, middleman, advocate, and even entrepreneur, in a complex economic web where not only do the frontiers between state and market become blurred, but also where their cross-cutting structures become closely intertwined and their behavioural modes become less and less easy to distinguish. In such complex conditions, the state is sometimes structurally fragmented, sometimes capable of strategic action—but increasingly caught up in and constrained by cross-cutting global/transnational/domestic structural and conjunctural conditions. Thus, although the problems faced by all capitalist industrial states have given rise to certain similarities of response, significant divergences remain. Different states have different sets of advantages and disadvantages in the search for international competitiveness. They differ in endogenous structural capacity for strategic action both domestically and internationally. They differ in the extent to which their existing economic structures, with or without government intervention, can easily adapt to international conditions. And they differ in their vulnerability to international and transnational trends and pressures.[17]

The Scope and Limits of the Competition State

One dimension of convergence, however, is that states and state actors—seemingly voluntarily—have given up a range of crucial policy instruments. In this context, states are less able to act as 'strategic' or 'developmental' states and become more 'splintered states'.[18] One result is that state actors and different agencies are increasingly intertwined with 'transgovernmental networks'—systematic linkages between state actors and agencies overseeing particular jurisdictions and sectors, but cutting across different countries and including a heterogeneous collection of private actors and groups in interlocking, unevenly developed cross-border policy communities.[19] These transgovernmental policy networks can also help to set actors and agencies within the *same* state into increased policy competition with each other, further reinforcing wider transnational linkages. The functions of the state, although central in maintaining domestic and global stability alike, are increasingly residual in terms of the range of policy instruments and outcomes they entail.

In international terms, states, in pursuing the goal of competitiveness, are increasingly involved in what John Stopford and Susan Strange have called 'triangular diplomacy', consisting of the complex interaction of state-state, state-firm, and firm-firm negotiations.[20] But this concept must be widened further. Interdependence analysis has focused too exclusively on two-level games. Although this is an oversimplification, I argue that complex globalization has to be seen as a structure involving (at least) *three*-level games, with third-level (transnational) games including not only 'firm-firm diplomacy' but also transgovernmental

networks and policy communities, internationalized market structures, transnational cause groups, and many other linked and interpenetrated markets, hierarchies, and networks. Thus the actual amount of government imbrication in social life can increase while the power of the state to control specific activities and market outcomes continues to diminish.

On the one hand, financial globalization and liberalization have intensified pressures for governments to increase monitoring financial markets, criminalize insider trading, stabilize failing banks, combat money laundering, and the like. The growth of competing authorities with overlapping jurisdictions does not reduce interventionism; it merely expands the range of possibilities for splintered governments and special interests to carve out new fiefdoms, both domestically and transnationally, while undermining their overall strategic and developmental capacity—what has been called 'neo-medievalism'.[21] On the other hand, while some countries, because of their infrastructure, education systems, workforce skills, and quality-of-life amenities, are able to attract mobile, foot-loose capital of a highly sophisticated kind, others may increasingly have to depend on low-wage, low-cost manufacturing or agricultural production. Indeed, such changes may well destabilize less-favoured states, whose already fragile governmental systems will be torn by the ascendancy of religious, ethnic, or other grassroots loyalties. Today's revival of nationalism is not of the state-bound, nineteenth-century variety; it is more elemental, and leads to the breakup of states rather than to their maintenance.

If we want to look for an alternative way of understanding the competition state, probably the best place to look is at American state governments. These governments can claim only a partial loyalty from their inhabitants, and their power over internal economic and social structures and forces has been limited indeed. They have been required to operate over the course of the past two centuries in an increasingly open continental market. Their taxing and regulating power has been seriously constrained in many spheres by the expansion of the weight and the legal prerogatives of the federal government. However, at the same time, their ability to control development planning, to collect and use the tax revenues they do impose (as well as offering tax incentives and subsidies), to build infrastructure, to run education and training systems, and to enforce law and order gives these subnational states a capacity to influence the provision of immobile factors of capital in significant ways—indeed, more so than many governments in developing countries.

The attempt to make the state more 'flexible' has moved a long way over the past decade or so, not only in the United States and Britain, where deregulation, privatization, and liberalization have evolved furthest, but also in a wide range of other countries. The 'ratchet effect'—the term used by Mrs Thatcher's guru Sir Keith Joseph for what was once called 'creeping socialism', i.e., that each attempt to use the state to achieve a new discrete policy goal ratchets up the size and unwieldiness of the state as a whole—has been turned on its head. In a globalizing world, the competition state is more likely to be involved in a process of competitive deregulation and creeping *liberalization*.

Conclusion: Globalization and the Competition State as Paradoxes

The central paradox of globalization itself—of the displacement of a crucial range of economic, social, and political activities from the national arena to a cross-cutting global/transnational/domestic field of action—is that rather than creating one big economy or one big polity, it also divides, fragments, and polarizes. While the potential for monopolization certainly exists, especially in particular sectors with large economies of scale, it is increasingly in the interests of national governments—or is seen by political actors of all sorts, including voters—to prevent that kind of monopolization and to promote the international competitiveness of a wide range of domestic firms and economic activities in a more open world. In this striving for competitiveness, convergence and divergence are two sides of the same coin. Whether the forces of convergence will lead to a complex but stable pluralistic world based on liberal capitalism and the vestiges of liberal democracy[22] or the forces of divergence and inequality are creating a more volatile and fragmented world remains to be seen. International security has become more complex, too, with the trend towards social fragmentation, civil wars, and terrorism undermining the capacity of nation-states to provide the kind of shield they have represented in the past—what I have elsewhere called the 'New Security Dilemma'.[23] Whatever direction the future takes, however, political strategies and projects will increasingly become multi-layered and globally oriented—whether on the right ('globalization' in the sense of pursuing economic efficiency in a liberalized world marketplace) or on the left (a regeneration of genuinely internationalist socialism). The postmodern irony of the competition state is that rather than simply being undermined by inexorable forces of economic globalization, politics is becoming not only the engine room but also the steering mechanism of a political globalization process that in the future will increasingly drive and shape the context—and the substance—of economic, social, and cultural globalization.

Notes

1. For an intelligent though perhaps overstated critique of the concept of globalization, see Paul Hirst and Grahame Thompson, *Globalization in Question: The International Economy and the Possibilities of Governance*, 2nd edn (Oxford: Polity Press, 1999).

2. P.G. Cerny, 'Globalization, Governance, and Complexity', in Aseem Prakash and Jeffrey A. Hart, eds, *Globalization and Governance* (London: Routledge, 1999), 184–208.

3. Karl Polanyi, *The Great Transformation: The Political and Economic Origins of Our Time* (New

York: Rinehart, 1944).

4. Reinhard Bendix, *Nation-Building and Citizenship: Studies of Our Changing Social Order* (New York: Wiley, 1964).

5. James O'Connor, *The Fiscal Crisis of the State* (New York: St Martin's Press, 1973).

6. Susan Strange, *Casino Capitalism* (Oxford: Blackwell, 1986).

7. P.G. Cerny, *The Changing Architecture of Politics: Structure, Agency, and the Future of the State* (London and Newbury Park, Calif.: Sage, 1990).

8. Saul Estrin and Peter Holmes, *French Planning in Theory and Practice* (London: Allen & Unwin, 1982).

9. The distinction between comparative advantage and competitive advantage is a central theme of John Zysman and Laura d'Andrea Tyson, eds, *American Industry in International Competition* (Ithaca, NY: Cornell University Press, 1983).

10. David Osborne and Ted Gaebler, *Reinventing Government: How the Entrepreneurial Spirit Is Transforming the Public Sector, from Schoolhouse to Statehouse, City Hall to the Pentagon* (Reading, Mass.: Addison-Wesley, 1992); Patrick Dunleavy, 'The Globalisation of Public Services Production: Can Government Be "Best in World"?', *Public Policy and Administration* 9, 2 (Summer 1994): 36–64.

11. Jeffry A. Frieden, 'Invested Interests: The Politics of National Economic Policies in a World of Global Finance', *International Organization* 45, 4 (Autumn 1991): 425–51.

12. P.G. Cerny, 'The Limits of Deregulation: Transnational Interpenetration and Policy Change', *European Journal of Political Research* 19, 2/3 (Mar.–Apr. 1991): 173–96.

13. John Zysman, *Governments, Markets, and Growth: Financial Systems and the Politics of Industrial Change* (Ithaca, NY: Cornell University Press, 1983); Chalmers Johnson, *M.I.T.I. and the Japanese Miracle: The Growth of Industrial Policy, 1925–1975* (Stanford, Calif.: Stanford University Press, 1982).

14. Steven K. Vogel, *Freer Markets, More Rules: Regulatory Reform in Advanced Industrial Countries* (Ithaca, NY: Cornell University Press, 1998); Vivien A. Schmidt, *From State to Market? The Transformation of French Business and Government* (Cambridge: Cambridge University Press, 1996).

15. Michael Moran, *The British Regulatory State: High Modernism and Hyper-Innovation* (Oxford: Oxford University Press, 2003).

16. John Zysman, 'The Myth of a "Global" Economy: Enduring National Foundations and Emerging Regional Realities', *New Political Economy* 1, 1 (1996): 157–84; cf. Louis W. Pauly and Simon Reich, 'Enduring Differences in the Era of Globalization: National Structures and Multinational Corporate Behavior', *International Organization* 51, 1 (1997): 1–30.

17. Axel Hülsemeyer, ed., *Globalization in the 21st Century: Convergence and Divergence* (London: Palgrave, 2003).

18. Howard Machin and Vincent Wright, eds, *Economic Policy and Policy-Making under the Mitterrand Presidency, 1981–84* (London: Pinter, 1985).

19. Anne-Marie Slaughter, *The New World Order* (Princeton, NJ: Princeton University Press, 2004).

20. John Stopford and Susan Strange, *Rival States, Rival Firms: Competition for World Market Shares* (Cambridge: Cambridge University Press, 1991).

21. P.G. Cerny, 'Neomedievalism, Civil War and the New Security Dilemma: Globalisation as Durable Disorder', *Civil Wars* 1, 1 (Spring 1998): 36–64.

22. Francis Fukuyama, *The End of History and the Last Man* (New York: Free Press, 1992).

23. P.G. Cerny, 'Terrorism and the New Security Dilemma', *Naval War College Review* 58, 1 (Winter 2005): 11–33.

Suggested Readings

Cerny, P.G. *The Changing Architecture of Politics: Structure, Agency, and the Future of the State.* London and Newbury Park, Calif.: Sage, 1990.

Frieden, Jeffry A. 'Invested Interests: The Politics of National Economic Policies in a World of Global Finance', *International Organization* 45, 4 (Autumn 1991): 425–51.

Hirst, Paul, and Grahame Thompson. *Globalization in Question: The International Economy and the Possibilities of Governance.* Oxford: Polity Press, 1996.

Hülsemeyer, Axel, ed. *Globalization in the 21st Century: Convergence and Divergence.* London: Palgrave, 2003.

Moran, Michael. *The British Regulatory State: High Modernism and Hyper-Innovation.* Oxford: Oxford University Press, 2003.

Osborne, David, and Ted Gaebler. *Reinventing Government: How the Entrepreneurial Spirit Is Transforming the Public Sector, from Schoolhouse to Statehouse, City Hall to the Pentagon.* Reading, Mass.: Addison-Wesley, 1992.

Polanyi, Karl. *The Great Transformation: The Political and Economic Origins of Our Time.* New York: Rinehart, 1944.

Prakash, Aseem, and Jeffrey A. Hart, eds. *Globalization and Governance.* London: Routledge, 1999.

Reich, Robert B. *The Work of Nations: Preparing Ourselves for 21st-Century Capitalism.* New York: Knopf, 1991.

Vogel, Steven K. *Freer Markets, More Rules: Regulatory Reform in Advanced Industrial Countries.* Ithaca, NY: Cornell University Press, 1998.

Zysman, John. *Governments, Markets, and Growth: Financial Systems and the Politics of Industrial Change.* Ithaca, NY: Cornell University Press, 1983.

Web Sites

European Commission, DG Competition: http://europa.eu.int/comm/competition/index_en.html

United States Trade Representative: www.ustr.gov/index.html

Chapter 27

Negotiating Globalization
The Foreign Economic Policy of the European Union

Michael Smith

The European Union (EU)[1] represents a paradox in a globalizing political economy. At a time when processes of integration at the global level are both widely noted and felt by policy-makers in the national and global arenas, the EU expresses a strong, highly institutionalized, and expanding variety of regional integration, in both the political and economic spheres.[2] As a result, it can be seen in at least three ways in relation to globalization processes. First, it serves as a barrier against globalization, capable because of its continental scale and strong institutions of resisting the forces of global integration. Second, it is a site for globalization, providing an integrated continental political economy within which globalizing forces can work untrammelled by national authority. Finally, the EU can be seen as a promoter of globalization, in the sense that it actively encourages the globalizing activities of European corporations and other actors. Each of these tendencies has arguably been intensified during the past decade. Having moved decisively in the late 1980s and early 1990s towards the creation of a single market for its existing members, during the late 1990s and early 2000s the EU moved further in two directions: on the one hand, 11 of its members agreed in 1998 to initiate a single currency, the euro, and by 2004 the currency was operating in full for 12 members of the 'eurozone'; on the other hand, 1998 also saw the opening of negotiations with what, in May 2004, became 10 new member states, with others to follow. In addition, the moves towards further definition of a Common Foreign and Security Policy (CFSP) and Common European Security and Defence Policy (CESDP) for the Union, in the context of the Amsterdam Treaty (1997), the Nice Treaty (2000), and the Constitutional Treaty signed in late 2004, demonstrated progress in the area not merely of economic security and regulation, but also of 'high politics' and an eventual defence policy. Such developments have raised in new forms the globalization/regionalization tension inherent in processes of economic integration, and have given new dimensions to the notion of an EU foreign economic policy.

But how valid is the notion of 'foreign economic policy' for the EU, and for the EU's role in a globalizing world? After all, the concept of foreign policy itself implies the existence of a central governing authority and, by extension, the existence of a state. While the nature of state structures and authorities can vary widely between national contexts, thereby creating difficulties for the conduct of foreign policy analysis, the EU seems to raise special problems. First, the EU indisputably has international presence and international effects, but are these systematic enough and purposeful enough to constitute a form of foreign economic policy or international economic policy? In the course of exploring this issue, one is led to a second set of questions, about the effectiveness and impact of policy itself. How effective is the process of policy formation and execution within the Union? How, and how well, does the EU translate its economic potential into economic and political effects? The issue is not simply one of the mechanics of policy formation and implementation; rather, it concerns the characteristics of the EU as a governance system and the ways in which it is possible to distinguish between the ability to form relationships and the capacity to carry out policy. As such, it gets to the heart of the EU's status, as a structuring factor or as an active presence, in the global arena.

This area of inquiry thus also holds important implications for the study of responses to globalization. If we assume that the EU needs a foreign economic policy in order to hold at bay or to manipulate the forces of globalization—the 'barrier' function mentioned above—this can lead to a view of the Union as a quasi-statist concentration of material and institutional power, competing with other such concentrations on an intercontinental scale. But if we assume that the EU as a regional governance system is part of an emerging system of global economic and political governance, we are led to explore the ways in which, first, the EU's external economic policies reflect its penetration by forces in the global economic order—the 'site' function—and second, the ways in which the EU's regional experiences can be diffused or used to exert leverage at the global level—the 'promoter' function. In reality, pure cases of each function are likely to be rare or non-existent. Foreign economic policy in the EU is likely to reflect a continuous and complex negotiation in which aims and interests, functions and impacts are intermingled.[3] This chapter sets out to explore how this negotiation process emerges and is managed within the EU and the implications for the global/regional balance.

Does Statehood Matter? The EU, Foreign Economic Policy, and the Global Arena

As already noted, the concept 'foreign economic policy' carries with it a conventional component of statehood or governmental authority. One of the problems in analyzing the EU is therefore the extent to which it measures up to established criteria of statehood and whether this matters in either conceptual or practical terms. Much of the literature on IPE has as a central focus the issue of statehood and

the relationship between statehood and processes of production and exchange in the global political economy; the EU thus presents a test of this literature from a distinctive but highly significant angle. To put it crudely, analysis of the EU enables the analyst to ask the question, in a focused and empirically substantial way, if statehood matters.[4]

To pursue this question, it is important first to address the issue of statehood today in the IPE. This chapter conceives of statehood as a variable in the international political economy, and also accepts that 'government' often does not take place exclusively through the agency of competitive national states. In consequence, the notions of foreign policy and foreign economic policy also need amendment. Conventionally, these would be seen as the embodiment of national aims and interests, pursued through the mobilization and application of national resources. In the case of foreign economic policy, the aims and the means would be defined as economic, although the ultimate goals would be implicitly political or concerned with security. The contemporary era demands that we question this rather restrictive and privileging view of the processes. A revised version would focus not so much on the mobilization of national governmental power so much as on the building of networks for action, which may or may not coincide with purely national boundaries. It would also focus on the role played by regulatory structures and rules at both the subnational and transnational levels, providing a framework for the pursuit of goals by a variety of public and private actors. This does not mean that the notion either of foreign policy or of foreign economic policy 'disappears'; rather, it recognizes that actions with meaning and effect can be produced by a range of actors and from a variety of sources, among them revitalized national authorities.[5]

Importantly, it is within this framework that the status and impact of the European Union are most salient, suggesting that the EU is in many ways a reflection of precisely these changed conditions. Many of the established views of the EU, though, tend to subject it to the tests of a traditional model of foreign economic policy and to identify the ways in which the Union falls short of the implied standards of statehood. Thus, there has been a strong focus on the economic 'weight' of the EU and on the undeniable fact that there is no direct translation of economic raw material into economic or political 'muscle'. Other analyses have focused on the extent to which the Community has become 'state-like' in conventional ways, on how it has supplanted state powers in particular domains such as trade. By implication, in areas where this has not happened, the EU cannot provide for its citizens the range of services that can be provided by 'real' states, either at home or abroad. We have just noted, though, that this kind of conventional analysis, both of statehood and of policy, is open to criticism. In the light of the revised analysis proposed above, what can now be said about the EU, its international status and its policy potential?

The EU is quintessentially a mixed system of participation, regulation, and action, epitomized by its 'three-pillar' institutional structure: the first pillar containing the European Community with its economic powers and procedures, the second containing the CFSP, linked now with elements of the CESDP, and the third containing provisions for justice and home affairs. Although it can be said that on the one hand the European Commission represents the basis for an eventual European government with supranational powers and on the other the member states in the Council of Ministers symbolize the continuity or even the dominance of conventional state power, the reality is a complex and multi-layered set of networks that constitute powerful mechanisms of regulation and behaviour modification. The areas of Community activity in which either the Commission or the Council of Ministers has exclusive policy competence are relatively few, and are particularly limited in the external domain, where trade policy has traditionally been cited as the example of shared competence. This situation was reaffirmed after the conclusion of the Uruguay Round in 1993, when the European Court of Justice confirmed that trade in services or matters of intellectual property were subject to shared competence between Commission and Council within the Community framework.[6] While the Nice Treaty and then the Constitutional Treaty later extended Community competence effectively to all areas covered by the WTO, there is no doubt that the policy process still reflects a complex division of powers and responsibilities. The converse of this is that there are also few areas in which the member states themselves can claim untrammelled power, either precisely because of their membership in the EU or because of the global spread of interdependence and interpenetration. In addition, the impact of interpenetration means that the notion of a privileged external or foreign policy domain is itself difficult to maintain. Finally, the increasingly close linkage between security policy and economic policy and the pervasiveness of politicization in the global political economy mean that the supposed limitation of the first pillar to 'low politics' is difficult to argue, although the process of linkage and politicization itself causes undoubted policy problems.[7] This issue is given added weight, as already noted, by the extension of EU policies with the growth of the CFSP and CESDP, and also by the 'securitization' of issues such as migration, which fall technically within the justice and home affairs domain of EU activity. The challenge of managing political/economic issues that cut across the 'three pillars' has already been felt by the EU in areas such as economic sanctions, but this is likely to become more taxing in the next few years as the EU's security presence extends.

As a result of these developments, the EU has much to offer the analyst of foreign economic policy. It combines elements of several layers of action and influence: subnational, intergovernmental, transnational, and in some areas supranational. It possesses a complex set of institutions that provide a powerful framework for continuous bargaining and for the adjustment of differences between member states and other groupings. In this sense, although the EU can be evaluated in terms of power and the inability to translate economic weight into tangible effects, such analysis is in part misguided; what really demands attention is the way in which and the extent to which the EU facilitates the achievement of joint objectives through predominantly economic and diplomatic means, and how it promotes effective communication and negotiation between member states and other groupings.

Analysis of foreign economic policy in the EU context must also take account of the multi-layered and sectorally specific nature of policy determination. There is a continuous competition, with well-established rules, for leverage within the Union, and at the same time an attempt to realize national or sectional objectives through EU means. It is important to recognize that this does not make the EU unique: the above description of the 'pulling and hauling' within the EU could be applied in many respects to the United States and other federal or fragmented government systems. In the case of the EU an important question must be asked about the extent to which it 'captures' or contains the economic or political activities of its members and other groupings, but this is not in principle different from similar questions arising from the permeability of national political and economic systems.

Power and Process in the EU's Foreign Economic Policy

The argument so far has identified three coexisting characteristics of EU foreign economic policy, each with its echoes in the broader literature of IPE and links to processes of globalization. First, the process is that of a multi-level game played according to distinct but intersecting rules in a number of sectors. Second, one of the principal features of the process is the constant adjustment of state policies and the interaction of national preferences with the institutions of the Union itself in a complex bargaining process. Third, the EU operates not only to provide a framework for the expression and adjustment of state and other interests, but also to structure the global political economy and thus to form an institutional expression of major forces within the global system. Whether this makes the EU into either a 'partial state' or a 'quasi-state' is an impor-

tant question. No less important is the empirical issue: what does the EU do and what roles does it perform within the global political economy?

As has been noted, the conversion of economic weight into economic and political effects is one of the great continuing problems of foreign economic policy at the EU level. One constraint on the effectiveness of this conversion process is the Union's institutional structure. The division of influence and competence between the member states and the EU's institutions, particularly the Commission, is a central driving force in the Union as a whole, but it has particular implications for external policy activities. In a formal sense, it is difficult if not impossible for the EU to operate collectively without a consensus in the Council of Ministers and without a convergence of views between the Council and the Commission. This is encapsulated most clearly in the conduct of trade negotiations such as those under the WTO. Here, the Commission can negotiate on behalf of the Community, but only on the basis of a mandate provided by the Council of Ministers under Article 113 of the Treaty of Rome (now Article 133 of the consolidated Treaty on European Union). Not surprisingly, such a mandate can restrict the capacity of EU negotiators to react flexibly and creatively to events or to initiatives from other negotiating partners. In the WTO context, things are further complicated by the fact that although the Commission may negotiate on behalf of EU member states, those states themselves are individually represented in the organization.[8]

There is a further dimension to the constraints exercised by the EU's division of powers. Quite apart from the limitations on external policy-making that arise from the Union's 'constitution', the impact of globalization and interpenetration means that external and internal policies are intimately linked. In agriculture, for example, the EC's negotiating position in the WTO is inseparable from the difficulties of reforming the Common Agricultural Policy (CAP)—an issue that engages national sensitivities and on which national governments have very strong views. Thus, from the mid-1990s, the attempts to find a basis for agreement on agricultural issues in the WTO were fundamentally affected by the national problems faced by the French, the Germans, and others with powerful farm lobbies. These reached a head in the problems experienced by the Doha Development Round, and especially the stalemate reached in the Cancún Ministerial Meeting of Autumn 2003, where the inability of the EU to concede on matters of agricultural export subsidies was a potent element in the eventual failure. In other areas there is a similar if often less dramatic linkage between levels: for instance, the development of EC policies on high technology is decisively influenced by the positions of national authorities with 'national champions' and by the development of cross-national business alliances, and this feeds inexorably into the Community's stance in relation to disputes with the United States and Japan. Likewise, the development of an EU negotiating position on so-called 'open skies' agreements with the United States has for many years come up against the entrenched preferences of member states and in particular their view of 'national flag carriers'.

The development of European institutions since the Single European Act during the mid-1980s, and later the Treaty on European Union (in force since 1993, modified at Amsterdam and Nice), promised to make decision-making and the 'conversion process' less constrained through the introduction of majority voting in the Council of Ministers and a clearer specification of the ground rules. They also promised a more effective role for the European Parliament in the conduct of external relations through the exercise of its powers of assent on international agreements. But even after the Amsterdam and Nice treaties the situation remains one in which the vital treaty-making and negotiating powers lie between the Commission and the Council, for example on WTO agreements. With the introduction of the euro as a single currency during 1999, the situation was further complicated, first by the fact that not all EU member states were initially members of 'euroland', and second by the need for co-ordination between the different structures and processes set up in com-

mercial and monetary policy[9] The enlargement of the EU in 2004 actually meant that in a 25-member Union the 'euroland' countries were suddenly in a minority, although several of the new members wished to join at the earliest opportunity. This brings us again to the distinctiveness of the EU. How different is the process of divided decision-making in the EU from that in, say, the United States, where Congress has considerable powers over trade policy and related areas and where the Federal Reserve holds sway over monetary policy? Both the EU and the United States are known to be difficult international negotiation partners, but is there anything distinctive in the fact that the division of powers in the EU is between a supranational and an intergovernmental body rather than between an executive and a legislature? Further, in the light of enlargement, will it become more difficult to do business with and through the EU as it absorbs the implications of a near-doubling of membership, in numbers if not in economic or political weight?

The decision-making and 'conversion' problems identified here also link with the types of resources mobilized by the EU for external action. From the outset, the Community (the 'first pillar') had certain important powers in trade policy, particularly those relating to market access and the Common Commercial Policy; these have been added to over the years, with such mechanisms as anti-dumping regulations and rules of origin giving the Union a powerful trade policy armoury. Add to this the treaty-making power, which has been exercised to enter into association agreements and other relationships with 'outsiders', and there is the clear basis for a partial but powerful foreign economic policy. Thus, in the case of the Lomé Conventions and their successor the Cotonou Convention of 2000, the EU has constructed a complex web of links with developing countries;[10] equally, the development of links with the European Free Trade Association (EFTA) countries led to the conclusion of a major agreement on the European Economic Area in 1991, while the newly democratizing states of Central and Eastern Europe were introduced to the EU network through the so-called 'Europe Agreements' during the early 1990s. In the latter two cases, the deepening of the economic and political links has led to membership in the EU itself, with Sweden, Finland, and Austria entering in 1995 and eight Central and East European countries becoming members after extended negotiation between 1998 and 2004.

Alongside these assets and resources, the EU also experiences severe constraints in the area of external policy. From the outset, the EU has faced the delicate problems surrounding the transfer of legal, financial, and other resources from the national to the European level and the limitations to EU autonomy even when such transfers can be agreed. For its internal policies, the EU relies on an uneasy blend of transfers from national governments, allocation by the Commission, Council, and Parliament, and implementation by the same national governments as originally transferred the resources; thus it is not surprising that the claims for a *juste retour* or 'fair return' have affected such areas as regional policy, and that the arguments over 'hard resources' such as money have been accompanied by equally severe tensions over 'soft resources' such as legal powers and institutional rules. This contest intersects with some of the central processes of globalization, such as investment by large corporations or the regulation of service provision across national boundaries, which have local as well as regional, national, and European implications. In external policy, although the Commission can be delegated to negotiate or to implement rules, there are uncertainties about the level of commitment of national authorities, especially when it comes to the political and economic costs of agreement. The mobilization of resources at the EU level is thus always political; while the development of routines or institutional habits may dilute the confrontation, there are always potential barriers to effective action or to the expansion of Commission competence.

A logical consequence of the features already noted is that the Union exercises power predominantly at the 'soft' end of the spectrum, as opposed to the 'hard' or coercive power taken to be the ultimate sanction available to state authorities. But as Joseph Nye has pointed out, states themselves, including the most powerful states, depend increasingly on 'soft' power to achieve outcomes in an interdependent and globalizing world. The capacity to co-opt, to enmesh in procedures and institutions, and to influence by contact and example is a growing part of the state's armoury, and it is a part in which the EU is well practised.[11]

It is thus possible to argue that the EU plays a powerful shaping role in the global political economy, both by developing structured commercial ties with its neighbours and competitors and by shaping the expectations of others in negotiation or diplomacy. In an increasingly globalized and turbulent world political economy, it might be argued that this capacity will become both more significant for the EU and more significant for its partners and targets during the early years of the twenty-first century. The EU as a 'community of law' has both inherent limitations and attractions, and can offer and deny rewards such as market access or privileged dialogue. The financial crises and related issues of trade and development that characterized large parts of the global political economy in the late 1990s and early 2000s were such as to place a large premium on institutional order, and on precisely the assets in which the EU is richest.

In a turbulent political economy, this can be and has been a powerful magnet for outsiders. The very fact that the EU is not a state like other states has attracted third parties, whether in the Middle East, the Asia-Pacific, Latin America, or elsewhere, to engage in dialogue and economic institution-building.[12] In the conditions of Europe after the end of the Cold War, the EU appeared as an island of stability and prosperity, and as a source of both economic and political advancement. But this in itself was a potent challenge to the EU's foreign economic policies, since the then European Community had existed for all of its life under the constraints of a divided Europe and prospered on the basis of exclusion and privilege rather than co-optation and inclusion. The ability to 'capture' neighbouring countries is thus an uncomfortable asset: how many, how, and when? It is not at all surprising that the EC response through the

'Europe Agreements' and other channels was initially uncertain and that suspicions in the new democracies were aroused by the view that Community membership is a privilege to be bought at a high price and over an extended period. When the EU published its *Agenda 2000* document as the basis for policy reform in the context of enlargement during 1997, it was also apparent that the process of negotiation with the candidates for membership would be accompanied by intense negotiation among the existing members themselves. The results of these tensions between the 'EU order' and the demands of the outside world were thus paradoxical and likely to remain so: increasing attractiveness, demands for access if not membership, and an EU response veering between the acceptance of responsibility as a 'regional superpower' and a form of conservative paralysis. The eventual enlargement of 2004, while in many ways a triumph of the EU's political/economic diplomacy, has raised further questions about the extent to which the 'new EU' will be able to escape the demands of achieving consensus among 25 members and fulfill what some see as its destiny as an 'economic superpower'.

The implication of the discussion here is that for the EU, foreign economic policy revolves as much around process as around substance. The process is one of continuous negotiation at the European level, where policy determination and policy output constitute an almost seamless web, and where the feedback between processes of internal bargaining and international action can be extremely difficult to disentangle.[13] Two distinct phenomena can be identified here, each of crucial significance to the international activity of the EU and of interest in the broader analysis of globalization. On the one hand, there is what might be termed a process of 'externalization', through which the internal bargaining between member states and within institutions spills over or is projected into the global arena. The example of agricultural policy already cited is one of the most salient in this respect, given the direct linkage between the reform of the CAP and the demands not

only of global trade negotiations but also of interregional agreements or of the enlargement of the Union itself. This is likely to be a crucial focus of tensions as the EU confronts the logic of its extension during the coming years, since it connects closely with the need for budgetary reform and the implications of the single European currency as EMU takes effect.

Other examples are not hard to find. During the 1990s, the internal effort to reach a consensus on support for the EU semiconductor industry frequently spilled over into the attempt to regulate access to the European market, and thus into relations with the United States and Japan, while the efforts to construct a regime for air transport in the EU have intersected at several points with international forces. A key development will be how such specific high-technology or regulatory issues come together and how the EU can shape the external implications of its increasingly unified but also enlarged markets. In turn, this links with a further area of 'externalization'. During the late 1990s, it also became evident that regulatory competition posed distinctive problems. 'Internal' EU efforts to regulate the growth of electronic commerce, for example, inexorably led to tensions with the United States in particular, while successive episodes in the application of EU competition rules to cross-national business alliances demonstrated the complexities of dealing with powerful firms at the same time as powerful governments.[14] This picture was made even more complex by the fact that after the attacks on the United States on 11 September 2001 and the Bush administration's declaration of the 'war on terror', there was an inevitable and intimate link between 'national security' and the provision of financial and other services. Given the continuing development of the EU's role in 'hard security' matters, there is bound to be a coming together of sensitive issues that can be loosely described as those of 'economic security'.

While the process of 'externalization' links the internal affairs of the EU with the global political economy, there is a parallel process of 'internalization', through which external developments and external actors can become part of the EU bargaining process and used either by member states or the Commission and other institutions as a factor in the determination of policy. During the implementation of the Single Market Program, during the early 1990s, US officials went so far as to call for a seat at the table for negotiation of EC measures—a rather dramatic way of expressing the need not just to be in the European market but also to be involved in the generation of rules and regulatory regimes crucial to its operation.[15] Although this was a politically charged episode, the SMP also involved intense efforts by US and Japanese multinational corporations to gain access to decision-making, arguably more effective because they were less confrontational. The other side of the 'internalization' coin is that the threat of external penetration of the process can be used by EU lobbies and member governments in defence of their own interests. Thus, the origins of the SMP itself lay partly in the perception by European industrial lobbies that international trends threatened the competitive position of the EC, a perception that could be used to drive internal reform in the shape of the Single European Act, and to influence the SMP in detail. Perhaps more dramatically, the perceived threat of political and economic collapse in Central and Eastern Europe in the early 1990s fed directly into bargaining over market access, which enabled those countries and their sponsors to engage with the EC policy process more or less effectively. It was apparent that such pressures would be affected during early 2000s by the combination of external financial turbulence, the 'war on terror', and the potential held by EMU, both as a 'safe haven' for assets and as a lever of potential political influence. To put it crudely, would the EU be able to operate as a new 'financial superpower', and what would be the costs and benefits of this status?

The conception of the EU as a continuous—and continuously reshaped—bargain is an important avenue for the analysis of policy, which adds to the evaluation of the Union's power resources and their deployment. The added elements of 'external-ization' and 'internalization' are not unique to the EU, but the EU does provide fertile ground for their occurrence, given its multi-layered and relatively open policy framework. If for no other reason, these processes are important inasmuch as they express political intervention in the decision-making arena—by 'insiders' (EU member governments, lobbies), by 'outsiders' (governments, multinationals, other international organizations), or by both acting in the context of global networks. In each such case, as Susan Strange has pointed out, the identification of a 'European' interest or line of policy can be put in question by the emergence of complex global alignments and cross-cutting interests.[16]

This discussion leads into consideration of a final element in the EU's foreign economic policy: the distinctive pressures and opportunities created by the Union's development of a complex governance system centred on regulatory and institutional structures. This set of structures, as already noted, plays an important part in shaping policy-making. But it is possible to view it in another light, exploring how the Union's regulatory and governance structures provide a potential asset for the pursuit of global objectives. There are two dimensions to this issue. In the first place, there is an increasing perception of the Union as an effective 'model' for the management of capitalist societies, based roughly on a modified social market economy as opposed to the free-market capitalism of the 'American model'. If this is indeed the case, then it is only a short step to the argument that the 'EU model' can be used to shape developments in the outside world, buttressed by the legal base of the treaties and their impact on growth and stability in Western Europe. Thus, the negotiation of the European Economic Area in 1990–1 demanded of the EFTA countries a reshaping of their economic and regulatory structures so that they could become compatible with the Community. Indeed, the reshaping was so profound that a number of members decided it was better to apply for full membership and thus full access to EC decision-making. The 'Europe Agreements' of 1991–2 in respect of Central and East European countries also gave evidence for the argument that the 'EC model' could be used to capture new adherents, with much the same results, although there were also strong political incentives driving the countries concerned to make their applications for membership. After the 2004 enlargement, the 'new neighbours' of the EU in the former Soviet Union and the Mediterranean will also be increasingly affected by the gravitational pull of the (now continental-sized) Union. The new 'model' constituted by EMU, as has been argued, could prove a powerful source of leverage—as well as a source of responsibilities—in the new millennium.

Second, the success of market regulation and integration in Western Europe is often seen by EU officials as providing the base for reshaping global regulatory regimes. The SMP provided such an impetus in respect of areas such as technical standards and public procurement within the context of the GATT. Within the WTO, the EU has acted in major sectoral negotiations such as those on financial services, telecommunications, and information technology to build coalitions on which important agreements could be based (often in juxtaposition to the stance taken by the United States). The 'muscle' available to the Europeans depends by implication on the success of the EU method internally and the effectiveness of its own regulatory structures. A number of analyses have drawn attention to the growth of 'competition among rules' as a central process of the relations between industrial societies; in this process, the existence in a given industry or sector of different regulatory structures gives a basis for attempts to lever open domestic economic activities, to the benefit of those whose rules are the most widely adopted or attractive. By this means, the interpenetration of notionally separate national economies can become more intense, and equally clearly, the more 'successful' regulatory structures can create regional or national advantage. The position of the EU in this respect is critical, reinforced by increasing market integration and by the 'capture' of ever-larger parts of the European economic space, and

expressed in the incentives created for outsiders by the unified market. This has been recognized by outsiders such as the American and the Japanese governments, but also and at least as significantly by firms and other 'private' organizations; such recognition has in the past few years been intensified by the imminence and then the reality of EMU. Whether the EU is capable through its decision processes of capitalizing on the leverage given by the 'Community model' and controlling market access or financial resources effectively in an increasingly globalized world is, in the light of the earlier discussion, an open question, but one that will be vital to the global economic order in the twenty-first century.

Conclusion: The European Union and the Global Political Economy

This chapter has focused on two interrelated aspects of the European Union's external economic policies. (1) Can the EU have a 'foreign economic policy' in the conventional sense of the word? (2) How effective are the forms of power and the decision processes that lie behind foreign economic policy in the Union, and what impact does the EU have in a globalizing world? The answers to both these questions are qualified, but no less significant for that. In the first place, the EU cannot be said to possess a 'foreign economic policy' in a traditional state-centric form; but the nature of the Union and of the global political economy have changed in such a way as to cast considerable doubt on the utility of the conventional conception of foreign economic policy. The EU, therefore, is as much a reflection of the new reality as it is a challenge to an entrenched notion. In the second place, evaluation of the EU's policy effectiveness in terms of its satisfaction of traditional state-centred criteria is misplaced. Just as the EU reflects new realities in the conception of foreign economic policy, so does it demand new criteria for the evaluation of policy effectiveness, based on the mobilization of predominantly 'soft' power, on the attractiveness of its negotiating and regulatory structures, and on the multiple roles played by the EU in the global political economy. Three central roles can be identified for the EU in relation to processes of globalization: those of 'barrier', 'site', and 'promoter'. While conceptually separable, in policy terms these roles are often closely interrelated, and they encapsulate many of the tensions between global and regional integration processes; within the EU, as illustrated by many of the examples cited in this chapter, they constitute a major focus for a continuous negotiation and renegotiation, both at the level of policy sectors and at the level of institutional understandings.

In this light, the EU is not necessarily the only possible model of a new form of foreign economic policy, but it is a challenge to conventional categories and a phenomenon that should make us look seriously and critically at prevailing assumptions—not least, those encapsulating notions of order and stability in the global political economy. The EU has often been the object of fears or suspicions on the part of outsiders, as the potential core of a 'fortress Europe' or as the major building block for a world of competing super-regions. This is indeed one possible future direction for the EU, but the Union will not construct that future by its own efforts alone; the roles of the United States, Japan, and China will also be crucial, as will the efforts of transnational groupings and mechanisms of global governance. At least as powerful is the image of the EU as a major contributor to global governance, encouraging the building of transnational networks and providing a model of continuous negotiation that is one way of coping with the emergence of a global political economy.

Notes

1. In general, this chapter adopts the term 'European Union' for all uses except two: first, those where the reference is clearly to the European Community (the 'first pillar' of the EU; see below); second, where the reference is clearly to the period before 1993 when the Treaty on European Union came into force.

2. For a general discussion of this tension, see William D. Coleman and Geoffrey R.D. Underhill, 'Introduction', in Coleman and Underhill, *Regionalism and Global Economic Integration* (London; Routledge, 1998). See also Björn Hettne, Andràs Inotai, and Osvaldo Sunkel, eds, *Globalism and the New Regionalism* (Basingstoke: Palgrave/Macmillan, 1999).

3. See Michael Smith, 'Foreign Economic Policy', in Walter Carlsnaes, Helene Sjursen, and Brian White, eds, *Contemporary European Foreign Policy* (London: Sage, 2004); Alasdair Young, *Extending European Cooperation: The European Union and the 'New' International Trade Agenda* (Manchester: Manchester University Press, 2002).

4. See Susan Strange, *States and Markets*, 2nd edn (London: Pinter, 1994); Peter Dicken, *Global Shift: Transforming the World Economy*, 4th edn (London: Paul Chapman, 1998); Brigid Laffan, Rory O'Donnell, and Michael Smith, *Europe's Experimental Union: Re-thinking Integration* (London: Routledge, 2000), ch. 3.

5. See Smith, 'Foreign Economic Policy'.

6. See I. Macleod, I.D. Hendry, and Stephen Hyatt, *The External Relations of the European Community* (Oxford: Oxford University Press, 1996), Part 1; Piet Eeckhout, *External Relations of the European Union: Legal and Constitutional Foundations* (Oxford: Oxford University Press, 2004).

7. See Michael Smith, 'Does the Flag Follow Trade? "Politicisation" and the Emergence of a European Foreign Policy', in John Peterson and Helene Sjursen, eds, *A Common Foreign Policy for Europe? Competing Visions of the CFSP* (London: Routledge, 1998).

8. See Grainne de Burca and Joanne Scott, eds, *The EU in the WTO: Legal and Constitutional Issues* (Oxford: Hart, 2001). A similar though not identical situation exists in other intergovernmental organizations. See Coleman and Underhill, 'Introduction'.

9. See Amy Verdun, ed., *The Euro: European Integration Theory and Economic and Monetary Union* (Lanham, Md: Rowman & Littlefield, 2002).

10. See Martin Holland, *The European Union and the Third World* (Basingstoke: Palgrave/Macmillan, 2002).

11. See Joseph S. Nye Jr, *Bound To Lead: The Changing Nature of American Power* (New York: Basic Books, 1990), ch. 5; Joseph S. Nye Jr, *Soft Power: The Means to Success in World Politics* (New York: Perseus Books Group, 2004).

12. See Mario Telo, ed., *The European Union and New Regionalism* (Aldershot: Ashgate, 2001).

13. See Michael Smith, 'European Union Commercial Policy: Between Coherence and fragmentation', *Journal of European Public Policy* 8, 5 (2001): 787–802.

14. See Michael Smith, 'The European Union as a Trade Policy Actor', in Brian Hocking and Stephen McGuire, eds, *Trade Politics*, 2nd edn (London: Routledge, 2004).

15. See Brian Hocking and Michael Smith, *Beyond Foreign Economic Policy: The United States, the Single European Market and the Changing World Economy* (London: Pinter/Cassell, 1997).

16. Susan Strange, 'Who Are EU? Ambiguities in the Concept of Competitiveness', *Journal of Common Market Studies* 36 (1998): 101–14.

Suggested Readings

Coleman, William D., and Geoffrey R.D. Underhill. *Regionalism and Global Economic Integration*. London: Routledge, 1998.

de Burca, Grainne, and Joanne Scott, eds. *The EU in the WTO: Legal and Constitutional Issues*. Oxford: Hart, 2001.

Dent, Christopher M. *The European Economy: The Global Context*. London: Routledge, 1997.

Dicken, Peter. *Global Shift: The Internationalization of Economic Activity*, 4th edn. London: Paul Chapman, 1998.

Eeckhout, Piet. *External Relations of the European Union: Legal and Constitutional Foundations*. Oxford: Oxford University Press, 2004.

Hine, R.C. *The Political Economy of European Trade*. London: Harvester Wheatsheaf, 1985.

Hocking, Brian, and Michael Smith. *Beyond Foreign Economic Policy: The United States, the Single European Market and the Changing World Economy*. London: Cassell/Pinter, 1997.

Kahler, Miles. *International Institutions and the Political Economy of Integration*. Washington: Brookings Institution, 1995.

Piening, Christopher. *Global Europe: The European Union in World Affairs*. (Boulder, Colo.: Lynne Rienner, 1997.

Smith, Michael, and Stephen Woolcock. *The United States and the European Community in a Transformed World*. London: Pinter for the Royal Institute of International Affairs, 1993.

Tsoukalis, Loukas. *The New European Economy Revisited*. Oxford: Oxford University Press, 1997.

Wallace, William. *Regional Integration: The West European Experience*. Washington: Brookings Institution, 1994.

Young, Alasdair. *Extending European Cooperation: The European Union and the 'New' International Trade Agenda*. Manchester: Manchester University Press, 2002.

Web Sites

European Commission: www.europa.eu.int/

European Commission Delegation in Washington: www.eurunion.org/

Chapter 28

Globalization and the Transformation of the German Model

Sigurt Vitols

In the 1970s and 1980s West Germany was widely seen as an attractive national model for other advanced capitalist economies for responding to problems in the global economy, including slower growth, greater financial instability, and increasing competition from developing countries. In contrast with other countries that relied mainly on either markets or state-directed industrial policy to deal with these challenges, the 'German Model' was based on a co-operative (or 'corporatist') approach to industrial modernization. This corporatist approach involved a partnership among the state, business, and trade unions in developing and implementing new policies. This model performed impressively on a number of indicators, including a high export surplus, low unemployment, and high income equality.

In the mid-1990s, however, a marked increase in unemployment and a setback in company profitability and export performance initiated a debate on whether these corporatist institutions were flexible enough to deal with the growing challenges of the future. This chapter reviews the major features of the German model and the new challenges it is facing: German unification, the continued transformation of global product and capital markets, European integration, and a crisis in the welfare state stemming from demographic shifts and low labour market participation. One of the responses to these problems was increasing criticism of German institutions and the call for a more deregulated system along Anglo-Saxon lines. This criticism could be heard mainly from the business community and the conservative-liberal govern-

ment in power through most of the 1980s and 1990s. However, the continued strong position of labour in the industrial relations system and the victory of a social democratic-green party coalition in national elections in 1998 and 2002 have sustained the corporatist approach to problem-solving at the company and national level. Nonetheless, the modest success of this approach (in comparison with the 1970s) has cost the social democratic party much popular support and strained its relationship with the trade unions. These difficulties have raised the prospects for a victory of the conservative-liberal party coalition in the next federal election and a more market-based approach to policy-making and implementation.

Characteristics of the German Model

The deep oil crisis recession of 1973–4 ushered in the end of the post-war 'golden age' of high-growth, low-unemployment capitalism. While all economies were affected by this recession, the policy response and subsequent economic performance differed greatly among the advanced industrialized countries. West Germany in particular received widespread attention as an attractive alternative to the market-oriented (neo-liberal) and state-directed (*dirigiste*) models of adjustment to slower worldwide growth, greater competition from developing countries, and financial instability. The term *Modell Deutschland*, which was originally coined by the German Social Democratic Party in their re-election campaign in 1976, came to symbolize adaptation to these new conditions

Table 1: Comparative Economic Performance, 1980–1990
Germany, US, UK, France, and OECD Average

	Germany	US	UK	France	OECD
Unemployment rate	5.8	7.0	9.7	9.0	7.2
Trade surplus/GDP	1.7	-1.6	-0.1	-1.1	-0.7
GDP growth per capita	1.8	1.9	2.4	2.0	2.2

SOURCE: OECD, Historical Statistics and National Accounts, various years.

through a strategy of export-oriented industrial modernization.[1] The success of this strategy can be seen most clearly in Germany's export performance; between 1970 and 1990, exports as a percentage of GDP increased from 21 to 32 per cent, the balance of trade was negative in only one year (1980), and the trade surplus increased from an annual average of 2.4 per cent in the 1970s to 3.2 per cent in the 1980s. In addition, Germany enjoyed good labour market performance; when using the standardized OECD figures, unemployment was lower than in Western Europe and the United States and the sharp trend towards wage and income inequality in most other industrialized countries was largely avoided.[2]

At the heart of this German model of adjustment was the upgrading of a broad spectrum of industrial sectors to concentrate production on higher-quality, specialized goods targeted towards premium domestic and world markets. This strategy, which has been variously named diversified quality production (Sorge and Streek), new production concepts (Kern and Schumann), and flexible specialization (Piore and Sabel), is based on a combination of building on traditional strengths—such as the technical ability and flexibility of skilled manual workers—and the rapid incorporation of new machinery and production methods. This capacity, which was visible as early as the end of the nineteenth century when Germany became an industrial leader in Europe, was strengthened after the first oil shock of 1973–4 through a mass upgrading of the skill

base and the rapid diffusion of a number of innovations, most notably the microchip.[3]

In his landmark study of the industrial profiles of 10 countries, Porter notes the exceptional broadness of the competitive advantage of Germany across a wide range of industrial sectors.[4] The most visible sector among these success stories is the automobile industry, which for millions of consumers worldwide has come to symbolize the craftsmanship and performance embodied in goods 'made in Germany'. The great expansion of production of traditionally low-volume luxury producers Mercedes-Benz and BMW to increase sales at the high end of the market is a significant story in and of itself. However, Germany's capacity to change has been most clearly demonstrated in the dramatic transformation of Volkswagen, which had been established expressly to mass-produce a low-cost car accessible to every household ('the Beetle'). After the first oil shock, Volkswagen radically changed its product market strategy by terminating production of the Beetle in Germany, introducing a range of new models aimed at significantly higher market segments, and purchasing the niche producer Audi. This example was repeated again and again, not only in sectors familiar in the literature in English, such as industrial machinery and chemicals, but also in steel, food processing, textiles, and wooden furniture.[5]

The joint contributions of business, labour, and the state were crucial for the success of the German model. At the danger of some oversimplification, these contributions occurred within an institutional framework that can be characterized as 'corporatist'. Unlike the neo-liberal market-based approach seen in countries like the United States and Britain, the state has supported a co-ordinated and proactive response to market forces. However, unlike the *dirigiste* state in countries such as France and Japan, the level of targeting of resources to specific sectors and companies ('national champions') in Germany has been low and initiatives have come mainly from the private sector.

Perhaps the most important contribution of the corporatist state is to support the collective organization of interest groups such as business and labour. The state provides associations with special privileges, including access to policy-making and representation vis-à-vis other associations. Furthermore, the state provides these associations with resources either directly through state funding or through the levying of membership fees. The strength of corporatism in Germany can be attributed both to cultural traditions and to strong federalist institutions, which contribute to a tradition of constructive compromise within the political system.

As a result of this support, business has a high capacity to co-ordinate and co-operate through a dense network of industry associations and local chambers of commerce and industry. Furthermore, since industrialization in the late nineteenth century, the state has encouraged the banks and insurance companies to acquire large shareholdings in industrial companies. These shareholdings, as well as interlocking board directorates, result in a dense network linking the largest companies, sometimes called 'Deutschland AG' (Germany, Inc.).[6] This co-ordination capacity through associations and through cross-shareholdings has helped business to pursue its collective interests in the political arena, to participate in the provision of collective goods important for restructuring such as skill formation, and to avoid the kind of destructive price competition that has plagued adjustment in other countries. This capacity has been critical in allowing the growth of an institutional infrastructure for competitive-

ness, for example, research institutes and day-release schools for the dual training system.

The corporatist approach extends into the industrial relations system. More than 80 per cent of employees are covered by collective bargaining between unions and employers' associations at the sectoral level. Most workers in larger companies are also represented at the plant level by works councils and at the firm level by employee representation on company boards. Perhaps best captured in the phrase 'conflictual partnership', labour has co-operated in the often drastic measures involved in adjustment without losing its capacity to pressure employers to take the 'high road' and to mobilize the rank and file when the integrity of the industrial relations system is threatened. The state has also reduced conflict by providing extensive early retirement subsidies to support restructuring in declining industries.

Although each of these three actors is potentially powerful enough to disrupt the system, they were rewarded for their co-operation throughout the 1970s and 1980s. Business enjoyed export success and reasonable profits, labour received high wages and a low level of income inequality, and the state experienced a strong balance of payments, moderate expenditures for labour market programs, and relatively low debt levels.

The German Model: Overwhelmed by New Challenges?

In the 1990s, however, a sense of crisis emerged in Germany and an extended debate ensued over whether the German corporatist system is capable of handling the new challenges started. These challenges include (1) the 'post-Communist' political order, particularly German unification, (2) continuing shifts in the global production and financial systems, (3) European integration, and (4) a crisis in the welfare state.

While all of these factors play a role in the current sense of crisis, the initial trigger was undoubtedly German unification in October 1990. At the time of unification productivity in East Germany was only one-third of the West German level, and its markets were concentrated in the Soviet bloc countries. Although there were great hopes in the early 1990s that eastern Germany could be built up as a commercial gateway between Western and Eastern Europe, the collapse of the Soviet economy led to the disappearance of these traditional markets. At the same time, the replacement of the East German currency with the Deutschemark—and thus the imposition of a single currency on all of Germany—removed the possibility of compensating for productivity differences through adjustments in the exchange rate. The corporatist wage-bargaining system in western Germany, which was transferred to the east, is based on a low level of wage inequality. Wage levels in eastern Germany rose rapidly as a result of this transfer, and the less productive companies in eastern Germany were therefore priced out of Western markets.

Adding to the adjustment problems was the fact that unification was mainly financed through fiscal transfers from western Germany, which resulted in a massive increase in federal debt. East Germans were allowed to exchange their money at parity (i.e., one east Mark for one Deutschemark), which provided them with a large amount of cash to satisfy their pent-up demand for Western consumer goods. Although this initially created an economic boom, with GDP growth exceeding 5 per cent in 1990 and 1991, the German central bank (the Bundesbank) was unhappy with this debt-financed boom and increased interest rates. As a result of these high interest rates and a worldwide slowdown in demand, Germany experienced a sharp recession in 1992–3. GDP decreased by more than 1 per cent in 1993, which was a particularly rapid deceleration considering that GDP growth was above 5 per cent in 1990 and 1991. Economic growth since then has

Figure 1: Annual Growth in German GDP, 1987–2003

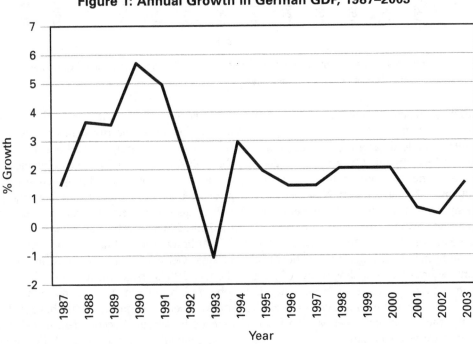

Year

SOURCE: OECD, Historical Statistics and National Accounts, various years.

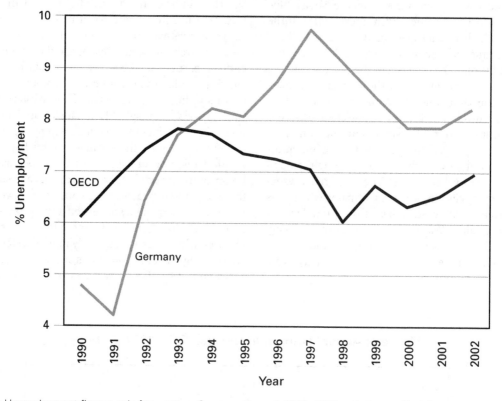

Figure 2: Unemployment Rate in Germany and OECD, 1990–2002

Note: Unemployment figures only for western Germany through 1992; 1993 and after, unified Germany.
SOURCES: OECD statistics, standardized unemployment rates.

been sluggish, averaging somewhat below 2 per cent per year (see Figure 1).

This unfavourable development in economic growth has been accompanied by a dramatic deterioration in the employment situation. Throughout the 1970s and 1980s West Germany had an unemployment rate significantly below the OECD average. However, in 1994 the unified German rate surpassed the OECD average and has remained stubbornly high since then. The OECD rate, in contrast, has trended downward (Figure 2). Although some of the increase in Germany is attributable to the collapse in employment in eastern Germany, there also has been a significant deterioration in western Germany.

The sense of economic crisis was not isolated to eastern Germany, however. World market shares

of Germany's core 'medium-tech' industries—autos, chemicals, industrial machinery, and electronics—were slipping throughout the first half of the 1990s, particularly relative to Japanese competition. Production and employment in high-tech areas such as information technology and biotechnology also remained underdeveloped relative to the United States and Great Britain.[7]

Although the profitability and competitiveness of large German companies have improved since the mid-1990s crisis, this has not led to significant job creation in Germany. One reason is that major improvements in productivity have led to less demand for labour. A second reason is that many of these companies have accelerated their attempts to internationalize. Company internationalization involves moving production closer to consumers in more dynamic markets, such as North America and Asia, rather than exporting goods produced in Germany. This reduces exchange rate risk and also makes it easier to incorporate customer demands into production. Another aspect of internationalization is the transfer of production to Eastern Europe, where labour is significantly cheaper. A final reason is that increasing demands of financial investors—particularly foreign pension and mutual funds—for 'shareholder value' have led to a reallocation of funds within the firm away from labour in favour of profits and dividends. The exposure of German companies to pressure from foreign investors has been increased by the fact that, since the mid-1990s, the large banks have been reducing their shareholdings in industrial companies. As a result companies in the network 'Germany, Inc.' are exposed to the threat of hostile takeovers and have to adopt shareholder value to increase their share prices in order to decrease their attractiveness as takeover targets. Motives for the banks' sale of shares include pressure to raise funds and also to avoid conflicts of interest in investment banking activities, such as mergers and acquisitions.[8]

The third major challenge for the German model is European integration. The European Single Market initiative and European Monetary Union (EMU) are European responses to the globalizing economy. However, both of these at the same time constrain Germany's ability to respond to its domestic economic problems, particularly unemployment. One constraint is pressure for deregulation in telecommunications and transportation, both of which are areas where the public sector provided large amounts of employment. A second constraint is the increasing fiscal burden for Germany, the 'paymaster' or largest net contributor to the European Union. The EU budget has increased dramatically due to the establishment of structural and regional funds to help the newer, less-wealthy 'peripheral' countries in the EU such as Portugal, Spain, Ireland, and Greece deal with change caused by the internal market.

However, the greatest EU constraint on national economic policy-making is undoubtedly the Maastricht Treaty, which lays the groundwork for the EMU and the single European currency, or euro. This treaty imposes strict criteria for fiscal and monetary discipline as prerequisites for countries participating in the EMU. Most significant among these is the requirement that government deficits not exceed 3 per cent of GDP. While intended to encourage convergence among member countries and confidence in the stability of the new currency, at the same time these criteria have restricted Germany's ability to use deficit spending and loose monetary policy to encourage economic growth and employment creation. Although Germany and a handful of other European countries are currently exceeding the 3 per cent limit, deficit spending (and thus government stimulus of the economy) would undoubtedly be much higher in the absence of this limit. Ironically, these measures were insisted upon by the German government (at the behest of the Bundesbank) during the Maastricht single currency negotiation process in order to keep *other* countries fiscally sober.

A final challenge for the German corporatist model is a crisis in the social security system and the welfare state. Germany has had relatively generous programs for unemployment insurance, retirement and disability pensions, and health care. Industrial conflict in the 1980s and early 1990s was reduced in part by early retirement programs, which allowed redundant workers in their late fifties and early sixties to go directly into retirement rather than unemployment. The unemployment rate was also kept down by one of the lowest female labour force participation rates in the OECD and the exceptionally long period of time involved in getting a degree in higher education relative to other countries. Finally, the birth rate has plummeted at the same time that the average life expectancy has increased, leading to a demographic crisis for the pay-as-you-go public pension system.

Since most of these programs are financed through employer and employee contributions, indirect labour costs (i.e., costs of labour other than direct wages) rapidly increased during the 1980s and 1990s to over 40 per cent of wage costs. Employers have argued that although direct wage increases in the last decade have been moderate, the increase in indirect labour costs has made it increasingly uneconomical to locate production in Germany. This has increased pressure to reform core principles of Germany's social security system, including solidarity between the generations, low levels of inequality, and reduction of vulnerability to market forces and structural change.

The Response to New Challenges

One response within Germany to these challenges, which has been strongest among the business community and the liberal Free Democratic Party (FDP), is to demand the reform of German institutions more along the lines of the Anglo-Saxon neo-liberal or market model. These critics blame strong unions, high labour costs, extensive regulations, and the government bureaucracy for the increasing unattractiveness of *Standort Deutschland* (the German production location). Businesses claim that they face a major cost disadvantage relative to other countries due to high wages, social security contributions, and taxes on business. Strong unions, works councils, and dismissal protection legislation have constrained flexibility in the use of labour. Because wage levels are set through industry-level bargaining, employers complain that they cannot design incentive systems within the firm needed to motivate employees. Finally, the business community has argued that the state bureaucracy has imposed unnecessary barriers on innovation, most notoriously in strict regulations on genetic research.

These critics eye the 'American model' with envy. However, implementing reforms is easier said than done in a corporatist system, where many interests have the power to veto proposals, or at least to water them down substantially. In 1996, then-Chancellor Helmut Kohl announced an initiative to cut unemployment in half by the year 2000. To achieve this goal he pushed through legislation to weaken dismissal protection, to lower the statutory minimum requirement on employers for sick pay from 100 per cent to 80 per cent of normal pay, to reduce unemployment and income assistance benefit rates and eligibility for early retirement pensions,

and to deregulate financial markets and increase the supply of venture capital. In addition, commissions were established to develop proposals to reduce the cost burden on employers through the fundamental reform of the tax and social security systems. However, there was remarkably little progress on implementing these measures, in part because of opposition groups within the governing coalition. For example, more radical labour market reform was blocked by the Christian Democratic trade unionists' group, CDA (Christian Democratic Employees).

In the collective bargaining arena, the increasing desire of large companies to offer customized incentives to highly skilled workers and lower the wages of the unskilled led to proposals to weaken significantly the cornerstone of the German system of co-ordinated bargaining, the sectoral-level collective agreement (*Flächentarifvertrag*).[9] Impatient with the pace of reform, record numbers of companies left or threatened to leave employers' associations in order to negotiate company-level agreements. This phenomenon of *Verbandsflucht*, which has been particularly strong in eastern Germany and during the 1992–3 recession, raised the spectre of the loss of the co-ordinating capacity of capital, one of the cornerstones of the German model.

As previously discussed, German businesses have made remarkable progress in restructuring. More efficient 'lean production' methods of manufacturing developed by the Japanese have been adopted on a widespread basis in sectors such as automobiles and electronics. In order to deal with exchange rate fluctuations and to be nearer to customers, many larger companies have expanded their production facilities in the United States, Latin America, and Asia. Finally, a number of larger companies have adopted new organizational and strategic concepts such as 'shareholder value' to boost profitability and improve their market position.

Criticism of German institutions from the government coalition also became more muted as the 1998 national elections approached. The governing centre-right parties had an interest in claiming that economic conditions were improving as a result of their policies. Furthermore, these parties ran into a credibility problem with the electorate when making the case for another term in office after relatively little progress in reform during their 16 successive years in government.

A final rejection of the neo-liberal model was provided by the resounding rejection by the electorate of the governing coalition in the October 1998 elections. Instead, majority support was given to the German Social Democratic Party (SPD) and the green party (Bündnis 90/Die Grünen). These parties support a more activist and less anti-trade union approach to economic modernization than their centre-right predecessors. However, the need to reduce the budget deficit to below 3 per cent of GDP, per the Maastricht Treaty, as well as the increasing financial burden of the welfare state forced the coalition to implement a number of unpopular measures to cut costs. The unpopularity of these measures may lead to defeat of the coalition in the next federal election.

One of the major initiatives of the red-green coalition was a strengthening of works councils through a reform of the Works Constitution Act (Betriebsverfassungsgesetz) in 2001. This new law strengthened the rights of existing works councils and also made it significantly easier to organize works councils in sectors dominated by small firms or branches, such as retail, hotels, and restaurants. A second initiative was a reform of the pension system (the so-called Riester reforms, named after the Minister of Labour at the time), which reduced the level of public pension provision and encouraged private savings. Unlike 'defined contribution' private pension systems in countries like the United States and Britain, which shift many financial market risks to the employee, the Riester reforms required that at least the paid-in capital be guaranteed by the plan providers. Furthermore, unions are required to be involved in the negotiation of industry-wide pension plans, such as the *Metall Rente* plan established in the metalworking sector.

The most sustained efforts of the red-green coalition have undoubtedly been in the area of labour market policy. In his election campaign in 1998, the social democratic candidate for chancellor, Gerhardt Schröder, promised to make job cre-

ation his main priority. Shortly after his election Schröder established the Alliance for Jobs (Bündnis für Arbeit), a tripartite institution based on a co-operative approach of business, labour, and the state to discuss, develop, and implement solutions to economic and employment problems. The Alliance was based on the hope that Germany can repeat the positive experiences with a corporatist solution developed in the Netherlands. Within a tripartite context, the Dutch unions agreed to wage moderation by the unions, the state agreed to make labour market institutions more flexible, and employers agreed to increase employment, particularly part-time employment in the service sector. The result had been a significantly lower unemployment rate and higher level of employment generation in the service sector in the Netherlands than in Germany.

Although the Alliance for Jobs was hindered by disagreements within both the trade unions and the employers' camps and its achievements have been quite modest, a number of proposals discussed within the context of the Alliance have subsequently been incorporated into legislation. The most significant of these measures has been a restructuring of labour market policy, including a reduction in active labour market measures, a liberalizing of the use of temporary agency workers, and a reduction in the generosity of unemployment insurance and welfare payments. The measures have been named the Hartz Laws, after the chairman of the commission set up to reform labour market policy. Interestingly enough, the liberalization of temporary agency work was accompanied by the requirement that trade unions conclude collective bargaining agreements for workers in that sector. The reduction of unemployment and welfare benefits has been particularly controversial, accompanied by a series of 'Monday demonstrations' in major cities reminiscent of 1989 and the fall of the Berlin Wall.

Although the social democratic-green coalition has been arguably more successful in labour market and social policy reforms than the previous right-liberal coalition, it appears that these measures have cost the social democrats considerable electoral support. In 2004, a particularly heavy year in terms of regional and local elections, the social democrats lost majority control in some of their key strongholds and set records in a number of jurisdictions for their worst post-war electoral performance.

Conclusion

The German national model of adjustment to new global challenges came to prominence in the 1970s and 1980s. This corporatist model—based on cooperation between the state and highly organized business and labour interests—was able to contribute successfully to the modernization of a wide variety of manufacturing industries. In the 1990s, however, the ability of this model to deal with four challenges—German unification, continued shifts in global production and consumption systems, European integration, and the crisis of the welfare state—was increasingly questioned. Segments of the business community and the liberal party suggest that Germany should reject its corporatist institutions in favour of a more market-oriented Anglo-Saxon approach to problem-solving.

Since the peak of economic problems was reached in the mid-1990s, however, support for such a neo-liberal model has decreased. Businesses, particularly large multinationals, have managed to regain profitability by implementing more efficient means of production and by

increasing their presence in the Americas and Asia. The liberal-conservative coalition, which was able only partially to implement a deregulatory approach, was resoundingly defeated in national elections in October 1998. The red-green coalition has taken a much more activist and less anti-trade union approach to combatting the problem of mass unemployment, as symbolized by the establishment of the tripartite Alliance for Jobs. This reaffirmation of the corporatist tradition in Germany has also received strong affirmation from the experience of other European countries.

Although the corporatist model of industrial relations and policy-making has enjoyed only limited success in dealing with the significant challenges that Germany currently faces, at the same time the public is skeptical that alternatives such as deregulation based on the neo-liberal model would perform significantly better. The party that has most strongly supported this alternative, the liberal party (FDP), has rarely gained much more than the 5 per cent of the votes it needs in the federal elections to get into the German parliament. Instead, the Christian Democratic Party, which emphasizes a more paternalistic and less pro-market approach to social and economic policy, has been the main alternative to the social democrats. The corporatist model of industrial relations and policy-making will therefore probably continue to exist until the unlikely event that the liberal party becomes the strongest party in Germany.

Notes

1. A. Markovits, ed., *The Political Economy of West Germany: Modell Deutschland* (New York: Praeger, 1982).

2. OECD, *Employment Outlook 1993* (Paris: OECD, 1993); OECD, *Employment Outlook 1994* (Paris: OECD, 1994); W. Carlin and D. Soskice, 'Shocks to the System: The German Political Economy Under Stress', *National Institute Economic Review* 159 (1997): 57–76.

3. See A. Sorge and W. Streeck, 'Industrial Relations and Technical Change: The Case for an Extended Perspective', in R. Hyman and Streeck, eds, *New Technology and Industrial Relations* (Oxford: Blackwell, 1988); H. Kern and M. Schumann, *Das Ende der Arbeitsteilung?* (Munich: Verlag C.H. Beck, 1986); M. Piore and C. Sabel, *The Second Industrial Divide: Possibilities for Prosperity* (New York: Basic Books, 1984).

4. M.E. Porter, *The Competitive Advantage of Nations* (New York: Free Press, 1990).

5. W. Streeck, *Industrial Relations in West Germany: A Case Study of the Car Industry* (London: Heinemann, 1984); P. Katzenstein, ed., *Industry and Politics in West Germany* (Ithaca, NY: Cornell University Press, 1989).

6. M. Höpner, 'The Politics of the German Company Network', *Competition and Change* 8, 4 (1984): 10–31.

7. Deutsches Institut für Wirschaftsforschung, *FuE-Aktivitäten, Außenhandel und Wirtschaftsstrukturen: Die technologische Leistungsfähigkeit der deutschen Wirtschaft im internationalen Vergleich* (Berlin: Duncker & Humblot, 1996).

8. Höpner, 'Politics of the German Company Network'.

9. Carlin and Soskice, 'Shocks to the System'.

Suggested Readings

Carlin, Wendy, and David Soskice. 'Shocks to the System: The German Political Economy under Stress', *National Institute Economic Review* 159 (1997): 57–76.

Deeg, Richard. *Finance Capitalism Unveiled: Banks and the German Political Economy*. Ann Arbor: University of Michigan Press, 1999.

Hall, Peter A., and David Soskice, eds. *Varieties of Capitalism: The Institutional Foundations of Comparative Advantage*. Oxford: Oxford University Press, 2001.

Streeck, Wolfgang. *Social Institutions and Economic Performance: Studies of Industrial Relations in Advanced Industrialized Countries*. London: Sage, 1992.

Vitols, Sigurt, ed. 'Made in Germany: The Transformation of the German Model?', *Competition and Change* Special Issue, 8, 4 (2004).

Wever, Kirsten S. *Negotiating Competitiveness: Employment Relations and Organizational Innovation in Germany and the United States*. Cambridge, Mass.: Harvard Business School Press, 1995.

Web Sites

DGB (Trade Union Confederation): www.dgb.de

DIW (German Institute for Economic Research): www.diw-berlin.de

German Bundesbank: www.bundesbank.de

German Corporate Governance Network: www.gcgn.net

German parliament: www.bundestag.de

Hans Böckler Foundation: www.boeckler.de

Max Planck Institute for the Study of Societies: www.mpi-fg-koeln.mpg.de

Social Science Research Center, Berlin: www.wz-berlin.de

Chapter 29

The Political Economy of the UK Competition State
Committed Globalism, Selective Europeanism

Andrew Baker

One of the most prominent debates in recent international political economy scholarship has concerned the extent to which state authority has been challenged by a process of globalization.[1] However, there is a growing appreciation that zero-sum dualistic debates over the extent to which states have lost power to global markets, or about the degree of global economic integration and the constraints this places on states, are not particularly enlightening when it comes to understanding the complex realities of globalization. This chapter does not set out to verify globalization theses about the lesser or greater power of states, their capacity for action, or their degree of policy autonomy. Rather, the state is seen as one of numerous interconnected and interpenetrated fields of political action and contestation that has undergone degrees of change and transformation in accordance with the particular national setting under consideration, the balance of political forces therein, the structure of the domestic political economy, and, most crucially, the way these arrangements interact with the wider global political economy. The focus in this chapter is on changing patterns of British state-society relationships and how they relate to globalization both as a discourse and as a politically engineered process of market opening.[2]

In many respects, the British case represents the archetypal example of state transformation from a Keynesian welfare state that attempted to promote national welfare by insulating aspects of national economic activity from the international economy, engaging in welfare spending and seeking to deliver full employment, to something resembling an outward-looking neo-liberal competition state that attempts to promote free-market forces internationally and make economic activities located in the national territory more competitive in international or transnational terms.[3] These changes have been bound up with the strategic use of globalization as a discourse by British political elites and with policies that have reconfigured not only British society, but also the global economy and the set of rules and norms governing it. The British state has a complex, reciprocal, and mutually reinforcing relationship with changes in the global political economy and an inherent circularity to this makes it difficult to identify cause and affect. However, UK state-society transformation is rooted in the particular nature of the historical development of British capitalism and its social, cultural, and institutional foundations. These social, cultural, and institutional factors explain why the United Kingdom has been a fervent advocate and promoter of globalization, and a particularly Anglo-Saxon form of neo-liberal globalism at that, while engaging rather selectively with economic regionalism in the form of the European Union.

The chapter is divided into three sections. The first section looks at both the cause and effect of the transformation of the UK state from a Keynesian welfare state to something resembling a neo-liberal competition state. The next section looks at the current UK political economy—the so-called Anglo-Saxon model—and examines its relationship with the wider global political economy and 'globalization'. The final section looks at the political economy of the 'New' Labour government in power since 1997, evaluates the legacy of Blair's so-called 'third way', and looks at Britain's position in relation to Europe and the United States on economic governance issues.

The Transformation of the State in the UK

The classic characterization of post-war political economy is contained in John Ruggie's phrase 'embedded liberalism',[4] which promoted a liberal international trading order accompanied by a restrictive financial order that insulated national economies from financial disruption and 'hot flows' of money. A liberal international economic order was embedded in national policy-making that facilitated social consensus and wealth redistribution. The UK largely followed Keynesian countercyclical demand management macroeconomic policies aimed at full employment, involving some consultation with big business and trade unions in the post-war period. Active social policies, including redistributive transfer payments and investment in public services, characterized the UK Keynesian welfare state. Industries such as steel, coal, and shipbuilding were either state-owned or heavily state-funded. Trade unions, despite fragmentation and weakness, made notable advances for their membership in terms of wages and working conditions.

The late 1970s, however, saw a paradigmatic shift.[5] Keynesianism was abandoned and a monetarist approach advocating free markets and neoclassical economic doctrines was adopted. Keynesianism in Britain had been unable to respond to domestic problems and a changing international economic context. Traditional reflationary responses stoked inflation and resulted in economic stagnation, major payments imbalances, and exchange rate crises. These problems were themselves partly the result of decisions by the UK government that caused the restrictive post-war financial order to unravel.

First, the UK government allowed the City of London to act as a dollar-financed base for US corporations operating in Europe. These 'Eurodollar' markets weakened the fixed exchange rate scheme negotiated at Bretton Woods, resulting in the United States gradually abandoning its commitment to guarantee the gold–dollar parity.[6] Sterling floated from June 1972, and became vulnerable to speculative pressures in the foreign exchange market. Second, liberalization measures in 1971 increased the cohesion of national corporate bond markets, enabling operators in these markets to refrain from purchasing UK government bonds.[7] Faced with difficulties in financing ambitious Keynesian-style public expenditure programs, successive governments were forced to pursue more restrictive monetarist policies involving interest rate rises and/or public expenditure cuts. The nadir came in 1976 with a balance-of-payments crisis that led to the Labour government arranging an IMF loan to ease state liquidity problems. IMF conditionality accentuated public expenditure cuts and rising interest rates that were already being implemented.

Middle- and working-class incomes had been squeezed against a backdrop of growing industrial unrest. Proposals for tax cuts, restrictions on trade unions, and the end of state support for uncompetitive nationalized industries became increasingly popular. Monetarist ideas and policies were appropriated by the Conservative Party and presented as a means of addressing the UK's economic problems. The demise of Keynesianism in the UK should, therefore, be understood in terms of specific national economic problems, a national climate of ideas that reflected this, and the existence of political forces able to exploit such a situation, albeit this was made possible by an international context of exchange rate disruption and rising international capital mobility.

In May 1979, the election of Margaret Thatcher led to a radical free-market agenda that shifted the social basis of the British state in the direction of finance capital and other mobile factors of production. This involved new priorities such as a growing focus on the control of inflation rather than economic growth or full employment.

Systematic attempts were made to 'roll back the frontiers of the state', cutting public expenditure and privatizing unprofitable nationalized industries. Public-sector efficiency was encouraged through the market mechanisms of the 'New Public Management', resulting in 'contracting out' and a growing commodification of the state. Finance was both liberalized and internationalized through abolition of foreign exchange controls in 1979 and removal of bank lending restrictions in 1980. The so-called 'big bang' in the City of London in 1986 broke up 'gentlemanly capitalism' and allowed aggressive foreign entrants into the financial services market.[8] More generally, labour market deregulation gave business a progressively freer hand, and there were sustained attacks on the powers of trade unions, made easier by their relatively weak institutional and legal position compared to their continental European counterparts.

Since Margaret Thatcher's election successive British governments have followed what amounts to an outward-looking competitive cost-cutting strategy, designed to expose British business to international competition and attract foreign direct investment. The continued capacity to attract inward investment and to protect British investments abroad has become integral to British economic success and this is essential for British political parties hoping to win elections. The state itself underwent a reorientation. The Treasury exerted increasing control on spending departments,[9] and Keynesian planning agencies were progressively abolished. More recently we have seen a progressive increase in the Bank of England's role in monetary policy.

In short, the British state has reoriented itself to ensure that a combination of deregulation, cost reduction, and macroeconomic discipline are prioritized over other economic objectives. This signals to transnational investors that the UK is a friendly competitive environment as welfare ministries with domestic constituents have become increasingly subordinated to the Treasury, the Bank of England, and financial market discipline.[10] The interests and concerns of internationally

mobile capital have been prioritized over those of domestic capital and labour and have been more effectively represented at the heart of key government agencies.[11] This has been accompanied by a discernible 'internationalization' in the most important economic sectors, as the UK economy has been opened up to foreign investment. The institutional and regulatory frameworks of the British state increasingly concentrate on the 'residual' function of providing the most appropriate institutional and legal foundations for the operation of what are perceived as efficient global markets: 'Britain's competitive position on the world market depends on a policy of financial stability to maintain and improve the conditions of exchange on the world market itself.'[12] This idea of a 'residual state' can easily be confused with less state intervention.[13] The crucial point is that the *reasoning* and *justification* for intervention have narrowed and state intervention in the UK increasingly lacks any wider sense of social and economic concerns.

Globalization and the Political Economy of Anglo-Saxon Capitalism

The 1980s reforms changed the structure of the British political economy. The always influential City of London became the UK's flagship industry and principal wealth earner. The UK also became dependent on FDI to modernize its manufacturing infrastructure, with far-reaching implications for patterns of wealth accumulation, cultural values, and the distribution of power in British society. An 'open economy' emerged in the UK wherein liberalization, privatization, and deregulation were implemented with relative ease because of historically weak trade unions (in European terms), the traditionally prominent position of finance capitalism and the City of London, and a liberal ideological and philosophical tradition that was suspicious of state intervention and social engineering. What emerged during the 1980s was an advanced form of British nineteenth-century laissez-faire capitalism, with the 1945–70s Keynesian interlude appearing, in retrospect, as the exception rather than the rule.

Michel Albert referred to the Anglo-American model of the late twentieth century as Atlantic capitalism.[14] It revolves around two key premises. First, each individual is assumed to be a rational, self-interested calculator of personal utility, and this utility maximization makes markets efficient. Second, markets are assumed to be most efficient when individuals have the fewest impediments to the pursuit of profit and a situation of near-perfect competition decides outcomes. These principles are on display through the Anglo-American concept of 'shareholder value'.

'Shareholder value' takes a narrow view of corporate enterprise based on profit maximization for individual shareholders, with share prices constituting the chief indicator of business success. This prioritization of share values and short-term private gain as the basis for organizing a society has a host of implications for labour market governance, corporate governance, and the character of financial and public sectors. People's livelihoods and futures become a function of stock markets that often behave in a volatile and speculative fashion. Senior managers boost share values by cutting costs and passing this on to workforces either by cutting wages or by making people redundant. It is no coincidence that countries prioritizing shareholder value also tend to have the weakest forms of labour market regulation, low levels of worker participation in corporate decision-making, and the lowest labour costs in the industrialized world. Although ordinary wages are low in relative terms, senior executives in the UK are the most handsomely rewarded in Europe, with salaries often linked to successful share performance and share options. Consequently, stark social and economic inequality is a feature of UK society. Wages are determined largely by supply and demand, and trade unions and employees have limited opportunity to participate in either firm or state decision-making. Through the UK's flexible labour market and its low (by European standards) wages, Britain has found a niche in a global system of production as a relatively 'low-cost' branch plant for foreign multinationals and as a supplier of cheap menial labour for the service sector.[15]

There is also a fierce market for hostile corporate takeover in the UK that acts as a means of boosting ailing companies' share value or consolidating the market position of successful enterprises. Moreover, the proportion of profits paid out to shareholders in the UK is typically three or four times higher than in Germany. The rewards of production are typically consumed by shareholders rather than reinvested in the production process. Private gain is prioritized over productivity levels and any sense of the social role of companies. As a consequence, the kind of investment that characterizes German or Japanese manufacturing (see Chapter 28 by Vitols and Chapter 33 by Hughes) does not exist to any great extent in the UK. The financial and manufacturing sectors have arm's-length relations in the UK, with the financial sector more interested in stock market and foreign exchange activity, where rewards are potentially greater, than in acting as a source of financing for industry. It is no coincidence that UK productivity levels remain low by European standards[16] and that, to an extent, capitalism in the UK has undergone a process of 'financialization'.[17]

The changing nature of UK political economy is also heavily bound up with globalization, in terms of both extraterritoriality and economic internationalization and as a discourse. First, the principle of shareholder value provides an incentive to globalize corporate strategies. Corporations whose futures depend on share value cannot afford to be vulnerable to an economic downturn in one continent or territory. Consequently, they disperse their economic activities around the globe. At the same time, the *ascendancy* of shareholder value as a principle for organizing society owes much to a globalization discourse that implies that only the most competitive companies survive in a global market environment, with the priority placed on shareholder value being the most effective route to competitive corporate efficiency.

Through the promotion of shareholder value, the UK is more heavily integrated into a global circuit of capital than any other country in the world. In the UK stock market, some 30 per cent of shares are held by foreign, mainly American, investors. By 2001 the leading City investment banks were the American firms Goldman Sachs, Morgan Stanley, and Merrill Lynch. European, Japanese, and US institutions dominate the City, and, hence, investment banking, the UK's flagship industry, is *not* British but largely foreign-owned. The total stock of inward direct investment in Britain, taken as a percentage of GDP, is higher than in any other G-7 country. Furthermore, the UK manufacturing sector has often deployed plant, equipment, and capital abroad simply to protect the profit levels of its owners. UK overseas investment is higher as a percentage of GDP than for any other G-7 country and Britain is home to more multinationals than any country except the United States (which is, of course, *much* larger). For some this has constituted a process of deindustrialization, in which there is a growing disjuncture between British capital and the British economy.[18] Certainly, high levels of outward investment have meant that instead of producing manufactured goods and exporting them, British investors have increasingly consumed rewards from overseas investments, resulting in a more active service sector. Consequently, for both the major political parties, a continued ability to attract foreign direct investment and to protect British investments abroad has become synonymous with successful economic performance. In short, once UK governments took up the mantra of free markets and prioritized profits and shareholder value, they reconfigured British society. In the British context, globalization assumed a mutually reinforcing dynamic and became a self-fulfilling prophecy. On the one hand, key British state-society coalitions promoted notions of shareholder value by citing competitive global pressures, but as they did so significant interests within these coalitions also became more dependent on the performance of the global economy, on further market opening, and on national policies that followed the 'no alternative' anti-inflationary and low-cost logic of a liberalized global economy. In addition to these developments, the social basis of support for the principle of shareholder value and the privileged position of the City of London have become broader as a consequence of the rise of equity-linked pension and mortgage plans that have connected a wider swath of the British electorate's fortunes and wealth to the performance of increasingly globalized financial markets. British political parties hoping to win elections have to be sensitive to such developments.

Second, the above developments have resulted in the UK 'competition state' (see Chapter 26 by Cerny) pursuing a committed Anglo-Saxon form of globalism evident in two discourses employed by the UK government. The first is what Hay and Rosamond have called 'globalization as external economic constraint'.[19] It implies a world of near-perfect capital mobility sparking an intense struggle for locational competitiveness based on cost reduction, welfare retrenchment, and labour market deregulation. UK governments have used this discourse to convince a domestic audience that there is no alternative to macroeconomic discipline and market-conforming deregulation if national competitiveness is to be maintained. The second discourse is what Hay and Rosamond call 'globalization as a desirable yet contingent outcome'.[20] This discourse presents globalization as desirable, but acknowledges that it has a fragile and contingent quality and therefore needs protection and promotion. Unlike the first discourse, the principal target audience for this second discourse is not the domestic electorate but other states in various international forums. It is a discourse frequently used in British foreign economic policy and is part of an effort to garner support for the institutionalization of a neo-liberal regime of global governance.[21] UK political elites tailor globalization discourse to suit the audience they are addressing. This is a direct result of the political economy of UK capitalism and reflects the interests of dominant state-society coalitions. This point will be explored further below.

In contrast to this commitment to globalization, the UK has been more selective in its support for 'Europeanism' and European integration. For example, on the one hand, the UK was an enthusiastic supporter of the predominantly neo-liberal Single Market Program as an increased market opportunity for British business.[22] On the other hand, entrenched 'Euroscepticism' gave Britain a reputation as an 'awkward partner' among its EU neighbours.[23] This is partly explained by the special relationship with the United States, but there is also a political economy explanation: UK political elites are suspicious of the European social model as potentially represented by the European integration process. The UK thus sought 'opt-outs' on European Monetary Union and the Social Chapter, and criticized the Common Agricultural Policy continuously. For the UK state, EU integration is exogenous, the work of 'others', and is addressed in terms of the defence of national interest rather than participation in a shared European project.[24] In short, in contrast to its committed globalism, the UK competition state has displayed a very selective Europeanism.

The Political Economy of New Labour

The election of a Labour government in May 1997 might have implied a break with the neo-liberal conservatism of the previous 20 years. However, the New Labour 'project' is consistent with all of the features of UK political economy outlined above—a preference for a style of Anglo-Saxon capitalism emphasizing neo-liberal shareholder value, the strategic political use of globalization in discourse, and a rather selective engagement with Europe and the European Union.

During 18 years in opposition the British Labour Party gradually shifted to the right of the political spectrum. Discourses of globalization and competitiveness were used to justify this 'modernization' process. In power, the Labour government has implemented a series of measures designed to promote competence and transparency in monetary policy, labour market flexibility, human capital formation, and welfare to work. New Labour has defended the least regulated labour market in the OECD.[25] The Labour Party has made repeated election pledges not to raise taxation and has taken means testing in the welfare system further than even Conservative governments dared, extending this to disability benefits. The core of New Labour's political economy, however, has been the

establishment and maintenance of anti-inflationary credibility (e.g., the Bank of England was granted operational independence), spending targets, and a fiscal golden rule that prevents borrowing to finance current expenditures.

It is interesting to observe the discourse that has accompanied this bid for macroeconomic credibility. One of the principal motivations behind the new framework has been the recognition that 'global capital markets immediately punish any government which strays from the macroeconomic straight and narrow.'[26] British policy-makers used globalization and the implications for competitiveness that flowed from this to argue for central bank independence and macroeconomic soundness, while other European states were justifying the move to central bank independence in terms of *European* monetary integration. Crucially, by citing national competitiveness, the Labour government could also claim that it was acting out of concern for the national interest and for British firms and their employees, rather than simply placating international financial markets.[27]

While using the language of non-negotiable external constraint with the electorate, New Labour's international policy also implies that globalization is a contingent process that requires further institutionalization. The UK government has sought to institutionalize the so-called 'Washington Consensus' of open markets and sound money policies, as advocated by multilateral agencies such as the IMF for most of the last two decades.[28] For the most part, this governance regime reflects US preferences for a global economy in its own image and on its own terms,[29] but the UK has similar sets of international preferences to those of the United States largely due to a shared Anglo-Saxon 'financialized' form of capitalism. The empowerment of a Bank of England–Treasury–City of London coalition effectively replicates in the UK the dominant position of the Wall Street–Treasury axis in the United States.[30]

Following successive emerging market financial crises in the second half of the 1990s, investment banks in the City feared that many countries affected by speculative financial flows might well attempt to reintroduce capital controls or seek to prevent their initial removal, so denying investors access to their markets.[31] Consequently, New Labour participated fully in the 'global financial architecture' proposals that emerged from the Asian financial crisis of 1997–8 and even provided some degree of intellectual leadership with the intent of institutionalizing capital account liberalization and creating a set of global norms and practices compatible with financial liberalization.[32] Recent British initiatives have included Chancellor Gordon Brown's proposals for the IMF to adopt codes of practice for fiscal and monetary transparency, designed to increase the information available to market participants, to discipline national policy, and to 'lock in' the principles of sound money and open markets. This creates institutional as well as market imperatives for policies compatible with and conducive to a liberalized financial order. Notably, these codes of practice are the international counterpart to the domestic commitment to orienting fiscal and monetary policy towards discipline, stability, and transparency.[33]

More generally, New Labour has pushed for a reconfiguration of the regional (European) and global economic orders in accordance with the imperatives of the Anglo-Saxon model. UK representatives at WTO gatherings have argued vehemently that the worst thing the developing world could do is resurrect trade barriers.[34] In relations with Europe, the most frequent argument forwarded by New Labour is that European labour costs need to be reduced and that the achievement of labour market flexibility is central to European competitiveness. Gordon Brown has encouraged his fellow European finance ministers to follow the UK deregulatory example, promoting the Anglo-Saxon labour market model while claiming interest in further EU integration. As the Labour government tries to sell the European Constitutional Treaty to the British public, its approach is selective and resists anything that might improve UK labour standards. This has precipitated an angry response from British trade unions, which have argued that the government is only interested in the EU as a free trade zone and is more concerned with pushing the Americanization of the British labour market.[35]

The selective Europeanism of New Labour has been most evident in its continued refusal to join the euro zone. Happy to portray euro membership as a technical issue, New Labour maintains that the time is not right for the UK to join. Gordon Brown's so-called five tests enable the Treasury to control the debate and to argue the tests have not yet been met. In reality, these tests are little more than a series of headings,[36] which makes it difficult to assess whether they have been definitively passed or not and if membership might be desirable. Of course, there are some legitimate concerns about UK entry, not least the sensitivity to exchange rate concerns and the UK economy's sensitivity to short-term interest rate adjustments in a context of highly liberalized credit markets and high levels of consumer indebtedness. However, New Labour has shown little appetite for reviewing British credit and lending practices because these practices have largely fuelled economic growth over the last five years and delivered higher standards of living for the electorate.

Those arguing in favour of the euro tend to see the issue in altogether broader terms than these technical questions. In particular, they see the decision on the euro as a crucial conjuncture in the historical development of British capitalism. For them, the decision provides a historic opportunity to break the iron grip of neo-liberalism and American-style Atlantic capitalism in the UK and move towards a more socially oriented European form of capitalism that takes manufacturing, the rights of workers, and public services seriously.[37] This argument maintains that by creating a potential master currency in the form of the euro, European states have given themselves more leeway to pursue expansionary monetary and fiscal policies and wrestle some macroeconomic autonomy back from global financial markets. Unfortunately, the current policy frameworks for monetary union in Europe, the Fiscal Stability and Growth Pact, and the design of the European Central Bank (ECB) have not been particularly conducive to macroeconomic expansion.

But advocates of euro membership argue that now that the new currency has established itself, the time is right for the UK to join and participate in the debate on *reform* of these frameworks, particularly as unrest with the fiscal stability pact is growing in continental Europe. In contrast to the euro zone, the UK's margins for macroeconomic manoeuvre are restricted. Sandwiched between the euro and the dollar, the band of market tolerance for UK monetary and fiscal policy is less than for the euro zone simply because of the size of the economies involved. The argument is therefore that euro zone membership would give the UK greater capacity to invest in public services, to raise taxes, and to protect its own workers without macroeconomic risks. Manufacturing would benefit from lower interest rates and, most crucially, from greater exchange rate stability brought about by euro entry. This is undoubtedly an optimistic assessment, and euro membership is an unavoidably political decision. Yet questions about the sort of society and public services Britons want, and whether the economy exists solely for the benefit of shareholders and investors as in the United States or whether it should be informed by a more socially grounded distinct European vision, have hardly been broached in the public debate on the euro in the UK. This kind of circumscribed public discussion has been politically convenient for New Labour and has enabled it to avoid taking tough decisions on the nature of the consumer credit market in the UK, allowing record levels of consumer indebtedness to fuel the New Labour economic success story.

However, our assessment of New Labour is incomplete until we consider that Gordon Brown's recent investment in public services in Labour's second term has been a *genuine* act of redistribution, though probably insufficient to reverse 25 years of neglect of the public realm in the UK. Crucially, the truth about Blair, Brown, et al. and their brand of New Labour is more subtle than simply labelling them descendants of the Thatcherite legacy. They *do* want improved public services, less discrimination in every walk of life, and a more just form of capitalism in which employers take social responsibility seriously. Yet at the same time, because they have accepted the Anglo-Saxon model of capitalism created in the UK

under Thatcher, these goals have proved elusive. The so-called third way has attempted to marry two incompatible value systems—Anglo-Saxon conservatism and European social democracy.[38] In the UK, conservatism is deeply entrenched in the structures of the competition state and continues to prevail over social democratic inclinations.

Conclusion

Currently, the political economy of the British state is considerably different from the post-war Keynesian welfare state. The transformation to a 'competition state' has been bound up with ongoing processes of market liberalization that have shifted the social basis of the state and created one of the world's most open economies. An Anglo-Saxon model of capitalism has emerged based on shareholder value, which creates incentives for corporate enterprises to globalize their activities and for decision-makers to strive to lower costs. As this has happened key economic actors and societal interests have become dependent on an open world economy. UK governments have responded by strategically employing two globalization discourses—one of external economic constraint for a domestic audience; the other, for an international audience, of a contingent globalization in need of protection and promotion. In contrast, the UK has adopted a somewhat selective form of Europeanism that is again derived from the imperatives of the Anglo-Saxon model of capitalism. There was enthusiasm for the liberalized single European market, but suspicion of supranationalism and of the European social model. This selective Europeanism has been most evident in the stifling of public debate on European Monetary Union and of its political significance for the future of British society.

The discussion of the British case in this chapter has demonstrated how globalization is not something that exists independently of the state. Globalization has developed because certain state agencies, acting on behalf of specific social forces, have actively promoted it. As they have done so, new structural pressures, ideas, and discourses, which further constrain states, have been promoted and invoked. Globalization has not heralded the 'retreat of the state'. The state remains a strategic contested terrain, control of which is pivotal to world order. An approach that acknowledges how states and markets are mutually constitutive, comprising integrated ensembles of governance, as advocated by the editors of this volume, is therefore a fruitful approach to the study of political economy in a globalized era. Applying such an approach to the UK case has demonstrated how the emergence of an Anglo-Saxon form of capitalism has been bound up in a mutually reinforcing fashion with the emergence of a UK competition state. Anglo-Saxon capitalism and the UK competition

state constitute an integrated ensemble of market-state governance that simultaneously promotes and is representative of a neo-liberal form of globalization. Finally, until New Labour embraces Europeanism and views markets as instruments for the achievement of public purpose, as well as for the generation of profits, where social co-operation is seen to be as important to economic success as individual competition, then social justice will remain a secondary consideration in the political economy of the UK competition state.

Notes

I am grateful to Phil Cerny and Richard Woodward for helpful comments on an earlier draft of this chapter.

1. For different perspectives, see S. Strange, *The Retreat of the State: The Diffusion of Power in the World Economy* (Cambridge: Cambridge University Press, 1996); P. Hirst and G. Thompson, *Globalization in Question* (Cambridge: Polity Press, 1996); L. Weiss, ed., *States in the Global Economy: Bringing Domestic Institutions Back In* (Cambridge: Cambridge University Press, 2003); G. Garrett, *Partisan Politics in the Global Economy* (Cambridge: Cambridge University Press, 1998).

2. Globalization has multiple meanings and causes. For a discussion of the complex nature of globalization, see J. Scholte, *Globalization: A Critical Introduction* (London: Palgrave, 2001).

3. P. Hall, 'Policy Paradigms, Social Learning and the State: The Case of Economic Policy Making in Britain', *Comparative Politics* (Apr. 1993): 275–96. For more on the competition state, see Chapter 26 by Cerny and P. Cerny, 'Paradoxes of the Competition State: The Dynamics of Political Globalization', *Government and Opposition*

(Spring 1997): 251–74.

4. J. Ruggie, 'International Regimes, Transactions and Change: Embedded Liberalism in the Postwar Economic Order', *International Organization* 36, 2 (1982): 379–415.

5. Hall, 'Policy Paradigms, Social Learning and the State'.

6. R. Gardener, *Sterling-Dollar Diplomacy in Current Perspective* (New York: Columbia University Press, 1981).

7. M. Moran, *The Politics of Banking* (London: Macmillan, 1988).

8. M. Moran, *The Politics of the Financial Services Revolution: The USA, UK and Japan* (London: Macmillan, 1991).

9. C. Thain and M. Wright, *The Treasury and Whitehall: The Planning and Control of Public Expenditure* (Oxford: Clarendon Press, 1995).

10. R. Cox, 'Global Perestroika', in R. Miliband and L. Panitch, eds, *The Socialist Register* (London: Merlin Press, 1992).

11. A. Baker, '*Nébuleuse* and the "Internationalisation of the State" in the UK? The Case of HM Treasury and the Bank of England', *Review of International Political Economy* 6, 1 (1999): 79–100.

12. W. Bonefield, A. Brown, and P. Burnham, *A Major Crisis? The Politics of Economic Policy in Britain in the 1990s* (Aldershot: Dartmouth, 1995), 187.

13. M. Moran, *The British Regulatory State: High Modernism and Hyper Innovation* (Oxford: Oxford University Press, 2003).

14. M. Albert, *Capitalism against Capitalism* (London: Whurr Publishers, 1993).

15. For example, a comparatively low skills base resulting from the absence of a comprehensive training system means that Japanese firms locate their assembly plants in the UK but their research and development facilities in Germany. Low-paid service-sector work is most evident in the explosion of call centres in the UK.

16. The UK *has* enjoyed higher growth levels but these have been fuelled in part by an explosion in consumer indebtedness and a boom in house prices rather than being based on sustainable increases in productivity performance, which remains quite poor. See Andrew Graham, 'The UK 1979–95: Myths and Realities of Conservative Capitalism', in C. Couch and W. Streeck, *Political Economy of Modern Capitalism* (London: Sage, 1997), 117–32.

17. Financialization can be defined as the increasing dominance of the finance industry in the sum total of economic activity, of financial controllers in the management of corporations, of financial assets among total assets, of marketized securities and particularly equities among financial assets, of the stock market as a market for corporate control in determining corporate strategies, and of fluctuations in the stock market as a determinant of business cycles. R. Dore, *Stock Market Capitalism: Japan and Germany versus the Anglo-Saxons* (Oxford: Oxford University Press, 2000).

18. D. Coates, *The Question of UK Decline* (Hemel Hempstead: Harvester Wheatsheaf, 1994).

19. C. Hay and B. Rosamond, 'Globalization, European Integration and the Discursive Construction of Economic Imperatives', *Journal of European Public Policy* 9, 2 (2002): 147–67.

20. Ibid.

21. For discussion of G-7 finance ministries and central banks, see A. Baker, *The Group of Seven:* *Finance Ministries, Central Banks and the Politics of Global Financial Governance* (London: Routledge, 2005); A. Baker, 'The G7 as a Global "Ginger Group": Pluralateralism and Four-Dimensional Diplomacy', *Global Governance* 6, 2 (2000): 165–89.

22. See Chapter 21 by van Apeldoorn.

23. S. George, *An Awkward Partner: Britain in the European Community* (Oxford: Oxford University Press, 1998).

24. Hay and Rosamond, 'Globalization, European Integration'.

25. For more on this, see D. Coates and C. Hay, 'The Internal and External Face of New Labour's Political Economy', *Government and Opposition* 36, 4 (2001): 444–72.

26. E. Balls, 'Open Macroeconomics in an Open Economy', *Scottish Journal of Political Economy* 45, 2 (May 1998): 122.

27. C. Hay and M. Watson, 'The Discourse of Globalization and the Logic of No Alternative: Rendering the Contingent Necessary in the Political Economy of New Labour', *Politics and Policy* 31, 3 (2003): 289–305.

28. The term 'Washington Consensus' was first coined by John Williamson. See Williamson, 'What Washington Means by Policy Reform', in Williamson, ed., *Latin American Adjustment: How Much Has Happened?* (Washington: Institute for International Economics, 1990). See also J. Stiglitz, *Globalization and Its Discontents* (London: Penguin, 2002).

29. On US structural power, see S. Strange, *States and Markets* (London: Pinter, 1994). Also see P. Gowan, *The Global Gamble: Washington's Faustian Bid for Global Dominance* (London: Verso, 1999).

30. Ibid.; Baker, 'Nébuleuse and the "Internationalisation of the State".

31. Confidential interview with HM Treasury official, Jan. 1998.

32. J. Best, 'From the Top Down: The New Financial Architecture and the Re-embedding of Global Finance', *New Political Economy* 8, 3 (Nov. 2003): 363–84. Also see A. Baker, 'The G7 and Architecture Debates: Norms, Authority and Global Financial Governance', in G. Underhill

and X. Zhang, eds, *International Financial Governance Under Stress: Global Structures versus National Imperatives* (Cambridge: Cambridge University Press, 2003), 324–42.

33. Coates and Hay, 'The Internal and External Face of New Labour's Political Economy'.

34. Gordon Brown has played a leading role in proposals for debt relief for the poorest of less-developed economies, but the main thrust of New Labour reform proposals concerning international institutions such as the World Bank and the IMF has been the codes of practice referred to above.

35. D. Simpson and T. Woodley, 'We Can't Back a Yes Vote', *The Guardian*, 30 June 2004.

36. The five tests are sustainable convergence with the euro zone; sufficient flexibility; impact on investment; impact on the City; impact on employment. The fourth test heading reveals the centrality of the City in the political economy of the UK.

37. The most erudite and coherent expression of this position is W. Hutton, *The World We're In* (London: Little, Brown, 2002).

38. See ibid. On the contradictions in post neo-classical endogenous growth theory and the difficulty in reconciling its view on markets and competitiveness with the pursuit of social justice, see Hay and Coates, 'The Internal and External Face of New Labour's Political Economy'.

Suggested Readings

Baker, A. *'Nébuleuse* and the "Internationalisation of the State" in the UK? The Case of HM Treasury and the Bank of England', *Review of International Political Economy* 6, 1 (1999): 79–100.

Coates, D., and C. Hay. 'The Internal and External Face of New Labour's Political Economy', *Government and Opposition* 36, 4 (2001): 444–72.

Graham, Andrew. 'The UK 1979–95: Myths and Realities of Conservative Capitalism', in C. Couch and W. Streeck, *Political Economy of Modern Capitalism*. London: Sage, 1997, 117–32.

Hay, C., and M. Watson. 'The Discourse of Globalization and the Logic of No Alternative: Rendering the Contingent Necessary in the Political Economy of New Labour', *Politics and Policy* 31, 3 (2003): 289–305.

Hutton, W. *The World We're In*. London: Little, Brown, 2002.

Web Sites

Bank of England: www.BankofEngland.co.uk
Department of Trade and Industry: www.dti.gov.uk
European Union: www.europa.eu.int
Foreign and Commonwealth Office: www.fc.gov.uk

HM Treasury: www.hm-treasury.gov.uk
International Monetary Fund:
   www.imf.org/external/country/GBR/index.htm

Chapter 30

Transition Economies

Annette Freyberg-Inan

Since 1996, the term 'transition economy' has been applied by the World Bank to those economies that have been undergoing a change from dependency on central planning and public ownership to more reliance on market mechanisms and private ownership of the means of production. Included among the transition economies have usually been those in Central and Eastern Europe (CEE), the newly independent states of the former Soviet Union (FSU), and some economies in East Asia, notably Vietnam and the People's Republic of China.

What does it mean to speak of transition economies and why are they a special category? The term 'transition', of course, implies that these economies are moving from one state of affairs to another, that is, from an economy with more state control and intervention to a more market-oriented and capitalist system. However, the term itself is problematic. One problem is that the term 'transition' clearly implies an end point—there can be no economies permanently in transition. Thus, for some countries, such as Belarus or Romania, where a so-called transition has dragged on for over 15 years, the term becomes increasingly questionable. At some point we need to consider the possibility that these economies are not in transition any more at all but may have become something that should receive a name of its own. In other words, the term 'transition' can distract us from properly understanding what is going on in these countries *right now*, because it leads us to focus instead on a supposedly desired future situation, which might never actually materialize.

The second problem with the term is that it implies a common goal for all transition economies and it is also frequently assumed that the way to reach this goal must be similar for all these countries. This criticism is the same that is raised against the 'modernization' paradigm more generally.[1] Thus, the question is whether there is only one way to develop, and whether all countries should try to emulate those considered relatively successful today, such as Germany and the Netherlands. Do the different historical, geographic, and cultural circumstances of different countries not matter for the way they evolve? And can we simply assume that people everywhere even *want* to live in the same way, namely, in *our* way, which is, after all, far from perfect? Clearly, there are different ways of organizing societies and, according to plentiful literature on contrasting varieties of capitalism,[2] there are different ways of organizing market-based economies successfully.

The bottom line is that when we hear or use the term 'transition economy' we should ask ourselves towards *what* exactly and *why* and *how* these countries are in transition. When we take a closer look, it also becomes immediately apparent just how difficult and fraught with problems such a process is, especially in today's context of profound world economic change. As students of international political economy, we should not only study theory but need to look at what happens 'on the ground' in the real world in different specific contexts. To have anything worthwhile to say to policy-makers, we need to link the theoretical knowledge developed by the field with a solid grasp of what happens in specific regions and countries around the world. This chapter will help us to understand those parts of the world that have emerged from some form of Communism to find themselves struggling to stay afloat in rapidly integrating regional and global markets.

The Problem of Multiple Transitions

The most important underlying premise of the field of study of political economy is that politics and economics are intrinsically connected. This means that the way we organize and run an economy is always a political decision. Even if many outcomes (such as employment rates and prices) are determined mainly by market mechanisms, it is still a political decision to leave such outcomes up to market mechanisms and not to regulate them differently. Vice versa, political economists also believe that politics and political decisions are very much affected by economic factors, such as the distribution of resources in a society. Political power and economic power tend to go hand in hand, and particular ways of organizing a society politically tend to be associated with particular forms of economic organization. For example, the organizational form considered normal and exemplary in the Western world today is some form of open market economy in some form of representative liberal democracy. Some states have had a form of both for many years, some are resisting the trend, but many are in one way or another attempting to develop both democratic and capitalist institutions and cultures.

It is therefore important to keep in mind that transition economies are always at the same time transition *polities*,[3] emerging from a totalitarian praxis that sought to subordinate most aspects of human life to the political norms of the state. They are now reorganizing their economies while simultaneously trying to establish and consolidate some form of democracy, and thus are always undergoing at least a double transition. The transition is 'at least' a double one because it is frequently argued that deep and sustainable political and economic change requires supporting cultural changes as

well. Few people like to hear that their culture is not fit for democracy or market competition, but it is frequently suggested that countries in the FSU, for example, have not yet developed the cultural prerequisites to 'join with the West' in a community of democratic states and open economies. A large and interesting body of literature revolving around the concepts of 'civil society' and 'social capital' looks into what the cultural prerequisites of democracy and market economy (and thus of transition) may be.[4] The point here is that economic transition should always be viewed in context as an encompassing historic change in these countries that involves economic plus profound political and frequently cultural reorganization. In the section on dilemmas of transition below, more will be said about the problems of multiple transition. But first we must take a look at transition countries in their contemporary regional and global contexts, contexts that create particular challenges for their domestic reorganization.

Transition Economies in a Globalizing World

Today's transition economies find themselves in an especially difficult context of rapid regional and global economic integration, both of which are proceeding so quickly that many states cannot properly reflect upon them in their desire to harness integration trends properly. Consider the world into which the 'post-Communist' countries emerged after the end of the Cold War in 1989. Marxist-inspired recipes for organizing economies were very much discredited by people's own experiences of oppression and deprivation, and also by the apparent success of more liberal models. Citizens in the newly post-Communist countries wanted above all to have better lives as quickly as possible by emulating some form of capitalism instead. Thus, it is probably fair to say that there was a widespread consensus in these countries that some kind of transition should take place towards more market-based economies with more private ownership. But ordinary people in those countries, and even elites, frequently knew little or disagreed about what specific form such a transition should take and what kind of system precisely they wanted to install. After all, they had no real-life experiences of and lacked knowledge about running market economies.

That was the first reason, though perhaps not the most important, why decision-makers in the transition countries tended to look outside their own countries for examples and advice about what to do. They looked for advice to those countries they considered economically most successful and also culturally most similar, and those were (at least for CEE and the FSU) the Western industrialized countries in Europe and North America. A second reason for a general international reorientation for many transition countries was that they had suddenly lost the interdependencies of the COMECON system (Council for Mutual Economic Assistance), which the Soviet Union had set up as the socialist integration network. It did not work very well and served essentially the interests of the USSR, but its loss—often combined with a dislike of continued close co-operation with Russia—was significant in sending these countries looking for other trade partners.

Another, more important reason why external Western advice became so influential was that Western actors, ranging from NGOs via national governments to international organizations, actively worked to exert their influence. Partly this was out of goodwill, to support these countries in their efforts to create better lives for their citizens and join the community of democratic and affluent states. Self-interest was also involved, however, because the Western countries and actors were keen on markets for their goods and services, investment opportunities, sources of cheap labour, or military allies. It is difficult to separate the nobler from the baser reasons for support for transition countries, because in most decisions to help both have played a role.

All these countries generally received similar advice from their most influential Western partners, such as the International Monetary Fund (IMF), the European Commission, the World Bank, or the US government. The advice was to restructure their economies as quickly as possible according to the guidelines of neo-liberal economic theory (even if the foreign countries giving advice were evidently *not* doing so themselves!).[5] This meant (1) 'privatization', or selling state-owned enterprises to private owners; (2) 'liberalization', or removing internal constraints on the free operation of market mechanisms; and (3) 'integration', or opening their economies to the outside world by abolishing external barriers to trade and financial flows. In the European Union (EU) and all around them barriers to trade and financial flows were being reduced. This was the age of economic integration, and transition economies were caught up in the tide. Economic integration took the simultaneous forms of regionalization and globalization. Regional agreements, such as the Central European Free Trade Agreement and the EU, became building blocks of larger free trade areas.

This process of opening up to other and more affluent economies had its benefits of course: it brought imports onto the shelves of supermarkets in Warsaw, Sofia, and Moscow of which the citizens there had long only dreamt. It brought investment into those countries, and it gave them better chances to export their own products and services to the outside world as well. Especially the last two factors could also stimulate recovery and growth within these economies, which had emerged from the Cold War with aging and inefficient industrial and agricultural, and underdeveloped service, sectors.

But the same recipe also contained problems. Over and over again the European Commission stressed that to join the EU the transition countries of CEE needed to develop 'a functioning market economy as well as the capacity to cope with competitive pressure and market forces within the Union'.[6] This was not only a formal criterion for EU accession, but a vital requirement to be able to compete economically with the rest of the world. Inasmuch as the transition countries had opened up their economies to the outside world, they had to compete with it. What does being able to compete mean for these countries in today's context? It is perhaps easiest to approach this question the other way around, by asking what we would *not* consider a sign of successful economic integration.

One complaint that is frequently heard from citizens in transition countries is that their countries are being 'bought' by foreigners. If the purchasing power of local citizens is much lower than that of foreign investors, which remains the case for nearly all the original transition economies, and if access to investment opportunities is fully liberalized, then foreigners will end up owning many of the attractive assets (factories, land, and retail outlets) in the transition countries. Sometimes considered foreign domination, this is certainly a form of foreign influence and it conflicts with the local desire for freedom and self-determination after decades of oppression. Thus privatization is not perceived as fully successful if ownership has in large part passed from the hands of, let us say, the Polish state to those of Western European and American shareholders. The problem is that Polish investors could not compete. Of course, most economists would say that shareholder nationality does not matter as long as companies improve efficiency, employ Poles, pay taxes, and reinvest in Poland. But aside from the fact that these outcomes cannot be ensured, most ordinary citizens would not agree with the economists' disregard for cultural sensitivities. Who has economic power also has political power, and citizens may fear that through economic domination their fates are too strongly affected by members of other communities.

For citizens, being 'competitive' means having sufficient means to invest in their own economies and to consume the imported goods on the shelves, the presence of which is otherwise rather meaningless to them. For an economy, being competitive means producing goods and services that can be successfully exported and can compete with imports on the domestic market. Even a country with low domestic purchasing power will be flooded with imports if it has no competitive products to offer. The reason is that large (almost inevitably foreign) multinational companies can afford to make losses for a few years until local purchasing power increases. Then local familiarity with foreign brand names will reward the companies for their patience, to the detriment of domestic producers who cannot employ the same strategy. Even though in many product categories there was no serious domestic competition at the beginning of transition, still many needs of people were previously fulfilled by domestically produced, if often inferior, solutions. When these domestic solutions could not compete, local businesses and the jobs they provided found themselves in a precarious position. At the same time, imports produced upward pressure on prices, creating problems for consumers.

A third element of competitiveness consists in a country's attractiveness to investment. Among the transition economies, although not exclusive to them, there is rather fierce competition for investment from abroad. Among the most important factors to support attractiveness to investors are political stability and legal transparency, a well-educated and trained workforce, and a tax structure acceptable to private business. These factors do not seem very controversial, and countries can work to improve them. However, the measure of improvement depends on the starting point, and the problems are often evident while solutions remain elusive. Investment is usually kept lower than it would otherwise be by corruption, legal instability, and a general lack of reliability of the institutions needed to support a market economy.[7]

Furthermore, the solutions to investment or economic growth impasses are not as straightforward as they might at first seem. For example, tax reform is politically a highly sensitive and contestable process, which involves many trade-offs. Balancing this process requires reflection and negotiation, rather than, for example, simply ceding to self-interested advice coming from investors' councils and business associations. Moreover, attractiveness to investment is also affected by factors beyond a country's control, such as geographic location or historical ties. The relatively rapid and successful transition of countries like the Czech Republic and Hungary is in no small part due to their immediate proximity to Germany and Austria and the enormous amount of money that entered these countries from the West as a consequence.

While this discussion of the general problems of transition could easily be extended, we will now move on to a discussion of the concrete experiences of several transition countries. It will become clear that while experiences differ from place to place, the general dilemmas of transition are shared. They will be summarized in the concluding section.

Transition Economies around the Globe

This section will take a closer look at the transition countries in Central and Eastern Europe and the former Soviet Union.[8] China, which entered the WTO in 2001 and has achieved a high degree of integration into the capitalist world economy after a long process of transformation, is of course a very important transition economy as well; it is dealt with elsewhere in this volume.[9]

For the countries in the FSU and CEE, the transition to market economy began quite suddenly and unexpectedly with the fall of the Berlin Wall in 1989 and was pushed forward by the enforcement of liberal economic 'shock therapy' by Boris Yeltsin and other leaders in the region. The hopeful term 'transition economy' can veil the fact that the expansion of capitalism to these countries has in practice proven to be brutal and problematic, especially for ordinary citizens. New elites (which were frequently largely identical to the old) promised their citizens to establish economic efficiency and entrepreneurial freedom as soon as the first free elections were being organized. In fact, they were often more interested in personal benefits from transition and economic integration and worked principally to maintain their old privileges after the 'transition' by a corrupt disposal of the state-owned assets. This phenomenon was widespread, especially in Russia, where a few individuals became extravagantly wealthy at public expense. To be sure, the privatization of state-owned enterprises also involved employee share ownership, but in practice shareholding ordinary citizens did not gain real decision-making power. That remained with the new-old elites and the new major shareholders with whom they colluded. Of course, these practices were not praised from abroad, but they were largely tolerated by Western elites, who seemed more concerned with a quick economic

integration of the new markets into the regional and global economy than with making sure the process was managed to the benefit of the affected peoples as a whole.

Central and Eastern Europe

Eight CEE countries recently joined the European Union after a difficult (and arguably incomplete) transition, and more are in the waiting room. The ambition of EU membership has driven most of their governments since the end of the Cold War, and the leadership in all CEE transition countries, independent of their political party leanings, came generally to accept and adopt the recipes for transition that came and still come from the IMF, the World Bank, and the European Bank for Reconstruction and Development (EBRD), as well as from the European Commission. These powerful institutions saw no need for a questioning of their guidelines for successful transition, simply expecting the transition countries to accept the (admittedly uncomfortable) reforms if they wished to receive aid for the process. This often generated a political backlash for fragile incumbent governments trying to balance their populations' abstract desire for EU membership with people's dislike of the practical effects of reforms. Thus, historically speaking, governments in CEE states have stood a very small chance of staying in office for more than one term.[10]

What policy advisers sitting in Washington or in Brussels found difficult to understand were the real effects 'on the ground' of the reforms they advocated. For example, while domestic companies in transition countries have remained largely unable to afford technological innovation and thereby remain competitive, increasing dependencies on imports of multinational companies have vastly increased trade deficits and upset current account balances. Foreign direct investment poured into the banking sectors in these countries (except for Slovenia, 50–90 per cent of all bank capital in these countries is in foreign hands). This has made it difficult for older state-owned firms, which are often still the largest employers, to obtain credit needed to maintain or recover efficiency.[11] The new markets have become open and profitable playing fields for transnational capital and corporations, but domestic enterprise and especially public sectors have been at a chronic disadvantage.

The radical economic change also constituted a social disaster for large parts of the population. Previously, the provision of many basic goods, including housing and utilities, along with child care, educational, health, and cultural services, had been part of public social services. The breakdown of the state and the severe reduction of public expenditure under 'shock therapy' drastically reduced all these services. So did privatization, because the large state-owned enterprises had frequently provided housing, child care, and the like. The more general commercialization of their societies was in itself a major change for citizens. State-owned firms had hidden huge underemployment, but now if one was not competitive on the labour market, one faced marginalization. This amounted quite literally to a breakdown of social security, prompting also a rise in crime.

Where previously there was full (if under-) employment in planned economies, there is now structural unemployment of up to 20 per cent of the working population (in Macedonia, Bosnia, and Serbia-Montenegro, but also in EU applicant countries Croatia and Bulgaria and new EU members Poland and Slovakia). The situation may further deteriorate before it can improve because some of the large state-owned enterprises, on which the well-being of entire regions can depend, have yet to be restructured even in the most successful transition economies. Fear of the future is reflected in low birth rates across the region and in the emigration of especially the young and highly educated (the so-called 'brain drain').[12] In the year 2002 the World Bank concluded that in CEE states poverty had reached greater proportions and greater rates of increase than in most of the rest of the world. Its report notes that the indicators for social services, especially in the health sector, have deteriorated most rapidly in Southeast Europe and the FSU. Life

expectancy is relatively low (for Albanian men, for example, only 64 years of age), and child mortality is high, especially in Bosnia and Romania but also more generally in the European southeast. The World Bank comes to the sobering conclusion that even though before the economic transformation these countries had the lowest levels of social inequality in the world, inequality has increased significantly, sometimes drastically. Poverty and inequality combined foster domestic social and political discontent, leading to potential destabilization and violence, such as in the former Yugoslavia.

The transition countries that have fared best had better pre-transition conditions, stayed out of wars (e.g., Slovenia versus other former Yugoslav states), and did not accept advice from Western partners quite as uncritically (which they could afford politically since they were the more attractive markets and investment locations). Often these same countries also received the most international support, which makes it difficult to say precisely which factors are responsible for their relative success. Poland, for example, was the first CEE country to register post-1989 economic growth, at least partly due to a massive negotiated foreign debt reduction at the beginning of the 1990s. Other factors contributing to relative success of the liberal reform process are previous levels of industrialization (the higher the better) and the characteristics of the political institutions before, during, and after Communist times. The quality of government and legal institutions, combined with an earlier history of industrialization, had a profound positive effect on such prerequisites of market economic success as levels of personal initiative and entrepreneurship. Location has also been very important, including proximity to the EU and to large urban areas (especially Prague and Budapest), which attracted most foreign investment. This increased economic disparities within as well as between countries. Aside from a growing gap between rural and urban populations, gaps have also been growing between different occupational groups (those with jobs that are in demand in the new economic context and those with jobs that are not). Joining the ranks of the unlucky are all the weaker groups in society, such as the elderly and unemployed, but also children, who suffer from rapid decreases in public support.

The Former Soviet Union

Growing socio-economic inequality and a drastic decline of the health, educational, and other public sectors also characterize transition in the FSU, which fragmented in 1989. Legal changes in 1988 began the process of private capital accumulation and the emergence of quasi-private companies. In Russia, privatization was steered deliberately to keep foreign investors at a distance, but the desired effect of a publicly controlled and equitable transformation did not materialize. On the (somewhat) positive side there are now many small and medium-sized private enterprises (often tax-evading) through which millions of employees gain a much-needed private income. However, in Russia in 1991 (and over time elsewhere) privatization laws heralded an opaque process that redistributed public wealth into the hands of a few members of the former Soviet *nomenklatura* who risked a switch into business life, while company shares initially issued to employees have long been sold off. A few huge industrial and financial conglomerates have obtained the de facto sway over the Russian economy and are contesting public authority. All attempts to introduce a 'soft' or social capitalism in the FSU, such as there were, must by now be considered to have failed. States like Belarus, Uzbekistan, and Turkmenistan, which have largely resisted reforms altogether, face economic collapse.

Income inequalities in Soviet times were rather small despite the privileges of the *nomenklatura*, but have grown rapidly since the collapse of the Soviet Union. Official Russian data show that in 1992 the income of the top 10 per cent of the population was eight times that of the bottom 10 per cent; by 2000 it was 13.8 times as much. Billions of dollars have been illegally transferred abroad by the nouveau riche, who send their children to (foreign) private schools and universities and use private health services, helping to generate a two-class society.

The sudden liberalization of prices in early 1992, combined with currency reform, yielded high inflation (especially in Georgia and Armenia) that ruined the savings of many in the lower socio-economic strata. Continual non-payment of salaries and pensions accompanied the reform process, hitting those who had most benefited from the previous system of redistribution (e.g., pensioners, teachers, and the military). The number of the 'new poor' is difficult to estimate. Depending on time of measurement and country it seems to lie between 20 and 40 per cent of the population. The figures are not entirely reliable, being based on average incomes and regional price baskets and excluding undeclared sources of income (such as illegal work or the cultivation of small plots of land).

What is clear is that the proportion of people living under the poverty line has at least doubled and in some areas (such as Georgia and Moldova) increased fourfold between 1988 and 1999. Mass emigration and a decline in school attendance have resulted, and the number of households with a television or refrigerator has declined drastically. In some FSU countries there is no secure electricity network outside the capitals. In giant Russia the situation is diverse and difficult to summarize. The people are surprisingly adaptable and economic dynamism is not absent; household equipment and housing quality have improved. However, the situation of some entire regions is catastrophic (especially the north of Siberia and areas dependent on mining or the textile industry). Signs of dire poverty—such as street children and begging pensioners in the cities—are increasing. Very worrisome is an above average mortality rate for men as well as children. Simultaneous rising inequality and poverty interact with other serious socio-political problems in many of the FSU countries. According to the World Bank, seven of them seriously risk 'failed state' status as result of excessive debt and an explosive growth of the population (Kyrgyzstan and Uzbekistan), ethnic conflict (Armenia, Azerbaijan, Moldova), or outright civil war (Georgia, Tajikistan).

Regionalization and globalization affect the FSU just as much as they do CEE. However, EU membership is not a realistic target (except, of course, for the Baltic states, which are already members) and Russian interests are central. A free trade area founded in 1993 unites the markets of Russia, Belarus, Kazakhstan, Kyrgyzstan, and Tajikistan (which have a customs union and since 2000 form the Eurasian Economic Community), plus Uzbekistan, Georgia, Armenia, Azerbaijan, and Moldova. Ukraine and Turkmenistan are more loosely associated. The countries around the Black Sea (Russia, Ukraine, Moldova, Georgia, Armenia, and Azerbaijan) also co-operate in a special regional arrangement, as do clusters of states in the Baltic region, the Caucasus, and Central Asia. All these states belong to the so-called Commonwealth of Independent States (CIS), which was founded in 1991 to maintain some level of co-operation after the dissolution of the USSR. Although not comparable to the EU, some observations can be made about the CIS as a whole to illustrate the changing position of its members in the world economy.

Mutual CIS and world trade linkages have changed since the dissolution of the Soviet Union. Imports of primary goods (especially grain) have been reduced, and imports of consumer goods and raw materials for producing consumer durables have increased significantly. This shows the increased importance of domestic demand as well as the crisis of Russian industry. As in Soviet times, raw materials (especially oil and gas) and primary industry products (especially steel and other metals) still form a disproportionate 43 per cent share of exports. The CIS as a whole generally runs a trade surplus, its size ($68 billion in 2000) depending strongly on the oil price. The significance of CIS trade with Western Europe is increasing (in 2000, 40 per cent of total CIS foreign trade was with Western Europe), while trade with Eastern Europe has declined. The EU had already secured a 34 per cent share of the total CIS foreign trade volume before the enlargement of 2004. Since the 2004 enlargement it accounts for about half. In 2000, Germany alone delivered 18 per cent of all imported consumer goods (and 49 per cent of

motor vehicles). The growth potential of the CIS is far from exhausted. In spite of a great enthusiasm for Western cars, for example, between 1992 and 2000 only 2,000 vehicles were imported per year.

At the same time, each CIS state is creating its own regional trade patterns with non- CIS partners: Turkmenistan and the Caucasus states are trading increasingly with Iran and Turkey, and Kazakhstan with China. Ukraine has reoriented from Russia towards Germany and Poland, with Azerbaijan also more strongly oriented towards Western Europe (especially Italy and France, which together accounted for 55 per cent of its exports in 2000). With the exception of Belarus (strongly focused on Russia) and Tajikistan, the former Soviet republics have opened op their economies to the wider world and are conducting an ever greater part of their foreign trade with markets outside the CIS, whose proportion of CIS total trade volume already amounts to 70 per cent.

This suggests a diminished position for Russia, though as a large and accessible market it is still important (especially for states with close bilateral ties, such as Tajikistan and Belarus, but even where ready alternatives for trade were found, such as in the case of Ukraine). The CIS states remain the main markets for some Russian products, and the Russian economy continues to depend on the CIS for some crucial imports, such as cotton, food, and metals. A genuine economic recovery in Russia would certainly exert a positive influence on the entire CIS. Russia's evident importance for security also continues to affect economic relations in the region. Countries facing conflict or closed borders with Russia (as in the Caucasus) have had to look elsewhere for markets after a historical dependence on Russia.

The economic situation in individual CIS states differs and this is partially due to the different levels of interest they arouse among foreign investors. For example, for the period 1989–2000 per capita foreign direct investment (FDI) amounted to $23 in Tajikistan and $571 in oil-rich Kazakhstan. Although the largest total amount went to Russia ($12 billion), FDI per capita there was only $85. Foreign investors, who seem mainly interested in oil, also prefer to invest where they can more easily exert control. This is the case in Kazakhstan and Azerbaijan rather than in Russia (where the Kremlin-Yukos oil company affair, for example, has shaken investor confidence).

A discussion of post-Soviet political economy would be incomplete without examining the oil and gas sector, which dominates the transition in the former Soviet Union. Oil and gas exports helped to stabilize Russia economically and are an important foreign policy resource to put pressure on dependent, debt-ridden CIS countries. The sector also attracts foreign investors looking for ways to loosen the stranglehold of the Russian economic and political elite on these resources, attempting to influence domestic politics to this end as well.

Most deposits of oil and gas in the FSU can be found in Russia and the states around the Caspian Sea. The sector constitutes 45 per cent of Russia's export earnings and a large part of its government revenue. After the economic crisis of 1998, the oil and gas industry led economic recovery. The privatization process in this sector has largely bene- fited Russian monopolies and remains subject to state control; foreign conglomerates have been kept out. The Russian mega-enterprises (Gasprom, Lukoil, and Yukos) founded powerful financial and industrial holdings that managed to stabilize production in spite of limited finances and technical deficits. They also increasingly began to operate in the 'near abroad' and Eastern Europe. Several non-oil states, such as Belarus, Ukraine, and Moldova, have in the meantime accumulated huge debts to Russia. With state support, the Russian companies are pushing for these debts to be transformed into investments in strategic acquisitions (refineries and distribution networks for oil and electricity generation)—a trusted method for exchanging political for eco- nomic domination. 'Pipeline politics' have also led to tensions between Russia and the West. Other oil- and gas-producing FSU states have tried to route their resources away from Russian territory (through which pipelines used to run) using investments from US and European MNCs; this

trend has been actively opposed by Russia, which would rather retain control over regional trans- portation networks.

Unfortunately, the possession of oil and gas is no guarantee for the economic and social develop- ment of a country. It is easy for elites to reap the profits from production. In Azerbaijan a few per- sons have become fabulously rich from oil, yet there are only one–two hours of electricity per day outside of the capital. Countries without such resources, however, can be even worse off. In Georgia, Moldova, and Ukraine, debt due to the lack of independent energy resources has con- tributed significantly to a deterioration of the eco- nomic situation, which Russia has sought to exploit. Otherwise struggling Belarus is in a privi- leged position in this respect because of its espe- cially close relations with Russia, which sells it oil and gas far below world market prices.

This brief look at the role of oil and webs of influence in the FSU, as well as East–West rivalries, indicates that important relationships in the inter- national political economy are inseparable from, and take place within, the dynamics of classic international *realpolitik*.

Dilemmas of Transition

Diversity is a central feature of transition economies. How three dilemmas, shared by all of these transition economies, are resolved is crucial to the fate of the people in these countries, and such resolution (or lack of resolution) links up with our quest for answers to broader questions of contemporary global governance.

The first dilemma is created by the conflicting desires to open up to the world and emulate appar- ently successful (usually Western) models, and to ensure independence and self-determination. Transition countries generally accept the need for progressive integration into regional and global markets (as well as, inevitably, also polities and cul- tures). Integration is also proactively supported by Western governments and international institu- tions. On the other hand, the people in transition countries are wary of foreign influence and protective of their cultural identities and particularities. The tension between increasing transnational integration and the desire to preserve a singular identity is something that the transition countries share with the rest of the globalizing world. However, they are in a particularly vulnerable position for at least two reasons. First, they depend massively on outside, usually Western actors for material and ideational support. Second, they suffer from an identity deficit after decades of oppression inside the Soviet bloc. Only now do people in countries like Albania and Georgia get a chance to find out *who they are* as a people in relative freedom. And immediately they find themselves merging in significant ways with other communities with which they are unfamiliar and who hardly care to understand them. Tragically, the timing of their emergence into self-determination has been such that their self-determination has become intensely difficult.

The second shared dilemma is created by the conflicting demands of global economic adjustment versus social equity and peace. As illustrated above, neo-liberal shock therapy has increased social disparities and poverty beyond anything known under Communism. The promise of liberal economics is that these problems constitute a painful but necessary adaptation, and that transition and other economies will eventually be collectively much better off. However, ordinary people are only too aware that, as John Maynard Keynes once famously remarked, 'in the long run we are all dead.' In the short run, it is difficult to persuade people that it made sense to overthrow Communism if they are worse off afterwards than they were before, it is difficult to gain support for democratic processes that do not deliver welfare gains, and it is difficult to maintain domestic social peace in the face of massive suffering and obvious inequity.

The third dilemma is related to the second: the 'dilemma of the double transition'. To hear politicians speak about the transition countries, one might be led to believe that transition to market economy and democracy go hand in hand—that the 'normal' and exemplary kind of country of today is one that is both. However, there is much

evidence that marketization and democratization can actually conflict with one another. The historical experience of Western Europe, North America, and newly industrialized Asia points to marketization first, followed by social and political upheaval, with democratization and social equity coming later. In many of the transition countries, the vast majority of the population actually wants a strong welfare state and mixed economy model. If they lived in genuine democracies, they would achieve this goal. But they do not. Few elected governments survive more than one term, while technocrats abroad and across the political spectrum in their capitals evidently believe they know better what is good for the people (at least in the famous long run) than the people do themselves.

In the short run this belief seems to justify manipulating public opinion through populist rhetoric and targeted interventions, so that people will bear with the reform process as specified by elites. But even if we believe that the elites really know best how to organize the economy (and we certainly are not obliged to believe that) it must be seen that by running the reform process in this manner they are undermining the development of democratic culture. If people are to learn how to govern themselves, they must be given some meaningful chance to do so. As is true for all kinds of education, teaching democracy requires some degree of trust in the students. The lack of attention to this fact suggests that democracy is not quite as important a goal as marketization, at least not for many of the important proponents of reforms.

How have the transition countries reacted to these dilemmas so far? One response they all seem to share is that they have largely accepted the inevitability of neo-liberal adaptation. This adds to the problems surrounding democratization, as it is difficult to practise democracy if there are seemingly no choices to be made. Those countries that are today deemed most successful from the Western perspective are those that have accepted the neo-liberal advice and often outperformed the advisers at their own game. They have liberalized their economies drastically and have created investment environments that manage to draw business away from Western Europe and other advanced economies. For example, the introduction of low corporate taxes in the new EU member states has angered some governments in the old EU, who complain about unfair competition. In the short run, while government revenue is forgone through lower taxes, countries such as Slovakia and Slovenia can benefit by attracting capital and jobs. However, it is unclear how long this sort of competitive underbidding is sustainable. If standards of living and therefore labour costs rise enough in the new member states, 'footloose capital' will look yet elsewhere for new opportunities, and it may become apparent that proactive solidarity in the defence of public welfare would have served both East and West better than pursuing competitive development strategies. The latter is creating (increasingly also in the West) deeply divided societies: the nouveau riche versus the new poor; technocrats or outright criminals who become decision-makers versus electorates they try to manipulate or repress. Ameliorating these divisions will prove crucial for the possibility of the peaceful and equitable coexistence of the peoples on this planet.

While there is widespread agreement on the problems of transition, there is no consensus among scholars or practitioners on what the transition countries and their partners should have done differently or should do differently henceforth. Some common ground might be visible in the recent institutional turn in transition economics. 'Market fundamentalism' has mostly been abandoned and there are widespread calls to focus support for transition economies on the development of legal and institutional underpinnings of markets. Law and its proper enforcement have proven critical to success in privatization and the generation of entrepreneurship, and effective industry has been recognized to depend on labour market governance and systems of social protection.

Notes

1. See, e.g., Alvin Y. So, *Social Change and Development: Modernization, Dependency and World-System Theories* (London: Sage, 1990). See also the country chapters in this volume.
2. For a good overview of this kind of scholarship, see, e.g., Peter A. Hall and David Soskice, eds, *Varieties of Capitalism: The Institutional Foundations of Comparative Advantage* (Oxford: Oxford University Press, 2001).
3. The word 'polity' is used to refer to the material structures that produce political decisions, such as governmental institutions. A country is a 'polity' in the sense that it is defined by a certain political institutional arrangement.
4. A classic is Robert Putnam, *Making Democracy Work* (Princeton, NJ: Princeton University Press, 1994). Putnam's suggestions concerning the cultural prerequisites of successful liberal democracy have by now been frequently applied to the post-Communist countries.
5. The fact that Western countries were sometimes not following their own advice suggests that to do so was more difficult and/or more contested than they claimed in their relations with CEE.
6. This demand was part of the so-called Copenhagen criteria. These were criteria established at the European Council meeting in Copenhagen in 1993, which stated clearly, although in rather general terms, what countries had to do to become new members of the EU. On the situation of the new and prospective EU member countries, see also Chapter 27 by Smith and Chapter 21 by van Apeldoorn.
7. The economy of Albania, for example, took a nosedive after several large pyramid schemes collapsed in 1996–7. In other countries, such as Romania, investment funds were also brought down by mismanagement and/or corruption, leaving many people ruined and seriously weakening investor confidence.
8. All statistics presented without attribution in this section come from Le Monde Diplomatique, ed.,

Atlas der Globalisierung (Berlin: taz, 2003).

9. See Chapter 34 by Breslin and Chapter 24 by Higgott.

10. See, e.g., Richard Rose and Beil Munro, *Elections and Parties in New European Democracies* (Washington: Congressional Quarterly Press, 2003).

11. In the past, such companies could obtain supportive credits from state-owned banks.

12. Of course, fluctuations in birth rates and migration patterns also have other reasons. Labour emigration from the transition economies, especially in Eastern Europe, in countries like Moldova or Romania, is substantial, and these countries' economies are strongly supported by so-called 'remittances' (money sent home by people working outside the country). Politics are affected directly as well, because there are fewer proactive (and frequently educated and critical) people at home who participate in it.

Suggested Readings

Balcerowicz, Leszek. *Socialism, Capitalism, Transformation.* Budapest: Central European University Press, 1996.

Eatwell, John, Michael Ellman, Mats Karlsson, Mario Nuti, and Judith Shapiro. *Transformation and Integration: Shaping the Future of Central and Eastern Europe.* London: Institute for Public Policy Research, 1995.

Haggard, Stephan, and Robert R. Kaufman. *The Political Economy of Democratic Transitions.* Princeton, NJ: Princeton University Press, 1995.

Web Sites

Stockholm Institute of Transition Economics: www.hhs.se/SITE/SITE.htm

Transitions Online: www.tol.cz/

World Bank Site for Research on Transition Economies:
http://econ.worldbank.org/topic.php?topic=24

Chapter 31

The United States and Globalization
Struggles with Hegemony

Bruce E. Moon

Most nations can only react to globalization, but the United States, as the system's dominant economic and political actor, is also able to affect the speed and character of the globalization process itself. By promoting the institutions that integrated national economies after World War II, it appears that the US acted as predicted by hegemonic stability theory (HST).[1] As American economic dominance later faded, the global system drifted away from the coherence of its original Bretton Woods design. The result is a chaotic patchwork of inadequate governance at the system level, while the management of trade relations has fallen increasingly to the regional level. Both patterns lend credence to HST explanations centred on the relative decline of the hegemonic power, but they tell only part of the story. America's distinctive foreign policy tradition and peculiar political, economic, and social structure offer a further explanation for the character of the globalization that has emerged. The idiosyncratic vision and reluctant hegemony of the United States also explain why globalization's core institutions lie in crisis while the negotiations to rescue them stagger on the verge of collapse.

At the end of World War II, the United States exhibited the two most important characteristics required of a candidate to champion global liberalism.[2] First, it possessed the dominance that affords a hegemon both the greatest incentive and the greatest capacity to advance globalization. As the most productive economy, it was the most likely to benefit from open goods markets. As the largest source of both supply and demand for capital it was also the most likely to exploit open capital markets. Its power could be used to persuade or co-opt a majority of nations, compel most of the remainder, and isolate the few dissenters. Second, the liberalism of the American domestic economy demonstrated that 'its social purpose and domestic distribution of power was favourably disposed toward a liberal international order.'[3] However, America's dominance is accompanied by a profound isolationism that induces episodic and inconsistent unilateralist impulses. Furthermore, American liberalism is coloured by unique circumstances that make the US commitment to it only skin deep. The effects of these eccentricities were discernible in the Bretton Woods design but eventually became dominant in both American policy and the global regime it sponsored. Today they threaten the continued viability of the international architecture that has governed the process of globalization for more than half a century.

Hegemonic, but Isolationist

No account of American foreign policy can ignore the monumental shadow cast by the deep historical isolationism of the United States.[4] From its colonial period onward, the United States has displayed hostility to foreign pressures and an abiding antipathy towards multilateral policies and supranational institutions.[5] This isolationism has been overcome only occasionally by extraordinary exigencies, most notably the combination of military, political, and economic challenges to the immediate post-war order in Europe. Even then, the American commitment to a global institutional order has been reluctant and sporadic. The much-criticized unilateralism of the George W. Bush administration is thus hardly new, but it does greatly accentuate one thread among several that make up the US foreign policy tradition.

This profound disinterest in foreign affairs has been sustained by a frequently overlooked economic reality: until quite recently the American economy has been relatively unaffected by developments elsewhere in the global economy. The historic insulation of the American economy from the global one stems from the size and physical remoteness of the US market, which relies less on trade than virtually any other in the world.[6] For most nations, of course, a small foreign sector would imply proportionately small external influence, but the overwhelming size of the US market means that even a modest percentage of American GNP constitutes a sizable share of global economic activity. In the early 1950s, for example, the United States controlled about 20 per cent of global trade, yet American exports constituted less than 5 per cent of US GNP. By contrast, a century earlier hegemonic Great Britain controlled a similar percentage of global trade, but that trade constituted about half of its total economy.

This odd pattern of dominance has crosscutting implications for the ability of the United States to embrace its theoretical role of global hegemon. It had the power to shape the international system's fundamental structure but little need to do so to protect either the national economy or the interests of subnational groups. This autonomy allowed the United States to be inattentive to systemic issues or to subordinate its economic interests to security concerns. When the US *was* engaged with questions of system design, it could easily afford to indulge the interests of others—as expected of a hegemon—because that seldom required much sacrifice of its own modest stake. However, this left the system vulnerable to the re-emergence of America's natural isolationism whenever the pressure to lead abated, as when the demise of the Cold War weakened the security motivations that sustained Bretton Woods. More recently, the US invulnerability to the global economy has evaporated—and with it the last vestiges of the American commitment to sacrifice narrow national interest in favour of global leadership.

Liberal, but Myopic

Minimal external reliance also affected the character of American liberalism, even though theory identifies some groups that normally oppose free trade and, in most nations, would lobby for a compromise on globalization. The modern trade theory of Heckscher-Ohlin (H-O) implies that inefficient sectors of the economy will suffer losses from trade, but with such a small import-competing sector, protectionist pressures from business were modest. The Stolper-Samuelson theorem predicts that trade will harm unskilled labour, but that group is notoriously poorly represented by structures of American political power.[7] Unlike the European working class, which has been championed economically by a strong trade union movement and defended politically by resultant social democratic parties, unskilled labour in the United States has been divided by ethnic identification, language, and region, leaving it politically impotent and economically vulnerable. Mobilization is especially difficult because American labour lacks even identification as the working class, preferring the moniker of 'middle class'. As such, American workers have always been about as likely to be pulled to upper-class as lower-class views.[8] The vibrancy of the American economy and the flexibility of its labour markets also allowed the minor adjustments required by external competition to be shifted almost entirely to the unorganized working class. Thus, US foreign economic policy had a built-in liberal inclination because its unusually small foreign sector was made up of elements either economically invulnerable to foreign competition or politically powerless to resist it.

Largely unchecked by contrary domestic forces, American liberalism has become theoretically rigid and ideologically extreme. Ever since

Cordell Hull's influential plea for free trade as the key to international peace in the 1940s, US rhetoric has associated free markets with material prosperity, stability, justice, democracy, human rights, international peace, and more. As James Fallows puts it:

> The Anglo-American system of politics and economics, like any system, rests on certain principles and beliefs. But rather than acting as if these are the best principles, or the ones their societies prefer, Britons and Americans often act as if these were the *only possible* principles and no one, except in error, could choose any others. Political economics becomes an essentially religious question, subject to the standard drawback of any religion—the failure to understand why people outside the faith might act as they do.[9]

Herein lies a contradiction. Though a passionate proselytizer, the United States maintains a more shallow commitment to liberalism than nations whose small market size makes trade openness inevitable or those for which it represents a conscious acceptance of its mixed welfare implications. Nor is it as stable as in those nations where it has evolved as a strategic compromise among powerful political actors. As a result, American systemic designs are not as complex and attentive to side effects as would be expected from a hegemon more deeply affected by the system it created.

As American economic supremacy has eroded since the 1970s, greater vulnerabilities have produced dislocations in scattered industries, most prominently in textiles, steel, and autos. But no ideological current or organized opposition exists to frame these as inevitable consequences of globalization requiring fundamental accommodation. Rather than instances of the trade-offs endemic to an open economy, they have been interpreted as reflections of 'cheating' by other nations. They have thus triggered narrow sectoral responses of protectionism that have left intact the rhetorical commitment to liberalism, but the widely perceived hypocrisy has sharply eroded the legitimacy of the American claim to benign hegemony.

Bretton Woods

Fifty years ago, the combination of American hegemonic credentials and fortuitous circumstances were sufficient to fashion a system to meet the delicate balance between national and systemic needs. The primary goal—to rekindle economic growth by restoring trade to levels reached before the catastrophic decline of two-thirds during the Great Depression of the 1930s—placed multilateral liberalization through trade negotiations within the General Agreement on Tariffs and Trade (GATT) at the system's core. However, the key to the success of Bretton Woods—and the sharpest contrast with the current system—was the recognition that liberalization also brought problems and constraints that not only undermined its benefits but threatened the capacity of individual nations to embrace it.

Thus, the Bretton Woods design acknowledged the sacrifices required of nations in order to liberalize and contained various provisions for easing those burdens. GATT allowed nations to demand access to foreign markets for their exports as compensation for the dislocations of imports, thus providing political cover for shaky governments to withstand protectionist pressures and creating domestic constituencies to balance them. The negotiation process enabled nations to liberalize trade at a pace compatible with resolving the domestic political and economic problems it created, and GATT itself included a number of escape clauses that recognized the inherent tension between liberalization and other domestic economic goals. The International Monetary Fund (IMF) not only prescribed stable exchange rates but also offered resources to member states to facilitate their co-operation in maintaining them: its lending facilities provided an alternative to exchange rate devaluation and protectionism for nations feeling balance-of-payments pressures. Finally, the World Bank offered longer-term funding to rebuild war-torn economies that otherwise could not survive international competition, most notably from the United States. American unilateral and bilateral policy towards Europe, especially the Marshall Plan and the temporary tolerance of European protectionism, greatly augmented these arrangements, perhaps dwarfing them in effect.

The system as a whole was coherent and realistic, allowing nations to move towards free capital and goods markets at their own pace. They fashioned arrangements that were consonant with their own priorities and circumstances but generally reflected 'the compromise of embedded liberalism'.[10] That is, trade was relatively free in order to gain the benefits associated with the theory of comparative advantage, whereas the dislocations produced by that trade were mitigated by domestic welfare policies and labour market regulations that would distort the economy less than protectionist alternatives. The challenge 'to devise a form of multilateralism compatible with the requirements of domestic stability'[11] was not seen as a lofty aspiration, but rather as an absolutely essential requirement to achieve any kind of workable system at all. Without the flexibility it provided, nations would not have agreed to the obligations implicit in acceptance of Bretton Woods initially, nor would they have been capable of meeting them subsequently. At stake was the very political legitimacy of the state itself, which had to achieve economic prosperity but also maintain enough control over the domestic political economy that its claim to being responsive to the citizenry was seen as plausible.

Still, Bretton Woods, with a sparse institutional component that contained no permanent trade organization, a monetary authority with sharply limited enforcement capacity, and an underfinanced development bank, represented as minimal a core as could be squared with the label of 'system'. If the profound threats of the 1940s made some institutional structure absolutely imperative, the American influence was responsible for its minimalist character. Proposals for an IMF and World Bank with a broader charge and expanded powers fell victim to American antipathy towards intrusive supranational institutions that would challenge US

policy autonomy. During heated negotiations over the charter for the International Trade Organization, the United States blocked provisions that would give the organization greater authority over domestic economic policies and a larger role in adjudicating trade policy disputes, yet permit nations greater freedom to adopt protectionist measures. Even so, the American Congress refused ratification, the result of a coalition of free trade purists who thought the agreement too illiberal and isolationists who thought it too internationalist. Thus, the tariff reduction negotiations of the skeletal GATT became the only instrument for regulating global trade. Subsequently, the system was to drift further from the compromises necessary for its founding and closer to the American vision of proper (that is, minimal) economic management.

The American Vision

Even in the face of increasing evidence of its flaws, the United States remains committed to a global system in line with its unique ideological vision—liberalism without support from institutions that mitigate the adverse consequences of the globalization it produces. The dilemma, faced squarely at Bretton Woods but neglected since, is put most plainly by a leading *proponent* of globalization: 'the most serious challenge for the world economy in the years ahead lies in making globalization compatible with domestic social and political stability—or to put it even more directly, in ensuring that international economic integration does not contribute to domestic social *dis*integration.'[12] The threat arises from the significant distributional consequences that attend massive trade and capital flows. Immediate dislocations[13] create tensions and contribute strongly to the politically and socially divisive income inequality that has been well documented in recent years.[14] Furthermore, 'globalization engenders conflict within and between nations over domestic norms and the social institutions that embody them.'[15] The most obvious issues concern the potential for a 'race to the bottom' in labour standards, environmental protection, competition policy, and child labour policy.

None of these problems needs to undermine the case for global liberalization, however, because most admit of governmental amelioration. Indeed, that is precisely the direction taken by 'the compromise of embedded liberalism' in the Bretton Woods era: 'societies were asked to embrace the change and dislocation attending international liberalization. In turn, liberalization and its effects were cushioned by the newly acquired domestic economic and social policy roles of governments.'[16] Over the longer term, however, the unencumbered capital mobility of contemporary globalization affords an exit option to capital owners that gives them unprecedented bargaining leverage over nation-bound actors. Workers face declines in wages, benefits, and working conditions and suffer the costs of increasing insecurity. Meanwhile, the difficulty of taxing footloose capital severely undermines the capacity of governments to provide social insurance or, indeed, to raise the revenues required to address *any* of the problems exacerbated by globalization. Further, regulation to advance environmental or other social goals becomes increasingly infeasible.

When the capacities of national governments to cope with such problems have been sharply reduced, one option is to augment national capacities with international ones. Another is to free governments to balance these pressures as they see fit and even to facilitate their creative choices. For example, the proposed Tobin tax on foreign exchange transactions would raise funds to support international efforts while reducing the destabilizing short-term capital flows that have been implicated in economic crises in East Asia and Latin America. The capital controls that have been used successfully in otherwise liberal economies such as Chile could be countenanced. Instead, the contemporary system has bound nations even more tightly to liberal orthodoxy and contributed further to the crisis of political legitimacy unleashed when governments are unable to insulate their citizens from the effects of global markets.[17]

Currency crises in Mexico, Russia, Thailand, Malaysia, Indonesia, Korea, and Argentina demonstrate what may be the most significant weakness of the current system's devotion to capital mobility—the monetary pressures that arise from the Mundell-Fleming constraint that a nation cannot simultaneously achieve the three goals of capital mobility, exchange rate stability, and monetary policy autonomy. Fidelity to the first of these is enforced by both the Washington Consensus that governs World Bank/IMF policy and the power of capital markets themselves to demand the freedom to engage in capital flight as a condition for not exercising that right. States forced to choose between the remaining two goals must hope that domestic economic and political needs do not require the exercise of real autonomy and that exchange rate volatility does not escalate beyond the tolerable. The foreign exchange reserves of even the largest economies are now inadequate to move appreciably the exchange rate, and the absence of a central institution to perform that role leaves domestic economies to adjust very painfully to rapid movements of capital.

In the face of accumulating evidence that excessive capital flows have become injurious to global welfare, a more attentive hegemon might try to rein in global finance. The United States has instead pushed hard for *further* liberalization of capital markets. In trade negotiations, American initiatives have emphasized the financial services sector, where US comparative advantage remains dominant. It has insisted on removal of national barriers to foreign investment that would constrain the expansion of American-based multinational corporations, among the few powerful American actors that rely heavily on the global economy.

In discussions of system architecture, the United States has favoured the weakening of international institutions that challenge private-sector operations with public oversight. For example, while the global financial system appeared poised on the brink of collapse in the autumn of 1998, disappointment with the IMF's management of the Asian crisis led the isolationist American Congress to seek the demise of the IMF rather than a change in its policies.[18] The Meltzer Commission appointed by Congress subsequently recommended a greatly reduced role for both the World Bank and the IMF in crisis-lending and a virtual end to their funding of long-term development outside Africa.[19] Congress refused to fund an extension of the IMF and also refused to make good on more than $1 billion in back dues owed to the United Nations. Worse yet for the image of a benign hegemon, Congress offered to meet financial obligations to the UN only in return for veto power over the reproductive health agendas of UN agencies (e.g., to bar any mention of abortion). As Diana Tussie notes, 'The United States has often interpreted a rule-based order to mean the extension of American rules and procedures to the rest of the world.'[20]

It is arguable whether the unresponsiveness of American policy to the costs implicit in accelerating globalization results more from design or neglect. Two sets of explanations—one centred on isolationism and the other on a striking narrowness of strategic vision—converge. Certainly, the American image of a successful international economic system is decidedly less regulated and institutionalized than others. In line with standard liberal theory, it seeks to decrease governmental control of cross-border transactions, confident that the resulting increase in flows will advance prosperity. When problems arise (as in Mexico, Southeast Asia, and Russia), it is content with ad hoc responses that maintain hegemonic autonomy rather than rely on global institutional authority.

It is also true that the United States is poorly positioned to design ways of resolving or coping with costs of globalization it does not feel. The United States has little experience with ameliorating trade-induced dislocations, unlike Europe, where generous welfare provisions have long complemented protectionism to afford security to the working class. Indeed, the division of authority between levels of government makes it difficult for the United States to integrate trade policy, which is enacted by the federal government, with welfare and education policy, which are largely functions of state and local government.

On the finance side, the United States is even less familiar with the challenges of coping with volatile and uncomfortable capital flows that plague developing countries. The United States cannot appreciate the complex effects of exchange rate movements on other nations because its own small foreign sector transmits so few impacts on price levels or output. It is ironic that the financial imbalances that most threaten the global economy of the twenty-first century stem from the twin deficits of the only nation that seems blind to them. Massive capital flows to fund the US budget deficit and the US trade deficit rob the rest of the world of investment funds while American officials seem intent on appropriating the slogan of *MAD* magazine's Alfred E. Neuman, 'What, me worry?'

Rising Vulnerability, Declining Hegemony

Since the 1970s, when the United States began to experience a changing pattern of comparative advantage, the uniqueness of the American experience with globalization has eroded. In 1970, trade was a smaller share of GDP in the United States than in any other developed country. Indeed, by one measure it was barely half that in the second most insulated nation, Japan. Since then, trade has grown rapidly in the United States, though the US economy remains much less exposed to foreign trade than most, with an export share about a third of the average European level.

The expansion in trade volume has been dramatic, but its unbalanced character has most changed the political dynamic of policy discussions. Greater opportunities in the export realm certainly have benefited high-technology goods and financial service sectors, among others. However, the United States has lost competitiveness in basic manufacturing, especially in industries whose well-paying blue-collar jobs have provided much of the vaunted social mobility that remains central to America's self-image, such as autos and steel. Moreover, with the widely publicized outsourcing of white-collar jobs, the impact of declining competitiveness is no longer restricted to odd corners of the economy or to the margins of the political system. A $500 billion annual trade deficit in recent years is testimony to how widespread is the vulnerability of American firms and American workers to the foreign competition unleashed by globalization.[21]

Public opinion surveys reveal the effect: reduced enthusiasm for globalization and a decline in uncritical acceptance of its benefits. Most telling is that in a 2002 poll only 14 per cent of the American public thought that their country should 'actively promote' further globalization, whereas 15 per cent favoured 'trying to reverse it', 24 per cent opted for 'trying to slow it down' and 12 per cent were 'not sure'. While such attitudes hardly seem indicative of a hegemon committed to liberalization, overall attitudes towards globalization do remain mildly positive, with 35 per cent favouring 'allow it to continue'.[22] Other surveys reinforce this picture of ambivalence, with marked increases in caution evident even since the late 1990s. A 2004 PIPA survey revealed that 40 per cent thought globalization was mostly positive, 19 per cent mostly negative, and 39 per cent equally positive and negative. In a broad survey of 19 countries, the people in 11 of these displayed a more positive attitude towards globalization than did the American public.[23]

It is not hard to see the source of such mixed feelings. By a 55–30 per cent margin, globalization is thought to be good for American companies, but by a 51–32 per cent margin it is seen as bad for the job security of American workers.[24] Nor does the American public share the attitudes of a hegemon willing to sacrifice the national interest for global welfare. When asked if 'rich countries have a moral responsibility to help poor countries develop', a vast majority of Americans agreed, but the percentage was lower than in 14 of 19 countries. Perhaps most telling in light of the stalled global negotiations over protectionism in agriculture is the response in the same survey to this scenario: 'Rich countries could reduce poverty in developing countries by allowing them to sell more food and clothing products to rich countries. In rich countries this would lower prices for food and clothing but would also mean significant job losses in these industries. Would you support or oppose rich countries allowing more food and clothing imports from developing countries even if it meant significant job losses in rich countries?' Support for this position in the United States was dead last among 19 nations.

Such public attitudes have had effects on policy. The United States has become less attentive to matters of system structure, allowing the World Trade Organization (WTO) negotiations to founder since the 1999 ministerial conference in Seattle that heralded the emergence of anti-globalization forces. Instead, Washington has pursued its increasingly narrow self-interested goals through aggressive unilateralism and regional arrangements.

The Multilateral Agenda

As its dominance has eroded, the United States has continued to promote liberalism, but it is now less likely to champion initiatives justified by global welfare considerations, particularly if they require sacrifice of national goals or ideological purity. Its agenda has narrowed to those areas in which American economic interests are directly involved. With its advantages on the capital side of the ledger intact, the United States has been most active in promoting liberalization on investment issues. Indicative was the abortive effort to enact a Multilateral Agreement on Investment (MAI), the centrepiece of which was the quintessential American position that foreign investors should be guaranteed national treatment—that is, virtually all national restrictions on foreign direct investment should be prohibited.

At the same time, the most prominent negotiations over the terms of globalization have been stalled and rudderless. The 1999 Seattle meeting was meant to launch the 'millennial round' of trade negotiations, the first since the formation of the WTO in 1994, but public protests turned it into the 'battle in Seattle'. The 'tear-gas ministerial' ended prematurely and in embarrassing chaos, not least because of tepid American leadership in response to the opposition of trade unions, environmental activists, and development advocates. Rather than seek a reasoned accommodation within the framework of acknowledged costs and benefits of global-ization, the WTO instead avoided controversy by holding the 2001 ministerial in Doha, Qatar, where public protests are banned.

Virtually no progress was made in Doha or in the following ministerial at Cancun in 2003. At issue was the unwillingness of both the United States and the European Union to liberal-ize trade in the agricultural goods that sustain the livelihoods of a majority of the globe's popu-lation. Even while traditional trade issues of major interest to less-developed nations remain unresolved, the US has shifted increasingly to auxiliary issues such as trade-related investment measures (TRIMs), the protection of intellectual property rights, and trade in services (especially financial). Rather than grant the legitimacy of the concerns of developing countries, the American representative attributed the collapse of the Cancun talks to 'a culture of protest'.[25]

If the hesitancy of the US to compromise on agriculture was damaging, its inability to per-suade the EU to do so either finally doomed Cancun. It could not exert the leadership expect-ed of a hegemon in part because security issues now cut differently than they did during the Cold War. Once, the United States provided security guarantees to Europe that earned it favourable considerations in economic negotia-tions. Now, the Bush administration's 'war on terror' demands that other nations contribute to American security, which reverses the leverage of the parties. Furthermore, America's global lead-ership had always been sustained by the Cold War image that international architecture was required to maintain national security. The end of the Cold War allowed the United States to return to its historic propensity to seek a naive combination of economic benefits but political disengagement, best exemplified by George Washington in his farewell address: 'The great rule of conduct for us in regard to foreign nations is, in extending our commercial rela-tions[,] to have with them [the nations of Europe] as little political connection as possible.'

Aggressive Unilateralism

As the US stake in the global economy has grown, American policy has followed a dual strategy. Efforts to promote opportunities for American exporters and foreign investors remain concentrat-ed in the multilateral drive to remove the barriers of others, while its unilateral and bilateral policies have increasingly *erected* such barriers to protect American firms that compete with imports. While other nations have criticized this pattern as hypo-critical, Washington justifies its unilateral actions as consistent with its systemic philosophy because they are designed to compensate for the unfair trade practices of others.[26]

Indeed, while the tariff rates that apply to most favoured nations have remained quite low, non-tariff barriers (NTBs) targeted against particu-lar nations have risen. They have taken several forms, some fully in accord with GATT rules and even consistent with liberal principles. Section 201 of the Trade Reform Act of 1974 implement-ed GATT's Article 19 escape clause, which permits nations to suspend tariff reductions in industries suffering from sudden increases in imports, regardless of cause. This escape clause has not been frequently used, no doubt because it under-mines the American case for systemic liberalism. After all, it permits a nation to protect its own industries through a so-called 'safeguard action' even when no wrongdoing by foreign competi-tors is even alleged. Article 19 also requires that competitors be compensated for the suspension of tariff benefits. The United States has felt more free to employ Section 301 (and its extension in the 1988 Trade Act dubbed 'Super 301') because it is designed to target particular countries found to be engaging in 'unjustifiable, unreasonable or discriminatory' trading practices. It authorizes countervailing duties to offset illegal dumping by foreign manufacturers or to compensate for unlawful subsidies by foreign governments. As such, these actions can be squared with the idea of 'fair trade' even if their consistency with 'free trade' is more dubious.

Competitors object to these actions for many reasons. They contend that these provisions are often invoked not in pursuit of any defensible principles, but for protectionist or even outright political purposes. They cite the Bush administration's imposition of 30 per cent tariff rates on steel imports from selected countries in the spring of 2002. They were narrowly targeted on certain categories of steel products in order to generate electoral support in key steel-producing states. Even though the tariffs were imposed pursuant to Section 201, many of the public justifications for it were couched in the accusatory language of Section 301. The action itself was based on such flimsy legal ground that its eventual rejection by a WTO dispute resolution panel was regarded as a foregone conclusion by almost all experts. The subsequent withdrawal of the tariffs was accompanied by political rhetoric that again implied that foreign cheating was involved.

Critics allege that such actions are invoked unpredictably and in bad faith, hoping to deter completely proper competition by threatening successful competitors with the rigours of the US legal process and potential retaliation. It has become common for Washington to threaten use of such 'fair trade' actions in order to require competitors to reduce exports through 'voluntary' export restraints (VERS), the most prominent of which was the 1980s agreement that restricted the import of Japanese autos.[27] This has led some to conclude that 'the greatest potential for the erosion of multilateralism lies in the ability of the powerful to heavy-ride rather than in the small and weak to free-ride.'[28] By playing on the ambiguity of 'free trade' and 'fair trade', these policies have enabled the United States to champion free trade and deny its disruptive impact, yet simultaneously protect its most vulnerable industries.

The Rise of Regionalism

Another dimension of recent US trade policy can be seen in a similarly ambivalent light. In a departure from the expectation that a hegemon would support a global trade regime, the United States has displayed a tolerance and, recently, even a *preference* for regional trade systems. The clearest example is the Canada–United States Free Trade Agreement, which evolved into the North American Free Trade Agreement (NAFTA) during the 1990s. Many liberal critics saw this as a rejection of multilateralism and a dangerous step towards regional trade blocs eventually bound to compete along mercantilist lines. In contrast, the United States claimed that NAFTA affirmed its commitment to a hegemonic role of cajoling and bullying others to support multilateral liberalism—because NAFTA was a bargaining ploy to counter regionalism in Europe and thus re-energize the then-languishing Uruguay Round of GATT talks.

Such arguments remain prominent a decade later. As the chief US negotiator, Robert Zoellick, put it in the fall of 2003, 'the key division at Cancun was between the can-do and the won't-do. For over two years, the US has pushed to open markets globally, in our hemisphere, and with subregions or individual countries. As WTO members ponder the future, the US will not wait: we will move towards free trade with can-do countries.'[29] The results have been dramatic. At the time, the United States had only four partners in free trade agreements (FTAS): Israel and Jordan in bilateral arrangements in addition to Canada and Mexico through NAFTA. By 1 January 2004 two more FTAS had entered into force—with Chile and Singapore—and, in the first six months of 2004, negotiations were completed with nine more countries: Australia, Morocco, Bahrain, the Dominican Republic, and the five nations of the Central America Free Trade Area. New and pending FTA partners, taken together, would constitute America's third largest export market and the sixth largest economy in the world. FTA negotiations began in the same period with Colombia, Ecuador, Bolivia, Panama, Peru, Thailand, and the five nations of the Southern Africa Customs Union. Negotiations continued on a Free Trade Area of the Americas that would bind together the entire hemisphere.

Clearly, the United States is far more satisfied with regional schemes than with being the mythical hegemon of HST. Frustration with the pace of global negotiations may be one factor, but the themes of this chapter suggest another interpretation—that regional agreements create liberalization structured along the lines favoured by the American vision but blocked by competing perspectives, especially in Europe. NAFTA, which lacks not only a secretariat but even an identifiable physical location, embodies the American ideal of a regime without institutions. It contrasts dramatically with the rich tapestry woven of the EU's multiple agencies, which are meant to mitigate the effects of liberalization and thus facilitate its extension and deepening.[30] In fact, America's bilateral initiatives with weaker states constitute a divide-and-conquer strategy not available in multilateral global settings. As nation after nation signs on, the pressure builds on others not to be left out of the lucrative US market. Thus, they accept provisions—such as those that open markets to foreign investment under highly favourable terms—that would not have been approved within the WTO, where nations can bargain as a unit.[31]

Contemporary Globalization: A Patchwork of Inadequate Governance

A regime committed to a neo-liberal brand of globalization has severe limitations. It is less stable than one built to withstand such economic forces as destabilizing capital flows. It is less resilient than one that accommodated predictable political forces like dissenting nations and subnational interests. In this sense, the American position is dangerous even to those it supports. It has been said that the America's 'multilateral agenda is increasingly the MNCs' agenda: intellectual property rights, standards, and, in the future, competition policy.'[32] However, globalization's downside effects could produce a political backlash that would undermine the system itself.

Instead of exploring alternatives, the United States has hoped to silence dissenters by portraying globalism as natural, inevitable, and irreversible. To the contrary, the 1920s demonstrate that when globalization is seen as a source of problems by citizens not convinced of its benefits, it can be reversed with breathtaking speed. Or, as Rodrik notes, 'social disintegration is not a spectator sport—those on the sidelines also get splashed with mud from the field.'[33]

In short, the explanation for recent evolution of the system lies in the peculiar character of American hegemony. Only an ideological hegemon would fail to see the need for more aggressive action and only an isolationist one would fail to act on it. As a result, it appears that America's peculiar vision of its hegemonic role is as grave a threat to globalization as its diminished hegemony.

Notes

1. Robert Gilpin, *The Political Economy of International Relations* (Princeton, NJ: Princeton University Press, 1987), 72–92.
2. John Ruggie, 'International Regimes, Transactions, and Change: Embedded Liberalism in the Postwar Economic Order', *International Organization* 36, 2 (1982): 382.
3. Ibid. For the generally unregulated character of 'Anglo-Saxon' capitalism, see James Fallows, 'How the World Works', *Atlantic Monthly* (Dec.

1993): 61–87.
4. Cecil V. Crabb Jr, *Policy-makers and Critics: Conflicting Theories of American Foreign Policy*, 2nd edn (New York: Praeger, 1986).
5. Evidence that the United States eschewed global leadership for half a century after its economic dominance entitled it to such a role includes the refusal to join the League of Nations and to co-operate at the World Economic Conference in London in 1933. The persistence of this attitude

was demonstrated in the 1970s when President Nixon unilaterally dissolved the fixed-rate monetary order that threatened American policy autonomy.

6. Exports account for slightly over 10 per cent of US GNP early in the twenty-first century, roughly a third of the average for European states. The United States has relied on foreign capital to balance perpetual trade deficits but it has not been forced to alter policy to attract it.

7. Because the United States is capital-abundant and labour-scarce, H-O anticipates that labour-intensive sectors would be harmed by trade. Stolper-Samuelson, an extension of H-O, expects free trade to harm unskilled labour regardless of the sector in which it is employed.

8. With the decline of manufacturing, a working class that could be mobilized to fashion a compromise between the benefits and costs of globalization has shrunk further. The rise of the white-collar service sector and high technology, together with the widespread distribution of equity issues through 401K and mutual funds, has swollen the size of the self-identified capitalist class.

9. Fallows, 'How the World Works', 65. His inclusion of Britain seems misplaced, except during the Thatcher period.

10. For an elaboration, see Ruggie, 'International Regimes, Transactions, and Change', 379–415.

11. Ibid., 399.

12. Dani Rodrik, *Has Globalization Gone Too Far?* (Washington: Institute for International Economics, 1997), 2.

13. For example, 'under typical parameters, lowering of a trade restriction will result in $5 or more of income being shuffled among different groups for every $1 of net gain.' Ibid., 30.

14. See William R. Cline, *Trade and Income Distribution* (Washington: Institute for International Economics, 1997), for a survey of the expansive literature on this effect.

15. Rodrik, *Has Globalization Gone Too Far?*, 5.

16. John Ruggie, 'At Home Abroad, Abroad at Home: International Liberalization and Domestic Stability in the New World Economy', *Millennium: Journal of International Studies* 24, 3 (1995): 508.

17. This is exacerbated when international financial institutions dictate policy, especially since the privatization urged as part of the Washington Consensus is widely seen as undemocratic, moving power from elected and accountable officials to unelected, unaccountable, foreign actors.

18. Designing a more humane globalization requires a combination of attributes not to be found in Congress, where internationalists are almost exclusively liberal whereas opponents of the market are both protectionist and isolationist.

19. The International Financial Institution Advisory Commission (IFIAC) report, released in 2000, is available at: <www.house.gov/jec/imf/meltzer.htm>.

20. Diana Tussie, 'Multilateralism Revisited in a Globalizing World Economy', *Mershon International Studies Review* 42 (1998): 189.

21. The resulting piles of debt—government, corporate, and household—must someday require a staggering economic adjustment that is sure to generate an intense political backlash to globalization. But not yet.

22. Pew Research Center survey, 19 Aug.–8 Sept. 2002, reported in 'Americans and the World' by the Program on International Policy Attitudes (PIPA), a joint program of the Center on Policy Attitudes and the Center for International and Security Studies at the School of Public Affairs, University of Maryland. Available at: <www.americans-world.org/digest/global_issues/globalization/rawdata/GlobalizationNewData.pdf>.

23. The poll by GlobeScan surveyed 18,797 people in Argentina, Brazil, Canada, Chile, China, France, Germany, Great Britain, India, Indonesia, Italy, Mexico, Nigeria, Russia, South Africa, Spain, Turkey, Uruguay, and the United States. Available at: <www.pipa.org/OnlineReports/Global_Issues/globescan_qnnre_06_04.pdf>.

24. Chicago Council on Foreign Relations survey, June 2002, reported in 'Americans and the World' by the Program on International Policy Attitudes (PIPA): <www.americans-world.org/index.cfm>.

25. 'America Will Not Wait for the Won't-Do Countries', *Financial Times* (London edn), 22 Sept. 2003, 23.
26. It is amazing that the 'unfair competition' interpretation has survived in the face of overwhelming evidence that the American competitiveness problem is not confined to a few products or a few countries. US imports are about 50 per cent greater than its exports and its annual trade deficit has exceeded $500 billion in recent years.
27. Indeed, Canadian enthusiasm for the Canada–US agreement, the precursor to NAFTA, owed much to its binational trade dispute resolution panels, which could block arbitrary American actions.
28. Tussie, 'Multilateralism Revisited', 190.
29. 'America Will Not Wait', 23.
30. Without a class-based system of political representation, the best-organized opposition has come from progressive organizations such as environmental groups. They have joined with elements of the right to emphasize the potential threats to national autonomy represented by the WTO and NAFTA's binational dispute resolution panels rather than distributional consequences.
31. Mary Lou Malig, 'War: Trade by Other Means: How the US Is Getting a Free Trade Agreement Minus the Negotiations', *Focus on Trade* 101 (July 2004). Available at: <www.focusweb.org/pdf/fot101.pdf>.
32. Stephen Haggard, 'Commentary', *Mershon International Studies Review* 42 (1998): 196.
33. Rodrik, *Has Globalization Gone Too Far?*, 7.

Suggested Readings

Block, Fred L. *The Origins of International Economic Disorder*. Berkeley: University of California Press, 1977.

Blumenthal, Sidney. 'The Return of the Repressed: Anti-Internationalism and the American Right', *World Policy Journal* 12 (1995): 1–13.

Gilpin, Robert. *The Political Economy of International Relations*. Princeton, NJ: Princeton University Press, 1987.

Goldstein, Judith. 'Ideas, Institutions, and American Trade Policy', *International Organization* 42, 1 (1988): 179–217.

Helleiner, Gerald. 'Transnational Enterprises and the New Political Economy of U.S. Trade Policy', *Oxford Economic Papers* 29, 1 (1977).

Kennedy, Paul. 'The (Relative) Decline of America', *Atlantic Monthly* (Aug. 1987): 29–38.

Kindleberger, Charles. *The World in Depression 1929–39*. Berkeley: University of California Press, 1973.

Pauly, Louis. *Who Elected the Bankers? Surveillance and Control in the World Economy*. Ithaca, NY: Cornell University Press, 1997.

Rogowski, Ronald. 'Political Cleavages and Changing Exposure to Trade', *American Political Science Review* 81, 4 (1987): 1121–37.

Web Sites

Program on International Policy Attitudes: www.pipa.org

Federal Reserve Bank: www.federalreserve.gov
United States Trade Representative: www.ustr.gov

Chapter 32

Politics and Markets in East Asia
Is the Developmental State Compatible with Globalization?

Mark Beeson

One of the most remarkable and surprising aspects of international economic development in the post-World War II period has been the rise of East Asia. A region that observers like Karl Marx and Max Weber once regarded as synonymous with a form of incurable 'Oriental' backwardness rapidly transformed itself into the most dynamic economic region on the planet. Even the financial and political crises that hit parts of the region in the late 1990s failed to stop the broadly based processes of economic expansion that had taken hold in East Asia or to erase the very real gains made there over the preceding 30–40 years. The big question, of course, is how did much of East Asia manage to pull off such a feat? This is an especially important question at a time when some observers think that the sorts of 'interventionist' policies associated with East Asia's most successful phase of development are no longer compatible with an increasingly integrated international political economy.

In addressing these issues the first part of this chapter initially provides a brief overview of both the 'developmental state' at the centre of East Asia's rapid growth and the precise circumstances that allowed it to flourish. The important point that emerges here is that East Asia's most successful economies were not just the beneficiaries of enlightened and effective public policy—although that plainly helped—they were also advantaged by a specific, possibly unique, set of geopolitical circumstances that allowed the distinctive, close relations between political and economic forces that are so characteristic of the region. In short, East

Asian-style state-led development was feasible for much of the post-war period because it was tolerated by the United States, the hegemonic power of the era, and because the expanding world economy facilitated export-oriented industrialization. Neither of these fundamental preconditions look as certain or benign at present. To illustrate how this change has come about, the second part of the chapter examines a number of factors—some domestic, some external—that have significantly undermined both the efficacy and legitimacy of the developmental state in East Asia. Nevertheless, the central argument of this chapter is that, even in an increasingly global political economy, states still have the potential capacity to influence economic outcomes significantly. Whether such interventions are considered to be appropriate, useful, or effective will remain as much a normative judgement as a 'technical' one, but in the case of the less economically developed southeast part of the region at least, effective state-led development may still have a critical role to play.

The Developmental State in Historical Context

At the outset it is important to acknowledge that the evolution of the state as the definitive form of political organization in 'the West' and latterly the rest of the world is intimately associated with the emergence and global spread of capitalism.[1] While there may be important and continuing differences in the way broadly capitalist economic systems are organized in different parts of the world, to operate effectively and with certainty, participants in *any* sort of market economy are highly dependent on political authorities to provide the basic institutional and legal infrastructure markets alone cannot supply. One of the defining public policy questions of the past couple of decades—a question given greater urgency by the rapid economic transformation of much of East Asia—has been about the extent and nature of the state's role. To understand the precise nature of the part played by the state in East Asia's general development and why such a role might no longer be considered feasible or appropriate, we need to place the entire developmental experience in its specific historical context. In this regard, a number of internal and external factors have had a decisive influence in shaping the overall environment within which the developmental state emerged in East Asia.

The defining feature of the international order in the aftermath of World War II was the Cold War confrontation between the United States and the Soviet Union. As far as the emergence of the developmental state in East Asia was concerned, this geopolitical standoff was crucial for a number of reasons. First, and most importantly, the intense struggle with the Soviet Union meant that the United States privileged security issues and the cultivation of successful capitalist allies over questions of ideological purity. In the context of East Asia this meant that throughout the Cold War successive American administrations were prepared to overlook political practices and forms of economic organization of which they did not necessarily approve. Even though the distinctive forms of social organization that emerged in East Asia might not have accorded with the creation of the sort of liberal international order American policy-makers wanted to create, these were tolerated if they helped consolidate the capitalist camp. The second reason why the Cold War environment was so conducive to the developmental strategies of those East Asian nations aligned with the

United States was that American power, aid, and assistance underpinned the 'golden age' of postwar capitalism from which a number of East Asian states were able to benefit.[2]

The potential importance of these interconnected regional and transnational or systemic factors can be seen in the case of the archetypal and pioneering developmental state: Japan. Whatever problems Japan may currently be experiencing, its metamorphosis from the devastation of its wartime defeat to become the second largest economy in the world within the space of about a quarter of a century was historically unprecedented and remains a stunning achievement. Although its neighbours South Korea and Taiwan have subsequently managed to achieve even more rapid rates of economic development and industrialization, they did so by following a Japanese blueprint of state-led development[3] rather than the sort of neoliberal, market-centred orthodoxy that has become so influential across much of the Western world and which is so assiduously promoted by the United States and key institutional allies like the International Monetary Fund.

How did Japan do it? At the centre of Japan's post-war renaissance was what Chalmers Johnson famously dubbed the developmental state.[4] In essence, the 'secret' of Japan's success was that it was *planned*. Powerful bureaucratic agencies like the Ministry of International Trade and Industry (MITI) and the Ministry of Finance systematically attempted to implement a vision of long-term economic expansion and upgrading to provide the basis for a modern industrial economy. They were able to do so for a number of reasons that merit emphasis: most fundamentally, Japan's post-war political and bureaucratic elites not only had the requisite desire to guide the course of development, they also had the capacity. At a pragmatic level, the idea of 'state capacity' simply means a particular government's ability to conceive and implement policy. At a conceptual level, however, the notion of state capacity directs our attention towards the precise circumstances, tools, strategies, and relationships that distinguish and effectively constitute different national approaches to successful economic development. It is worth briefly spelling out the manner in which these relationships have been conceptualized, as they can help us to understand the basis for, and possible merits of, state intervention, both in the past and in the context of an increasingly integrated international political economy.

In one influential reading of economic development, the chief variable determining successful and unsuccessful development outcomes is state policy, the effectiveness of which is determined by the degree of 'embedded autonomy' the state enjoys. The state must establish 'institutionalised channels for the continual negotiation and renegotiation of goals and policies',[5] which are sufficiently close to allow it to implement policy but not so close that it is 'captured' by vested economic interests. When the developmental state was at its most effective and successful in Northeast Asia during the 1950s, 1960s, and 1970s, the ability of the state in Japan, Korea, Taiwan, and even Singapore in Southeast Asia to establish 'pilot agencies' to guide development and implement policy was clearly a crucial part of their respective economic expansions.[6] While all of this may have been couched in the rhetoric of 'the national interest' and was made easier by the perceived need for nationally based economic development in the face of growing international economic competition, it is important to recognize that East Asian states had powerful policy tools at their disposal that made the co-operation of indigenous business more likely: access to cheap capital, protection from external competition, and assisted access to export markets were all levers that states could use to ensure business compliance with governmental goals.

It is also important to stress that in much of East Asia 'strong' states were not looked on with alarm, nor were their interventions in the economic process regarded as illegitimate. This was especially true when rapid economic growth appeared to validate such strategies and the 'late' developer status of the region as a whole meant that policies

necessary for 'catching up' were comparatively easy to formulate.[7] Consequently, much of East Asia was able to replicate the experience of the 'developed' world, facilitate industrial development through technological adaptation, and integrate national economies into the wider international system on favourable terms through a judicious use of trade and industry policies. The situation presently confronting the political elites of East Asia is a good deal more complex and the concomitant role for states is less clear. The current challenges can be summed up in one word: globalization.

East Asia in an Era of Globalization

'Globalization' is, of course, what social scientists like to refer to as an 'essentially contested concept'. Although its meaning may not be as clear as we might like, its extent contested, and its precise periodization unclear, globalization nevertheless is a convenient shorthand for a number of processes that have become more influential and intense over the last few decades. For the purposes of this chapter globalization is taken to refer to the array of social, political, and economic processes that transcend national borders and reflexively connect hitherto discrete parts of the world in new and complex ways.

As far as East Asia is concerned, the most important aspect of those processes subsumed under the globalization rubric has been economic. Although East Asia generally and the role of the developmental state in particular are powerful reminders that economic and political processes are inseparable, mutually constitutive forces,[8] it is still useful to highlight a number of developments that can be considered as primarily economic. To make this point clearer, two further analytical distinctions are necessary. First, it is important to distinguish between the 'real' or industrial economy and the financial sector, the latter being manifest principally in a range of transnational capital flows and the operations of international money markets. Both industrial restructuring and the spectacular growth of the financial sector have had a powerful impact on the East Asian region and the capacity of states to manage, or indeed take advantage of, forces that emanate from outside formerly discrete national economies. The second point to highlight about the East Asian region and the differential impact of global forces is that the region itself is far from homogeneous and is characterized by great variations in developmental outcomes and state capacities. It is possible, however, to make a very broad-brush distinction between those countries of Northeast Asia discussed above, which industrialized in the early post-war period, and the 'late-late' industrializers of Southeast Asia, which did not generally experience significant industrialization until about 20 years ago. With these caveats in mind, it is possible to identify a number of transnational trends and forces that have been influential not only in shaping economic outcomes but also in helping to determine the role of regional states.

International Restructuring and East Asia

There is little doubt that East Asia as a whole has benefited enormously from the transformation of trade and production in the real economy that has taken place in the post-war period. The economic expansion that occurred in North America and Western Europe created lucrative new markets that provided the basis for successive waves of export-oriented industrialization, initially in Japan and the rest of Northeast Asia, and more recently in Southeast Asia. This remarkable, regionally based transformation attracted increased scholarly attention, which highlighted the crucial role of the state in encouraging the development of export-oriented indigenous industries while simultaneously protecting domestic markets from foreign competition.[9] Inevitably, perhaps, those countries running growing trade deficits with East Asia became increasingly disgruntled. Throughout the 1980s, as concerns about the relative performance of the American economy became a prominent issue, enormous political pressure was placed on Japan in particular to reform its economy and open up to foreign competition.

The point to emphasize, therefore, is that while many of the decisions that drove the process of post-war international restructuring were taken by the heads of multinational corporations in the private sector, they did so in a politically conditioned environment. While the connection between state actors and the private sector may have been most overt and institutionalized in East Asia, American foreign policy was also clearly intended to advantage politically powerful 'national champions' in the United States. In other words, all states are interested in trying to give advantage to indigenous firms in an increasingly competitive international environment; the big question is about the guiding rationale that informs policy. Understood in this context, globalization is not simply a process determined solely by what Marxists might describe as the logic of capital accumulation, or—more simply—by the imperatives of international corporate competition. On the contrary, states—in the politically powerful industrialized economies, at least—have a continuing capacity to shape the national and transnational regulatory frameworks within which such processes occur.[10]

The result of this interplay between political and corporate power at both the national and transnational levels is complex and occasionally paradoxical. On the one hand, a surprising degree of continuity and distinctiveness exists in the style of corporate activities in countries like Japan and South Korea, where large industrial conglomerates continue to dominate the economic landscape and long-term relationships remain important.[11] On the other hand, long-run changes in the overall international political economy—often the result of precisely the sort of political reformist pressures previously mentioned—have begun to unravel the entrenched, institutionalized relationships between corporate players and between the economic and political actors that have been such a central part of many East Asian political economies. In Japan, for example, long considered to be the most distinctive, non-market-oriented system in Asia, there is compelling evidence that its famous *keiretsu* networks of interconnected corporate entities are being eroded by increased levels of foreign ownership and the fact that governments can no longer offer such attractive incentives to, or constraints over, powerful corporations, which now have an increasing global logic and can easily raise capital on international financial markets.[12]

While the deeply institutionalized basis of the distinctive forms of capitalism found in the region will ensure that a radical transformation of national political practices and economic structures is simply not possible in the short-term,[13] longer-term forces clearly are eroding national distinctiveness and identification. This can be seen in the development of East Asia's other unique form of economic and social organization—'Chinese' capitalism. The dominance of ethnic Chinese business interests in a number of Southeast Asia economies, such as Indonesia, Malaysia, Thailand, and the Philippines, has long been recognized, as has the importance of personal connections in consolidating economic and political relationships. Significantly, however, globalization in general and the recent economic crisis in particular appear to have engendered a significant change in both the attitudes of many Chinese business people and the strategies they employ as a consequence. Yeung argues that globalization is being used discursively 'as an external "objective" force to discipline corrupted and statist economies in the region'.[14] This is especially significant in a Southeast Asian context where political and economic power has frequently fused to create a pattern of 'embedded mercantilism', in which the state has protected local business from external competition in a mutually rewarding symbiosis.[15] If 'domestic' business now considers that the logic of international restructuring means that alliances with local political elites no longer offer the benefits they once did, and may in fact have become liabilities, this calls into question the sustainability of existent patterns of political and economic organization and the concomitant role of the state.

Given the frequently self-serving if not unambiguously corrupt nature of business–government relations in parts of East Asia, their erosion may not seem to be such a bad thing. Certainly, powerful external agencies like the IMF, the World Bank, and the United States Treasury Department were keen to attribute the economic crisis of the late 1990s to problems of indigenous governance and corporate organization, rather than to systemic problems within the wider international political economy.[16] While 'crony capitalism' clearly has been a problem in parts of the region, it needs to be emphasized that not only were the causes of the crisis much more complex than orthodox IMF-style analyses imply, but it has been persuasively argued that in some circumstances what the less-developed economies of Southeast Asia actually need is more state 'intervention' rather than less.[17] To see why, we need to look at the other major element of economic globalization, the financial sector.

The Financial Sector in East Asia

The financial sector is the area of international economic activity that has become most 'global' and mobile, and has grown enormously in scale and scope. One of the most important theoretical and pragmatic questions to emerge from this transformation has been about its possible impact on the state, with some observers considering that the 'structural' power of global finance heralds an inevitable diminution of state power.[18] For a region in which the state has sought to play an active role in economic management, this is potentially a major challenge to both the traditional style of governance and to the legitimacy of the state itself as a consequence.

The potential significance of this point becomes clearer when we remember how the most successful development state operated at the height of its powers. One of the reasons Japanese state officials were able to implement their plans for the development of the 'strategic' industries that would provide the backbone of a modern industrial economy was because they had leverage over domestic business. Until the 1970s, the Japanese financial system was relatively insulated and autonomous. In such circumstances, MITI and the Ministry of Finance were able to recycle Japan's famously high levels of domestic savings to targeted domestic industrial sectors and businesses. Business co-operated because it had access to capital at 'artificially' low interest rates, which gave it a potentially important advantage over established rivals elsewhere. Governmental control of the domestic banking system ensured that indigenous financial institutions co-operated in providing funds to industry, something that helped to consolidate the close ties between industrial and financial capital that was so characteristic of Japan during the boom years.

It is difficult to generalize about the financial systems of a region as diverse as East Asia, which contains countries at very different levels of economic development, to say nothing of highly diverse political systems and state capacities. What we can say, however, is that across much of the region the Japanese exemplar, high domestic savings rates, and a general desire to accelerate the development process led to broadly similar patterns of state intervention in Korea, Taiwan, China, Singapore, Indonesia, Thailand, and Malaysia, with states repressing interest rates, directing credit, and using capital controls to guide the course of economic development.[19] Although there may be important differences in places like Korea and Singapore, where foreign capital has played a more important part in development, in resource-dependent Indonesia, where the price of oil has critically influenced government autonomy, and in China, which is still nominally Communist, the overall contrast between East Asia and the market-oriented Anglo-American economies is still striking. The key question is whether changes in the increasingly integrated international financial sector will inevitably undermine state autonomy and the concomitant capacity to influence economic outcomes.

In this regard, the financial crises of the late 1990s revealed the different ways East Asian economies had already integrated with the wider international system and raised important questions about the state's role in this process. The crisis itself has generated a voluminous literature

and there is no intention of adding to this here,[20] but it is important to note a number of issues the crisis highlighted. First, the biggest economy in the region—that of Japan—was already experiencing economic difficulties that predated the crisis by nearly a decade. Although Japanese officials plainly made a number of 'mistakes' in their management of the rise and fall of the 'bubble economy', it is significant that the bubble itself emerged in the wake of the liberalization of Japan's financial sector. Old relationships between industrial and financial interests in Japan had already begun to weaken as corporations accessed offshore finance.[21] Heightened competition in a liberalized domestic environment fuelled dubious lending practices and rampant speculation in property and equity markets. As a consequence, the 'Japanese model' began to unravel. It is important to recognize, however, that this unravelling had Japanese origins: the shift to deficit financing by the Japanese government from the 1970s onward made liberalization and a diminution of governmental control almost inevitable.[22] In addition, increasingly self-serving relationships between business and government meant that much of the money raised by successive Japanese governments was wasted on politically powerful lobby groups rather than broader developmental goals.

Even if Japan's problems were largely indigenously generated, the problems confronting other countries often had a significant external component. Indeed, the second point to make about the Asian crisis is that those countries worst affected were also the most exposed to the international financial system. Although there undoubtedly were problems with 'crony capitalism' in South Korea, Thailand, Malaysia, and Indonesia, which led to Japanese-style policy mistakes and a misallocation of resources, there is now widespread agreement that 'excessively rapid financial and capital market liberalization was probably the single most important cause of the crisis.'[23] Inadequately regulated domestic financial markets and institutions, combined with a frequently poor understanding of the implications that flow from opening the capital account, led to a rapid buildup of foreign debt—especially short-term—establishing the preconditions for capital flight, chaos, and crisis.

The other factor the crisis highlighted that had particular implications for East Asia's developmental states was the rise of other non-state actors as centres of power and authoritative decision-making. Not only did the IMF play a (generally resented and much criticized) high-profile role in managing the crisis, but it became apparent that other actors—emerging market managers and the credit rating agencies that informed them—had become pivotal players influencing the movements of mobile financial capital.[24] Significantly, and despite much post-crisis talk about the need to reform the 'international financial architecture', which was widely blamed for the rapid and destructive unfolding of the crisis, little has changed. This is not surprising: the ability of 'Wall Street' to influence American policy and the pivotal role the United States continues to play in shaping the rules of the international financial game mean that the prevailing order is likely to continue despite concerns about its stability and impact.[25]

This is all the more remarkable when we consider that the third major point to emerge from the crisis is that those countries least affected were also least integrated into the international financial system. China's currency was non-convertible, Hong Kong maintained a currency board, while Taiwan's formidable foreign exchange reserves, high domestic savings, and relatively independent financial regulators rendered it relatively immune to external pressures.[26] However, all this may change. China, for example, is coming under increased pressure from the United States to 'float' its currency in the hope that this will rectify the latter's chronic trade deficit. Given that a similar policy towards Japan in the 1980s led to the development of the bubble economy and did little to fix the trade imbalance, there is no reason to suppose such a policy will succeed in China's case. What it does illustrate, however, is that the international economic system will continue to be shaped by the actions of powerful nations and that such power

may be exercised indirectly. China's accession to the World Trade Organization under terms and conditions established by the most powerful capitalist countries exemplifies the new order in which East Asian states find themselves increasingly constrained by powerful intergovernmental agencies and non-state actors.[27]

The End of the Developmental State?

Thus, the state in East Asia, like its counterparts elsewhere, is having to come to terms with processes of globalization that threaten to undermine its capacity to influence the course of economic development. In the Anglo-American economies, such as the United States, Britain, and Australia, this is not necessarily such a problem. On the contrary, the apparent diminution of state power and influence over the economy is entirely in keeping with a neo-liberal ideology that normatively privileges markets over governments, and state policy has actually encouraged this diminution. In East Asia, by contrast, where the legitimacy and authority of ruling elites frequently hinge on their capacity to deliver economic growth, if states are generally in retreat then this presents a more fundamental challenge to a region that has risen to prominence in large part as a consequence of state activism.

In deciding whether East Asia's developmental state is in terminal decline, two questions loom large. First, is it certain that states generally are losing their capacity to act effectively and authoritatively? Second, does the developmental state in particular have a limited lifespan, after which it should be reconfigured if it is not to become self-serving and counterproductive? These are plainly large questions and answers to them can only be sketched here.

As far as the state of the state is concerned, the East Asian experience serves as a cautionary reminder that generalization is difficult. While the countries of Northeast Asia may have had a highly developed ability to devise and implement policy, in much of Southeast Asia state sovereignty was frequently incompletely realized even before the processes associated with globalization intensified.[28]

Nevertheless, a number of scholars have argued that globalization has done little to undermine either the capacity of or the necessity for states to shape economic outcomes. Linda Weiss, for example, suggests that states have retained a considerable degree of 'room for manoeuvre' in policy-making and that 'globalization also contributes to the expansion of governing capacities through both the transformation of public-private sector relations and the growth of policy networks.'[29] Certainly this might seem to apply to many 'developed' economies where (even in the Anglo-American countries) governments generally account for an increasing share of economic activity and an array of non-governmental or quasi-state agencies facilitate new modes of governance and state influence. In parts of East Asia, however, where the non-state sector is not as well developed or independent, claims about the potential reconfiguring of public-private relations look more dubious.[30]

In such circumstances, therefore, what much of Southeast Asia in particular needs is *more* state capacity and intervention rather than less. There are two compelling reasons for advancing this argument. On the one hand, as Ha Joon Chang has pointed out, all those states that have successfully developed sophisticated industrial economies have done so with the assistance of developmental states.[31] This applies to both interventionist East Asian governments like Japan, *and* to the original industrializing nations like Britain and later the United States. The degree of collective amnesia about their own historical development on the part of many in the West consequently makes the advocacy of economic liberalization and a winding back of the developmental state in East Asia hypocritical at best, self-serving and discriminatory at worst. Put simply, political elites in the developed world and the powerful non-state and intergovernmental agencies that constitute the international regulatory architecture are effectively depriving developing nations of an important mechanism for promoting development—a mechanism their predecessors used to facilitate their own economic expansion. This is especially troubling since the historical

record also suggests that, even though Southeast Asian states have had less capacity to develop and implement industrial developmental policies than their Northeast Asian counterparts, there is, as Jomo points out, 'little doubt that the structural transformation and industrialization of these economies have gone well beyond what would have been achieved by relying exclusively on market forces and private sector initiatives.'[32]

Of equal importance in the contemporary, increasingly integrated international economy—and this is the second major argument in favour of enhanced state capacity and continuing intervention in economic activity—governments need to manage and oversee the manner in which small, vulnerable economies are integrated with the potentially volatile and highly destabilizing flows of mobile capital that emanate from the world's capital markets. Indeed, governments in the developing world need to think carefully about whether flows of financial or portfolio capital are useful at all. Discriminating between and developing suitable policy responses towards long-term direct foreign investment and short-term flows of highly mobile, speculative capital are central to this process. In short, as far as many developing economies are concerned, an effective, relatively independent and non-corrupt developmental state is still a potentially critical part of economic progress and serves as a mechanism for mediating global forces.

Creating and maintaining the sort of ideal-typical state–business relationship described by the likes of Evans and Weiss is plainly not a simple matter, however. Not only are such strategies at odds with the prevailing ideological climate and likely to be challenged by powerful international actors, but there are legitimate concerns about whether they are achievable without creating self-serving and corrupt relationships. The experience of Japan suggests that however effective the developmental state may be initially, there is a very real danger that it will be captured by vested interests, making it an obstacle to, rather than a promoter of, much needed reform. The Japanese case also suggests that once the developmental state has effectively done its job and 'caught up' with established industrial economies at the leading edge of production and knowledge, it is far from clear that state planners are any wiser about the course of future technological development than the private sector.[33] In other words, there are limits to what states can do, specific circumstances in which planned development seems to be effective, and a danger of entrenching a counterproductive institutional inertia where the relationships between political and economic elites are inadequately monitored and transparent, or where they linger on past their expiry dates.

Ultimately, therefore, the relative long-term decline of the state may be inevitable and not a bad thing. The East Asian experience reminds us that the price of state-led development can be authoritarianism, corruption, and an often cavalier attitude towards human rights and the environment. The extent to which the destruction of protective coastal mangrove forests and coral reefs to make room for tourist and aquaculture development in Southeast Asia contributed to the devastation and loss of life from the Asian tsunami at the end of 2004 is a case in point. Moreover, political and economic theorists have rightly drawn attention to both the conceptual and normative problems that revolve around nationally based frameworks of understanding and action.[34] Nevertheless, if parts of the world that are presently 'underdeveloped' economically are to experience rising living standards and be integrated into the global economy on more favourable terms, the historical record strongly suggests that states continue to be critically important: even in an era of globalization, states retain a significant potential capacity to influence domestic economic outcomes and the way broadly conceived national economic spaces are articulated with the wider global system. Consequently, if parts of the developing world—not just in Southeast Asia, but also in Eastern Europe, Latin America, and especially Africa—are to move up the ladder of economic development, they may still need to employ some of the same sorts of co-ordinated, interventionist, state-led strategies that underpinned Northeast Asia's rise during its most successful period.

Whether they will have the necessary sort of domestic capacity and permissive international environment that might allow them to do so is, of course, another question. At a time when the United States is no longer constrained by wider geopolitical imperatives and much more willing to act unilaterally in pursuit of what it takes to be its national interest, then it is entirely possible that the international ideational and political environment will remain hostile to state activism, despite compelling evidence that for some countries it may still be the key to successful economic development.

Notes

1. Charles Tilly, *Coercion, Capital, and European States* (Oxford: Blackwell, 1990).
2. Richard Stubbs, 'War and Economic Development: Export-oriented Industrialization in East and Southeast Asia', *Comparative Politics* 31, 3 (1999): 337–55.
3. Japan's colonization of Taiwan and South Korea helps to explain both its own direct influence and the wider political economy of regional development. For a seminal discussion, see Bruce Cumings, 'The Origins and Development of Northeast Asian Political Economy: Industrial Sectors, Product Cycles, and Political Consequences', *International Organization* 38, 10, (1984): 1–40.
4. Chalmers Johnson, *MITI and the Japanese Miracle: The Growth of Industry Policy 1925–1975* (Stanford, Calif.: Stanford University Press, 1982).
5. Peter Evans, *Embedded Autonomy: States and Industrial Transformation* (Princeton, NJ: Princeton

University Press, 1995), 12.

6. Linda Weiss and John M. Hobson, *States and Economic Development: A Comparative Historical Analysis* (Oxford: Polity Press, 1995). See also Adrian Leftwich, *States of Development: On the Primacy of Politics in Development* (Oxford: Polity Press, 2000).

7. On late development, see A. Gerschenkron, *Economic Backwardness in Historical Perspective* (Cambridge, Mass.: Belknap Press, 1966).

8. See Edmund T. Gomez, ed., *Political Business in Asia* (London: Routledge, 2002).

9. There is an enormous literature on the 'Asian miracle', but in addition to those works already cited, see Robert Wade, *Governing the Market: Economic Theory and the Role of Government in East Asian Industrialization* (Princeton, NJ: Princeton University Press, 1990); World Bank, *The East Asian Miracle: Economic Growth and Public Policy* (Oxford: Oxford University Press, 1993).

10. Just how much influence states retain is a hotly contested issue. For important competing perspectives, see Linda Weiss, *The Myth of the Powerless State* (Ithaca, NY: Cornell University Press, 1998), and Susan Strange, *The Retreat of the State: The Diffusion of Power in the World Economy* (Cambridge: Cambridge University Press, 1996).

11. Paul N. Doremus, William W. Keller, Louis W. Pauly, and Simon Reich, *The Myth of the Global Corporation* (Princeton, NJ: Princeton University Press, 1998).

12. T.J. Pempel, *Regime Shift: Comparative Dynamics of the Japanese Political Economy* (Ithaca, NY: Cornell University Press, 1999).

13. See Mark Beeson, 'Theorising Institutional Change in East Asia', in Beeson, ed., *Reconfiguring East Asia: Regional Institutions and Organisations after the Crisis* (London: RoutledgeCurzon Press, 2002), 7–27.

14. Henry Wai-chung Yeung, 'Economic Globalization, Crisis and the Emergence of Chinese Business Communities in Southeast Asia', *International Sociology* 15, 2 (2000): 266–87.

15. Kanishka Jayasuriya, 'Southeast Asia's Embedded Mercantilism in Crisis: International Strategies and Domestic Coalitions', in A. Tan and J. Boutin, eds, *Non-Traditional Security Issues in Southeast Asia* (Singapore: Select Publishing, 2001), 26–53.

16. See, e.g., Stanley Fischer, 'The Asian Crisis: A View from the IMF', address to Midwinter Conference of the Bankers' Association for Foreign Trade, Washington, 22 Jan. 1998. Available at: <www.imf.org/external/np/speeches/1998/012298.htm>.

17. Joseph Stiglitz, 'The Role of International Financial Institutions in the Current Global Economy', address to the Chicago Council on Foreign Relations, Chicago, 27 Feb. 1998. Available at: <http://web.worldbank.org/WBSITE/EXTERNAL/NEWS/0,,contentMDK:20024294~menuPK:34474~pagePK:34370~piPK:34424~theSitePK:4607,00.html>.

18. David Andrews, 'Capital Mobility and State Autonomy: Toward a Structural Theory of International Monetary Relations', *International Studies Quarterly* 38 (1994): 193–218; Strange, *Retreat of the State*.

19. Grahame Thompson, 'Financial Systems and Monetary Integration', in Thompson, ed., *Economic Dynamism in the Asia-Pacific* (London: Routledge, 1998), 83–111.

20. See, e.g., R. Robison et al., eds, *Politics and Markets in the Wake of the Asian Crisis* (London: Routledge, 2000).

21. Kent E. Calder, 'Assault on the Bankers' Kingdom: Politics, Markets, and the Liberalization of Japanese Industrial Finance', in M. Loriaux et al., *Capital Ungoverned: Liberalizing Finance in Interventionist States* (Ithaca, NY: Cornell University Press, 1997), 17–56.

22. Andrew Leyshon, 'Under Pressure: Finance, Geo-economic Competition and the Rise and Fall of Japan's Postwar Growth Economy', in S. Corbridge, R. Martin, and N. Thrift, eds, *Money, Power and Space* (Oxford: Blackwell, 1994), 116–45.

23. Joseph E. Stiglitz, *Globalization and Its Discontents* (New York: Norton, 2002), 89.

24. For a discussion of the role of ratings agencies in particular and the shift in authority to the private sector more generally, see A. Claire Cutler et al., eds, *Private Authority in International Affairs*

(Albany, NY: SUNY Press, 1999).

25. See Mark Beeson, 'East Asia, the International Financial Institutions and Regional Regulatory Reform: A Review of the Issues', *Journal of the Asia Pacific Economy* 8, 3 (2003): 305–26.

26. For useful case studies of the crisis and its impact on the region's financial sectors, see Gregory W. Noble and John Ravenhill, *The Asian Financial Crisis and the Architecture of Global Finance* (Cambridge: Cambridge University Press, 2000).

27. The extent of this process is indicated by China having to rewrite parts of its constitution to comply with WTO regulations. See Joseph Fewsmith, 'The Political and Social Implications of China's Accession to the WTO', *China Quarterly* 167 (2001): 573–91.

28. Mark Beeson 'Sovereignty under Siege: Globalisation and the State in Southeast Asia', *Third World Quarterly* 24, 2 (2003): 357–74.

29. Linda Weiss, 'Introduction: Bringing Domestic Institutions Back In', in Weiss, ed., *States in the Global Economy: Bringing Domestic Institutions Back In* (Cambridge: Cambridge University Press, 2003), 19.

30. Mark Beeson, 'Globalisation, Governance, and the Political Economy of Public Policy Reform in East Asia', *Governance* 14, 4 (2001): 481–502.

31. Ha Joon Chang, *Kicking Away the Ladder: Development Strategy in Historical Perspective* (London: Anthem Books, 2002).

32. K.S. Jomo, 'Rethinking the Role of Government Policy in Southeast Asia', in J.E. Stiglitz and S. Yusuf, eds, *Rethinking the East Asia Miracle* (Washington: World Bank, 2001), 461–508.

33. Mark Beeson, 'Japan's Reluctant Reformers and the Legacy of the Developmental State', in Anthony Cheung and Ian Scott, eds, *Governance and Public Sector Reform in Post-Crisis Asia: Paradigm Shift or Business as Usual?* (London: Curzon Press, 2003), 25–43.

34. On the normative and political issues raised by globalization, see David Held, *Democracy and the Global Order* (Cambridge: Polity Press, 1995). On conceptual issues raised by transnational economic integration, see Stephen J. Korbin, 'Economic Governance in an Electronically Networked Global Economy', in R.B. Hall and T.J. Biersteker, eds, *The Emergence of Private Authority in Global Governance* (Cambridge: Cambridge University Press, 2002), 43–75.

Suggested Readings

Beeson, Mark, ed. *Reconfiguring East Asia: Regional Institutions and Organisations after the Crisis.* London: RoutledgeCurzon Press, 2002.

Berger, Mark T. *The Battle for Asia: From Decolonization to Globalization.* London: Routledge, 2003.

Chang, Ha Joon. *Kicking Away the Ladder: Development Strategy in Historical Perspective.* London: Anthem Books, 2002.

Katz, Richard. *Japan: The System That Soured.* Armonk, NY: M.E. Sharpe, 1998.

Leftwich, Adrian. *States of Development: On the Primacy of Politics in Development.* Oxford: Polity Press, 2000.

Stiglitz, Joseph E., and Shahid Yusuf, eds. *Rethinking the East Asian Miracle.* Washington: World Bank, 2001.

Weiss, Linda, ed. *States in the Global Economy: Bringing Domestic Institutions Back In.* Cambridge: Cambridge University Press, 2003.

Woo-Cumings, Meredith ed. *The Developmental State,* Ithaca, NY: Cornell University Press, 1999.

Web Sites

Asia Recovery Information Center: http://aric.adb.org/
Asia Source: www.asiasource.org/index.cfm
Asia Times: www.atimes.com/atimes/Front_Page.html
East and Southeast Asia, Annotated Directory of

Internet Resources: http://newton.uor.edu/Departments&Programs/AsianStudiesDept/index.html

Chapter 33

Japan, East Asian Regionalization, and Selective Resistance to Globalization

Christopher W. Hughes

Globalization, defined as the de-territorialization of social space and manifested in the diffusion of technology and neo-liberal economics, is generally thought to exert strong convergence tendencies on different national and regional modes of capitalism. East Asia is now increasingly viewed as no exception to this convergence thesis. The financial crises of 1997–8 are seen to have exploded the myth of the 'East Asian Miracle' and to have revealed the incapacity of the 'developmental state' model, characterized by formal and informal government intervention in the market, to cope with the stresses of globalization. Consequently, in the post-financial crisis period, many East Asian economies are now viewed as moving along a development trajectory that dictates the retreat of the state from the market and greater convergence with Anglo-American modes of capitalism.

Similarly, Japan's exceptionalism as an advanced industrial economy is also seen to have failed to escape the onslaught of globalization and convergence pressures. Japan, despite its developed status and sheer size as the second largest national economy in the world, and despite its identity as the originator of the developmental state model and as the most successful example of an alternative to the Anglo-American form of capitalism, has been heavily buffeted by the forces of globalization. Japan's prolonged economic recession since the early 1990s, its parlous financial sector, the increasing woes of sections of its once seemingly invincible manufacturing industry, and the perceived bungling of economic policy by its

bureaucratic elite have forced restructuring on Japan and an acceptance of declining state capacity to intervene in the private markets. Indeed, certain observers have argued that globalization represents the third major opening and transformation of Japanese society in the modern era. Globalization is seen to follow in a line of successive openings of Japan to external social forces. External influence is viewed as having begun with the first opening of the Meiji Restoration of 1868, which ended Japan's self-imposed isolation and initiated a process of modern state-building and imperialism. The second opening, the Allied occupation (1945–52), brought about demilitarization, democratization, and a multiplication of the number of producers in the spheres of agriculture and industry. Globalization now carries the potential for Japan of the decoupling of the public and private spheres and dismantlement of the pre-eminent model of the developmental state.

In turn, globalization is believed not only to have begun to create significant economic and social change within Japan itself, but also to have had a deleterious impact on Japan's role in structuring the East Asian regional political economy. Japan, although engaged in efforts in the past to foster the developmental state model within East Asia, is now thought to have a declining capacity and commitment to perpetuate this model in the region, beset as it is by its own economic problems and difficulties in maintaining variants of this model domestically. Hence, the Japanese state might be viewed as not only retreating domestically in the face of globalization, but also retreating from fostering state-led models of capitalism in East Asia and from organizing the region to deal with the onset of globalization. Consequently, some observers predict that Japan will increasingly be obliged to cede economic leadership in the region to the United States or, more likely, China, which may be better equipped and more willing to bear the costs of influencing the pattern of regional economic development.

This chapter seeks to correct this view and to provide a more sophisticated and nuanced approach concerning the convergence effects of globalization on Japan's domestic economy and the East Asian states, as well as in regard to Japan's role in organizing the region in an era of globalization. To be sure, globalization has had a fundamental impact on the developmental model in Japan and across the region, and Japan's attempts to organize the regional economy are under severe stress. However, Japan certainly has not been passive or totally impotent in responding to globalization, and the Japanese state has determined not to let the attendant pressures of globalization run untrammelled. Japan has sought to lead a quiet and selective resistance movement, not to exclude but to mould globalization to its own advantage and to the advantage of other East Asian states.

Japanese Perspectives on Globalization

Japanese views of globalization are clearly multiple, reflecting the pluralistic nature of its society and the policy agents involved in devising responses to this complex phenomenon. The particular focus here is on the attitudes to globalization of Japan's elite bureaucratic actors, and to a lesser extent its political and business actors. These actors have been important in the past in determining the course of Japan's engagement with the global and regional economies, and they remain today the leading Japanese actors in this task. Hence, any investigation of Japan and globalization, although not complete by looking just at these agents, must at least start at this point.

Reflecting the complexity of Japanese society, these actors hold a variety of views concerning globalization. In fact, many leading policy actors, and particularly the Ministry of Economy, Trade and Industry (METI) and Ministry of Finance, appreciate that Japan has long been a central player in the globalization process in East Asia, and that globalization presents for Japan many positive opportunities for evolving its economy. Japan's massive expansion of private foreign direct investment (FDI) in East Asia, triggered by the 1985 Plaza Accord and upward revaluation of the yen, was a powerful motive force for the integration of the Japanese and East Asian economies and for the further integration of the latter into the global economy. METI policymakers, since and before the Plaza Accord, have understood also that globalization and its associated features—the diffusion of technology, the mobility of capital, outsourcing, and the creation of transnational production networks—offer the opportunity for Japanese industries to move segments of their activities offshore in order to maintain their international competitiveness.

At the same time, though, METI and Ministry of Finance officials and other policy actors have recognized that globalization is a double-edged sword in terms of its economic and other effects. Japanese concerns about globalization first arose with the 'hollowing out' debate of the early 1990s, centred on fears that the majority of Japan's industrial base would be transplanted to offshore production sites in East Asia. Nevertheless, it was the East Asian financial crisis that fully alerted Japanese policymakers to the risks of the free flow of globalization forces in the region. The conversion of the original financial crisis into a full-blown economic crisis threatened to undo Japan's carefully fostered trade and production networks in the region. The impact of the crisis even appeared to impinge directly on Japan by contributing to a domestic financial panic in late 1997 with the collapse of a major regional bank and securities house. Moreover, for Japan's policy-makers the financial crisis and the intervention of the International Monetary Fund (IMF) demonstrated that globalization produces strong convergence pressures, is a threat to the developmental state model, and can be heavily weighted against the developmental aspirations of East Asian states. Finally, the escalation of the crisis into social, political, and security crises in states such as Indonesia was taken as a demonstration that globalization has the potential to destabilize the entire region.

The conclusion drawn from these events by Japan's policy-makers has thus been that globalization, while a positive force in many circumstances, also needs to be carefully managed by states and its worst excesses mitigated. Japan's approach to the management of globalization, once again reflecting the pluralistic interests of its policy system, has been mixed. At times, as in the case of domestic banking reform, the Japanese state has been involved in attempts to hold back the tide of globalization through massive state intervention and de facto nationalization of banks, thus producing an actual advance of public–private co-operation. More usually, however, the Japanese state has sought to manage globalization not by throwing up barriers to the inflow of external globalization forces but by attempting to create structures that channel or filter, and thereby ameliorate, the impact of globalization. In other contexts this has been termed a policy of 'permeable insulation' for Japan, whereby the Japanese state seeks to insulate its domestic political economy from the shocks of globalization while allowing in those aspects of the globalization process it deems to be beneficial.[1] This chapter expands this concept by suggesting that, increasingly, Japanese government objectives are not just to insulate Japan's own economy but also that of East Asia as a whole. In recent initiatives since the East Asian financial crisis, Japan has experimented with sponsoring regional structures that can fend off the unwelcome penetration of globalization. This may best be viewed as a process of selective resistance. These structures are not designed to close the region to external linkages, as this would clearly contravene the fundamental interests of Japan and its East Asian neighbours in maintaining region-wide and subregional projects that can attract external capital and access to external markets. Instead, these structures are designed to provide an interface to allow both the inflow of globalization forces and the preservation of key aspects of the developmental state model in the region. In this way, the intent is to provide a new layer of permeable insulation for the East Asian states and a further double layer of permeable insulation for Japan. In turn, these initiatives are also clearly aimed at preserving Japan's leadership in the economic sphere in East Asia.

The Japanese state has worked to preserve or to develop anew two principal forms of regional structure. The first is a structure for the regional division of labour. In the wake of the financial crisis Japan has sought to re-gear the division of labour and, through official development assistance (ODA) and free trade agreements (FTAS), to strengthen the developmental economies of the region, with the final aim of consolidating Japanese strengths in manufacturing in East Asia and globally. The second structure is that of financial and monetary co-operation in the region. In this regard, Japan has assisted in the creation of new institutions and mechanisms to minimize the possibility of any repetition of the damaging 1997–8 financial crisis and to insulate Japan's own domestic economy as it undergoes a painful and slow process of financial sector reform.

Japan's attempts to manage globalization would seem very much in keeping with its past history of dealing with pressures that have forced open a hitherto closed national economy. As is well known, in the previous openings of the Meiji Restoration and Allied occupation, Japan displayed the knack of accepting from the West those features of a modern economy and society that it saw as advantageous, and at the same time projected the concept that it had managed to preserve much of its indigenous national characteristics. This chapter does not attempt a prediction of the final outcome of globalization for Japan and the region, nor does it attempt to assess fully the likelihood of current regional initiatives succeeding in insulating Japan. However, it does address the question of what types of obstacles Japan currently faces in organizing structures for the division of labour for financial co-operation in the region, especially with regard to its own willingness to shoulder the costs of regional development and the issue of competition from a rising China.

Japan and the Regional Division of Labour

Japan's initial efforts to create structures to insulate its own domestic economy and the East Asian states from the extremes of globalization have been centred on the regional division of labour for production. Japan's strategy in essence has been based on the recognition that globalization's potential for transnational production generates shifts in comparative advantage among states, with a concomitant trend towards the relocation of industries wholesale or in part to lower-cost developing countries. Globalization thus exerts significant pressure on the competitiveness of Japanese manufacturing industry. Japan's policy-makers have long known that comparative advantage is not necessarily a preordained economic fact and that it can be manipulated and enhanced through government policies and subsidies. Nevertheless, Japanese policy-makers have been forced to accept that the shifts in comparative advantage brought about by globalization are too great to be resisted outright and are beyond the resources of individual national governments. Instead, Japan, alongside continuing attempts to engineer comparative advantage in its favour, has looked to harness globalization to its own ends. The government has sought to do so by encouraging a managed process of transplanting or outsourcing Japanese private manufacturing industry to the East Asia region. In certain cases, this has taken the form of the transplant of large sections of declining industries; in others, the aim has been to transplant or outsource only those elements of production that are labour-intensive and thus of high cost in Japan, while retaining technology-intensive and high-earning production in Japan. Hence, the Japanese government's overall objective has been to utilize the potentialities of globalization and transnational production to maintain the competitiveness and profits of Japanese corporations, and

subsequently to use regionalized production as a means to dampen the potentially larger and direct impact on Japan of globalization unmediated by any form of regional insulation.

Moreover, at the same time that Japan has sought to use the regionalization of production to maintain its own competitiveness, it has also viewed this process as a means to assist the development of the East Asian regional economy. Japan's transplanting and outsourcing of production is seen to be important in providing capital, technology, and management systems to boost the developmental states of East Asia, as well as initiating greater intra-regional production and trading links, thus holding out for the first time the possibility of an integrated region.

Japan's regionalization strategy to cope with globalization has taken more concrete form in its plans for guiding the establishment of a regional division of labour. As noted earlier, Japan has long been interested in fostering regionalized production as a means to preserve its international competitiveness. Since the 1950s the Japanese government has provided financial assistance for private-sector FDI in East Asia, in part to secure natural resources for manufacturing. Since the 1970s and the first upward realignment of the value of the yen, FDI has been directed increasingly to promote the movement offshore of heavy industries facing increasing domestic labour and environmental costs.[2] Similarly, the Plaza Accord, yen appreciation, and the surge in outflows of FDI, although presenting concerns about the 'hollowing out' of Japanese industry, came to be viewed as an opportunity to organize regional production in a such a way that Japanese industry could maintain its international competitiveness and high-value exports, while the development of the East Asian states would be assured through their engagement in lower-end production activities complementary with those of Japan.

Japan's best-known plan for the organization of regional production to mediate the impact of globalization is that of the 'flying geese model' and its variant of 'production cycles'.[3] According to these models, as championed by METI in the late

1980s, the appreciation of the yen and rising labour costs in Japan should have been expected to lead to the transfer of technology and older exporting industries from Japan to East Asia. The East Asian states were then to use these investments and technologies to produce for export to Japan and other regions, and in turn to move up the production cycle in Japan's wake. The patterns of Japanese FDI and regional production post-Plaza Accord and in the early 1990s appeared to support the predictions of this model. Japan's FDI concentration shifted in succession from the four newly industrialized economies of Taiwan, South Korea, Hong Kong, and Singapore (the NIES-4) to the ASEAN-4 (Thailand, Indonesia, Malaysia, and the Philippines) and then to China, and this was seemingly mirrored by the successive entry of these states into ever higher echelons of the production ladder in products such as textiles, chemicals, consumer electronics, and automobiles. Meanwhile, in line with this model Japan was thought to remain the 'lead goose', passing down uncompetitive industries while remaining at the highest value end of the production chain. The implication of the model was thus that Japan was able to counter the effects of globalization on its domestic economy by creating a regional division of labour that simultaneously preserved the international competitiveness of Japanese industry and delivered orderly development to the East Asian states.

Japan's views of regionalization and the establishment of a vertical regional division of labour as the key to reducing the impact of globalization were further revealed by METI's New Aid Plan. This purveyed the vision of an integrated regional production order centred on Japan, and with Japan allocating to individual East Asian states the industrial sectors in which they should seek to develop and to supply products to complement Japanese industry.

Japan's flying geese model as a depiction of the division of labour in East Asia has been heavily criticized. In many ways, it is seen as a type of Japanese propaganda designed to reinforce the impression that Japan will perpetually remain at the top of the production ladder and other states must inevitably follow its leadership. Just as importantly, this model has been challenged by a 'complex production' links model that contends that even though the transfer of production technology may take place between Japan and East Asia, the cost of industry start-ups and the difficulty of mastering new technologies are so great that these countries ultimately remain dependent on Japanese technology and cannot close the production cycle to create their own fully fledged industries.[4] Instead, according to this model, Japan has put in place in East Asia a system of hierarchical complex production links that are connected vertically backward to Japan due to the dependence on exports of Japanese technology, and vertically forward to the United States due to its continuing position as the main extra-regional and most valuable export market for East Asian manufactures.[5] In accordance with this view, much of the intra-regional investment and trade within East Asia can actually be accounted for not by independent trade between individual states in finished products in which they enjoy a comparative advantage, but by trade controlled by or linked to Japanese subsidiaries based in East Asia and consisting of products such as components for eventual assembly in Japanese-made manufactures, which are then exported to other regions. Thus, the implication of these criticisms of the flying geese model is that it does not deliver complete economic development to those East Asian states to which it is directed.

The complex production model is perhaps a more accurate depiction of Japan's reaction to the onset of globalization in East Asia since the mid-1980s than the flying geese model. It might be argued that the complex production model is somewhat static in its analysis of the regional division of labour and that there is increasing evidence of the genuine diffusion of Japanese technology to production bases in East Asia that may enable the eventual closing of production cycles. Nevertheless, the model is perceptive in pointing out that even though Japanese policy has assisted in the creation of a vertical division of labour that promoted regional integration and functioned to insulate Japan's domestic economy, this has not always worked to the full advantage of the development strategies of the East Asian states.

These criticisms appear to have been borne out in part by the East Asian financial crisis. Although the financial crisis gained momentum through the withdrawal of 'hot money' from the region, one of its original triggers was investors' fears that the fundamentals of the newly industrialized economies, and especially the ASEAN states, had deteriorated due to a declining ability to maintain export competitiveness. The NIEs faced increasing competition from Japanese products in higher-value exports, while the ASEAN states at the lower and middle echelons of the production ladder faced the rapidly rising mega-competitor of China, which was taking increasing shares of external technology and industrial investment previously channelled towards ASEAN.[6]

Hence, Japan's promotion of a regional division of labour did not appear to have been successful in delivering the orderly pattern of growth to East Asia that the flying geese model suggested. Instead, the regional states, and in particular the ASEAN states, found themselves squeezed between Japanese and Chinese competition and, lacking any insulation of their own, fully exposed to the competitive pressures of globalization that threatened to undermine their developmental strategies.

Japan's subsequent reaction in the wake of the financial crisis has been to acknowledge certain defects in the execution of its original plans for the regional division of labour. Nevertheless, the thrust of its policy has been to preserve the basic model for regional production and at the same time to instigate modifications that not only continue to ensure the insulation of Japan's domestic economy but also offer a degree of greater insulation from globalization for the developmental states of the region.

Japan has been forced to accept that China's potential as a site for offshore production, reverse imports, and export to third countries means that it can no longer be placed at the bottom of a regional division of labour. Japanese policy has thus become increasingly oriented to supporting growing economic complementarities between Japan and China and to supporting the necessary vertical movement of China up the production chain. Indeed, Japanese policy now acknowledges that there may be increasing horizontal competition between Japan and China in certain products. At same time, though, as Japan is prepared to accept the reality of China's growing presence within the regional production order, it has seen the need to temper this with renewed efforts to strengthen ASEAN's role. Japan, aware of the criticisms that insufficient technology transfer may have undercut the regional and global competitiveness prior to the financial crisis, has since laid out a series of ODA packages designed to boost the technology and management skills within the ASEAN states. Japanese support has taken the form of aid for individual states, as well as for initiatives to close the development gap within ASEAN, such as the ASEAN's 2020 Vision and the Mekong Delta Development Plan. Similarly, Japan has also been highly supportive of ASEAN's attempts to further economic integration through the ASEAN Free Trade Area (AFTA) process, viewing this as a means for ASEAN to counter the competitive pressures of globalization. Just as importantly, AFTA is also seen to provide Japanese industry with an important sub-regional production base, especially for the sourcing of components, which can balance against the rising strength of China and further maintain Japan's international competitiveness.[7]

Finally, Japan's continued ambition to orchestrate the regionalization of production in order to mitigate the impact of globalization on itself and on the developmental states of East Asia is revealed by its current FTA strategy. Japan's motivations for the pursuit of bilateral and multilateral FTAS with the states of East Asia are complex and various. Japan signed its first FTA with Singapore in the form of the Japan–Singapore Economic Partnership Agreement (JSEPA) in 2002 and is currently engaged in negotiations or the study of FTAS with Thailand, the Philippines, Malaysia, Vietnam, and South Korea. Added to this, Japan's hope is to convert these bilateral agreements into a full-scale multilateral Japan–ASEAN FTA and Comprehensive Economic Partnership (CEP).

In part, the trade liberalization aspects of the FTAs, although meeting with strong opposition from sections of the domestic economy, especially agriculture, are designed by METI to open Japan selectively to greater competition and to force restructuring as a jolt towards domestic recovery.[8] However, liberalization in itself is clearly not the final or the main objective of Japan's FTA strategy. The liberalization measures inherent to the FTAs are just one component of a broader strategy to consolidate the regional division of labour. Japan's FTA arrangements are notable in that they are designed to be subsumed into wider comprehensive economic agreements that include not just trade liberalization but also 'industrial harmonization' among Japan and East Asian partners, including areas such as sharing information on financial flows, human resources, information technology, and the provision of technical assistance to small and medium-sized enterprises.[9] In essence, therefore, Japan sees trade liberalization and the FTAs within the CEP as a means of lowering barriers to trade among Japan and ASEAN members. The lowering of barriers, it is believed, will complement and eventually go beyond AFTA's existing efforts and, combined with measures for industrial harmonization, will reinforce existing strategies to foster ASEAN as a production base for Japanese industry. Consequently, Japan is not suddenly acting as a convert to wholesale liberalization in the pursuit of FTAs, but (following on from its approach to Asia-Pacific Economic Co-operation [APEC], which was concerned more with aid and development co-operation than trade liberalization per se) is once again implementing policies of managed liberalization and transnational production in order to promote development, maintain the regional division of labour, and insulate its economy.[10]

Japan and Financial and Monetary Co-operation in East Asia

Japan's ambitions for organizing the East Asian regional economy also experienced major shocks in the aftermath of the 1997–8 crisis. As is now well known, Japan attempted a regional response to the financial crisis in the shape of proposals in the autumn of 1997 for a US$100 billion Asian Monetary Fund (AMF). However, the initiative foundered due to a lack of sufficient preparation and political will by Japan and opposition from the United States, which feared that the AMF would undermine IMF (International Monetary Fund) conditionality, as well as opposition from China, which was anxious not to allow Japan to exercise overt leadership in the region. In turn, the failure of Japan's AMF initiative contributed to the necessity of the states of the region to accept IMF intervention and thus the start of the dismantlement of the developmental state model in East Asia. Moreover, as already noted, Japan's financial sector, despite its vast size, was shaken by the escalation of the crisis in late 1997. Hence, Japanese policy-makers became aware that Japan's domestic economy was neither invulnerable to the direct impact of the financial crisis and globalization, nor was it invulnerable to the indirect impact of the globalized finance via the havoc wrought on the East Asian economy and the downturn in the prospects of many key trading and production partners.

Japan's subsequent response in the wake of the crisis, in a similar fashion to the production sphere but starting from a shorter history and lower basis of co-operation, has been to sponsor the creation of regional structures to insulate its own financial sector and those of the developmental states of East Asia. The essence of Japan's strategy yet again has been not to attempt to close off the region to globalized finance. Instead, it has sought to establish organizations and other mechanisms that can mediate the worst excesses of unconstrained financial flows, while attempting to accrue the maximum benefits from access to global capital in order to boost Japanese and regional growth.

Japan thus followed up its aborted AMF proposal with the New Miyazawa Initiative in October 1998, a US$30 billion program designed to dispense funds bilaterally to East Asian states to assist them to strengthen their financial systems to cope with the fallout of the crisis. Japan disbursed via the Japan Bank for International Cooperation a total of US$3 billon to Indonesia, US$2.5billion to the Philippines, US$3 billion to Thailand, US$4.4 billion to Malaysia, and US$8 billion to South Korea.[11] These funds were used to guarantee sovereign bonds issued by the East Asian states, which could then be used to recapitalize ailing banks and corporations in the region. It is notable that these funds were offered on softer conditionality than the IMF programs, and the clear intention of the New Miyazawa Initiative was not to seek massive structural reforms in line with the IMF, but to seek to give the East Asian states the necessary breathing space to reorganize their export and investment policies so that a revamped development model could be relaunched. Indeed, it is striking that one of the largest beneficiaries of the New Miyazawa Initiative was Malaysia, which had refused IMF intervention and implemented economic stimulus measures that were exactly the opposite of IMF policy prescriptions in other East Asian states. Hence, Japan's strategy in the late 1990s was clearly to use its financial and ODA resources to enable the East Asian states to insulate themselves from the effects of the crisis.

In the period following the worst impact of the crisis, Japan's insulation strategy has further developed to include not only immediate crisis prevention measures, but also measures to strengthen long-term regional financial and monetary co-operation that should contribute to mitigating the future impact of globalization on developmentalism. Japan's first area of concentration has been to build on the start made by the New Miyazawa Initiative and to foster the creation of a regional liquidity fund. Japan has provided financial support and technical knowledge for the establishment since 2001 of the Chiang Mai Initiative. This is a region-wide bilateral currency swap facility within the framework of the ASEAN + 3, which is designed to fight off future financial crises in the region. At present the Chiang Mai Initiative remains small in scale, with the swap agreements on average only around US$1–$3 billion (although each of Japan's individual bilateral agreements tops US$3 billion and in the case of South Korea is US$7 billion); reliant on bilateral agreements for its operation; and linked to IMF conditionalities, as the region

lacks an effective surveillance mechanism to ensure the correct usage of funds dispensed.[12] Nevertheless, it does represent an important step forward in attempts at regional self-help in the financial sphere and to lessen the grip of the IMF and neo-liberalism on the developmental policies of the East Asian states. Moreover, many observers see the Chiang Mai Initiative as a step towards eventually achieving by an alternative route the establishment of some form of AMF-type organization in the future. Japan's instrumental role in supporting the Chiang Mai Initiative thus shows that it is quietly reversing some of the inroads of untrammelled globalization in the East Asia region.

Japan's second area of concentration in the financial sphere has been investigating the establishment of a common currency arrangement, especially one that may provide a major role for the internationalization of the yen. Japanese policymakers have in large part attributed the financial vulnerability of the East Asian states to their usage of the US dollar as the principal unit of exchange for trade and investment, which thus exposes their level of international competitiveness to fluctuations in the value of the dollar. Japan's government has argued that it would be more beneficial for the East Asian states to use a basket of currencies or Asian Currency Unit, including possibly the dollar, the euro, and the yen, to level out exchange rate fluctuations and the impact on their international competitiveness.[13] Japan has consequently provided technical assistance for the study of these proposals within the APT framework and the Asia–Europe Meeting.

Japan's efforts to create a regional common currency arrangement and to internationalize the yen carry clear potential benefits for the region to reduce its exposure to global currency fluctuations. At the same time, they offer a potentially valuable insulation for Japan's domestic economy. Japan is also hit by currency fluctuations that affect its ability to source components at stable prices within the region and impact on its international competitiveness. The internationalization of the yen would provide a more stable trade and investment environment in East Asia for Japan to maintain its competitiveness.[14] In addition, the greater use of the yen in East Asia would enable Japan to extend its capital markets into the region and enable it to procure at a reduced exchange rate the finance necessary to fund its government debt and the slow reform of its domestic banking sector; although this could also carry the risk of exposing Japan's previously largely closed financial markets to external pressures.[15] Hence, once again, regionalization is seen as a way by Japan's policy-makers to counter the effects of globalization.

The third area of Japan's concentration on regional financial co-operation is linked to the second, and aims to assist the development of a common bond market in East Asia. Japanese analyses of the causes of the crisis often fix upon the dependence of the East Asian states on extra-regional loans and 'hot money' as engendering a high degree of vulnerability to global finance. Japan's policy has been to support investigation within the APT and through bodies such as the Executives' Meeting of East Asia-Pacific Central Banks of the development of a regional bond market, which will tap the massive savings resources of the region and wean the states of the region off this external dependence.[16] As noted above, Japan favours greater usage of East Asian funds in order to insulate both the regional states and itself from the pressures of globalization.

Conclusion

Although globalization may have strong convergence tendencies in regard to Japan and the East Asia region and has placed increasing pressure on the developmental state model, Japan is not prepared to abandon the model or to allow its economic leadership in East Asia to be challenged without considerable resistance. Japanese government resistance has been selective and has not taken the form of attempts to create a closed domestic economy or region in the face of globalization. Instead, it has endeavoured to manage and channel globalization in such a way that what are seen as its negative aspects are to some degree dissipated, and its positive aspects are turned to the benefit of the developmental strategies of Japan and the East Asian states. Japan has pursued this strategy of permeable insulation for the management of globalization through formally instituted and informal regionalization. Japanese government plans for the regional division of labour have been designed to maintain Japan's international competitiveness through the exploitation of low-cost production and trading platforms in East Asia. Increasingly, however, Japan's plans are now also designed to assist the insulation of the East Asian states themselves, in order to add a double layer of insulation for Japan's economy. Meanwhile, Japanese government plans in the financial sphere have focused on the creation of a liquidity fund, a common currency arrangement, and regional bond market that can assist the region to fend off the risks involved with the globalization of finance and further cushion Japan's own economy.

Hence, even if the pressure from globalization for convergence appears increasingly relentless in East Asia, its progress is certainly not being facilitated by any absence of Japanese attempts to mount a regional resistance to it. Indeed, it is still possible that its progress may be further slowed. Japan's gradual recovery from 2003 onward and the renewed growth of many of the states in the region since the end of the 1990s suggest that the developmental model is certainly not yet down and out.

As noted at the beginning of this chapter, my purpose has not been to make firm predictions about the likely success of Japanese strategy over the long term. However, it is clear at this stage that if Japan is to attempt to continue to resuscitate the developmental model it will need to grapple with a range of problems that may form the key to any future success. The first issue that Japan may have to address is how far it is willing to bear the costs of supporting a developmental state model into the future. As is well known, Japanese and East Asian economic growth in the past was in large part made possible by the willingness of the United States to open its markets to the region's manufactured goods as part of its program to sponsor friendly capitalist regimes during the Cold War. In the post-Cold War era the United States still demonstrates a continued, if declining, willingness to maintain market access, and one of the primary factors in explaining the recovery of the East Asian states after the financial crisis has been their ability to export to the US market. However, as the American trade deficits with Japan, East Asia, and particularly China continue to mount in the next few years, that country's commitment to market access and thus the sustainability of the developmental model will increasingly come into question. In this instance, it will be up to Japan to decide whether it will take up the mantle of the United States and be prepared to act as the market of last resort. At present its trade with East Asia is expanding, but much of this is still intra-firm trade among Japanese subsidiaries located in the region. Japan is yet to convert itself into a true consumer of East Asian manufactures and thus a principal support of the export-led developmental state model. If Japan does not develop consumption power to complement its existing production power in the region, then globalization and neo-liberal capitalism may further wrest control of the East Asian economy.

Likewise, Japan's FTA strategy in terms of its trade liberalization aspects may also prove problematic for sustaining the developmental state in the region and insulating its own economy. Japan's predilection for first tackling bilateral FTAs before achieving multilateral FTAs may backfire. Its negotiation of individual FTAs with each partner in the region, designed to protect different domestic interests within Japan, necessarily sets up added obstacles to extending these agreements across the region multilaterally. Moreover, protectionist agricultural interests in Japan may yet hamstring the progress of FTAs. Hence, the effect may be more to encumber Japan's corporations in their search for production platforms and international competitiveness, rather than to facilitate their operations.

Finally, Japan needs to face more directly the challenge of China. Japan–China economic complementarities mean that these two economies will increasingly become locked together, with benefits for both. Indeed, recent trade friction, in part resulting from the success of reverse imports to Japan by Japanese firms manufacturing in China, should be taken as a sign of the growing forces for interdependence among them. Nevertheless, Japan will need to accept that China is unlikely to remain subordinate to Japan in many economic sectors in the regional division of labour and that it will have to find new concepts of regional organization to account for this. Furthermore, Japan will face increasing political competition from China with regard to the creation of bilateral and region-wide FTAS and financial co-operation. Japan is already perceived to be lagging behind China in the drive for liberalization in the region, and China maintains a de facto veto on the greater use of the yen in the region for fear that this could create a yen bloc. In addition, China's yuan over the longer term could threaten the place of the yen as the likely unit of common currency to substitute for the dollar. Hence, Japan's attempts to organize the region and to insulate its own economy could yet be frustrated by China. The important hope must be that Japan and China will actually step up their joint co-operation to avoid unnecessary rivalry in the region and to pool their resources so as to mitigate the impact of globalization on East Asia's developmental aspirations.

Notes

1. Ulrike Schaede and William Grimes, 'Introduction: The Emergence of Permeable Insulation', in Schaede and Grimes, *Japan's Managed Globalization: Adapting to the Twenty-First Century* (New York: M.E. Sharpe, 2003), 6–8.

2. Mireya Solís, 'Adjustment Through Globalisation: The Role of State FDI Finance', in Schaede and Grimes, *Japan's Managed Globalization*, 103–6.

3. For an influential academic discussion of the

production cycles variant of the flying geese model, see Bruce Cumings, 'The Origins and Development of the Northeast Asian Political Economy: Industrial Sectors, Product Cycles and Political Consequences', *International Organization* 38, 10 (1984): 1–40.

4. Bernard Mitchell and John Ravenhill, 'Beyond Product Cycles and Flying Geese: Regionalization, Hierarchy and the Industrialization of East Asia', *World Politics* 47, 2 (1995): 171–209.

5. Walter Hatch and Kōzō Yamamura, *Asia in Japan's Embrace: Building a Regional Production Alliance* (Cambridge: Cambridge University Press, 1996).

6. Christopher W. Hughes, 'Japanese Policy and the East Asian Currency Crisis: Abject Defeat or Quiet Victory?', *Review of International Political Economy* 7, 2 (Summer 2000): 235.

7. METI, *Tsūshō Hakusho 2003* (White Paper on International Trade) (Tokyo, 2003), 186–7.

8. Munakata Naoko, 'Nihon no FTA Senryaku' (Japan's FTA Strategy), in Soeya Yoshihide and Todoroko Masayuki, eds, *Gendai Ajia to Nihon 1: Nihon no Higashi Ajia Koso* (Japan and Contemporary Asia 1: Japan's Vision of East Asia) (Tokyo: Keiō Gijuku Daigaku Shuppankai,

2004), 153–6.

9. Urata Shuichiro, 'Nihon–Shingaporu Shinjidai Keizai Renkei Kyotei' (Japan–Singapore Economic Partnership Agreement for a New Age), in Urata Shuichiro, ed., *Nihon no FTA Senryaku* (Japan's FTA Strategy) (Tokyo: Nihon Keizai Shimbunsha, 2004), 81–6.

10. John Ravenhill, *APEC and the Construction of Pacific Rim Regionalism* (Cambridge: Cambridge University Press, 2001).

11. Todokoro Masayuki, 'Ajia ni okeru Chiki Tsuka Kyoryoku no Tenkai' (Regional Monetary Cooperation in Asia), in Soeya and Totoroko, eds, *Gendai Ajia to Nihon 1*, 119.

12. Ibid., 120.

13. METI, *Tsūshō Hakusho 2003*, 180.

14. William Grimes, 'Internationalization as Insulation: Dilemmas of the Yen', in Schaede and Grimes, *Japan's Managed Globalization*, 56.

15. Nobuhiro Hiwatari, 'Embedded Policy Preferences and the Formation of International Arrangements after the Asian Financial Crisis', *Pacific Review* 16, 3 (2003): 331-60.

16. METI, *Tsūshō Hakusho 2003*, 178-9.

Suggested Readings

Hatch, Walter, and Kozo Yamamura. *Asia in Japan's Embrace: Building a Regional Production Alliance.* Cambridge: Cambridge University Press, 1996.

Katzenstein, Peter, and Takashi Shiraishi. *Network Power: Japan and East Asia.* Ithaca, NY: Cornell University Press, 1997.

Krauss, Ellis S., and T.J. Pempel. *Beyond Bilateralism: US–Japan Relations in the New Asia-Pacific.* Stanford, Calif.: Stanford University Press, 2004.

Schaede, Ulrike, and William Grimes. *Japan's Managed Globalization: Adapting to the Twenty-First Century.* New York: M.E. Sharpe, 2003.

Web Sites

Japan Information Access Project: www.jiaponline.org/
Japan Policy Research Institute: www.jpri.org

Ministry of Economy, Trade and Industry: www.meti.go.jp/english/
Ministry of Finance: www.mof.go.jp/english/

Chapter 34

China and the Political Economy of Global Engagement

Shaun Breslin

Not that long ago China was all but irrelevant to the functioning of the global political economy. Although China emerged from the relative isolation and autarky of the Maoist period with the assumption of de facto power by Deng Xiaoping in 1978, it was not until 1993 that China really became a significant entity in terms of global trade and foreign direct investment (FDI) flows.

How times change. By the end of 2003, official Chinese figures showed that the Chinese economy reached US$1.4 trillion, making it the sixth biggest economy in the world.[1] It had foreign currency reserves of US$403.3 billion, second only to Japan, and was the fourth biggest exporter in the world with a foreign trade surplus of at least US$26 billion. In 2002, China surpassed the United States for the first time as the world's largest recipient of non-stocks and shares FDI, with actual FDI in 2003 standing at US$53.5 billion.

In an era when it is often difficult to find toys, clothing, and computer-related equipment that do not bear the 'Made in China' stamp, it is worth remembering that China is a relative newcomer to the global economy. And despite China's current international economic profile, it has not always been an easy task to convince everybody in China of the wisdom of a policy of economic engagement, or what the Chinese refer to as 'economic opening' (jingji kaifang). By and large, the Chinese economy under Mao Zedong looked to itself to provide for itself, and viewed the capitalist global economy with not so much suspicion as outright hatred. The first step in changing this perception came in 1978,

when Deng Xiaoping relegated class struggle and the advancement of Communism to the Chinese Communist Party's (CCP) secondary task behind the goal of economic development. At this stage, ideologically and perhaps psychologically, many in the Chinese leadership were not yet ready for a full insertion into the capitalist global economy. As such, four Special Economic Zones (SEZs) were established with special rights to conduct international economic relations at Zhuhai, Shantou, and Shenzhen in Guangdong province and Xiamen in Fujian. When Hainan Island was later separated from Guangdong to become a province in its own right, it was established as the fifth SEZ. If, as some feared, economic contacts would inevitably lead to political contamination through the spread of bourgeois ideas, then this ideological pollution could be strictly contained.

Ideological considerations over the wisdom of insertion into the global economy lost ground once encouraging inward investment proved to be a highly successful means of capital accumulation. Local leaders from other cities lobbied the central leadership to be allowed at least some of the privileges afforded to the SEZs, resulting in a further 14 coastal cities being 'opened' in 1984.[2] Two years later, the central government moved to improve the investment environment to encourage even more capital inflow in what became known as the '22 regulations'. These regulations created a more attractive environment for FDI by reducing fees for labour and rent, providing tax rebates for exporters, and so on. This move considerably increased the attraction of investing in China—particularly investment to produce exports for other markets. While foreign-invested enterprises accounted for only 2 per cent of exports and 6 per cent of imports before 1986, the figure increased to around half of all trade by the end of the century.

In many respects it was not until 1992 that China really began to engage with the global economy in a significant way. In an inspection tour of development in southern China in 1992, Deng Xiaoping praised the emergence of proto-capitalist practices in open areas and called for further opening. Following Deng's exhortations, the CCP declared in October 1992 that China now had a 'socialist market economy'—the ideological battle appeared to have been won, and this victory was given further force when 1993 saw more FDI flood into China than in the preceding 14 years of reform put together. A trade deficit in 1992 was turned into surplus as exports doubled in the space of five years on the back of FDI growth.

Winners and Losers

But if ideology and a resistance to the capitalist international economy were decreasingly significant in policy debates, other more practical considerations continued to have a massive impact on how China was inserted into the international economy. Promoting exporting industries had proved to be a highly successful means of generating growth. Rural reform in China had released excess workers from the land, many of whom found employment in small-scale township and village enterprises (TVEs), which accounted for around a third of all exports in the 1990s. Foreign-invested enterprises (FIEs) also generated new jobs and economic growth without the need to find domestic sources of investment. Chinese economists estimate that every 100 million yuan (US$12.05 million) of exports provides 120,000 jobs—on this basis, over 52 million jobs in 2003 were supported by export-based industries.[3] But the key question for policy-makers was whether domestic producers could compete with imports from more efficient foreign producers if the Chinese market became fully integrated into the global economy.

Thus, a dualistic trade regime was created: on one side, a relatively liberal *internationalized* export system built on supporting exporters and encouraging FDI to produce exports for external markets; on the other, a relatively protected domestic system with domestic producers protected from international competition through high tariffs and quotas, the lack of currency convertibility, state-set exchange rates, and strictly limited external access to domestic financial markets.[4] In its own terms, the strategy was a great success. Domestic producers were freed from the challenges of competition, while exporters were given an advantageous position to develop external markets—not least after the devaluation of the yuan or renminbi (RMB) in 1994 made exporting from China to the West increasingly profitable. Furthermore, the closed nature of the Chinese financial system meant that China was not affected by the financial crises that caused so much damage to other East Asian economies in 1997. As Yu Yongding put it:

> For many years, observers have criticized China's slowness in developing financial markets and liberalizing its capital account. The Chinese government itself was also worried by the slow progress. Rather theatrically, the disadvantage has turned into advantage. Owing to capital controls and the underdevelopment of financial markets and the lack of sophisticated financial instruments, such as stock futures and foreign exchange forwards, RMB escaped the attack by international speculators.[5]

Not surprisingly, the strategy created concern outside of China—particularly as China's trade surplus with the United States and other Western countries continued to grow. This concern was given a political airing every year in the United States prior to the annual vote on whether to allow China normal access to the US market. But while this provided an opportunity for groups to raise objections to China—not just on economic grounds, but more fiercely in calls for trade sanctions unless China improved its human rights regime—the vote always went in China's favour.

Joining the WTO

Given the success, in its own terms, of this policy of engaging while protecting, it was something of a surprise when the Chinese leadership signed a deal with the United States in 1999 that paved the way for entry into the World Trade Organization (WTO) in 2001. Or more correctly, it was a surprise that they agreed to join the WTO on terms that, theoretically at least, should reduce much of the protection previously afforded to domestic producers.

In order to join the WTO, prospective members must gain the acceptance of any existing member that requests a bilateral agreement.[6] In China's case, the most important bilateral partners were the United States and the European Union,[7] and the specific terms of Chinese entry owed much to the criteria that they laid down. But the Chinese authorities did not have to accept these criteria and did not have to join the WTO, so why did they decide to loosen the dualistic trading regime that had apparently served China so well in previous years?

The answer is partially found in the desire to stabilize access to key markets in the West and to avoid the uncertainty created by the annual vote on Chinese trade in the US Congress. It is also partly found in a Chinese desire to shape the future rules of world trade from inside the WTO, as opposed to looking on powerlessly from the outside. But the main explanation is found in the changing conception of some Chinese leaders of what was best for the Chinese economy. For Zhu Rongji, the then Prime Minister, protecting domestic producers from competition was doing nothing to promote greater efficiency and the rationalization of the Chinese economy. Previous attempts at greater domestic reform had met with resistance from domestic actors, mainly but not only at the subnational level, who did not share his vision. Zhu's push for WTO

entry, then, can be seen as representing an ideological acceptance of the efficacy of neo-liberalism as the best way of generating long-term sustainable growth within China. And the most effective way of promoting this approach within China was to use an external agreement to enforce liberalization on reluctant domestic actors.

Joining the WTO did not result in the total liberalization of the economy overnight. In addition to the phasing in over time of a number of the reforms, many of the officials who were sceptical about liberalization before WTO entry are now charged with making the Chinese economy WTO-compliant. Some are concerned about the loss of the 'bureaucratic power base'[8] that would result from implementing WTO criteria, while others are more concerned about the potential impact on rural incomes and urban unemployment. As a result, WTO agreements have been interpreted and implemented in ways that have at times undermined the liberalizing logic of the 2001 WTO agreement.

So we should be wary of assuming that WTO entry has massively reduced the capacity of the Chinese leadership to control China's own economic destiny in the face of WTO-inspired liberalization agendas. But in terms of intention, and partially in execution, joining the WTO marks a key turning point in China's relationship with the global political economy

The Investment-Trade Nexus

One of the most striking features about China's position in the global political economy is the extent to which FDI has contributed to China's economic growth. Cumulative FDI into China since 1978 passed the US$400 billion figures at the start of 2003, with China accounting for around 20 per cent of global FDI in developing countries. Unlike other developing states in East Asia, China has not attracted large amounts of 'hot capital'—not least because of the still relatively closed nature of the Chinese financial sector combined with the lack of currency convertibility—with almost all FDI being in productive capacity.

FDI into China takes two forms—market-accessing investment and investment for export production. The latter dominates FDI into China, accounting for at least two-thirds of all FDI, and FIES account for over half of all Chinese trade. For market-based investors, the main pull is access to a market of over 1.3 billion Chinese consumers. Of course, the reality is that only a small proportion of the Chinese population earn enough money to buy the more expensive goods produced by foreign firms in China. The real market is probably something in the region of 150 million—not inconsiderable in itself—but the future potential market that China might provide is the attraction for many.

Cheap labour remains a dominant reason for export-based investors. For example, wages in the Chinese textile industry are just 4 per cent of comparable Japanese manufacturing wages. The UK shoe manufacturer, Doctor Martens, relocated its production from the UK, where wages were just under US$2,000 a month, to China, where workers get just US$100 a month plus accommodation and work almost 50 per cent longer each week.[9] Even when the cost of transporting raw materials to China and finished goods back to the West are added on, production costs can be massively lowered by shifting manufacturing to China.

But it is not all about cheap labour. As noted above, manipulating exchange rates to keep exports cheap has also attracted FDI. Although this increases the price of imported components used in the production of exports, investors find it relatively easy to negotiate tax rebates and export subsidies as China's numerous local governments and development zones compete with each other to attract investment. Indeed, as China joined the WTO, most imports came into China tariff-free in the form of components that were processed and subsequently re-exported as finished goods.[10] Cheng and Kwan also point to the importance of a physical infrastructure that facilitates the quick and easy flow of components into China and finished goods out.[11] In this respect, the Chinese government (both local and national) has spent huge amounts of money facilitating international economic interaction through the construction of roads and harbours.

It is difficult to overstate the importance of this FDI-export nexus for the Chinese economy. Annual average growth rates of around 8 per cent would have been unattainable; those areas engaged in export production have the highest per capita GNP rates; it has had a positive impact on balance of payments and foreign currency reserves; FDI has created new jobs, upgraded skills, raised factor productivity, increased technology transfer, and encouraged reform of domestic Chinese industries. The investment-trade nexus for overall growth has been most important when what we might call the domestic economy has slowed. The declining profitability of TVEs (over 70 per cent were in debt by 1999) combined with the restructuring of the state-owned sector and an attack on inflation after 1994, resulted in annual negative growth in retail and consumer price indexes between 1998 and 2003. Massive government spending (both through a budget deficit and through directed lending via the banking system) helped maintain overall growth rates, but the major source of growth—and in particular the source of new jobs—during this period was foreign-invested export industries.

The FDI-trade nexus is also important for students of international political economy as it raises a number of critical questions that have relevance not just for the way we think about China but also for how we think about the functioning of the global political economy in general. Given the importance of importing components into FIES to produce goods for export, it is perhaps not surprising that China's coastal provinces with good international transport links account for the vast majority of both FDI and exports. Indeed, China's engagement with the global economy is characterized by a massively uneven spatial distribution. Nearly 90 per cent of cumulative FDI since 1978 has gone to just eight coastal provinces and cities—Guangdong, Shanghai, Jiangsu, Fujian, Shandong, Tianjin, and Liaoning. Guangdong province has been the single biggest recipient, though its share of investment has declined as more FDI has moved to other coastal areas such as Shanghai and Liaoning. There are even large disparities within individual provinces. Over half of all the investment into Liaoning province goes to the city of Dalian, while investment in Guangdong province is concentrated on the area around the Pearl River delta. In terms of exports, these eight coastal provinces account for 95 per cent of the exports of FIEs in China, and the most successful township and village enterprises are also found in the region. Trade dependency (trade as a percentage of GDP) is around 10 per cent in the 19 interior provinces, but nearly 75 per cent on the coast and 356 per cent in Guangdong.[12]

Growth and Development

For many domestic and external observers, rapid growth built on the investment-trade nexus is one of China's most impressive achievements of the post-Mao era. And the good news for proponents of neo-liberalism is that the figures suggest that the most open and liberal areas of China have the fastest growth and most wealth. Nevertheless, there is recognition in China that rapid economic growth can generate significant political problems. For example, there is concern over the consequences of the uneven spatial distribution of growth. Inequality as measured by the gini coefficient has risen dramatically in recent years from 0.288 in 1981 to 0.46 in 2002. China ranks at fifth in the list of most unequal economies, and has recorded the fastest-growing rates of inequality in the world in the last two decades. Of course, not all of this inequality can be put down to engagement with the global economy—the single biggest indicator of how well-off people are in China remains whether they live in and off the countryside or in an urban area. But the uneven impact of China's insertion into the global economy has played its part.

The Chinese government has tasked itself with balancing growth among regions by promoting the development of western China and the old industrial heartlands of state-planned China, which are now commonly referred to as China's 'rust belt'. But the Chinese leadership's ability to control China's own economic destiny is not what it was in the old days when state ownership and state planning dominated. The importance of foreign invest-

ment as a source of capital accumulation means that the investment decisions of foreign companies have a profound impact on what happens in the Chinese economy. The Chinese leadership might want to move the focus of investment to the west and might want to change the nature of economic activity, but the reality of life in the global political economy is that governments alone cannot dictate what is produced, how it is produced, or where it is produced. As Camilleri has argued:

> The greater international division of labour with transnational corporations, evidenced in increasing intra-firm trade and investment flows, shows how the engine of industrial restructuring is increasingly driven by transnational objectives and strategies. . . . States will no doubt continue to perform a number of important administrative and legitimizing functions in the management of economic activity, but their ability to control, let alone plan, the industrial restructuring process is diminishing.[13]

In theoretical terms, we need to consider what we mean by international economic integration. Whether we take geography or economic sectors as the starting point, only parts of China have become integrated into the global economy. And as FIEs in China rely heavily on imported components in the exports from China, there has been a remarkably small footprint or trickle-down from FDI onto other parts of the economy. The value of exports from FIEs actually surpassed the value of their imports for the first time in 1998—though this is a very rough indicator as it includes all imports, not just those used to produce exports. Even since 1998, the value of imports of FIEs has remained at about 98 per cent of the value of exports. If we look at the processing trade alone, then figures from the China Association of Enterprises with Foreign Investment show that imports accounted for 86.5 per cent of the value of FIE processing trade exports in 2000. Imported components are particularly important in high-tech industries. The overwhelming majority of foreign producers in China continue to source their high-tech components overseas, primarily from Southeast Asia, Taiwan, and Japan. As Chinese exports of high-tech goods increased, so, too, did imports of components for high-tech commodities. For example, when the Chinese authorities reported a 58.3 per cent increase in the export of high-tech goods in August 2004, they also announced a 40.7 per cent increase in high-tech imports. While the growth of exports was faster than the growth of imports, the value of exports at US$83.8 billion was still less than the value of imports (mainly integrated circuits and digital-control machine tools) at US$86.46 billion.[14] Thus, in many respects those internationalized parts of China can have more linkages with external economies than with other parts of China itself. As such, we need to consider whether international economic integration can actually generate national economic fragmentation.

A second issue we need to consider is whether growth and development are necessarily the same things. For example, while economic growth has been surging in China, access to decent health, education, and welfare services in large parts of rural China has been declining. Furthermore, if the jobs being created in FIEs largely entail putting together components imported from other countries, where is the development of skills, knowledge, and technology that could create the basis for long-term sustainable economic development? In its extreme form, this can lead to what is termed 'technology-less growth', in that the technology base of the national economy is not advanced as economic growth occurs through the assembly of external productive forces rather than through domestic productive forces. Of course, wholly technology-less growth is a pure type that is not reflected in reality. Participation in the global economy has seen a technological upgrading. But the technological and developmental spillovers of export-oriented growth remain to be attained in many areas.

Many of the jobs that have been created in FIEs are low-skilled and low-paid ones, often or usually employing young women recruited from China's interior. Working hours are long and conditions often or usually are poor, with safety considera-tions ignored in the push to meet deadlines. For the workers, there is not a choice between these jobs and better-paid jobs with better working conditions elsewhere. Lack of training and skills means that the choice is between these jobs or no jobs, with millions of others willing to take up any vacancy. The mobility of international capital also means that investors, if production costs get too high, can easily pack up and move to cheaper sites—in another part of China or in other developing states emphasizing low-cost comparative advantage to attract investment.

Power and Production

Indeed, China has already become a beneficiary of the mobility of international capital. Economic growth is not a zero-sum game. Just because China grows, it does not necessarily mean that other countries suffer. But there is a strong line of thought that suggests that China's growth is detrimental to the economic fortunes of other states. For example, the Japan External Trade Organization found a correlation between the rise of Chinese exports to the United States and Japan of specific goods and the decline in exports of those same goods from Malaysia, Thailand, Indonesia, and the Philippines. Malaysia's Mahathir Mohamad has aired his concern that 'There's not much capital going around. Whatever there is gets sucked in by China',[15] and it has been claimed that 16,000 jobs were lost in Penang alone in 2002 as major high-tech producers move capacity to China.[16] And most analysts suggest that joining the WTO will only increase China's competitive advantage as an export site for investors, particularly in the textiles sector. The potential problem for late-developing states emphasizing low costs as a means of attracting investment to spur export-led growth is that an even later developer with even lower costs might erode their comparative advantage.

Nor is it just other developing states that are concerned about the impact of Chinese growth. As a report from the World Economic Forum noted: 'From Tokyo to Milan, from Mexico City to Chicago, everyone is wondering whether China can continue to grow so fast and how their own jobs and businesses will be affected if it does.'[17] Concern grows in Hong Kong, Japan, and Taiwan that their economies have become 'hollowed out' as the manufacturing bases move to China. And cheap imports from China were largely blamed for the loss of 270,000 US textile and apparel jobs, about a quarter of the workforce in these sectors, in the space of two years.[18]

China's emergence as a major international economic player clearly has massive significance for the global political economy. But we need to take more care when we think about the relationship between significance and power. Economic growth driven by the FDI-trade nexus has provided tax revenues that help fund increased military spending. China's huge foreign currency reserves are also being channelled into buying US treasury bonds, in part at least funding the US budget deficit. And as Williams argues, this gives China a degree of power: 'if push came to shove over, for example, the Taiwan Strait, all Beijing has to do is to mention the possibility of a sell order going down the wires. It would devastate the US economy more than any nuclear strike the Chinese could manage at the moment.'[19]

The Chinese market is important for some producers and will increase in importance in the future. Notwithstanding entry into the WTO, the Chinese authorities still have the power to restrict access to its market. For example, the provision of tax rebates to domestic producers of semiconductors protected Chinese producers from the full impact of international competition (and led to the United States making the first official complaint against Chinese policy to the WTO in 2004). But while it is important for specific producers in specific industries, the Chinese market has nowhere near the same structural power as that of the United States, or even of the EU.

Domestic Chinese companies are also beginning to have an important global role. Lenovo (formerly Legend) is emerging as a power in the domestic computer industry while the Hai'er Group is developing an international profile in white consumer goods, such as kitchen appliances.

China is also becoming increasingly important in outward investment to other economies—primarily in East and West Asia. Outward investment may only have been just over US$2 billion in 2003, but the trend is ever upward.

But for the time being at least, much of China's international economic presence remains dependent on external factors. On one level, it depends on continued demand in the major markets of the West. Interpreting direction of trade figures from China can be difficult due to the large amounts of exports to Hong Kong that are subsequently re-exported to third countries. But we can roughly calculate that two-thirds of all exports from China finally end up in the US, Japan, or the EU. On another level, it largely depends on investment decisions made by foreign companies to fuel its export growth. If we add domestic Chinese producers who produce under contract for export using imported foreign components with the exports of FIEs, then we can suggest that at least 60 per cent of Chinese exports are produced by or for external companies. And although first impressions suggest that investment from the rest of East Asia primarily drives China's export growth, a closer examination reveals the importance of non-regional actors and interests.

Foreign Indirect Investment

FDI from 'developed' states into China has increased in recent years, not least as a result of increased market access in the wake of China's WTO entry. Nevertheless, a dominant theme throughout the literature on FDI in China is the significance of investment that comes from the rest of Asia in general and from 'Chinese Asia' in particular. Houde and Lee calculate that between 1993 and 1998, Hong Kong provided over half of all investment into China, Taiwan nearly 8 per cent, and Singapore around 4.5 per cent.[20] Similarly, Charles Wolf calculates that 'two-thirds [of all investment has] come from "overseas" Chinese, especially overseas Chinese in Taiwan, Hong Kong, and Southeast Asia.'[21] If we add investment from Japan, then the figure for Asia as a whole rises to nearly 80 per cent, with Europe and North America each accounting for between 7 and 9 per cent depending on which figures are used.

Some care is necessary when interpreting these statistics. Probably around a quarter of all investment into China originates from China itself and is routed through Hong Kong to take advantage of the special incentives afforded to foreign investors. And in recent years we have seen an extraordinary rise of investment from the British Virgin Islands (now the second biggest source of FDI in China), the Cayman Islands, and Bermuda. Available evidence suggests that this is predominantly a result of Taiwanese and Hong Kong companies incorporating in these tax havens.

Not surprisingly, the extent of Asian investment in China, combined with the concomitant trade flows, has led many to focus on intra-Asian economic regionalization as a new driving force in the global political economy. For example, one strand in the literature emphasizes the importance of links between expatriate Chinese businesses in the Chinese diaspora and investment into China. This literature concentrates on the 'bamboo networks'[22] that link Chinese family businesses to China's growing international economic relations. The emphasis here is on cultural ties between ethnic Chinese across Asia and the Chinese 'homeland'—ties of loyalty and trust, cultural understanding, common language, and also closer ties with government officials than those afforded to non-Chinese.

Another strand in the literature emphasizes the emergence of an integrated economy spanning a 'Greater China' economic space that includes the national boundaries of 'Chinese' territories—Macao, Hong Kong, Taiwan, and the People's Republic of China. The term 'Greater China' remains a contested one with no clearly accepted understanding. Not least, there is the question of whether this integrated economy includes all of China or just those coastal provinces that dominate China's international economic relations. Even then, some argue that the low level of economic interaction between

China's 'internationalized' provinces suggests that there is not a single region[23] but a number of overlapping sub- or micro-regions.

It is for this reason that Naughton's framework provides the most efficacious understanding of Greater China—primarily because he eschews a definitive definition and instead deploys a fluid multi-level approach.[24] At the lowest level, there is a Greater China circle that covers the most intense level of integration—that between Hong Kong and the Pearl River delta of Guangdong. The second level of integration covers the most internationalized provinces of China (Guangdong and Fujian), Hong Kong, and Taiwan. The highest level circle, which has yet to see full integration, could comprise the three Chinese economies in total, that is, all of China as well as Hong Kong and Taiwan.

While it is right and important to consider these regional processes and their implications for national politics, there is a danger that the emphasis on regional processes misses the salience of extra-regional actors. In particular, we need to consider the way that companies in Hong Kong, Singapore, and Taiwan play the role of intermediaries between China and the global political economy, suggesting that processes of regionalization are themselves often dependent on global processes. If we think about the way that production of individual goods has become increasingly internationally fragmented in production networks, then we can find evidence to suggest that non-Asian economic interests have played a much bigger role in the Chinese economy—particularly in the last few years—than studying bilateral trade and investment figures will ever be able to reveal.

On a very basic level, international companies have long been routing their investment into China through subsidiary offices in Hong Kong. The use of subsidiaries in Hong Kong is a particularly important element in Japanese investment in southern China. Although sorting through the statistics is an inexact science, Matsuzaki has estimated that about 80 per cent of Japanese FDI in Hong

Kong is subsequently reinvested in Guangdong province alone, showing up on the FDI statistics as investment from Hong Kong.[25]

We should also consider the importance of original equipment manufacturing (OEM)—a system where companies produce goods under licence deals with other companies. The best and most important example is in the Taiwanese computer industry. Around 70 per cent of all computer-related goods produced by Taiwanese firms are based on OEM contracts with foreign firms—primarily from the United States and Japan.[26] Most significantly for the discussion here, Taiwanese computer companies have embraced this changing manufacturing structure and located themselves as key links in the production chain. At a 'higher' level, they sign OEM agreements to produce computers using foreign technology and operating platforms. At a 'lower' level, they have outsourced the low-tech and low value-added elements of production to China to maintain cost efficiency.[27]

Such OEM-based investment from Taiwanese companies in the computer industry is now a major source of Taiwanese investment in China. Indeed, nearly three-quarters of China's computer-related products are produced by Taiwanese companies, which are themselves dependent on OEM contracts with Japanese and US companies.[28] As such, the regional economic integration taking place across national borders in Greater China is the end stage of a production process that spans the most industrialized global economies such as the United States and Japan, intermediate states such as Taiwan, and developing states like China.

Another increasingly important source of FDI into China is subcontracted investment. Here, third-country investors do not invest in China either directly or through regional offices, but instead subcontract production to investment companies within the East Asia region itself. In these cases, investment figures for China will show a transfer from the intermediary company's country and not from the original investor country. A second type of subcontracting is where the third-country company subcontracts to a regional intermediary, which then produces in China on a contract basis. In these cases, no investment will be recorded as the transactions are on a processing fee basis, even further disguising the original investors' involvement in the Chinese economy. Such investment has been a major element in Western companies' involvement in China in textiles, clothing and shoes, toys, and more recently, electronics. For example, the Pou-Chen company in Taiwan produces about one in seven of the world's sport shoes in its factories in China (and now Vietnam) on contracts with foreign companies—Nike, Reebok, New Balance, Adidas, Timberland, Asics, Puma, Hi-Tec, Lotto, LA Gear, Mitre, and so on. FDI figures for China will show another Taiwanese project, but the real originators of this investment are located elsewhere.

Major investment companies such as the Swire Group and the Jardine Matheson Group have long acted as intermediaries between China and the global economy. Perhaps less well known are the plethora of Hong Kong-owned companies such as Li and Fung, which act as intermediaries in the global supply chain. More recently, Taiwanese companies have also developed such an intermediary role in accessing China through companies such as Pou-Chen, BenQ, and Hon Hai Precision Industry.[29]

There are four main reasons why these intermediary companies have established themselves as a link between foreign producers and China. First, Rodrik has noted a tendency to subcontract to countries with poor labour standards rather than invest there directly.[30] This assertion is supported by interviews with what must remain an unnamed intermediary company in Hong Kong. Certain US-based companies, which again must remain unnamed, use subcontracting through Hong Kong because they fear that being associated with sweatshop production would severely damage their image (and therefore sales) at home.

Second, the intermediary companies market themselves as matchmakers with specialist expertise and specialist knowledge of China—

technical, cultural, and linguistic. Third, the contract manufacturers have established reputations as reliable partners and are seen as more reliable than Chinese producers. They can manage the entire production process from sourcing raw materials to the delivery of finished goods on time and at good quality. Fourth, subcontracting production means that multinational producers do not need to employ their own workforce, pay them pensions, and keep them on when economic times get hard. Brand-name producers can simply increase or decrease their orders to contractors as the market demands.

Many of the world's leading brand-name producers simply do not produce anything themselves any more. The headquarters company concentrates on establishing the brand name, marketing, and advertising while devolving the actual production process to reliable subcontractors. And while it has long been a feature of the production of toys, textiles, and clothing, it is now also 'one of the fastest growing segments in the IT [information technology] industry'.[31] In the IT industry, five major contracting companies of North American origin now play a pivotal role in the production of consumer electronics—Solectron, Flextronics, SCI, and Jabil Circuits from the United States and Celestica from Canada.[32]

As China has become the 'world's outsourcer of first resort',[33] it has become engaged in this global division of production—typically at the low-tech and low value-added processing stage. Singapore Flextronics, for example, invests in China on behalf of Microsoft, Motorola, Dell, Palm, and Sony Erickson. In all these cases, the 'Made in China' brand will appear on the product—a product that carries a non-Chinese brand name—but the investment and trade figures will show inter-Asian trade and investment.

Regional economic integration is taking place but is more dependent on actors and interests from outside the region than the statistics initially suggest. Similarly, the Chinese economy is clearly becoming more important for the global political economy—but again, Chinese economic growth,

and export growth in particular, is more reliant on extra-regional actors than appears at first sight. The prima facie evidence suggests that US companies have been much more engaged with the Chinese economy than the investment and trade figures suggest, albeit through third-party actors. The evidence also suggests that Japanese companies have been even more important than previous studies have indicated. If you want to test this idea, check clothing, electronics, and so on and see where they are made. If they say 'Made in China', look at the brand name and think what country you identify that brand name with. If you are surprised that you have a Chinese product, it's because you were buying the item based on its brand name, not its nationality.

But how can we really identify the nationality of a specific product? If a plastic toy says 'Made in China', but it is produced for a US company by a Taiwanese contractor using imported raw materials from the Middle East and Japan, can we really say that it is Chinese? If we buy a computer with an American brand name using Taiwanese components sourced through a company in Singapore and assembled in China, what is its nationality? So perhaps it is wrong to ask if China—or the United States or Japan—has economic power. Instead, we might consider how transnational production networks spanning different political boundaries provide another denationalized source of power in the global political economy.

Competition from China might indeed have led to the loss of jobs in the United States in some areas. But some US-based companies are reaping the rewards of China's growth through lower costs and increased profits. So, too, are the individuals and investment companies that own shares in these companies. Some Japanese workers have been losing their jobs as production (particularly in the textiles and apparel industries) moves to China, but Japanese companies have maintained and increased their profits by outsourcing production to China—often through intermediary companies in Taiwan and Hong Kong—and Japanese consumers are reaping the benefits through cheaper prices. Focusing on the nation-state as the unit of analysis when it comes to considering economic competition—and who wins and who loses— misses the point. It depends on which groups you are looking at within individual nation-states.

Conclusion

The above analysis suggests that while China is clearly important for the global political economy, we need to be careful not to equate importance and significance with power. China's insertion into the global political economy could not have occurred without the actions of Chinese government officials at both the national and local levels. But how this insertion has evolved owes as much to the interests and actions of external non-state actors as it does to the decisions and policies of Chinese state elites.

The speed at which China has changed over the last two decades has at times been bewildering. Even if the pace of change slows, we have to be aware that the China of tomorrow will be very different from the China of today. For the time being, Chinese economic growth is heavily unbalanced in terms of the dependence on exports as an engine of growth and in terms of the distribution of the benefits of this growth within China. Developing the domestic economy as a market for itself would reduce the dependency on external factors for economic growth. It might also reduce regional inequalities—although the evidence to date is that the new middle class with disposable income and materialistic aspirations disproportionately live in the cities in eastern China.

For the time being, Chinese export industries typically occupy labour-intensive low value-added stages of global production processes. Other countries in East Asia previously emphasized low value-added production, but subsequently developed domestic industries and moved to more advanced higher value-added stages of the production process. Having emulated other regional states in the initial process of insertion into the global economy, the challenge for Chinese policy-makers and business elites is now to emulate those regional states that successfully altered their production structures and participation in the global economy.

Notes

1. Under Purchasing Power Parity calculations, China's economy in 2002 stood at around US$6 trillion, making it the second biggest economy in the world.

2. Carol Lee Hamrin, *China and the Challenge of the Future: Changing Political Patterns* (Boulder, Colo.: Westview Press, 1990), 83.

3. 'China's Foreign Trade Has Ripple Effects', *People's Daily*, 28 Mar. 2004.

4. Barry Naughton, 'China's Trade Regime at the end of the 1990s', in Ted Carpenter and James Dorn, eds, *China's Future: Constructive Partner or Emerging Threat?* (Washington: Cato Institute, 2000), 235–60.

5. Yu Yongding, 'China's Macroeconomic Situation and Future Prospect', *World Economy and China* 3 and 4 (1999): 15.

6. China did not reach an agreement with Mexico, but Mexico agreed to allow Chinese entry as long as it could retain restrictions on Chinese imports.

7. The EU acts as a single actor on behalf of EU member states in such WTO negotiations.

8. David Murphy, 'Car Makers Worry China Is Planning a U-Turn', *Wall Street Journal*, 31 July 2003.

9. Dan Roberts and James Kynge, 'How Cheap Labour, Foreign Investment and Rapid Industrialisation Are Creating a New Workshop for the World', *Financial Times*, 4 Feb. 2003.

10. Nicholas Lardy, *Integrating China into the Global Economy* (Washington: Brookings Institution, 2002).

11. Leonard Cheng and Yum Kwan, 'What Are the Determinants of the Location of Foreign Direct

Investment? The Chinese Experience', *Journal of International Economics* 51, 2 (2000): 379–400.

12. 'China's Foreign Trade Has Ripple Effects'.

13. Joseph Camilleri, *States, Markets and Civil Society in Asia-Pacific* (Cheltenham: Edward Elgar, 2000), 66.

14. 'China's Hi-Tech Exports up 58.3 percent in January–July', *People's Daily,* 11 Aug. 2004.

15. Clay Chandler, 'Coping with China: As China Becomes the Workshop of the World, Where Does That Leave the Rest of Asia?', *Fortune,* 16 Jan. 2003.

16. Erik Eckholm, with Joseph Kahn, 'Asia Worries about Growth of China's Economic Power', *New York Times,* 24 Nov. 2002.

17. Xavier Sala-I-Martin, *Global Competitiveness Report: Executive Summary* (Geneva: World Economic Forum, 2003), 11.

18. David Barboza, 'Textile Industry Seeks Trade Limits on Chinese', *New York Times,* 25 July 2003.

19. Ian Williams, 'China–US: Double Bubbles in Danger of Colliding', *Asia Times,* 23 Jan. 2004.

20. Marie-France Houde and Hak-Loh Lee, *Main Determinants and Impacts of Foreign Direct Investment on China's Economy,* OECD Working Papers on International Investment No. 2000/4 (Paris: OECD, 2000), 7.

21. Charles Wolf, *Straddling Economics and Politics: Cross-Cutting Issues in Asia, the United States, and the Global Economy* (Santa Monica, Calif.: Rand Corporation, 2002), 134.

22. Murray Weidenbaum and Samuel Hughes, *The Bamboo Network: How Expatriate Chinese Entrepreneurs Are Creating a New Economic Superpower in Asia* (New York: Simon & Schuster, 1996).

23. Katsuhira Sasuga, 'The Dynamics of Cross-Border Micro-Regionalisation between Guangdong, Taiwan and Japan: Sub-national Governments, Multinational Corporations and the Emergence of Multi-Level Governance', Ph.D. thesis (University of Warwick, 2002).

24. Barry Naughton, 'Introduction: The Emergence of the China Circle', in Naughton, ed., *The China Circle: Economics and Electronics in the PRC, Taiwan, and Hong Kong* (Washington: Brookings Institution, 1997), 3–37.

25. Y. Matsuzaki, 'Hon Kon: tai Chu kyoten to shite no genjo', in K. Ishihara, ed., *Chugoku Keizai no Kokusaika to Higashi Ajia* (Tokyo: Ajia Keizai Kenkyusho, 1997), 160, cited in Katsuhiro Sasuga, *Microregionalism and Governance in East Asia* (London: Routledge, 2004).

26. Sasuga, *Microregionalism and Governance in East Asia.*

27. Shin-Hong Chen, 'Global Production Networks and Information Technology: The Case of Taiwan', *Industry and Innovation* 9, 3 (2002): 249–65.

28. Sasuga, *Microregionalism and Governance in East Asia.*

29. Boy Luthje, 'Electronics Contract Manufacturing: Global Production and the International Division of Labor in the Age of the Internet', *Industry and Innovation* 9, 3 (2002): 227–47.

30. Dani Rodrik, *Has Globalization Gone Too Far?* (Washington: Institute for International Economics, 1997), 46.

31. Luthje, 'Electronics Contract Manufacturing', 228–9.

32. Ibid., 227–47.

33. Stephen Roach, 'Global: China's Heavy Lifting', *Morgan Stanley Global Economic Forum,* 6 Mar. 2002.

Suggested Readings

Fewsmith, Joseph. 'The Political and Social Implications of China's Accession to the WTO', *China Quarterly* no. 167 (2001): 573–91.

Lardy, Nicholas. *Integrating China into the Global Economy.* Washington: Brookings Institution, 2002.

Studwell, Joe. *The China Dream: The Quest for the Last Great Untapped Market on Earth.* New York: Grove Press, 2003.

Tseng, Wanda, and Harm Zebregs. 'Foreign Direct Investment in China: Some Lessons for Other

Countries', *International Monetary Fund Policy Discussion Paper*, No. PDP/02/03, 2002. Available at: <www.imf.org/external/pubs/ft/pdp/2002/pdp03.pdf>.

Yasheng, Huang. *Selling China: Foreign Direct Investment during the Reform Era*. Cambridge: Cambridge University Press, 2003.

Zweig, David. *Internationalizing China: Domestic Interests and Global Linkages*. Ithaca, NY: Cornell University Press, 2002.

Web Sites

Chinese Ministry of Commerce:
  http://english.mofcom.gov.cn/
Institute of World Economics and Politics, Chinese Academy of Social Sciences:
  www.iwep.org.cn/english/index.htm
Royal Institute of International Affairs, China Project:
  www.riia.org/index.php?id=272

Shaun Breslin, on-line publications:
  www2.warwick.ac.uk/fac/soc/pais/staff/breslin/research/
Taylor Fravel's Chinese foreign policy portal:
  www.stanford.edu/%7Efravel/chinafp/toc.htm
US Trade Representative:
  www.ustr.gov/World_Regions/North_Asia/China/Section_Index.html

Contributors

Bastiaan van Apeldoorn Senior Lecturer in International Relations, Department of Political Science, Free University, Amsterdam (Netherlands)

Andrew Baker Lecturer, School of Politics and International Studies, Queen's University, Belfast (UK)

Mark Beeson Senior Lecturer in International Relations, School of Political Science and International Studies, University of Queensland (Australia)

Steven Bernstein Associate Professor, Department of Political Science, University of Toronto (Canada)

Shaun Breslin Associate Fellow, Asia Research Centre, Murdoch University; Professor, Department of Politics and International Studies, and Research Associate, Centre for the Study of Globalisation and Regionalisation, University of Warwick (UK)

Brian Burgoon Assistant Professor, Department of Political Science, University of Amsterdam (Netherlands)

Philip G. Cerny Professor of Global Political Economy, Center for Global Change and Governance and Department of Political Science, Rutgers University—Newark (US)

Geeta Chowdhry Professor of Political Science and Director, Ethnic Studies Program, Northern Arizona University (US)

Robert W. Cox Emeritus Professor, Department of Political Science, York University (Canada)

Sarah Eaton Doctoral Student, Department of Political Science, University of Toronto (Canada)

Henry Farrell Assistant Professor, Department of Political Science and Center for International Science and Technology Policy, Elliott School of International Affairs, George Washington University (US)

Annette Freyberg-Inan Assistant Professor, Department of Political Science, University of Amsterdam (Netherlands)

H. Richard Friman Professor, Department of Political Science, and Director, Institute for Transnational Justice, Marquette University (US)

Eric Helleiner Canada Research Chair in International Political Economy, International Development Studies Program, Trent University (Canada)

Richard Higgott Professor of International Political Economy, Department of Politics and International Studies, and Director, Centre for the Study of Globalisation and Regionalisation, University of Warwick (UK)

Christopher W. Hughes Senior Research Fellow and Deputy Director, Centre for the Study of Globalisation and Regionalisation, and Reader in International Politics, Department of Politics and International Studies, University of Warwick (UK)

Helge Hveem Professor in International Politics, Department of Political Science, and Director of the Centre on Technology, Innovation and Culture, University of Oslo (Norway)

Michael Krätke Reader, Department of Political Science, University of Amsterdam (Netherlands)

Marianne Marchand Professor of International Relations, Department of International Relations and History, Co-ordinator of the MA Program in the Study of North America, Universidad de las Américas, Puebla (Mexico)

Pamela K. Mbabazi Dean and Senior Lecturer, Faculty of Development Studies, Mbarara University of Science and Technology (Uganda)

James H. Mittelman Professor, School of International Service, American University (US)

Bruce E. Moon Professor, Department of International Relations, Lehigh University (US)

Jens Ladefoged Mortensen Assistant Professor, Department of Political Science, University of Copenhagen (Denmark)

Robert O'Brien LIUNA/Enrico Henry Mancinelli Professor in Global Labour Issues, Department of Political Science, and Associate Director, Institute on Globalization and the Human Condition, McMaster University (Canada)

Louis W. Pauly Canada Research Chair and Director, Centre for International Studies, University of Toronto (Canada)

Nicola Phillips Lecturer and Hallsworth Research Fellow, Department of Government, University of Manchester (UK)

Tony Porter Professor and Chair, Department of Political Science, McMaster University (Canada)

Austina J. Reed Doctoral Student, Department of Political Science, McMaster University (Canada)

Winfried Ruigrok Professor and Director of the Research Institute for International Management, University of St Gallen (Switzerland)

Herman M. Schwartz Professor, Woodrow Wilson Department of Politics, University of Virginia (US)

Susan K. Sell Associate Professor, Department of Political Science and Elliott School of International Affairs, George Washington University (US)

Timothy M. Shaw Professor of Commonwealth Governance and Development and Director of the Institute of Commonwealth Studies, University of London (UK)

Michael Smith Professor of European Politics, Department of Politics, International Relations and European Studies, Loughborough University (UK)

Jonathan Story The Shell Fellow in Economic Transformation and Professor of International Political Economy, INSEAD (France)

Richard Stubbs Professor, Department of Political Science, McMaster University (Canada)

Geoffrey R.D. Underhill Chair of International Governance, Department of Political Science, University of Amsterdam (Netherlands)

Sigurt Vitols Senior Research Fellow, Social Science Research Center, Berlin (Germany)

Michael C. Webb Associate Professor, Department of Political Science, University of Victoria (Canada)

Sandra Whitworth Associate Professor of Political Science and Women's Studies and Deputy Director, York Centre for International and Security Studies, York University (Canada)

Index

actors, 16–18; EU and, 307–8; private, 112, 183–94, 211–19; rational, 10–11; state, 211, 213–19; WTO and, 178–9; *see also* agents

Afghanistan, 44, 273, 275, 276

Africa, 356–65; child labour in, 233; conflict in, 362–3; constitutional abuses in, 361; democratic development states in, 356, 357, 358; diasporas in, 363; 'global governance' and, 363; infrastructure projects, 361–2, 365; investment in, 358–9, 361, 364–5; 'many', 356, 357; mining in, 359, 363, 364; pharmaceuticals and, 190–1; regionalization and, 299, 356–65; retail sector in, 364; women in, 91

Africa, Caribbean, Pacific (ACP)–Lomé agreement, 299

African Capacity Building Foundation, 364

African Development Bank, 356, 361

African Economic Research Consortium, 364

African Growth and Opportunity Act, 360–1

African Peer Review Mechanism, 361

'African Renaissance', 357, 358–60

African Union (AU), 357

agency: private, 302; regionalization and, 299–300, 302; state, 302; structured, 183–94

agents, 4–5, 16–18; structure-agent question, 6, 8, 15–19; *see also* actors

Aggarwal, Vinod, 277

'agrarian question', 223

agriculture: capitalist, 56, 57, 82, 223; EU and, 390–1, 393; Latin America and, 193, 336, 337; NAFTA and, 320–1, 324; peasant-based, 223, 225, 226, 227; standards in, 174–5; subsidies, 192, 193, 390; tobacco, 358, 363–4; trade in, 438; WTO and, 192–3

Albert, Michel, 411

Alliance for Jobs, 405, 406

Al-Qaeda, 276–7

'American' model, 404

Amin, Samir, 357, 365

Amorim, Celso, 192, 193

Amsterdam school, 31

analysis: levels of, 5–6, 30, 32

anarchy, 5–6, 19; critique of globalization and, 69–70; in realist tradition, 11

Andean Counterdrug Initiative, 281, 283

Anderson, Perry, 236

Anglo American (company), 359

Angola, 357–8, 359

Annan, Kofi, 67

anti-globalization movement, 48, 77–8, 167, 226, 294, 437–8

Antigua, 218

Argentina, 148, 333, 334, 337–9

Armenia, 425

arms, illegal, 273–6

Asad, Talal, 235

Ashanti Goldfields, 359

Asia: capitalism in, 292; child labour in, 233; financial crises in, 65, 154, 155, 187, 301, 344, 345–8, 352; regionalization and, 290, 301, 244–54, 454–63; women in, 91; *see also* East Asia

Asia–Europe dialogue process (ASEM), 345

Asian Bond Fund (ABF), 351

Asian Currency Unit, 461

Asian Development Bank (ADB), 350

Asian Monetary Fund (AMF), 81, 346, 347, 350–2, 460

'Asian values', 81, 239

'Asian Way', 345

Asia–Pacific Economic Co-operation (APEC), 299, 345–7, 349, 350, 352, 460

Asia–Pacific region, 154, 155, 156; as artificial, 346; *see also* Asia; East Asia

Association for Monetary Union in Europe (AMUE), 308

Association of Southeast Asian Nations (ASEAN), 299, 301, 345, 349, 350–1, 459, 460; –China FTA, 349; Economic Community (AEC), 349; Free Trade Area, 349, 350, 450; Plus Three (APT), 291, 347, 349, 350–1, 461

Association pour une Taxation des Transactions financières pour l'Aide aux Citoyens (ATTAC), 294

Australia, 348–9

authority: global finance and, 141–3; market-based v. society-based, 170, 180; regionalization and, 295, 300–1, 302

automobile industry: Africa, 361; Germany, 399; NAFTA